THE NATIONAL INSTITUTE OF
ECONOMIC AND SOCIAL RESEARCH

Economic and Social Studies

XXI

INDUSTRIAL GROWTH
AND
WORLD TRADE

The National Institute of Economic and Social Research is an independent, non-profit-making body, founded in 1938. It has as its aim the promotion of realistic research, particularly in the field of economics. It conducts research by its own research staff and in co-operation with the universities and other academic bodies. The results of the work done under the Institute's auspices are published in several series, and a list of its publications up to the present time will be found at the end of this volume.

INDUSTRIAL GROWTH
AND
WORLD TRADE

*An Empirical Study of Trends in Production,
Consumption and Trade in Manufactures from 1899-1959
with a Discussion
of Probable Future Trends*

BY

ALFRED MAIZELS

CAMBRIDGE
AT THE UNIVERSITY PRESS
1971

PUBLISHED BY

THE SYNDICS OF THE CAMBRIDGE UNIVERSITY PRESS

Bentley House, 200 Euston Road, London, NW1 2DB

American Branch: 32 East 57th Street, New York, N.Y. 10022

ISBN 0 521 05662 4

First Edition 1963
Reprinted 1965, 1971

First printed in Great Britain by Metcalf and Cooper Ltd., London, E.C.2
Reprinted in Great Britain by Lewis Reprints Limited, London and Tonbridge

CONTENTS

INTRODUCTION AND SUMMARY OF FINDINGS

PART I
PATTERNS OF INDUSTRIAL GROWTH AND TRADE

A*

78675

PART II

TRENDS AND RELATIONSHIPS

PART III

COMMODITY GROUPS

PART IV
PROSPECTS AND CONCLUSIONS

APPENDICES

LIST OF TABLES IN THE TEXT

LIST OF FIGURES

LIST OF TABLES IN THE APPENDICES

Appendix A   THE TRADE NETWORK TABLES

'IMPORTS' OF MANUFACTURES: TOTALS BY COMMODITY GROUP
AND TOTALS BY COUNTRY OF ORIGIN, AT CONSTANT PRICES, 1899-1955

Industrial countries

Semi-industrial countries

Non-industrial countries

PREFACE

The idea of undertaking a new study on industrialization and international trade developed during the years 1953–55, when my colleagues and I in the Board of Trade were reconsidering the implications for the British economy of the more important long-term changes that were taking place in the outside world. The growth of manufacturing industry in our overseas markets in the primary-producing countries had already modified the character of our export trade very substantially, and there seemed little doubt that it would continue to exert a profound influence on our external economic position.

A detailed study of the effects of overseas industrialization on Britain's economic structure and development seemed to me to be vitally important for any realistic assessment of our future export prospects. A study on these lines interested the National Institute of Economic and Social Research, and through the generosity of the Leverhulme Foundation I was able to join the Institute's staff for this purpose. The study, as it developed, assumed a wider perspective than had originally been envisaged. The effect of overseas industrialization on Britain is, after all, only one aspect of the changing economic relations between the industrial countries as a whole and the primary-producing areas. This more general aspect of the mutual adjustments which are necessary between major economic areas of the world developing in different ways and at different speeds forms the principal theme of this book. Against this background, the varying fortunes of Britain and of the other main industrial countries can be appropriately assessed.

The statistical material available on long-term movements in international trade in manufactured goods was, however, quite inadequate for the sort of analysis that was required, and a completely new set of trade network tables was compiled for selected years back to the end of last century. This proved a heavy task and the time taken to produce this basic set of tables inevitably delayed the analytical part of the study. The new material provided should, incidentally, be of use to other workers in this field.

Throughout the greater part of the research, I was particularly fortunate in having the close assistance and support of Mr L. F. Campbell-Boross and Mr R. W. Thomas. Together, they were responsible for compiling the detailed trade network tables and the majority of the tables in the text, as well as helping on numerous other statistical matters which arose in the course of the research. The detailed argument at many points in the study has also benefited from the numerous fruitful discussions which developed in the course of our work.

Mr L. F..Campbell-Boross has also been responsible for the general editing of the statistical material to its final form.   I am also indebted to Mr G. F. Ray for assembling the data on tariff levels pre-war and post-war, which were used in Chapters 6 and 7, and for valuable advice on the design of many of the charts used.

Some offshoots of the study have already been published.   A new calculation of the growth of industrial production and productivity in Australia since before the first World War was published in *The Economic Record* for 1957, and a study of comparative productivity in Australian and Canadian manufacturing industries appeared in the same journal in 1958.   A paper on *The Effects of Industrialization on Exports of Primary-producing Countries* was read to the Cardiff meeting of the British Association, Summer, 1960, and subsequently published in *Kyklos* in 1961.   With the kind agreement of the editor of *Kyklos*, this paper, with some amendment, has been incorporated in Chapter 5 of the present book, while Chapter 12 is a somewhat revised version of an article on trends in world trade in durable consumer goods which was published in the *National Institute Economic Review* for November 1959.   On the methodological plane, consideration of various methods of 'deflating' the value series in the trade network tables to arrive at the underlying volume movements led to the writing of a note on *Unit Value and Volume Indices in Inter-Area Trade*, which was published in the *Journal of the Royal Statistical Society* (Series A) for 1959.   An earlier draft of the book was accepted in 1962 as a dissertation for the Ph.D. degree in the University of London.

My intellectual debt to my colleagues at the National Institute is great, and particularly so to Mr Christopher T. Saunders, the Director of the Institute, whose constructive criticisms have influenced the analysis and presentation of almost every chapter of the book.   I am also indebted to Mr D. A. Rowe for much stimulating discussion on various mathematical aspects of the study.   Of many other colleagues from whose helpful criticisms I have benefited, I would mention Mr W. Beckerman, Mr L. F. Campbell-Boross, Mr W. M. Corden, Mrs M. F. W. Hemming, Mr R. L. Major, Mr R. R. Neild, Mr K. V. Pankhurst, Mr G. F. Ray, Mr A. D. Smith, Mr R. W. Thomas and Mr C. Winsten.   I am also most grateful to Mrs A. K. Jackson, the Secretary of the Institute, for her close interest at all times in furthering the work on this project and in the presentation of the material for publication. Miss A. A. Clarke, the Institute's former Librarian, gave constantly helpful and efficient support in providing innumerable publications at short notice, while Miss M. J. Harington, the present Librarian, helped with the proofs and general editing.   My thanks are also due to Mr W. A. B. Hopkin who, when Director of the National Institute, not only arranged for me to the join Institute's staff as a Senior Research Fellow, but also took an active interest in the planning stages of the research.

I am especially grateful to Mr A. K. Cairncross and Professor E. Devons for their penetrating and critical comments on the argument and methods of analysis at numerous points throughout the book. Valuable comments on chapter drafts were received also from Sir Donald MacDougall, Professor C. P. Kindleberger, Mr H. G. Aubrey, Mr S. Dell, Mr H. R. Fisher, Mr Hal B. Lary, Mr D. Shaw and Mr A. P. Zentler, from the Steel, Engineering and Housing Division of the Economic Commission for Europe, Geneva, and from former colleagues in the Board of Trade. I am also much indebted to Mrs Winifred Moss for some valuable suggestions on the first draft of the book.

Mrs H. Brew and Miss S. Hunt helped in the earlier stages of the study. The large amount of computing work was undertaken by the Institute staff, particularly by Miss J. Vallily, Miss M. Bickel and Miss B. Leighton, to all of whom I must express my appreciation, as well as to Mrs J. Ray for drawing the charts. Miss A. Ruston, Miss K. Garnett and Miss J. Goodman all helped at various times to type chapter drafts, the final draft being typed by Mrs R. E. Wiffen.

This record of acknowledgements would be incomplete without a reference to the use of statistical source material. Mr J. A. King, the Librarian of the Royal Statistical Society, was kind enough to loan to the Institute the Society's copies of the 1899 and 1913 trade returns of the main industrial countries, while Mr K. A. Mallaber, the Board of Trade Librarian, and his staff in the Statistics Library, also gave willing assistance. Thanks are also due to several members of the staff of the Board of Trade Statistics Division for their active interest in the course of the research.

A. M.

NATIONAL INSTITUTE OF ECONOMIC
AND SOCIAL RESEARCH

December 1962

Certain inconsistencies in the British export figures as originally published in this book were pointed out by Dr A. G. Ford of the University of Warwick. These figures, and in fact those for some other countries, included re-exports for some years only which made the time-series misleading. This has now been corrected throughout the text and tables by excluding all re-exports. The general conclusions remain unaltered.

February 1969   A.M.

CONVENTIONS AND SYMBOLS

Countries

Names of countries are those which were in use in 1955.

'Southern Dominions' denotes Australia, New Zealand and (the present Republic of) South Africa in the aggregate.

'Soviet countries' denotes the Soviet Union, Eastern Europe and China in the aggregate, though in some cases the figures also include the other Asian communist countries.

'Germany' for post-World War II denotes West Germany, unless stated otherwise.

Units

All values are given in terms of United States dollars.

All quantities are in metric units.

A 'billion' denotes one thousand million.

Trade values are f.o.b. exporting country, unless stated otherwise.

Details in tables may not add to totals because of rounding.

Symbols

    ..   not available or not applicable.

0   less than half the unit stated.

—   nil.

INTRODUCTION AND SUMMARY OF FINDINGS

1. AIMS

The main aim of this book is to analyse the long-term relationship between industrial growth and international trade in manufactured goods. Several distinct aspects of this relationship can be separately considered. In particular, it is useful at the outset to distinguish the problems of industrialization in a primary-producing country such as India or Brazil, and the impact of such industrialization on that country's trade, from the continuing industrial advance of a mature industrial country and the consequent effects of this on trade. In the first example, industrialization sets in motion quite new economic forces, involving a greater or lesser transformation of the social and economic balance of the country. Such profound changes may substantially affect the export potential as well as the import demand, of the industrializing country; and are likely to do so in different ways, or to a significantly different extent, from the continued economic development of an industrial country with a population enjoying a relatively high level of income.

Since the intention was to analyse the main trends in world trade since the end of last century, it was necessary to consider the economic growth of all the main trading countries. In general, the experiences of the industrializing primary-producing countries are separated from, and contrasted with, those of the industrial countries of Western Europe, North America and Japan, and—wherever possible—with those of a selection of less-developed countries which have not yet begun to industrialize. To some extent, also, the development experiences of some of the present industrial countries in the early years of this century may be a pointer to how some of the present primary-producing countries might develop in the future, though clearly much caution is needed before any conclusions can be drawn from the analogy.

The method of approach has thus been to attempt to explain the trends in world trade in manufactured goods by industrial and economic changes in the main importing countries. Such changes are not, of course, the only factors influencing trade; in certain periods, other factors—changes in trade restrictions or in a country's foreign exchange earnings due to changes in the terms of trade, or in foreign demand conditions, for example—may be the major influences. The outstanding analytical problem is to eliminate, if possible, the influence of such extraneous factors, so that the net effect of industrial growth on imports can be adequately assessed. Since the imports of manufactures into both the industrial and primary-producing countries are supplied very largely by the industrial countries themselves, the analysis of import trends is, in effect, an explanation of trends in exports of manufactures from the industrial countries.

A secondary objective has been to analyse the trends in exports from each

B

of the main industrial countries separately. The industrialization of the primary-producing countries has resulted not only in a shift in the pattern of their import trade which has affected all the industrial countries generally; it has also resulted in a substantial degree of import-substitution which has adversely affected the export trade of some of the industrial countries much more than that of others. Here it is necessary to distinguish the effects of such import-substitution from the effects of competition between the industrial countries, and from the indirect effects of industrialization on imports through its effects on real incomes.

Finally, it was hoped that the underlying relationships between economic growth and imports of manufactures which were found for the past half-century could be used, with suitable modifications, to assess the prospects for growth and trade over the coming decade or so. Such an assessment has been made on the basis of alternative assumptions about the future rates of economic growth in the main industrial countries and about the probable future relationship between imports and consumption of manufactured goods.

2. THE ANALYTIC BACKGROUND

The general problem of how the industrialization of primary-producing countries affects the economies of the older industrial countries has been discussed on many previous occasions since the beginning of the century. Curiously enough, views on the problem have tended—with few exceptions— to polarize into opposing schools of thought: those who viewed the industrialization of primary-producing countries with some alarm, and those who welcomed it as a basis for the further expansion of the world economy. The exponents of the former view usually based their argument on one or both of the following propositions: that as primary-producing countries industrialized, Britain and other industrial countries lost their traditional export markets for manufactured goods; and that, at the same time, local industries in primary-producing countries absorbed raw materials which would otherwise be used by the industrial countries.

In Britain, the loss of traditional markets for textiles was, indeed, a major and obvious cause of the economic difficulties of the 1920's. 'The most obvious and immediate effect' of the growth of local manufacture, stated the Balfour Committee in 1925, 'is, of course, a restrictive one. Goods that formerly found a ready sale in a particular market are now wholly or partially excluded by the competition of the locally produced article under the protection of an import tariff'[1]. The Committee considered, however, that two qualifications were necessary to their main thesis. The first was that new manufacturing industries set up in Britain's main export markets were likely to be concentrated

[1]*Survey of Overseas Markets*, Committee on Industry and Trade, H.M.S.O., London, 1925.

on the production of the simpler classes of manufactures. This would lead to a shift in the pattern of overseas demand towards higher-quality goods, in which Britain specialized. The second qualification was that new industries create new needs for plant and materials and that, as income grows with expanding production, expenditures will increase and this will tend to increase the demand for imports. The Committee's view was that the growth in the demand for plant and materials would not of itself be sufficient to offset the loss of the market for the final product, but they were careful to leave open the crucial question of whether the subsequent increase in incomes would offset the effect on imports of the process of import substitution.

This generally pessimistic view of the effects of industrialization in 'overseas markets' appeared to be confirmed by the events of the 1930's. The world economic crisis of 1931 was immediately followed by a host of trade restrictions of all kinds. At the same time, local manufacturing was greatly stimulated in many important markets outside Europe and North America, and in the older industrial countries a number of industries (particularly textiles) were adversely affected by this development. The link between unemployment in the export industries and the growth of secondary industry abroad inevitably coloured the thinking of many British economists at that time.

Very similar arguments to these were, in fact, put forward by the Economics Committee of the Royal Commission on Population in 1950[1]. The Committee argued that industrialization in countries suffering from rural over-population 'offers by far the most promising means of raising the standard of life . . . The improvement in the standard of life may give rise to a demand for imports of new types; and it is sometimes argued that by supplying this demand, and also by supplying the investment goods required during the process of industrialization, Great Britain might obtain compensation for the loss of her traditional lines of export trade. But this compensation is most unlikely to be more than partial. It cannot be assumed that the total imports of the country in which industrialization takes place will be maintained in undiminished volume. Still less can it be assumed that the new imports will be obtained from the particular countries which supplied the old imports displaced by industrialization. Nor is it probable that the new imports will be wholly industrial products; insofar as they consist of food or other primary commodities, the difficulties of an industrial exporting country will be aggravated rather than relieved'.

These views were paralleled in the academic discussions by arguments, such as those put forward in the 1930's by the late Lord Keynes and Professor D. H. Robertson, based on the doctrine of comparative costs[2]. Keynes argued, for

[1]Papers of the Royal Commission on Population, Vol. III, *Report of the Economics Committee*, H.M.S.O., London, 1950, pp. 10–13.
[2]These arguments can be traced back to Robert Torrens (*An Essay on the Production of Wealth*, London, 1821), who argued that as 'newer' countries progress in population,

example, that the spread of technical progress among the nations of the world tends to narrow the differences in relative costs of production between one country and another, and thus reduces the scope for specialization through international trade[1]. Robertson used a similar argument to explain the shrinkage in world trade in textiles[2].

More recently, Dominguez[3] has argued that the process of economic growth will lead to a reduction in the division of labour between industrial countries. Economic growth involves changes both in the pattern of demand and in the pattern of output. Since resource-endowments are likely to differ, economic growth implies a different pattern of demand for the products of each country. Assuming that each country has an initial specialization, the change in demand pattern implies the emergence of surplus capacity in one country, provided that labour is not mobile between countries. This surplus capacity can be taken up only if the range of production is extended into the speciality of the other country; such an extension would, however, imply a contraction in the trade between the partner countries. This argument is, however, based wholly on the effects of growth on the *pattern* of demand; but economic growth implies also an increase in the *level* of demand, and if aggregate demand rose rapidly enough, this could offset the effects of the change in pattern, and prevent the emergence of surplus capacity.

Dominguez also argues that, to the extent to which the primary-producing countries succeed in industrializing, their imports of certain simply-fabricated manufactures will contract, and this will make it somewhat more difficult for the older industrial countries to obtain primary commodities in the desired volume[4]. This line of thought is similar to that expressed by the Economics Committee of the Royal Commission on Population.

These various arguments have all been belied by the course of events since the early 1950's. The past decade has witnessed a faster rate of industrial growth and a faster rate of increase in the intra-trade of the industrial countries than at any previous period since the beginning of the century. The view that industrialization of the primary-producing countries (especially the less-

the law of diminishing returns will ensure that the cost of their primary produce will rise, while with rising productivity of labour the cost of production of manufactures in such countries will fall. Thus, relative differences in costs between old and new countries become evened up, and international trade is eventually 'confined to those peculiar articles, in the production of which immutable circumstances of soil and climate give one country a permanent advantage over another'. See Professor J. Viner's address to the Manchester Statistical Society (*The Prospects for Foreign Trade in the Post-War World*, June 1946), in which he discusses Torrens' argument at some length.

[1] J. M. Keynes, 'National Self-Sufficiency', *Yale Review*, Vol. 22, No. 4, June 1933.

[2] D. H. Robertson, 'The Future of International Trade', *Economic Journal*, Vol. 48, No. 189, March 1938. See also Professor J. Viner, *op. cit.*, for a critical review of the arguments put forward by Keynes and Robertson.

[3] L. M. Dominguez, *International Trade, Industrialization and Economic Growth*, Pan-American Union, Washington, D.C., 1954.

[4] L. M. Dominguez, *op. cit.*, page 153.

developed ones) is ultimately to the benefit of the older industrial countries (as well as to the industrializing countries themselves) is one that is now generally accepted both by governments and by economists.

Yet this conclusion had already been reached nearly twenty years ago by the late Folke Hilgerdt in his classic study of the effects of industrialization on international trade[1]. This study provided, for the first time, a systematic review of the empirical evidence on the subject, from the beginnings of the modern industrial era in the 1870's to the outbreak of the second World War. The more important of Hilgerdt's conclusions can, perhaps, be summarized as follows:

1. Industrialization increases the productivity of labour, and the resulting greater supply of manufactured goods tends to stimulate the production of primary produce for sale. Thus, industrialization tends to increase a country's ability to export and in this way it helps to finance increased imports of manufactures.

2. This process of simultaneous industrial growth and trade expansion was disrupted in the 1930's by the disintegration of the world economy. The real danger to the further growth of trade, therefore, is not industrialization but the failure to abolish restrictions on international trade.

Hilgerdt's *schema* of industrialization leading to increased exports, which are then used to finance a greater volume of imports, was founded—securely enough—on the historical development of the main industrial countries up to 1930. Yet it is precisely this assumption of the necessary inter-action of industrialization and export growth which has seemed most open to question from the experiences of many industrializing primary-producing countries since 1945. The major limitation on growth in these countries has generally been the insufficiency of foreign exchange to purchase essential 'developmental' imports. Hilgerdt's conclusion thus appeared to need re-examination in the light of the post-war evidence which is now available.

Moreover, the statistical material presented by Hilgerdt suffered from major limitations which inevitably restricted the scope of his analysis. The first was that the statistics related essentially to the more advanced industrial countries of Europe and North America, only five primary-producing countries— Australia, Chile, India, New Zealand and the Union of South Africa—being included in the analysis. Second, Hilgerdt's material related solely to the movements in production and trade of manufactured goods as a whole, though shifts in the commodity pattern of trade in manufactures have been no less significant than changes in the total. The present study attempts to extend Hilgerdt's analysis in both these directions: a fairly wide range of 'less-developed' countries is included in the analysis, while separate series have been compiled for the main groups of manufactured goods.

[1] *Industrialization and Foreign Trade*, League of Nations, Geneva, 1945.

Much of the statistical analysis in this book is based on least-squares regression techniques. This approach owes a good deal in inspiration to Professor H. B. Chenery's well-known analysis of cross-country differences in output and trade patterns in a recent period[1]. The new trade data compiled during the present study have allowed the calculation of time-series regressions, as well as cross-country ones; the results indicate fairly conclusively that the latter are, in some important cases, misleading guides to the changing pattern of international trade.

Professor Chenery's has hitherto been the only comprehensive attempt, since Hilgerdt's study, to analyse the relationships between industrial growth and foreign trade. There have, however, been a number of valuable studies of particular aspects of the development of world trade, especially its changing commodity-pattern and changes in the share of world exports held by individual industrial countries. Among these latter studies, those by Baldwin, Cairncross, Kindleberger, Svennilson and Tyszynski are worthy of special mention: detailed references and comment will be found in Chapters 7 and 8. Several detailed studies in this field have also been made in recent years by the United Nations and its regional Economic Commissions[2], as well as by the G.A.T.T. secretariat[3].

3. PLAN OF THE BOOK

The greater part of the analysis in this book is based on two new sets of statistical series. The first, described in Appendices A to D, consists of a detailed subdivision of exports of manufactures from the main industrial countries by commodity group, distinguishing a wide range of countries of destination. These 'Trade Network' tables relate to selected years of relatively good trade from 1899 to 1959. The figures are, as near as possible, internationally comparable, being derived by re-classifying the original trade statistics of the exporting countries on to the basis currently in use by the United Nations. The original figures in national currencies have all been converted into U.S. dollars at current prices, by using the average rates of exchange for the relevant years; and into 'constant' prices by deflating the current value series by indices of export unit values (see Appendix B).

The countries of destination were chosen so as to include all the main industrial countries and a majority of the industrializing primary-producing countries. In addition, a selection of primary-producing countries which have

[1]H. B. Chenery, 'Patterns of Industrial Growth', *American Economic Review*, Vol. 50, No. 4, Sept. 1960.

[2]See, in particular, *Processes and Problems of Industrialization in Under-Developed Countries*, United Nations, New York, 1955; *World Economic Survey, 1956* and *1961*, United Nations, New York, 1957 and 1962; *Economic Survey of Latin America, 1956*, United Nations, New York, 1957.

[3]Annual Reports (particularly *International Trade, 1956, 1957–58* and *1959*, G.A.T.T., Geneva, 1957, 1959 and 1960, respectively).

not yet begun to industrialize was included in order to contrast their trading experience with that of the industrializing group. The Soviet Union was also distinguished separately in view of its very different development over most of the period considered.

In order to confine the considerable volume of statistical extraction, classification and computation work within manageable limits, some countries had to be excluded from the Trade Network tables, although their inclusion would otherwise have been desirable. The most important of these exclusions, measured in terms of value of their foreign trade, are some of the smaller European countries: Austria, Denmark and Finland, for example, in Western Europe, and the countries of Eastern Europe outside the Soviet Union. Thus, the new statistical series for the 'industrial countries' relates to a rather narrower definition of countries than is usually adopted, though this is not likely to have distorted, to any significant extent, the broad trends over the past half-century, nor the relationships found between trade and economic growth. The excluded countries are, however, included in their appropriate groups in some parts of the analysis.

The second set of statistics consists of estimates of gross domestic product, the net output of manufactures and the gross value, free of duplication, of consumption of non-food manufactures for those countries included in the Trade Network tables for as many of the selected years as possible (see Appendices E and F).

The construction of these basic series allowed an analysis to be made of the relation between import growth and economic expansion in the various importing areas. Before starting such an analysis, however, it seemed necessary to inquire into certain aspects of industrialization and economic growth which form the general setting of the whole study. This inquiry is the main purpose of the three chapters in Part I.

The first aspect considered is the relation between the expansion of manufacturing industry and general economic growth, which is discussed in Chapter 1. This is followed by an examination of historical patterns of change within the manufacturing sector, together with an attempt to deduce from the evidence a 'typical' historical pattern (Chapter 2). The third aspect considered is whether the material assembled could be used in some way to classify countries according to the level of industrialization that they have achieved. In Chapter 3, a broad classification is suggested, based both on the statistics of manufacturing output and on the composition of the export trade of different countries.

Having examined the evidence on industrial growth, and classified countries into broad groups, the stage is set for an analysis of the main trends and of the various influences at work insofar as these can be quantified. This is the purpose of Parts II and III. The discussion in Part II is confined to the more general aspects, the commodity groups being left over for detailed treatment in Part III. A broad review is first made of the long-term trends in international trade with which the book is mainly concerned (Chapter 4). This is followed by a discussion of the effects of industrialization on exports from primary-producing countries (Chapter 5) and of industrial growth on imports of manufactures (Chapter 6). The next chapter deals with trends in commodity trade patterns, distinguishing the main markets, while Chapter 8 considers secular changes in the share of the world market for manufactures held by each of the main industrial countries. Part III, as already mentioned, deals in greater detail with the main commodity groups (Chapters 9-14). The following chapter (Part IV—Chapter 15) attempts to assess possible future trends in world trade in manufactures on the basis of the past relationships already revealed, and of a number of specific assumptions, and discusses the implications of these trends for the economic policies of the industrial countries. Finally, in Chapter 16, some general conclusions suggested by the study are reviewed.

4. SUMMARY OF FINDINGS

Industrialization and economic growth

There have been several 'rounds' of industrialization in the primary-producing areas of the world since the beginning of the century. Shortages in supplies of manufactured goods during the two World Wars stimulated local production, while during the 1930's the deterioration in the terms of trade of these countries and the network of trade restrictions which grew up forced many governments to foster secondary industries behind tariff protection to safeguard living standards and to keep down unemployment. Since 1945, there has been another spurt of industrial development, partly as a result of economic planning in many of the less-developed countries. Nevertheless, manufacturing production in the 'low-income' continents of Latin America, Africa and Asia by 1959 totalled little more than 10 per cent of that in North America, Western Europe and Oceania.

Though industrialization may not be the appropriate policy for economic growth in every country, it seems that in many—probably the majority—of the less-developed countries, industrialization is the key to economic progress. The main causal connection, as suggested in Chapter 1, is that industrialization tends to raise physical output per head in the economy. There are several ways in which this comes about, and these tend to operate simultaneously. First, with industrialization the share of manufacturing in national output increases. Since the average product per worker is higher in manufacturing than in agriculture in low-income countries, this shift in the pattern of output will raise total commodity output per head in the economy. Second, with the progress of industrialization, productivity in the manufacturing sector itself tends to increase relatively rapidly, compared with progress in other sectors.

Increasing manufacturing output will often be accompanied by economies of scale (within plants and in industry generally), by increases in capital assets employed, and by the development of new skills and attitudes to work. Finally, the level of productivity in the rest of the economy may be raised as a result of industrialization (by increasing the supplies of farm equipment and fertilizers to agriculture, for example; or, more indirectly, by improving transport facilities, educational levels, and so on).

Changes in the pattern of output

Industrialization also involves changes in the pattern of manufacturing output. As income levels rise, the pattern of demand changes and the growth of industry responds to this. The main features of the typical change in demand pattern are a relatively rapid growth in demand for capital goods, chemicals and durable consumer goods, and a relatively slow expansion in demand for food, textiles and clothing (Chapter 2). Apart from demand influences, changes in the pattern of output also depend on the resource endowments of the industrializing country—which are likely to vary substantially from one country to another—and the extent to which economies of scale accrue as output is expanded in particular industries.

However, the influence of the indigenous natural and human resources on the pattern of economic growth can be greatly modified by the relative ease or difficulty of transporting resources to and from other countries, and of increasing the population by immigration, as well as by government intervention. With so many variable influences at work modifying the effects of the uneven distribution of resources among different countries, it might be expected that the pattern of industrial growth which actually develops in any one country would differ significantly from that of other countries. However, there are other influences which tend to make the industry-pattern of growth broadly similar in countries at similar stages of industrialization. First, as already mentioned, the pattern of demand tends to change in a similar way in such countries. Second, manufacturing tends to be restricted in the earlier phases of industrialization by the available level of skill and organizational ability to the simpler processes, which are typical of the consumer industries. Third, the size of the market tends to be too small in the earlier stages of industrialization to justify the establishment of optimum-sized plants in a number of industries, particularly in the chemicals and capital goods field. With the progress of industrialization, new skills and organizational abilities emerge, while the expanding market allows new industries to be profitably established.

The industrial development of the economically advanced countries provides empirical evidence of the existence of a common broad pattern of growth. Taking the historical changes in output patterns in the industrial countries since the end of last century, regression equations were computed to show the association between the rate of growth in each main industry group and the rate of growth in the gross domestic product. This provides a quantitative assessment of the association between economic growth and the pattern of manufacturing output. The results show a fairly sharp fall in the relative importance of food processing and textiles in the earlier stages of growth, with a continued, though reduced, rate of decline thereafter. Metals and engineering products show the reverse movement, with a declining rate of growth (relative to the total) as the later stages of development are reached. Chemicals production shows an uninterrupted rise, while the miscellaneous group of manufactures first rises and then tends to fall slowly in relative importance.

This picture is based on the common evolution of manufacturing in the main industrial countries; the calculation thus presupposes a wide variety of resources and an expanding market. It does not necessarily describe how industry will develop in any given country, particularly where resources are limited or where the market is restricted. Nor does it imply any necessary sequence in the pattern of growth. Now that aid and technical know-how are available in substantial amounts to less-developed countries, a wider choice of development-pattern is possible, including development of some engineering industries in the earlier stages of industrialization. Such development on a broad industrial front would accelerate the changes in the industrial pattern revealed by the present analysis.

A broad classification of countries

The net value of manufacturing production per head of the total population is taken as a statistical measure of the level of industrialization in any country (Chapter 1). This is combined with an indicator of the degree of industrialization of exports (taken as the proportion of 'finished' manufactures in total exports) to derive a broad classification of countries into 'industrial', 'semi-industrial' and 'non-industrial' which is convenient for the analysis of international trade trends (Chapter 3). The following criteria, admittedly arbitrary, have been used (based on the position in 1955):

	Industrial	Semi-industrial	Non-industrial
Net value of manufacturing production per head ($ at 1955 prices) ..	Over 150	30–350	Under 15
Finished manufactures as proportion of total exports (percentage) ..	Over 15	Under 15	Negligible

In the industrial group are both large countries like the United States, Britain and West Germany, and small ones like Belgium and the Netherlands. Canada and Japan are both borderline cases but are included here in the industrial area. Other borderline cases are India and Israel, both of which are classed as semi-industrial, while Pakistan is also included here since the pre-war figures for undivided India cannot be split to compare with present boundaries. The semi-industrial group thus contains countries at very different levels of industrialization. The two main sub-groups included, apart from India/ Pakistan, are (a) the 'countries of recent settlement', such as Australia, New Zealand and South Africa, which have already reached a relatively mature phase of industrialization, and (b) countries where industrialization is a much more recent development, such as Brazil, Chile, Turkey and Yugoslavia. In the later analysis, the various sub-groups are discussed separately wherever possible. The non-industrial group includes countries such as Southern Rhodesia and Egypt, which have already begun to industrialize, as well as a large number of under-developed countries, which have not, or whose manufacturing output is still very small. The countries in the Soviet group are excluded from this classification, and are treated separately wherever possible.

The industrial countries as here defined contained 28 per cent of the total population of the world outside the Soviet countries in 1959, but consumed about 82 per cent of all non-food manufactures in that year. The semi-industrial countries had 40 per cent of the total population and accounted for some 13 per cent of consumption of non-food manufactures. The corresponding proportions for the non-industrial areas were 32 per cent for population and only 5 per cent for consumption. The relative importance of the non-industrial areas was, however, considerably greater in terms of imports of manufactures. In 1959, they took in aggregate about 25 per cent of world imports of manufactures (excluding imports by the Soviet area), compared with about 20 per cent by the semi-industrial countries, and 55 per cent by the industrial countries.

The main trends

In a review of the movement in world trade over the past half-century (Chapter 4), four main trends became apparent. First, the long-term movement in world trade in manufactures has been closely related to that in world manufacturing production. There was a break in the relationship in the 1930's, but in historical perspective this appears as a discontinuity due to special factors (trade and currency restrictions) which depressed the level of trade in those years.

Second, before 1939, a relative increase in the volume of trade in manufactures, compared with primary products, was normally associated with a reverse movement in the relative prices of these two groups. Since the second World War, however, a relative expansion in the volume of trade in manufactures has been accompanied by a worsening of the terms of trade for primary products. Some of the possible reasons for this are examined in Chapter 4, and the implications of this recent trend for the future are discussed in Chapter 15.

Third, trade between the industrial countries has increased faster since 1950 than any other sector of world trade. It seems likely that this was, in part, a reversion to a more 'normal' relationship between the intra-trade of the industrial countries and their total output of manufactures. Trade in manufactures *within* the industrial continents (i.e. between Canada and the United States, and between countries of Western Europe) has increased faster than that *between* these continents. Of exports of manufactures to outside countries, those to semi-industrial countries have risen much more slowly than those to non-industrial ones.

Fourth, against this background of secular expansion, imports of manufactures into three important trading countries—Britain, India and Argentina—have tended to stagnate over the period covered by the analysis[1], thus helping to retard the rate of growth in world trade. The fact that India and Argentina are also important examples of industrializing primary-producing countries has appeared to support the view that industrialization in such countries necessarily tends to reduce exports (or, at least, reduces the potential growth in exports) and so limits the increase in imports which can be achieved.

Effect of industrialization on exports

This view is examined (in Chapter 5) in relation to the experience of the semi-industrial countries, comparing a pre-war period (1937–38) with a post-war one (1955). Two methods of analysis were used. The first considers the movement in exports from each semi-industrial country from pre-war to post-war, in relation to (a) the movement in world trade in the same 'bundle' of goods, and (b) the movement in that country's average export prices (unit values) compared with that in world trade in the same 'bundle' of goods[2]. A regression analysis shows that the very different movement in exports from different industrializing countries since pre-war is closely related to the different commodity-patterns of their exports. The introduction of an index of manufacturing production, or an index of the relative importance of manufacturing in the gross domestic product, did not improve the statistical result. It seems reasonable to conclude that, in general, the secular change in exports of these countries from pre-war to post-war was not significantly associated with their rate of industrialization.

The second approach was to contrast the experience of the semi-industrial countries as a group with that of the non-industrial countries. The results gave striking confirmation of the previous conclusion. The volume of exports from the non-industrial countries in 1955 of commodities directly competitive

[1] The period covered here generally ends in 1959. British imports of manufactures rose substantially in 1960 and 1961.

[2] This approach has been subject to some criticism, which is further discussed in Chapter 5 (page 125).

with the exports of the semi-industrial countries was only 5 per cent above the 1937–38 level. This is not significantly different from the 1 per cent increase calculated for the semi-industrial countries. By contrast, the exports of other primary products from the non-industrial countries rose by over 120 per cent in volume in the same period.

This evidence does not support the view that the rate of export growth of the semi-industrial countries was, as a general rule, retarded by the process of industrialization. If there was a 'supply limitation' due to industrialization, why then were the exports of similar products from the non-industrial countries affected in similar degree? This is not to claim that in particular countries, at particular periods, industrialization has not, in fact, retarded exports— several well-known examples can in fact be quoted of industrialization resulting in a retarded growth in exports—but it cannot be claimed that it must necessarily do so.

Effect of industrial growth on the total volume of imports of manufactures

Changes in the volume of imports of manufactures are considered here as the resultant of two influences: changes in the level of consumption of manufactures and changes in the proportion of consumption which is met by imports. Levels of consumption per head are closely related to levels of real income per head. Estimates are presented in Chapter 6 of apparent consumption of manufactures per head in a wide range of countries for selected years back to 1899. Regression calculations indicate that in most countries consumption of manufactures rises at an appreciably faster rate than real income.

The discussion of the relative share of imports in consumption is conducted, for technical reasons, in terms of the import-content of 'supplies', which are defined as production plus imports of manufactures. It is shown that the import-content declines with the progress of industrialization, at least up to a point where a fairly mature level of industrialization has been reached. The rate of decline is likely to be influenced by a number of different factors; those considered here are (1) the size of the country, (2) the degree of import restric- tions, (3) the relative importance of exports in the economy, and (4) the level of industrialization.

Small countries are likely to be more dependent on imports than large ones, both because their range of natural resources available for industrial develop- ment is likely to be more restricted, and because they may have too small a home market for the efficient operation of optimum-sized plants. In general, it seems that the import-content is inversely associated with population size in countries in a similar stage of economic development.

Import restrictions (protective tariffs, quotas, discrimination, exchange regulations, etc.) are a major method of influencing the import-content of supplies. Though statistical difficulties of measuring the degree of restriction applied prevent any precise conclusions being drawn, it appears from a relatively crude analysis for a sample of countries that the height of the duty on imports of manufactures is not related to the import-content of supplies. Country differences in tariff heights tend to reflect differences in costs of manufacturing production, so that where production is high-cost, tariffs tend to be relatively high also.

Countries which have relatively large export sectors will tend to rely more heavily on imports for their supplies of manufactures than will countries with relatively small export sectors. Statistical analysis for a recent year confirms this.

The influence of the fourth factor—the level of industrialization—is obscured by the effect of the other three on the import-content of supplies. To find the net effect of industrialization, multiple regression equations were calculated, based both on time series and on cross-country data for a recent year.

The results of the analysis can be summarized as follows. Industrialization leads to increased real income per head (unless abnormal circumstances are at work), and this in turn raises demand for manufactures per head (which, in the semi-industrial countries, rises by $1\frac{1}{2}$–2 times the rate of growth in real income per head). With the progress of industrialization, the import-content falls until —as already mentioned—a fairly mature level of industrialization has been reached. The rate at which the import-content has fallen in the industrial and semi-industrial countries in the past is in the region of 40–60 per cent of the rate of increase in manufacturing production per head. For example, if the import-content was 40 per cent, an increase of 100 per cent in manufacturing production per head would tend to be associated with a reduction in the import-content to about 15–25 per cent; had the initial import-content been say, 33 per cent, the final proportion would have been 13–20 per cent. Thus, in the semi-industrial countries, a 10 per cent increase in real income per head would be associated with an increase of some 17–20 per cent in consumption of manufactures per head. The corresponding rise in production of manufactures per head would, however, result in a fall in the import-content of supplies by some 10–15 per cent from its initial level, or considerably less than the percentage rise in per caput consumption. The implication is that there would be an increase of 5–10 per cent in the volume of imports of manufactures per head. These are, of course, average relationships based on past trends on the assumption that industrialization has no adverse repercussions on the capacity to import; they do not necessarily show how imports would move in the future with continued industrial growth.

The estimates of consumption levels, combined with the long-term series for foreign trade, enable the movement in imports of manufactures to be divided into two parts. The first, a positive factor, is the effect of the growth in demand for manufactured goods on the level of imports. The second, normally negative, results from the substitution of home production for imports. Over the period from 1913 to 1959, the import-substitution effect was considerably greater in the semi-industrial countries than in the industrial ones, while the expansion in demand was less. For both reasons, therefore, the increase in the volume of imports was much larger for the industrial countries. For the period 1950–59, about one-half of the increase in the imports of manufactures into the industrial countries can be attributed to the expansion in demand, the other half resulting from the rise in the import-content (which was artificially depressed by trade and currency restrictions in the early 1950's) to more 'normal' levels. This suggests that in the 1960's, if we can assume that 'normality' had been approximately restored by 1959, this sector of trade might grow at only about half the rate of the past decade, in relation to the rate of growth in real income in the industrial countries. However, a new factor which might result in a more rapid growth in trade is the move towards closer economic integration on a regional basis, at any rate in Western Europe; the possible impact of such integration on the import-content of supplies is discussed further in Chapter 9.

Trends in the commodity-pattern of trade in manufactures

Changes in the commodity-pattern of world trade in manufactures since the beginning of the century have been drastic and unambiguous. The outstanding trends, in volume terms, have been a relatively rapid growth in trade in machinery, transport equipment and chemicals, and a relatively rapid decline in textiles and clothing. Of the remaining groups, metals and miscellaneous manufactures have shown little change relatively to the total, but 'other metal goods' have been declining.

These results, which are discussed in Chapter 7, are generally similar to those arrived at in several previous studies based on current values of exports. The main difference is that on the current value basis, chemicals show no significant upward trend as a percentage of the total, while there is only a moderate uptrend for transport equipment. This method of analysis thus gives a distorted picture of the underlying trends in 'real' (or volume) terms. The difference arises because unit values of exports of chemicals and transport equipment have fallen appreciably in relation to those of other manufactured goods over the past 30 years or more.

Fundamentally, this is because technological progress tends to be faster in expanding industries than in stagnant or contracting ones, with consequent effects on relative unit costs, and on relative export prices. In the transport equipment industry, for example, the mass production of passenger cars and trucks in the 1920's resulted in a substantial decline (some 20 per cent) in export unit values between 1913 and 1929, whereas there was a rise of about 45 per cent in the unit value of exports of all other manufactures. The rapid expansion in production, allied with technological progress, in the chemical industry since the early 1950's is another example of the same process; in this period, there were price reductions for several important chemical products.

Though the groups which are relatively stagnant or contracting tend not to be involved in new technical developments to the same extent as the expanding groups, even in textiles there have been notable technical advances since the war in the development of synthetic fibres and improved finishes for cotton fabrics.

These general trends in the world trading pattern are reflected in the patterns of imports into the main groups of countries. The shift in pattern towards the expanding groups has, however, been much sharper in the semi-industrial countries than in the industrial or non-industrial groups in the period since 1950. This is due essentially to the beginnings of industrialization in India and Pakistan and to industrial growth in Latin America, and to restrictions in these, and other, semi-industrial countries on imports of 'less essential' goods such as textiles. The pattern of import duties imposed by industrializing countries generally reinforces this trend; duties tend to be relatively low on capital equipment and chemicals and relatively high on consumer manufactures.

The earlier analysis has shown that for manufactured goods both the pattern of demand and the pattern of output are systematically related to the process of economic growth. The implication is that the pattern of imports of manufactures is also related to growth. This has been demonstrated directly by a series of regressions of import volume per head on real income per head for the industrial and semi-industrial countries. The regression for each commodity group related to the 'selected years' from 1899 to 1955. The results for the industrial countries show that per caput imports of transport equipment (other than passenger road vehicles) rose, on average, some $2\frac{1}{2}$ times as fast as per caput real income; passenger road vehicles rose 1.8 times as fast, while machinery and chemicals rose $1\frac{1}{2}$ times as fast. At the other extreme, there was an absolute decline in imports of textiles and clothing per head, but no significant statistical relationship with real income changes appeared. In the semi-industrial countries, the pattern of change is much more diversified, though very generally the pattern is similar to that for the industrial countries; as was to be expected, the decline in textiles has been much greater in relation to economic growth in the semi-industrial than in the industrial countries.

The general commodity pattern of change in supplies of manufactures which is associated with economic growth is not, however, causally related to the tendency of the import-content of supplies to fall in the earlier stages of industrialization. This is because there is no necessary or unique relationship between a country's import dependence on any one commodity and the rate at which supplies of that commodity increase as the economy expands.

Competition and import-substitution in the world market

Trends in world trade in manufactures are examined in Chapter 8 from the point of view of the several exporting countries. The outstanding change since 1899 has been the secular decline in Britain's share of the total, from one-third before the first World War to about one-sixth by 1959. The principal gainer has been the United States (one-eighth to one-fifth of the total). Both the United States and Britain have lost ground since 1950 to Germany and Japan. Of the other main industrial exporters, France suffered a severe relative decline in the inter-war period, but her share of the total recovered after the devaluations of the franc in 1958 and 1959.

These changes in relative market shares reflect, in the main, changes in the competitive positions of the different exporting countries; the influence of variations in the area and commodity patterns of trade in manufactures has generally been small. Price is an essential element in competitive power, but there are considerable difficulties in measuring changes in the relative export prices of different countries. The approach used here—the limitations of which are discussed in some detail in Chapter 8—is to construct for each main industrial country new series of unit values of exports from competing countries, based on a standardized commodity group weighting. The results of some regression calculations showed that relative shares of the world market were negatively associated with movements in relative export prices. These results do not imply, however, that price is necessarily the predominant component of competitive power. The non-price factors—technological progress, quality and design, delivery delays, credit terms, sales push, and so on—also play a major part in the competitive process.

A general hypothesis advanced is that long-term shifts in relative competitive power in the widest sense may reflect changes in the rates of economic growth of the various industrial countries. Since exports are also an important part of total demand for final output in most industrial countries, a change in competitive power—which implies a change in export sales—will itself affect the rate of growth in industrial production. Thus, exports interact in a dynamic way with the growth of the whole economy.

There has, in fact, been a remarkably close relationship over the past 60 years in the relative growth rates of the main industrial countries and their shares of the world export market in manufactures. This may have arisen, in part, because faster growth tends to be associated with higher productivity and lower costs, and with an increased range and variety of new products; the more slowly growing country will thus tend to become less competitive. At the same time, the movement in exports will tend to reinforce the underlying trend in the economy. Thus, the relative stagnation in British exports in the inter-war period had a major retarding effect on the growth of the British economy, while the retardation in growth itself reacted adversely on Britain's competitive position. The connection between economic growth and competitive power can also work through changes in government policy. Countries which are growing relatively fast will tend to have a relatively fast growth in imports and government policy may have to be adjusted—by a currency devaluation, in the last resort—to achieve the required increase in exports to finance this growth.

Changes in the export performance of the different industrial countries have also been influenced by import-substitution arising from industrial growth in the importing countries. The burden of import-substitution, in this sense, has fallen very unequally on the different industrial countries. In the semi-industrial countries, Britain has been easily the main loser. Before the second World War, the development of the Indian textile industry, with the consequent sharp contraction of a main market for British cotton textiles, had been the major influence. Since 1950, the industrial expansion of Australia has been the biggest single element in the import-substitution against British exports.

The relatively severe loss through import-substitution suffered by Britain in the semi-industrial markets may well have had an important depressive influence on her competitive position generally. If, as argued earlier, a slowly growing economy is likely to be less competitive than fast growing ones, part of the loss in Britain's competitive share of world exports may have been an indirect result of import-substitution. The United States, by contrast, though also suffering a large import-substitution loss (mainly in Latin America), has improved its competitive position appreciably since the first World War. The major factor here has been the rapid expansion of the United States economy which, because exports are relatively very small (unlike the position in Britain), was not significantly retarded by the import-substitution overseas.

PROSPECTS AND POLICIES

What are the future prospects for trade in manufactures? Two main aspects considered in Chapter 15 are, first, the prospects for the total volume of such trade and, second, the commodity pattern which is likely to emerge.

Total volume of trade in manufactures

A quantitative assessment of probable trends in the volume of trade in manufactures can be made on the basis of some of the relationships found for the past, and of specific assumptions about the future growth of real income and of likely changes in the import-content of supplies. Assuming that the import-content in the industrial countries will continue to rise over the next decade, mainly as a result of economic integration in Western Europe, it is estimated that the imports of manufactures by the industrial countries—in effect, their intra-trade—in the period 1970–75 would be 100–103 per cent higher than in 1959, if real income per head in each country rose by 3 per cent per annum, compound, that is, by almost 50 per cent over the period as a whole. If the rate of growth continued to be slower in the United States (where the import-content is low) than in Western Europe, though the average remained at 3 per cent, the rise in imports of manufactures would be greater than this, possibly as high as 150 per cent above the 1959 level.

Estimates of imports by the primary-producing countries are even less definitely related to income trends. However, if real incomes per head rise by 2 per cent per annum, compound, that is, by about 30 per cent over the whole period, the volume of imports of manufactures in 1970–75 might be in the range of 125–175 per cent of the 1959 level for the semi-industrial countries and perhaps 150–190 per cent for the non-industrial ones.

On the basis of the various assumptions made, the total volume of world trade in 1970–75 might average about double the 1959 level; this compares with an assumed increase of about 70 per cent in total real income of the industrial countries. The greater part of the expansion in trade is likely still to be in the intra-trade of the industrial countries.

Even if the rate of growth in real income per head in the primary-producing countries is only 2 per cent per annum, compared with the 3 per cent assumed for the industrial countries, they will face a major problem in finding adequate foreign exchange to pay for the imports of capital goods and other manufactures they will require. Their exports of primary produce (other than oil) to the industrial areas are unlikely to rise more than two-thirds as fast as the rise in the real national income of the industrial countries in total. On this basis—which is probably an optimistic one—a rate of growth of 2 per cent per annum would require the net capital inflow into the primary-producing areas to be almost doubled from the level of some $7 billion a year in the late 1950's to about $13 billion in the period 1970–75. For the rate of growth of real income per head to be increased to 3 per cent a year, the net capital inflow in 1970–75 would then have to be in the region of $18 billion.

Commodity patterns

Past trends in the commodity pattern of trade in manufactures can be projected into the future in various different ways. Alternative methods used in Chapter 15 show broadly similar results, though with one important exception— textiles. For this group, a mechanical projection of past trends would show the extinction of all trade by 1975. But it is more plausible to assume that trade in textiles will continue to be of some importance; indeed, the textile trade among the industrial countries might well expand, rather than decline.

Generally, however, past trends in commodity patterns may be expected to continue. By 1970–75, machinery and transport equipment might represent 45–50 per cent of total trade in manufactures (39 per cent in 1959), while for chemicals the proportion might rise to 16–18 per cent from 13 per cent in 1959. The various estimates depend to some extent, however, on the pattern of economic growth in the various main importing regions. A faster rate of growth in the United States than in the other industrial countries, for example, would tend to reduce the relative importance of capital goods and chemicals in world trade. A higher rate of growth in the small, compared with the large, industrial countries would accentuate the present general trends in the commodity pattern of trade in manufactures.

Policies in the industrial countries

There are three fields in which policy changes by the industrial countries would benefit the balance of payments of the primary-producing countries and so make possible an increase in their rate of economic growth.

The first line of action would be to introduce, or reinforce, policies designed to speed up growth in the industrial countries themselves. An increase in the average annual rate of growth in the industrial countries from, say, 4 to 5 per cent per head per annum would probably lead to a rise of some $3 billion (at 1959 prices) in the total export earnings of the primary-producing countries by the early 1970's. This should be sufficient to meet about half the latter's payments gap so long as the assumed rate of growth in their real incomes per head does not exceed 2 per cent per annum. This is a purely arithmetical calculation, which ignores the difficulties which would be caused by a continuing widening of the income gap between the industrial and primary-producing areas.

A second approach would be the reduction in government restrictions on imports from the primary-producing countries. In 1958, about 9–10 per cent of consumption of food and feedingstuffs in North America and Western Europe was imported. If tariffs and quotas on imports were relaxed to allow the import proportion to rise to 16–17 per cent, this would have added another $5–6 billion in 1959 to the export earnings of the primary-producing countries, while by 1970–75 the additional income would be about $8 billion. A further gain—though a relatively small one as yet—would result from relaxing restrictions on trade in manufactured products.

Finally, the flow of capital to the less-developed areas might be increased. In 1959, the net capital outflow from the industrial countries represented little more than 1 per cent of their total national product. An increase by a further ½ per cent would imply an addition by 1970–75 of $6 billion (at 1959 prices) to the capital outflow that can otherwise be assumed. However, interest payments on the mounting total of capital investments may well grow so large as to threaten the external viability of the developing countries. Some concerted effort, possibly of an international character, therefore seems required to minimize the future burden of interest charges on the less-developed countries.

Of these various measures, the relaxation of trade restrictions on imports from primary-producing countries appears to be the most immediately practicable. Indeed, in the context of world economic growth, such relaxation seems a more important objective than economic integration among the industrial countries themselves. However, in the longer term, even complete freedom of trade would need to be supplemented by industrial development in many of the primary-producing countries for them to ensure the achievement of a fast rate of economic growth.

CHAPTER 1

INDUSTRIAL GROWTH, PRODUCTIVITY AND REAL INCOME

1. THE GROWTH OF MANUFACTURING INDUSTRY

The first half of the present century witnessed the spread of the modern industrial system from the older industrial areas of Western Europe and the United States to an increasing number of the traditional primary-producing countries. The growth of factory industry in the primary-producing areas has been mainly confined to countries in which the market economy predominates, and which are dependent, to a greater or lesser extent, on foreign capital investments. However, even in countries with large subsistence sectors, such as many African and South-East Asian countries, there has been a substantial increase in the processing of local materials. This spread of factory production was, of course, most uneven; there was a rapid growth in industrial production in some countries and virtually none at all in others.

Nevertheless, several distinct spurts in the rate of industrialization of the primary-producing areas were generally noticeable over the past half-century. The first was generated, during the first World War, by the shortage of supplies of manufactured goods of all kinds available to the non-industrial countries. Many of these countries were forced to start up local manufacturing plants, a good proportion of which continued to flourish after the war behind tariff walls, or as the result of other forms of government support[1].

The next 'round' of industrialization followed closely on the world economic crisis of 1930–31. Two of the main features of the crisis were particularly disadvantageous to the primary-producing countries: there was a drastic deterioration in their terms of trade while, at the same time, their main customers—the industrial countries—set up a complex system of trade and currency restrictions. The result was that the majority of primary-producing countries found themselves in serious balance-of-payments difficulties, and many of them adopted a policy of promoting secondary industry development at home, with tariff protection, in order to safeguard their standard of living, and to keep unemployment down.

A third spurt in the industrialization process can be traced during the second World War, for much the same reasons as those operating in the first World War. Again, the pace of development was very uneven, some countries

---

[1] In its *Survey of Overseas Markets* (H.M.S.O., 1925, p. 9) the Committee on Industry and Trade (the 'Balfour Committee') expressed the opinion that 'the widespread development of home manufactures to meet needs formerly supplied by imported goods is by general consent one of the outstanding features of the post-war economic situation, and this is perhaps the most important permanent factor tending either to limit the volume or to modify the character of British export trade'.

achieving considerable increases in industrial output, while others expanded only to a small extent.   In the six years 1939 to 1945, manufacturing production was more than doubled in Southern Rhodesia, and rose by two-fifths in Mexico and the Union of South Africa, by almost one-third in Brazil, one-quarter in Argentina, by one-sixth in Chile and New Zealand and by one-seventh in India and Turkey.

In the early post-war period, moreover, there were two additional forces making for an intensification of the industrialization process in the primary-producing areas, the first of a transient nature, but the second of permanent importance.   The transient factor was the possession by many underdeveloped countries at the end of the war of substantial amounts of accumulated reserves of foreign currency, with which development plans could be financed.   In most cases, these accumulated foreign currency reserves were largely exhausted by 1950.   This was only partly due to an increase in the volume of purchases of manufactured goods abroad; in part, it was due also to the considerable rise in the prices of manufactured goods after 1947.   Several primary-producing countries had a second 'round' of windfall accumulation of foreign exchange during and immediately after the Korean War, when commodity prices soared to new heights; but, once again, the new-found prosperity was short-lived.

The more permanent feature in the situation has been the realization by a large number of underdeveloped countries that industrialization and economic progress can be speeded by conscious planning.   Planners, like other mortals, can and do make mistakes; but there is little doubt that, in a number of countries since the end of the war, government policy has been more effectively directed than previously towards the creation of the pre-requisites for economic growth. One result has been a general increase in the pace of industrialization in the underdeveloped countries of the world.

Manufacturing production in the less-developed continents is still, however, only a small fraction of that in the economically advanced areas.   In 1937, the latter (North America, Western Europe and Oceania) produced about nine times the manufacturing output of the former (Latin America, Asia and Africa), though by 1959 the ratio had been reduced to seven to one (see Table 1.1). Of the increase of some $165 billion at 1955 prices[1] in the net value of manufacturing production in the world (excluding the Soviet countries) between these two years, about £140 billion, or nearly nine-tenths, was produced in the economically advanced continents.

The major part of the expansion in manufacturing production in the more developed areas between 1937 and 1950 occurred in North America.   Over this period, the net value of manufacturing production in the United States

---

[1]Throughout this book, changes in the volume of production and trade are usually expressed in terms of value at constant (1955) prices.   For a discussion of methods, see Appendices A, B and E.

Table 1.1. *World production of manufactures by continent,[a] 1937–59*

Net values, in $ billion at 1955 prices[b]

	1937	1950	1955	1957	1959	Change from		
						1937 to 1950	1950 to 1955	1955 to 1959
North America	50.5	97.8	121.9	126.7	133.2	+ 47.3	+ 24.1	+ 11.3
Western Europe	50.2	62.6	88.2	97.0	105.8	+ 12.4	+ 25.6	+ 17.6
Oceania	1.8	3.1	4.0	4.4	5.2	+ 1.3	+ 0.9	+ 1.2
Sub-total	103	164	214	228	244	+ 61	+ 51	+ 30
Latin America[c]	4.2	8.1	10.5	11.7	13.9	+ 3.9	+ 2.4	+ 3.4
Asia	6.9	6.3	11.3	15.2	18.6	− 0.6	+ 5.0	+ 7.3
of which Japan	*2.8*	*1.7*	*4.0*	*5.8*	*7.4*	*− 1.1*	*+ 2.3*	*+ 3.4*
Africa	0.5	1.6	2.3	2.5	2.8	+ 1.1	+ 0.7	+ 0.5
Sub-total	12	16	24	29	35	+ 4	+ 8	+ 11
TOTAL	115	180	238	257	279	+ 65	+ 58	+ 41

Sources: Table E.3; *Patterns of Industrial Growth, 1938–1958*, United Nations, New York, 1960; *Monthly Bulletin of Statistics*, United Nations, New York.

[a]Excluding the Soviet countries.
[b]See Appendix E for discussion of the concept of 'net value' of manufacturing production.
[c]Including the Caribbean.

Table 1.2. *Annual rates of growth in manufacturing production, 1937–57*

Percentage, compound

	1937–50	1950–55	1955–57	1937–57
North America	5.2	4.5	1.9	4.7
Western Europe	1.7	7.1	4.9	3.3
Oceania	4.3	5.2	4.9	4.6
Latin America	5.2	5.3	5.6	5.3
Asia	−0.6	12.4	16.0	4.1
Total, excluding Soviet countries	3.6	5.7	3.9	4.2
U.S.S.R.	7.3	13.0	10.5	9.0
Eastern Europe	3.0	12.2		6.2
China	0.9	20.8		7.5
Total, Soviet countries[a]	5.0	13.1		7.8

Sources: Table 1.1 and *World Economic Survey, 1958*, United Nations, New York, 1959.

[a]The indices for Soviet countries relate to industrial production as a whole. They are based on official statistics of gross output, and are therefore known to have an upward bias.

rose by some $45 billion (90 per cent), at 1955 prices[1], representing nearly three-quarters of the total increase in the three economically advanced continents. During the 1950's, however, the larger part of the expansion took place in Western Europe. Nonetheless, by the end of the decade, North American manufacturing production was something like one-quarter greater than the Western European total, whereas in 1937 these two continents had produced much the same output of manufactured goods[2].

In the less-developed continents, considerable progress has been made since before the war in Latin America and in many countries elsewhere. Manufacturing production in Latin America almost doubled from 1937 to 1950, and rose by a further 70 per cent from 1950 to 1959. In Asia (excluding Japan), production in 1950 was only marginally above the pre-war level, but from 1950 to 1959 it rose by about one and a half times. Indeed, over this last decade, the rise in manufacturing output in Asian countries (excluding Japan) accounted for about half the total expansion in the less-developed areas.

Rates of industrial growth in the Soviet countries have generally been considerably greater than in the rest of the world (Table 1.2). Comparably high growth rates have, however, also been achieved since 1950 in countries like West Germany and Japan, where output in the early post-war period had yet not recovered from wartime dislocations.

2. INDUSTRIAL GROWTH AND PRODUCTIVITY

The industrialization process does not mean merely that production of manufactured goods increases; its importance lies particularly in the general association which appears to exist between industrialization and productivity. If industrialization does, in fact, lead to an overall increase in labour productivity in the economy, real incomes will rise and this will affect both the volume of demand, including demand for imported goods, and the commodity pattern of demand, which again is likely to affect imports.

There may, of course, be circumstances in which industrialization would not lead to a rise in the overall productivity of resources used in a given economy. In conditions of full employment, a diversion of resources to manufacturing industry from other activities will result in a higher total product only if the marginal productivity of the diverted resources is greater in manufacture than in their former employment. In a primary-producing country, dependent on exports for a substantial part of total income, real income may in some circumstances be lower if resources are diverted to manufacturing than it would be if the resources were used to increase income from agricultural exports and

[1]See Table E.3 for the detailed country estimates.

[2]These and similar comparisons made in this chapter depend to a considerable extent on the rate of exchange used to convert national currencies into United States dollars. All the comparisons of manufacturing production in this book are based on estimates of purchasing-power parity rates in 1955: see Appendix F for details.

so pay for additional imports of manufactures[1]. However, there is frequently a limit to the extent to which export income can be increased by producing more agricultural goods for export markets, because such exports generally face an inelastic world demand, so that the price falls more than in proportion to the rise in quantity.

Similarly, if there is a surplus of labour in agriculture, it might be more profitable in a number of cases to re-settle the surplus population on reclaimed land, or land otherwise made available for cultivation, rather than to attempt to absorb them in manufacturing industry. But in many underdeveloped countries there is a shortage of cultivable land, and economic growth inevitably involves a process of industrialization.

Indeed, for countries which do possess the pre-requisites for industrial growth, in the form of natural resources and labour potential, there appears to be a general positive association between the degree of industrialization attained and the overall output per head of the occupied population. This does not necessarily imply that the greater the degree of industrialization attained, the higher the productivity of all resources used, including land and capital as well as labour. If industrialization is based on a diversion of capital from agriculture to manufacture, the productivity of land, but not of labour, is likely to fall. If, however, industrialization is associated with a general increase in the supply of capital—which is likely to be the more usual case—the productivity of both labour and land is likely to rise. If economies of scale accrue as industry grows, or if the developing country is more suited, because of its natural resources, to manufacturing than to agriculture, then industrialization will also be accompanied by an increase in the productivity of capital.

Output of physical commodities per head in the economy can rise with the progress of industrialization, for several reasons. The first is that labour productivity tends to be higher than in primary production, so that the average rises merely because the relative size of the labour force in the secondary sector increases[2]. The second factor operating—as is shown later—is that with the increasing industrialization of an economy, labour productivity in manufacturing itself tends to rise and, in an underdeveloped economy, tends to rise faster than productivity in agriculture[3]. Finally, the introduction of new techniques, and the development of new skills and managerial ability, which accrue with industrialization, will tend to spread over into other sectors, including primary production, and so stimulate efficiency there also. This last

[1]See P. T. Bauer and B. S. Yamey, *The Economics of Underdeveloped Countries*, Cambridge University Press, 1957, pp. 237 ff. for a discussion of the pitfalls in the crude argument that industrialization must necessarily lead to higher real income.

[2]Tertiary production is not considered here, since this book is concerned essentially with production and trade in physical commodities.

[3]In economically advanced countries, productivity per head in agriculture may rise faster than in manufacturing. This appears to have been the case in both Canada and the United States since the war.

factor is more qualitative in nature than the first two, and so is much more difficult to isolate and measure. There is, however, some statistical evidence on the operation of the first two factors.

Relative labour productivity in manufacture and agriculture

A word of caution is first necessary about statistics of the relative values of output of manufactured and agricultural products.   In the majority of industrial countries, agricultural production is protected against competition from imports to a far greater extent than are manufactured goods. This discrimination results in a higher net value of production by farms than the same physical output would have had in conditions of free competition.   The consequence is that the apparent productivity of labour in agriculture, relatively to that in manufacture, is inflated in the industrial countries generally.   The reverse tends to be true in primary-producing countries; there, secondary industry tends to profit by protection and the statistics thus tend to overstate the relative productivity advantage of manufacturing compared with agriculture.   Differences in the net value of production per head in manufacturing and in agriculture thus reflect differences in factor incomes as well as differences in productivity.

Another difficulty which also may affect comparisons of this kind is that in many underdeveloped countries the subsistence sector of the economy is relatively large and consists essentially of agricultural production for local consumption by the producer and his family.   Even apart from the problem of the valuation of such subsistence production, there is also the difficulty of making reasonably accurate estimates of the quantities involved.   It seems likely that the official estimates of the net value of agricultural production in a number of underdeveloped countries underestimate the contribution of the subsistence sector, so that the ratio of manufacturing productivity to agricultural productivity is, to this extent, overstated[1].

A further statistical difficulty relates to the recorded number of persons engaged in the different occupational groups.   The difficulty is most acute for agriculture, in which part-time work, particularly by members of the farmer's family, is widespread in most countries.   In underdeveloped countries, moreover, the distinction between occupations is sometimes blurred, for example when farmers also engage in trading[2].

---

[1]The *rate* of growth of agricultural production in countries with a subsistence sector may, however, be overestimated, since official methods of estimating output are likely to be improved as agriculture is progressively drawn into the market economy.   Equally, the rate of growth in manufacturing may be overestimated in countries where handicraft output is declining (as a result of the growth in factory production) and is not included in the official production statistics.

[2]See Bauer and Yamey, *The Economics of Underdeveloped Countries*, ch. III for a detailed discussion of this and similar difficulties in international comparisons of income per head.

Nonetheless, the difference in the net value of output per head in manufacture, compared with agriculture, is so wide in a majority of countries for which the relevant statistics are available, that it seems reasonable to conclude that, in spite of the various qualifications that have to be made, the difference is generally a real one and does not arise from a statistical illusion. Of some forty countries for which relative net values of output per head in manufacture and agriculture can be calculated for 1950[1], all but five showed higher figures for manufacture; in almost half the countries the figure for manufacture was more than double that for agriculture (see Table 1.3). In seven countries the ratio exceeded 3.0; in some of these countries, the relatively low productivity in agriculture may be, in part, a result of the statistical underestimation of output to which reference was made earlier.

At the other extreme come Australia and New Zealand, where wool farming is a highly productive industry in relation to numbers of persons employed[2], and the United Kingdom, where farming is both highly protected and highly mechanized. If, however, the subsidy element is deducted from the net income of British agriculture, the net value per head is lower than in manufacture[3]. Also in this group showing a relatively highly productive agriculture are the two Andean countries of Ecuador and Peru; their presence here is due essentially to the fact that a substantial part of their total output of manufactured goods comes from handicraft and homecraft workers, whose productivity is far below the average factory level[4]. The movement out of handicrafts and into factory production is a most important factor in increasing productivity in the manufacturing sector in the early stages of industrialization.

It is not perhaps surprising that real output per head generally tends to be higher in manufacturing than in agriculture. Even in Canada, which has a large-scale and efficient farming industry, the value added per gainfully employed person in agriculture is little more than one-half of that in manufacturing[5]. One major reason for the difference is that more capital is

---

[1]This was about the last year for which the occupational distribution of the population was available for most countries at the time of writing.

[2]The average net value of output per head in agriculture and allied occupations in the early 1950's was about one-half higher, in Australia, and two-thirds higher, in New Zealand, than in manufacturing.

[3]In 1954, the gross product of agriculture, forestry and fishing was £766 million, and net subsidies received amounted to £169 million. (See *Input-Output Tables for the United Kingdom, 1954*, Studies in Official Statistics, no. 8, H.M.S.O., London, 1961.) If subsidies are deducted, the gross product falls to £597 million, or £514 per person employed, compared with £700 per person employed in manufacturing industries in that year. This comparison is, however, unrealistic because, without subsidies, agricultural employment and production on marginal land would be reduced, and gross product per head would be higher than £514, though probably it would remain below the average for manufacturing.

[4]See *Economic Bulletin for Latin America*, Vol. 2, No. 1, February 1957, United Nations, Santiago, for a discussion of the special position of the Andean countries in this respect.

[5]This proportion relates to 1950, but even in 1900 the relative output per occupied person in agriculture was only half that in manufacturing (see O. J. Firestone, 'Canada's Economic

employed per head in manufacturing than in most, if not all, agricultural activities. In Canada, for example, the value of machinery available per head

Table 1.3. *Relative labour productivity in manufacture and agriculture and the proportion of the occupied population engaged in agriculture, 1950*

Ratio of labour productivity in manufacture to that in agriculture	Percentage of occupied population in agriculture				
	Under 20	20–39	40–59	69–79	80 and over
Under 1.0	Australia*a* New Zealand*b* United Kingdom		Ecuador	Peru	
1.0–1.9	Austria Belgium Canada Netherlands	Argentina Chile Denmark Ireland Puerto Rico Sweden	Costa Rica Greece Paraguay Spain	Egypt Honduras Pakistan	
2.0–2.9	United States	France Norway West Germany	Colombia Finland Italy Portugal	Brazil India	
3.0 and over		Luxembourg	Japan Mexico Union of South Africa Venezuela	Philippines	Turkey

Sources: Statistical Yearbook, 1957, United Nations, New York, 1957, and *Yearbook of National Accounts Statistics, 1957,* United Nations, New York, 1958.

[a]1954.
[b]1951–52.

in manufacturing was about 3.7 times the corresponding figure in agriculture in 1900 though the ratio had been reduced to 1.4 by 1950[1]; although the higher amount of depreciation of capital assets in manufacturing than in agriculture must also be allowed for, the difference in capital available per head in the two sectors is still very large. Another important element is that economies of scale are more likely to be greater in manufacturing, though there may be

Development, 1867-1953', in *Income and Wealth, Series VII,* International Association for Research in Income and Wealth, London, 1958).

[1]Firestone, 'Canada's Economic Development, 1867-1953', Tables 71 and 82 and footnote, p. 231. The values are 'book values', not replacement costs.

particular exceptions to the general rule. This may allow manufacturing production to grow more rapidly than agricultural output, and may allow manufacturing productivity to be greater where there is a large manufacturing sector than where there is a small one.

The evidence of Table 1.3 appears also to indicate that the productivity differential in favour of manufacturing tends to be greater in the less-developed countries (taking these as countries with a high proportion of the occupied population in agriculture) than in the more advanced countries ; and that this differential tends to decline as an economy becomes more industrialized. This relationship is, however, partly the result of the statistical bias mentioned earlier, whereby relative incomes of agriculture are apparently increased in industrial countries, and reduced in primary-producing countries.

Productivity growth in manufacturing

The second factor tending to increase output per head in the economy as industrialization progresses is that as the scale of manufacturing production rises, productivity in manufacturing tends to rise also. Increasing the volume of production will often generate economies of scale, both within the average plant and in manufacturing industry generally; the growth in the manufacturing complex also normally involves a commensurate increase in capital assets used per head; while the development of new processes implies also the development of skills in production and management.

The output of manufactured goods per head of total population—which is a major determinant of the standard of living—can be increased in any of three ways. First, by increasing the effective participation of the population in the labour force; second, by increasing the proportion of the total labour force employed in manufacturing; and, third, by increasing the productivity of those employed in manufacturing. In many underdeveloped countries, the social and economic transformation involved in industrialization will increase the work participation rate; but there are clearly limits to the extent to which a rising standard of living can depend on this factor. In the long run, the two other factors are likely to be the major elements in increasing output of manufactures per head.

Some insight into the underlying relationships involved can be gained by comparing the relative productivity of labour in different countries at one time with their respective ratios of manufacturing to total employment. Estimates of the net value of manufacturing production per head have been made for 25 countries at different stages of economic development in 1950, or an adjacent year, and are shown in Table 1.4. The range between production per head in the most advanced countries and that in the least advanced is very great. Taking the figures for net value of production per head of persons employed in manufacturing, which can be taken as a crude indicator of relative labour productivity, the five countries in the bottom group in Table 1.4 all had outputs per head of one-tenth or less of that in the United States[1]. The differences are even larger when the comparison is based on manufacturing output per head of the occupied or total population, the outputs per head of the five least-advanced countries being under 3–4 per cent of that in the United States. This greater discrepancy arises because in the less-developed areas a much smaller proportion of the population—both total and occupied—is engaged in manufacturing industry.

The difference in the proportion of the occupied population engaged in manufacturing between the most advanced and least advanced countries is much less, proportionately, than the difference in productivity levels. Thus, the simple average proportion of the occupied population in manufacturing in the five least advanced countries (7 per cent) is one-quarter of the United States level, compared with well under one-tenth for manufacturing productivity. This relatively crude test indicates that productivity is the more dynamic of the two factors in the growth in the availability of home-produced manufactures per head of the population as an economy industrializes. By contrast, the differences in the work-participation rates are relatively small, except in the very early stages of industrialization.

The general relationship between manufacturing productivity and the proportion of the occupied population engaged in manufacturing can more readily be seen from Fig. 1.1. The relationship shown is not, however, an easy one to describe in precise terms; the scatter of positions could, in fact, be described statistically by any one of a number of different curves. There is, moreover, one qualification to be borne in mind: as an economy becomes progressively more industrialized, the proportion of the occupied population engaged in manufacturing does not rise indefinitely—there is an effective limit, which may already have been reached by a number of countries. This limit comes into operation for two reasons. First, as the economy grows and incomes rise, the demand for workers in 'service' occupations, such as teachers, doctors, typists, government officials, etc., increases as fast as, or faster than, the demand for manufactured goods[2]. Secondly, the productivity increase in manufacturing tends to outstrip by far the corresponding productivity increase in the distribution of goods from factory to consumer; thus, workers tend to be absorbed in distribution to match the increased flow of industrial products[3]. If the demand

---

[1]Such comparisons inevitably contain an appreciable margin of error, but are useful as illustrative of the orders of magnitude involved. Though the net values have been based on estimated purchasing power parity rates, they have not been corrected for differences in the industry structures of the different countries. For further discussion of the statistical basis of the estimates, see Appendix E.

[2]See C. Clark, *The Conditions of Economic Progress*, 3rd ed., London, 1957, pp. 492–5, for a detailed discussion of this phenomenon.

[3]See H. Barger, *Distribution's Place in the American Economy since 1869*, Princeton, 1955 (especially ch. 3).

Table 1.4.   *Occupied population engaged in manufacturing and net value of manufacturing production per head*, 1950

	Total popula-tion	Proportion of occupied population		Net value of manu-facturing pro-duction	Net value of manufacturing production per head		
		In total popula-tion	Engaged in manu-facturing		Engaged in manu-facturing	Occupied popula-tion	Total popula-tion
	(*millions*)	(*percentage*)		(*$ billion at 1955 prices*)	(*$ at 1955 prices*)		
United States	151.7	39	27	91.9	5730	1535	605
Canada	13.7	38ᵃ	26	5.85	4380	1120	425
Sweden	7.01	44	32	2.98	3050	965	425
United Kingdom	50.3	45ᵃ	37	19.1	2260	845	380
Belgium-Luxembourg	8.94	41ᵇ	37	3.18	2320	865	355
Denmark	4.27	48	26	1.34	2500	650	315
Australia	8.18	42ᶜ	27ᶜ	2.50	2740	725	305
New Zealand	1.91	38ᵃ	24ᵃ	0.52	3030	725	275
Norway	3.27	43	26	0.81	2240	575	245
West Germany	47.8	46	31	10.9	1610	500	230
France	41.7	47ᵈ	24ᵈ	8.67	1860	445	210
Netherlands	10.1	40ᵇ	24ᵇ	2.05	2120	510	205
Finland	4.01	49	21	0.58	1420	295	145
Argentina	17.2	41ᵇ	22ᵇ	2.46	1600	355	145
Italy	46.6	44ᵃ	22ᵃ	4.63	1030	230	100
Ireland	2.97	43ᵃ	15ᵃ	0.29	1570	235	100
Chile	6.07	34ᵉ	19	0.35	845	160	55
Mexico	25.8	32	12	1.36	1420	170	55
Brazil	52.0	33	13ᵍ	2.06	925ʰ	120	40
Colombia	11.3	32ᵃ	12	0.40	915	110	35
Turkey	20.9	58	6	0.43	590	35	20
Egypt	20.4	44ᵇ	8	0.30	460	35	15
Philippines	19.9	39ᶠ	6	0.18	400	25	9
India	358.3	28ᵃ	9	2.03	220	20	6
Pakistan	75.0	29ᵃ	6	0.13	90	6	2

Sources: Tables E.3, E.4 and E.7; *Statistical Yearbook, 1957*, Table 6, United Nations, New York; *Monthly Bulletin of Statistics*, United Nations, New York.

ᵃ1951.
ᵇ1947.
ᶜMean of 1947 and 1954 Census results.
ᵈMean of 1946 and 1954 Census results.
ᵉ1952.
ᶠ1948.
ᵍIncluding construction and electricity, gas, etc.
ʰUnderstated (see *g*).

for 'service' workers rises fast enough, and/or the rise in productivity in distribution is relatively slow, it is likely that, after a certain stage of economic development has been reached, the proportion of the occupied population in manufacturing will actually fall off. Thus, as countries approach their effective limit—which may differ from one country to another—this path to increasing output of manufactures per head becomes progressively obstructed and they have to rely increasingly on the productivity element to raise their real income (in terms of manufactured goods produced at home).

Typical paths of industrial growth

These considerations would lead one to expect either of two 'typical' paths of development to operate in the majority of industrializing countries. The first

Fig. 1.1. Relation between proportion of occupied population in manufacturing and manufacturing production per person, 1950

Semi-logarithmic scale

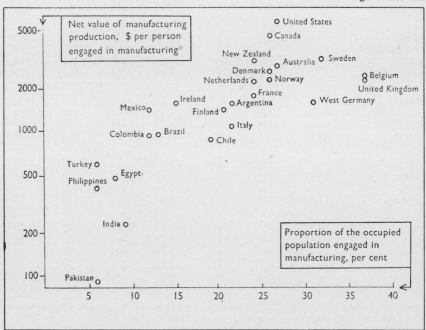

*Valued at 1955 prices.

would be a substantial increase in the relative size of the labour force in manufacturing in the early stages of industrialization, unaccompanied by any big increase in productivity; this might perhaps be the case if a large number of small manufacturing plants were set up, distributed over a wide area. Only at a much later stage of development would a cumulative increase in productivity be attained. This path of development is depicted by curve A in Fig. 1.2. The second 'typical' path is where a sharp rise in productivity can be achieved in the early phases of industrialization, as in curve B; this might happen if, for example, there is a substantial switch from handicraft to factory production, or if production can quickly become more capital-intensive and workers and managements can quickly increase their respective skills. At a fairly advanced stage of economic development, as already mentioned, the proportion of the occupied population engaged in manufacturing might fall off, as is indicated, for example, in curve C.

Fig. 1.2. Typical paths of development of manufacturing industry

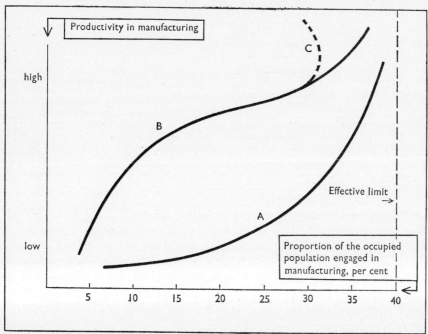

The actual paths of development of particular countries may not, of course, follow either of the 'typical' cases very closely. The lack of statistical data, moreover, prevents the calculation being done over a long period of years for more than a small number of countries. But for four countries with very different economic structures and rates of growth—Colombia, France, Japan and the United States—the evidence bears out the hypothesis that in general both paths of development mentioned above are followed at the same time (see Fig. 1.3).

The paths shown by these four countries represent empirical illustrations of

Fig. 1.3.   Development paths in four countries, 1870–1959

Semi-logarithmic scale

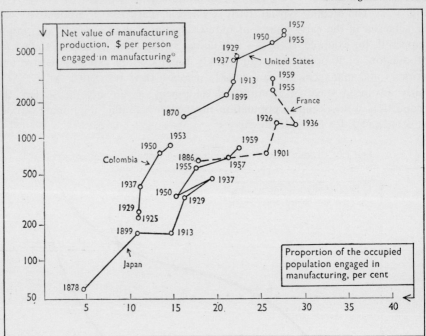

*Valued at 1955 prices.

possible patterns of development in particular countries in particular periods. They do not represent 'laws of growth' which every country is supposed to follow.   There is no reason, for example, why a country which had arrived at path C should not revert to path B for a period of years and then, once more, follow path C.   This seems to be, roughly speaking, what happened in the United States.   From 1899 to 1937, that country appeared to be virtually on path C, but was pushed back on to path B by the impetus of wartime production and full employment.   From 1955, the evidence—though scanty—indicates that the United States may now be back on path C, though at a higher level of productivity and of manufacturing employment in relation to the occupied population than in the period up to 1937.   The development in Colombia seems to be following path B, handicrafts being still of considerable importance in 1950[1].   Japan's development has been closer to A, while France since the late 1930's appears to have entered phase C.   Great Britain has not been included in Fig. 1.3 because the corresponding data cannot be carried back much earlier than 1850, by which time Britain already had a fairly well-developed manu-

[1] About 70 per cent of the manufacturing labour force in that year were handicraft workers.

facturing sector. Indeed, in 1851 the proportion of the occupied population in manufacturing was virtually the same as in 1951—almost 40 per cent—

Table 1.5.   *Ratio of manufacturing to agricultural net product and net value of manufacturing per head of population, 1955*

	Ratio of manufacturing to agricultural net product	Net value of manufacturing per head of population ($)		Ratio of manufacturing to agricultural net product	Net value of manufacturing per head of population ($)
United States	6.74	695	Chile	1.33	75
Sweden	3.20	465	Greece	0.57	70
United Kingdom	7.81	460	Mexico	1.00ᵃ	60
Belgium-Luxembourg	4.33	460	Brazil	0.72	50
Canada	2.96	440	Japan	1.05	45
West Germany	5.11	405	Colombia	0.42	45
Australia	1.20	350	Lebanon	0.78	35
Denmark	1.49	325	Turkey	0.30	30
New Zealand	0.98	325	Costa Rica	0.26	30
Norway	2.07	315	French Morocco	0.43	25
Netherlands	2.71	270	Peru	0.52	25
France	1.70	265	Ecuador	0.42	20
Austria	2.60	255	Philippines	0.32	15
Finland	1.28	205	Egypt	0.35	15
Israel	1.83	170	Belgian Congo	0.43	15
Italy	1.35	150	Federation of Rhodesia and Nyasaland	0.31	15
Argentina	1.32	145	Honduras	0.17	15
Ireland	0.70	115	Ceylon	0.11	10
Union of South Africa	1.49	115	Indonesia	0.20ᵃ	10
Spain	0.93	105	Thailand	0.28	10
Portugal	1.07	95	South Korea	0.20	8
Venezuela	1.43	95	India	0.30	7
Yugoslavia	1.33	85	Kenya	0.23	7
Puerto Rico	1.27	85	Pakistan	0.20	5
			Burma	0.26	5

Sources: Table E.4; *Yearbook of National Accounts Statistics, 1959*, United Nations, New York, 1960; *Patterns of Industrial Growth, 1938–1958*, United Nations, New York, 1960; *Economic Survey of Europe, 1956*, ch. VII, United Nations, Geneva 1957; *Secondary Industry Bulletins*, Commonwealth Bureau of Statistics, Canberra.

ᵃApproximate estimates.

Fig. 1.4.   Ratio of manufacturing to agricultural product and manufacturing
production per head of population, 1955

Double logarithmic scale

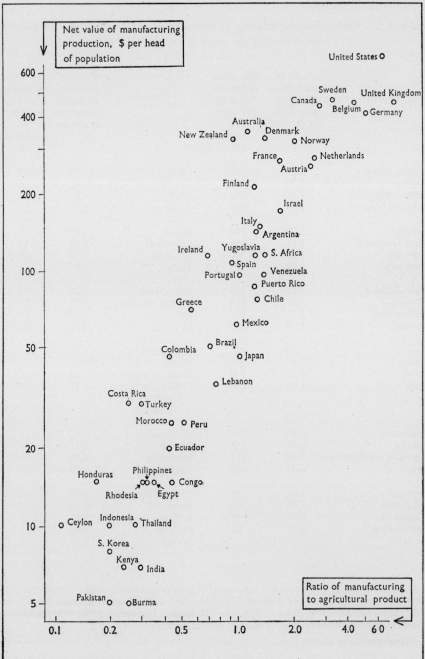

though there had been some decline in the intervening century[1]; the evidence thus indicates that Britain has been on path C for at least a century.

The value of output of manufactures per head of the population is a useful indicator of the stage of industrial development that has been reached by different countries. Fig. 1.4 and Table 1.5 show the position in 1955 for about fifty countries classified not only by manufacturing output per head, but also by the relative size of their manufacturing and agricultural products. The distribution is more or less continuous from Pakistan and Burma at the lower end to the United States at the other. Nonetheless, some broad divisions can be made between the 'highly industrialized' countries (say, those with over $250 per head in 1955), the 'moderately industrialized' (say, $50–$250 per head), and those having a low degree of industrialization (say, under $50 per head). Countries having a relatively large agricultural sector, such as Australia, New Zealand and Denmark, can be considered as in the same stage of industrialization, on this criterion, as countries like Austria and the Netherlands, where agricultural output is much smaller in relation to manufacturing production.

3. INDUSTRIALIZATION AND THE GROWTH OF REAL INCOME

The association between industrialization and economic growth so far discussed has been essentially in terms of the output of physical goods, manufactures and agricultural produce, though the argument would in principle cover mining, construction and other work resulting in the production or transformation of physical goods. Since physical goods form a large part of the total flow of real income, an increase in their production resulting from industrialization will also mean a rise in real income.

However, as already indicated, the 'services' element of real income can also be expected to increase with industrial growth. In particular, an expansion of transport services is an almost essential pre-requisite of growth in agriculture and manufacturing industry. The demand for many other services (education, health, etc.) also tends to rise with the growth in incomes; indeed, better health and education can also be regarded as essential pre-requisites of economic growth. Though there may be a decline in some services (e.g. domestic service) as an economy grows, the total contribution made by the service sector as a whole is likely to expand.

If we take as our measure of real income the gross domestic product[2] valued at 1955 prices, we find that the expansion in manufacturing output between

---

[1]See C. Clark, *The Conditions of Economic Progress*, 3rd ed., p. 514. Clark's figures include electricity and gas, which are excluded here.

[2]The gross domestic product differs from the gross national income by the amount of the net inflow of factor income from abroad. This difference is not, however, large enough to distort the very broad comparisons made here.

1937 and 1957 represented two-fifths of the expansion in the total product of Western Europe, and one-third of that of North America and of Oceania. For Asia, outside the Soviet countries, the proportion was one-quarter; for Japan alone it was as high as 45 per cent. Excluding Japan, manufacturing contributed about one-fifth of the rise in total output in Asian countries over the twenty years, the same proportion as for Latin America (Table 1.6).

Table 1.6. *Share of manufacturing in expansion of gross domestic product,* 1937–57

	1937–50	1950–55	1955–57	1937–57
CHANGE IN GROSS DOMESTIC PRODUCT	($ *billion at 1955 prices*)			
North America	+133	+73	+15	+221
Western Europe	+ 31	+55	+23	+109
Oceania	+ 6	+ 1	+ 1	+ 8
Latin America[a]	+ 20	+11	+ 6	+ 37
Asia[b]	+ 8	+16	+ 8	+ 32
SHARE OF MANUFACTURING IN EXPANSION OF GROSS DOMESTIC PRODUCT	(*percentage*)			
North America	36	33	30	34
Western Europe	40	47	38	43
Oceania	22	69	50	33
Latin America[a]	20	22	19	20
Asia[b]	− 6	31	52	26

Sources: Tables 1.1, E.1. and related data.

[a]Including the Caribbean.

[b]Approximate estimates, excluding Soviet countries.

These estimates relate, of course, only to the *direct* contribution of manufacturing to the national output. There may also be large *indirect* gains as, for example, when the growth of manufacturing affects the demand for—and output of—other sectors such as transport, construction and commercial and financial services. In some cases, agricultural or mining output may also be expanded as an indirect result of the expansion in manufacturing. This would happen if the expanded manufacturing industries require greater quantities of raw materials and fuels, or if real incomes rise and, consequently, the demand for locally-grown food rises also. The causality may, of course, work in the other direction, and manufacturing may expand as a result of expansion in the output of agricultural or mining products, the increased incomes in the latter sectors financing an expansion in demand for manufactured goods.

It also seems broadly true that there is a positive association between the relative importance of manufacturing in the economy and the level of real income *per head*; and this association seems to hold—again in a general way—both across countries at a given time and for single countries over a long period. Taking a very broad picture of the position in a recent year, it seems that real product per head in North America and Western Europe was many times higher than in Latin America, Asia and Africa, all of which are considerably less industrialized (Table 1.7). The two main industrial continents, North America and Western Europe, contain 28 per cent of the world's

Table 1.7. *World population, gross domestic product and manufacturing production, 1955[a]*

	Population	Gross domestic product		Manufacturing as proportion of gross domestic product
		Total	Per head	
	(*millions*)	(*$ billion*)	(*$*)	(*percentage*)
North America	182	387	2130	32
Western Europe	314	257	820	34
Oceania	15	17	1150	23
Latin America	183	57	310	18
Asia	862	76	90	15
Africa	216	30	140	8
TOTAL	1770	825	465	29

Sources: The Future Growth of World Population, United Nations, New York, 1958; *Demographic Yearbook, 1958*, United Nations, New York, 1958; Tables 1.1. and E.1 and related estimates.

[a]Excluding the Soviet countries with a total population of about 930 million in 1955.

population outside the Soviet countries, but produce almost 80 per cent of the total product, and almost 90 per cent of total output of manufactures. In Oceania, however, total product per head exceeds the West European average, though the relative importance of manufacture is considerably less. The association is clearly not a simple one since, as already mentioned, the causal connection can work in either direction and, moreover, many other factors influence real income.

The positive association between the share of manufacturing in the total product and the level of product per head is also apparent in the economic growth of the industrial and semi-industrial countries (see Fig. 1.5). Though the *level* of real product per head varies enormously for countries with similar manufacturing shares, the *rate* of growth for a given change in the manufacturing shares does not vary so greatly for the majority of countries. The implication seems to be that, while for some countries optimum progress may

Fig. 1.5.   Share of manufacture in gross domestic product in relation to gross
domestic product per head, 1913–57

Semi-logarithmic scale

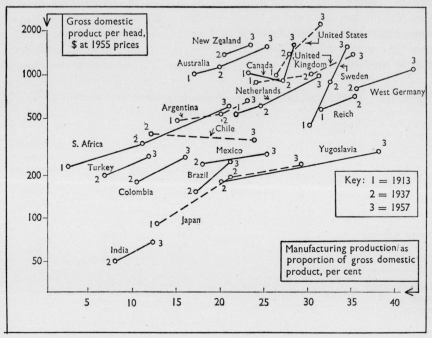

lie in the expansion of sectors other than manufacture, for a great many
countries in the underdeveloped areas industrialization will remain the major
dynamic element in economic growth.   To the extent to which this is so, the
causal relationship is likely to operate through the increase in productivity
which was discussed in the previous section.

CHAPTER 2

PATTERNS OF INDUSTRIAL GROWTH

1. DEMAND PATTERNS AND RESOURCE ENDOWMENTS

The different ways in which the pattern of industry develops in different countries depends on many factors. But some general rules can be identified. First, there are certain general patterns for the increase in demand as income grows; the growth of industry will show some response to these. Second, the pattern of industrial growth will depend partly on a country's endowment in natural and human resources, though the rate and order in which these are developed is influenced by changes in transport costs, by population trends and by outside factors such as the investment of foreign capital.

Demand patterns

Changes in demand patterns are affected not only by growth as such, but by changes in tastes, in relative prices, and in other economic factors, and these differ considerably from one country to another. Nonetheless, when changes in the pattern of demand are compared in countries at different stages of economic development, some general pattern can be discerned. Such a generalized picture of how the pattern of demand for manufactured goods changes with economic growth can be obtained either by tracing how the pattern changes over time in different countries, or by cross-section analysis of expenditure-patterns of different income groups ('within-country' comparisons), or by comparing the different patterns of consumption of manufactured goods at one point of time in a range of countries at different stages of economic development ('between-country' comparisons). A summary of the results of such analyses as are available, covering a range of countries at different levels of development, is given in Table 2.1. The co-efficients for the different commodity groups are only very broadly comparable, however, since several different methods of calculation were involved.

The broad picture that emerges can be taken as a valid representation of how the pattern of demand for manufactures changes with the rise in real income. The important features are the relatively rapid rise in demand for capital goods, chemicals and durable consumer goods, and the relatively slow expansion in the demand for food, beverages and tobacco, and for textiles and clothing. This is, of course, a highly generalized picture, based in the main on the historical experience of the industrial countries of Western Europe and North America. The actual pattern of change in demand with economic growth in a particular country may well be different.

There are two further qualifications. First, the income elasticities may not

Table 2.1.   *Estimates of income-elasticities of demand for major groups of manufactured goods, based on multi-national data*

	Single year		Time series
	Between countries	Within countries ('cross section')	
Food and beverages (excl. alcoholic drink)	0.5[a]	0.6	0.8[c]
Tobacco	0.9[a]	..	..
Metals	..	..	1.2[d]
Machinery and transport equipment (excl. passenger cars)	..	..	1.5–2.0[e]
Chemicals	..	..	2.1[f]
Durable consumer goods	2.1[a g]	..	2.7[c]
Textiles	0.5[h]	..	0.8[i]
Clothing	{ 0.8 / 0.9[j] }	1.2	{ 0.7[c] / 0.8[i] }
Other manufactures	..	1.6[k]	..
TOTAL Excluding food, beverages and tobacco	1.3[l]	..	1.4–2.0[m]

Sources: M. Gilbert, *et al.*, *Comparative National Products and Price Levels*, O.E.E.C., Paris, 1958; H. S. Houthakker, 'An International Comparison of Household Expenditure Patterns, Commemorating the Centenary of Engel's Law', *Econometrica*, Vol. 25, No. 4, Oct. 1957; *Economic Survey of Europe in 1958*, United Nations, Geneva, 1959; 'Report by the F.A.O. Secretariat on Fiber Consumption Trends' in *Studies of Factors Affecting Consumption of Textile Fibers*, International Cotton Advisory Committee, Washington, 1960; Chapters 6, 9, 10, 11 and 12 (present book).

[a] M. Gilbert, *et al.*   The co-efficients were calculated for the year 1950 with respect to differences between a number of O.E.E.C. countries and the United States in total private *consumption*, after allowing for differences in relative prices.

[b] H. S. Houthakker.   The co-efficients are based on a detailed analysis of family expenditure surveys in a number of countries.

[c] *Economic Survey of Europe in 1958.*   The co-efficients shown are medians of the ratio of the increase in per caput consumption from 1950 to 1957 to the increase in per caput total private consumption in the same period for 13 or 14 Western European countries.

[d] Chapter 9.

[e] Chapter 10.

[f] Chapter 11.

[g] 'Household goods' (i.e. furniture, incl. floor coverings, equipment and appliances, and household and personal supplies and equipment).   The authors did not regard this calculation as satisfactory, partly because the form of the demand equation was unsatisfactory, and partly because consumption levels in 1950 were still considerably influenced by post-war restrictions.

[h] F.A.O. Secretariat Report.   Mean result for 1953–57.   Co-efficient relates to weight of per caput fibre consumption.

[i] F.A.O. Secretariat Report.   Time series, 1953–57 for textiles and 1950–57 for clothing. Co-efficient for textiles relates to weight of per caput fibre consumption.

[j] F.A.O. Seeretariat Report.   Co-efficient relates to consumers' expenditure on clothing in 9 Western European countries.   Mean of result for 1950–57.

[k] Total consumers' expenditure *minus* food, clothing and footwear and housing (incl. fuel and light).

[l] Chapter 6 (Table 6.3).

[m] Chapter 6 (Table 6.2).

in fact be the same at all levels of income. At low income levels, a rise in income may generate a more rapid expansion in demand for the 'essentials' of life—food and clothing, in particular—than is indicated by the 'average' co-efficients shown here; while at high income levels, consumption may be much nearer saturation point for many items, and demand may expand at a relatively slower rate than indicated.

The second qualification is that the calculated income-elasticities based on time-series have not been corrected for price changes. This is of some importance, since the relatively 'newer' goods, such as transport equipment and chemicals, have tended to fall in price relatively to the older, more traditional products, such as textiles, over the last forty or fifty years. This would in itself tend to stimulate the demand for 'newer' goods at the expense of other goods, the degree of stimulation depending on the magnitude of the price-elasticity of demand. To the extent, however, that such price movements are *systematically* related to economic growth, they may be expected to occur in the future, as in the past. To this extent, the time-series co-efficients show how demand changes with economic growth in general, rather than simply with changes in income.

Resource endowments

Changes in demand patterns are not, however, the sole influence on changes in the pattern of output. As an economy grows, its ability to produce different commodities changes, and this is reflected in changes in relative costs of production in different lines. Industries or firms which can reduce their relative costs will tend to expand their output, and the reverse process will occur in the high-cost plants.

Such changes in relative production costs depend partly on what may be called the 'resource endowments' of the growing economy, and partly on the extent to which economies of scale accrue as production is expanded. The resource endowment in the narrower sense consists simply of the natural features of the country, i.e. its location, climate and vegetable and mineral wealth. The vast differences in these alone would account for great differences in patterns of output. In a wider sense, the resource endowment includes human as well as inanimate resources. Here again, there are extremely wide variations to be found in both the quantity and quality (in terms of education, skill, etc.) of human resources in different countries, and these variations also explain much of the differences in the relative production costs noted above, and thus in the patterns of output in different countries. If the natural resource endowment of a country is suitable for industrialization, the local population can usually adapt in time to the needs of economic growth. This adaptation involves the acquisition of new skills and implies a fall in the relative cost of skilled labour in the more rapidly growing sectors. Thus, in general, changes in relative costs which occur as a result of the acquisition of new skills will tend to reinforce the changes in output pattern that would occur as a result of changes in demand alone.

However, the influence of the indigenous natural and human resources on the pattern of economic growth can be greatly modified by the relative ease or difficulty of transporting resources, and of increasing the population by immigration. Countries with no mineral resources, for example, are less likely to develop a steel industry than are countries with ore deposits; nevertheless, some countries without iron ore or bauxite can develop a metallurgical industry if they have abundant supplies of cheap fuel and can readily import the ore. Though 'heavy' industries, like steel or cement, tend to be located in areas where the cost of transporting the raw materials is relatively low, the cost of transport of the finished product to the market is also a factor influencing the location of a plant.

The 'light' industries, such as textiles, many food processing industries and metal wares, on the other hand, depend very largely on the availability of suitable labour, sufficiency of capital and, very often, proximity to local markets. These 'footloose' industries tend to develop as a conglomeration of small-scale units and, since the optimum size of plant is much lower than for the 'heavy' industries, they are likely to be found in most developing countries, including those with small populations and relatively restricted markets[1]. Even where transport costs are such as to make the establishment of an industry uneconomic in a given country, it may still be profitable to establish a particular process there, usually the assembly of imported parts and components. This would apply where the parts (such as motor car chassis) can be transported over long distances at a cost which is small in relation to the value of the assembled product.

The pattern of industrial growth may also be substantially influenced by government intervention, either directly in the form of an economic Plan, or indirectly through discriminatory import restrictions or other measures. The particular growth pattern will thus depend on a complex interplay of influences, reflecting *inter alia* not only the indigenous availability of resources, but also the relative cost of importing materials from particular sources and of exporting finished products to particular markets. Different combinations of these influences are likely to result in somewhat different patterns of industrial growth in different countries. However, there are other influences which tend to make the industry-pattern of growth broadly similar in countries at similar stages of industrialization.

The first of such 'unifying' influences is that the pattern of demand tends to change in a similar way in countries at broadly the same level of industrializa-

---

[1]For a detailed analysis of the characteristics of industries which are 'footloose', 'rooted' (to sources of materials) and 'tied' (to market areas), see the pioneer work of P. Sargant Florence, *Investment, Location and Size of Plant*, Cambridge, 1948, and *The Logic of British and American Industry*, London, 1953.

tion; and, as already mentioned, this influences the pattern of industrial development. Second, in the early phases of industrialization, the levels of skill and of organizational ability set limits to the type of industrial process that can profitably be undertaken. Generally speaking, this means that the simpler forms of manufacturing, which are typical of the consumer industries, tend to be developed before the more complex processes involved in, say, capital goods industries. Third, the size of the market—measured in terms of national expenditure—tends to be too small, in the earlier stages of industrialization, to justify the establishment of optimum-sized plants in a number of industries, particularly in the chemicals and capital goods fields. These limitations on the supply side tend to be relaxed as industrialization develops, because new industrial skills and organizational abilities emerge and the wider market allows new industries to be profitably established. Thus, while different countries must be expected to differ considerably in the detailed way in which their industries grow because of specific national features, there are good reasons to expect that some broad pattern of growth can be discerned among countries at the same stage of industrialization. The evidence for such a general pattern of growth is examined below.

2. THE CHANGING PATTERN OF MANUFACTURING PRODUCTION

Shifts in output patterns have been much more marked in the larger industrial countries, which have a wide variety of resources and substantial home markets, than in the smaller industrial countries or in the industrializing primary-producing countries. The process is more readily identifiable in the economically advanced countries, most of which have statistics of industrial production going back to the early years of this century.

Comparing Britain with the other O.E.E.C. countries and the United States (Table 2.2), a remarkable similarity is apparent in the movement of the industrial output pattern. In each area the relative importance of the food processing industries has declined to about one-half the relative shares held at the beginning of the century, while the percentage share of the textile industry has declined to about one-third of its former size. The relative importance of the metal product industries, on the other hand, has risen sharply and there has also been a marked increase in the share of chemicals. There was little change in the percentages for basic metals, but the miscellaneous group has fallen relatively, particularly in the United States. It is evident that the metal products (i.e. engineering) industries constitute the most dynamic sector in industrial growth. This sector has risen faster in relative importance in the United States than in Western Europe, or in Britain, since the beginning of the century, and this reflects the greater industrial expansion in the United States in this period. Since 1929, however, the relative growth in metal products has been greater in Britain than in the other two areas.

The change in pattern has been more dramatic in Japan. In 1880, Japan had no modern engineering industry, and only a small production of metals and chemicals; in this pre-industrial phase, two-thirds of total manufacturing output consisted of foodstuffs and beverages (see Table 2.3, in which the percentages are on a 'net' basis). The next twenty years saw a rapid expansion in the textile industries. Textile production, at one-third of the total in 1900,

Table 2.2. *Changes in the pattern of manufacturing production in O.E.E.C. countries, United Kingdom and United States, 1899–1959*

Percentage[a]

	1899 or 1901[b]	1913	1929	1937	1955	1959
Food, beverages and tobacco						
O.E.E.C.[c]	27	19	15	15	13	12
United Kingdom	27	20	18	16	14	14
United States	24	20	14	15	11	11
Basic metals						
O.E.E.C.[c]	7	11	11	11	10	9
United Kingdom	7	7	7	8	8	8
United States	9	10	10	9	9	7
Metal products						
O.E.E.C.[c]	16	24	27	27	32	32
United Kingdom	16	19	25	29	38	38
United States	10	13	33	31	41	41
Chemicals						
O.E.E.C[c]	5	6	11	12	15	18
United Kingdom	6	6	8	7	12	13
United States	5	6	8	10	13	15
Textiles						
O.E.E.C.[c]	23	18	14	13	9	8
United Kingdom	16	19	12	11	6	5
United States	20	19	11	12	8	8
Other manufactures						
O.E.E.C.[c]	22	22	22	22	21	21
United Kingdom	28	29	30	29	22	22
United States	32	32	24	23	18	18
TOTAL MANUFACTURES IN EACH AREA	100	100	100	100	100	100
Volume of manufacturing production						
O.E.E.C.[c]	100	168	216	241	429	525
United Kingdom	100	135	160	220	367	400
United States	100	180	352	360	870	940

Sources: V. Paretti and G. Bloch, 'Industrial Production in Western Europe and the United States, 1901 to 1955', *Banca Nazionale del Lavoro Quarterly Review*, No. 39, Dec. 1956; *Industrial Statistics, 1900–1959*, O.E.E.C., Paris, 1960.

[a]Based on value added at constant (1955) prices.

[b]1899 for United States; 1901 for O.E.E.C. countries.

[c]Excluding United Kingdom.

Table 2.3. *Changes in the pattern of manufacturing production in Australia, Canada and Japan*, 1880–1959

Percentage

		1880	1900	1913ᵃ	1929	1953	1959
Food, beverages and tobacco							
Australia		..	..	24	23	14	14
Canada	Gross	27	30	25	24	..	..
	Net	..	..	..	13	14	15
Japan		65	36	26	15	10	7
Basic metals							
Australia		..	..	..ᵇ	6	4	6
Canada	Gross	..ᵇ	..ᵇ	..ᵇ	..	..	..
	Net	..	..	..	7	8	9
Japan		6	4	3	7	12	11
Metal products							
Australia		..	..	24	21	36	35
Canada	Gross	6	6	9	20	..	..
	Net	..	..	..	31	29	26
Japan		..	2	15	15	24	39
Chemicals							
Australia		.	..	4	8	7	9
Canada	Gross	3	2	2	4	..	..
	Net	.	..	..	6	8	10
Japan		8	11	10	20	15	15
Textilesᶜ							
Australia			..	17	16	15	12
Canada	Gross	13	14	12	10	..	..
	Net	..	..	..	6	5	5
Japan		11	32	30	25	14	11
Other manufactures							
Australia		..	..	31	26	24	23
Canada	Gross	52	48	52	42	..	..
	Net	..	..	..	36	36	36
Japan		10	15	16	18	25	17
TOTAL MANUFACTURES IN EACH AREA		100	100	100	100	100	100
Volume of manufacturing production							
Australia		..	..	100	145	370	565
Canada		24	55	100	190	455	540
Japan		8	53	100	250	530	1,170

Sources: Secondary Industry Bulletins, Commonwealth Bureau of Census and Statistics, Canberra; *Quarterly Survey*, Australia and New Zealand Bank, Ltd.; A. Maizels, 'Trends in Production and Labour Productivity in Australian Manufacturing Industries', *Economic Record*, Vol. 33, No. 65, Aug. 1957; O. J. Firestone, *Canada's Economic Development* (*Income and Wealth*, Series VII, London, 1958); *Industrial Statistics, 1900–1959*, O.E.E.C., Paris, 1960; K. Ohkawa, *The Growth Rate of the Japanese Economy since 1878*, Tokyo, 1957.

ᵃ1910 for Canada.

ᵇIncluded in 'Metal Products'.

ᶜIncluding Clothing.

almost equalled the output of the food, etc. industries in that year, and became Japan's largest industry in the decade before the first World War. Since the beginning of the century, however, the relative size of the textile industry in Japan has been falling with the growth of the metals, engineering and chemical industries. By 1959, Japan's industrial pattern was very similar to that of Western Europe and the United States.

A broadly similar pattern of change can be traced in Australia and Canada, two of the very few other countries for which a comparable statistical analysis is possible over a considerable period of time. For the period 1880–1929, the Canadian percentages are based on figures of gross output; this inflates the importance of the food and beverage, textiles, and miscellaneous industries, where materials are costly relative to wages and overheads, and reduces the importance of engineering and chemicals for the opposite reason. This does not, however, detract from the usefulness of the gross output figures for measuring the changes over time. The most important change in the period up to 1929 was the sharp relative expansion in engineering; chemicals also increased somewhat in relative importance. After 1929, it was chemicals which showed the most rapid expansion; food and metals also expanded, but there was a decline in the relative size of the engineering group. Taking all three 'expanding' groups together (i.e. metals, metal products and chemicals), the proportion in 1959 (45 per cent) was virtually identical with that in 1929.

In Australia, engineering was relatively of some importance even before the first World War (though the absolute size of the industry was small by modern standards), and this sector has shown a considerable relative expansion since then; by the 1950's, its relative importance was similar to that in Western Europe. Textiles have shown a downward trend in relative importance, but for chemicals the upward trend was slight. This is because the percentages in Table 2.3 are based on current values, and the increase in chemicals production since the 1930's was associated with a fall in prices of chemicals relative to prices of other manufactures. On a volume basis, Australian chemical production increased at an average annual rate of 6.9 per cent, compound, from 1936/7–38/9 to 1947/8–49/50, compared with 4.1 per cent for all manufacturing, excluding energy, and at a rate of 6.4 per cent, compound, from 1947/8–49/50 to 1953/4–54/5, compared with 6.2 per cent for the total[1].

That these shifts in industry pattern are closely related to economic development can also be seen if we compare the economically more advanced continents with the less-developed ones in a recent year (see Table 2.4). In Latin America, for example, metal products accounted for only one-tenth of manufacturing production in 1953, as against one-third in the more advanced areas. At the same time, the relative importance of food processing and textiles was considerably higher in Latin America than in the more advanced areas. The

[1] A. Maizels, 'Trends in Production and Labour Productivity in Australian Manufacturing Industries', *Economic Record*, Vol. 33, No. 65, August 1957.

Table 2.4. *Pattern of manufacturing production in the main Continents*, 1953

Percentage[a]

	North America	Europe[b]	Oceania	Latin America	Asia[c]	Africa[d]
Food, beverages and tobacco	11.0	13.6	18.6	32.1	15.3	15.8
Basic metals	8.9	8.3	4.3	5.7	7.1	11.7
Metal products	36.3	32.2	32.8	11.6	17.1	24.3
Chemicals[e]	9.8	10.1	6.8	13.8	11.2	13.6
Textiles	4.3	10.2	5.9	12.0	17.7	7.3
Clothing, footwear and made-up textiles	5.5	5.2	7.2	5.9	6.0	7.3
Wood	4.5	4.4	7.9	4.4	7.4	4.8
Paper and printing	8.7	6.4	6.7	4.0	5.0	5.3
Rubber and leather	2.2	2.2	3.0	2.8	3.2	2.3
Non-metallic mineral products	3.0	4.6	4.4	5.4	5.1	6.0
Other manufactures	5.8	2.8	2.4	1.7	3.9	1.6
TOTAL MANUFACTURING	100	100	100	100	100	100
Manufacturing production as proportion of world total	55.9	33.6	1.6	3.4	4.4	1.1

Source: *Patterns of Industrial Growth, 1938–1958*, United Nations, New York, 1960, p. 453.

[a]Based on value added.
[b]Excluding Soviet countries.
[c]Excluding China and Middle East.
[d]Including Middle East.
[e]Including petroleum and coal products.

industry pattern in Asia and Africa appears to have been 'intermediate' between those of Latin America and the more advanced areas, insofar as can be judged by the relative importance of the metal products, food processing and textile industries.

The Hoffmann ratio

This general relationship between industrial growth and the industry-pattern of output is a field of inquiry which has been pioneered by Professor Hoffmann. In his well-known study of the growth of industrial economies[1], Hoffmann has defined several distinct 'stages' of industrialization in terms of the ratio of the net output of the consumer goods industries to that of the capital goods industries. According to Hoffmann, in the first stage of industrialization the consumer goods industries are of major importance, their net output being on

[1]W. G. Hoffmann, *The Growth of Industrial Economies*, Manchester University Press, 1958. This is a revised and expanded version of Professor Hoffmann's *Stadien und Typen der Industrialisierung*, Jena, 1931.

average five times as large as that of the capital goods industries. In the second stage, the ratio is reduced to about $2\frac{1}{2}$: 1, while in the third stage the net outputs of the two groups are approximately equal. Finally, in the fourth stage, the consumer goods industries are left far behind by the rapidly growing capital goods industries.

On Hoffmann's definitions, the United States had reached the second stage of industrialization by the middle of the nineteenth century, whereas this stage was reached by Britain, France, Germany, Belgium and Switzerland only towards the end of the century. By 1914, both the United States and Sweden had reached the third stage (where the two sectors of industry were approximately of equal importance), whilst the other industrial countries of Europe and Japan and Australia were still in the second stage; New Zealand, Brazil and Chile, however, were in their first stage of industrialization at that time. By the later 1930's, most of the industrial countries of Europe had reached, or were approaching, Hoffmann's third stage, and by the 1950's the United States, Britain and Germany could be said to have reached the fourth stage. By this time, Canada, Australia and Japan were in the third stage, while India, the Philippines and South Korea had reached the second stage. Some of the less-developed Asian countries (for example, Taiwan and South Vietnam) could be considered still to be in the first stage of industrialization[1].

The calculation involved in the Hoffmann ratio is, however, open to some statistical criticism, because the definitions of 'capital goods' and 'consumer goods' are, to some extent, arbitrary and have to be fitted rather imperfectly to the different commodity classifications in use by different countries; and because the ratio excludes altogether the important group of intermediate products, which are, strictly speaking, neither 'capital' nor 'consumer'. Nonetheless, the movement in the Hoffmann ratio is a useful summary description of the way in which industrialization influences the pattern of output.

However, as an indicator of the stage of industrialization reached by different countries, the Hoffmann ratio has two major limitations. First, it relates solely to the 'balance' within the manufacturing sector, whereas one of the characteristics of industrialization is the growth in the relative importance of manufacturing in the developing economy. Second, it makes no allowance for differences in productivity levels between different countries. It would be stretching definitions too much, for example, to conclude from the fact that the Hoffman ratios for New Zealand and South Korea are similar—as they

---

[1]Developments in China appeared rapid in the mid-fifties. The Hoffmann ratio, based on the *gross* output of 'consumer goods' to 'producer goods' industries, fell from 2.5 in 1949 to 1.4 in 1953, 1.2 in 1955 and 0.9 in 1957. These figures exclude the output of handicrafts; taking these into account, the Hoffmann ratio would reach 1.0 by 1962, the end of the second five-year plan, if the planned targets for industrial output are reached by then. If they are, China would have passed through all the main 'stages', on Hoffmann's definitions, in roughly a decade. (See *Economic Bulletin for Asia and the Far East*, Vol. 9, No. 3, December 1958, p. 11.)

appear to be—that the 'stage' of industrialization in any realistic sense is the same in these two countries[1].

These limitations arise in part because Professor Hoffmann was seeking a *single* measure of the significance of the industrialization process. It is, however, more useful analytically to trace the association between industrialization and the relative magnitudes of each of the main manufacturing industries, and this is attempted in the following section.

3. THE GENERAL PATTERN OF MANUFACTURING GROWTH

The relative rates of growth in individual industries over time can readily be compared by use of official indices of production for the main industrial countries back to about 1900. Unfortunately, data for similar long-term comparisons are available for few other countries. The analysis in this section is therefore confined to industrial growth in the main industrial countries of Western Europe and North America.

Since the object here is to relate the pattern of industrial growth to the general economic development of the economy, it is assumed that the two are inter-related in a specific way. The general assumption made is that value added per head in any given industry, measured at constant prices, is a function of total national product (income) per head.

For the main industrial countries, estimates of the net value of manufacturing production in 1955 (as given in Table E.3 on page 535) were sub-divided into six major industry groups, using data recently published by the United Nations[2]. Estimates for other selected years were then derived by applying the appropriate indices of production for each group to the 1955 figures; the seven years selected were those shown in Table E.3, covering years of good business activity in the period from 1899 to 1957. The resulting net values at 1955 prices were converted to a per caput basis and for each commodity group a regression equation was computed, using per caput real income as the independent variable, covering all the principal industrial countries and all seven years together[3]. Each equation was thus based on sixty or more 'observations'. The regression co-efficient of the income variable represents

---

[1]Both these objections to the Hoffmann ratio are met by the use, as in Chapter 1, of the net value of manufacturing production per head of population as an indicator of the stage of industrialization.

[2]*Patterns of Industrial Growth, 1938-1958*, United Nations, New York, 1960. The data given in the appendices of this publication have been adjusted as far as possible to a standard industrial classification and allow also for small establishments·excluded from industrial censuses.

[3]A double logarithmic form was used as follows:

$$\log V = \log \beta_0 + \beta_1 \log Y$$

where V is value added per head, Y is real national product per head, β_1 is the mean slope of the regression lines for the individual countries in the calculation, and $\log \beta_0 = $ mean $(\log V) - \beta_1$ mean $(\log Y)$.

the mean 'growth elasticity' of that commodity group, for all the main industrial countries, over a period exceeding fifty years. The growth elasticity represents the effect of income, not only on the demand for the products of a particular industry, but also on relative costs of production in different lines insofar as these are related to economic growth.

For a recent year (1955), separate cross-country regressions were also computed for each commodity group, using a relationship recently advanced by Professor H. B. Chenery[1], who calculated 'growth' and 'size' elasticities from regression equations for major economic sectors and for a number of manufacturing industries. Professor Chenery's equations related to one period (average of 1952–54), the relationship assumed being that per caput value added is a function of per caput income and population size[2]. The co-efficient of the income variable is the growth elasticity, as for the time-series regressions, while the co-efficient for population is termed the size elasticity. The latter indicates the net effect of the size of the market both on costs and on the derived demand for the output of particular industries arising from import-substitution in other sectors[3].

The introduction of population size into the cross-country regressions is necessary because of the vast differences in size of market in different countries, affecting the opportunity for cost reductions with industrial growth. For the time-series regressions, however, a better 'explanation' of the changing pattern of production was obtained by omitting the size factor[4].

Two main conclusions seem to emerge from the results of the regressions (Table 2.5). First, the pattern of industrial growth has consisted, to a marked degree, of a shift towards chemicals, metals and engineering. Chemicals, the fastest growing industry, was expanding four times as rapidly as textiles which, together with food processing, was growing at a lower rate than real income. Expressed as a percentage of the growth co-efficient for manufacturing as a whole, the co-efficients for the different industry groups in order of magnitude are: chemicals, 194; metal products, 156; metals, 120; miscellaneous manufacturing industries, 92; food, beverages and tobacco, 62; textiles, 47. These great differences in rates of growth imply an enormous shift in the pattern of industrial output from a low-income economy to a high-income one.

Second, the growth co-efficients based on the single-year regressions are significantly different from those based on time-series for food processing,

---

[1]H. B. Chenery, 'Patterns of Industrial Growth', *American Economic Review*, Vol. 50, No. 4, September 1960.

[2]Professor Chenery used the double logarithmic form:
$$\log V = \log \beta_0 + \beta_1 \log Y + \beta_2 \log N$$
where V is per caput value added, Y is per caput income and N is population size. The growth elasticity is then β_1 and the size elasticity is β_2.

[3]H. B. Chenery, 'Patterns of Industrial Growth', p. 631.

[4]This was so because the movements over time in population size and in income per head are auto-correlated for individual countries.

Table 2.5. *Regressions of manufacturing production on income and size,*
1955 *and* 1899–1957

	Period[a]	Income		Size[b]		R^2
		Co-effi-cient	Standard error	Co-effi-cient	Standard error	
Food, beverages and tobacco	1955	1.10	± 0.08	− 0.14	± 0.06	0.889
	1899–1957	0.78	± 0.05			0.858
Metals	1955	1.68	± 0.25	0.44	± 0.20	0.652
	1899–1957	1.52	± 0.13			0.718
Metal products	1955	1.97	± 0.13	..	..	0.904
	1899–1957	1.96	± 0.12			0.824
Chemicals	1955	1.31	± 0.17	..	..	0.721
	1899–1957	2.44	± 0.13			0.883
Textiles	1955	0.93	± 0.13	..	..	0.666
	1899–1957	0.59	± 0.09			0.553
Other manufacturing industries	1955	1.50	± 0.10	..	..	0.921
	1899–1957	1.16	± 0.07			0.863
TOTAL	1955	1.45	± 0.06	0.07	± 0.05	0.930
	1899–1957	1.26	± 0.05			0.910
TOTAL EXCLUDING FOOD, BEVERAGES AND TOBACCO	1955	1.49	± 0.07	0.10	± 0.05	0.943
	1899–1957	1.44	± 0.06			0.897

Sources: Tables E.3 and E.7; *Patterns of Industrial Growth, 1938–1958* United Nations, New York, 1960; *Industrial Statistics, 1900–1959*, O.E.E.C., Paris, 1960; national production statistics.

[a]For the 1955 cross-country regressions, some 30 countries were included in the commodity group calculations, and 48 countries in the calculation for the total. For the time-series regressions, the data related to selected years from 1899 to 1957 covering from 7 to 10 countries (according to the commodity group concerned); all these time-regressions thus covered over 60 'observations' each.

[b]A size variable (total population) was omitted from the time-regressions. For the cross-country regressions, the size co-efficient is shown only where it is significantly different from zero at the 95 per cent confidence level.

chemicals and the miscellaneous group at the 1 per cent level of significance, and differed significantly for textiles at the 5 per cent level. The difference is particularly great for chemicals, for which the single-year growth co-efficient was lower than that for all manufacturing, including food[1], whereas on the time-series basis, the chemicals co-efficient was about 70 per cent higher. This marked difference appears to result largely from the fact that in the less-developed countries included in the single-year regression, 'chemicals' consist mainly of simply-processed goods, such as soap, candles, matches and paint. These countries, therefore, tend to have a relatively high chemicals output in

[1]Professor Chenery's cross-country 'growth co-efficient' for chemicals (1.66), though slightly higher than that for total manufacturing (1.44), was appreciably below those for machinery (2.80) and transport equipment (2.33).

relation to their national incomes, but the output pattern is very different from that of the chemical industries in the economically advanced countries. Because of such differences in output patterns between countries at different stages of development, the single-year cross-country regressions can give a misleading picture of the underlying growth elasticities.

The 'size effect' derived from the single-year regressions appears to be significant in only two industry groups, metals and food, beverages and tobacco[1]. For metals, the size co-efficient indicates that a 10 per cent variation in population size between different countries tends to be associated with a difference of about $4\frac{1}{2}$ per cent in metal production per head after allowing for differences in per caput income levels. For food, beverages and tobacco, the relationship is inverse, a 10 per cent variation in population size being associated with a variation of about $1\frac{1}{2}$ per cent in the opposite direction in food, etc. output per head[2].

Table 2.6.   *Changes in pattern of manufacturing production with growth in income per head*

$ at 1955 *prices and percentages*

	Income per head									
	$100		$250		$500		$750		$1000	
			(Net value of production per head)							
Food, beverages and tobacco	8.8	*40*	17.9	*33*	30.8	*26*	42.3	*21*	52.9	*18*
Metals	0.7	*3*	2.9	*5*	8.4	*7*	13.5	*7*	23.9	*8*
Metal products	0.9	*4*	5.6	*10*	21.9	*18*	48.4	*24*	85.4	*29*
Chemicals	0.1	*0*	0.9	*2*	5.0	*4*	13.4	*7*	26.9	*9*
Textiles	5.7	*26*	9.9	*18*	14.9	*13*	19.0	*10*	22.5	*8*
Other manufactures	6.0	*27*	17.2	*32*	38.4	*32*	61.4	*31*	85.6	*29*
TOTAL	22.2	*100*	54.4	*100*	119.4	*100*	198.0	*100*	297.2	*100*

Source: Based on time series regressions in Table 2.5.

The typical pattern of expansion in manufacturing industry[3] can be derived from the time-series regressions summarized in Table 2.5. The results (Table 2.6 and Fig. 2.1) show a fairly sharp fall in the relative importance of food processing and textiles in the earlier stages of growth of the present industrial countries (from $100–$250 real product per head), with a continued, though reduced, rate of decline thereafter. Metals and metal products show the

[1]Professor Chenery, however, derived 'size co-efficients' which were significantly different from zero for 9 out of 15 industry groups; for total manufacturing, his size co-efficient is 0.20 ($\pm$0.05), as against 0.07 ($\pm$0.05) shown in Table 2.5.

[2]Professor Chenery's 'size co-efficients' for food and beverages and for tobacco were, however, not significantly different from zero.

[3]This corresponds to 'normal' output in Professor Chenery's scheme.

reverse movement, with a declining rate of relative growth as the later stages of development are reached. Chemicals show an uninterrupted rise, while the miscellaneous group first rises (up to about $250–$500 per head) and then tends to fall slowly in relative importance. The pattern of growth in Fig.

Fig. 2.1. Typical patterns of growth in manufacturing industries

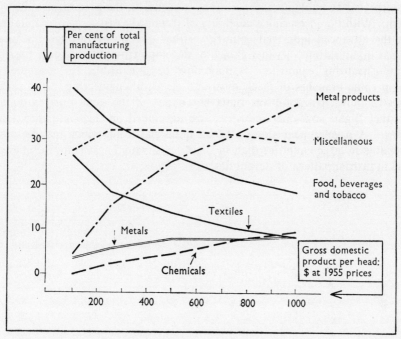

2.1 cannot necessarily be projected back to earlier stages of economic development, though it does strongly suggest that at the beginning of the industrialization process (say, between $50 and $75 per head), textiles, food and miscellaneous (presumably light consumer) industries will play the major rôle. This is generally borne out by an examination of the present industrial structure in a number of underdeveloped, but industrializing countries, as well as by the Japanese example mentioned earlier. At these earlier stages of industrialization, manufacturing is generally confined to the processing of primary products (such as grain milling, spinning yarn or smelting metals) and, at a later stage in development, to the simple transformation of materials (such as clothing, footwear, furniture or paper)[1]. A more mature phase of industrialization can be said to commence with the production of capital equipment based on machine technology.

[1]*Processes and Problems of Industrialization in Under-Developed Countries*, United Nations, New York, 1955, pp. 8-9.

This picture is based on the common evolution of manufacturing in the main industrial countries, covering an income range beginning at about $100 per head. The underlying calculation implies a development based on a fairly wide variety of resources, and on an expanding market. It does not necessarily describe the actual internal development of any given country, particularly one which is limited in resources or has a restricted home market. Nor should it be interpreted as implying any necessary sequence in the pattern of industrial growth. With the increasing availability of technical assistance and capital aid from the advanced industrial countries, either directly or through the international organizations, a wider choice of development-pattern is now possible for industrializing countries. It may now be practicable, for example, to develop some branches of mechanical and electrical engineering in the earlier phases of industrialization—as India has done—at the same time as textiles and other 'light' consumer industries are developed on the more traditional pattern. A development along a broad industrial front, which may be more practicable in large countries than in small ones, would accelerate the changes in the industrial pattern of output described above.

CHAPTER 3

INDUSTRIALIZATION AND THE STRUCTURE OF FOREIGN TRADE

1. INDUSTRIALIZATION AND EXPORTS

In this chapter the ways in which industrialization has affected the development of exports and imports are described in broad terms. Several of the points made are developed more fully in later chapters.

In all the main industrial countries, the relative importance of manufactures[1] in total exports has increased over the past sixty years (see Table 3.1). An increasing degree of 'industrialization of the export structure' is, indeed, to be expected as a consequence of industrial growth. For some countries, such as Canada, Sweden, the United States and Japan, the proportion of exports consisting of manufactured goods has risen sharply over the past half-century; most of the Canadian increase came in the 1920's, whereas the Japanese transformation came after the second World War. By the end of the 1950's, the proportion of manufactured goods in the export trade exceeded 60 per cent for all but two (Canada and Netherlands) of the countries included in Table 3.1. For five countries (Belgium-Luxembourg, Switzerland, United Kingdom, West Germany and Japan) the proportion exceeded 80 per cent.

The relative importance of manufactures in exports shows a much greater variation among the primary-producing countries. Chile, for example, depends on manufactures, as here defined, for about three-quarters of her export sales, while over one-half the total exports from Israel and the Congo consists of manufactures. On the other hand, for the majority of primary-producing countries, manufactures represent only a small fraction, often under 5 per cent, of their total exports.

However, in Chile and the Congo, the 'manufactures' consist essentially of smelted or refined non-ferrous metals, which are the product of a specialized sector of industry consisting of a relatively few (foreign-owned) plants. Similarly, over one-half of Mexico's exports of 'manufactures' consist of simply-processed base metals. Thus, the export of 'manufactures' does not necessarily reflect the development of the industrialization process in the sense of an economic transformation of the economy through the establishment of a large-scale base of manufacturing production. There are many other primary-producing countries whose manufactured exports consist mainly of the first stages of processing of locally produced agricultural commodities or minerals.

---

[1] 'Manufactures' in foreign trade are defined here as those goods included in the United Nations' *Standard International Trade Classification*, Sections 5 to 8, inclusive, but excluding United States 'special category' exports. For further discussion see Appendices A and D.

Table 3.1. *Share of manufactures in exports from the industrial countries,*
1899–1959

	Percentage of total exports[a]					Total exports 1959 ($ billion)
	1899	1913	1929	1955	1959	
Belgium-Luxembourg	46	45	73	80	83	3.29
France	55	58	68	64	74	5.62
Germany	70	72	78	86[b]	89[b]	9.80[b]
Italy	41	45	58	62	69	2.90
Netherlands	..[c]	..[c]	38	48	52	3.61
Sweden	30	41	43	53	63	2.21
Switzerland	75	77	84	92	92	1.69
United Kingdom	80	77	77	82	84	9.31
Canada	9	12	37	48	44	5.37
United States	30	35	48	62	61	15.70[d]
Japan	42	49	49	87	88	3.45

Sources: Tables A.1, A.3 and related data.

[a]Based on current values.
[b]West Germany.
[c]Not available.
[d]Excluding special categories.

The relationship between industrialization and the commodity pattern of exports can be seriously obscured for countries substantially engaged in exporting a very restricted range of simply processed goods. No very accurate method can easily be devised to separate the simply processed goods, which are little more than an extension of agriculture and mining, from those more elaborately processed[1]. But the former group consist essentially of *intermediate products*, i.e. goods intended for further processing: smelted metal exported for refining and use in engineering production, for example, or simple chemicals for further processing in the chemical and allied industries. A much more accurate picture of the incidence of industrialization can be obtained by excluding these intermediate products from the definition of exports of manufactures. The residual consists of *finished goods* in the sense that they are not normally subject to a further process of manufacture. The main categories of finished manufactured goods are machinery and transport equipment; cutlery, implements and other metal products; drugs, fertilizers, paints and other chemical products used mainly outside manufacturing industry ; textile fabrics

[1]The League of Nations' Committee of Statistical Experts recommended in 1935 the adoption of a *Minimum List* of commodity headings for international trade statistics. The Committee also recommended the use, as a subsidiary classification, of a list of headings based on stage of fabrication and end-use, but this latter classification did not come into general use.

Table 3.2. *Degree of industrialization in production and in exports in 1955*

	Production of manufactures per head ($)	Manufactures as proportion of total exports		Exports of finished manufactures ($ million)
		All manufactures	Finished manufactures	
		(*percentage*)		
INDUSTRIAL COUNTRIES				
Belgium-Luxembourg	460	80	35	965
Denmark	325	27	23	240
France	265	64	38	1845
Western Germany	405	86	65	3999
Italy	150	62	47	873
Netherlands	270	48	31	822
Norway	315	51	17	107
Sweden	465	53	33	577
Switzerland	480	92	76	994
United Kingdom	460	82	65	5270
Canada	440	48	11	464
United States	695	62	48	6418
Japan	45	87	64	1281
SEMI-INDUSTRIAL COUNTRIES				
Australia	350	11	6	100
New Zealand	325	1.2	0.4	3
Union of South Africa	115	29[a]	11	99
India	7	37	31	399
Argentina	145	5.4	0.4	4
Brazil	50	1.4	0.4	5
Chile	75	76	1.4	7
Colombia	45	1.1	0.6	4
Mexico	60	25	3	26
Israel	170	56	25	22
Turkey	30	4.1	0.4	1
Yugoslavia	85	38	13	33
NON-INDUSTRIAL COUNTRIES				
Belgian Congo	15	53	0.8	4
Burma	5	3.0	0.4	1
Egypt	15	6.4	3	12
Pakistan	5	5.1	5	19
Philippines	15	2.2	1.4	5
Thailand	10	1.4	1.1	4

Sources: Tables A.1, A.46 to A.68, and Table E.4; *Yearbook of International Trade Statistics, 1957*, United Nations, New York, 1959; and national trade statistics.

[a]Excluding fissionable materials.

Note: The figures for exports of finished manufactures are approximate for some of the semi-industrial and non-industrial countries.

D

and made-up goods, including clothing; and a wide range of miscellaneous manufactures, including a substantial proportion of consumer goods such as footwear, books and stationery, pottery and glassware, etc.[1]

The proportion of exports consisting of (a) all manufactures and (b) finished manufactures in a recent year—1955—is given in Table 3.2 for about thirty countries covering very different stages of industrial development. The proportion of finished manufactures in total exports is very small for the countries specializing in non-ferrous metals (Chile, Mexico and the Belgian Congo). For Yugoslavia the proportion of manufactures in the total is considerably reduced when intermediates (mainly base metals) are excluded, but Yugoslavia's exports are much more diversified than those of the countries specializing in metals, finished manufactures representing about one-eighth of her total exports in 1955. Among the countries classed as semi-industrial or non-industrial, only India and Israel depend substantially (more than one-fifth) on finished manufactures for their export income.

Among the countries of Western Europe and North America, the greatest deductions for intermediates are made for Belgium-Luxembourg (intermediates —mainly metals—consisting of 45 per cent of total exports), and Canada and Norway (about 35 per cent each). At the other extreme, the deduction for Denmark is under 5 per cent.

2. A CLASSIFICATION OF INDUSTRIAL, SEMI-INDUSTRIAL AND NON-INDUSTRIAL COUNTRIES

The relationship between the stage of industrial development (as measured by the net value of production of manufactures per head of population) and the degree of 'industrialization' of the export trade (as measured by the proportion of exports consisting of finished manufactures) can be employed to classify countries into broad groups convenient for the analysis of the effects of industrialization on foreign trade. The relationship involved can be seen more clearly in Fig. 3.1. The distribution of countries is essentially a continuous one and any demarcation inevitably involves arbitrary decisions. Nonetheless, some broad groupings of countries seem to suggest themselves, as indicated by the broken curves in Fig. 3.1.

The first group distinguished consists of the industrially advanced countries of Western Europe[2] and the United States. All of these countries produced at least $150 of manufactured goods per head (net value) in 1955, and their exports of finished manufactures accounted for at least one-sixth (mostly over

---

[1] See Appendix D for precise definitions of both intermediate products and finished manufactures.

[2] Austria, Denmark and Finland, which are not separately shown in Table 3.2, would also be in this group.

one-third) of total exports. Japan is a special case; though her net value of production per head is relatively small, her export trade structure is essentially similar to that of the industrial countries of Western Europe and the United States. Moreover, Japan is one of the very few countries (Britain is another) where industrialization has from the beginning been built up largely on an export trade in manufactures. For an analysis of export trade, therefore, it is reasonable to include Japan in the first group, henceforth termed the *industrial* countries.

The second group consists of countries which produced over $75 and not

Fig. 3.1. Degree of industrialization in production and exports, 1955

Semi-logarithmic scale

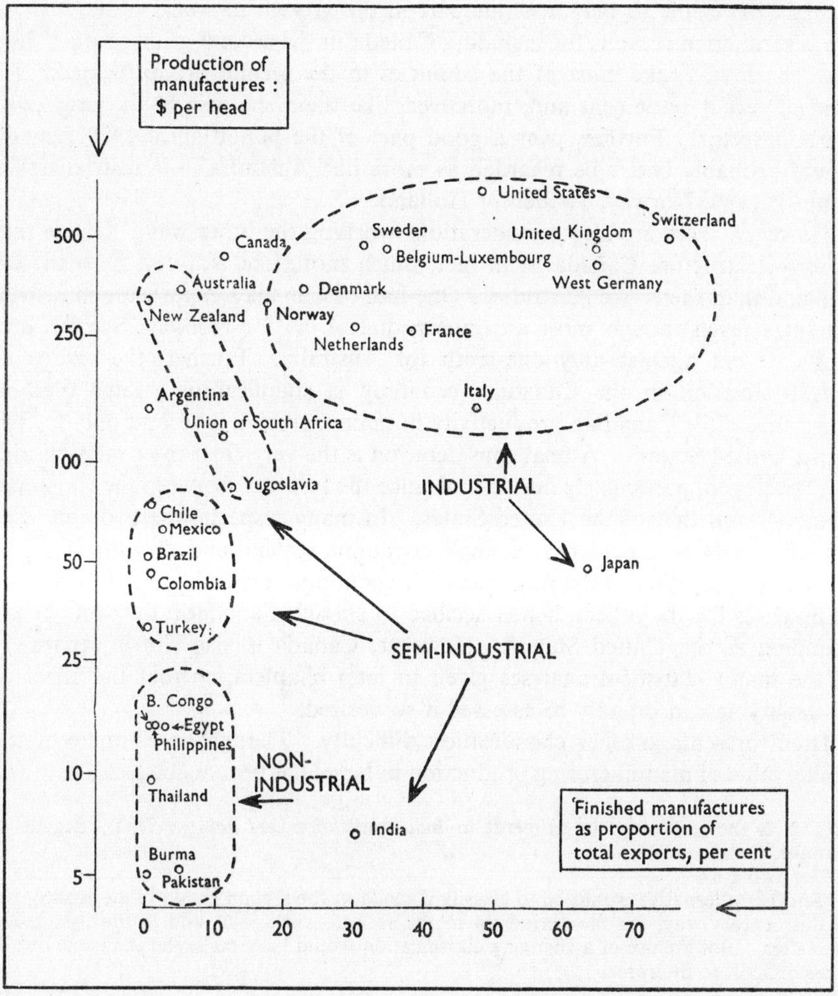

more than $350, net value of manufactures per head in 1955, and where exports of finished manufactures accounted for under 15 per cent of their total exports. The upper limit of production has been chosen so as to exclude Canada, which is clearly a borderline case and is discussed further below. Apart from Yugoslavia, the countries in this group, which also includes Argentina, are all 'countries of recent settlement'[1]. The degree of industrialization achieved by Australia and New Zealand, on the criteria used here, is as great as in many of the advanced countries of Western Europe but, unlike the latter, they still depend predominantly on primary products for the great bulk of their export earnings.

Canada falls between these first two groups, on the definitions adopted, and so could reasonably be included in either. The choice is important because Canada has come to play a major part in the growth of world trade. There are several good reasons for including Canada in the second group, rather than with the first. Like most of the countries in the second group, Canada is a land of recent settlement and, moreover, like them she also has a large agricultural sector. Further, over a good part of the period since 1900 Canada would probably better be regarded as more like Australia in industrialization than like, say, Norway, Sweden or Holland.

However, there are also considerations working the other way. One is that in export structure Canada is, in fact, much more like Norway, Sweden and Holland than she is like Australia. One-half of Canada's exports are industrial products (even though most are intermediates), as for Norway, Sweden and Holland, but against only one-tenth for Australia. Further, the degree of industrialization in the Canadian economy is significantly greater than in Australia, while Canadian productivity in manufacturing is second only to that in the United States[2]. A final consideration is the very close inter-relation that has developed, particularly during and since the last war, between the Canadian economy and that of the United States. In many respects, the two countries can effectively be regarded as a single economic system, and they are likely to grow closer together in the future as their economies expand. For this reason, as much as for the others, it was decided to classify Canada in the same broad grouping as the United States[3]. However, Canada is also shown separately in the major statistical analyses given in later chapters, so that the effect of re-classifying can broadly be assessed if so desired.

Israel presents another classification difficulty. Though an estimate of the dollar value of manufacturing production in Israel has been made (see Table 3.2)

[1]This is the term used by Hilgerdt in *Industrialization and Foreign Trade*, League of Nations, Geneva, 1945.

[2]See Table 1.4.

[3]Another alternative would be to classify Canada in the second group in the earlier part of this century, say, for the period up to the second world war, and in the first group thereafter. But the use of a changing classification would have made the statistical results more difficult to interpret.

this is, in fact, little more than an order of magnitude in view of the peculiarities of the Israeli price structure and the artificially maintained rates of exchange[1]. The estimate indicates that Israel's per caput production of manufactures in 1955 was probably much the same as Argentina's, but was substantially lower than that of Australia or New Zealand. The degree of industrialization of Israel's export trade is, however, considerably greater than that of Argentina, Australia or New Zealand, and is comparable with that of some of the smaller industrial countries of Western Europe. From this point of view, it would be quite reasonable to classify Israel in group 1 (the industrial countries). However, though her industrial development has been remarkably rapid since 1950, Israel is still a very young country with a high immigration rate, and in this respect she is much more like the countries of recent settlement than she is like the industrial countries of Western Europe. On balance, it seemed best to classify Israel with the countries in group 2, rather than with the industrial countries[2].

In the third group are countries producing in 1955 a per caput net value of manufactures between $30 and $75, and whose exports of finished manufactures were under one-tenth of their total exports. These are mostly countries in which industrialization is a fairly recent development, and they export very little finished manufactures at all.

For convenience of statistical presentation in later chapters, both the second and third groups will often be combined under the heading *semi-industrial* countries[3], though data for individual countries, or groups of countries, are also given where appropriate. This general grouping for semi-industrial countries is also used to include India, which produced less than $10 per head net value of manufactures in 1955, but whose exports are much more 'industrialized' than those of the Latin American countries or of the three Southern Dominions in this group. In fact, India seems to be related to the other semi-industrial countries in much the same way as Japan is related to the other industrial countries.

Finally, in group 4, we have countries which produced in 1955 not more than $15 per head net value of manufactures and exported negligible amounts of finished manufactures or none at all. These are countries in a very early stage of industrialization, and they are generally dependent on imports for a high proportion of their supplies of finished manufactures. In the subsequent discussion, these are referred to as the *non-industrial* countries, though in fact some of them (for example, Egypt) are in an early phase of industrialization. Exceptionally, Pakistan—which falls in this last group—is considered jointly

[1]For this reason, Israel is not shown in Fig. 3.1; if it had been included, it would have been approximately half-way between South Africa and the Netherlands.
[2]The classification of Israel makes little difference to the totals for the various groups of countries in view of her relatively small amount of trade in manufactured goods.
[3]Portugal, Spain, Greece and Ireland are not shown separately in Table 3.2 but would also fall into this group.

with India, because the two cannot be separated in the pre-war statistics.

Fig. 3.1 relates to one year only, but it has implications for the way in which the export pattern tends to change over time with the progress of industrialization. In the earlier stages of industrialization, certainly in groups three and four, and for some countries in group two also, local manufacturing output is of an import-saving character, being directed almost entirely towards the home market. After this stage is reached—which can be roughly characterized as the 'European level of industrialization'—then the product of home manufacturing industry tends to spill over into the export market, and there is a marked tendency for the share of finished manufactures in total exports to rise as industrialization progresses.

This general picture seems to be confirmed by Table 3.3, which shows the corresponding movement over time for a number of countries. There are, however, exceptions to the general rule that finished manufactures become of importance in exports only after a certain 'European' stage of industrialization has been reached. The two obvious exceptions are India and Japan, but Italy prior to 1939 was also exceptional in this respect. In India and Japan particularly, the export structure reflects the output pattern of large-scale factory industry, while total home output of manufactures in each case consists also of a substantial volume of handicraft work and produce of small-scale manufactures operated at a low level of productivity.

A similar classification into 'industrial' and 'semi-industrial' cannot be done

Table 3.3. *Finished manufactures as proportion of the total exports of selected countries, 1899–1959*

Percentage

	1899	1913	1929	1955	1959
Belgium-Luxembourg	23	21	37	35	36
France	43	44	47	38	48
Germany	49	46	54	65[a]	65[a]
Italy	17	31	41	47	54
Netherlands	..[b]	..[b]	29	31	34
Sweden	15	23	26	33	40
Switzerland	59	61	64	76	76
United Kingdom	59	58	57	65	64
Canada	7	6	14	11	11
United States	18	22	37	48	48
Japan	22	31	44	64	74
India	8	13	19	31	34

Sources: Tables A.1 and A.46 to A.68 and related data.

[a]West Germany.

[b]Not available.

on these criteria for the Soviet countries because comparable estimates of production of manufactures cannot be made very accurately in terms of United States dollars[1].   However, information is available about the pattern of exports from these countries (see Table 3.4).   Czechoslovakia and East Germany have the most highly 'industrialized' pattern of exports in terms of the proportion of manufactured goods in the total; indeed the East German percentage in 1959 was exceeded only by a small number of Western industrial countries.   The corresponding percentages for finished manufactures only were, of course, somewhat smaller—in 1958, about two-thirds for East Germany and about three-fifths for Czechoslovakia (much the same as for West Germany, Britain and Japan).   In 1958, too, about one-third of Poland's exports were finished manufactures, while for the Soviet Union the proportion was one-quarter. Though the Soviet Union's proportion of finished manufactures in total exports is appreciably lower than for most of the larger industrial countries of the West, her export trade in manufactured goods has grown considerably more rapidly since 1955 than the total manufactured exports of the Western industrial countries.

Table 3.4.   *Exports of manufactures from Eastern Europe and the Soviet Union, 1955–59*

	Value of exports of manufactures			Manufactures as proportion of total exports	
	1955	1959	Index, 1959	1955	1959
	($ billion, f.o.b.)		(1955 = 100)	(percentage)	
Czechoslovakia	0.92	1.44	157	78	83
East Germany	1.11	1.87	167	87	88
Hungary	0.33	0.49	149	55	64
Poland	0.36	0.54	152	38	47
Soviet Union	1.36	2.31	170	39	43

Sources: Yearbook of International Trade Statistics, 1960, Vol. I, United Nations, New York, 1962; *Economic Survey of Europe, 1957* and *1960*, United Nations, Geneva, 1958 and 1961.   The figures include some estimates.

3. INDUSTRIALIZATION AND IMPORTS

The relative importance of manufactures in total imports

Unlike the effect on exports, the effect of industrialization on the proportion

[1]The Soviet Union and Czechoslovakia would certainly qualify for inclusion in the 'industrial' group and probably East Germany, Hungary and Poland would also.   The other countries of Eastern Europe (except Albania) would probably qualify as 'semi-industrial'.   China appears to have moved rapidly from 'non-industrial' to 'semi-industrial' in the 1950's (see footnote on page 50).

of imports consisting of manufactures varies considerably from country to country and from one period to another. This is because the import pattern of an industrializing country is heavily dependent on its resource-endowment, as well as on its developing pattern of demand. Thus, in countries which are deficient in petroleum and coal, for example, the development of demand resulting from industrialization inevitably involves a sharp rise in fuel imports. Most countries of Latin America have found the rising cost of fuel imports a heavy burden on their balance of payments since 1950[1]. Equally, industrialization may result in an increased demand for food (for example, by the expanding urban population), and this may have to be met largely by imports.

In the semi-industrial countries as a group, the proportion of imports consisting of manufactures was, however, virtually the same in 1955 as it was in 1913 (Table 3.5). The main changes were the greater relative importance of fuels in the later year, and the reduced importance of food in total imports.

Table 3.5. *Relative importance of major commodity groups in imports of countries classified by stage of industrialization, 1913 and 1955*

	Year	Food	Fuels	Indus-trial materials	Manu-factures	Total imports
		(Percentage of total imports)				*($ billion, c.i.f.)*
Industrial countries[a]	1913	29	5	34	32	14.1
	1955	25	12	26	37	53.3
Russia/U.S.S.R.	1913	19	7	32	41	0.7
	1955	15	8	23	49	4.1
Semi-industrial countries[b]	1913	16	6	8	69	2.6
	1955	8	11	10	70	10.8
Rest of world	1913	33	6	13	47	1.9
	1955	18	11	9	61	11.2
TOTAL	1913	28	5	28	38	19.3
	1955	21	11	21	46	79.3

Sources: Yearbook of International Trade Statistics, 1958, Vol. I, United Nations, New York, 1960, and national trade statistics for the 1955 figures; P. Lamartine Yates, unpublished data sheets for *Forty Years of Foreign Trade,* London, 1959, for the 1913 figures.

[a]Belgium-Luxembourg, France, Germany (West Germany in 1955), Italy, Netherlands (1955 only), Sweden, Switzerland and United Kingdom ; Canada and United States ; Japan.

[b]Australia, New Zealand and Union of South Africa ; India and Pakistan ; Argentina, Brazil, Chile, Colombia and Mexico ; Israel (1955 only), Turkey and Yugoslavia (1955 only).

[1]Between 1948-50 and 1957-58, for example, the volume of fuel imports into Latin America rose by 72 per cent, as against an increase of only 37 per cent in total import volume (*Economic Bulletin for Latin America,* Vol. 4, No. 2, October 1959).

Manufactures are, however, relatively more important in the imports of these countries than in those of the non-industrial countries, and substantially more important than in the imports of the industrial countries. This seems to indicate that the proportion of manufactures in total imports tends to diminish after the early stages of industrial development have been passed.

Notable declines in the proportion of manufactures in imports have, in fact, occurred for several of the industrial countries. The United States is an outstanding example. In 1850, 70 per cent of her imports consisted of semi-manufactures and finished manufactures[1]. By the 1870's the proportion was reduced to about 45 per cent, and by the 1890's to 40 per cent[2]. The industrialization of the United States resulted in a sharp switch in favour of imports of crude materials, and this process continued into the early decades of the present century.

Japan is another country where the proportion of manufactures in imports has been sharply reduced during the earlier period of industrialization. In 1900, manufactured goods accounted for 48 per cent of Japan's imports, and for 43 per cent in 1913, whereas by 1959 the proportion had been reduced to only 21 per cent. The change has been due in the main to the development of the Japanese textile industry. In 1900, textiles represented one-fifth of all imports, but by 1913 they had been reduced to only 5 per cent and after 1930 they were negligible[3]. For Italy, too, the fall in the manufactures' proportion has been appreciable: from 43 per cent in 1900 to 32 per cent in 1955, though the proportion rose by 1959 to 36 per cent. The reduction since 1900 resulted largely from the substitution of home textiles for imports, though there was also a fall in the relative importance of miscellaneous consumer goods in total imports.

However, there have also been some marked increases since 1900 in the proportion of manufactures in total imports, particularly for Belgium (28 per cent in 1900 and 54 per cent in 1959), Sweden (37 and 63 per cent) and Switzerland (41 and 63 per cent). On the other hand, for Britain (22 and 26 per cent), France (25 and 32 per cent) and the United States (35 and 44 per cent), the increases in the proportion of manufactures have been very modest.

These different tendencies among the industrial countries reflect the fact that the smaller countries inevitably tend to specialize, while the larger ones produce virtually the whole range of manufactured goods. Thus, the smaller industrial countries depend heavily on the larger ones for increases in their requirement of manufactures, so that as their economies expand the proportion of manufactures in their total imports tends to rise. The inter-dependence of the

[1] The United States classifications of 'semi-manufactures' and 'finished manufactures' do not correspond with the definition of 'manufactures' used here.

[2] Decade averages.

[3] R. E. Baldwin, 'The Commodity Composition of Trade: Selected Industrial Countries, 1900-1954', *Review of Economics and Statistics*, Vol. 40, No. 1, February 1958, Part 2, Supplement.

industrial countries in manufactured goods is examined further in the next section.

The pattern of imports of manufactures

Industrial growth has had a marked influence on the commodity pattern *within* the manufactures group of imports. This is one of the main subjects discussed later in some detail[1], and only a brief review of the main trends is necessary at this stage. Industrialization has a double impact on the pattern of imports of manufactured goods, since it influences both the pattern of demand and the pattern of import-substitution. On the demand side, there are two distinct effects. First, the development of manufacturing industries in countries at an early stage of industrialization inevitably involves a relative increase in the demand for capital equipment and intermediate products for the construction and operation of the new industries; since both have a high import-content, industrial development results in increased imports of these goods. Second, as incomes rise, consumers' demand will switch towards durable goods and other goods with high income-elasticities, while the demand for other goods, which may include textiles, clothing and food, will rise less slowly. Again, insofar as consumer durables have higher import-contents than, say, clothing and food, this shift in demand patterns will also affect the commodity pattern of imports.

Industrialization also affects the pattern of import-substitution. As indicated earlier, the development of textiles and other light consumer industries tends to be of major importance in the earlier stages of industrial growth, while a more mature phase begins with the large-scale production of capital goods[2]. Thus the shift in the pattern of output in the earlier stages of industrialization tends to diverge from the shift in the demand pattern described above. This divergence is likely to result in a drastic contraction in imports of textiles and other consumer goods where import-substitution comes into play, in relation to imports of capital goods and intermediate products.

Moreover, as industries develop, a definite sequence of processes tends to be adopted. In the earlier stages, manufacturing may depend to a considerable extent on imported parts and components, or on imported semi-processed goods (such as yarns), whereas at a later stage—when labour skills are more developed and the home market is more extensive—complete production from the raw material to the final product may be introduced. This general sequence may, of course, apply more to some industries or countries than to others. Insofar, however, as it has any general application among industrializing countries, it is likely to reinforce the tendency for the pattern of imports of manufactures to shift towards intermediate products in the earlier phases of

[1]See Chapter 7.
[2]See page 55.

the industrialization process, though not perhaps in the later.

In fact, the share of intermediates in total exports of manufactures from the industrial[1] to the semi-industrial countries rose from about 20 per cent in 1929 to about 25 per cent in 1955. Over this period there was, however, virtually no change in the relative importance of intermediates in exports of manufactures to industrial countries and to the rest of the world (excluding the Soviet Union). Though changes over time in this proportion have been small, or negligible, the fact that intermediates play a much more important rôle in imports into the industrial countries than into the other groups supports the view that in the long run industrialization tends to result in a shift in the import pattern towards intermediate products. As will be seen later, the relatively high proportion of intermediates in the imports of the industrial countries is mainly due to the import pattern of the three largest industrial countries[2]—Britain, West Germany and the United States.

The most important shift in commodity pattern of imports since the beginning of the century, however, has been within the field of finished manufactures. The share of capital goods has increased dramatically in all areas; in 1955, it was highest in Soviet imports, at three-fifths of total imports of manufactures, and lowest in the industrial countries, at rather more than one-quarter (Table 3.6). At the same time, there has been a sharp contraction in the share of textile fabrics, particularly in the semi-industrial countries, where the share of miscellaneous manufactures (largely consumer goods) has also been drastically curtailed as a result of import-substitution.

4. INTER-DEPENDENCE OF THE INDUSTRIAL COUNTRIES IN MANUFACTURED GOODS

The smaller[3] industrial countries tend to specialize in production, as already indicated, rather than to produce the whole range of manufactures. Professor Kuznets has suggested three reasons why this should be so[4]. First, most countries with small populations, Professor Kuznets argues, tend to have more limited natural resources than countries with large populations. This proposition may not be universally true, particularly in underdeveloped countries, but it seems to be generally valid for the developed industrial countries[5]. A second

[1]The figures relate to exports from the main industrial countries and India.
[2]I.e. the three largest outside the Soviet Union.
[3]No precise statistical criterion of 'smallness' is needed at this stage. The distinction between 'small' and 'large' industrial countries is further developed in Chapter 6; see also Chapter 15.
[4]S. Kuznets, 'Economic Growth of Small Nations', in *Economic Consequences of the Size of Nations*, Proceedings of a Conference held by the International Economic Association, London, 1960.
[5]See, however, Dr K. W. Rothschild's illuminating comments on Professor Kuznets' paper (in *Economic Consequences of the Size of Nations*, page 353). Dr Rothschild argues that natural resources are not randomly distributed, but are in fact highly concentrated, so that a small country can be as well-endowed with them as a large country.

Table 3.6. *Exports[a] of manufactures to countries classified by degree of industrialization, subdivided by stage of fabrication and end use,* 1899, 1929 *and* 1955

Percentage[b]

Commodity group[c]	Year	Industrial countries	Semi-industrial countries	U.S.S.R.[d]	Rest of world	Total
Intermediate products	1899	37.4	18.4	34.9	27.2	31.4
	1929	38.1	19.6	19.5	21.4	28.9
	1955	38.7	25.5	14.8	21.8	30.4
Finished manufactures	1899	62.6	81.6	65.1	72.8	68.6
	1929	61.9	80.4	80.5	78.6	71.1
	1955	61.3	74.5	85.2	78.2	69.6
Capital goods	1899	9.4	11.8	35.7	11.9	11.5
	1929	17.7	23.8	59.2	20.1	20.3
	1955	28.4	43.4	60.0	32.2	32.8
Textile fabrics	1899	19.5	34.1	2.4	26.5	23.2
	1929	13.0	22.1	2.3	22.1	17.5
	1955	5.8	6.8	—	11.0	7.7
Other finished goods	1899	33.7	35.7	27.0	34.4	33.9
	1929	31.2	34.5	19.0	36.4	33.3
	1955	27.1	24.3	25.2	35.0	29.1
ALL MANUFACTURES	1899	100.0	100.0	100.0	100.0	100.0
	1929	100.0	100.0	100.0	100.0	100.0
	1955	100.0	100.0	100.0	100.0	100.0

Sources: Tables A.5, A.7, A.9, A.11 and national trade statistics.

[a]Exports from 11 industrial countries and India (see Appendix A for details).
[b]Based on current values, f.o.b., exporting countries.
[c]See Appendix D for definitions of these commodity groups.
[d]Russia in 1899.

factor is that small countries tend to have a limited domestic market which makes the establishment of some industries uneconomic. This is because in such industries, for example, aircraft, motor vehicles or heavy electrical equipment, the small domestic market could not support even the minimum scale of plant which would be necessary for profitable operation, while 'heavy reliance on foreign markets is not a sound base for many industries'[1]. There are, of course, notable exceptions to this, such as the Swiss watch, pharmaceutical and precision engineering industries or the Belgian steel industry, which rely mainly on the export market. In such cases, the home industry has been built up on a considerable degree of specialization and, in the Swiss case, a high level of

[1]Kuznets, 'Economic Growth of Small Nations', *op. cit.*, p. 17.

skilled craftsmanship. Nonetheless, though there is a range of industry in which specialization for export may be profitable, the extra risks of selling in export markets may be too great in other industries, particularly those—such as Professor Kuznets mentions—in which exceptionally large capital investments are involved.

Finally, a small country may more readily possess a relative abundance of a few natural resources, in relation to its population or its requirements, and it may therefore find it profitable to build up its manufacturing activities on this basis. Canadian, Norwegian and Swedish paper and board exports, and Belgian steel exports are examples of such resource-oriented specialization. Though Professor Kuznets had in mind the possible comparative advantages which a small country might have in any economic activity, the point applies with equal force within the manufacturing field alone.

The pattern of specialization among the smaller industrial countries is a very diverse one in terms of particular commodities, as is to be expected in view of the differences in magnitude and variety of their natural resources, their different manufacturing traditions, their variation in ease of access to export markets, and so on[1]. There is, however, more uniformity if specialization is thought of in terms of the degree of fabrication of exports of manufactures. In these terms, there are some important contrasts between some of the small industrial countries and some of the large ones.

By relating the relative importance of finished goods in total imports to that in total exports of manufactures, a definite 'ordering' of countries appears, as can be seen from Fig. 3.2, which relates to the position in 1955 (this general pattern also applies to the period since then). At one extreme are Canada and Belgium-Luxembourg (Norway is also in this group), whose imports of manufactures are mostly in finished form, and whose exports are largely intermediates; at the other extreme, the reverse is true for Britain, West Germany and the United States. Between these extremes are France, Sweden and the Netherlands, whose trade in finished goods represents about the same proportion (about 60 per cent) of trade in manufactures both for imports and exports; and Italy, Switzerland and Japan, whose exports consist of a higher proportion of finished goods than do their imports.

These differences in the structure of foreign trade were much less marked before the first World War than they were in 1955 (see Table 3.7), or are now. In the intervening period, the relative importance of finished goods in total imports of manufactures has fallen substantially in Britain and the United States, while at the other end of the distribution, the share of intermediates in

[1]That there is, in fact, a significantly higher concentration by commodity group in the exports of small developed countries than in those of large developed countries has been demonstrated statistically by Dr M. Michaely. If, however, all small countries are compared with all large ones (including under-developed countries in each group), the degree of commodity concentration on exports is much the same in each (M. Michaely, *Concentration in International Trade*, North-Holland Publishing Co., Amsterdam, 1962).

Fig. 3.2.   Finished manufactures as proportion of total trade in manufactures
of the main industrial countries, 1955

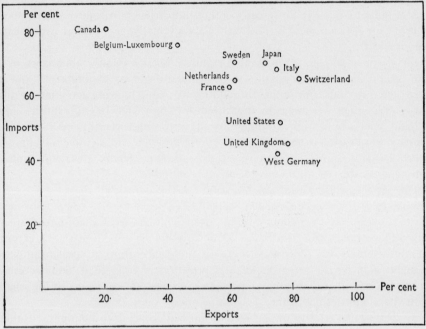

Canadian exports of manufactures has considerably increased.   In general, the
degree of specialization among the industrial countries, as indicated by the
degree of fabrication in the foreign trade structure, seems to have increased
significantly over the past four decades.

Belgium-Luxembourg, Canada and Sweden depend heavily on the major
industrial countries (Britain, France, West Germany and the United States)
for export markets for their intermediate products; in 1955, nearly two-thirds
of their exports of intermediates went to these four industrial countries
(Table 3.8)[1].   By contrast, only one-third of their exports of finished manufactures went to the four large industrial countries in that year.   At the same
time, these smaller countries (Belgium-Luxembourg, Canada, Norway and
Sweden) depend heavily on the four major industrial countries for their imports
of finished manufactures; in 1955, about 85 per cent of their imports in this
category came from these four countries.

The four major industrial countries, for their part, are not nearly so
dependent on the small industrial countries for markets.   In 1955 four
small industrial countries (Belgium-Luxembourg, Canada, Norway and
Sweden) took only 20 per cent of the exports of both intermediates and

[1]A similar analysis is not available for Norwegian exports of intermediates and finished
goods by destination.

Table 3.7 *Finished manufactures as proportion of total trade in manufactures of the main industrial countries, 1913 and 1955*

Percentage

	Imports[a]		Exports	
	1913	1955	1913	1955
Belgium-Luxembourg	62	75	46	44
France	59	62	76	60
Germany	43	41[b]	63	76[b]
Italy	63	67	70	76
Netherlands	53	63	..	63
Sweden	55	69	57	63
Switzerland	59	63	79	83
United Kingdom	64	43	76	79
Canada	75	80	52	22
United States	69	50	62	77
Japan	62	68	63	73
TOTAL	61	61	68	69

Sources: Tables A.15 to A.26; and A.46 to A.68.

[a]That is exports from other industrial countries and India to the countries listed. For further details see Appendix A.
[b]West Germany.

finished manufactures from the four larger countries, while Italy, Japan, Switzerland and the Netherlands together took only 10 per cent. Moreover, the intra-trade among the four supplied almost one-half of their total imports of finished goods, and though the corresponding proportion was lower for intermediates, it was still substantial (30 per cent). The countries classified in the middle group of industrial countries in Table 3.8 (i.e. Italy, Japan, Netherlands and Switzerland), depend largely on the four major industrial countries for their imports, both of intermediates and of finished manufactures.

This structural inter-dependence of the smaller industrial countries on the larger ones necessarily has a major influence on the rate of growth in the intra-trade among the industrial countries, as well as on the degree to which economic growth in the major industrial nations is transmitted to the smaller countries.

Though this type of inter-dependence—which is based essentially on differences in size of the various industrial countries—explains much of the pattern of trade in terms of the proportion of intermediate products to finished manufactures, it does not go very far in explaining the level or the pattern of trade in finished manufactures themselves. Here, it seems likely that demand factors play a more important rôle in determining trade patterns, while resource-endowments are relatively less important than for trade in intermediates. Providing international trade in finished manufactures is free of governmental

Table 3.8. *Exports of intermediate products and finished manufactures from the industrial countries by destination, 1955*

$ *billion, f.o.b.*

Exports from

Exports to	Belgium-Luxembourg, Canada, Sweden	Italy, Netherlands, Switzerland	France, United Kingdom, United States, West Germany	Japan	Total
INTERMEDIATE PRODUCTS					
Belgium-Luxembourg, Canada, Norway, Sweden	0.15	0.11	1.05	0.01	1.32
Italy, Japan, Netherlands, Switzerland	0.35	0.07	0.77	0.01	1.20
France, West Germany, United Kingdom, United States	2.07	0.39	1.15	0.06	3.68
Semi-industrial countries	0.23	0.14	1.17	0.18	1.71
Rest of world	0.39	0.26	1.63	0.20	2.48
WORLD TOTAL	3.19	0.96	5.78	0.47	10.39
FINISHED MANUFACTURES					
Belgium-Luxembourg, Canada, Norway, Sweden	0.22	0.39	3.57	0.04	4.22
Italy, Japan, Netherlands, Switzerland	0.34	0.20	1.61	0.02	2.16
France, West Germany, United Kingdom, United States	0.65	0.80	1.64	0.33	3.41
Semi-industrial countries	0.26	0.47	4.05	0.17	4.95
Rest of world	0.53	0.84	6.67	0.72	8.77
WORLD TOTAL	2.01	2.69	17.53	1.28	23.51

Source: Working sheet for Tables A.78 and A.79.

restrictions, the great diversification in consumer tastes can by itself explain a good deal of the trade expansion in this sector[1].

[1] S. B. Linder has recently advanced the theory that trade in manufactures is most intensive between countries with similar patterns of demand. Since the pattern of demand is determined, to a large extent, by a country's average income level, Linder argues that trade in manufactures should be most intensive between countries with similar average income levels. His statistical tests of this theory are, however, inconclusive both for total trade and for trade in manufactures alone (see S. B. Linder, *An Essay on Trade and Transformation*, Wiley, New York, 1961). This may be, in part, because for intermediate products the resource-endowments of different countries are a major determinant of the pattern of trade, while for finished manufactures the different sizes of the home markets of countries at similar income levels will also influence the pattern of output, and thus of trade, for reasons given earlier.

5. EXPORTS OF MANUFACTURES FROM THE SEMI-INDUSTRIAL COUNTRIES

Though the greater part of the expanding output of manufactures in an industrializing country can be expected to replace imports on the home market, manufactures may also be of great importance in helping the expansion of exports. Britain, Japan, India and, to a lesser degree, Israel, have all developed their economies on the basis of a relatively large export of manufactured goods. For countries which have traditionally relied on primary products for their export income, a development of export trade in manufactures has proved of assistance in financing the import of other manufactures needed for economic growth. The development of an export trade in manufactures may, indeed, be found essential for such countries in the future if exports of primary products and the inflow of long-term capital fail to expand enough.

So far, however, relatively few countries outside the main industrial areas have developed any substantial export trade in finished manufactures. Among these are India and Israel, already mentioned, and Australia, South Africa and Yugoslavia, among the countries included in our 'semi-industrial' group;

Table 3.9. *Exports of manufactures from the semi-industrial countries, 1937–59*

$ million, f.o.b.

	1937	1948	1955	1957	1959
Australia	51[a]	137	184	260	240
New Zealand	6[b]	5[b]	9	16	26
Union of South Africa[c]	21	145	268	315	379
India	} 196	566	471	607	542
Pakistan		..	21	42	73
Argentina	18	50	53	58	46
Brazil	3	54	20	18	18
Chile	115[b]	215[b]	364	326	335
Colombia	0	4	7	6	7
Mexico	80	187	200	190	198
Israel[c]	..	10[d]	49	78	103
Turkey	3[b]	11[b]	14	11	11
Yugoslavia	18	54	96	176	246

Sources: International Trade, 1956, Table 32, G.A.T.T., Geneva, 1957; *Yearbook of International Trade Statistics, 1960,* Vol. I, United Nations, New York, 1962; and national trade statistics.

[a]Year beginning 1 July 1937.
[b]Partly estimated.
[c]Including diamonds.
[d]1949.

other such countries are Hong Kong (textiles and apparel) and Egypt (cotton textiles).

India's exports of manufactures consist very largely of cotton and jute goods, but Israeli exports, though relatively small, cover a wide range, from cut and polished diamonds, the largest single item, to textiles and clothing, passenger cars and rubber tyres. Australia has developed an export trade in machinery and transport equipment, metal goods and chemicals; South Africa exports

Table 3.10. *Exports of manufactures from semi-industrial and non-industrial countries, and Soviet countries, 1953 and 1958*

$ million, f.o.b.

Exports from	Year	Capital goods	Consumer goods	Base metals	Other manufactures	Total
Dollar Latin America	1953	4	39	100	55	200
	1958	12	43	85	85	225
Other Latin America	1953	1	10	285	100	395
	1958	5	8	290	90	390
Overseas Sterling Area	1953	115	780	550	430	1875
	1958	145	875	480	520	2020
Overseas Associates of Continental Western Europe	1953	18	12	220	70	320
	1958	20	10	190	110	330
U.S.S.R., Eastern Europe and China[a]	1953	60	125	30	160	375
	1958	335	260	250	410	1225
Other semi-industrial and non-industrial countries	1953	105	120	55	280	560
	1958	150	170	80	490	890
TOTAL	1953	305	1085	1240	1095	3725
	1958	665	1365	1375	1705	5110

Source: International Trade, 1959 (Table IV), G.A.T.T., Geneva, 1960.

[a]Excluding the intra-trade of these countries. In 1958, the intra-trade in all commodities, manufactures and primary products amounted to $8,510 million, or 71 per cent of the total exports of $12,010 million from these countries.

diamonds, machinery, chemicals, apparel and a range of other manufactured goods; while Yugoslavia exports a fairly wide range, including chemicals, textiles and electric machinery. Exports of finished manufactures from the semi-industrial countries still represent only a small fraction—under 2 per cent—of the comparable total for the industrial countries. In recent years, exports of manufactures from the semi-industrial countries have been in total about

75 per cent above the pre-war volume, the biggest increases being achieved by Australia, South Africa, India/Pakistan and Chile (see Table 3.9).

For the period from 1953 to 1958 a detailed analysis of the export trade of the semi-industrial and non-industrial areas is available in the annual reports of G.A.T.T. Over this period, exports of manufactures from these areas (including, however, the Soviet countries) rose from 3.7 to 5.1 billion dollars (see Table 3.10). Excluding the Soviet group, exports of manufactures from the semi-industrial and non-industrial areas rose by some 15 per cent to $3.9 billion in 1958, but since this was a period of great expansion in world trade, their exports expressed as a proportion of exports of manufactures from the industrial countries[1] fell from 12 to 9 per cent over the period. The main reason for this relative fall was the decline in the value of exports of non-ferrous metals to the United States[2]. Of the other main commodity groups, the biggest increase since 1953 was in miscellaneous manufactures, the smallest being in capital goods.

Exports from the Soviet countries showed a substantial increase between 1953 and 1958, the rise in exports of capital goods ($275 million) being particularly notable. Though exports of capital goods from Soviet countries represent a very small fraction of world trade in this category (about 2 per cent in 1958), they are more highly concentrated on markets in the underdeveloped areas than are exports from the industrial countries[3].

The relatively small scale of exports of finished manufactures from the semi-industrial areas reflects two quite separate limiting factors. The first, already mentioned, is that in the earlier phases of industrialization, manufacturing output substitutes for imports and is thus not available for export. The second limitation is that the industrial countries—which are easily the main consumers of manufactures in the world—have generally restricted the importation of manufactures from the less-developed areas by tariffs, quotas or other protectionist measures[4]. Such measures have been effective in restricting imports of cheap textiles, apparel and other lightly-processed goods having a high labour-content, and in which the less-developed countries concerned have a cost advantage. Import restrictions on such manufactures act both to limit

---

[1]Using the G.A.T.T. definition of industrial countries (i.e. North America, European Economic Community, European Free Trade Association and Japan).

[2]The main reason was that the 'traditional' non-ferrous metals (copper, lead and zinc) were subject to substitution on a large scale in the United States by aluminium and plastics during the 1950's (see J. A. Rowlatt and F. T. Blackaby, 'The Demand for Industrial Materials, 1950-57', *National Institute Economic Review*, No. 5, September 1959).

[3]Three-quarters of exports of capital goods from Soviet countries went to non-Soviet semi-industrial and non-industrial countries in 1958, as against one-half of those from the Western industrial countries.

[4]The United Kingdom is exceptional in allowing free entry for manufactures originating in less-developed Commonwealth countries (for example, Indian textiles and Hong Kong textiles and apparel). However, even here, some restrictions on the level of imports (based on voluntary agreements) are in force.

the rate of industrial growth which can be achieved in some of the less advanced countries, and to reduce the real income of the industrial countries themselves, since more costly home-produced goods are consumed instead. The import policy of the industrial countries with regard to such products of the less developed areas is likely to become of greater importance in the future with the progress of industrialization in those areas[1].

[1]This problem is discussed further in Chapter 15.

CHAPTER 4

TRENDS IN WORLD TRADE IN MANUFACTURES

1. PRODUCTION AND TRADE IN MANUFACTURES AND PRIMARY PRODUCTS

Since the beginning of this century, world production of manufactures per head of the population had almost quadrupled by the late 1950's, whereas for primary products the rise was only some 50 per cent (see Table 4.1)[1]. In the period up to the first World War, the volume of international trade expanded at roughly the same rate as world production. This was true for both manufactures and primary commodities. But, as Fig. 4.1 shows, in the inter-war period large divergencies appeared between the trend in production and that in international trade[2].

The later 1920's was a period of rapid economic growth, both world production and world trade in primary produce, in the period 1926–30, averaging nearly one-quarter above the 1913 levels. In manufactures, however, there was a much sharper growth in production than in trade—about 40 per cent as against less than 15 per cent. This was partly the result of the faster expansion in the United States economy than in Western Europe (the United States being more self-sufficient as regards foreign trade), and partly the result of import-substitution in all the main industrial countries[3].

The major break, however, in the relationship between world production and trade came with the economic crisis of 1930–32, and with its aftermath of trade and currency restrictions. The re-expansion, when it came, was based on a sharp re-alignment of the pattern of output in the majority of industrial countries with a substantially reduced level of trade in industrial products. This major discontinuity in the relationship of production and trade can be traced right up to about 1950, which marks the beginning of rapid economic expansion in Western Europe.

The discontinuity of the 1930's was sharper for manufactures than for other

[1]There has also been a rapid expansion in the output of the 'service' industries; this is neglected here, since this chapter is concerned essentially with physical commodities.

[2]Too much reliance must not be placed on index numbers extending over such a long period, and small movements are unlikely to have much significance. In particular, it should be noted that the index of world production of manufactures probably contains a downward bias in the period before 1913, because most of the national index numbers of production in the first decades of the present century were based to a substantial extent on data of consumption of materials so that insufficient allowance was generally made for the increased volume of work done per unit of materials consumed. The more rapid growth in production than in trade in manufactures, which was such a marked feature of the inter-war period, may well have been present *before* 1913 also. The index for primary products is not affected by this type of bias.

[3]The effect of import-substitution in the industrial countries on the volume of trade in manufactures is discussed in some detail in Chapters 6 and 8.

goods. Between 1929—a peak year—and the bottom of the Depression, in 1932, world industrial production fell by one-third and world trade in manufactures by two-fifths; but though production recovered by 1937 to one-tenth higher than the 1929 peak, trade in manufactures in 1937 was still some 15 per cent lower. By contrast, the volume of world trade in primary products had fallen only by about one-eighth from 1929 to 1932, and by 1937 had just exceeded the previous (1929) peak, though as a proportion of world production, the 1937 trade volume was still lower than in 1929. As is shown later, these divergent movements were closely associated with inverse movements in relative prices.

Table 4.1.   *World trends in population, production and trade, 1876–1959*

Index numbers, 1913 = 100

	Population[a]	Production		Trade volume		Trade unit values[b]	
		Manu-factures	Primary produce	Manu-factures	Primary produce	Manu-factures	Primary produce
1876–80	79	25	..	31	31	102	104
1896–1900	90	54	76[c]	54	62	82	77
1911–13	99	95	93	94	97	98	98
1926–30	111	141	123	113	123	145	128
1931–33	117	110	120	81	116	100	68
1934–35	120	133	125	84	114	117	85
1936–38	124	158	135	100	125	120	93
1948–50	145	238	156	132	116	233	259
1951–53	151	297	176	178	133	248	289
1954–56	158	341	191	216	156	244	271
1957–59	166	381	203	251	182	259	257

Sources: Industrialization and Foreign Trade, League of Nations, Geneva, 1945; W. A. Lewis, 'World Production, Prices and Trade, 1870–1960', *Manchester School*, Vol. 20, No. 2, May 1952; E. Lerdau, 'Stabilization and the Terms of Trade', *Kyklos*, Vol. XII, 1959, Fasc. 3; Sir D. MacDougall, *The World Dollar Problem*, London, 1957; *Statistical Yearbooks* and *Monthly Bulletin of Statistics*, United Nations, New York.

[a]From 1948, the indices exclude the Soviet countries.
[b]In terms of current U.S. dollars.
[c]1900.

In the 1950,s the trend in world trade was sharply upward for both major segments of world trade. Moreover, for the first time this century, the volume of trade has expanded at a faster rate than world production. A major factor here has been the rapid economic growth in Western Europe since 1950 and the progressive reduction in import restrictions and other barriers to trade.

Fig. 4.1.   Trends in world* production and trade in manufactures and primary products, 1876–1959

Volume indices, 1913 = 100
Semi-logarithmic scale

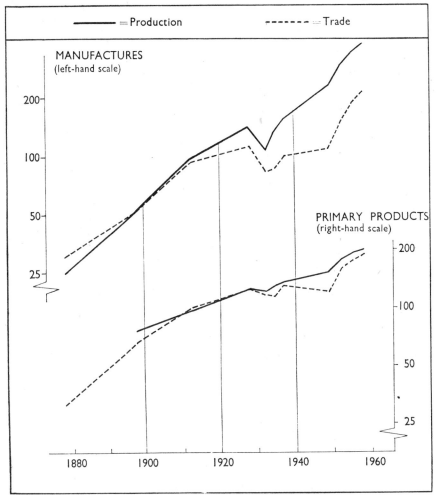

*Excluding production and exports of the present Soviet countries so far as possible.

Western Europe is highly dependent on imports, relatively to the United States, and the different rates of growth in the two areas explain a good deal of the difference in the long-term trends of world production and trade. An important additional factor which has retarded the rate of growth in trade in primary products has been the widespread adoption of agricultural protectionism by the industrial countries.

G

Price trends

As already mentioned, the smaller contraction of trade in primary products than in manufactures during the 1930's was closely associated with a much sharper relative price fall. Similarly, the greater expansion in the volume of world trade in manufactures than in primary products since 1938 has been associated with a relatively smaller rise in unit values. In the inter-war period, this inverse association was particularly close though, as can be seen from Fig. 4.2, it can also be traced back to the period from the 1890's to 1913[1].

The degree of inverse association between relative volumes and relative unit values cannot be expected to remain unchanged over time, since the relationship depends on the relative rates of change in world demand and supply of both manufactures and primary products. These, in turn, reflect changes in more fundamental factors such as the supply and productivity of labour and capital in different areas and lines of production, and changes in real incomes and divergencies in the income-elasticities of demand for various types of commodity[2].

The relationship between the relative volumes and the relative unit values of manufactures and primary products has, in fact, changed considerably since the 1890's. In the period 1891–1913, the rise in the relative volume of manufactures (14 per cent) was double the fall in their relative unit value (7 per cent). From 1926–30 to 1931–33, however, the relative fall in volume was less than the relative rise in price (24 as against 30 per cent); while from 1931–33 to 1936–38, the relative changes were almost the same (14 per cent for volume and 12 per cent for price). Thus, in the inter-war period, a given price rise in manufactures relative to primary products had a smaller adverse effect on the relative volume of manufactures traded than was the case prior to 1914.

Since 1948, however, there appears to have been a *positive*, not an inverse, association between relative volumes and unit values, and in this respect the post-war period has been in marked contrast with the two earlier periods. This new development has two related aspects; a rapid growth in the *volume* of world trade in manufactures relatively to other goods; and a tendency, over the period since 1948, for the *prices* of primary products to rise slightly, and then to fall, in relation to those of manufactures.

The expansion in the relative volume of trade in manufactures in the post-war period appears to have been due essentially to two main factors. The first was a

---

[1]This inverse association resulted in a relatively stable proportion, in *value* terms, of world trade in manufactures to total world trade from the 1890's up to 1938.

[2]Different projections of the future trend in the terms of trade between manufactures and primary products can be obtained according to the functional relationships assumed to exist between the relevant variables, and according to the assumed or calculated magnitudes of the various parameters. For examples of such projections see M. K. Atallah, *The Long-Term Movement of the Terms of Trade between Agricultural and Industrial Products*, Netherlands Economic Institute, Rotterdam, 1958

temporary phenomenon: the economic dislocation and reconstruction of the
West European economy in the early post-war years. The period 1948–50
was clearly abnormal insofar as the supply of manufactured goods was still
severely limited and it was only after the mid-1950's that the 'seller's market'
in manufactures generally disappeared.

Fig. 4.2.   Changes in relative unit value and volume of world trade in
manufactures and primary products, 1876–1959

Indices, 1913 = 100

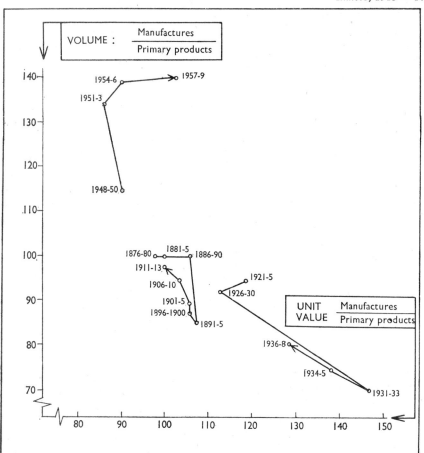

The other factor, of a more permanent character, has been a retardation in
the rate of growth in demand for primary products in relation to manufactured
goods. A shift in the balance of world demand towards manufactured goods
seems to be an inevitable accompaniment of economic growth. But the shift
that has occurred since 1945 appears to have been much sharper than previously.

In part, it has been a consequence of the industrialization of many primary-producing countries, which has resulted in a marked increase in their demand for capital equipment and semi-finished manufactures. But the more important developments have occurred within the industrial countries themselves. There, too, the balance of demand has shifted towards the 'growth' sectors of engineering and chemicals; and it is precisely in these that the raw material content per unit of output is lower than in other major industries, such as textiles, clothing and food processing. Consequently, the shift in the pattern of output has resulted in the demand for raw materials in total lagging behind industrial growth. Second, there has been a noticeable trend, in many major industries, to produce a given volume of manufactures from a progressively smaller volume of materials. Finally, and of extreme importance, the development of synthetic substitutes for various natural primary products since the war has made very considerable inroads into the demand for the typical exports of the primary-producing countries[1].

In the period up to 1939, economic expansion in the industrial countries tended to result in increased demand for primary products. A great many industrial materials and foods are subject to inelastic supply in the short run, while in the expansionary phase of the cycle the supply of manufactures increases. The terms of trade during expansion thus tended, with a varying time-lag, to turn in favour of primary products. During the economic expansion of the 1950's, however, the technological and other factors mentioned above were inhibiting the growth in demand for primary products, and so preventing the 'normal' swing in the terms of trade against manufactures[2].

The network of trade

The rapid growth of Western Europe since 1950 is also reflected in a great expansion of trade between the industrial countries in this period. As will be seen later, this expansion in intra-trade can be considered very largely as a return to a more 'normal' relationship between the intra-trade of the industrial countries and total world trade.

By 1959, the intra-trade of the industrial countries accounted for about 40 per cent of total world trade, compared with only about 33 per cent in 1950. In 1959, some two-thirds of the intra-trade consisted of manufactures (Table 4.2), which implies that a substantial proportion of the intra-trade consisted of an exchange of manufactures for other manufactures[3]. The intra-trade of

[1]The effect of these developments on the export earnings of the primary-producing countries is considered in more detail in Chapter 5.

[2]There were, as already mentioned, other factors affecting the relative volumes and unit values of manufactures and primary products in world trade.

[3]The magnitude of this exchange of 'manufactures for manufactures' is not, however, given by the difference between the $28.8 billion of intra-trade in manufactures and the $16.0 billion of intra-trade in primary products shown in Table 4.2. The true figure can be calculated only from the detailed figures of trade between individual countries.

the industrial countries in manufactures in 1959 represented almost one-half of total world trade in this category, while their intra-trade in primary products represented one-third of the total.

Table 4.2. *Network of trade in manufactures and primary products between industrial, primary-producing and Soviet countries, 1959*

$ *billion, f.o.b.*

| | Exports from | | | |
Exports to	Industrial countries[a]	Primary-producing countries[b]	Soviet countries	Total
INDUSTRIAL COUNTRIES[a]				
Manufactures	28.8	2.5	0.8	32.1
Primary products	16.0	18.5	1.6	36.1
PRIMARY-PRODUCING COUNTRIES[b]				
Manufactures	17.4	1.3	0.6	19.3
Primary products	4.0	5.5	0.4	9.9
SOVIET COUNTRIES				
Manufactures	1.7	0.1	6.3	8.1
Primary products	0.6	1.0	4.1	5.7
TOTAL				
Manufactures	47.9	3.9	7.7	59.5
Primary products	20.5	25.0	6.1	51.6

Source: International Trade, 1960, G.A.T.T., Geneva, 1961.

[a]North America, Western Europe (including Finland, Spain and Yugoslavia) and Japan.
[b]Rest of the world, excluding Soviet countries.

The other main interchange of goods is between the industrial countries and the primary-producing areas. This consists mainly of exports of manufactures from the industrial countries in exchange for imports of primary products. In 1959, this trade amounted to some $17½–18½ billion each way; in total, about one-third of world trade in all commodities. Of the other flows of trade shown in Table 4.2, the most important are the exports of primary products (including surplus disposals by the United States) from the industrial to the primary-producing countries; the interchange of primary products between the primary-producing countries; and the intra-trade among the Soviet countries.

In the present study, attention is focused essentially on the export trade in manufactures from the main industrial countries. Relatively little is said about the other streams of trade, including exports of manufactures from the primary-producing and Soviet countries. Manufactured goods exported by the primary-producing countries consist in the main of non-ferrous metals and textile products; these are referred to in the relevant commodity chapters (9 and 13). Exports from the Soviet group are not analysed in great detail, though they are referred to where this seemed to be relevant to the discussion in various chapters; some of the factors which would affect their future trend are discussed in Chapter 15.

Since we are primarily concerned with the effects of industrial growth on the exports of manufactures from the industrial countries, it is necessary to attempt an explanation of the movement in the demand for manufactured goods in the main importing areas. Hitherto, studies in this field have been severely handicapped by the lack of long-term series, on a comparable basis, relating to imports of various categories of goods into countries at different stages of industrialization[1]. Furthermore, comparable series relating to the movement in the consumption of manufactures in different countries appeared also to be completely lacking. Accordingly, it was decided to mould the present study around two new sets of statistical series. The first, designed to remedy the gap in our knowledge about long-term movements in trade in manufactures, is described briefly in the following section. The second set of statistics relates to the apparent consumption of non-food manufactures in a wide range of countries for the same selection of years for which the new trade data were computed. The methods used in estimating the consumption series are described in detail in Appendix E; the results are first introduced in Chapter 6.

2. THE TRADE NETWORK TABLES

The subsequent analysis of trade movements in this book is based on a set of statistics showing the change over the period 1899–1959 in the value and estimated volume of exports by the main industrial countries[2] and India to a wide range of countries, including the industrial and semi-industrial countries (as defined in Chapter 3), a selection of non-industrial countries, and the Soviet Union. Exports from these twelve countries accounted for 77 per cent of total world exports of manufactures in 1959, and 88 per cent of the total, if exports from the Soviet countries are excluded. For the period before the second World War the corresponding percentages would be even higher.

The statistics relate to selected years only, namely 1899, 1913, 1929, 1937, 1950, 1955, 1957 and 1959, which were chosen as years of relatively good trade[3]. No individual year can, however, be fully representative of its immediate period, and a year of 'relatively good' trade in one period may not be so regarded in another period. The years selected here are, nonetheless, believed to give a good representation of the long-term trend in world trade

---

[1]Hilgerdt's study, for example, covered only five countries outside North America, Europe and Japan, while his series related to manufactured goods in total, with no commodity division (*Industrialization and Foreign Trade*, League of Nations, Geneva, 1945).

[2]Belgium-Luxembourg, France, Germany, Italy, Netherlands, Sweden, Switzerland, United Kingdom, Canada, United States and Japan. Austria, Denmark and Finland were excluded to reduce the statistical extraction and computation involved.

[3]The figures for 1957 and 1959 have not been compiled in such detail as those for the earlier years.

with the following major exceptions. World trading conditions were very different in 1937, and to some extent also in 1950, from those in the other selected years. In 1937, the measures of trade control and restriction which followed the economic depression of the early 1930's were still in full operation. In 1950, quantitative import restrictions and supply shortages were still affecting trade, though the Korean War did not seriously distort the pattern until the following year. World trading conditions since 1955 have been more comparable with those in 1929 than with the intervening years selected, and the comparison with 1929 is therefore more revealing of the underlying trends.

One other major qualification needs to be made at the outset. The estimates of changes in the volume of trade in a period of over half a century inevitably contain a fair margin of error; only really marked differences in trend are significant. The method of compiling the basic tables is set out in some detail in Appendices A and B; these, together with Appendices C and D, also give the main statistical results. In the following discussion, the term 'imports' (in quotation marks) is applied to figures based on the exports of partner trading countries.

3. EXPORTS FROM THE INDUSTRIAL COUNTRIES

The proportion of manufactured goods in the total exports of the industrial countries has increased substantially since the early period of industrialization in the last century. By the beginning of the present century, about one-half of the exports of the eleven countries included in our 'industrial' group consisted of manufactures; the proportion rose to three-fifths by 1929, to two-thirds by 1950 and 1955, and to almost three-quarters by 1959. In volume terms, the disparity in rates of growth in exports of manufactures and of primary products from the industrial countries is more striking. By 1959, for example, the volume index for manufactures was roughly two-and-a-half times the 1913 level, whereas that for primary products was higher only by two-thirds (Table 4.3). By comparison, the volume of exports from non-industrial countries, consisting in the main of primary commodities, was well over double the 1913 level in 1959[1].

However, the greater expansion in exports of primary products from the non-industrial countries, compared with those from the industrial countries, was entirely due to developments prior to the war. By 1950, there had been a dramatic reversal: exports in that year from the industrial countries were somewhat higher than in 1937, but those from the non-industrial areas were lower by almost 20 per cent, mainly as a result of the dislocation of the economies of a number of South-East Asian countries during the war and the early

[1]A major part of this expansion has been due to petroleum and minerals exported to the industrial countries (see *Economic Survey of Europe for 1957*, Economic Commission for Europe, Geneva, 1958, and recent annual reports of G.A.T.T.).

post-war period. In the following decade, there was little change in the relative position established by 1950, exports of primary commodities from the industrial countries rising by about 55 per cent in volume from 1950 to 1959, whereas exports from other countries rose in total by about 65 per cent. The latter expansion contained some 'once-for-all' element of recovery from the economic aftermath of the war.

The decline since before the war in the share of world exports of primary products held by the non-industrial countries has been associated with a rise

Table 4.3. *Value, volume and unit value of exports from industrial and other countries, 1899–1959*

	1899	1913	1929	1937	1950	1955	1957	1959
EXPORTS FROM INDUSTRIAL COUNTRIES[a]								
Value ($ billion)								
Manufactures	3.1	6.5	11.9	9.1	20.1	33.9	42.9	45.3
Primary products	2.6	5.1	7.4	5.0	11.1	15.4	18.9	17.8
Total	5.7	11.6	19.4	14.1	31.2	49.3	61.8	63.1
Volume (indices, 1913 = 100)								
Manufactures	56	100	138	115	143	200	237	253
Primary products	64	100	109	92	105	136	158	165
Total	59	100	127	106	128	175	206	217
Unit value (indices, 1913 = 100)								
Manufactures	85	100	133	122	216	261	278	276
Primary products	81	100	134	108	206	222	236	212
Total	83	100	132	115	210	244	260	251
EXPORTS FROM OTHER COUNTRIES[b]								
Value ($ billion)	2.7	5.7	10.3	9.3	24.2	33.4	37.1	36.7
Volume (indices, 1913 = 100)	66	100	148	161	133	186	204	218
Unit value (indices, 1913 = 100)	72	100	122	102	320	315	319	295
TOTAL EXPORTS								
Value ($ billion)	8.4	17.3	29.7	23.4	55.4	82.7	98.9	99.8
Volume (indices, 1913 = 100)	62	100	135	127	130	179	205	218
Unit value (indices, 1913 = 100)	78	100	127	106	247	268	281	265

Sources: Tables A.1 to A.4, A.80 and related data; W. A. Lewis, 'World Production, Prices and Trade, 1870–1960', *Manchester School*, May 1952; *Statistical Yearbook, 1959*, United Nations, New York, 1960.

[a]Exports from 11 countries only: Belgium-Luxembourg, France, Germany (West Germany for 1950–59), Italy, Netherlands (including estimated figures for 1899 and 1913), Sweden, Switzerland, United Kingdom; Canada and United States; Japan. In 1959, these countries accounted for 95 per cent of the manufactures and 86 per cent of the primary products exported from the wider group of industrial countries shown in Table 4.2.

[b]Residual; excluding exports from Soviet countries, 1950–59.

in the relative prices of their exports. From 1937 to 1950, their export unit values rose by about 215 per cent in total compared with an increase of only 90 per cent for primary products exported by the industrial countries. At first sight, it would seem that the fall in the share of the world market for primary products held by the non-industrial countries since before the war has resulted directly from the sharper rise in their export prices. This is, indeed, the conclusion drawn from the figures by Professor Cairncross[1]. However, as will be seen later[2], the exports from the non-industrial countries consist of a very different 'product-mix' from those of the industrial countries, and this difference in commodity pattern appears to be a major reason for the different export experience of the two groups of countries.

Table 4.4. *Trade of the industrial countries in manufactures and primary products, 1899–1959*

$ billion at 1955 prices

	Manufactures		Primary products		Total intra-trade	Total exports to rest of world	Total
	Intra-trade	Exports to rest of world	Intra-trade	Exports to rest of world			
1899	5.04	4.50	5.99	1.21	11.03	5.71	16.74
1913	8.52	8.43	8.42	2.85	16.94	11.28	28.20
1929	11.05	12.37	9.00	3.32	20.05	15.70	35.75
1937	7.82	11.60	7.78	2.57	15.60	14.18	29.78
1950	9.98	14.30	8.15	3.73	18.14	18.03	36.17
1955	15.99	17.91	10.36	4.99	26.35	22.90	49.25
1957	19.24	20.97	12.32	5.48	31.56	26.46	58.01
1959	22.34	20.51	12.51	6.10	34.85	26.61	61.46
Change in period							
1899–1913	+3.48	+3.93	+2.43	+1.64	+5.91	+5.57	+11.46
1913–29	+2.53	+3.94	+0.58	+0.47	+3.11	+4.42	+7.55
1929–37	−3.23	−0.77	−1.22	−0.75	−4.45	−1.52	−5.97
1937–50	+2.16	+2.70	+0.37	+1.16	+2.54	+3.85	+6.39
1950–59	+12.36	+6.21	+4.36	+2.37	+16.71	+8.58	+25.29
1929–59	+11.29	+8.14	+3.51	+2.78	+14.80	+10.91	+25.71

Sources: Tables A.2 and A.4 and related data.

Up to the early 1930's, the greater part of the expansion in exports from the industrial countries was directed towards the rest of the world. The intra-trade among the industrial countries themselves accounted for rather less than half the total increase (Table 4.4). This was also true of the trade in manufactured goods, in which the intra-trade accounted for just under one-half

[1]A. K. Cairncross, 'International Trade and Economic Development', *Kyklos*, Vol. 13, Fasc. 4, 1960.
[2]See Chapter 5.

of the increase from 1899 to 1913, and for two-fifths of that from 1913 to 1929. For primary products, however, the growth in the intra-trade was greater in absolute terms, over this period, than the rise in exports to non-industrial countries (though the *rate* of increase in the latter was greater). The trade restrictionism of the 1930's affected the intra-trade far more severely than exports to non-industrial countries. By 1937, exports of manufactures in total were 15–20 per cent lower than the 1929 peak, the contraction in the intra-trade accounting for four-fifths of the total decline; similarly, the intra-trade suffered the major part (three-fifths) of the decline in exports of primary products from the industrial countries in this period (though the *rate* of decline in exports to non-industrial countries was greater than that in the intra-trade).

Fig. 4.3.   Trends in exports of manufactures from the industrial countries, distinguishing the intra-trade from exports to the rest of the world, 1899–1959

Volume indices, 1899 = 100
Semi-logarithmic scale

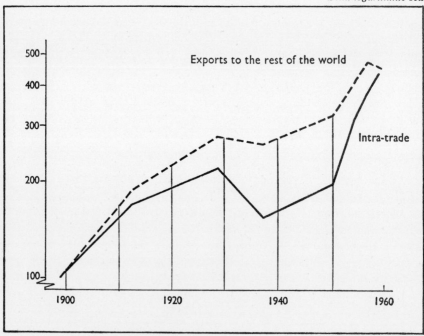

The greater contraction, during the 1930's, in the intra-trade than in exports to outside countries appears to have been due in large measure to the creation by the industrial countries of greater barriers to freedom of trade than those created at that time in the rest of the world. The progressive relaxation of trade barriers in the 1950's—which, however, applied in the main to industrial rather than to agricultural products—could therefore be expected *per se* to result in a greater increase in the intra-trade than in exports to outside countries, even if the rates of economic growth in the industrial and primary-producing areas had been the same. The fact that the rate of economic growth was higher in the industrial countries does not diminish the importance of the movement towards freer trade and payments, which has been such a marked feature of the period. In the event, the rise in the volume of intra-trade in manufactured goods from 1950 to 1959 accounted for as much as two-thirds of the total trade expansion in this category, a far higher proportion than had ever before been achieved. However, if 1959 is compared with 1929, before trade restrictions and controls become widespread, a rather smaller proportion (three-fifths) of the increase in total trade in manufactures was in the intra-trade, compared with under one-half in the period before 1913.

The same conclusion is reached if one considers the relative rates of growth of the two streams of trade (see Fig. 4.3). Though the rate of growth has been faster in the intra-trade since 1950, this is seen to be essentially an offset to the greater relative contraction in that trade between 1929 and 1937 and to its delayed post-war recovery. By 1959, both the intra-trade and exports to outside countries seem to be close to a long-term trend based on the movement from 1899 to 1929. The trade experience of the 1950's must therefore be considered as reflecting, in part at least, some exceptional factors of a temporary character[1].

The following sections, which relate to manufactured goods only, deal separately with the intra-trade of the industrial countries and with their exports to other areas of the world.

4. THE INTRA-TRADE OF THE INDUSTRIAL COUNTRIES

Several distinct streams of trade can be distinguished in the intra-trade of the industrial countries. For convenience, we can divide this group of countries into four, namely, the United Kingdom, the Continental countries of Western Europe, North America and Japan, and examine the trends in trade between each of the four. In addition, of course, there is the important trade between the Continental West European countries themselves and between Canada and the United States.

In the period since 1913, the greatest expansion in trade in absolute terms has been in the intra-trade of Continental Western Europe. This accounted for two-fifths of the entire expansion in the intra-trade of all industrial countries (Table 4.5). There was also a sharp increase in trade between Canada and the

---

[1]An assessment of the probable magnitude of these exceptional factors is made in Chapter 6, while the implications for the future growth of trade between the industrial countries are discussed further in Chapter 9.

E

United States, particularly after the second World War, the increase since 1913 accounting for one-quarter of the total increase in the intra-trade. This was easily the most rapidly-growing stream of trade, the volume of interchange of manufactures in 1959 between the two North American countries being over seven times the 1913 total. Trade in manufactures between Western Europe and North America has grown at a slower rate than either of these. Nonetheless, the expansion in the 1950's has been an impressive one, and by 1959 the volume was not far short of three times that in 1913. Trade between Japan and the other industrial countries was severely depressed in the early post-war years, but by 1955 it had recovered to the pre-war level and by 1959 had reached a volume some three-and-a-half times the 1913 total. By contrast, the trade between Britain and Western Europe, though increasing during the 1950's, was no higher in 1959 than in 1913.

Table 4.5. *Intra-trade[a] of the industrial countries in manufactures*, 1899–1959

$ billion at 1955 prices

	Intra-European		Intra-North American	Inter-continental		Total
	United Kingdom-Continent	Intra-continental		Europe-North America	Japan-Europe and North America	
1899	2.00	-1.44	0.16	1.24	0.20	5.04
1913	2.64	2.81	0.54	2.08	0.45	8.52
1929	2.29	3.76	1.56	2.78	0.64	11.05
1937	1.45	2.39	1.09	2.13	0.76	7.82
1950	1.61	2.96	2.49	2.62	0.30	9.98
1955	2.06	5.73	3.72	3.75	0.73	15.99
1957	2.27	7.15	3.89	4.59	1.34	19.24
1959	2.50	8.50	3.98	5.76	1.60	22.34
Change in period						
1899–1913	+0.64	+1.37	+0.38	+0.84	+0.25	+3.48
1913–29	−0.35	+0.95	+1.02	+0.70	+0.19	+2.53
1929–37	−0.84	−1.37	−0.47	−0.65	+0.12	−3.23
1937–50	+0.16	+0.57	+1.40	+0.49	−0.46	+2.16
1950–59	+0.89	+5.54	+1.49	+3.14	+1.30	+12.36
1929–59	+0.21	+4.73	+2.42	+2.98	+0.96	+11.30

Sources: Table A.4 and related data.

[a]The figures represent the total of trade in both directions.

United Kingdom trade with the Continent

The exceptional trend in Britain's share of the intra-trade within Western

Europe appears to be due almost entirely to the failure of her imports of manufactures from the Continent to expand with her economic growth since the early 1930's. This is, perhaps, the more surprising since before the Great Depression Britain's 'imports' of manufactures from the Continent had been considerably more buoyant than her exports to that area (see Table 4.6 and Fig. 4.4). Before 1913, indeed, the rate of increase in Britain's 'imports' was considerably higher than in her exports, while from 1913 to 1929 the fall in her 'imports' was under 10 per cent, whereas her exports to the Continent in 1929 were some 20 per cent lower in volume than in 1913. Virtually the whole of this latter reduction was in exports to Germany and France; exports to Germany in 1929 were about 45 per cent lower in volume than in 1913, while those to France were nearly 30 per cent down[1].

Table 4.6. *Trade in manufactures between the United Kingdom and Continental Western Europe, 1899–1959*

$ *billion at 1955 prices*

	1899	1913	1929	1937	1950	1955	1957	1959
United Kingdom exports	0.94	1.08	0.87	0.61	1.12	1.25	1.38	1.39
United Kingdom ' imports '	1.06	1.56	1.43	0.84	0.50	0.81	0.89	1.11

Sources: Table A.4 and related data.

During the early 1930's, Britain's trade with the Continent was slashed in both directions, but the cut in her imports was very much greater than in her exports. By 1933, both industrial activity and foreign trade had begun to increase again, and there was a substantial expansion in both between that year and 1937. Nevertheless, the ratio of imports to total consumption of manufactures in Britain never recovered to the pre-Depression level. The trade contraction of the early 1930's bore particularly heavily once again on trade with France and Germany. British exports of manufactures both to Germany and France in 1937 were down by two-fifths from the 1929 figures. In the reverse direction, British 'imports' from Germany were down by one-half, while those from France (nearly half of which consisted of textiles in 1929) were down by two-thirds between these two years[2]. There seems little doubt that this severe contraction in Britain's trade with her European neighbours was largely a result of the general rise in tariff levels and the introduction of other trade restrictions in the early 1930's.

In the early post-war period, British imports of manufactures from the

[1]The main reason for these reductions was the sharp contraction in British exports of textiles. In the case of Germany, this was one result of the increase in the level of German import duties after the first World War.

[2]About half the fall in the volume of exports of French manufactures to Britain between 1929 and 1937 was in textiles, but the major part of the decline in German shipments to Britain was in base metals, machinery and other metal goods.

Continent were generally limited by import licensing arrangements, but after 1953 a sharp upward movement occurred, particularly in fully fabricated manufactures. Nonetheless, even in 1957 the volume of Britain's 'imports' of manufactures from the Continent exceeded those of 1937 only by a slight margin and were almost 40 per cent below the 1929 peak. The subsequent expansion in 'imports' brought the 1959 total to three-quarters of that in 1929. By contrast, British exports of manufactures to Western Europe in 1957 were more than double the 1937 volume and almost 60 per cent higher than in 1929. There was a fall in 1958, however, and a recovery in 1959 back to the 1957 level. Thus, the sharp expansion in Britain's imports of manufactures from the Continent between 1955 and 1959 could be regarded, in large measure, as a return to a more 'normal' relationship between such imports and economic activity in Britain[1].

Fig. 4.4.   Trade in manufactures between the United Kingdom and
Continental Western Europe, 1899–1959

$ *billion at* 1955 *prices*
Semi-logarithmic scale

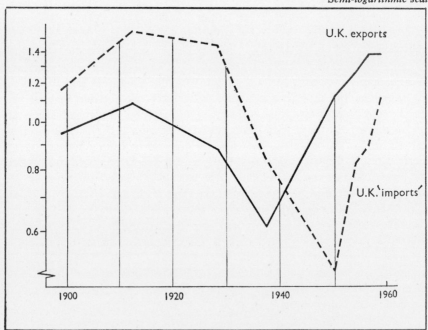

Intra-trade of Continental Western Europe

Germany has traditionally been the principal single supplier of manufactures

[1]Between 1959 and 1961 there was a further substantial rise (30–40 per cent) in the volume of British imports and exports of manufactures in trade with Western Europe.

to the markets of Continental Western Europe. She supplied nearly one-half the total intra-trade of these countries in 1913 and about two-fifths in 1929 and 1937 and again in 1957 (Table 4.7). West German exports in 1959 were double the figure for the whole of Germany in 1929, and about treble that for the same territorial area. During the 1950's, West German exports of manu-

Table 4.7. *Intra-trade of Continental Western Europe in manufactures,*
1913–59

$ billion at 1955 prices

Exports to	Year	Exports from			
		France	Germany*a*	Other Western Europe*b*	Total
France	1913	—	0.34	0.21	0.55
	1929	—	0.28	0.26	0.53
	1937	—	0.10	0.25	0.35
	1950	—	0.08	0.28	0.36
	1955	—	0.27	0.43	0.70
	1957	—	0.45	0.54	0.99
	1959	—	0.53	0.52	1.05
Germany*a*	1913	0.21	—	0.40	0.61
	1929	0.28	—	0.37	0.64
	1937	0.02	—	0.31	0.33
	1950	0.09	—	0.29	0.38
	1955	0.27	—	0.70	0.97
	1957	0.29	—	0.84	1.13
	1959	0.50	—	1.31	1.81
Other Western Europe*c*	1913	0.54	1.07	0.31	1.92
	1929	0.74	1.29	0.57	2.59
	1937	0.27	0.86	0.58	1.71
	1950	0.45	0.71	1.06	2.23
	1955	0.56	1.86	1.64	4.06
	1957	0.58	2.49	1.97	5.04
	1959	0.76	2.73	2.15	5.64
TOTAL	1913	0.75	1.41	0.92	3.08
	1929	1.02	1.56	1.19	3.77
	1937	0.29	0.96	1.14	2.39
	1950	0.54	0.79	1.64	2.96
	1955	0.83	2.13	2.77	5.73
	1957	0.87	2.94	3.35	7.16
	1959	1.26	3.26	3.98	8.50

Sources: Tables A.15–A.22 and related data.

a West Germany only in 1950–59.
b Belgium-Luxembourg, Italy, Netherlands, Sweden and Switzerland.
c As in note *b*, *plus* Norway.

factures to France increased rapidly, but comparing 1959 with 1929 the proportionate increase in exports was much the same to France and to the smaller
Continental countries.

In the period up to 1929, exports from France accounted for about one-
quarter of intra-Continental trade in manufactures.   In the 1930's, however,
there was a sharp contraction in French exports of manufactures—the result
of a change in the structure of demand (particularly the encroachment of rayon
on the traditional French silk fabric trade), of tariff increases in some of
France's more important markets, and also of the over-valuation of the franc
in the earlier part of the decade.   By 1937, French exports were down to only
one-eighth of intra-Continental trade in manufactures.   Moreover, French
exports to her neighbours were very slow to rise in the post-war period, but a
fillip was given by the devaluations of the franc in 1957 and, particularly, in
1958.   By 1959, French shipments of manufactures to West Germany were
higher than in 1957 (or 1929) by three-quarters, while her sales to the other
Continental countries had just exceeded the previous (1929) peak.

Since 1929 there has been a strong tendency for the exports from the smaller
countries of Western Europe to become increasingly important in intra-
Continental trade in manufactures.   In 1959, the aggregate exports of Belgium-
Luxembourg, Italy, Netherlands, Sweden and Switzerland to countries in
Continental Western Europe were nearly three-and-a-half times the corresponding 1929 volume (Table 4.7).   Trade among the smaller countries has
increased fastest of all, comparing 1959 with 1929, the most rapidly growing
sector being trade between Belgium-Luxembourg and the Netherlands—the
countries of the Benelux Customs Union[1].   Between 1950 and 1959, the
expansion in trade between the Benelux countries accounted for two-fifths of
the total increase of some $1,100 million (at 1955 prices) in the intra-trade of
the smaller countries of Western Europe.

The rapid expansion of trade in manufactured goods within Continental
Western Europe since 1950 is, to a large extent, a reflection of the growth in
the national economies of the countries of this area.   The progressive
liberalization of trade, carried out under the auspices of the O.E.E.C., was
also of considerable importance in facilitating the increase in trade[2].   An
outstanding feature of the period since 1950 has been the growth in West

[1]The ordinary customs duties between Belgium-Luxembourg and the Netherlands were
abolished as from 1 January 1948.   But the expansion of trade between the three countries
of the Benelux Union was restricted by the Dutch payments deficit with Belgium up to 1952.
The economic background to the building of a full economic union of the Benelux countries
is discussed at some length by Professor J. E. Meade, *Negotiations for Benelux: An
annotated Chronicle, 1943–1956*, Princeton Studies in International Finance, No. 6, Princeton
University, 1957.

[2]There is no evidence, however, that the formation of the European Economic Community
has led to any significant expansion in the intra-trade of Western Europe (see R. L. Major,
'The Common Market: Production and Trade', *National Institute Economic Review*,
No. 21, August 1962.)

Germany's trade with other Continental countries; taking the trade in both directions together, this accounted for about 70 per cent of the total increase, from 1950 to 1959, in the intra-trade of Continental Western Europe in manufactured goods. The West German economy is oriented towards foreign trade to a greater extent than are its Continental neighbours; this can be seen from Fig. 4.5, which shows a much higher ratio of growth in trade to growth in the total real product in West Germany than in other Continental countries.

This development in West Germany is in marked contrast to that during the Nazi regime before the war. Germany's real product was increasing substantially in the later 1930's and by 1937 had exceeded the 1929 pre-Depression level by some 15 per cent. The volume of her trade in manufactures with other Continental countries in Western Europe, however, was reduced by about 40 per cent in the same period. This was largely the result of the efforts of the German government to create an autarkic war economy, independent of imports of strategic materials and manufactured goods. Moreover, for political reasons, there was some considerable diversion of trade away from Western Europe to countries in South-East Europe and Latin America. Thus, if a comparison is made with 1937, we find that the volume of intra-continental Western European trade in manufactures had risen two-and-a-half times by 1959, whereas the total real product of the countries concerned[1] was higher by only about 65 per cent. However, if we compare 1959 with 1929, the picture is very different; trade in manufactures rose by about 125 per cent in volume, as against an increase of 90–100 per cent in real product. The somewhat greater rise in trade than in real product since 1929 is due entirely to Germany; this has resulted largely because the post-war economy of West Germany has become more highly dependent on production for export markets than was that of the pre-war Reich. Excluding Germany, both the total real product and the volume of intra-trade in manufactures of the countries of Continental Western Europe in 1959 were rather more than double the 1929 level.

The rapid expansion of the intra-trade in manufactures in Western Europe since 1950 thus reflects not only the expansion in real output mentioned earlier. It is also, in part, a reversion to a more 'normal' relationship—particularly for Germany—between production and trade in manufactured goods.

Intra-North American trade

The rapid expansion of trade between the United States and Canada has been an outstanding feature of world trade over the past half-century. The upward trend has been particularly rapid since the late 1930's (see Fig. 4.6), reflecting the great economic expansion that has taken place in both countries. The increase in this two-way flow of trade between 1929 and 1959 accounted for 20 per cent of the total increase in the intra-trade of the industrial countries,

[1]Including the whole of Germany in 1937, but only West Germany post-war (see Table E.1).

H   WT

Fig. 4.5.   Trade in manufactures within Continental Western Europe in relation to Real Product, 1899–1959

Volume indices, 1899 = 100
Semi-logarithmic scale

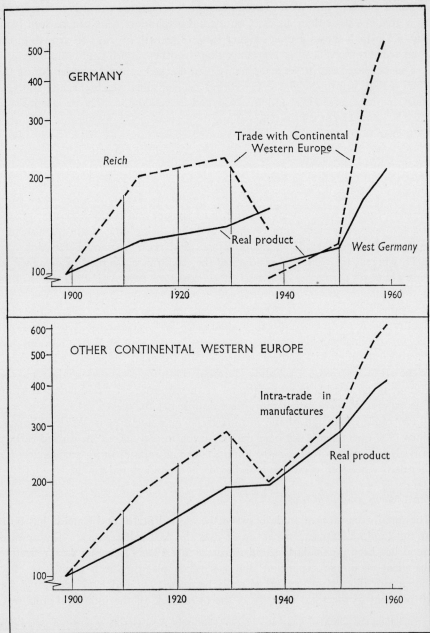

compared with 45 per cent from 1913 to 1929. The fall in the proportion reflects the sharp expansion in intra-trade in Continental Western Europe mentioned above.

The increase in this stream of trade between 1929 and 1959 was shared about equally by United States exports to Canada and by Canadian exports to the United States. The exports from the United States to Canada are, however, much more highly fabricated on average than those moving in the reverse direction. Over half the increase in United States exports of manufactures to Canada between 1929 and 1959 was accounted for by machinery and transport equipment, whereas some two-thirds of the corresponding increase in Canadian exports to the United States consisted of non-ferrous metals and newsprint.

Trade between Western Europe and North America

This flow of trade represents one-quarter to one-fifth of the total intra-trade in manufactures among the industrial countries. In the period up to 1929, the flow in each direction between the two Continents increased at roughly the same pace, as can be seen from Table 4.8. Exports from Europe to North America suffered much more sharply in the Great Depression than did the

Fig. 4.6. Trade in manufactures between Canada and United States, 1899–1959

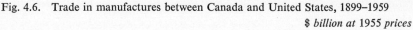

$ *billion at 1955 prices*

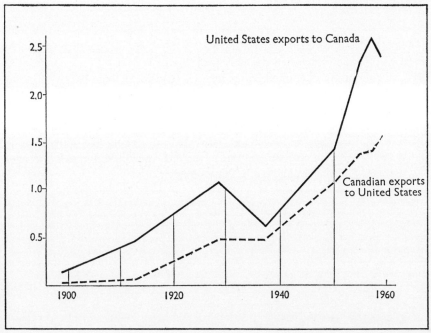

reverse flow. United States imports of manufactures were cut back sharply between 1929 and 1932, while the recovery in the next five years did not regain the previous peak level. By 1937, exports of manufactures from Western Europe to the United States were some 40 per cent lower in volume than in 1929, whereas total United States 'imports' of manufactures were lower by

Table 4.8. *Trade in manufactures between Western Europe and North America*

$ *billion at* 1955 *prices*

	Exports from Western Europe to North America			Exports from North America to Western Europe		
	From United Kingdom	From Continent	Total	To United Kingdom	To Continent	Total
1899	0.32	0.34	0.66	0.29	0.28	0.57
1913	0.54	0.62	1.16	0.36	0.56	0.92
1929	0.56	0.84	1.40	0.58	0.80	1.38
1937	0.41	0.47	0.88	0.68	0.58	1.26
1950	0.66	0.64	1.30	0.36	0.96	1.32
1955	0.69	1.24	1.93	0.63	1.19	1.82
1957	0.96	1.67	2.63	0.60	1.36	1.96
1959	1.24	2.67	3.91	0.58	1.27	1.85

Sources: Table A.4 and related data.

about 20 per cent[1]. Japan was the only industrial country whose exports to the United States in 1937 (consisting mainly of textiles and other consumer goods) considerably exceeded the 1929 peak level.

Part of the failure of United States imports to recover their 1929 volume by 1937 was due to the increase in the United States tariff under the Hawley-Smoot Law of 1930. This Law increased the rates of duty, which were already generally high, and also resulted in an increase in the proportion of imports subject to duty. The major factor, however, influencing the movement in United States imports of manufactures in the inter-war period appears to have been the variation in real income in that country[2].

[1]This is a greater decline than appears to be shown by the United States official import statistics. Total imports of finished manufactures into the United States are estimated to have been 10 per cent lower in volume in 1937 than in 1929, while 'semi-manufactures' were down by 7 per cent (D. D. Humphrey, *American Imports*, Twentieth Century Fund, New York, 1955, table 3). The definition of 'manufactures' used here differs in some respects (e.g. by the exclusion of petroleum) from the United States definitions of 'finished manufactures' and 'semi-manufactures', while the latter would also include imports from semi-industrial and non-industrial countries (e.g. tin metal from Malaya and refined copper from Chile) which are excluded from the figures given in the present chapter.

[2]See D. D. Humphrey, *American Imports*, ch. 4, and H. Neisser and F. Modigliani, *National Incomes and International Trade*, University of Illinois Press, 1953, pp. 280-2.

In the reverse direction, exports from the United States to Western Europe in 1937 were about 40 per cent below the 1929 volume, but this fall was partly offset by a sharp increase over the period in Canadian shipments of non-ferrous metals to Britain.

Since 1950, trade between Western Europe and North America has increased rapidly. By 1959, exports from Western Europe to North America were treble the 1950 volume; the reverse flow, however, was higher by only two-fifths. In 1950, West Germany's exports were only just starting their post-war expansion, so that it is not surprising that Germany accounted for as much as one-third of the total increase, from that year to 1959, in Western Europe's exports of manufactures to North America. Britain's share of the increase was under one-quarter (see Table 4.8). In the second part of the decade, from 1955 to 1959, Britain and West Germany accounted for equal proportions (nearly 30 per cent each) of the total increase in shipments from Western Europe to North America. The major part of the expansion was in exports to the United States, with passenger cars as the most dynamic single element[1].

Exports of manufactures from North America to Western Europe, by contrast, have showed no marked trend either way in the latter half of the 1950's (Table 4.8). By 1959, exports to Britain were somewhat lower than in 1955 or 1957 and only about equal to the volume achieved in 1929. Exports to the Continent in 1959, however, were 60 per cent greater than in 1929.

The static nature of the British market for North American manufactures in the post-war period has been due in the main to discrimination against 'dollar' imports. Restrictions on dollar imports into Britain were eased in 1958, and in 1959 they were abolished over a wide range of goods. A specially computed 'index of control'[2] of imports, showed a gradual fall in the degree of

United Kingdom imports from dollar area

	1950	1953	1955	1957	1959	1960
Index of control[a]	99	92	74	69	8[b]	
Volume of imports of manufactures from the United States	100	103	111	119	127	255

Sources: G. F. Ray, 'British Imports of Manufactured Goods', *National Institute Economic Review*, No. 8, March 1960; *Report on Overseas Trade*, 1961, *passim*, H.M.S.O., London.
[a]Index relates to mid-year position.
[b]Position at end of January, 1960; there were further relaxations in February, 1960.

[1]This expansion in Western Europe's exports to the United States was followed by a sharp setback after the spring of 1960 as a result mainly of a contraction in American demand for foreign cars.
[2]This index shows the value of 'controlled' imports (i.e. imports on government account plus private imports under licence) as a percentage of all imports of manufactures (see 'A Statistical Summary of the Extent of Import Control in the United Kingdom since the War', by M. F. W. Hemming, C. M. Miles and G. F. Ray, *Review of Economic Studies*, Vol. 26, No. 2, February 1959).

restriction of imports from dollar sources between 1953 and 1957, followed by a substantial relaxation in 1958 and virtual abolition of discrimination by early 1960. As a result, British imports of manufactures from North America rose sharply in 1960; imports from the United States rose by 100 per cent, compared with 1959, while those from Canada rose by 40 per cent.

Thus, by 1960 Britain's import market for North American manufactures had grown, compared with 1929, by much the same proportion as had the import market of Continental Western Europe.

Trade between Japan and other industrial countries

This trade accounts for about 7 per cent of the total intra-trade in manufactures among the industrial countries. Before the war, Japanese imports of manufactures greatly exceeded Japanese exports to other industrial countries (see Fig. 4.7). The gap was considerably narrowed in the 1930's, mainly as a result of the depreciation of the yen, and since 1950 Japanese exports have been somewhat larger than imports in trade with other industrial countries. The rate of expansion in Japan's trade since 1950 has been exceedingly rapid; by

Fig. 4.7.   Trade in manufactures between Japan and other industrial
countries, 1899–1959

$ *billion at* 1955 *prices*

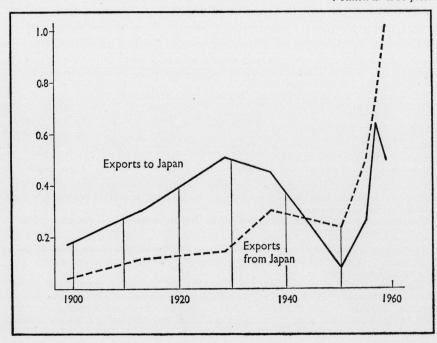

1959, the volume of Japanese exports to other industrial countries was not far short of three times the 1937 level, whereas 'imports' from those countries were higher by only one-third.   Even so, this flow of trade has remained relatively small, accounting, for example, for little more than 5 per cent of the increase in the total intra-trade of the industrial countries between 1937 and 1959.

5. EXPORTS FROM THE INDUSTRIAL COUNTRIES
TO THE REST OF THE WORLD

Over the past half-century, exports of manufactures to the semi-industrial countries have expanded at a much slower rate than have those to non-industrial countries.   Exports to the latter group[1] in 1959, for example, were more than treble the 1913 volume, whereas those to semi-industrial countries in total were only two-thirds higher than the earlier figure (Table 4.9).   In absolute terms, the expansion in exports to the non-industrial countries was two-and-a-half times that to the semi-industrial ones between 1913 and 1929, whereas it was four times for the expansion from 1929 to 1959.

The semi-industrial countries

The failure of this group to expand its imports of manufactures as fast as those of the non-industrial countries was largely due to the stagnation in the level of import demand by India until 1955 and 1956, when the import require-ments of the first Five-Year Plan began to impinge on the Indian balance of payments.   Up to that time, India's import experience had been quite different from that of the other semi-industrial countries, as can be seen from Fig. 4.8. Indeed, by 1955 'imports' of manufactures into India and Pakistan together were actually about 10 per cent lower in volume than they had been in 1913; even by 1957, they were only some 15 per cent up on 1913 in spite of the con-siderably higher level of economic activity in the later year.   The Indian 'shortfall' appears to have two main causes: first, the acute shortage of foreign exchange to finance the level of imports required under the various Five-Year Plans and, second, the fact that local development has had a greater import-saving character than in most other countries.   The effect of local industrializa-tion on the level of imports is examined further in Chapter 6.

Imports of manufactures into the three Southern Dominions and the semi-industrial countries of Latin America have both shown a marked upward trend since the turn of the century.   An apparent difference (see Fig. 4.8) is that the movement in imports was upward in the Southern Dominions in the 1930's, whereas in Latin America the level of 'imports' in 1937 was still con-

[1]Taking the movement in exports to non-industrial countries as being indicated by the figures in the last column of Table 4.9, though these also include some industrial markets.

Table 4.9. 'Imports'[a] of manufactures by the semi-industrial countries, U.S.S.R. and the rest of the world, 1899–1959

$ billion at 1955 prices

| | Semi-industrial countries | | | | | | |
	Southern Dominions[b]	India/ Pakistan	Latin America[c]	Others[d]	Total	U.S.S.R.	Rest of world[e]
1899	0.64	0.70	0.65	0.10	2.09	0.39[f]	2.25
1913	1.08	1.22	1.56	0.23	4.10	0.69[f]	4.13
1929	1.53	1.13	2.28	0.26	5.20	0.36	7.01
1937	1.71	0.80	1.66	0.32	4.48	0.31	7.07
1950	2.27	0.89	2.37	0.49	6.02	0.12	8.50
1955	2.63	1.07	2.38	0.66	6.74	0.15	11.30
1957	2.45	1.41	2.71	0.59	7.16	0.28	13.85
1959	2.32	1.21	2.53	0.75	6.81	0.37	13.62
Change in period							
1899–1913	+ 0.44	+ 0.52	+ 0.91	+ 0.13	+ 2.01	+ 0.32	+ 1.91
1913–29	+ 0.45	− 0.09	+ 0.72	+ 0.03	+ 1.10	− 0.34	+ 2.72
1929–37	+ 0.18	− 0.33	− 0.62	+ 0.06	− 0.72	− 0.05	+ 0.06
1937–50	+ 0.56	+ 0.09	+ 0.71	+ 0.17	+ 1.54	− 0.19	+ 1.43
1950–59	+ 0.05	+ 0.32	+ 0.16	+ 0.26	+ 0.79	+ 0.25	+ 5.12
1929–59	+ 0.79	+ 0.08	+ 0.25	+ 0.49	+ 1.61	+ 0.01	+ 6.61

Sources: Table A.4 and related data.

[a]'Imports' from the industrial countries and India.
[b]Australia, New Zealand and the Union of South Africa.
[c]Argentina, Brazil, Chile, Colombia and Mexico only.
[d]Palestine/Israel (except in 1899 and 1913), Turkey and Yugoslavia (Serbia in 1899 and 1913).
[e]Mainly non-industrial countries. Figures derived as residue from world totals.
[f]Russia.

siderably below the 1929 peak. However, the rise in the former case was essentially due to the exceptional experience of the Union of South Africa, which benefited from the rise in the price of gold in the early 1930's as well as from expanding world demand for some of its main export products. The volume of 'imports' of manufactures into the Union in 1937 was some two-thirds higher than in 1929, whereas Australia—which was heavily affected by the economic difficulties of the 1930's—reduced its 'imports' of manufactures by 15–20 per cent in the same period.

The movement since 1937 in 'imports' of manufactures into the Southern Dominions and Latin America has been strikingly similar. Taking an average of the 1955 and 1957 figures, both areas had increased their volume of 'imports' of manufactures by one-half since 1937; in both areas, too, 'imports' fell off somewhat between 1957 and 1959. Among the Latin American countries, however, the trend in Argentina's imports since the war has been in marked

Fig. 4.8. 'Imports' of manufactures into India/Pakistan, Southern Dominions
and Latin America, 1899–1959

Volume indices, 1899 = 100
Semi-logarithmic scale

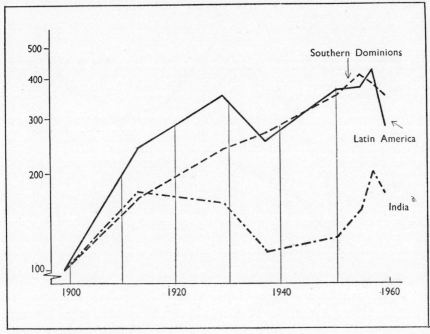

*Including Pakistan, 1950–59.

contrast with the trend for the rest (see Fig. 4.9).   Argentina, like India, is
evidently a special case, and both are discussed in greater detail in the next
two chapters.   Here, it suffices to point out that if both Argentina and India
are excluded, the upward trend in 'imports' of manufactures into the semi-
industrial countries was not very much less, taking the whole period up to
1955, than was that for the non-industrial countries (Table 4.10); though in the
later 1950's the trends diverged because of the fall in imports by the semi-
industrial countries mentioned earlier.

The Soviet countries

Russia and China were important markets for the Western industrial countries
before the first World War.   In 1913, for example, these two countries took
one-quarter of all imports of manufactures by countries outside the industrial
and semi-industrial areas as here defined (Table 4.11).   Over one-half of
Russia's imports of manufactures before the first World War consisted of metals

Fig. 4.9.   'Imports' of manufactures into Argentina and other semi-industrial
countries in Latin America, 1899–1959

Volume indices, 1899 = 100
Semi-logarithmic scale

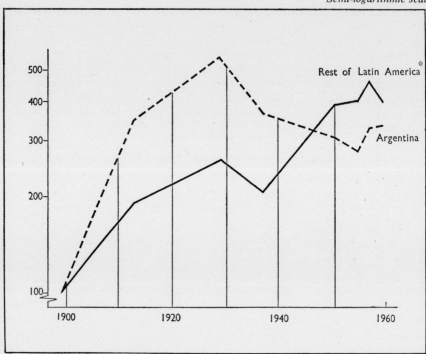

*Brazil, Chile, Colombia and Mexico.

and engineering goods[1], though the greater part of Chinese imports consisted
of textile products.

Trade between the West and the Soviet Union was disrupted by the Civil
War and did not reach any substantial amount until the late 1920's.   After the
beginning of the first Five-Year Plan in 1928, Soviet imports of machinery,
metals and transport equipment began on a fairly large scale and continued
up to the second World War.   Since the war, Soviet imports of manufactures
from the West have been lower, in volume terms, than they were in the 1930's;
in 1955, they were under one-half of the volume taken by Czarist Russia in
1913[2].   Since 1955, however, there has been a substantial increase in imports

[1]See Table A.39.
[2]Exports of manufactures to the Soviet Union from the main industrial countries and
India in 1955 were, however, only 20-25 per cent of the comparable 1913 volume (Table
A.39).   In 1955, these countries accounted for only about half the total value of manufactures exported to the Soviet Union by the rest of the world (other than Eastern Europe
and China).

Table 4.10. *Volume of 'imports' of manufactures into the semi-industrial and non-industrial countries, 1899–1959*

Indices, 1899 = 100

	1899	1913	1929	1937	1950	1955	1959
Total, semi-industrial countries	100	196	250	215	288	322	326
India[a] and Argentina	100	213	250	170	168	180	205
Total, *less* India[a] and Argentina	100	183	250	250	380	430	420
Total, non-industrial countries[b]	100	183	312	314	378	502	605

Sources: Tables 4.9, A.13 and A.81.

[a]Including Pakistan for 1950–59.
[b]Final column of Table 4.9.

of manufactures from the West into both the U.S.S.R. and other countries of Eastern Europe. From 1955 to 1960, for example, imports of manufactures into both areas rose from about $700 million to about $2,000 million. The volume of manufactured imports into the U.S.S.R. alone in 1960 was almost certainly in excess of the 1913 level.

China's imports of manufactures from the West fell off during the 1930's, mainly as a consequence of the war with Japan, and have remained relatively small ever since. China took about one-quarter of the 1913 volume in 1955 though, as with the Soviet Union, the volume of trade with Western countries grew in the late 1950's considerably. China's imports of manufactures from Western countries in 1960 were more than double the 1955 volume, their share of China's total imports of manufactures (including imports from the U.S.S.R. and Eastern Europe) rising from 14 to 26 per cent between these years.

Other countries

The totals for exports to the 'rest of the world' given previously relate in the main to non-industrial countries outside Europe. A comparison of the long-term trends for the main groups of countries can be made by relating actual imports in a recent year (1955) with the figures for 1913 compiled by Lamartine Yates[1].

For this purpose, the non-industrial countries outside Europe have been grouped according to their main export product in 1955 (Table 4.11). The outstanding change over the period has been the sharp expansion in imports of manufactures by countries exporting petroleum and other minerals and, to a lesser extent, by those exporting tropical beverage crops. Among the oil countries, Venezuela is particularly important as a market for manufactures, her 'imports' in 1957 being about ten times the 1929 volume. Substantial increases have also occurred in the other major oil-producing states—Iran, Iraq, Saudi Arabia and the Persian Gulf Sheikhdoms. The oil and mineral

[1]P. Lamartine Yates, *Forty Years of Foreign Trade*, London, 1959.

Table 4.11.   *Imports of manufactures into countries not classified as 'industrial'
or 'semi-industrial', 1913 and 1955*

	1913		1955		Approx. volume in 1955
	($ million, (percentage) c.i.f.)		($ million, (percentage) c.i.f.)		(1913 = 100)
SOVIET COUNTRIES	696	32.7	890	7.1	..
Russia/U.S.S.R.	295	13.8	347	2.8	45
Eastern Europe[a]	117	5.6	357	2.8	..
China	284	13.3	186	1.5	25
OTHER COUNTRIES IN EUROPE[b]	548	25.7	2510	20.0	..
EXTRA-EUROPEAN COUNTRIES exporting mainly[c]	886	41.6	9165	72.9	400
Petroleum[d]	58	2.7	1475	11.7	1000
Other minerals[e]	86	4.0	1466	11.7	675
Coffee, tea and cocoa[f]	145	6.8	1872	14.9	525
Other foods[g]	194	9.1	1684	13.4	350
Rubber[h]	249	11.7	1083	8.6	170
Other agricultural raw materials[i]	154	7.2	1248	9.9	320
Manufactures[j]	..	..	336	2.7	..
TOTAL	2130	100	12565	100	230

Sources: For 1913, P. L. Yates, unpublished data sheets compiled for *Forty Years of Foreign Trade*, London, 1959.   For 1955, *Yearbook of International Trade Statistics, 1957*, United Nations, New York, 1958;   *Monthly Bulletin of Statistics*, March 1961, United Nations, New York, and national trade statistics.

[a]Bulgaria and Rumania only in 1913; in addition, Albania, Czechoslovakia, Hungary and Poland in 1955.

[b]Austria-Hungary in 1913, Austria in 1955; Republic of Ireland in 1955 only; Channel Islands, Denmark, Finland, Greece, Iceland, Portugal and Spain in both years.

[c]The countries listed in the following footnotes relate to the 1955 figures.   Those for 1913 are not fully comparable for all groups of countries because of boundary changes in some cases.

[d]Iran, Iraq, Kuwait, Netherlands Antilles, Sarawak and Brunei, Saudi Arabia, Trinidad and Venezuela.

[e]Belgian Congo, Bolivia, Cyprus, Federation of Rhodesia and Nyasaland, Morocco, Peru, Sierra Leone, South Korea, Surinam and Tunisia.

[f]Angola, British East Africa, Ceylon, Costa Rica, Dominican Republic, Ecuador, El Salvador, Ethiopia and Eritrea, French Cameroons, French West Africa, Ghana, Guatemala, Haiti, Madagascar and Nigeria.

[g]Algeria, Barbados, British Guiana, Burma, Cuba, Formosa, Honduras, Jamaica, Jordan, Lebanon, Mauritius, Panama and Thailand.

[h]Indo-China, Indonesia, Liberia and Malaya.

[i]Egypt, French Equatorial Africa, Mozambique, Nicaragua, North Borneo, Paraguay, Philippines, Sudan, Syria and Uruguay.

[j]Hong Kong.

Note: Imports into Soviet countries in 1955 are exports to these countries from the rest of the world; valuation is f.o.b. *plus* 10 per cent for U.S.S.R. and Eastern Europe, and *plus* 15 per cent for China.

exporters, together with countries exporting coffee, tea and cocoa, took over one-half of all imports of manufactures into the non-industrial primary-producing countries in 1955. Countries exporting mainly agricultural raw materials expanded their imports of manufactures least of the various primary-producing groups[1].

Finally, there is a small group of European countries which were excluded from both the 'industrial' and 'semi-industrial' classifications[2]. Taken as a group, their relative importance as markets for manufactured goods has declined over the period since 1913, though they still account for about one-fifth of all manufactured imports into the 'rest of the world'.

6. THE MAIN TRENDS

This survey of the movement of world trade over the past half-century has revealed several major trends. First, the long-term movement in world trade in manufactures has been closely related to that in world manufacturing production. There was a break in the relationship in the 1930's, but in historical perspective this appears as a discontinuity due to special factors (i.e. trade and currency restrictions) operating to depress the level of trade in that period.

Second, the depression in world trade volume in the 1930's and the expansion in the 1950's was largely in manufactured goods. Before the second World War, a relative increase in the volume of trade in manufactures, compared with primary products, was normally associated with a reverse movement in the relative prices of these two groups. Since the second World War, however, a relative expansion in the volume of trade in manufactures has been accompanied by a net *increase* in the prices of manufactures in relation to an average of primary product prices. Some of the possible reasons for this change have been set out earlier; whether or not the present relationship is likely to continue in the future is discussed further in Chapter 15.

Third, in the trade expansion of the 1950's, the intra-trade of the industrial countries increased faster than any other sector of world trade. This was, in part, a reversion to a more 'normal' relationship between the intra-trade of the industrial countries and their total output of manufactures. Within the total intra-trade, however, the several streams of trade showed very different long-term tendencies. The most dynamic sectors have been the 'internal' exchanges *within* the two industrial continents, that is, the trade between Canada and the United States on the one side, and that among the Continental countries of

[1]Changes in the volume of 'imports' of manufactures into a selection of non-industrial countries in the period 1929-55 can be seen from Tables A.40-A.45.
[2]This group includes some countries (e.g. Austria and Denmark) which could be regarded as 'industrial'; and others (e.g. Greece and Portugal) which could be classed as 'semi-industrial'. These were all excluded from the detailed analysis in order to keep the volume of statistical extraction and computation work within reasonable limits. They are, however, included in the appropriate groups in some of the estimates presented in Chapters 6 and 15

Western Europe on the other. Trade *between* the industrial continents has increased at a slower pace. Of exports to outside countries, those to semi-industrial countries have tended to rise at a substantially lower rate than those to non-industrial ones.

Fourth, against this background of secular expansion, imports of manufactures into three important trading countries—Britain, India and Argentina—have tended to stagnate over the greater part of the period covered in this analysis, thus helping to retard the rate of growth in world trade. It was not until the late 1950's that imports of manufactures into Britain and India began to rise substantially. For Britain this was partly due to liberalization of import restrictions; while for India it reflected in the main an increase in inflow of aid and long-term capital. Imports into Argentina varied in an erratic manner from year to year in the later 1950's. The long period of stagnation in imports into India and Argentina did, however, appear significant at the time since they are also important examples of industrializing primary-producing countries. Their experiences thus appeared to support the view that industrialization in such countries necessarily tends to restrict exports, and so limits the increase in imports which can be achieved. This thesis is examined in more detail in the next chapter. Here, it suffices to point out that, on the historical evidence, both India and Argentina appear to be exceptional cases, in this respect, among the semi-industrial countries, just as Britain has been among the industrial ones.

CHAPTER 5

INDUSTRIALIZATION AND EXPORTS[1]

Though the main theme of this book is the relationship of economic growth— more particularly, industrialization—to imports of manufactured goods, we must digress at this point to consider the effects of industrialization on exports. The reason for this is that the process of industrialization may affect the availability of goods for export, and thus the export earnings of the industrializing country. Since, over a period of years, an expansion in imports has to be matched by a corresponding expansion in the buying power of exports, any substantial variation in the latter resulting from industrialization will affect the level of imports indirectly *via* the effect on exports.

Before proceeding to discuss the impact of industrialization on imports of manufactures, in Chapter 6, it is therefore necessary to assess whether the indirect effect on imports, *via* export availabilities, is generally a major factor to be taken into account.

1. EXPORT LEADS AND LAGS

In principle, three distinct relationships can be envisaged between the export sector and the whole economy in the process of economic development : exports can be the ' leading ' sector, i.e. they can provide the dynamic stimulus to growth in the rest of the economy ; or they can be a ' lagging ' sector as, for example, if development concentrates on the domestic market and the demand for imports outstrips the capacity to import ; or, finally, economic development may give rise to an expansion in supplies of export goods which is sufficient to pay for the increase in imports which is required.[2]

The economic growth of Britain in the nineteenth century is usually given as the classic example of exports as the ' leading ' sector. Japan, in the very early stages of industrialization, also seems to have developed mainly through the expansion of exports. Other examples, quoted by Kindleberger, are Sweden and Denmark after 1880, Switzerland, the Low Countries and Canada from 1900 to 1913, and Canada after 1945[3].

In general, small countries, or countries with limited natural resources, are more likely to find that economic growth can be accelerated by export specialization than are large countries or countries with a wide variety of natural resources.

---

[1]This chapter is a revised and somewhat extended version of an article entitled 'The Effects of Industrialization on Exports of Primary-producing Countries', *Kyklos*, Vol. 14, 1961, Fasc. 1.

[2]See C. P. Kindleberger, *Economic Development*, New York, 1958, Chapter 14, for a more detailed analysis of these three foreign trade 'models'.

[3]Kindleberger, *op. cit.*, pp. 245–252.

The extent to which resources in a developing economy can profitably be invested in export industries depends on the relative elasticities of supply and demand for imports and exports. If home supplies of primary goods are elastic and foreign demand is expanding (petroleum is perhaps the classic example), then exports almost inevitably become the ' leading ' sector.

Exports will, however, tend to lag behind if the traditional export products have a low supply elasticity and are not benefiting from expanding foreign demand. If new export products can successfully be developed, the lag may be overcome, but only a minority of developing countries may have both the resources and the flexibility in economic organization to achieve this. The export ' lagging ' type of development appears to be a very general one since 1945 among the industrializing countries which depend mainly on primary produce for their export earnings. Apart from the early post-war years, when accumulated holdings of foreign exchange were being spent, and a brief period during and immediately after the commodity price-inflation associated with the Korean War, the great majority of industrializing countries outside Europe and North America have been almost continuously faced with balance of payments difficulties and with an insufficient inflow of foreign capital investment.

To the extent that such payments difficulties have been due to an ' unbalanced ' growth, in the sense of over-concentration on development for the home market at the expense of exports, it can be said that the type of industrialization which has occurred has itself set limits to the rate of economic growth that could be achieved without further external aid. The difficulty is to determine whether, and to what extent, the post-war payments difficulties of industrializing countries were, in fact, due to industrial growth at home rather than to unfavourable economic conditions in the outside world.

2. TRENDS IN EXPORTS FROM THE SEMI-INDUSTRIAL AND NON-INDUSTRIAL COUNTRIES

Before further discussion of this question, it will be helpful to consider some of the main trends in the exports of the industrializing primary-producing countries (the ' semi-industrial ' countries) and of other primary-producers (the ' non-industrial ' countries). The salient facts are now well known as a result of recent studies, particularly those of G.A.T.T.[1] and the United Nations[2]. The G.A.T.T. analysis shows that from 1928 to 1955, the volume of exports from both industrial and primary-producing countries rose by nearly 40 per cent, but if petroleum is excluded the rise in exports from the latter group was under 20 per cent. Further evidence of the slower rate of growth of exports from the primary-producers than from the industrial countries is shown by the

[1]*International Trade, 1956* and subsequent years, G.A.T.T., Geneva.
[2]See, in particular, *World Economic Survey, 1958*, United Nations, New York, 1959, and *Economic Survey of Europe, 1957*, United Nations, Geneva, 1958.

fall in the percentage share of the former in world exports. If the oil countries are included, the percentage fell only marginally from 34 in 1928 to 31 in 1957 ; but excluding the oil countries, the fall was from 32 to 24 per cent over the period[1].

The main reason for this relative decline was the low rate of growth in exports from the industrializing group of primary-producing countries (the relevant statistics are examined later in this chapter). This discrepancy is the obverse of the ' lagging ' role played by the export sector in the economies of these countries, which was mentioned earlier. A considerable literature already exists on the possible causal influences at work in the apparent association between industrialization, the lag in the export sector of the economy and the slower rate of growth in exports than in exports from non-industrializing countries. The arguments invoked can conveniently be grouped according to whether they place emphasis on a deficiency in world demand for the exports of the industrializing primary-producing countries, or on a deficiency in the supply of those exports to the world market.

(a) Demand-deficiency

Perhaps the most powerful advocate of the demand-deficiency theory was the late Professor R. Nurkse. In his last discussion of the problem[2], Nurkse argued that the lag in exports of the less developed countries was ' mainly a reflection of relative sluggishness in external demand emanating from the great industrial consumers '[3]. The causes of this sluggish growth in the demand for imports of primary products on the part of the industrial countries has also been the subject of several empirical studies in recent years[4]. The principal factors at work appear to have been (i) a shift in the pattern of output in the industrial countries in favour of engineering, chemicals and other industries and services which have a low import-content, relatively to textiles and other industries which have a high import-content ; (ii) agricultural protectionism in the industrial countries, which has proved in practice more difficult to reduce than trade restrictions on manufactures ; (iii) a secular trend towards reduced usage of primary materials per unit of output of manufactures ; and (iv) a substantial substitution of synthetics for imported natural materials.

Nurkse did not, however, deny that in some countries domestic policies have resulted in restrictions on supplies of primary produce for export. But he considered that such policies in certain cases were themselves reactions to unfavourable demand conditions in the export market[5].

[1] *Trends in International Trade*, G.A.T.T., Geneva, 1958.
[2] R. Nurkse, *Patterns of Trade and Development*, The Wicksell Lectures, 1959, Stockholm.
[3] *Ibid.*, p. 26.
[4] See, for example, recent annual reports of G.A.T.T. and 'The Demand for Industrial Materials, 1950–1957' in the *National Institute Economic Review*, No. 5, Sept. 1959.
[5] *Op. cit.*, p. 26.

I

(b) Supply-deficiency

The opposing view, that the failure of primary-producing countries to expand their exports more rapidly is due to the process of industrialization, is a more traditional one and is still fairly widely held.   In its cruder form, the argument is that industrial growth in these countries will involve the consumption of greater quantities of their own agricultural produce, thus restricting supplies for the export market[1]. This line of thought, however, ignores the influence of price increases in stimulating the output of primary products.

A more sophisticated argument in general support of the supply-deficiency viewpoint has recently been expressed by Professor A. K. Cairncross[2], who points out that the failure of industrial countries to expand their imports of primary products between 1937 and 1957 in proportion to their economic growth, or to their consumption of manufactures, must have been due, in part at least, to the price factor.   The prices of exports from the non-industrial countries have risen since pre-war by almost half as much again as the prices obtained by industrial countries for their exports of primary produce[3].   The sharper rise in prices of exports from the non-industrial countries, Professor Cairncross argues, ' reflected the acute pressure on supplies of primary produce in a fully-employed economy—a pressure that continued because of the low elasticity of supply of this produce '.   Professor Cairncross further argues that this low elasticity was ' aggravated by the concentration of effort in many under-developed countries on industrialization rather than agricultural development '.

The various theoretical arguments have been considerably illumined in recent years by the very valuable statistical analysis of world trade movements to be found in the annual reports of G.A.T.T.   The 1955 G.A.T.T. report included a detailed statistical analysis of the factors on the demand side which were mainly responsible for the 'export lag' of the primary-producing countries[4]; but the expanded analysis in the subsequent reports supported the view that the lag in exports was due, in part at least, to the process of industrialization in the primary-producing countries.   This more recent analysis is of considerable importance, since it is so far the only comprehensive statistical analysis of the problem that has been available.   Moreover, if its conclusion is generally valid,

---

[1]This was, for example, the argument put forward by the Economics Committee of the Royal Commission on Population (*Report of the Economics Committee*, H.M.S.O., London, 1950, p. 13).

[2]A. K. Cairncross, 'International Trade and Economic Development' (*Kyklos*, Vol. 13, 1960, Fasc. 4).

[3]The unit value index for exports of primary produce from the main industrial countries was **218** in 1957 (1937 =100), whereas the corresponding index for exports from non-industrial countries in 1957 was **313** (see Table 4.3).   The latter includes a small proportion of manufactured goods, but this does not seriously affect the result.   Prices of primary product exports fell off between 1957 and 1959, but compared with pre-war there was still a large difference between the two indices: **196** (1937 =100) for the industrial, and **289** for the non-industrial, countries.

[4]*International Trade, 1955*, G.A.T.T., Geneva, 1956, especially pp. 6–15 and 206–211.

the implications are particularly serious for those under-developed countries now in an early phase of industrialization.

However, it would seem that the G.A.T.T. analysis does not take sufficiently into account some major factors—particularly on the demand side—which influence an industrializing country's exports, and that when these are included in the analysis the trend of development appears to fit in more closely with Nurkse's line of argument than with that put forward by Cairncross.

3. THE G.A.T.T. ANALYSIS

The 1956 G.A.T.T. report contains a detailed analysis of the position in world trade of industrializing countries outside North America, Europe and Japan[1]. For this purpose, eight countries (Argentina, Brazil, Mexico, Australia, India, South Africa, Finland, and Yugoslavia) were taken as the group of ' semi-industrialized ' countries, and their collective trading experience was compared with that of the non-industrial world. The main results are summarised in Table 5.1.

Table 5.1. *Exports from semi-industrial and non-industrial countries,*
1938 and 1955

	1938	1955	1955 volume index
	(*percentage of world exports*)		(*1937–38 = 100*)
Semi-industrial countries	11.7	9.8	95
Non-industrial countries	26.1	26.3	158
Total	37.8	36.1	134

Source: Based on Tables 3 and 4 of *International Trade, 1956*, G.A.T.T., Geneva, 1957.

The fall in the combined share held by these two areas in world trade since 1938 is seen to be due entirely to the reduced relative importance of the exports of the semi-industrial countries. This, in turn, reflected a fall in the volume of exports to industrial countries. By contrast, the non-industrial countries were exporting nearly 60 per cent more, in volume, in 1955 than in 1938. After examining the development of agricultural, mining and industrial production in different countries, the G.A.T.T. report concluded that the failure of the exports of the semi-industrial countries to expand at a fast rate was closely connected with the rapid growth in their industrial activities[2].

The analysis was considerably developed in the two subsequent annual reports of G.A.T.T., in particular by an attempt to include in the analysis both the effects of trade discrimination by importing countries, and the effects of

[1] *International Trade, 1956*, G.A.T.T., Geneva, 1957.
[2] *Ibid.*, pp. 16–17.

differences in the commodity-pattern of exports of the main industrializing countries. As regards the former, the extremely useful concept of 'shelter' was introduced[1]. A sheltered country is defined as one enjoying a privileged position in its main export market; conversely, an unsheltered country enjoys no special privilege of entry in its main export market, but may well be discriminated against by one method or another. As regards the latter, non-industrial countries were grouped according to their main export products.

For each group of countries classified in this way the increase in total export proceeds since 1928 was calculated in terms of U.S. dollars. A summary of the results is given in Table 5.2.

Table 5.2.   *Indices of export proceeds of countries grouped according to commodity composition, presence or absence of shelter and degree of industrialization, 1928–1956*

Indices, 1928 = 100

Countries exporting mainly	Year	Unsheltered		Sheltered	
		Semi-Industrial[a]	Other	Semi-Industrial[b]	Other
Non-tropical foods	1937	75	—	—	96
	1950	107	—	—	206
	1956	93	—	—	276
Agricultural raw materials	1937	—	84	73	106
	1950	—	164	173	243
	1956	—	187	184	277
Tropical foods	1937	74	64	—	90
	1950	284	287	—	180
	1956	312	403	—	398
Minerals	1937	—	79	84	594
	1950	—	134	230	274
	1956	—	236	393	1090

Source: Condensed version of Table 5, *International Trade, 1957–58,* G.A.T.T., Geneva, 1959.

[a]Non-tropical foods—Argentina; tropical foods—Brazil.

[b]Agricultural raw materials—Australia, India (including Pakistan), Mexico; Minerals—Union of South Africa.

The sheltered non-industrial countries have clearly done much better than the other groups of countries, except for countries exporting tropical foods. The export performance of the unsheltered semi-industrial countries has been the least satisfactory. The conclusion reached by the 1957/58 G.A.T.T. report from this analysis is that 'both the stage of industrialization and the presence or

[1]This concept is, in fact, the same as the 'regional trading' discussed in the earlier G.A.T.T. report for 1953.

absence of shelter seem to affect the course of export proceeds within each of the four commodity groups of countries'[1]. Though the report stresses that there are special factors at work in each country, it concludes that, nevertheless, 'such special factors appear not to be strong enough to blur completely the effect of the three factors investigated'[2]. This tends to support the conclusion reached in the 1958 report (the 'Haberler Report') that industrialization is a significant factor in the long-term tendency for the exports of the semi-industrial countries to rise more slowly than those of non-industrial countries.

Though the G.A.T.T. analysis is extremely useful for an assessment of the long-term trends, it is subject to two limitations. The first is that the four-fold commodity grouping is so wide as to be of very little use for comparing the export performance of different groups of countries. For example, Table 5.2 shows a much slower rate of growth in exports from semi-industrialized sheltered exporters of minerals (which group includes only the Union of South Africa) than from the non-industrialized sheltered exporters in that commodity group. The divergence appears to be due mainly to the growth in copper exports from Rhodesia and the Belgian Congo, and it is difficult to see how it can usefully be attributed to industrialization in South Africa. The second limitation is that no allowance has been made for the influence of price changes on the demand for exports of the primary-producing countries. In the following sections an attempt is made to build on the G.A.T.T. analysis by extending it to cover these two points.

4. INDICES OF WORLD ABSORPTION AND OF RELATIVE
EXPORT PRICES

The first limitation mentioned above can be overcome, in principle, only if specific allowance is made for the particular commodity pattern of exports from each industrializing country. One way of making such allowance is to construct an index of world absorption (or disappearance) for each country's particular ' bundle ' of exports, and to relate its actual export performance to this index. This would obviate the need for a broad grouping of countries according to the nature of their characteristic export product—a procedure which, as indicated above, can be most misleading. In practice, of course, indices of world absorption of different groupings of commodities are difficult to construct, because of the scarcity of the relevant statistics, even if we are quite clear what it is we are trying to measure.

Two alternative meanings of ' world absorption ' appear in fact to be relevant to the immediate problem. The first would relate to the movement in world *consumption* of the particular ' bundle ' of exports from a given country, the second would relate to world *trade* in that export ' bundle '. The consumption

[1]*Ibid.*, pp. 20–22.
[2]*Ibid.*, p. 29.

concept is the fundamental one, and would include both imports into the main industrial areas and the supply of natural and synthetic materials produced in those areas. ˙

However, for many primary commodities, statistical series for world consumption are difficult to collate on a reliable basis, and it was decided to make use instead of the second concept mentioned above, namely, world trade movements, the statistics for which are much more readily available. It should be noted, however, that changes in ' absorption ' in this sense reflect not only changes in consumption, but also the effects of competition from natural and synthetic substitutes produced in the industrial countries. Thus, this concept relates essentially to the volume of imported primary commodities by the main industrial countries, though in fact the statistics usually available relate to total world imports (outside the Soviet countries). Moreover, the use of world trade movements as the basis of an index of absorption implicitly assumes that the exporting country being considered is not the only effective source of supply of its particular export ' bundle ', so that if its exports are in fact restricted this would not affect the trend in world trade. This corresponds fairly closely to the position for the majority of the countries and commodities included in the present analysis. There are, however, one or two exceptional cases which are mentioned later.

For a selection of eleven industrializing countries, indices of world trade were calculated for the particular ' bundle ' of exports of each country, relating the base period chosen (the average of the years 1937 and 1938) with the year 1955. These periods were chosen so as to be comparable with the series given in the ' Haberler Report ', though the latter also extend back to 1928. The indices relate to both value and volume and cover as large a sample as possible of the primary commodity exports of each country. The indices were calculated on both pre-war and post-war weighting, but only the former set is presented here[1].

[1]The formulae used are as follows, where small letters p and q represent price and quantity of exports from a given country, and capitals P and Q represent the corresponding world exports of a given commodity, the subscripts 0 and 1 representing the base and current periods, respectively:

Value index of world trade

$$= \frac{\Sigma\left(p_0 q_0 \cdot \dfrac{P_1 Q_1}{P_0 Q_0}\right)}{\Sigma(p_0 q_0)} = \frac{\Sigma(s_0 \cdot P_1 Q_1)}{\Sigma(s_0 \cdot P_0 Q_0)}$$

the aggregations being made over all the separate commodities, where

$s_0 = \dfrac{p_0 q_0}{P_0 Q_0} = $ country's share of world exports of a given commodity, by value, in the base period.

Volume index of world trade

$$= \frac{\Sigma\left(p_0 q_0 \cdot \dfrac{Q_1}{Q_0}\right)}{\Sigma(p_0 q_0)} = \frac{\Sigma(s_0 \cdot P_0 Q_1)}{\Sigma(s_0 \cdot P_0 Q_0)}$$

The index of world trade used here is simply the movement in world exports of the individual primary commodities exported by a given country from 1937-38 to 1955, weighted by the relative importance of each commodity in the country's export trade in the base period. This can also be looked at as measuring how the exports of each country would have changed over this period, if its share of world exports of each commodity had been the same in 1955 as it had been pre-war. Hence, a comparison of the appropriate world trade index with the comparable index of actual exports shows to what extent each country has suffered a loss, or enjoyed a gain, of its average pre-war share of the world import market. The indices for actual exports are calculated in the usual way, the volume index being base-weighted to maintain comparability with the corresponding volume index of world trade[1].

Relative price movements

The second limitation of the G.A.T.T. analysis mentioned above can be met by relating the movement in the prices of exports from an industrializing country to the corresponding price movements in (a) exports of the same, or closely competing, commodities from other primary-producing countries, and (b) supplies of locally-produced natural or synthetic substitutes in the main consuming countries. For a complete explanation of changes in exports of primary products from particular countries, it would be necessary to take account of both these sources of competition, and a separate analysis would have to be made for each commodity.

This would, however, be too great a task to embark upon here and, in order to limit the scope of the statistical analysis, the present discussion is confined to (a) above ; that is, to relative movements in prices of exports from a given industrializing country, compared with similar commodities exported by other countries.   This is, of course, a substantial limitation though it does allow for an important part of the whole process of price competition in the primary commodity markets.

More specifically, the price factor considered here is defined as the movement in the unit value of exports of primary produce from a given industrializing country relatively to the unit value of world trade in the same ' bundle ' of

---

[1]Value index of actual exports $= \dfrac{\Sigma(p_1 q_1)}{\Sigma(p_0 q_0)}$

Volume index of actual exports $= \dfrac{\Sigma(p_0 q_1)}{\Sigma(p_0 q_0)}$

the aggregations being made over the separate commodity groups.

commodities[1]. This implies that different producing countries are competing in the world market, though in particular commodities the competition may be between different varieties or grades of the same product. The fact that some goods may be offered at an auction-type sale, rather than at a fixed price, does not invalidate the hypothesis that there is competition at the margin between different producing countries in the primary commodity markets[2].

Export unit value series were calculated for 1955 (the 1937-38 average being taken as 100) for the same eleven countries covered by the volume indices described earlier. As already indicated, a separate index was also calculated for each country for the movement in the unit value of world trade in its particular commodity ' bundle '.

5. A STATISTICAL ANALYSIS OF EXPORTS IN RELATION TO INDUSTRIALIZATION

The main results of the various calculations are given in Table 5.3. The total indices for each country include various minor items as well as the primary commodity exports shown separately. The relative importance of the sample in total exports varies a good deal ; it is highest in Colombia and Brazil, and lowest in Yugoslavia, which has a very diversified export trade. Generally, the coverage is reasonably good enough to allow the computed indices to be taken as representative of exports of primary produce from each country in relation to world trade in its particular export ' bundle '[3].

[1]On the previous notation, the relevant indices are as follows:
Unit value of world trade (current weighted)
$$= \frac{\Sigma(p_1 q_1)}{\Sigma(p_1 q_1 \cdot P_0/P_1)} = \frac{\Sigma(s_1 \cdot P_1 Q_1)}{\Sigma(s_1 \cdot P_0 Q_1)}$$
where $s_1 = \dfrac{p_1 q_1}{P_1 Q_1} = $ country's share of world exports of a given commodity, by value, in the current period.
Unit value of actual exports (current weighted)
$$= \frac{\Sigma(p_1 q_1)}{\Sigma(p_0 q_1)}$$
all aggregations being made over the separate commodity groups.

[2]For an opposing viewpoint, see K. Bieda, 'The Causes of the Export Lag of the Industrializing Countries', *Kyklos*, Vol. 15, 1962, Fasc. 2.

[3]As mentioned earlier, there were one or two cases in which exports from a particular country were taken as representing world absorption also. Exports of saltpetre from Chile are counted both in the export index and in the world trade index for that country; an alternative procedure might have been to use world trade in nitrogenous fertilizers for the latter index. The other major case is the export of jute from India and Pakistan, for which the export index and the world trade index is virtually identical; there is no simple alternative here since a widening of the commodity definition to include close substitutes (for example, shipping sack paper) would have raised formidable statistical difficulties. To this extent, of course, the export and world trade indices are not, strictly speaking, independent variables. However, in both these cases, the offending commodity represents a relatively small proportion of exports.

Several interesting points emerge. Taking first the total export performance of all eleven countries, the table shows that the entire increase in export earnings[1] was due to price increases ; the volume of exports in 1955 was not significantly different from the 1937-38 average. Moreover, the increase in export earnings was closely in line with the increase in world trade in the commodities concerned. Over the period covered, the difference between the two value indices was only 3 per cent. In volume terms, there was a larger difference, actual exports falling short of the rise in world trade volume by 6 per cent, but this was partly offset by the fact that unit values of exports from the eleven countries had risen rather more than unit values in world trade for the same commodity ' bundles '. The greater part of the shortfall in export volume was attributable to Argentina ; excluding that country, the volume indices were virtually identical (111 for actual exports and 113 for world trade).

However, once we get away from the overall totals, the outstanding feature of Table 5.3 is the remarkable diversity of experience, between commodities and between countries. In terms of volume, the growth in world trade in petroleum has easily outstripped that in any of the other commodities included in the sample, while trade in hardwood, canned meat and diamonds has also expanded much faster than the average. At the other extreme, world trade in 1955 in maize, linseed, beef, butter, raw cotton and jute was in each case lower than the pre-war volume.

The dispersion in unit values was, however, greater than in volume. The post-war boom in the coffee and cocoa markets brought their prices by 1955 to, respectively, six times, and five times, the pre-war average. Unit values of canned meat, lead, copper and raw cotton had all risen by well above the average rate whereas, apart from the special case of gold, the rise was smallest for wheat, linseed, butter and hardwood, and was also below average for petroleum.

The combination of these very diverse movements in volume and unit value of the different primary products was responsible for extremely great variation in the market opportunities facing the different countries in terms of export income. This ranged from an increase of nearly six-fold in potential export income (as measured by the index for world trade value) for Colombia, and nearly four-fold for Brazil, to one of about 100 per cent for Argentina and New Zealand and about 150 per cent for Australia and India-Pakistan. Colombia's share of world petroleum exports has fallen sharply since pre-war, with the rise in Middle East supplies, but her share of world coffee exports has risen whereas Brazil's share has fallen substantially. Both Colombia and Brazil, however, gained tremendously from the very high relative prices of coffee in 1955.

Among the less fortunate countries, New Zealand has offset a poor market

---

[1]The rise of 183 per cent in the value of exports from the 11 countries, shown in Table 5.3 is practically identical with the G.A.T.T. figures for 8 semi-industrialized countries, which showed an increase of 184 per cent over the same period (*Trends in International Trade*, G.A.T.T., Geneva, 1958, p. 24).

Table 5.3. *Changes in the value and volume of selected exports from the semi-industrial countries compared with changes in world trade, 1937–38 to 1955*

	Exports from country specified				World trade		
	Proportion of total exports of primary products 1937–8 1955	Indices for 1955			Indices for 1955		
		Value[a]	Volume	Unit Value[a]	Value[a]	Volume	Unit Value[a]
	(*Percentage*)	(*1937–8 = 100*)			(*1937–8 = 100*)		
ARGENTINA							
Maize	21 3	18	6	300	97	41	237
Wheat (incl. flour)	18 27	234	123	190	251	138	182
Linseed and linseed oil	12 3	40	26[b]	154	116	63	184
Beef	11 9	128	43	298	190	72	264
Wool	9 13	238	69	345	323	117	276
Canned Meat	2 7	515	114	452	695	194	358
Total of sample	*84 77*	*141*	*62*	*227*	*193*	*88*	*211*
AUSTRALIA							
Wool	34 44	350	145	241	323	117	276
Wheat (incl. flour)	16 8	147	94	156	251	138	182
Gold	9 1	31	31	100	88[c]	88[c]	100
Butter	6 4	173	100	173	134	69	194
Lead and ores[d]	3 4	305	106	288	312[e]	103[e]	303[e]
Total of sample	*83 76*	*253*	*116*	*218*	*255*	*113*	*232*
BRAZIL							
Coffee	44 59	597	94	635	702	116	605
Cotton	18 9	222	70	317	215	71	303
Cocoa	4 6	654	105	623	520	99	525
Total of sample	*87 91*	*463*	*92*	*503*	*486*	*106*	*431*
CHILE							
Copper and ores	52 69	385	112	343	422[e]	117[e]	360[e]
Saltpetre	21 12	165	83	199	165[f]	83[f]	199
Total of sample	*77 82*	*306*	*99*	*310*	*313*	*101*	*314*
COLOMBIA							
Coffee	65 83	920	140	657	702	116	605
Petroleum	25 11	318	127	250	740	350	211
Total of sample	*98 98*	*707*	*132*	*537*	*673*	*173*	*488*
INDIA (incl. Pakistan)							
Cotton	18 11	148	52	285	215	71	303
Tea	13 15	271	121	224	269	111	242
Jute	8 9	268	84	319	222	82	271
Total of sample	*78 75*	*230*	*83*	*277*	*244*	*92*	*268*
MEXICO							
Silver and ores[d]	18 5	93	44	211	129[e]	64[e]	202[e]
Gold[d]	18 —	1	1	100	88[c]	88[c]	100
Petroleum	15 7	178	95	187	740	350	211
Lead and ores[d]	12[g] 7[g]	218[g]	70	311	312[e]	103[e]	303[e]
Coffee	4 11	1221	238	513	702	116	605
Cotton	2[g] 32[g]	754[g]	206	366	215	71	303
Total of sample	*79 74*	*359*	*121*	*296*	*325*	*140*	*300*
Total, less gold	*77 74*	*463*	*156*	*296*	*394*	*155*	*301*

Table 5.3.(cont.)

	Exports from country specified					World trade		
	Proportion of total exports of primary products		Indices for 1955			Indices for 1955		
	1937–8	1955	Value[a]	Volume	Unit Value[a]	Value[a]	Volume	Unit Value[a]
	(Percentage)		(1937–8 = 100)			(1937–8 = 100)		
NEW ZEALAND								
Butter	27	20	212	106	200	134	69	194
Wool	25	37	416	154	270	323	117	276
Mutton and lamb	18	16	268	142	189	205	106	193
Total of sample	*84*	*84*	*293*	*131*	*224*	*218*	*98*	*227*
TURKEY								
Tobacco	29	28	280	143	196	214	102	210
Hazel nuts	8	14	507	195	260	470	184	255
Cotton	5	15	770	247	312	215	71	303
Total of sample	*69*	*76*	*319*	*138*	*231*	*253*	*119*	*231*
UNION OF SOUTH AFRICA								
Gold	63	35	156	156	100	88	88	100
Wool	10	11	295	109	271	323	117	276
Rough diamonds	3	5	497	161	309	457[h]	190[h]	241[h]
Total of sample	*89*	*81*	*212*	*152*	*139*	*144*	*96*	*138*
Total less gold	*64*	*64*	*376*	*140*	*268*	*307*	*120*	*253*
YUGOSLAVIA								
Maize	10	—	1	—	375	97	41	237
Copper and ores	8	4	87	27	322	422[e]	117[e]	360[e]
Softwood	7	6	148	33	448	337	116	291
Wheat (incl. flour)	7	—	—	—	—	251	138	182
Hardwood	7	7	211	62	340	560	290	193
Lead and ores	5	7	301	92	327	312[e]	103[e]	303[e]
Tobacco	2	7	554	318	174	214	102	210
Total of sample	*57*	*52*	*161*	*59*	*272*	*303*	*125*	*245*
TOTAL (excl. gold)	81	80	283	101	286	292	107	279

Sources: Statistics of the Volume, Average Unit Value and Total Value of International Trade in Agricultural Products, Food and Agriculture Organization, Rome, 1956; and national trade statistics.

Only major export items are given separately; minor items are also included in the figures for total sample. The volume indices for the totals have 1937–8 weights and the unit value indices 1955 weights.

[a]In terms of United States dollars.
[b]Estimates based on oil equivalent.
[c]World production outside U.S.S.R. and semi-industrial countries, *plus* exports from U.S.S.R. (estimates) and semi-industrial countries.
[d]Estimates based on value and composition of mixed ores.
[e]Exports from producing countries only.
[f]Exports from Chile only.
[g]Adjusted official values.
[h]World production *minus* South African production *plus* South African exports.

opportunity by capturing a much greater share of the world market for each of her major exports, whereas Argentina which was also faced with intractable foreign demand conditions, lost more than she need have done. Australia expanded her export volume in virtually the same proportion as world demand for her exports, a gain in market share in raw wool being offset by a loss in wheat. Indian exports increased rather less than in proportion to world trade as a result of a loss of share in raw cotton ; this was mainly the result of pre-emption of cotton for home mills in 1955 though, of course, there was an offset in the much greater Indian export of cotton textiles in that year than in the pre-war period.

Yugoslavia is very much a special case among this group of countries. World trade in her pre-war export ' bundle ' rose by 25 per cent in volume from 1937-38 to 1955, yet her exports fell off by some 40 per cent. Only in tobacco were exports in 1955 greater than pre-war. Yugoslavia's major economic effort since 1945 has been directed to industrialization and the modernization of the economy ; from this point of view, the failure of exports to recover their pre-war level by 1955 appears to be a clear case of the ' supply deficiency ' argument mentioned earlier[1].

The other general effect of the varied changes in world demand for the different primary commodity exports, is that countries have tended to shift their export pattern away from commodities for which demand was contracting, or expanding less rapidly, to those for which a more rapid expansion had taken place. In this process, some of these countries, such as Australia and South Africa, had achieved a more diversified export pattern, but others had not ; overall, there was no significant change in the degree of concentration of exports in the commodities listed in Table 5.3.

These results indicate a fairly close association between the movement in world trade for individual commodities and the movement in exports from the different semi-industrial countries. This relationship is examined further in the next section, which also considers the effects on exports of relative prices, the presence or absence of ' sheltered ' markets, and of industrial growth in the exporting countries.

(a) *Influence of movements in world trade, relative export prices, and presence or absence of shelter*

The relationship between the movement in the volume of exports of primary produce from the semi-industrial countries since pre-war and the movement in world trade in the corresponding commodity groups and in relative export prices can be expressed in the form of a multiple regression equation. A linear

---

[1] Since 1955, exports from Yugoslavia have expanded at a rapid rate, the volume of exports in 1959 being about 80 per cent above the 1955 level.

logarithmic form was used, and the results for regressions using various combinations of the independent variables are summarised in Table 5.4.

Table 5.4. *Results of regressions of export volume on world trade index and relative export prices[a]*

Regression[b]	Co-efficient of			R^2
	W	$\dfrac{P_E}{P_W}$	S	
1. E on W	0.96 ($\pm$0.32)	—	—	0.532
2. E on W and $\dfrac{P_E}{P_W}$	0.97 ($\pm$0.28)	−1.71 ($\pm$0.94)	—	0.683
3. $\dfrac{E}{W}$ on $\dfrac{P_E}{P_W}$	—	−1.72 ($\pm$0.89)	—	0.318
4. E on W, $\dfrac{P_E}{P_W}$ and S	0.97 ($\pm$0.28)	−1.20 ($\pm$1.10)	0.06 ($\pm$0.06)	0.723

[a]Based on indices for 10 countries (all countries listed in Table 5.3 except Yugoslavia, which is excluded as a special case where the incentives of the world market were not operative, or only partially operative, in this period).
[b]E and W = logarithms of export volume, and of the volume of world trade, respectively.

$\dfrac{P_E}{P_W}$ = logarithm of ratio of unit value of exports to unit value of world trade.

S = presence or absence of shelter (taken in the calculation as unity for presence and zero for absence).

The regression co-efficient for the volume of world trade index is virtually unity, indicating that there has been no significant change in the share of world trade in their export specialities held by these industrializing countries over the period covered[1]. This, of course, is a generalized result, there being some appreciable diversity of experience in this respect among the different countries, as can be seen from Fig. 5.1. As was to be expected, the co-efficient for the relative price term is negative, equations 2 and 3 indicating a price-substitution elasticity in relation to competing exports from other countries of about −1.7[2].

A further regression was tried (equation 4 in Table 5.4), including a variable representing the presence or absence of 'sheltered' markets for the exports of

[1]An objection to this approach has been raised by Professor E. Devons ('Understanding International Trade', *Economica*, New Series, Vol. 28, No. 112, November 1961). Professor Devons argues that for some commodities, such as wool, the exports from four semi-industrial countries account for the bulk of world export trade in wool; and it is 'hardly surprising therefore that the export volume of wool from these countries, on average, approximates to the world total, some above and some below'. However, the fact that the semi-industrial countries *as a group* account for a large proportion of world trade in any particular commodity does not, by itself, invalidate the method used here, since the regression analysis is essentially a comparison of the exports of each semi-industrial country separately with those of all other countries, semi-industrial or otherwise.

[2]Since this represents a mean value for all the commodities covered, it is not, perhaps, surprising that the standard error ($\pm$0.9) is relatively high. The corresponding country price-substitution elasticities may, in fact, vary considerably.

each country. For this purpose, Australia, India (including Pakistan), Mexico, New Zealand and South Africa were counted in the 'sheltered' group; the rest were taken as selling in 'unsheltered' markets. This is, of course, only a very crude indication of the relevance of 'shelter' in the development of exports from these countries, since they may well be selling under sheltered conditions in some markets but not in others. For example, Britain would rank as a 'sheltered' market for the Commonwealth countries, whereas their exports to the United States and Continental Europe should be considered 'unsheltered'. For this reason, the result of the regression analysis, which shows that the presence or absence of sheltered markets had no significant influence on the development of exports from the semi-industrial countries, should be accepted with some reserve.

Fig. 5.1. Relation between computed export volume indices and world trade indices for semi-industrial countries, 1937–38 to 1955

Indices for 1955 (1937–38 = 100)

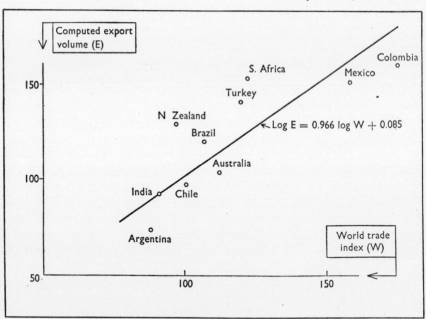

The line shows the net regression of export volume on the world trade index, based on equation 2 in Table 5.4, assuming that $P_E/P_W = 1$.

(b) *Influence of industrialization*

We can now consider whether there is any significant relationship between the export performance of an industrializing country and its rate of industrial development. There are several ways in which the latter can be measured. The main alternatives are to measure the rate of growth of manufacturing production or the rate of growth of the manufacturing sector in relation to that of the economy as a whole. Both measures are used here, indices being computed for 1955 compared with 1937. Table 5.5 summarises the results of regressions using these indices. The dependent variable for this purpose has been taken to be the ratio E/W; that is, it is proposed to measure the effect of industrial growth on changes in the *share* of the individual countries in world trade in their particular ' bundles ' of primary commodities.

Table 5.5. *Results of regressions of export volume on manufacturing production and relative export prices*

| Regression[a] | Co-efficient of | | | |
	M_1	M_2	$\dfrac{P_E}{P_W}$	R^2
10 *countries*				
5. $\dfrac{E}{W}$ on M_1	0.05 (± 0.27)	—	—	0.004
6. $\dfrac{E}{W}$ on M_2	—	0.28 (± 0.37)	—	0.068
7. $\dfrac{E}{W}$ on M_1 and $\dfrac{P_E}{P_W}$	0.26 (± 0.24)	—	-2.14 (± 0.96)	0.415
8. $\dfrac{E}{W}$ on M_2 and $\dfrac{P_E}{P_W}$	—	0.20 (± 0.33)	-1.64 (± 0.94)	0.353
9 *countries* (*excl. New Zealand*)				
9. $\dfrac{E}{W}$ on M_2	—	0.56 (± 0.29)	—	0.348
10. $\dfrac{E}{W}$ on M_2 a $\dfrac{P_E}{P_W}$	—	0.47 (± 0.28)	-1.10 (± 0.76)	0.519

[a]E, P_E, W and P_W defined as in Table 5.4.
M_1 = logarithm of index of manufacturing production.
M_2 = logarithm of ratio of index of manufacturing production to index of real domestic product.

The relationship between E/W and industrial growth is not statistically significant in any of the four regressions covering all ten countries. If New Zealand is excluded[1], the goodness of fit of the regressions is considerably improved, the co-efficient of M_2 (manufacturing sector in relation to the whole economy) being in the region of 0.5. The main point which emerges from Table 5.5. is that, if there *is* any significant relationship between E/W and either M_1 or M_2, it is a positive and not a negative one.

[1]The exclusion of New Zealand can perhaps be justified on the grounds that her export performance automatically benefited, to a much greater degree than any other country's, by the failure of Argentina to maintain her export supplies.

6. EXPORTS OF COMPETING PRODUCTS FROM THE INDUSTRIAL, SEMI-INDUSTRIAL AND NON-INDUSTRIAL COUNTRIES

So far, the export experience of the semi-industrial countries has been compared, in effect, with exports of similar commodities from all other countries without distinction. However, it is very relevant to the discussion of the ' demand-deficiency ' and ' supply-deficiency ' arguments to distinguish between the industrial and the non-industrial competitors of the semi-industrial countries. Since the exports of the industrial and the non-industrial countries might have changed differently, it might be misleading to compare their combined experience with that of the semi-industrial countries.

The distinction is a vital one when the comparison is made in terms of commodities, since the semi-industrial countries compete with the non-industrial countries mainly in tropical foodstuffs, non-ferrous metals, raw cotton and sugar, and with the industrial countries mainly in cereals, tobacco, raw cotton and raw wool, meat, non-ferrous metals, butter and sugar. Though there is a considerable amount of overlapping in the competitive pattern, there are also clearly defined areas in which the semi-industrial countries compete only with the industrial countries or only with the non-industrial ones.

The virtual stability in the total volume of exports of primary products from the semi-industrial countries between 1937-38 and 1955 conceals a sharp reduction in cereals offset by gains in beverages and tobacco and in textile fibres (see Table 5.6). The decline in cereals exports was mainly due to the drastic curtailment of maize exports from Argentina, while exports of maize from non-industrial countries also declined. On the other hand, exports of wheat from the industrial countries expanded by a very substantial amount as a result of the farm surplus position in the United States and the various commodity aid programmes.

Of the two large increases in exports from the semi-industrial countries, that in textile fibres was entirely in raw wool (the shortfall in Argentine shipments being more than offset by expansion in Australian and New Zealand exports), whereas the decline in exports from the other two groups of countries was in raw cotton. The other major increase in exports from the semi-industrial countries was in coffee and tea. In coffee, there was, however, a marked gain in the share of the world market taken by the non-industrial producing countries, but in tea the semi-industrial countries gained in market share over the period. The relative gain in coffee by the non-industrial countries was not, however, mainly the result of industrialization in their semi-industrial competitors; rather, it resulted from the switch in consumer demand to soluble coffee, for which African *robusta* varieties are more suitable than the *arabicas* produced in Latin America, and from the preferential treatment of coffee from the associated African territories imported into many of the expanding markets of Western Europe in the post-war period.

The prime importance of the commodity composition of trade of the different groups of countries can be seen even more clearly if we divide the exports of the non-industrial countries into two parts : the commodities directly competitive with those of the semi-industrial countries (as included in Table 5.6), and all other primary products. The contrast in export experience of the two commodity groups is most striking. Whereas the increase in export volume from 1937–38 to 1955 for the first, ' competitive ', group was only 5 per cent, compared with an increase of 1 per cent for the semi-industrial countries, the rise in export volume in the second, ' non-competitive ', group was over 120 per cent (see Table 5.7).

This further evidence also supports the view that the divergent rate of growth in exports from the semi-industrial and the non-industrial countries is closely

Table 5.6. *Exports of major groups of primary products^a from industrial, semi-industrial and non-industrial countries, 1955 compared with 1937–38*

		Industrial countries^b	Semi-industrial countries	Non-industrial countries	Total
				$ billion at 1955 prices	
Beverages and tobacco	1955	0.35	2.05	1.73	4.13
	Change from 1937–38	*+ 0.07*	*+ 0.23*	*+ 0.14*	*+ 0.44*
Meat	1955	0.20	0.53	0.01	0.74
	Change from 1937–38	*+ 0.11*	*− 0.03*	*− 0.02*	*+ 0.06*
Cereals	1955	1.50	0.58	0.06	2.14
	Change from 1937–38	*+ 0.51*	*− 0.43*	*− 0.11*	*− 0.03*
Non-ferrous metals	1955	0.28	0.69	0.60	1.57
	Change from 1937–38	*− 0.04*	*+ 0.03*	*+ 0.19*	*+ 0.18*
Textile fibres	1955	0.81	2.39	0.74	3.94
	Change from 1937–38	*− 0.62*	*+ 0.25*	*− 0.11*	*− 0.48*
Other primary products^c	1955	0.50	0.58	1.37	2.45
	Change from 1937–38	*− 0.06*	*0*	*+ 0.13*	*+ 0.07*
TOTAL	1955	3.64	6.82	4.51	14.97
	Change from 1937–38	*− 0.03*	*+ 0.05*	*+ 0.22*	*+ 0.24*

Sources: As for Table 5.3.

^{a}This table is confined to the principal exports of primary products from the semi-industrial countries, as listed in Table 5.3.

^{b}O.E.E.C. countries, North America and Japan,

^{c}Butter, sugar, linseed and cattle hides,

K   WT

Table 5.7.   *Exports of primary commodities from the non-industrial countries,*
1937–38 and 1955

	1937–38	1955	Volume in 1955
	($ billion at 1955 prices)		(1937–38 = 100)
1. Directly competitive with exports of semi-industrial countries[a]	4.29	4.51	105
2. Other primary commodity exports[b]	4.42	9.90	224
TOTAL	8.71	14.41	165[c]

Sources: International Trade 1956 (Table 4 and Appendix), and working data for Table 5.3.

[a] As in Table 5.6.

[b] Residue.

[c] This differs slightly from the corresponding volume index (158) published in *International Trade 1956* because of some difference in the countries included in the calculation.

connected with the different commodity-patterns of their exports. Moreover, for the period covered by the preceding analysis, there was no negative association *in general*, between industrial growth and export volume (though such an association would have been expected on the basis of the supply-deficiency view). The implication of the results seems to be that, at least for the period from 1937 up to 1955, the demand-deficiency argument has been nearer the truth than the supply deficiency argument, *if a broad generalization is sought.* It should be emphasized that this generalization relates to the behaviour of the semi-industrial countries in the aggregate over a particular period of time ; it does *not* imply that for particular countries, at some periods, industrialization has not had a retarding effect on the supply of primary commodities for export. Indeed, several specific examples of this have already been mentioned ; for example, Argentine maize, Indian raw cotton and Yugoslav cereals, non-ferrous metals and timber. Clearly, much depends on the type of industrialization and the general economic and monetary policy being pursued ; industrialization can just as well promote exports as retard them or, equally, have little or no significant influence on the total export volume. It cannot therefore be assumed that industrialization of a primary-producing country will, in itself, necessarily have adverse effects on the capacity to import and thus indirectly place limits on its domestic rate of economic growth.

CHAPTER 6

INDUSTRIALIZATION AND IMPORTS OF MANUFACTURES

1. THE CONSUMPTION OF MANUFACTURES

Industrialization, as we saw in Chapter 1, is closely associated with rising real income per head. It is also associated with an increase in the consumption of goods and services of all kinds, but particularly, perhaps, in the consumption of manufactured goods. The industrial areas still account for much the greater part of the total consumption of manufactures outside the Soviet countries. Before the war, in 1937, they consumed some 85 per cent of the world total, while by 1959 the proportion was about 80 per cent (see Table 6.1)[1]. The semi-industrial[2] countries increased their proportion of world consumption of manufactures from about 10 per cent pre-war to about 13 per cent in 1959, but there was no change in the proportion for the non-industrial countries—about 5–6 per cent of the world total both pre-war and in 1959.

The range between the developed and under-developed areas is much greater for per caput than for total consumption. Two features of the estimates in Table 6.1 call for special comment. First, there is a wide range in consumption of manufactures per head *within* the industrial and semi-industrial groups. Consumption per head in Japan, for example, was only about one-tenth that in North America in 1959 (the proportion was much lower than this in the earlier 1950's), while the per caput figure for India and Pakistan in 1959 was only some 6 per cent of the average for the three Southern Dominions. The second feature is that, irrespective of the *level* of consumption per head, there has been a general increase in per caput consumption in all areas since 1950. The percentage increase has been particularly marked in Japan, where production was abnormally low in 1950; in India, where successive Five-Year Plans have resulted in a sharp increase in demand for manufactured goods (particularly for capital equipment); and in the non-industrial areas generally[3]. The increase shown for the industrial countries of Western Europe from 1950 to 1959 ($175 per head or about 60 per cent) is heavily affected by the rapid recovery of West Germany from a low economic level in the earlier year. Compared with 1937,

[1]See Appendix E for a discussion of the statistical basis of the estimates in Table 6.1.
[2]The classification of countries in Table 6.1 is intended to be comprehensive, and the totals for 'industrial' and 'semi-industrial' countries are therefore not comparable with those given in earlier chapters. Table 6.1 includes Austria, Denmark and Finland with the industrial countries of Western Europe, and also includes a semi-industrial group of Western European countries. For the estimates for individual countries, see Tables E.5 and E.6.
[3]A part of the increase in the consumption of manufactures in the non-industrial areas since 1950 has consisted of equipment for the petroleum industry.

per caput consumption of manufactures had doubled by 1959 in the industrial countries, had more than doubled in the semi-industrial areas, while in the non-industrial areas the rise was a more modest one (about 75 per cent).

Table 6.1.   *Estimated apparent consumption of manufactures[a] in industrial, semi-industrial and non-industrial countries, 1937–59*

	Apparent consumption				Apparent consumption per head			
	1937	1950	1955	1959	1937	1950	1955	1959
	($ billion at 1955 prices)				($ at 1955 prices)			
INDUSTRIAL	143	211	287	328	315	435	560	605
Western Europe[b]	59.4	67.8	100.2	117.9	240	290	410	465
North America	81.0	141.0	181.5	200.0	580	855	1000	1025
Japan	2.9	1.9	4.9	9.6	40	25	55	105
SEMI-INDUSTRIAL[c]	16[d]	33	42	52	30[d]	50	58	70
Western Europe[e]	2.9[d]	9.1	10.4	13.8	90[d]	145	165	200
Southern Dominions	4.9	8.5	11.3	13.2	270	380	450	485
India/Pakistan	2.4	3.1	4.8	5.9	6	7	10	12
Latin America	5.4	11.1	13.5	17.1	65	100	105	125
NON-INDUSTRIAL	9	11	16	22	20	20	30	35
TOTAL[f]	168[d]	255	345	402	120[d]	155	190	210

Sources: Table E.5 and related data; Table E.7.

[a]Excluding food, beverages and tobacco; and imports of manufactures from Soviet countries and from non-industrial areas.

[b]Including Austria, Denmark and Finland as well as the group usually taken as 'industrial' (i.e. Belgium-Luxembourg, France, Germany (West Germany in 1950–59), Italy, Netherlands, Norway, Sweden, Switzerland and United Kingdom).

[c]Including Israel and Turkey.

[d]Excluding Spain.

[e]Greece, Ireland, Portugal, Spain and Yugoslavia.

[f]Excluding Soviet countries.

Real income changes

That these increases in the volume of apparent consumption of manufactured goods have been closely associated with changes in real incomes can readily be seen from Fig. 6.1, which includes a sample of ten countries at different stages of economic development. Though the industrial countries generally consume considerably greater quantities of manufactured goods in relation to income than do the semi-industrial countries, it would seem from this Figure that the *rate* at which the consumption of manufactures increases in relation to real income is not dissimilar in the two groups of countries.

A more accurate assessment of the relation between the rates of growth in consumption of manufactures and in real income can be obtained by regression analysis.   Regression equations were calculated, for eleven industrial and seven semi-industrial countries, of per caput consumption of manufactures on per caput real income for selected years from 1899 to 1957[1].   The resulting

Fig. 6.1.   Apparent consumption of manufactures per head in relation to gross domestic product per head in selected countries, 1899–1957

Double logarithmic scale

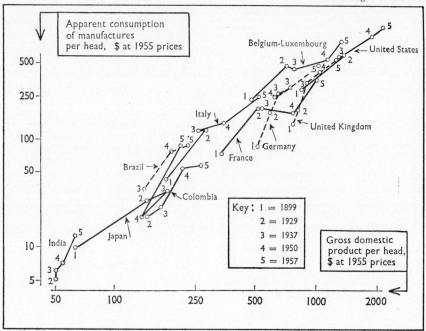

co-efficients (see Table 6.2) are mostly within the range of 1.3 to 2.0 for the industrial countries, and 1.7 to 2.1 for the semi-industrial countries.   For all eleven industrial countries, the combined co-efficient was 1.4, while for the semi-industrial group it was 1.7 (or 2.0, if South Africa is excluded)[2].

The higher co-efficient for the semi-industrial than for the industrial group implies that in the early phases of industrialization the demand for manufactures increases at a faster rate, in relation to income, than it does at a more mature phase.   A parallel difference appears when cross-country comparisons are made for a recent year (Table 6.3); however, in this case the differences between

---

[1]A double logarithmic form of equation was used.   Since no allowance was made for changes in the prices of manufactures in relation to other goods and services, the regression co-efficients overstate the underlying income elasticities if, as seems likely, there has been a general fall in the relative price of manufactures over the past half-century.

[2]See footnote [3] on page 51 for the form of equation used in these cross-country time series regressions.

Table 6.2. *Income co-efficients for consumption of manufactures based on time series*

	Period[a]	Income co-efficient	Standard error	R^2
INDUSTRIAL COUNTRIES				
Belgium-Luxembourg	1899–57	0.98	± 0.10	0.952
France	,,	1.25	± 0.25	0.836
Germany/West Germany	,,	2.16	± 0.37	0.895
Italy	,,	1.40	± 0.21	0.898
Netherlands	1929–57	1.95	± 0.36	0.908
Norway	1913–57	1.33	± 0.16	0.946
Sweden	1899–57	1.20	± 0.05	0.990
United Kingdom	,,	2.56	± 0.23	0.959
Canada	,,	1.39	± 0.09	0.978
United States	,,	1.26	± 0.11	0.963
Japan	,,	1.65	± 0.17	0.950
Total		1.39	± 0.06	0.884
SEMI-INDUSTRIAL COUNTRIES				
Australia	1913–57	1.77	± 0.27	0.912
New Zealand	1929–57	2.04	± 0.62	0.785
Union of South Africa	1913–57	1.35	± 0.23	0.893
India	1929–57	2.65	± 0.40	0.936
Argentina	1913–57	2.11	± 0.34	0.905
Colombia	1929–57	1.93	± 0.21	0.966
Yugoslavia	1937–57	2.03	± 0.55	0.872
Total		1.67	± 0.11	0.864
Total, excluding South Africa		2.00	± 0.13	0.898

Sources: Tables E.2 and E.6.

[a]The regressions were based on the estimates for selected years only (see Tables in Appendix E).   Thus, for the period 1899–1957, seven 'observations' were used; for 1913–57, six 'observations', and so on.

Table 6.3. *Income co-efficients[a] for consumption of manufactures based on cross-country regressions, 1955*

	No. of countries	Income co-efficient	Standard error	R^2
Industrial countries	15	1.16	± 0.08	0.955
Semi-industrial countries	17	1.36	± 0.19	0.915
Non-industrial countries	10	1.04	± 0.10	0.957
Total	42	1.28	± 0.05	0.955

Sources: Tables E.2 and E.6.

[a]Co-efficients based on double logarithmic regressions.   An additional variable (total population) was also used, but none of the resulting co-efficients was significantly different from zero.

the co-efficients for the several groups of countries are not statistically significant. It is of interest, however, that the co-efficients derived from time series tend to be higher than those based on cross-country comparisons, so that the use of the latter results would tend to underestimate the probable future level of demand for manufactures.

2. TRENDS IN THE IMPORT-CONTENT OF SUPPLIES

As industrialization proceeds from an earlier to a more mature phase, and as the demand for manufactures expands, the proportion of demand which can be met from home production tends to grow, and the 'import-content' of consumption tends to decline. This decline can be traced in nearly all industrializing countries. Unfortunately, the estimates presented here (Table 6.4) do not go back before 1899, by which time the industrialization process in Western Europe and the United States had already reached a relatively advanced stage. Nonetheless, even since the period before the first World War, the import content of supplies[1] of manufactures in the industrial countries has halved—from 11 to about 6 per cent.

Among the industrial countries, however, there are two fairly distinct groups: the larger countries, such as the United States, Britain, France and Germany, with a diversified industrial system, which now import only marginal quantities of manufactured goods; and the smaller industrial countries, which are still heavily dependent on imports for their supplies of manufactures[2]. For the large countries, the import-content of supplies was showing a downward trend even before the depression years of the early 1930's: it fell from 9 per cent in 1899 to 6 per cent in 1929. The trade restrictions of the 1930's caused a further fall, and by 1937 the proportion was only 4 per cent—a slight recovery from the abnormally low trade levels of the early 1930's. It should be noted, however, that for Britain the import-proportion in 1929 was no lower than at the beginning of the century; the big reductions in the import-content were confined to France, Germany and Japan. This diversity of experience might have been due, in part, to the later development by the three latter countries, compared with Britain and the United States, of a wide range of manufacturing industry behind substantial tariff barriers. For Britain, on the other hand, the import tariff was generally non-existent or negligible in this period, so that imports could expand in proportion to the growth in demand.

In the smaller industrial countries, the average import-content is about one-fifth of total supplies, and though there was a sharp reduction in the 1930's

[1] I.e., the proportion of imports of manufactures in total available supplies of manufactures, whether for home consumption or for export. The corresponding estimates for the import-content of home consumption would show the same trends.
[2] This distinction has some relation to that made in Chapter 3 between countries whose exports of manufactures are mainly finished and their imports mainly intermediates, and the countries where the reverse is true.

Table 6.4.   *Import-content of supplies^a of manufactured goods, 1899–1959*

Percentage and values in $ billion at 1955 prices^b

INDUSTRIAL COUNTRIES	1899	1913	1929	1937	1950	1955	1957	1959
Large								
France	12	13	9	7	7	8	8	6
Germany^c	16	10	7	3	4	6	6	7
Italy	11	14	11	5	8	7	8	8
United Kingdom	16	17	16	10	4	5	5	6
United States	3	3	2	2	2	2	2	3
Japan	30	34	21	11	3	5	7	4
Total	9	8	6	4	3	3	4	4
Total 'imports' of manufactures^d	*4.1*	*6.6*	*7.6*	*5.4*	*5.4*	*9.1*	*11.4*	*14.2*
Small								
Belgium-Luxembourg	26	24	19	11	14	15	17	15
Netherlands	..	..	52	41	33	32	35	33
Norway	..	35	38	36	33	32	34	34
Sweden	8	14	18	14	12	17	17	17
Canada	20	23	24	16	16	20	21	20
Total^e	..	..	26	18	18	21	22	21
Total 'imports' of manufactures^d	*1.4*	*2.8*	*4.3*	*3.1*	*5.3*	*7.9*	*9.2*	*9.4*
TOTAL^e	..	10–11	8	5	5	6	6	6
Total 'imports' of manufactures^d	*5.5*	*9.4*	*11.9*	*8.5*	*10.7*	*17.0*	*20.6*	*23.6*
SEMI-INDUSTRIAL COUNTRIES								
Australia	..	39	37	25	25	21	15	15
New Zealand	..	46	46	40	32	32	28	19
Union of South Africa	..	97	69	60	33	29	29	..
India	} 58	61	41	23 {	22	21	27	20
Pakistan					80	35	30	24
Argentina	..	81	51	32	16	14	15	17
Brazil	..	..	..	25	21	12	15	..
Chile	..	..	58	30	23	19	26	20
Colombia	..	..	90	59	49	51	37	..
Mexico	..	..	..	29	27	25	25	20
Israel	..	..	..	..	..	31	30	29
Turkey	..	..	..	..	33	29	20	..
Yugoslavia	..	..	..	14	7	7	6	6
Total	..	55–60	40–45	29	23	20	19	17–18
Total 'imports' of manufactures^d	*2.3*	*4.5*	*5.7*	*4.8*	*6.5*	*7.3*	*7.7*	*7.4*

Sources: Table E.5 and national trade and production statistics.

^a'Supplies' are defined as gross value of production of non-food manufactures, free of duplication, *plus* c.i.f. value of imports of 'finished' manufactures (i.e. goods not normally subject to further processing). See Appendix E for further discussion.

^bValuation is c.i.f., estimated from f.o.b. exporting country values.

^cWest Germany in 1950–59.

^dImports from the industrial countries and India only. Major exclusion consists of non-ferrous metals imported from semi-industrial and non-industrial areas.

^eExcluding Switzerland.

(from 26 to 18 per cent in 1929 and 1937, respectively), there has been a noticeable recovery since 1950, due essentially to developments in Sweden and Canada. In both these countries, manufacturing production has risen much less rapidly since 1950 than in the other countries in this group, while their imports have risen at much the same rate.

The average import-content of supplies in the semi-industrial countries, at about one-sixth, is now rather lower than in the smaller industrial countries, and the decline has been very much sharper than in the latter, particularly in the pre-war period. Before the first World War, the proportion was probably over one-half, but it was substantially reduced during that War, and again in the 1930's with the development of secondary industries in these countries. Among the individual countries, the import-content of supplies in 1959 was generally lower than in 1937; in some countries (for example, New Zealand, Argentina and Brazil), the decline was very considerable.

For the non-industrial countries, no very accurate figures can be given, but approximate estimates indicate that by the late 1950's, their average import-content of supplies was probably in the region of 50–60 per cent, somewhat less than in the immediate post-war period, but not significantly different from the pre-war position.

The rate of decline in the import-content of consumption will depend on a variety of factors, some internal to the growing economy, others originating in the outside world. Before discussing such possible factors, however, it is necessary to consider whether the process of economic growth itself, insofar as it involves changes in the pattern of demand and production, thereby contains some form of 'automatic' mechanism which reduces the average import-content of supplies. Such a mechanism would operate if the import-content of supplies in the relatively expanding commodity groups was lower than the import-content in the relatively declining groups. However, as is shown later[1], there is no systematic relationship between the rate of growth in supplies and the magnitude of the import-content, so that the changing pattern of supplies cannot by itself explain the secular movement in the average import-content of supplies.

Of the several possible factors which might have influenced the trend in the import-content, four are considered here: the size of the country, the stage of industrial development, the degree of import restrictions, and the relative importance of exports in the economy.

Size of country

Size is not an unambiguous concept. It can be defined in terms of area, population, income or even of natural resources. To some extent, area and resources are inter-related, since a country with a large area is more likely to

[1]See Chapter 7, pp. 185–7.

have a diversified base of natural resources than one with a limited territory. Even so, there may be exceptions as, for example, when a large country consists mainly of desert and a small one has coal and iron-ore deposits. The size of the population is a more meaningful index of economic size than is area, relative population size of different countries being a guide to the relative size of their internal markets. Since, however, income per head varies enormously, if we compare developed with under-developed countries, size of total population may be a misleading measure of market size in terms of effective demand.

Some countries are, of course, small in terms of all four criteria; others again, are large whichever basis is used. But, in general, it seems most sensible to distinguish large, medium and small countries, in terms of population size, in the economically advanced areas from the corresponding size categories in the under-developed world.

The relationship between a country's size and the extent to which it specializes in production was discussed in Chapter 3[1]. The reasons given there to explain why small countries tend to specialize in a restricted range of manufactures also help to explain why small countries are generally more dependent on imports

Table 6.5. *Import-content of supplies of manufactured goods in relation to population in selected countries, 1957*

Population (*million*)	Import-content of supplies (*percentage*)			
	Under 10	10–19	20–29	30 or over
Under 10		Australia Belgium Sweden	Chile New Zealand	Israel Norway
10–24	Yugoslavia	Argentina	Canada Union of South Africa	Colombia Netherlands
25–49	France Italy		Mexico Turkey	
50–74	United Kingdom West Germany	Brazil		
75–99	Japan		Pakistan	
100 or over	United States		India	

Sources: Tables 6.4 and E.7.

[1] See pages 69–71.

for their supplies of manufactures, than are large countries. The average income level in the small industrial countries is not significantly different from that in the large industrial countries, and the pattern of demand for manufactures is also not likely to be greatly different. The higher import-content of the smaller industrial countries thus reflects their relative specialization in production rather than any peculiarity in their demand pattern.

When we turn to examine the relationship between import-content and population size in a recent year (see Table 6.5), we do find a very general association between the two. At one extreme stands the United States, a large country on any criterion, with a very small dependence on imports; at the other extreme is Israel, where the opposite is true. There are, however, some large countries (India and Pakistan) which are heavily dependent on imports for their supplies of manufactures, while Australia—a small country on the population criterion—is much less dependent on imports than a good number of large countries. The high dependence on imports exhibited by India and Pakistan, and the low dependence of Australia, is much more likely to reflect the relative development of the manufacturing industries of these countries than the mere size of their populations. Taking only countries at a similar stage of development, however, it does seem that the import-content is inversely associated with population size.

Stage of industrial development

In previous chapters, the stage of industrial development has been taken to be reflected by the output of manufactured goods per head of population. One would expect, *a priori*, that with the growth of manufacturing output, a country would be able to substitute against imports to a greater or lesser extent, thus causing a fall in the import-content of supplies of manufactures. That this has been the case historically can be seen from Fig. 6.2, which shows the relationship separately for the large and small industrial countries and the semi-industrial and non-industrial countries. Had it been possible to extend the curve for the large industrial countries back to, say, 1870 it might possibly have overlapped that shown for the semi-industrial group. It may also be significant that at the other end of its range the curve for the semi-industrial countries is close to that for the non-industrial areas.

The general form of relationship suggested by Fig. 6.2 is that in the early stages of industrialization the import-content of supplies tends to fall sharply, while in the more mature phases, the import-content is low but fairly stable. Indeed, since 1950, the import-content has been rising in the industrial countries, though the rise has been small and the import-content had not by 1959 reached the 1929 level, in either the large or the small industrial countries. In the earlier phases of industrialization, the fall in the import-content reflects the process of import-substitution, usually behind tariff barriers or other forms of infant-industry protection. At some level of industrialization, the optimum size of plant may be reached, and home output may then substitute for imports without the help of protectionist devices. At a more mature level of industrialization, for example that reached at present in the main industrial countries of Western Europe and the United States, international trade is likely to be stimulated not only by rising total demand, but also by an increasing diversity in the detailed pattern of demand which tends to stimulate trade

Fig. 6.2.   Relation between manufacturing production per head and the import-content of supplies, 1899–1957

Semi-logarithmic scale

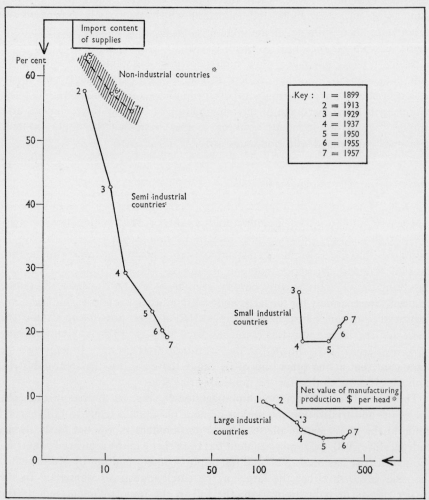

*Shading indicates very approximate estimates; net values are at 1955 prices.

between the industrial countries themselves.

Nonetheless, Fig. 6.2 needs to be interpreted with some caution, both because it represents the *average* relationship for a number of countries, and does not necessarily describe the way in which industrialization reacts on the import-content in any one of them separately; and because the movement in the import-content has been influenced by other factors as well as by industrialization.

Import restrictions

A major factor allowing the semi-industrial countries to achieve such a sharp reduction in their dependence on imported manufactures has been government

Table 6.6. *Average ad valorem rates of import duty on a sample[a] of manufactured goods in selected countries, 1937 and 1955*

	Unweighted			Weighted[b]		
	1937	1955	Index for 1955	1937	1955	Index for 1955
	(*Percentage*)		(*1937 = 100*)	(*Percentage*)		(*1937 = 100*)
INDUSTRIAL COUNTRIES						
Belgium-Luxembourg[c]	10.5	7.0	67	6.2	4.3	70
France	17.1	14.5	85	11.7	10.3	88
Germany[d]	14.3	9.4	66	10.0	5.8	58
Norway	14.3	10.7	75	10.1	7.6	75
Sweden	13.1	5.7	44	11.6	7.4	64
Switzerland	12.7	8.7	68	10.9	7.4	68
Canada[e]	15.8	12.5	79	13.7	11.1	81
Japan[c]	11.1	13.9	125	4.4	11.7	265
SEMI-INDUSTRIAL COUNTRIES						
Australia[e]	15.7	7.7	49	14.1	6.8	48
Union of South Africa[e]	11.8	7.7	65	10.0	6.8	68
India[e]	28.9	30.4	105	23.6	24.6	104
Brazil[f]	69.5	28.6	41	71.7	26.4	37
Chile[f]	33.5	39.1	117	35.9	36.2	101

Sources: Bulletin International des Douanes, Brussels (var. edns.); national tariffs and trade statistics.

[a]About 60 commodities of importance in international trade (see Table 7.13 for details).

[b]Weighted by value of imports in 1937.

[c]Based on a limited number of broad commodity categories.

[d]West Germany in 1955.

[e]Rates calculated by dividing total revenue collected on individual commodities by their import value.   Changes in the rates shown are therefore affected by changes in the proportion of imports entering under the British Preferential Tariff and the General Tariff, as well as by changes in the rates of duty themselves.

[f] Rates include 'additional taxes' and luxury taxes levied specifically on imports.

restrictions on imports competing with home manufacturing industries. As already mentioned[1], import restrictions were also of major importance in the contraction of imports by the industrial countries in the 1930's. Such restrictions take a variety of forms, among the more important being import duties, quantitative import restrictions, discriminatory exchange regulations, and tax reliefs and other fiscal benefits for local industries.

Import duties are the most widespread method in use for protecting local industry against competition from imports, and it is therefore worth considering how important, or effective, such duties are and whether there is any relation between the height of duty and the import-content of supply of manufactured goods. A major statistical difficulty arises, however, in any attempt to calculate the average height of the duties on any collection of imports, namely, that their effectiveness as a protection of home industry varies not with the value of goods imported, but with the value of goods *kept out*. There is, of course, no record of the goods kept out, only of those which come in over the tariff barrier. Even so, it would be possible, in principle, to calculate indices of average tariff heights for a number of countries at different periods, by applying to the different rates of duty weights approximating to the value of goods of each kind which were kept out by them[2]. The magnitude of such a calculation, however, puts it beyond the scope of the present book.

Another approach, cruder in form, was adopted to illustrate broadly the

---

[1]See Chapter 4, *passim*.

[2]If p is the duty-free import price of a given commodity, q the quantity imported and r the *ad valorem* rate of import duty, the duty-paid price is then $p' = p(1 + r)$ and the value of potential imports of that commodity kept out by the import duty is:

$$pq\left\{ \eta \cdot \frac{r}{1 + r} \right\}$$

where η is the elasticity of demand for imports of that commodity with respect to the duty-paid price; that is, $\eta = - \dfrac{dq}{dp'} \cdot \dfrac{p'}{q}$. These values of potential imports kept out will give a different set of weights from actual import values (pq) for the different commodities imported, since there is no reason to expect any systematic relationship between η and r, and the magnitude of each is likely to vary widely from one commodity to another. The average height of the import duty, weighted by potential imports kept out, is then:

$$D_1 = \frac{\Sigma pqr\left\{ \eta \cdot \dfrac{r}{1 + r} \right\}}{\Sigma pq \left\{ \eta \cdot \dfrac{r}{1 + r} \right\}}$$

summing over all commodities.

An alternative approach is to define the effective height of an import duty as the *proportion* of potential imports which it keeps out. On this definition, the average height of the import duty would be:

$$D_2 = \frac{\Sigma pq\left\{ \eta \cdot \dfrac{r}{1 + r} \right\}}{\Sigma pq\left\{ 1 + \eta \cdot \dfrac{r}{1 + r} \right\}}$$

again, summing over all commodities.

differences in average tariff levels and the changes in them since pre-war. For a selection of industrial and semi-industrial countries, the *ad valorem* duty equivalent was calculated for a standard list of about 60 manufactured goods, spread over the main commodity groups, for the two years 1937 and 1955. Both unweighted and weighted means (using import values in 1937 as weights for both years) were calculated—though as explained earlier, neither method is very satisfactory as indicating the average height of the tariff. Moreover, since several different methods of calculation were used, the mean tariff levels arrived at are not quite comparable across countries; small differences therefore have little meaning in this context.

Several broad conclusions emerge from the results of these calculations (see Table 6.6). First, tariffs are generally much higher in countries which have embarked on industrialization only in recent decades. In 1955, the unweighted means of the import duties (including internal taxes on imports) on the sample of manufactures ranged from about 30 to about 40 per cent for India, Brazil and Chile. Similarly, high rates of duty are generally found to be in operation in other primary-producing countries which are relative newcomers to industrialization[1]. On the other hand, in primary-producing countries having relatively old-established manufacturing industries, such as Australia and the Union of South Africa, the mean tariff level is not very different from those of many industrial countries in Europe.

Second, the incidence of the import tariff appears to have declined appreciably since pre-war in most countries. One reason is that where duties are specific, their *ad valorem* incidence falls as prices rise, and in most countries a proportion of the duties are specific in form.

Third, the height of the duty on imports has no apparent relation with the import-content of supplies of manufactures. *A priori* one would expect a high tariff to be associated with a low import-content, but the differences between countries in their dependence on imports are, if anything, reflected by a positive association with the height of the duty. Country differences in tariff heights tend to reflect differences in costs of production of manufactures, so that where local production is relatively new and high-cost, tariffs tend to be high.

The argument that tariff height should be inversely associated with the import-content of supplies has more substance when applied to the movement over time in particular countries. But the evidence (Tables 6.4 and 6.6) is inconclusive. For Japan and Chile, tariff increases since pre-war are associated with reductions in import content; but for Brazil and the Union of South Africa both the tariff level and the import-content fell. On the other hand, for several European countries, tariff levels were lower in 1955 than pre-war, and the import-content was higher.

One of the difficulties in interpreting the tariff level figures is that the tariff

---

[1]For example, Egypt, Turkey, Burma, and many Latin American countries.

is not the only obstacle to trade. A great many countries operate quantitative restrictions on imports in addition to the tariff, and it is not possible to estimate the *ad valorem* equivalent of such restrictions. The rise in the average level of the Japanese tariff since pre-war, for example, probably does not reflect the true ease or difficulty of importing into that country, since in 1937 imports were subject to a stringent licensing procedure, whereas in 1955 imports were on the whole much freer, though licensing was in force for non-dollar imports Equally, the fall in the Brazilian tariff gives a misleading impression; in 1955, Brazil operated a system of multiple exchange rates biased against the import of 'less essential' manufactures.

Insofar as changes in the tariff reflect changes in the relative competitive position of the local industry, they will also tend to be associated in a broad way with changes in the level of industrialization, which have been discussed earlier. The same applies to quantitative restrictions, insofar as these are used as permanent instruments of protection for local manufacturing industry[1].

Table 6.7. *Import-content of supplies of manufactured goods in relation to ratio of exports[a] to gross domestic product*, 1955

Ratio of exports[a] to gross domestic product (*percentage*)	Import-content of supplies (*percentage*)			
	Under 10	10–19	20–29	30–39
Under 10	United States	Brazil Chile India		
10–19	France Italy Japan		Australia Mexico	Israel
20–29	United Kingdom West Germany	Sweden	Canada	New Zealand
30–39		Belgium- Luxembourg	Union of South Africa	
40 or over				Netherlands Norway

Sources: Table 6.4, and *Yearbook of National Accounts Statistics, 1959*, United Nations, New York, 1960.

a Including exports of services.

[1] Quantitative restrictions applied for balance of payments reasons will, of course, depress the import-content until export incomes revive. Such restrictions can be considered as essentially temporary in character, and therefore fall outside our consideration of long-term movements.

Export orientation

Countries which have large export sectors in relation to their total economies will tend to rely more heavily on imports for their supplies of manufactures, than will countries where exports provide only a small part of the national income. Since there are very great differences between countries in the degree of export orientation of their economies this might, by itself, account for a good deal of the differences already noted in the import-content of supplies.

A comparison of the import-content in a recent year with the relative import-ance of exports in gross domestic product (Table 6.7) shows that a broad relationship of this kind seems to exist. Taking only the industrial countries, we find that after the export ratio exceeds about 25 per cent the import-content tends to rise with the export ratio. A similar positive relationship holds true for the semi-industrial countries, but at a higher average import-content level for a given export ratio.

The influence of changing export income over time on the import-content of supplies can also be of significance. A comparison of the movement between pre-war and 1957 however, does not show any very clear relation-ship. To some extent, this is no doubt due to the exclusion of services from the export figures (because the pre-war figures for these are either non-existent or unreliable in many cases); and to the fact that no allowance has been made for capital flows, which were probably more important, relatively to exports, in 1957 than they were pre-war. Probably, if these omissions could be repaired, the export ratio for India might not be very much lower in 1957 than it was pre-war[1]. On the other hand, the export ratio for the United States would be reduced if the greatly increased flow of capital (and military aid) in 1957 compared with 1929 were taken into account[2]; whereas the import dependence of the United States, at 2 per cent of supplies, was the same in both these years. When imports are as marginal as this, changes in the ratio of exports to national income are unlikely to be closely related to the import-content of supplies.

3. A STATISTICAL ANALYSIS OF THE EFFECTS OF INDUSTRIALIZATION ON IMPORTS OF MANUFACTURES

A more precise assessment of the various influences discussed above on the import-content of supplies can be obtained by multiple regression analysis. The effect of import restrictions cannot be included in this analysis, since no overall measure of such restrictions has been attempted, but the other three factors—size of population, stage of industrial development and export

---

[1]In 1957, India's export receipts amounted to 6.97 billion Rs., while net invisibles, private and official donations and long-term capital inflow together amounted to a further 2.04 billion Rs.
[2]The inclusion of invisibles, military aid and long-term capital outflow would reduce the export ratio for the United States in 1957 (1929 = 100) from about 80 to about 60.

Table 6.8. *Results of regressions of import-content of supplies of manufactured goods on 'deflated' exports, manufacturing production and size of population*

Regression[a]	Co-efficient[b] of			R^2
	E	P/N	N	
Semi-industrial countries				
1955	0.64	−0.45	−0.31	0.661
	(±0.32)	(±0.24)	(±0.14)	
1957	0.48	−0.44	−0.24	0.959
	(±0.09)	(±0.06)	(±0.04)	
1937–57 indices[c]	0.58	−0.53	0.06	0.814
	(±0.14)	(±0.15)	(±0.03)	
Industrial and semi-industrial countries				
1955	0.41	−0.40	−0.47	0.847
	(±0.18)	(±0.10)	(±0.08)	
1957	0.44	−0.47	−0.42	0.886
	(±0.16)	(±0.08)	(±0.07)	
Large industrial countries				
1913–29 indices	0.60	−0.51	−0.29	0.921
	(±0.21)	(±0.12)	(±0.08)	
Large and small[d] industrial countries				
1913–29 indices	0.30	−0.38	−0.16	0.750
	(±0.25)	(±0.24)	(±0.05)	

Sources: Tables 6.4, A1, E.1, E.4, and E.7; national export statistics; and *Yearbook of National Accounts Statistics*, 1959, United Nations, New York, 1960.

[a]E = index of deflated total value of exports (using unit value index of world trade in manufactures as deflator) divided by index of real gross domestic product. For the 1955 and 1957 cross-country regressions, E represents the proportion of exports (incl. services) in gross domestic product in that year.

P/N = net value of manufacturing production per head at 1955 prices (see Table E.4).

N = total population; for the time-series regressions, the mean of the population in the base and later years.

[b]All co-efficients derived from double-logarithmic equations.

[c]For the Union of South Africa, the export variable includes exports of gold.

[d]Belgium–Luxembourg, Sweden and Canada.

orientation—have been used to try to 'explain' changes in the import-content. Regression equations were calculated, using the double-logarithmic form, on both a cross-country and a time-series basis. The former covered both semi-industrial and industrial countries together, and the semi-industrial countries separately, and related to two recent years, 1955 and 1957. For the semi-industrial countries, adequate data were available for only one long-term comparison, 1937 to 1957. Regressions for the industrial countries, and for the large industrial countries alone, were also computed for the period 1913 to 1929; corresponding regressions for the industrial countries for later periods did not, however, yield statistically significant results, probably because for many of these countries the degree of import restriction was substantially different in 1929 from that of post-war years.

All these regressions provided good explanations of differences in the import-content of supplies (see Table 6.8). The co-efficient of P/N showed relatively little variation; for the cross-country regressions, this co-efficient varied from -0.40 to -0.47, and three of the four co-efficients were statistically significant at the 1 per cent level. For the semi-industrial countries, the corresponding co-efficient derived from the time comparison was just in excess of -0.5, as was also that for the large industrial countries for the period 1913–29. These results indicate that, in the earlier stages of industrialization, a 10 per cent increase in the volume of manufacturing production per head tends to be associated with a 4 or 5 per cent decline in the import-content of supplies of manufactured goods.

The co-efficient of E varied from about 0.4 to over 0.6 (omitting the result of the time-series regression for the large and small industrial countries, which had a large standard error). This indicates that, with manufacturing production per head and total population constant, a variation of 10 per cent in export income in relation to gross domestic product is likely to be associated with a 4–6 per cent variation in the same direction, in the import-content of supplies.

The influence of population size on the import-content is not, however, so clearly defined. The co-efficients derived from cross-country regressions indicated that, on average, a 10 per cent difference between countries in population size is associated with a difference in the other direction, of $2\frac{1}{2}$ to 4 per cent in the import-content. The time-series regression for the large industrial countries gave much the same result, but that for the semi-industrial countries did not. The results do appear, however, to bear out the general impression gained from Table 6.5 that there is an inverse association between size and import-content, allowing for differences in the stage of industrialization and the degree of export orientation of different countries. The possible reasons for this inverse association have been discussed earlier[1].

If we can accept a range of -0.4 to -0.6 for the co-efficient of P/N, we can summarize the analysis made of the effects of industrialization on imports of manufactures in countries in an early stage of industrialization by the following general propositions. First, industrialization leads to increased real income per head (unless abnormal circumstances are at work), and with growing income comes an increase in demand for manufactured goods, the rise in per caput demand being, on average, in the region of 1.7–2.0 times the rate of growth in real income per head in the semi-industrial countries[2].

Second, with the progress of industrialization, the proportion of demand met by imports falls off, the rate of fall being 0.4 to 0.6 times the rate of increase in manufacturing production per head. The implication of these results is that, on average, imports of manufactures will rise, since the percentage fall in

[1]See pages 138–9.
[2]See Table 6.2.

import-content is less than the percentage rise in supplies[1]. Thus, taking the average results arrived at, a 10 per cent increase in real income per head will result in an increase of 17–20 per cent in consumption of manufactures per head in the semi-industrial countries. At the same time, if the growth in income is induced by industrialization, the production of manufactures per head in the semi-industrial countries will rise, on average, by some 25–30 per cent[2]. Thus, the fall in the import-content will be about 10–15 per cent, or considerably less than the percentage rise in per caput consumption, implying a rise of some 5–10 per cent in the volume of imports of manufactures[3].

This illustration shows the average *net* effect of industrialization on the volume of imports of manufactures, assuming that population does not change significantly and that industrialization has no adverse repercussions on the capacity to import. If, however, export earnings fail, for other reasons, to expand during a phase of industrialization—or fail to expand sufficiently fast—

---

[1]The model implied in these general propositions can be set out as follows. The consumption function is assumed to take the form:

$$\frac{S}{N} = a\left(\frac{Y}{N}\right)^{\epsilon_1} \quad .. \quad .. \quad .. \quad .. \quad .. \quad (1)$$

where S represents the volume of supplies of manufactures, Y real income and N total population. It is assumed, for simplicity, that the effect of relative price changes on total consumption of manufactures can be ignored, and that there is a constant income-elasticity of demand, ϵ_1, which applies both to consumption and to supplies.

The import-content of supplies can be expressed as:

$$\frac{M}{S} = b\left(\frac{P}{N}\right)^{-\epsilon_2}\left(\frac{X}{Y}\right)^{\epsilon_3} \quad .. \quad .. \quad .. \quad .. \quad (2)$$

where M represents imports of manufactures, P production of manufactures and X exports of goods and services deflated by import prices.

By substituting (1) in (2), and expressing proportionate rates of change in the variables by the symbol $\wedge$, we have by differentiation:

$$\hat{M} = (\hat{Y} - \hat{N})\{\epsilon_1 - \rho\epsilon_2 + (\lambda - 1)\epsilon_3\}$$
$$+ \hat{N}\{1 - (\rho - 1)\epsilon_2 + (\lambda-1)\epsilon_3\} \quad .. \quad (3)$$

where $\rho = \dfrac{\hat{P}}{\hat{Y}}$ and $\lambda = \dfrac{\hat{X}}{\hat{Y}}$. The first term on the right-hand side of (3) indicates the effective relationship, on this model, between economic growth (measured by changes in real income per head) and the rate of change in imports of manufactures. The first parameter in brackets, ϵ_1, expresses the net effect of the change in home demand; the second term, $- \rho\epsilon_2$, shows the net import-substitution effect, while the final term, $(\lambda - 1)\epsilon_3$, shows the net 'balance of payments' effect. The second part on the right-hand side indicates the net effect of population changes on the rate of growth of imports of manufactures, with a constant level of per caput real income.

If industrialization proceeds without any adverse effects on the balance of payments— for example, if the capacity to import rises at the same rate as the real national product— then $\lambda = 1$, and

$$\hat{M} = (\hat{Y} - \hat{N})\{\epsilon_1 - \rho\epsilon_2\} + \hat{N}\{1 - (\rho - 1)\epsilon_2\}$$

[2]For the industrial countries, the rise would be 14–15 per cent (see Table 2.5).

[3]In terms of the previous model, this calculation assumes $\hat{N} = 0$ and $\lambda = 1$.

this would diminish the rate of growth in manufactured imports which would otherwise be attained.

To illustrate this possibility, if the volume of exports (and the capacity to import) of the industrializing country is assumed to be unchanged, the rate of growth in the volume of manufactured imports associated with industrialization would be reduced by about one-half[1] the rate of growth in real income per head. Applying this to the previous example of a 10 per cent rise in real income per head, the increase (5–10 per cent) in the volume of manufactured imports would be reduced by some 5 per cent. Thus, the change in manufactured imports would be in the range 0 to +5 per cent[2].

4. THE RELATIVE EFFECTS OF IMPORT-SUBSTITUTION AND DEMAND EXPANSION ON IMPORTS OF MANUFACTURES BY INDIVIDUAL COUNTRIES

The model used above for the analysis of the net effect of industrial growth on imports of manufactures over one or two selected periods could be applied, in principle, to each of a range of different countries for a number of different periods. This approach would, however, encounter serious difficulties in collating reliable historical series for the capacity to import for many countries and the scale of the task seemed to put it beyond the scope of the present chapter.

Instead, an analysis has been made of the magnitude of the import-substitution that has in fact taken place in the industrial and semi-industrial countries since 1913, whether this was due to industrialization as such, to changes in the relative importance of exports in the national product, or to any other causes. Import-substitution in this sense is a *gross* concept, in contrast with the *net* concept (import-substitution resulting from industrialization alone) which was considered previously.

---

[1] I.e. taking the co-efficient of E in Table 6.8 as 0.5 and putting $\lambda = 0$.

[2] If it is assumed that the parameters of the model are constants, and that population remains unchanged, the effect of variations in λ on the ratio $\dfrac{\hat{M}}{\hat{Y}}$ can be expressed by the linear function:

$$\frac{\hat{M}}{\hat{Y}} = k + \lambda \epsilon_3$$

where $k = \epsilon_1 - (\rho \epsilon_2 + \epsilon_3)$. For the values of the parameters adopted in the text, the mean value of k would be 0.2 for $\epsilon_3 = 0.5$; if ϵ_3 were as high as 0.7, k would be zero. Thus, for imports of manufactures to rise as fast as real income (that is, for $\hat{M} = \hat{Y}$), the capacity to import would have to rise over $1\frac{1}{2}$ times as fast as real income for $\epsilon_3 = 0.5$, and over $1\frac{1}{3}$ times as fast for $\epsilon_3 = 0.7$.

Gross import-substitution can be defined either as an absolute magnitude or as a relative one. The absolute concept would consider the entire increase in home output of manufactures as substituting for imports whereas, on the relative concept, only a greater proportionate increase in home output than in home consumption of manufactures would qualify as import-substitution. The two concepts would, of course, result in quite different results since they measure different things. If, for example, home production rises in the same proportion as home consumption, then there is no import-substitution on the second definition, though there is on the first.

The second, or relative, concept is the one used here because it is more logical, and because it corresponds closely with the definition of net import-substitution used earlier. The absolute concept is illogical, in the sense that it implies that the entire increase in home consumption of manufactures *could* be met by imports; but this cannot be so *ipso facto*, because the home economy is an industrializing one, substituting home production of manufactures for imported goods.

Gross import-substitution during a given period can be defined as the difference between actual imports at the end of the period and what they would then have been had they formed the same proportion of total consumption as at the beginning of the period; in the remainder of this chapter, 'import-substitution' is used in this 'gross' sense. The same calculation also gives a measure of the effect of demand expansion on imports, since this can be defined as the difference between imports of manufactures at the beginning of the period and what they would have been at the end had they changed in the same proportion as total consumption of manufactures[1].

This formulation is not quite accurate for the industrial countries, which have relatively large exports of manufactures since such exports, as well as home consumption, must be assumed to incorporate semi-manufactures. For these countries, the definitions of 'import-substitution' and 'home-demand' have been appropriately amended to make room for a third category, 'export demand', which is intended to indicate the effects of changes in exports of manufactures on the demand for imported semi-manufactured goods[2]. For

---

[1]The change in imports from a base to a current year can be written as
$$dM = m_1 S_1 - m_0 S_0$$
where m represents the import-content of supplies, S—as previously—denotes total supplies, the subscripts $_0$ and $_1$ referring to the base and current periods, respectively. This change can be divided into two elements, as follows:
$$dM = S_1(m_1 - m_0) + m_0(S_1 - S_0)$$
where the first term represents gross import-substitution, and the second the expansion in imports due to the increase in home demand.

[2]It has been assumed that the import-content of exports (in terms of semi-manufactures only) is the same as the import-content of production of manufactures. On this basis imports of intermediate products into each industrial country were allocated to production

the semi-industrial countries, exports of manufactures are relatively very small—except for India—and the problem does not really arise.   For India, the simpler formula has been used on the argument that imports of intermediate products into that country are intended essentially for use in output for the home market, rather than in exports.

The results show that import-substitution has been of major importance, since the beginning of the century, in both the industrial and semi-industrial areas; but that, in both, the adverse effect of import-substitution on trade in manufactures has been more than outweighed by the stimulation of expanding demand.

Comparing 1959 with 1913 (see Table 6.9), the import-substitution effect was considerably greater in the semi-industrial, than in the industrial, countries. For the former, import-substitution during the period was more than double their volume of imports of manufactures in 1913, whereas for the industrial

Table 6.9.   *Effect of import-substitution and of expansion in demand^a on 'imports' of manufactured goods, 1913–59*

$ billion, f.o.b. at 1955 prices

| | Total 'imports' in 1913 | Change due to | | | Total 'imports' in 1959 |
		Import-substitution	Expansion in demand	Total	
Industrial countries	8.9	− 3.1	+ 16.8^b	+ 13.7	22.6
Semi-industrial countries	4.1	− 8.9	+ 11.6	+ 2.7	6.8
Rest of the world	4.8	..	..	+ 9.2	14.0
Total	17.9	..	..	+ 25.5	43.4

Source: Working sheets for Table 6.1.

^{a}Import-substitution is defined as $S_1(m_1 - m_0)$, and the effect on imports of the expansion in home demand is defined as $m_0(S_1 - S_0)$, where S represents supplies and m is the proportion of supplies imported.   The subscripts $_0$ and $_1$ refer to the earlier and later year, respectively.

^{b}Of which, +0.8 relates to the expansion in export demand.

for export and for the home market, and the procedure described in the previous footnote was applied separately to each.   The change in total imports was thus divided into four elements:

$$dM = C_1(m_1{}^* - m_0{}^*) + m_0{}^*(C_1 - C_0) + E_1(n_1 - n_0) + n_0(E_1 - E_0)$$

where m^* represents the import-content of consumption of manufactures, n the import-content of exports, C the total consumption of manufactures and E exports.   The first and third terms can be taken together as representing the import-substitution effect; the second term represents the effect of changes in consumption on imports, while the final term represents the effect of changes in exports.

countries it was only about one-third as great as the 1913 total. Had the import-content of supplies in the semi-industrial countries remained unchanged between 1913 and 1959, their imports of manufactures in the latter year would have been higher than they actually were by some $9 billion (at 1955 prices), or 130–140 per cent. On the other hand, the expansion in demand was greater in the industrial areas, so that for both these reasons the increase in imports of manufactures from 1913 to 1959 was much greater for the industrial than for the semi-industrial countries. Exports accounted for only about 5 per cent of the increase in demand in the industrial countries.

A similar analysis is not possible for the 'rest of the world'; it can be assumed that a certain amount of import-substitution has taken place there also, but probably this was relatively small in relation to the growth of demand. A major influence at work in the less-developed areas has been the expansion of the petroleum industry; though confined to a few countries, this expansion has necessitated large shipments of oilfield equipment of various kinds from the industrial countries.

Changes in import restrictions

In the industrial countries, import-substitution was artificially accentuated in the 1930's by import restrictions, and some part of the expansion in the intra-trade of these countries during the 1950's was undoubtedly the result of the relaxation of such restrictions. Indeed, from 1950 to 1959 the *faster* rate of growth in imports than in consumption in the industrial countries accounted for almost as great an increase in their imports of manufactures as did the growth of demand (see Table 6.10).

Table 6.10) *Effect of import-substitution and of expansion in demand on 'imports' of manufactured goods between selected years, 1913–59*

$ billion, f.o.b. at 1955 prices

	Industrial countries			Semi-industrial countries		
	Import-substitution	Expansion in demand[a]	Total	Import-substitution	Expansion in demand	Total
1913–29	− 2.2	+ 4.5	+ 2.3	− 1.9	+ 3.0	+ 1.1
1929–37	− 5.1	+ 1.9	− 3.2	− 1.8	+ 1.1	− 0.7
1937–50	− 2.0	+ 4.1	+ 2.1	− 2.1	+ 3.7	+ 1.5
1950–59	+ 6.1	+ 6.3	+ 12.4	− 3.1	+ 3.9	+ 0.8
Total	− 3.1	+ 16.8	+ 13.7	− 8.9	+ 11.6	+ 2.7

Source: Working sheets for Table 6.1.

[a]Including export demand.

Had there been no trade liberalization in this period, trade in manufactures among the industrial countries would have expanded in any event because of the economic growth that took place. It is not possible to say with any precision how much of the growth in the intra-trade was due to one factor or the other. But an approximate answer can be derived from the movement in the import-content of supplies of manufactures discussed earlier (see Table 6.4). For the large industrial countries, 1950 appears to have been even more abnormal than 1937, and the rise of the import-content from 2.8 per cent in 1950 to 4.4 per cent in 1959 appears to reflect essentially a return to a more 'normal' relationship between production and trade. For the small industrial countries, there was also some recovery in the import-content of supplies after 1950, though the recovery was relatively much smaller than for the large countries, as can be seen from Table 6.4. However, the rate of growth in total supplies was also less than in the large countries, reflecting the latter's sharper rate of economic expansion[1]. Of the total increase of some $12–13 billion in the 'imports' of manufactures into the industrial countries, both large and small, between 1950 and 1959, about one-half can be attributed to the expansion in demand (as measured by total supplies available), the other half resulting from the rise in the import-content to more 'normal' levels.

It would seem from the earlier discussion that there is an underlying downward trend in the import-content of supplies of manufactures in the industrial countries, and that this trend was greatly accentuated by the restrictionism of the 1930's and early 1950's. If this were indeed the case, it could be argued that the import-content may well have reverted to somewhere near its 'trend' position by 1959, when most of the restrictions on the intra-trade of the industrial countries in manufactured goods had been removed. If this interpretation is even approximately correct, then we should expect the intra-trade in manufactures to grow in the coming decade at only about half the rate of the past decade, in relation to the rate of growth in supplies (or in real income) in the industrial countries. A new factor which might, however, result in a rather faster rate of growth in the intra-trade than would be expected on the basis of past trends alone is the establishment of freer trading groups (E.E.C. and E.F.T.A.) in Western Europe. The prospects here are discussed further in Chapter 15.

Even allowing for the rapid expansion of trade in the 1950's, the magnitude of the import-substitution that has occurred in the industrial countries since 1913 is somewhat surprising, since one might perhaps have expected that the phase of substantial import-substitution belonged essentially to the earlier stages

---

[1] Total available supplies of manufactures are estimated to have risen from $195 billion in 1950 to $320 billion in 1959 (at 1955 prices) in the large industrial countries, an increase of some 65 per cent. In the small industrial countries, the rise was from $30 billion to $45 billion, or 50 per cent.

of industrial growth. Moreover, the substitution effect was important in the industrial areas even in the 1920's, so that the import-restrictions of the 1930's, though of importance, cannot be the whole explanation. Four-fifths of the total import-substitution in the industrial countries from 1913 to 1959 occurred in Britain (see Table 6.11) where, as indicated earlier, it exceeded the expansion in demand, so that only in Britain, among the countries or groups shown, did the volume of 'imports' of manufactures show no increase between 1913 and 1959[1]. Economic development in Britain had unusually sharp adverse repercussions on imports; the import-substitution from 1913 to 1959 amounted to some 130 per cent of total 'imports' of manufactures in the earlier year, as against only about 50 per cent in Germany and the smaller European countries. The relative size of the Japanese import-substitution (about 240 per cent of the 1913 total) exceeded even the British, but this was to be expected since in 1913 the Japanese economy was in a relatively early stage of industrial development.

The contrast with Japan is all the more striking if one compares the rates of growth in the two countries. Over the period 1913–59, Britain's gross domestic product rose by only 65 per cent whereas Japan's rose by some 400 per cent (Table 6.11). Britain's rate of growth was considerably lower than in the other industrial countries also (including Germany, when allowance is made for territorial changes). The sharp import-substitution in Britain was therefore not caused by the upsurge of home production *per se*. As Fig. 6.3 shows, the divergence between the trends in Britain's home production and imports of manufactures came in the early 1930's, due in part to the imposition of a general import tariff[2]. In this period, both Britain and Japan gained an expansion of domestic output and income from competitive import restrictionism, and both countries succeeded in reducing their import-proportions to much nearer the levels attained earlier by the other big industrial countries (see Table 6.4).

Though a similar discontinuity in the relationship between production and imports also occurred at that time in the other industrial countries, the post-war period up to 1959 saw a substantial closing of the 'import gap' (that is, a return of imports to a more 'normal' relationship with production) in all the industrial

---

[1] The *actual* volume of imports of manufactures into Britain (as indicated by the official United Kingdom statistics) was, however, about two-fifths higher in 1959 than in 1913. This series includes imports from non-industrial countries (e.g. copper from Northern Rhodesia and Chile).

[2] This is also the conclusion drawn by M. FG. Scott, *A Study of United Kingdom Imports*, Cambridge University Press, 1963. Mr Scott suggests that Britain's price-elasticity of demand for imported manufactures is considerably larger than has usually been thought. The experience of 1931–32, when imports of manufactures fell by over 40 per cent in volume, while import unit values (including the tariff) rose by about 10 per cent relatively to prices of home produced manufactures, leads Mr Scott to an estimate of about −6.0 for the price-elasticity.

Table 6.11. *Effect of import-substitution and of expansion in demand on 'imports' of manufactures, in relation to changes in gross domestic product, 1913–59*

$ billion at 1955 prices

	Gross domestic product		'Imports' of manufactures				
			1959	Increase, 1913–59			
	1959	Increase, 1913–59		Import-substitution	Expansion in demand[a]	Total	
		(Percentage)					(Percentage)
INDUSTRIAL COUNTRIES							
France	47	+190	1.42	− 0.70	+ 1.21	+ 0.51	+ 56
Germany[b]	60	+ 60	2.43	− 0.07	+ 1.20	+ 1.13	+ 87
United Kingdom	69	+ 65	1.81	− 2.52	+ 2.39	− 0.13	− 7
Other Western Europe[c]	74	+230	7.45	−1.20	+ 6.03	+ 4.83	+184
Canada	29	+305	3.32	+ 0.36	+ 2.14	+ 2.50	+305
United States	396	+310	5.66	+ 1.77	+ 2.87	+ 4.64	+455
Japan	24	+405	0.50	− 0.76	+ 0.94	+ 0.18	+ 56
Total	700	+210	22.59	− 3.12	+ 16.78	+ 13.66	+153
SEMI-INDUSTRIAL COUNTRIES							
Southern Dominions	27	+300	2.32	− 2.56	+ 3.80	+ 1.24	+114
India/Pakistan	36	..	1.21	− 1.69	+ 1.68	− 0.01	− 1
Latin America[d]	44	..	2.53 }	− 4.62[f]	+ 6.11[f]	{ + 0.97	+ 62
Others[e]	15	..	0.75 }			{ + 0.52	+226
Total	122	..	6.81	− 8.87	+ 11.59	+ 2.72	+ 62

Source: Working sheets for Table 6.1.

[a]Including export demand.

[b]Whole of Germany in 1913 and West Germany in 1959. On the basis of the present territory of West Germany, the rise in gross domestic product from 1913 to 1959 was about 120 per cent.

[c]Belgium-Luxembourg, Italy, Netherlands, Norway, Sweden and Switzerland. The figures for 'import substitution' and 'change in demand' include approximate estimates for Switzerland (1913–57) and for the Netherlands (1913–29).

[d]Argentine, Brazil, Chile, Colombia and Mexico.

[e]Turkey in 1913 and 1957; Israel and Yugoslavia in 1959 only.

[f]Including approximate estimates for Brazil (1913–37), Chile (1913–29), Colombia (1913–29), Mexico (1913–37), Palestine/Israel (1929–50), Turkey (1913–37), and Yugoslavia (1929–37).

Note: The figures for 'import-substitution' and 'expansion in demand' were calculated for each of the periods shown in Table 6.10 and then aggregated. A direct comparison of 1913 with 1959 would yield somewhat different results.

Fig. 6.3.   'Imports' of manufactures in relation to manufacturing production
in the industrial countries, 1899–1959

Volume indices (1913=100), *semi-logarithmic scale*

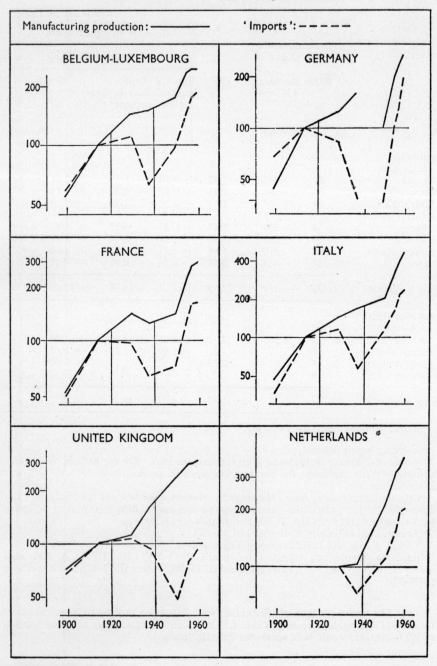

*Indices, 1929 = 100.

Fig. 6.3 (continued)

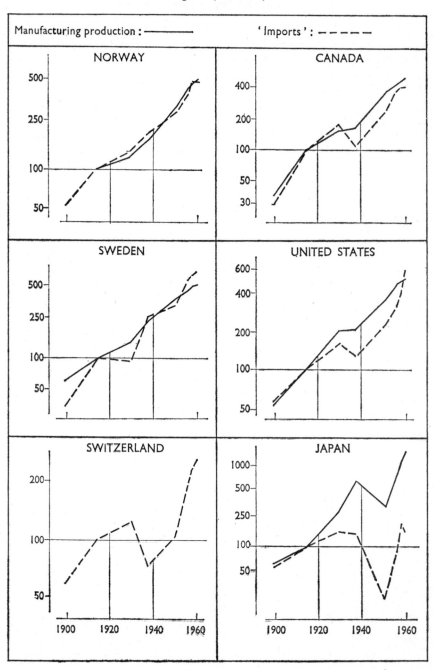

Manufacturing production : ———— 'Imports' : — — — —

Fig. 6.4.   'Imports' of manufactures in relation to manufacturing production
in the semi-industrial countries, 1899–1959

*$ billion, f.o.b. at 1955 prices,
semi-logarithmic scale*

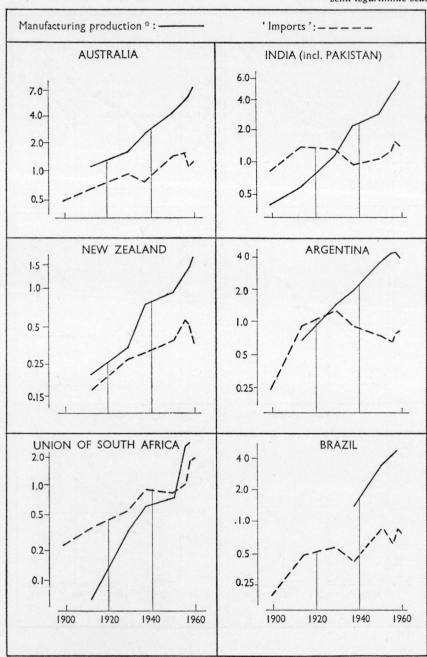

*Estimated gross values, free of duplication.

Fig. 6.4 (continued)

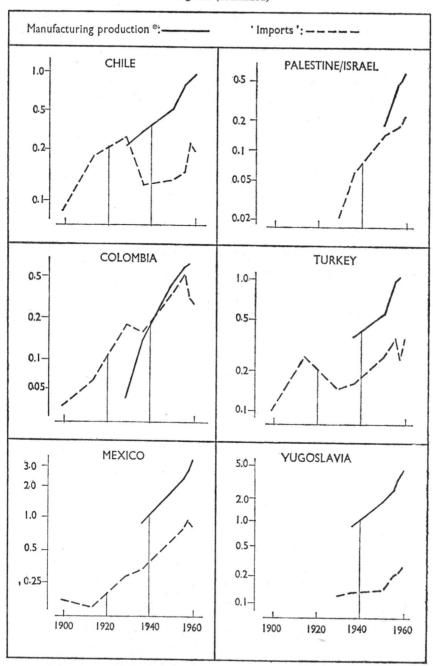

countries except Britain. In 1958, Britain liberalised a range of imports from the dollar area, previously restricted, and in 1959 ended all discrimination against dollar imports. Though imports of dollar goods rose substantially between 1958 and 1960, the liberalisation of dollar imports accounted for only a small part of the rise of over 50 per cent in the volume of British imports of manufactures in this period. A more important factor appears to have been a loss of competitiveness in many lines by British manufacturers compared with foreign concerns competing on the British market[1].

The United States alone, among the large industrial countries, showed no decline in its import-content of supplies of manufactures, comparing 1959 with 1913[2]. Indeed, between 1950 and 1959, United States 'imports' of manufactures rose at an appreciably faster rate than supplies; this was, in large part, associated with successful 'export drives' by Western European countries, particularly in passenger cars and other consumer durables.

In contrast to the development in the industrial countries, the semi-industrial countries continued the import-substitution process during the 1950's (Table 6.10); indeed, the pace of import-substitution appears to have increased in these countries since the Second World War. The main countries involved in this process since 1950 have been Australia, New Zealand, India, Brazil and Mexico; these five accounted for about four-fifths of the total import-substitution of $3.1 billion shown in Table 6.10. Some of these countries had also been prominent in the substitution of home output for imported manufactures in the inter-war period, as can be seen from Fig. 6.4.

The effect of demand expansion on imports has generally been greater, in volume terms, in the Southern Dominions and Latin America than in the other semi-industrial areas. During the 1950's, the five countries mentioned previously accounted for about 70 per cent of the total increase in 'imports' into the semi-industrial countries attributable to demand expansion.

All the semi-industrial countries experienced balance of payments difficulties during the 1950's. Insofar as these difficulties arose from changes in the world economy (for example, adverse shifts in foreign demand for their exports), rather than from their own industrialization process[3], only part of the import-substitution effected in this period is properly attributable to industrialization.

---

[1] G. F. Ray, 'British Imports of Manufactures', *National Institute Economic Review*, No. 15, May 1961.

[2] Canada is also shown as having a 'positive' import-substitution in Table 6.11, though her import-content in 1959 was lower than in 1913 (see Table 6.4). This difference arises because the figure in Table 6.11 is the aggregate of calculations made for four consecutive periods and the 'weighting' in the most recent (1950–59), when the import-content was rising, was much greater than in the two previous periods, when the import-content was falling.

[3] This seems to be a reasonable deduction from the general argument presented in Chapter 5.

Part would also have been due to import and currency restrictions designed to correct disequilibria in their balances of payments arising mainly, or partly from external causes.

M

CHAPTER 7

COMMODITY AND AREA PATTERNS OF TRADE IN MANUFACTURES

1. CHANGES IN THE COMMODITY PATTERN

Value basis

There have been drastic changes in the relative importance of the different groups of manufactures in world trade since the beginning of the century. The two outstanding changes have been the rise in machinery and transport equipment from 12 per cent of the total in 1899 to over 40 per cent sixty years later; and the fall in textiles and clothing over the same period from over 40 per cent to little more than 10 per cent (see Table 7.1). Thus, machinery and transport equipment now occupy the same importance in world trade in manufactures that textiles and clothing did at the beginning of the century.

Of the other groups, chemicals showed no change in relative importance up to 1929; there was an increase in the 1930's, and a further small increase in relative importance since 1950. No significant trend is apparent in the relative share of metals in the total, but the percentage for the miscellaneous group since 1950 is decidedly lower than before the war[1].

These results are essentially the same as those arrived at in the pioneering study by the late H. Tyszynski[2], in the subsequent contributions by Baldwin, Cairncross, Kindleberger, Spiegelglas, Svennilson and Yates[3], and by the Economic Commission for Europe and the G.A.T.T. secretariat[4], though the commodity classification used in the present book differs in several respects from those used previously[5]. Tyszynski fitted regression equations to the

---

[1]The inclusion of exports from the Netherlands from 1929 increases the percentage for machinery somewhat and reduces those for metals and transport equipment, but in no case is the trend significantly affected.

[2]H. Tyszynski, 'World Trade in Manufactured Commodities, 1899–1950', *Manchester School*, Vol. 19, No. 3, Sept. 1951.

[3]R. E. Baldwin, 'The Commodity Composition of Trade: Selected Industrial Countries, 1900–1954', *Review of Economics and Statistics*, Vol. 40, No. 1, Part 2: *Supplement*, Feb. 1958; A. K. Cairncross, 'World Trade in Manufactures since 1900', *Economia Internazionale*, Vol. 8, No. 4, 1955; C. P. Kindleberger, *The Terms of Trade, A European Case Study*, Wiley, 1956; S. Spiegelglas, 'World Exports of Manufactures, 1956 vs. 1937', *Manchester School*, Vol. 27, No. 2, May 1959; Ingvar Svennilson, *Growth and Stagnation in the European Economy*, United Nations, Geneva, 1954; P. L. Yates, *Forty Years of Foreign Trade*, London, 1959.

[4]*Economic Survey of Europe since the War*, United Nations Economic Commission for Europe, Geneva, 1953; various annual reports of G.A.T.T.

[5]The commodity classification used in the present book is based on the United Nations' *Standard International Trade Classification*. Previous studies of trends in world trade since 1900 have used either the *Brussels* classification, or some variant of the trade classification used by the United Kingdom before 1954.

Table 7.1. *Commodity pattern of world trade[a] in manufactures, 1899–1959*

Percentage

	Excluding Netherlands			Including Netherlands					
	1899	1913	1929	1929	1937	1950	1955	1957	1959
Metals	11.5	13.7	12.1	11.9	15.3	12.9	15.0	15.5	13.5
Machinery	8.0	10.4	13.9	14.5	16.0	20.7	22.3	24.1	24.8
Transport equipment	3.8	5.4	9.9	9.8	10.5	14.2	15.3	16.1	16.5
Passenger road vehicles	*0.3*	*1.7*	*3.7*	*3.6*	*3.8*	*4.1*	*4.8*	*4.7*	*6.0*
Other transport equipment	*3.5*	*3.7*	*6.2*	*6.2*	*6.7*	*10.1*	*10.4*	*11.4*	*10.5*
Other metal goods	7.0	6.5	5.9	5.9	6.5	4.9	4.8	4.4	4.2
Chemicals	8.3	9.1	8.4	8.5	10.6	10.5	11.4	11.0	12.0
Textiles and clothing	40.6	34.1	28.7	28.7	21.5	19.9	13.4	11.8	11.1
Yarns	*9.0*	*6.4*	*5.0*	*5.0*	*4.1*	*3.7*	*2.5*	*2.2*	*2.0*
Fabrics	*23.2*	*21.2*	*17.5*	*17.5*	*12.9*	*12.2*	*7.7*	*6.7*	*6.1*
Made-up goods	*8.4*	*6.5*	*6.3*	*6.2*	*4.6*	*3.9*	*3.2*	*2.9*	*3.0*
Other manufactures	20.8	20.7	21.1	21.0	19.5	17.0	17.9	17.1	17.9
TOTAL	100.0	100.0	100.0	100.0	100.0	100.0	100.0	100.0	100.0
Total in $ billion	*3.11*	*6.50*	*11.90*	*12.20*	*9.27*	*20.77*	*34.37*	*43.48*	*45.89*

Sources: Tables A.5 and A.80.

[a]Exports from 12 main exporting countries.

percentages for each of 16 commodity groups, taking time as the independent variable; the values of the regression co-efficients were then used to classify the groups into 'expanding', 'stable' and 'declining' categories, with the following results:—

Expanding: Motor vehicles, aircraft, etc.; industrial equipment; electrical goods; iron and steel; agricultural equipment.

Stable: Chemicals; miscellaneous materials; non-ferrous metals; non-metalliferous materials; books, films, etc.

Declining: Metal manufactures, n.e.s.; railways, ships, etc.; drink and tobacco; miscellaneous manufactures; apparel; textiles.

The newer forms of transport (cars, aircraft, etc.) were found to be the most rapidly expanding group, followed by machinery and iron and steel. Chemicals were found not to have increased their share—though an increase might have been expected—while, at the other extreme, the sharpest rate of decline was found in apparel and textiles.

This analysis has been carried forward to 1956 by Spiegelglas[1], who distinguished between the long-term trend, covering the entire period 1899–1956, and the short-term trend, covering the period 1937–56 only. For both periods, Spiegelglas presents regression co-efficients calculated in the same way as

[1]S. Spiegelglas, *Manchester School*, May 1959.

Tyszynski's. Some interesting differences emerge. The older forms of transport (railways, ships, etc.) and the miscellaneous group of manufactures, which Tyszynski had found to be declining, are now found to have a stable long-term trend as a percentage of world trade in all manufactures. Chemicals, which had been classed by Tyszynski as 'stable' are reclassified as 'expanding' by Spiegelglas[1]; moreover, the short-term trend (since 1937) for chemicals appears to have been definitely upward. In general, however, the trends since 1937 in the commodity pattern of trade appear to be a continuation of the longer-term trends already noted by Tyszynski.

Volume basis

Changes in the percentage shares of the different commodity groups, however, may be misleading for indicating trends in the volume of trade, because the average price movements in the various groups will differ considerably over a long period. These different price movements are discussed further below.

The trends in the volume of world exports of each main group of manufactures from 1899 to 1959 are shown in Table 7.2[2]. Up to 1913, the volume of trade in each commodity group expanded, the greatest rate of increase being in transport equipment, machinery and metals and the lowest in textiles and clothing. After the post-war slump, the recovery of the late 1920's also favoured transport equipment and machinery relatively to the other groups, while even by 1929 the volume of trade in textiles and clothing was no higher than in 1913. The great depression of the 1930's was accompanied by a much sharper contraction in world demand for capital goods than for consumer goods, but the recovery in the latter part of the decade once again favoured the former. By 1937, world trade in manufactures was still about one-sixth below the 1929 peak, in volume terms, chemicals, metals and transport equipment having achieved the greatest recovery. The volume of trade in textiles and clothing in 1937 was also one-sixth lower than in 1929, so that by volume this group had kept its share of the total, in marked contrast to the sharp fall indicated over this period in its percentage share of total value of trade; this was because of the fall in relative unit values of textiles and clothing.

[1]Tyszynski's regression co-efficient for chemicals was +0.017, while Spiegelglas's was +0.032. Unfortunately, neither author gives the standard errors of their co-efficients, so that it is not possible to say whether this difference is statistically significant. The results for the similar regression equations given later in this chapter (see Table 7.5) suggest that the difference between Tyszynski's and Spielgelglas's results for chemicals was not significant.
[2]These volume series are based on the detailed revaluations made for the trade network tables, separate unit value indices being used for each exporting country and each commodity group (see Appendices A and B). Similar attempts to examine trends in the volume of trade by commodity group were made by Baldwin (*op. cit.*, Table 3) and Yates (*op. cit.*, Table A.17); both used Kindleberger's unit value index for exports from industrial Europe to deflate current values of trade.

Table 7.2. *Volume of world trade^a in manufactures by main commodity group, 1899–1959*

	1899	1913	1929	1937	1950	1955	1957	1959
					Index numbers, 1929 = 100			
Metals	33	78	100	88	98	136	161	164
Machinery	26	64	100	78	132	188	228	238
Transport equipment	7	24	100	87	151	214	272	282
Passenger road vehicles	*1*	*19*	*100*	*84*	*115*	*179*	*212*	*276*
Other transport equipment	*11*	*26*	*100*	*91*	*173*	*234*	*307*	*284*
Other metal goods	45	80	100	72	78	94	100	96
Chemicals	37	81	100	93	142	242	298	356
Textiles and clothing	75	100	100	84	74	81	89	94
Yarns	*93*	*105*	*100*	*87*	*77*	*84*	*90*	*96*
Fabrics	*72*	*103*	*100*	*83*	*72*	*76*	*84*	*84*
Made-up goods	*69*	*86*	*100*	*83*	*78*	*91*	*104*	*122*
Other manufactures	40	76	100	84	93	137	159	174
TOTAL	41	72	100	83	104	144	171	182

Sources: Tables A.6 and A.80.

^aExports from 12 main exporting countries.

The post-war expansion has been associated with a continuation of the previous trends, with one major exception—chemicals. Transport equipment and machinery continued to expand faster than the average, while trade in chemicals—which had expanded roughly in line with the average up to 1929—has expanded fastest of all since 1950. The volume of trade in machinery and transport equipment in 1959 was in each case about three times the 1937 level, while trade in chemicals was nearly four times the pre-war figure; trade in metals and miscellaneous manufactures in each case about doubled. By contrast, trade in 'other metal goods' rose by about 30 per cent, but for textiles and clothing the volume of trade rose less than 15 per cent.

The contribution made by each commodity group to the expansion in total world trade in manufactures over the sixty years up to 1959 can be seen from Table 7.3. Machinery, transport equipment and chemicals together accounted for 45 per cent of the total increase in the volume of world trade in manufactures in the first half of the period, up to 1929, and for over 70 per cent of the total increase in the second half. Textiles and clothing had contributed 10 per cent of the increase from 1899 to 1929, but the volume in 1959 was still below the 1929 peak, easily the biggest decline being in fabrics. 'Other metal goods' also contributed nothing to the expansion in the total in the second half of the period.

Another, and perhaps more convenient, way of assessing the changes that have taken place in the relative volume of trade in the different groups is to express the volume indices for each group as a percentage of that for total

Table 7.3. *Changes in the volume of world trade*[a] *in the main groups of manufactures, 1899–1959*

$ billion at 1955 prices

	1899	1929	1959	Change from 1899 to 1929	Change from 1929 to 1959
Metals	1.26	3.78	6.20	+ 2.52	+ 2.42
Machinery	1.05	4.07	9.69	+ 3.02	+ 5.62
Transport equipment	0.17	2.45	6.92	+ 2.28	+ 4.47
Passenger road vehicles	*0.01*	*0.93*	*2.58*	*+ 0.92*	*+ 1.65*
Other transport equipment	*0.16*	*1.52*	*4.35*	*+ 1.36*	*+ 2.83*
Other metal goods	0.78	1.75	1.68	+ 0.97	− 0.07
Chemicals	0.60	1.62	5.75	+ 1.02	+ 4.13
Textiles and clothing	4.26	5.67	5.34	+ 1.41	− 0.33
Yarns	*0.94*	*1.01*	*0.98*	*+ 0.37*	*− 0.03*
Fabrics	*2.49*	*3.46*	*2.91*	*+ 0.97*	*− 0.55*
Made-up goods	*0.83*	*1.20*	*1.45*	*+ 0.07*	*+ 0.25*
Other manufactures	1.80	4.50	7.81	+ 2.70	+ 3.31
TOTAL	9.92	23.84	43.40	+ 13.92	+ 19.56

Sources: Tables A.6 and A.80.

[a]Exports from 12 main exporting countries. Figures for 1899 include estimates for the Netherlands.

Table 7.4. *World trade*[a] *in manufactures by main commodity group: relative volume indices*[b], *1899–1959*

Index numbers, 1929 = 100

	1899	1913	1929	1937	1950	1955	1957	1959
Metals	81	108	100	106	94	94	94	90
Machinery	63	89	100	94	127	130	133	131
Transport equipment	17	33	100	105	145	149	159	155
Passenger road vehicles	*2*	*26*	*100*	*101*	*111*	*124*	*124*	*152*
Other transport equipment	*27*	*36*	*100*	*107*	*166*	*163*	*180*	*156*
Other metal goods	110	111	100	87	75	65	58	53
Chemicals	90	112	100	112	136	168	174	196
Textiles and clothing	183	140	100	101	71	56	52	52
Yarns	*227*	*146*	*100*	*105*	*74*	*58*	*53*	*53*
Fabrics	*176*	*143*	*100*	*100*	*69*	*53*	*49*	*46*
Made-up goods	*168*	*119*	*100*	*100*	*75*	*63*	*61*	*67*
Other manufactures	98	106	100	101	89	95	93	96
TOTAL	100	100	100	100	100	100	100	100

Source: Table 7.2.

[a]Exports from 12 main exporting countries.
[b]Indices of actual volume expressed as percentages of index for total manufactures.

manufactures. The resulting series shows the volume change relative to that for all manufactures (see Table 7.4). On this basis, the various commodity groups can be classified into 'expanding', 'stable' and 'declining' categories. Regression equations were fitted to each relative volume series, with time as the independent variable, following the method used by Tyszynski. The results are given in Table 7.5, together with the corresponding coefficients for the current value percentages, both for the entire period 1899–1957 and for the shorter period since 1937[1].

Table 7.5. *Expanding, stable and declining commodity groups, 1899–1957*

	Long-term trend (1899–1957)		Short-term trend (1937–57)	
	Percentage of current value	Relative volume	Percentage of current value	Relative volume
Metals	+ 0.051[b]S	+ 0.079 S	− 0.003[b]S	− 0.541 D
Machinery	+ 0.276 E	+ 1.119 E	+ 0.383 E	+ 1.918 E
Transport equipment	+ 0.221 E	+ 2.525 E	+ 0.275 E	+ 2.546 E
Passenger road vehicles	*+ 0.073 E*	*+ 2.113 E*	*+ 0.049 E*	*+ 1.105 E*
Other transport equipment	*+ 0.142 E*	*+ 2.767 E*	*+ 0.224 E*	*+ 3.422 E*
Other metal goods	− 0.042 D	− 0.913 D	− 0.101 D	− 1.324 D
Chemicals	+ 0.046[b]S	+ 1.286 E	+ 0.029[b]S	+ 3.058 E
Textiles and clothing	− 0.476 D	− 2.123 D	− 0.467 D	− 2.438 D
Yarns	*− 0.106 D*	*− 2.664 D*	*− 0.092 D*	*− 2.601 D*
Fabrics	*− 0.282 D*	*− 2.125 D*	*− 0.298 D*	*− 2.672 D*
Made-up goods	*− 0.090 D*	*− 1.665 D*	*− 0.082 D*	*− 2.021 D*
Other manufactures	− 0.071 D	− 0.160 S	− 0.109 D	− 0.351 S

[a]Calculated by method of least squares; where the 1929 percentages differed according to whether the Netherlands were included or excluded, an additional variable was added, with value zero when Netherlands excluded and unity when included. The classification of the co-efficients indicated in the table is:

E = expanding   S = stable   D = declining

the definitions used being as follows:—

	E	S	D
Percentage of current value	over +0.05	+0.05 to −0.05	below −0.05
Relative volume	over +0.5	+0.5 to −0.5	below −0.5

[b]Not significantly different from zero.

The criteria used to distinguish the 'expanding', 'stable' and 'declining' categories are inevitably arbitrary ones. Most of the groups are clearly either 'expanding' or 'declining', but there are one or two borderline cases. All the co-efficients are significantly different from zero, except those for metals and chemicals based on percentages of current value. Some rather important

[1]This part of the analysis was completed before the 1959 figures became available; the inclusion of these would not, however, alter the results in Table 7.5 significantly.

Fig. 7.1. Expanding, stable and declining commodity groups[a] in world trade
in manufactures, 1899–1959

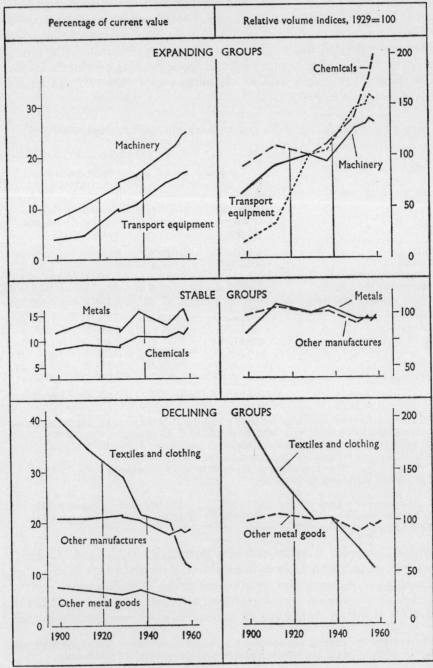

[a]Classification based on long-term trends.

differences emerge between the two methods of assessing trends in the com-, modity pattern of trade, the most important being that chemicals are 'expanding' on the relative volume basis, but are 'stable' as a percentage of the value of trade, whether the long-term or the short-term trend is considered.   Minor differences are that metals have been 'declining' on the relative volume basis since 1937, but were 'stable' on the percentage basis; and that, for both long and short periods, the miscellaneous group was found to be 'stable' on the relative volume basis instead of 'declining', as on the percentage basis (see Fig. 7.1).

A more detailed comparison of the long-term trends reveals further differences in the results according to which basis of calculation is used.   The outstanding difference is that whereas on the percentage basis the machinery and transport equipment groups have been expanding at roughly the same rate, on the volume basis the rate of growth in transport equipment is found to be more than double that of machinery (see the co-efficients in Table 7.5, and also Fig. 7.1).   The other major difference is that the decline in the relative importance of textiles and clothing is exaggerated by the use of value percentages.   The percentage co-efficient for this group, taking the long-term trend and ignoring signs (0.476),

Table 7.6.   *Volume and unit value changes in world trade[a] in manufactures, by main commodity group, 1899–1959*

Percentage

| | | Change from | | | | |
	Series	1899 to 1913	1913 to 1929	1929 to 1937	1937 to 1955	1955 to 1959
Metals	Volume	+135	+ 28	−12	+ 56	+20
	Unit value	+ 6	+ 26	+12	+133	0
Machinery	Volume	+146	+ 57	−22	+141	+26
	Unit value	+ 11	+ 53	+10	+115	+17
Transport equipment	Volume	+235	+325	−13	+145	+32
	Unit value	− 12	− 21	− 6	+118	+ 9
Other metal goods	Volume	+ 77	+ 26	−28	+ 31	+ 2
	Unit value	+ 11	+ 32	+17	+108	+16
Chemicals	Volume	+117	+ 23	− 7	+159	+47
	Unit value	+ 6	+ 36	+ 1	+ 54	− 5
Textiles and clothing	Volume	+ 33	0	−16	− 3	+16
	Unit value	+ 32	+ 53	−32	+138	− 5
Other manufactures	Volume	+ 88	+ 32	−16	+ 64	+27
	Unit value	+ 10	+ 42	−16	+108	+ 5
TOTAL	Volume	+ 78	+ 38	−17	+ 73	+26
	Unit value	+ 18	+ 33	− 9	+115	+ 6

Sources: Tables A.5, A.6 and A.80.
[a] Exports from 12 main exporting countries.

is more than double that for transport equipment (0.221), whereas on the relative volume basis it is actually lower (2.123 as against 2.525).

Volume and unit value

The reason for these divergent results is, of course, the very different movements in unit values of the various groups of commodities (see Table 7.6)[1]. There are two main reasons for these differences. First, technological progress tends to be faster in some industries than in others, with consequent effects on relative unit costs, and on relative export prices. Such technological changes tend to be more important in the expanding industries than in the contracting ones. Second, relative prices may change for purely competitive reasons; the obvious case is the sharp relative devaluation of the Japanese currency in the 1930's, which was a major factor in reducing world cotton textile prices relatively to prices of other manufactures.

The rapid development of trade in transport equipment from 1899 to 1929 is a clear case of the effect of technological development on price. The technical changes involved in mass production of motor vehicles and aircraft resulted in a substantial decline in unit costs of production over this period. Unit values of trade in transport equipment in 1929 were some 30 per cent lower than in 1899, when the volume of trade in this group was, of course, relatively small; over the same period, however, unit values of manufactured goods in total rose by 50–60 per cent. The rapid growth of chemical production and trade since 1945 is another example of the effect of technological progress on relative unit values. Between 1937 and 1955, the rise in unit values of chemicals and allied products was only just over 50 per cent, whereas that for all manufactures was 115 per cent. Rapid technological development, together with increasing competition in export markets, resulted during the 1950's in price reductions for several important chemical products (for example, penicillin and other antibiotics, and many plastic materials).

At the other extreme, those groups which are contracting tend not to be involved in new technical developments to the same extent as the expanding groups. However, even in textiles, there have been notable technical advances since the war in the development of synthetic fibres and improved finishes for cotton fabrics. So far, these newer products have tended to raise textile unit values, rather than reduce them, but in the longer run, they may well result in a higher volume of trade and a lower unit value than would otherwise have occurred.

The underlying relationship between rapid growth and greater technological development has resulted in a general inverse association between changes in

[1] It must be borne in mind, however, that the calculation of unit values (and consequently of volume indices) is inevitably subject to a considerable margin of error. Some of the qualifications are discussed in some detail in Chapter 8 (see pages 203–6).

the volume of trade and changes in unit values. For the period 1899–1913, the relationship between changes in volume and in unit values is extremely close (see Fig. 7.2), a 10 per cent rise in relative unit values being associated, on average, with a 23 per cent fall in relative volume[1]. A very similar result is obtained for the movement from 1913 to 1929, though in this case the relationship depends highly on the transport equipment group.

The slump of the 1930's caused a sharp fall in prices and volume of trade in several groups of manufactures. The behaviour of textiles and clothing and, to a lesser extent, of miscellaneous manufactures, is in marked contrast to that of the other commodity groups. For both these groups, the volume of world trade in 1937 was some 15 per cent below the 1929 peak; had the price-volume relationship been the same as for the other groups[2], the volume of trade in 1937 would have been 25 and 13 per cent higher, respectively, than in 1929, instead of about 15 per cent lower. These large differences were probably due to the fact that textiles and clothing, and a wide variety of miscellaneous consumer goods, suffered particularly heavily from increases in import duties and from quantitative import restrictions in the intervening period. The intensification of barriers to trade, however, was itself largely a reaction to the fall in unit values, which was in turn due substantially to export competition by the low-cost Japanese industry.

For the comparisons of 1955 with 1937, and 1959 with 1955, the goodness of fit of the regression equations was poor in each case. However, the inverse relationship of volume and unit value was still prominent in these periods.

Degree of fabrication

For a comparison of trade movements with industrial development, it is useful to distinguish intermediate products from finished manufactures[3]. Within the latter group, a division by end-use has been made into capital goods, durable consumer goods, textile fabrics[4] and other finished goods.

---

[1]Regression equations were calculated for each of the four comparisons shown in Fig. 7.2, using the form $\log v = \log a + b \log u$, where v = volume index and u = unit value index. The results were as follows:—

Period	b	R^2
1899–1913	$- 2.28 \ (\pm 0.40)$	0.865
1913–29	$- 1.91 \ (\pm 0.38)$	0.834
1929–37[a]	$- 0.79 \ (\pm 0.50)$	0.451
1937–55	$- 1.48 \ (\pm 0.94)$	0.332
1955–59	$- 0.93 \ (\pm 0.56)$	0.405

[a] Excluding textiles and clothing and miscellaneous manufactures.

[2]The regression equation gave a relatively poor fit, however.

[3]This distinction was discussed in general terms on pages 58–60; for detailed definitions, see Appendix D.

[4]The classification of textile fabrics presents a major difficulty, since these are sold both direct to consumers and also to factories for making up into clothing. For further discussion, see Appendix D, pages 517–8.

Fig. 7.2. Relation between volume and unit value indices by commodity group

Double logarithmic scale

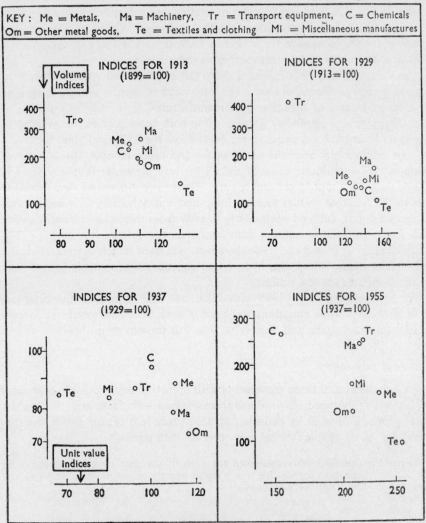

KEY : Me = Metals,   Ma = Machinery,   Tr = Transport equipment,   C = Chemicals
Om = Other metal goods,   Te = Textiles and clothing   Mi = Miscellaneous manufactures

The volume of world trade in both intermediate products and finished manufactures has risen at much the same rate since the beginning of the century[1]. By 1959, the volume of each was nearly $4\frac{1}{2}$ times the corresponding total in 1899 (see Table 7.7). Throughout the period, finished goods represented about 70 per cent of total trade in all manufactured goods, though there

[1]This is, in effect, the same conclusion that was reached by Tyszynski, Svennilson and Cairncross on the basis of value figures.

have been some variations, particularly during the 1930's, when the slump hit trade in finished manufactures to a greater extent than trade in intermediates.

The greatest changes have been within the finished manufactures category. Capital goods represented only one-sixth of the total of world trade in finished goods at the beginning of the century, but the proportion has risen substantially since then: to one-fifth in 1913, one-third in the inter-war years and to about one-half since 1950 (all proportions being based on 1955 prices). Durable consumer goods (mainly passenger cars), have also been expanding more rapidly than the total[1], while other finished goods have represented a falling proportion. Non-durable finished goods other than textile fabrics, though relatively less important now in the total than before the first World War, have expanded considerably in volume terms—by 1959 they were some three times the 1899 volume. Trade in textile fabrics has risen somewhat since 1950, but in 1959 was still about 20 per cent below the 1913 peak[2].

Table 7.7. *Changes in the volume of world trade[a] in manufactures, by degree of fabrication and end-use, 1899–1959*

$ billion, at 1955 prices

	1899	1929	1959	Change from 1899 to 1929	Change from 1929 to 1959
Intermediate products	3.10	7.22	13.65	+ 4.12	+ 6.43
Metals	1.26	3.78	6.20	+ 2.52	+ 2.42
Other	1.84	3.44	7.45	+ 1.60	+ 4.01
Finished manufactures	6.82	16.62	29.75	+ 9.80	+ 13.13
Capital goods	1.16	5.34	14.03	+ 4.18	+ 8.69
Durable consumer goods	0.15[b]	1.50	3.83	+ 1.35[b]	+ 2.33
Textile fabrics	2.49	3.46	2.91	+ 0.97	− 0.55
Other	3.02	6.32	8.97	+ 3.30	+ 2.65
TOTAL	9.92	23.84	43.40	+ 13.92	+ 19.56

Sources: Tables A.6, A.80, 12.1 and related data.

[a]Exports from twelve main exporting countries. Figures for 1899 include estimates for the Netherlands.

[b]Approximate.

2. COMMODITY PATTERN OF IMPORTS BY AREA

The shifts in the commodity pattern of world trade in manufactures described above have been a marked feature of the imports into both industrial and semi-industrial countries and into the non-industrial areas. Over the sixty

[1]See Chapter 12.
[2]See Table A.78 for fuller statistical detail.

years to 1959, for example, the relative importance of machinery and transport equipment in total 'imports' of manufactures rose from one-tenth to one-third in the industrial countries, from one-tenth to one-half in the semi-industrial countries, and from one-sixth to two-fifths in the 'rest of the world', which consists largely of non-industrial countries (see Table 7.8 and Fig. 7.3). Similarly, for textiles and clothing, the percentage was drastically reduced over the period in all three major groups of countries—and particularly so in the semi-industrial countries.

The shift in commodity pattern has, in fact, been much more drastic in the semi-industrial, than in the two other country groups. A simple way of comparing these shifts in commodity pattern over the period is to take the ratio of 'imports' of machinery, transport equipment and chemicals, the expanding groups, to those of textiles and clothing, the main contracting group. This ratio was lower for the semi-industrial countries than for the industrial ones up to the last war, exceeded it slightly in 1950 and since then has risen much more sharply.

Table 7.8.   *'Imports' of main commodity groups into industrial and semi-industrial countries and the rest of the world, 1899–1959*

Percentage[a]

		Metals	Machinery and transport equipment	Chemi-cals	Textiles and clothing	Other manu-fac-tures[b]	Total	Total value[c] ($ billion)
Industrial countries	1899	16	10	7	38	29	100	5.1
	1929	20	24	7	20	29	100	11.3
	1955	19	33	11	11	26	100	16.2
	1959	16	35	12	11	26	100	22.6
Semi-industrial countries	1899	8	11	3	55	23	100	2.1
	1929	12	31	4	30	23	100	5.2
	1955	13	48	11	11	17	100	6.7
	1959	11	50	14	9	16	100	6.8
Rest of the world	1899	11	17	6	44	22	100	2.8
	1929	12	31	7	26	24	100	7.4
	1955	11	38	12	17	22	100	11.5
	1959	13	39	15	15	18	100	14.0

Sources: Tables A.8, A.10, A.12 and related data.

[a] Based on values at 1955 prices.
[b] Including 'other metal goods'.
[c] Values at 1955 prices.

For the 'rest of the world', the ratio has risen less sharply since 1937 than for the two other groups, and by 1959 it was only about one-half the ratio for the semi-industrial countries.

Fig. 7.3. Relative importance of commodity groups in 'imports' into
industrial, semi-industrial and non-industrial countries, 1899–1959

Percentages of total

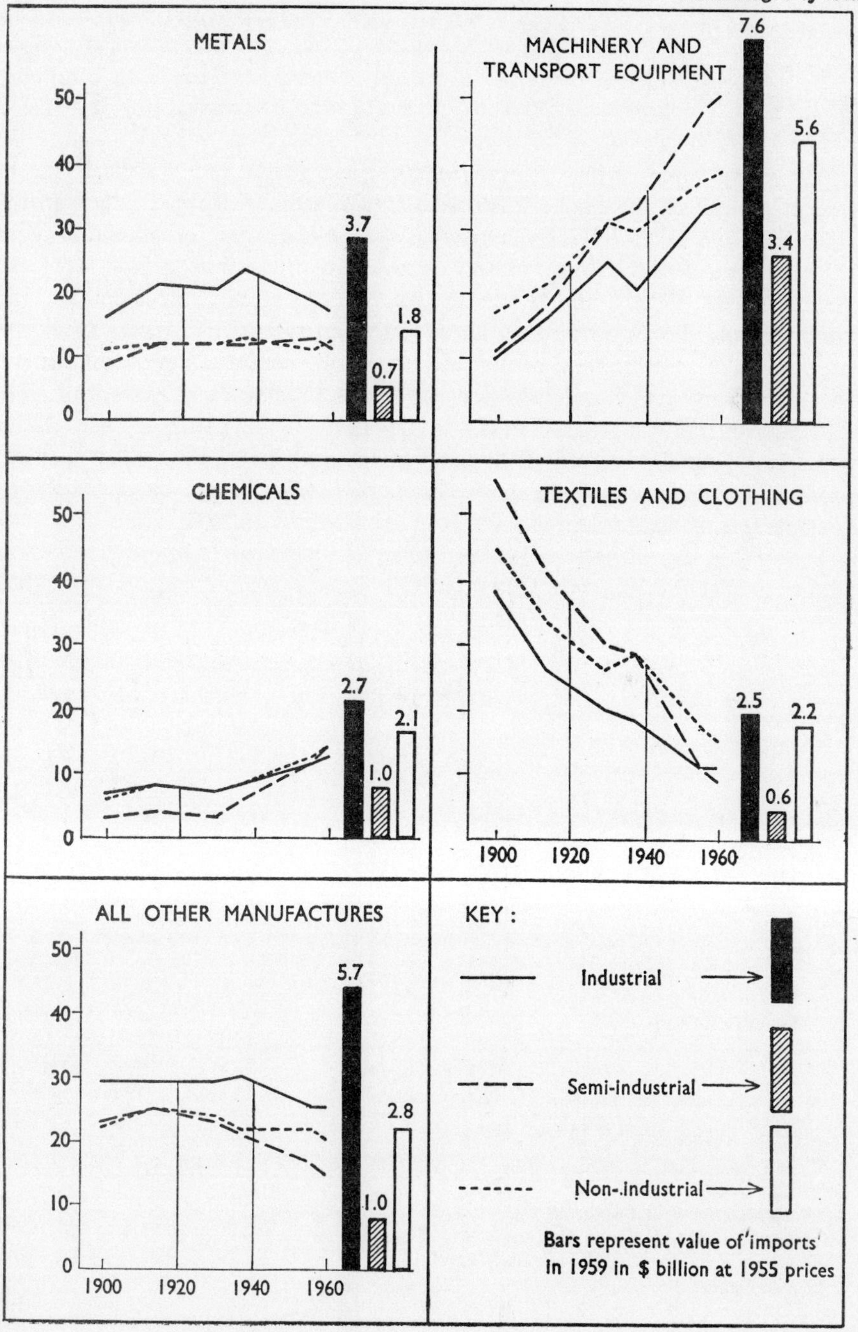

Ratio of 'imports' in expanding groups to 'imports' in textiles and clothing

Country group	1899	1913	1929	1937	1950	1955	1959
Industrial	0.5	0.9	1.6	1.7	2.7	4.0	4.2
Semi-industrial	0.3	0.5	1.2	1.4	2.8	5.4	7.2
Rest of world	0.5	0.9	1.5	1.3	2.2	3.0	3.5

The more rapid switch towards engineering goods and chemicals in the import-pattern of the semi-industrial countries than of the two other groups since 1950 (see Table 7.9) is due essentially to the beginnings of industrialization in India and Pakistan and to the considerable industrial growth of Latin America. By 1959, imports of textiles into both the Indo-Pakistan sub-continent and the industrializing Latin American countries formed a negligible proportion of total imports of manufactures. By contrast, the proportion for the three Southern Dominions was still substantial (nearly one-fifth). The difference in pattern is due mainly to the need of the poorer industrializing countries to restrict imports of 'less essentials' such as textiles (which they can produce for themselves), so as to maximise their foreign expenditures on development goods.

The shift in import-pattern has been generally much less in the large industrial countries (Table 7.10), since they supply by far the greater proportion of their

Table 7.9.   *'Imports' of selected commodity groups into semi-industrial countries,*
1899–1959

Percentage[a]

		Southern Dominions[b]	India/ Pakistan	Latin America[c]	Others[d]
Machinery and transport equipment	1899	12	7	13	5[e]
	1929	32	22	38	25
	1955	44	50	52	52
	1959	46	57	53	49
Chemicals	1899	5	1	5	5[e]
	1929	5	3	5	5
	1955	7	13	14	10
	1959	12	14	16	16
Textiles and clothing	1899	46	69	47	60[e]
	1929	30	44	22	29
	1955	20	7	4	9
	1959	18	4	3	4

Sources: Tables A.27–A.38 and related data

[a]Based on values at 1955 prices. 'Imports' of total manufactures into each group of countries = 100.
[b]Australia, New Zealand and the Union of South Africa.
[c]Argentina, Brazil, Chile, Colombia and Mexico.
[d]Turkey, Yugoslavia and Palestine/Israel.
[e]Turkey only.

Table 7.10. *'Imports' of selected commodity groups into industrial countries,*
1899–1959

Percentage[a]

		United King- dom	France	Ger- many[b]	Other Western Europe	United States	Canada
Machinery and transport	1899	6	19	20	13	2	13
equipment	1929	16	34	17	26	6	42
	1955	20	41	18	38	15	49
	1959	27	39	24	37	27	49
Chemicals	1899	8	7	7	7	9	7
	1929	7	6	8	7	7	5
	1955	14	14	11	11	8	9
	1959	16	15	11	15	6	10
Textiles and clothing	1899	34	30	41	32	53	27
	1913	22	10	28	19	26	17
	1955	10	5	19	12	13	8
	1959	12	4	19	12	11	10

Sources: Tables A.15–A.26 and related data.

[a]Based on values at 1955 prices. 'Imports' of total manufactures into each country = 100.
[b]West Germany in 1955 and 1959.

Table 7.11. *'Imports' of main commodity groups into non-industrial countries,*
1929 and 1955

Percentage[a]

Countries exporting mainly:		Metals	Machinery and transport equipment	Chemi- cals	Textiles and clothing	Other manu- fac- tures[b]	Total
Food[c]	1929	12	23	6	36	23	100
	1955	12	33	14	21	20	100
Agricultural raw	1929	10	20	8	39	23	100
materials[d]	1955	7	33	9	25	26	100
Petroleum[e]	1929	20	31	5	20	24	100
	1955	14	46	8	10	22	100
Other minerals[f]	1929	14	38	4	22	22	100
	1955	10	45	9	13	23	100

Sources: Tables A.40–A.45.

[a]Based on values at 1955 prices.
[b]Including 'other metal goods'.
[c]Egypt, Indonesia and Philippines.
[d]Burma, Cuba and Nigeria.
[e]Iran and Venezuela.
[f]Belgian Congo, French Morocco, Peru and the Federation of Rhodesia and Nyasaland (Southern Rhodesia in 1929).

own requirements of engineering products and chemicals. France, however, is exceptional insofar as her proportion of imports of engineering products (two-fifths in 1959) is much the same as for the smaller Western European countries. This is not because the French import-proportion of consumption is relatively high in engineering goods, but because it is unusually low in textiles and clothing, which has traditionally been a French speciality, and which has been heavily protected against competition from imports.

Table 7.12. *Changes in 'imports' of manufactures into industrial and semi-industrial countries and the rest of the world by major commodity group, 1899–1959*

$ billion at 1955 prices

		Industrial countries	Semi-industrial countries	Rest of world	Total
Machinery, transport equip-	1899–1929	+ 2.52	+ 1.59	+ 2.21	+ 6.32
ment and chemicals	1929–1959	+ 7.05	+ 2.51	+ 4.66	+ 14.23
Textiles and clothing	1899–1929	+ 0.33	+ 0.40	+ 0.68	+ 1.41
	1929–1959	+ 0.34	− 0.95	+ 0.28	− 0.33
Other manufactures	1899–1929	+ 3.33	+ 1.14	+ 1.72	+ 6.19
	1929–1959	+ 3.95	+ 0.05	+ 1.67	+ 5.66
TOTAL	1899–1929	+ 6.18	+ 3.13	+ 4.61	+ 13.92
	1929–1959	+ 11.33	+ 1.61	+ 6.62	+ 19.56

Sources: Tables A.8, A.10, A.12 and related data.

Comparable data for a number of non-industrial countries are available only for selected years from 1929 to 1955 (Table 7.11). The countries exporting petroleum and other minerals already had a fairly high proportion of imports consisting of engineering goods and chemicals even before the war, and this proportion increased markedly by 1955, particularly in the oil countries. However, the shift away from textiles and towards engineering and chemicals has also been important in countries specialising in exports of agricultural produce. In such countries, economic development would imply increasing demand for agricultural equipment, constructional plant and materials, fertilizers, drugs and other development goods for the non-manufacturing sectors.

Though the greatest shift in import-pattern has occurred in the semi-industrial countries, this group contributed least to the growth in world imports of the three expanding commodity groups over the period 1899–1959 (Table 7.12). In the first half of the period, up to 1929, the semi-industrial countries accounted for one-quarter of the increase in the volume of world imports of machinery, transport equipment and chemicals; in the second half, for one-sixth. The major contribution, particularly since 1929, has been made by the industrial

Table 7.13. *Average ad valorem rates of import duty[a] on a sample of manufactures in selected countries: main commodity groups, 1937 and 1955*

	Industrial countries				Semi-industrial countries			
	Low tariff[b]		High tariff[c]		Low tariff[d]		High tariff[e]	
	1937	1955	1937	1955	1937	1955	1937	1955
	(Average ad valorem rates)							
Metals[f]	5.2	2.9	6.1	5.3	6.6	2.7	34.6	24.9
Machinery[g]	11.0	7.6	14.9	11.6	11.5	7.6	22.9	23.2
Transport equipment[h]	21.3	11.6	26.6	19.6	20.1	9.2	32.8	27.6
Other metal goods[i]	11.9	8.9	16.8	12.9	18.4	12.3	113.8	49.6
Chemicals[j]	8.4	7.7	12.1	10.5	12.3	7.5	39.0	32.5
Textiles and clothing[k]	19.6	8.0	16.4	16.3	11.7	7.3	43.3	37.7
Other manufactures[l]	17.5	11.9	17.5	17.1	21.0	11.1	83.1	43.5
TOTAL	13.6	8.4	15.8	13.3	14.5	8.2	52.8	34.1
	(Percentage of total)							
Metals[j]	38	35	39	40	46	33	66	73
Machinery[g]	81	90	94	87	79	93	43	68
Transport equipment[h]	157	138	168	147	139	112	62	81
Other metal goods[i]	88	106	106	97	127	150	216	145
Chemicals[j]	62	92	77	79	85	91	74	95
Textiles and clothing[k]	144	95	104	123	81	89	82	111
Other manufactures[l]	129	142	111	129	145	135	157	128
TOTAL	100	100	100	100	100	100	100	100

Sources: Bulletin International des Douanes, Brussels (var. edns); national tariffs and trade statistics.

[a] Unweighted averages.

[b] Belgium-Luxembourg, Germany (West Germany in 1955), Sweden and Switzerland.

[c] Canada, France, Japan and Norway.

[d] Australia and the Union of South Africa.

[e] Brazil, Chile and India.

[f] Iron and steel bars, blooms, etc. sections, wire, sheet and pipes; copper manufactures; aluminium manufactures; nickel.

[g] Agricultural machinery; electric machinery; textile machinery; metal-working machine tools; typewriters; radio apparatus; gramophones.

[h] Passenger cars, motor cycles, bicycles and ships.

[i] Precision tools; bolts, nuts, screws, etc.; locks.

[j] Pharmaceutical and cosmetic products; specified chemicals (e.g. magnesium chloride and sodium phosphate); coal-tar derivatives; plastic materials; dyestuffs; colours, including synthetic; fertilizers; essential oils; soap.

[k] Staple fibre; cotton, wool and synthetic yarns and fabrics; wool carpets and rugs.

[l] Writing paper; rubber manufactures; portland cement; window glass and crude glass; footwear; electric lamps; toys.

countries. This is even more true of the group of miscellaneous manufactures, for which the industrial countries accounted for 70 per cent of the total expansion since 1929. This has resulted both from an increasing diversity of demand for consumer manufactures in the industrial countries, leading to an increase in intra-trade in such goods; and from a substantial degree of import-substitution in the semi-industrial countries. As already remarked, such import-substitution was greatest in textiles and clothing.

Tariff discrimination

These shifts in the pattern of imports have generally been supported by discriminatory tariffs protecting the development of local manufacturing industries. In the earlier stages of industrialization, the tariff on capital goods imports tends to be relatively low, and that on textiles and miscellaneous consumer manufactures—which can be produced locally—relatively high. Moreover, this general pattern of tariff discrimination, tends to be perpetuated as countries become more industrialized (see Table 7.13). For a sample of semi-industrial countries, the highest duty rates in 1955 were found in miscellaneous manufactures, including 'other metal goods', and this was true both for the low-tariff and the high-tariff countries. Similarly, metals and machinery attracted the lowest duty rates, relatively to the average, for both groups of countries, and chemicals were also charged at less than average rates.

In the industrial countries, the pattern of tariff discrimination in 1955 was generally similar to that of the semi-industrial countries, the main difference being a much greater relative discrimination, among both low-tariff and high-tariff industrial countries, against passenger cars.

Though tariff rates have generally fallen since pre-war in all commodity groups, they are still considerably higher in the lower-income (that is, the high-tariff) group of semi-industrial countries than elsewhere[1]. In 1955, the average rates on metals and textiles in these countries were nine and five times, respectively, the corresponding rates in the low-tariff semi-industrial countries included in the sample. For chemicals, 'other metal goods' and miscellaneous manufactures the rates were about four times, and for machinery and transport equipment about three times, those for the low-tariff semi-industrial countries. Tariff rates which are both high and discriminating against imports competing with local manufacturing output are evidently a typical feature of the industrialization process in under-developed countries.

3. THE PATTERN OF IMPORTS IN RELATION TO ECONOMIC GROWTH

The general patterns of change in demand and in output associated with economic growth have already been discussed in Chapter 2. It was shown there that both tend to shift towards engineering and chemicals as the economic

[1] Though the figures in Table 7.13 relate to 1955, there is little doubt that the same general relationship has been maintained since then.

Table 7.14. *Growth co-efficients based on time series for imports of manufactures into industrial and semi-industrial countries by main commodity group*

	Industrial countries		Semi-industrial countries	
	Growth co-efficient[a]	R^2	Growth coefficient[a]	R^2
Metals	0.79 ($\pm$ 0.16)	0.315	0.07 ($\pm$ 0.27)	0.002
Metal products	1.54 ($\pm$ 0.12)	0.789	1.29 ($\pm$ 0.23)	0.571
Machinery	1.47 ($\pm$ 0.13)	0.711	1.43 ($\pm$ 0.28)	0.523
Passenger road vehicles	1.81 ($\pm$ 0.28)	0.683	− 0.55 ($\pm$ 0.54)	0.046
Other transport equipment	2.48 ($\pm$ 0.19)	0.812	1.55 ($\pm$ 0.30)	0.497
Other metal goods	0.06 ($\pm$ 0.17)	0.002	1.41 ($\pm$ 0.34)	0.339
Chemicals	1.48 ($\pm$ 0.14)	0.706	1.19 ($\pm$ 0.28)	0.410
Textiles and clothing	− 0.22 ($\pm$ 0.19)	0.029	− 1.98 ($\pm$ 0.45)	0.359
Yarns	− 0.40 ($\pm$ 0.19)	0.074	− 0.12 ($\pm$ 0.51)	0.002
Fabrics	− 0.35 ($\pm$ 0.20)	0.059	− 2.14 ($\pm$ 0.56)	0.289
Made-up goods	0.02 ($\pm$ 0.23)	0.000	− 2.62 ($\pm$ 0.53)	0.495
Other manufactures	0.27 ($\pm$ 0.14)	0.073	− 1.33 ($\pm$ 0.35)	0.315
TOTAL	1.01 ($\pm$ 0.09)	0.672	0.22 ($\pm$ 0.25)	0.020

Sources: Tables A.15–A.38, E.2 and E.7.

[a]Regression co-efficients derived from time-series regressions of 'imports' per head on gross domestic product per head. For further explanation, see text.

system expands, and away from textiles, clothing and other 'non-durable' consumer goods. The implication is that the pattern of imports will also shift in this direction. That it has done so, historically, for world trade as a whole and for individual countries, has already been shown, but a positive demonstration of the relationship can be made by relating the pattern of imports directly to the growth in real product per head.

This has been done by a series of regressions for each main commodity group, relating the value of per caput 'imports' to per caput gross domestic product, both valued at 1955 prices. Each regression covered the selected years (1899–1955) for which the Trade Network tables were available (see Appendix A), and separate calculations were done for the industrial and the semi-industrial countries[1]. Similar regressions were not possible for the non-industrial countries because of general lack of historical series for real product.

[1]A double logarithmic equation was used as follows:

$$\frac{M}{N} = \beta_0 \left(\frac{Y}{N}\right)^{\beta_1}$$

using the same notation as previously. For the industrial countries, each regression covered 60 or more 'observations', except for passenger road vehicles (28) and other transport equipment (48). For the semi-industrial countries, the number of 'observations' varied between 30 and 50.

The results (Table 7.14) support the view that economic growth is associated with a drastic shift in the pattern of imports, as well as of demand and output[1]. In the industrial countries, the volume of imports of manufactures per head grew at about the same rate as real income per head over the period covered by the calculations. Imports of transport equipment (other than passenger road vehicles) have risen $2\frac{1}{2}$ times as fast as real income per head, while the ratio for passenger road vehicles was 1.8 and for machinery and chemicals 1.5. At the other extreme, imports of textile yarns and fabrics have fallen in relation to real income but there is no clear evidence of a close association between income and imports in this case, and there has been no significant movement either way for textile made-up goods (including clothing) and for 'other metal goods' (cutlery, tools, implements, etc.).

In the semi-industrial countries, the same general pattern emerges, though the rate of decline in textile fabrics and made-up goods has been considerably greater, in relation to economic growth, than in the industrial countries, and the rate of increase in transport equipment (other than passenger road vehicles) and chemicals considerably less. In passenger road vehicles and in miscellaneous manufactures, imports per head have tended to fall with economic growth. The downtrend for passenger road vehicles is not well established[2]; it probably reflects the fact that passenger cars are generally regarded as 'nonessential' by industrializing countries, which tend to restrict imports of them so as to allow relatively more 'development goods' to be bought abroad.

The downtrends in imports of textiles and miscellaneous manufactures into the semi-industrial countries reflect the growth of local manufacture of these products, which substitute for imports. The pattern is considerably more complicated than appears from Table 7.14, which gives merely the average relationship. There are, in fact, several distinct patterns of change in textiles, depending largely on the availability of locally produced fibre. One group of countries (Australia and Colombia) show an upward trend in yarn imports, but a downward trend in imports of fabrics and made-up goods. Another group (Argentina, Brazil, Chile and Mexico) show a downtrend in both, while for a third group (New Zealand and South Africa) both yarns and fabrics (though not made-up goods) have risen as income increased. These different

---

[1]No allowance has been made in these regressions for changes in the capacity to import of the countries included, since adequate statistical data were not available for the long time-period covered. In terms of the model used in Chapter 6, the co-efficient β_1 is equivalent to $\epsilon_1 - \rho\epsilon_2 + (\lambda - 1)\epsilon_3$. The regression formula would result in unbiased estimates of the combined income- and substitution-effects if variations in λ were not correlated with variations in $\dfrac{Y}{N}$. However, to the extent that ϵ_3 may differ significantly between commodity groups, variations in λ would have disproportionate effects on imports in each group. This point is considered further in Chapter 15 (see page 405).

[2]Since the proportion of the variance explained is very low and the standard error of the growth co-efficient is relatively high.

patterns are discussed in more detail in Chapter 13[1].

For the industrial countries, the import growth co-efficients are directly comparable with the production co-efficients given in Chapter 2[2]. The relationship, which is both positive and close, indicates that the rates of growth of *both* production and imports in the different commodity groups reflect the different rates of growth of demand in each. The fact that imports into the industrial countries tend to rise more rapidly for the commodity groups for which demand is also expanding fastest, is probably the result of several factors. Perhaps the most important is that production of capital equipment and chemicals—the more 'dynamic' groups—is more concentrated in a relatively small number of large industrial countries than is production of textiles or miscellaneous consumer manufactures. This means that the expansion in demand in all the other countries tends to spill over into imports of the expanding groups, whereas this does not happen to the same extent for the relatively declining commodity groups.

Moreover, *within* the expanding groups there may be more specialization among the industrial countries on a product basis than there is within, say, textiles. For example, Sweden tends to specialize, *inter alia*, in telephone, cable and electrical equipment, ball and roller bearings and typewriters; Switzerland in machine tools and electrical plant; and so on. To this extent, a general rise in demand in these groups is inevitably accompanied by a rise in demand for imports.

The general positive association between the rates of growth in production and imports of the different commodity groups can be seen for the industrial countries for each of a number of periods since 1913 (Table 7.15). The relationship between production and imports varied widely between the different periods; but in each period, the relationship between production change and import change was much the same for each commodity group, though there were some exceptions. From 1913 to 1929, production was growing faster

---

[1]A set of cross-country regressions for a recent year (1955) was also calculated for each commodity group; using the previous notation, the function used was:

$$\log \frac{M}{N} = \log \beta_0 + \beta_1 \log \frac{Y}{N} + \beta_2 \log N$$

following the approach used by Professor Chenery ('Patterns of Industrial Growth' *American Economic Review*, vol. 50, no. 4, Sept. 1960). The goodness of fit was high for machinery, transport equipment, chemicals and miscellaneous manufactures (R^2 generally exceeding 0.7 or 0.8), and fair for textiles (R^2 over 0.55). The growth co-efficients all had low standard errors and were all positive, ranging from 0.44 for 'other metal goods' to 0.73 for textiles and clothing and 0.98 for metals. These results bear a marked similarity to those presented by Professor Chenery (*op. cit.*, Table 4), but in view of the results of the time regressions they must be regarded as a misleading representation of how imports change with economic growth in individual countries. The misrepresentation is particularly acute in textiles because there is a positive cross-country association between per caput income and per caput imports, though at the same time the latter has declined in the majority of countries as the former has risen.

[2]See the co-efficients based on time-series in Table 2.5.

than imports in all groups, except textiles where it fell less. In the period of
trade restrictions in the 1930's there was a small gain in production, comparing
1937 with 1929, but big falls in 'imports' in every group. From 1937 to 1955,
the percentage increases in production and 'imports' were remarkably similar
in each commodity group, but in the following period the percentage rise in
'imports' outstripped that of production. It is an interesting phenomenon that
the abnormally high rate of growth in the intra-trade of the industrial countries
in the 1950's affected textiles and clothing, as well as the 'dynamic' groups—
metal products and chemicals.

Table 7.15. *Changes in commodity patterns of production and 'imports' of
manufactures in the industrial countries, 1913–59*

Percentage

Change from	Series[a]	Metals	Metal products[b]	Chemi- cals	Textiles and clothing[c]	Miscell- aneous	Total[d]
1913 to 1929[e]	P	+ 62	+156	+150	− 6	+ 37	+ 65
	I	+ 25	+ 40	− 4	−10	+ 26	+ 22
1929 to 1937	P	+ 4	+ 6	+ 21	+ 6	+ 11	+ 9
	I	− 26	− 36	− 17	−34	− 22	− 29
1937 to 1955	P	+ 93	+172	+194	+29	+ 59	+105
	I	+ 92	+194	+172	+28	+ 77	+109
1955 to 1959	P	− 4	+ 12	+ 28	+ 3	+ 16	+ 13
	I[f]	+ 19	+ 43	+ 47	+39	+ 17	+ 38
1913 to 1959	P	+210	+725	+ 1,040	+35	+180	+320
	I[g]	+110	+320	+ 220	+ 5	+120	+150

Sources: Tables A.8, A.15–A.25 and related data; *Industrial Statistics, 1900–1959*,
O.E.E.C., Paris, 1960.
[a]P = volume of production. I = volume of 'imports' from twelve main exporting
countries. All figures exclude Switzerland and Japan.
[b]Machinery, transport equipment and other metal goods.
[c]Production series relate to textiles only.
[d]Excluding food, beverages and tobacco.
[e]Excluding Canada and Netherlands throughout; excluding France and Germany for
chemicals.
[f]'Other metal goods' included in the miscellaneous group.
[g]Based on percentages for separate periods shown, so that country coverage is comparable
with production indices. For this reason, import percentages do not quite agree with
totals for the industrial countries given elsewhere.

A similar comparison of production and imports cannot be made for the
semi-industrial countries, and it would not be very relevant for the non-industrial
ones. However, as was shown above, the pattern of change in imports has
been broadly similar in these groups of countries. Since the pattern of change
in imports is associated with economic growth, the past trends in the commodity-
pattern of world trade may be expected to continue in future, though probably
in a modified form; this is discussed further in Chapter 15.

4. THE EFFECT OF CHANGES IN COMMODITY PATTERNS ON THE IMPORT-CONTENT OF SUPPLIES

The changes in production and imports of the different commodity groups set out in Table 7.15 imply corresponding changes in the import-content of supplies. It was shown earlier that as real incomes rise the commodity pattern of consumption of manufactures changes in a definite way[1]. This implies that if the import-content is relatively low in the 'growth' industries—engineering and chemicals—and relatively high in the 'declining' ones—for example, textiles—the process of economic growth would be accompanied by a falling average import-content of supplies due simply to the changing pattern of consumption. Conversely, with a high import-content in engineering and a low one in textiles, economic growth would by itself tend to generate an increase in the average import-content. It is important in interpreting the past trend in the import-content, as well as in assessing the possible future trend[2], to know whether there is in fact such a 'built-in' association between economic growth and the average import-content of supplies of manufactures.

Estimates of the value of supplies in each main commodity group can be made by adding imports to the gross output free of duplication in each country[3]. This calculation has been made for each of the industrial countries (except Japan and Switzerland, for which the relevant production indices are not available) for 1913 and each subsequent year shown in the Trade Network tables. For each of four periods from 1913 to 1959 the change in the import-content of supplies of manufactures is sub-divided in Table 7.16 into two parts, which can be attributed, respectively to[4]:

[1] See pages 41–43. The pattern of change in supplies is closely similar to that in consumption.

[2] The possible future trend in the import-content of supplies of various groups of countries is discussed in Chapter 15.

[3] The detailed procedure is set out in Appendix E. For capital goods and chemicals, some details of the calculations are given in Chapters 10 and 11, respectively. The estimates of gross output for the other commodity groups are subject to a fairly large margin of error, and are not given separately.

[4] The change from one year to another in a country's import-content of supplies can be written as:

$$\frac{\Sigma m_1 S_1}{\Sigma S_1} - \frac{\Sigma m_0 S_0}{\Sigma S_0}$$

where m represents the import-content of supplies in a given commodity group and S the total supplies, the subscripts $_0$ and $_1$ representing the base and current periods, respectively, aggregation being made over the various commodity groups. This change can be divided into the following elements:—

$$\frac{\Sigma m_1 S_1}{\Sigma S_1} - \frac{\Sigma m_0 S_0}{\Sigma S_0} = \frac{\Sigma m_1 S_1 - \Sigma m_0 S_1}{\Sigma S_1} + \left\{ \frac{\Sigma m_0 S_1}{\Sigma S_1} - \frac{\Sigma m_0 S_0}{\Sigma S_0} \right\}$$

The first term on the right-hand side measures the change attributable to changes in the import-content of supplies in each commodity-group (using current weights); the second term that attributable to changes in the pattern of supplies (using base weights).

(a) changes in the import-content of supplies in each of the separate commodity groups ; and

(b) changes in the commodity-pattern of supplies.

The results are shown separately for the United States, which has a

Table 7.16. *Changes in the import-content of supplies of manufactures attributable to changes in the import-content within commodity groups and to changes in the commodity pattern of supplies[a], 1913–59*

Percentages[b]

	1913–29	1929–37	1937–50	1950–59
UNITED STATES				
Change in import-content of supplies attributable to				
(a) Import-content within commodity groups	− 0.27	− 0.52	− 0.15	+ 1.26
(b) Commodity pattern of supplies	− 0.33	+ 0.06	− 0.14	− 0.13
Total[c]	− 0.60	− 0.46	− 0.29	+ 1.13
OTHER LARGE INDUSTRIAL COUNTRIES[d]				
Change in import-content of supplies attributable to				
(a) Import-content within commodity groups	− 2.04	− 3.22	− 1.50	+ 1.28
(b) Commodity/area pattern of supplies	+ 0.60	+ 0.17	+ 0.80	+ 0.17
Total[c]	− 1.44	− 3.05	− 0.70	+ 1.45
SMALL INDUSTRIAL COUNTRIES[e]				
Change in import-content of supplies attributable to				
(a) Import-content within commodity groups	..	− 5.44	− 1.42	+ 2.69
(b) Commodity/area pattern of supplies	..	− 0.86	+ 1.39	+ 0.32
Total[c]	..	− 6.30	− 0.03	+ 3.01

Sources: Tables 7.15 and A.15-A.25.

[a]'Supplies' are defined as in Table 6.4; see Appendix E for further discussion. Gross values of production, free of duplication, were estimated in terms of 1955 prices for each of the five main commodity groups shown in Table 7.15. The method used follows that for total non-food manufactures (see Appendix E), but the margin of error is likely to be considerably greater for the separate commodity groups than for the total.

[b]Based on estimated value of 'imports', c.i.f., valued at 1955 prices.

[c]These changes in the import-content of supplies do not in all cases correspond precisely with those derived from Table 6.4. The discrepancy arises because the latter is based on a single total of supplies of non-food manufactures for each country, excluding all inter-firm sales or transfers, whereas the total by commodity groups includes the value of sales or transfers between groups.

[d]France, Germany (West Germany in 1950 and 1959), Italy and the United Kingdom.

[e]Belgium-Luxembourg, Canada, Netherlands, Norway and Sweden.

significantly lower import-content than have the other industrial countries; the other large industrial countries (except Japan); and the small industrial countries (except Switzerland).

Two relevant conclusions can be reached from these figures. First, changes in the pattern of supplies have had only a relatively small effect on the movement in the import-content of supplies of manufactures in the industrial countries, at least since 1913[1]. Second, there has been no systematic association between the changing pattern of supplies and the average import-content; in some periods, the effect of the changing pattern has been to increase the import-content, in other periods to decrease it. This variable effect arises because there is no necessary relationship between a country's import dependence in any one commodity and the rate at which supplies of that commodity are increasing. Thus, the net effect of the changing commodity pattern tends to reflect haphazard and offsetting movements in the different countries and commodity groups.

[1] A similar calculation made for the period 1899–1913, though subject to a considerably greater margin of error, also showed that changes in the pattern of supplies were a relatively unimportant influence on the movement in the average import-content.

CHAPTER 8

EFFECTS OF COMPETITION AND IMPORT-SUBSTITUTION ON EXPORTS FROM THE MAIN INDUSTRIAL COUNTRIES

1. SHARES OF WORLD EXPORTS OF MANUFACTURES

The outstanding change since 1899 in the shares of the world market for manufactures held by the main industrial countries has been the secular decline in Britain's share from one-third in the period prior to 1914 to little more than one-sixth by the end of the 1950's (Table 8.1). The principal gainer has been the United States (one-eighth to one-fifth of the world total). Both the United States and Britain have been losing ground since 1950 with the re-emergence of Germany and Japan as major exporting nations. The German share of the world total remained between one-fifth and one-quarter in the period up to 1937. By contrast, West Germany's share has risen rapidly since 1950 ; in the early part of the 1950's this reflected a recovery of German export industries from a period of post-war reconstruction, but since 1956—when the West German share equalled the 1937 share of the same territory—her share has continued to rise. By 1959, West Germany's share, at 19 per cent, was second only to the United States, and was well above the comparable pre-war proportion. Of the other main countries exporting manufactured goods, France suffered a severe relative decline in the inter-war period, but has shown some recovery in the late 1950's, while the shares of both Canada and Japan have shown strong upward trends[1].

Another way of looking at the movement in relative shares is to compare the trend in the volume of exports from each country with that in the world total. The concept can conveniently be expressed in terms of indices of *relative* volume of exports, arrived at by dividing the country indices by that for the world total. The results of this calculation (Table 8.2) show a considerable diversity of experience among the different exporting countries. They nevertheless seem to fall into four broad groups (see Fig. 8.1). In the first group are Britain and France, both of which have experienced a substantial secular decline in the relative volume of their exports of manufactures. The decline for France has, however, been much less than for Britain, taking the period as a whole ; moreover, France's relative volume of exports has been rising since 1957, helped by the devaluation of the franc. The second group consists of countries (Belgium, India and Switzerland) whose relative volume indices show no marked upward or downward trend since the beginning of the century. The third and fourth groups consist of countries whose relative export volumes have shown a

---

[1]These various trends are essentially the same as those previously described by Tyszynski and others (see page 162).

Table 8.1. *Shares of the world market for manufactures, 1899–1959*

Percentage

Exporting country	Excluding Netherlands			Including Netherlands					
	1899	1913	1929	1929	1937	1950	1955	1957	1959
United States	11.7	13.0	21.0	20.4	19.2	26.6	24.1	25.3	21.0
Germany	22.4	26.6	21.0	20.5	21.8	..	..	..	..
West Germany	—	—	—	—	16.5[a]	7.0	15.3	17.2	18.9
United Kingdom	33.2	30.2	23.0	22.4	20.9	24.6	19.5	17.7	17.1
France	14.4	12.1	11.1	10.9	5.8	9.6	8.9	7.9	9.1
Japan	1.5	2.3	4.0	3.9	6.9	3.4	5.1	5.8	6.6
Belgium-Luxembourg	5.5	5.0	5.5	5.4	6.6	6.2	6.4	5.9	6.0
Canada	0.4	0.6	3.6	3.5	4.8	6.1	6.0	5.4	5.2
Netherlands	—	—	—	2.5	3.0	2.9	3.8	3.5	4.1
Italy	3.6	3.3	3.8	3.7	3.5	3.6	3.3	3.8	4.4
Switzerland	4.0	3.1	2.8	2.8	2.8	4.1	3.5	3.3	3.4
Sweden	0.9	1.4	1.8	1.7	2.6	2.8	2.7	2.8	3.0
India	2.4	2.4	2.4	2.3	2.1	3.1	1.4	1.4	1.2
TOTAL	100.0	100.0	100.0	100.0	100.0	100.0	100.0	100.0	100.0

Sources: Table A.5 and A.80.

[a]Approximate estimate. Exports from present area of West Germany in 1937 were taken as 71 per cent of total German exports in that year, and the residue was excluded from the total.

Table 8.2. *Relative volume indices[a] of exports of manufactures, 1899–1959*

Indices, 1929 = 100

Exporting country	1899	1913	1929	1937	1950	1955	1957	1959
United Kingdom	174	144	100	94	121	90	83	77
France	114	101	100	51	87	78	69	84
Germany	100	124	100	82	..	..	..	..
West Germany[b]	—	—	—	58	37	76	87	96
Other Western Europe	76	83	100	118	109	119	119	131
Belgium-Luxembourg	76	80	100	113	97	108	100	103
Italy	74	69	100	131	102	109	127	160
Netherlands	..	..	100	119	104	141	131	158
Sweden	36	69	100	166	181	158	172	171
Switzerland	112	120	100	89	101	109	110	109
Canada	14	19	100	149	153	154	141	139
United States	48	55	100	96	127	113	113	90
India	126	103	100	136	123	78	84	71
Japan	43	61	100	300	104	160	183	214
TOTAL	100	100	100	100	100	100	100	100

Sources: Table A.6 and A.80.

[a]Volume index of exports from specified country as percentage of total volume index for all countries listed.

[b]Based on exports from the whole of Germany in 1929.

Fig. 8.1.   Relative volume indices[a] of exports of manufactures from the main industrial countries and India, 1899–1959

Relative volume indices, 1929 = 100

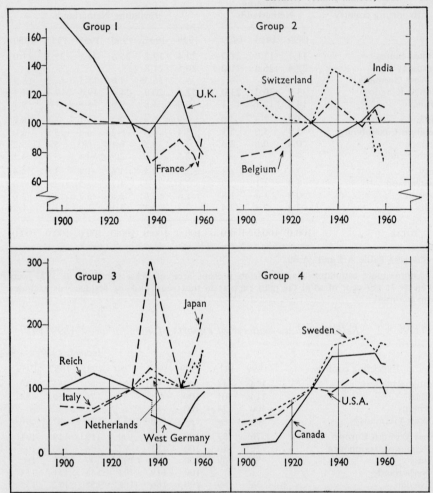

[a]Volume index of exports from each country, expressed as percentage of total volume index of world trade in manufactures.

distinct upward secular trend, but whereas the upward trend has been particularly marked since 1950 for the countries in the third group (Germany[1], Italy, Japan and the Netherlands), there has been a downward trend in this most recent period for those in group four (Sweden, Canada and the United States).

[1]Germany seems to be a special case since, as already mentioned, the export performance of West Germany since 1950 has been markedly different from that of the pre-war Reich. Thus Germany could equally well have been classified in group two.

2. SHARES BY COMMODITY GROUP AND MARKET

Commodity groups

The extent to which the main commodity groups contributed to the global trends in market shares is illustrated by Table 8.3 and Fig. 8.2. In the ' growth ' sector of machinery, transport equipment and chemicals, the United States showed the greatest expansion in market share from 1913 to 1929, though there was some relative decline thereafter in machinery and transport equipment, but not in chemicals (see Fig. 8.2). Britain's share fell dramatically in textiles and clothing, and modestly but, nonetheless, significantly in the miscellaneous group of manufactures ; her share of total exports of machinery, transport equipment and chemicals in 1959 was, however, marginally higher than it had been thirty years earlier.

Because of the change in area, West German exports are not strictly comparable with those of the Reich before the war. An approximate allowance for exports from the areas now incorporated into Eastern Europe can, however, be made on the basis of the German census of production for 1936 and the pre-war German transport statistics[1]. On this basis, the percentage shares of exports of the present area of West Germany in 1937 were approximately as follows for the main commodity groups (Reich percentages in brackets for the same year) : machinery, 21 (28) ; transport equipment, 13 (16) ; chemicals, 27 (32), textiles and clothing, 5 (11) ; all other manufactures, 18 (24). West Germany's share in 1959 was thus appreciably higher than the comparable 1937 figure for transport equipment and—at a lower level—for textiles and clothing, but was lower for chemicals.

Changes in the French share of exports have been relatively small in all the commodity groups. The main change has been a reduction in chemicals and in textiles and clothing since 1929. Two other important changes have been the expansion of Japanese exports in both the expanding and contracting commodity groups, and the notable progress of the smaller countries of Western Europe, both in machinery, transport equipment and chemicals and in miscellaneous manufactures[2].

The changing pattern of world production and trade in manufactures has been reflected in drastic shifts in the commodity pattern of exports from the main industrial countries, as can be seen from the lower part of Table 8.3. In 1913, a far higher proportion of the manufactured exports of the United States (over 40 per cent) and of Germany (about 35 per cent) than of the other industrial countries consisted of the ' expanding ' commodity groups. This reflected to a large extent the more dynamic character of the economies of these two countries,

[1]The relevant material is assembled and discussed in *Economic Bulletin for Europe*, Vol. 1, No. 3, 3rd Quarter, 1949, United Nations, Geneva, January 1950.

[2]Changes in market shares within each commodity group are discussed in some detail in Chapters 9 to 14.

Table 8.3. *Shares of world market by major commodity group, 1913–59*

Percentage

Commodity group		United Kingdom	France	Germany[a]	Other Western Europe[b]	Canada	United States	Japan	Total[c]	Total[c]
										($ *billion*)
Machinery, transport	1913	26.8	9.9	32.9	10.7	1.1	18.1	0.5	100.0	*1.62*
equipment and	1929	18.7	8.0	22.3	12.1	2.6	35.3	0.9	100.0	*3.96*
chemicals	1955	21.9	6.8	18.7	15.5	3.2	31.9	2.0	100.0	*16.83*
	1959	19.7	7.5	22.1	17.0	2.7	27.0	4.0	100.0	*24.43*
Textiles and clothing	1913	42.9	14.9	14.6	14.2	0.1	3.0	4.3	100.0	*2.22*
	1929	33.0	15.2	11.8	18.5	0.2	5.5	9.5	100.0	*3.51*
	1955	20.9	11.6	7.7	23.3	0.4	11.7	15.1	100.0	*4.59*
	1959	15.3	11.3	8.4	26.6	0.5	10.6	18.9	100.0	*5.09*
Other manufactures	1913	21.6	11.2	32.6	12.8	0.9	18.3	1.9	100.0	*2.66*
	1929	17.7	10.2	25.5	17.6	6.7	19.0	2.3	100.0	*4.73*
	1955	15.8	10.8	13.6	23.9	11.7	18.4	5.5	100.0	*12.95*
	1959	13.9	10.7	17.5	25.0	10.5	15.1	6.7	100.0	*16.37*
Total manufactures	1913	30.2	12.1	26.6	12.8	0.6	13.0	2.3	100.0	*6.50*
	1929	22.4	10.9	20.5	16.1	3.5	20.4	3.9	100.0	*12.20*
	1955	19.5	8.9	15.3	19.7	6.0	24.1	5.1	100.0	*34.37*
	1959	17.1	9.1	18.9	20.9	5.2	21.0	6.6	100.0	*45.89*
Machinery, transport	1913	22.2	20.3	31.0	20.9	42.8	34.6	5.2	25.0	
equipment and	1929	27.1	23.7	35.3	24.5	24.4	56.1	7.3	32.5	
chemicals	1955	55.1	37.2	59.8	38.4	25.6	64.8	19.5	48.9	
	1959	61.3	44.2	62.1	43.1	27.4	68.6	32.2	53.2	
Textiles and clothing	1913	48.5	41.9	18.8	38.0	2.4	7.8	62.1	34.1	
	1929	42.3	40.0	16.5	33.2	1.4	7.7	70.0	28.7	
	1955	14.4	17.4	6.7	15.8	0.9	6.5	39.6	13.4	
	1959	9.9	13.8	4.9	14.1	1.0	5.6	31.8	11.2	
Other manufactures	1913	29.3	37.8	50.2	41.1	54.8	57.6	32.7	41.0	
	1929	30.6	36.3	48.2	42.3	74.2	36.2	22.7	38.8	
	1955	30.5	45.4	33.5	45.8	73.5	28.7	40.9	37.7	
	1959	28.8	42.0	33.0	42.8	71.6	25.8	36.0	35.6	
Total manufactures in each year		100.0	100.0	100.0	100.0	100.0	100.0	100.0	100.0	

Sources: Tables A.46 to A.68 and A.80.

[a]West Germany in 1955 and 1959.
[b]Belgium-Luxembourg, Italy, Netherlands (except in 1913), Sweden and Switzerland.
[c]Including exports from India.

Fig. 8.2.   Shares of total exports by major commodity group,
1913, 1929, 1955 and 1959

Total exports in each commodity group = 100

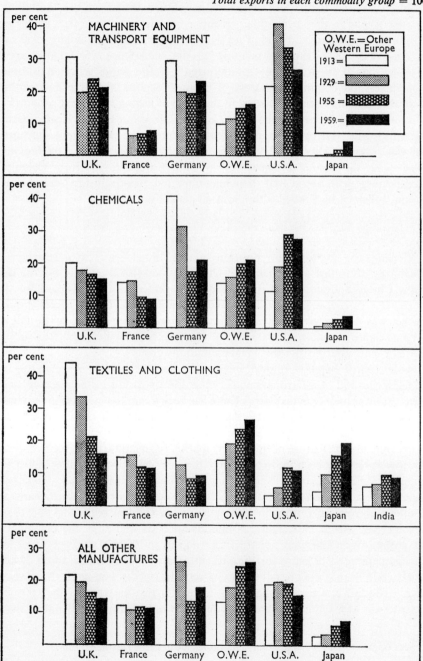

and their higher technical level. At the other extreme, Japan had only 5 per cent of her manufactured exports in the ' expanding ' groups in 1913.

Since that time, the pattern of exports has shifted away from the ' declining ' (textiles) group to the ' expanding ' groups in all the main industrial countries. Britain, in particular, had caught up with West Germany by the late 1950's in the relative size of the three ' expanding ' groups, while since 1955 Japan's export structure has been drastically ' modernized ', if this same criterion is used. Nonetheless, the commodity pattern of Japanese exports is still the least mature of all the large industrial countries, in the sense of having the lowest proportion of manufactured exports in the three ' expanding ' groups. The United States was still in the lead by 1959 (nearly 70 per cent in the ' expanding ' groups), but was followed very closely in this respect by Britain and West Germany. Then came the smaller countries of Western Europe (apart from Belgium-Luxembourg) with about half their manufactured exports in the ' expanding ' groups, followed by France with about 40 per cent.

The main markets

In *Canada*, the predominant position of the United States as a supplier of machinery, transport equipment and chemicals accounted entirely for the rise in the United States share of the Canadian market since 1913 (Table 8.4). In the reverse direction, the rise in Canada's share of the *United States* import market was almost wholly in newsprint and non-ferrous metals. The fall in Britain's share of that market since 1913 was mainly in textiles, while that in the German share affected all three main commodity groups.

In the *United Kingdom* import market, the rise in Canada's share was again in newsprint and non-ferrous metals, while the sharp fall in the French share since 1913 was mainly in textiles[1]. There has been a marked increase in the share of British imports of machinery, transport equipment and chemicals coming from the smaller European countries during the post-war period.

The outstanding feature of the import market for manufactures in *Continental Western Europe* has been the expansion of the share held by the smaller industrial countries : Belgium, Italy, Netherlands, Sweden and Switzerland. Together, these five countries accounted for one-fifth of total exports of manufactures to Continental Western Europe in 1929, but for one-third in both 1955 and 1959. This increase was in miscellaneous manufactures as well as in the machinery, etc. group. West Germany's share of this market in 1959 (29 per cent) exceeded the comparable 1929 share for the present area of that country (about 23 per cent), while France's share fell from one-sixth in 1929 to one-tenth thirty years later. The fall in France's share was mainly in textiles whereas the German increase was in machinery, transport equipment and chemicals. Britain's share

---

[1]See Chapter 13 for further discussion of the decline in French textile exports.

in both these years was the same (13 per cent), a fall in share in textiles being offset by a rise in machinery, etc.

Britain was the main supplier of manufactured goods to *Japan* before the first World War ; in 1913 over one-half of Japanese ' imports ' of manufactures were of British make. By 1929 the British component had fallen to one-quarter and by 1955 to one-tenth. This was in the main due to a loss of share by Britain in all three major commodity groups. There was a very substantial switch in the pattern of Japanese ' imports ' towards the machinery, etc. group (one-half the total in 1929, but three-quarters in 1959). The United States reaped almost the whole benefit from this switch, her expansion in this group accounting entirely for the increase in the U.S. share of Japanese ' imports ' of manufactures in the period since 1929. By 1955, the United States had just over one-half the Japanese market for imported manufactures, while Britain held one-tenth—just the reverse of the position in 1913. Between 1955 and 1959, there was a further slight gain in relative share by the United States, and a further slight loss by Britain.

Almost three-quarters of ' imports ' of manufactures into the three *Southern Dominions* in 1913 came from Britain, but by 1929 the proportion had fallen to three-fifths, partly as a result of the expansion in imports of machinery, etc. from the United States, and partly because of the relative contraction in imports of miscellaneous manufactures which came mainly from Britain. Britain's share in 1955 was the same as in 1929, a relative increase in the machinery etc. group being offset by relative declines elsewhere. Britain's share fell to one-half in textiles and miscellaneous manufactures.

There were several reasons for the decline in Britain's share of the Southern Dominions market since 1955. One reason was the erosion of tariff preferences in her favour ; another was the Trade Agreement between Australia and Japan in 1957, as a result of which Australian imports of Japanese textiles and other consumer goods rose sharply in 1959 and 1960. Further, discriminatory restrictions against imports of a range of dollar goods were in force in Australia and New Zealand in 1955, but were largely relaxed by 1959. However, the main gainers in these markets since 1955 have been West Germany and other Continental European countries, and the evidence indicates that their gains reflected their keen competitive position, together with some abandonment of individual preferences for British goods based on sentimental reasons[1].

Before the first World War, the *Indian* import market was very largely a British preserve. Britain supplied 85 per cent of India's imports of manufactures in 1899 and 80 per cent. in 1913. The greater part of the trade at that time was in cottons and other textile manufactures. The growth of factory production of cotton textiles in India in the 1920's was already adversely

[1]The evidence is discussed in some detail by R. S. Gilbert and R. L. Major, 'Britain's Falling Share of Sterling Area Imports', *National Institute Economic Review*, No. 14, March 1961.

Percentage

Table 8.4. *Shares of industrial, semi-industrial and non-industrial markets by major commodity group: 1913, 1929, 1955 and 1959*

Exports to	Exports from	Machinery, transport equipment and chemicals				Textiles and clothing				Other manufactures				Total manufactures			
		1913	1929	1955	1959	1913	1929	1955	1959	1913	1929	1955	1959	1913	1929	1955	1959
CANADA	United Kingdom	3.7	4.5	5.1	7.8	15.1	8.5	2.4	1.9	9.6	5.5	3.9	4.1	28.4	18.5	11.4	13.8
	United States	20.5	40.4	51.4	47.6	5.4	4.9	3.8	4.4	36.3	26.1	26.0	22.8	62.2	71.4	81.2	74.4
	Other countries	1.4	1.3	2.0	4.4	4.1	5.3	1.8	2.5	3.9	3.5	3.6	4.9	9.4	10.1	7.4	11.8
	Total	25.6	46.2	58.5	59.8	24.6	18.7	8.0	8.4	49.8	35.1	33.5	31.8	100.0	100.0	100.0	100.0
	Total in $ billion													*0.30*	*0.74*	*2.87*	*3.73*
UNITED STATES	United Kingdom	3.9	1.8	4.4	8.5	13.7	7.6	2.6	1.3	9.0	8.7	4.1	4.3	26.6	18.1	11.1	14.1
	France	2.0	1.2	1.1	3.6	8.5	5.1	1.0	0.5	3.3	4.4	2.4	2.8	13.8	10.7	4.5	6.9
	Germany[a]	10.9	5.9	4.5	8.3	7.6	4.1	0.4	0.5	12.1	9.4	5.6	6.1	30.6	19.4	10.5	14.9
	Other Western Europe[b]	1.7	2.0	3.8	5.5	5.6	4.9	2.6	2.1	3.1	8.4	12.2	11.9	10.4	15.3	18.6	19.5
	Canada	0.9	2.4	8.9	6.7	0.1	0.2	0.3	0.2	3.7	21.5	33.3	20.6	4.7	24.1	42.5	27.5
	Japan	0.2	0.5	0.7	2.5	2.3	1.7	4.3	4.3	2.0	1.8	5.6	8.4	4.5	4.0	10.6	15.2
	India	0.2	0.2	0	0.1	9.1	7.5	2.2	1.5	0.1	0.7	0	0.3	9.4	8.4	2.2	1.9
	Total	19.8	14.0	23.4	35.2	46.9	31.1	13.4	10.4	33.3	54.9	63.2	54.4	100.0	100.0	100.0	100.0
	Total in $ billion													*0.42*	*0.94*	*3.26*	*5.81*
UNITED KINGDOM	France	3.1	2.0	3.1	3.8	15.4	10.9	1.4	1.2	7.5	6.0	4.9	2.5	26.0	18.9	9.4	7.5
	Germany[a]	5.9	4.6	8.6	12.2	8.5	5.7	0.7	1.1	17.9	13.1	4.9	6.0	32.3	23.4	14.2	19.3
	Other Western Europe[b]	2.4	3.8	9.8	15.5	8.1	9.3	4.5	4.5	9.4	13.8	14.3	13.4	19.9	26.9	28.6	33.4
	Canada	0.2	1.0	2.0	3.0	0	0	0.1	0	0.5	3.1	16.8	13.2	0.7	4.1	18.9	16.2
	United States	5.5	9.3	10.8	9.7	0.6	1.2	0.1	0.3	10.5	10.3	10.6	6.8	16.6	20.8	21.5	16.8
	India	0.2	0.2	0.3	0.4	1.8	2.5	3.6	3.2	2.5	3.2	3.5	3.2	4.5	5.9	7.4	6.8
	Total	17.3	20.9	34.6	44.6	34.4	29.6	10.4	10.3	48.3	49.5	55.0	45.1	100.0	100.0	100.0	100.0
	Total in $ billion													*0.76*	*1.14*	*1.54*	*1.88*
CONTINENTAL WESTERN EUROPE[c]	United Kingdom	5.3	4.1	8.4	7.4	10.5	3.8	1.8	1.4	6.3	5.0	5.0	4.1	22.1	12.9	15.2	12.9
	France	3.7	4.1	2.9	4.0	4.2	5.6	1.7	1.5	6.6	6.6	5.4	5.2	14.5	16.3	10.0	10.7
	Germany[a]	9.3	10.8	15.1	17.1	5.2	5.0	1.8	1.6	16.4	14.2	8.8	9.8	30.9	30.0	25.7	28.5
	Other Western Europe[b]	4.4	5.7	11.9	13.7	6.3	5.9	5.9	5.6	7.5	10.2	15.9	15.5	18.2	21.8	33.7	34.8
	United States	3.0	7.0	8.2	7.3	0.1	0.3	0.5	0.5	9.6	6.1	4.6	2.9	12.7	13.4	13.3	10.7
	Other countries	0.3	0.3	0.7	0.7	0.8	4.2	0.3	0.5	0.5	1.1	1.1	1.2	1.6	5.6	2.1	2.4
	Total	26.0	32.0	47.2	50.2	27.1	24.8	12.0	11.1	46.9	43.2	40.8	38.7	100.0	100.0	100.0	100.0
	Total in $ billion													*1.66*	*2.70*	*8.24*	*11.74*

SOUTHERN DOMINIONS

United Kingdom	15.8	15.1	32.2	31.2	25.3	20.4	10.7	7.1	31.4	22.6	16.6	12.4	72.5	58.1	59.5	50.7
Germany[a]	1.2	1.5	3.4	7.8	0.5	1.1	0.8	0.9	3.6	2.7	1.9	2.1	5.3	5.3	6.1	10.8
United States	5.8	13.3	10.1	12.1	0.6	2.2	1.8	1.5	4.8	4.3	3.3	2.4	11.2	19.8	15.2	16.0
Japan	0.1	0.1	0.2	0.9	0.5	2.7	1.7	3.5	0.3	0.3	1.4	1.1	0.9	3.1	3.3	5.5
Other countries	2.3	3.9	4.9	7.2	4.8	5.0	5.2	3.7	3.0	4.8	5.8	6.1	10.1	13.7	15.9	17.0
Total	25.2	33.9	50.8	59.2	31.7	31.7	20.2	16.7	43.1	34.7	29.0	24.1	100.0	100.0	100.0	100.0
Total in $ billion													0.40	0.81	2.63	2.48

INDIA/PAKISTAN

United Kingdom	12.7	17.2	26.4	32.5	50.2	26.0	1.9	0.9	17.5	14.2	9.4	9.2	80.4	57.4	37.7	42.6
Germany[a]	1.9	2.9	12.2	17.2	2.2	0.8	0.5	0.7	4.4	4.2	3.0	3.1	8.5	7.9	15.7	21.0
United States	0.7	0.4	11.4	9.6	0.3	0.9	0.1	0.1	0.7	2.1	3.8	1.9	1.7	7.2	15.3	11.6
Japan	0.1	0.4	4.0	4.3	1.1	12.3	2.4	0.8	0.6	1.9	5.3	2.5	1.8	14.6	11.7	7.6
Other countries	0.8	2.3	8.9	9.4	3.6	4.6	3.3	0.7	3.2	6.0	7.4	7.0	7.6	12.9	19.6	17.1
Total	16.2	27.0	62.9	73.0	57.4	44.6	8.2	3.2	26.4	28.4	28.9	23.8	100.0	100.0	100.0	100.0
Total in $ billion													0.39	0.60	1.07	1.28

LATIN AMERICA

United Kingdom	7.9	6.3	3.5	5.4	13.2	8.9	0.4	0.1	10.2	6.5	1.6	2.2	31.3	21.7	5.5	7.7
Germany[a]	6.6	5.4	9.0	10.3	4.9	1.8	0.2	0.2	13.6	8.9	3.2	5.4	25.1	16.1	12.4	15.9
United States	7.2	23.9	37.1	40.3	1.1	3.2	1.3	1.1	7.0	10.7	11.6	8.9	15.3	37.8	50.0	50.4
Japan	—	0	1.2	1.4	0.1	0.4	0.4	0.1	0.1	0.1	3.8	1.7	0.1	0.5	5.4	3.2
Other countries	6.8	6.0	15.8	13.3	11.7	10.7	2.0	1.0	9.7	7.2	8.9	8.5	28.2	23.9	26.7	22.8
Total	28.5	41.6	66.6	70.7	31.0	25.0	4.3	2.5	40.5	33.4	29.1	26.8	100.0	100.0	100.0	100.0
Total in $ billion													0.56	1.12	2.38	2.75

REST OF WORLD[d] (mainly non-industrial countries)

United Kingdom	6.5	6.5	12.3	11.6	16.4	11.0	3.0	1.9	7.9	4.9	6.7	5.7	30.8	22.4	22.0	19.2
France	3.0	5.1	5.6	5.8	4.6	2.9	2.7	2.2	5.1	5.0	5.7	5.3	12.7	13.0	14.0	13.3
Germany[a]	9.8	7.4	8.4	11.2	4.6	1.1	1.0	1.0	13.1	11.6	4.6	5.7	27.5	20.1	14.0	18.0
Other Western Europe[b]	1.9	7.5	7.2	8.3	4.2	4.3	2.6	2.7	3.7	6.1	6.9	5.8	9.8	17.9	16.7	16.9
United States	3.4	9.0	14.1	12.8	1.9	1.8	2.7	1.7	4.2	6.4	5.7	5.0	9.5	17.2	22.5	19.5
Japan	0.2	0.1	1.9	4.5	4.0	4.1	3.7	3.6	1.6	1.6	2.4	2.5	5.8	6.2	8.0	10.6
India	0.1	0.1	0.1	0.1	3.5	1.9	1.8	1.3	0.2	0.1	0	0.1	3.8	2.1	1.8	1.5
Total[e]	25.0	36.7	50.1	54.9	39.2	27.1	17.5	14.5	35.8	36.2	32.4	30.6	100.0	100.0	100.0	100.0
Total in $ billion													1.54	3.58	11.31	14.51

Sources: National trade statistics.

[a] West Germany in 1955 and 1959.

[b] Belgium-Luxembourg, Italy, Netherlands (except in 1913), Sweden and Switzerland.

[c] Countries in [b] *plus* France, Germany and Norway.

[d] World *minus* industrial and semi-industrial countries and the U.S.S.R.

[e] Including Canada.

affecting the level of imports, and Britain was the main loser. There was a further sharp contraction in the 1930's, and by 1937 Britain's textile exports to India were only one-seventh of their 1913 volume[1]. Since Independence, India has emerged as a major exporter of cotton goods, her imports being negligible. On the other hand, Britain has made good some part of her loss of the textile market by increasing her share of India's imports of machinery, transport equipment and chemicals ; this group accounted for almost three-quarters of total ' imports ' of manufactures into the Indian sub-Continent in 1959 compared with only one-quarter in 1929. Japan's share of this market in 1959 was smaller than in 1955 and considerably less than in 1929 as a result of the contraction in the textile trade. Germany's share, on the contrary, is well above pre-war as a result of gains in the expanding machinery, etc. group.

For the semi-industrial countries of *Latin America*, the main changes since 1913 have been the increase in the United States' share and the decline in Britain's share. The United States' expansion has been almost entirely in machinery, etc., while Britain's decline here, as in India, has resulted mainly from the contraction in the textile trade, though she has also lost ground in the miscellaneous manufactures group as a result of United States competition. West Germany has gained in machinery but lost in the miscellaneous group, compared with pre-war, her share of the market in 1959 being the same as that held by the Reich in 1929.

In the *rest of the world*, consisting in the main of non-industrial markets, Britain's share fell slightly from 1955 to 1959 as a result of loss of share in all three major groups. There was an increase in West Germany's share of these markets in this period, mainly due to increasing exports of machinery, etc., but no change in the share held by the United States. Compared with 1929, however, the United States' share in 1959 was higher (increase in machinery, etc.), but Britain's share was lower (decline in textiles only partly offset by an increase in machinery, etc.). West Germany's share in 1959 was probably greater than the 1929 share held by the present area of that country.

Main elements in the movement of the volume of exports

The relative importance of these various changes in shares and in the commodity pattern of imports can more easily be seen from Table 8.5, which divides the changes in the value of exports of manufactures, measured at constant prices, into three parts, which can be attributed, respectively, to[2] :

[1] See Table A.76.

[2] The change from one year to another in exports from a single country can be written as

$$\Sigma s_1 v_1 - \Sigma s_0 v_0$$

where s represents that country's share of total exports of a particular commodity group to a given market, v the total value of exports of that commodity group to that market from all sources, the subscripts $_0$ and $_1$ representing the base and current periods, respectively, and

(a) the change in the size of the world market for manufactured goods as a whole (this measures how exports from each country would have moved if the area and commodity pattern of trade, and the share of individual markets, had remained unchanged) ;

(b) the change in the area and commodity pattern of trade (this measures how exports would have moved if the world total, and each country's share of each market, had remained unchanged) ; and

(c) the change in the share of each exporting country in imports of each commodity group into each market (this measures how exports would have moved if the world total, and the area and commodity pattern of trade, had remained unchanged).

Changes in shares due to variations in the area and commodity pattern of trade have in general been the least important element in the period since 1913. Comparing 1929 with 1913, for example, the area/commodity change was of importance only for the United States, and even here was of less importance than the expansion in world trade or the rise in the United States' share of individual markets. The lower level of British exports in 1929, than in 1913, was almost entirely due to loss of share, only partly offset by expanding world demand. Apart from the United States, significant gains in the share of individual markets from 1913 to 1929 were made by Canada and by the smaller industrial countries of Western Europe.

During the 1930's there was a sharp re-alignment of the competitive position of the main exporting countries, mainly as a result of differential currency depreciation. By 1937, Japan had achieved a major increase in her share of individual markets, compared with 1929, while Canada and the smaller European countries also increased their shares. The main losers in terms of ' competitive ' shares (as indicated by (c) in Table 8.5) were France[1], Britain and Germany.

Shares of world trade in 1950 were greatly distorted because of the delayed post-war recovery of Germany and Japan. Comparing 1955 with 1937, the main changes in the ' competitive ' share were increases for France and the

aggregation being made over the various commodity/market groups. This change can be divided into the three elements shown in Table 8.5 in various ways; the one used here is —

$$\Sigma s_1 v_1 - \Sigma s_0 v_0 = \left\{ \Sigma s_0 v_0 \left(\frac{\Sigma v_1}{\Sigma v_0} - 1 \right) \right\} + \left\{ \Sigma s_0 v_1 - \Sigma s_0 v_0 \left(\frac{\Sigma v_1}{\Sigma v_0} \right) \right\} + \left\{ \Sigma s_1 v_1 - \Sigma s_0 v_1 \right\}$$

The first term on the right hand side measures the change attributable to the movement in total world trade; the second, that part attributable to the change in the area and commodity pattern of trade (using base weights); and the third, that part attributable to changes in the share of individual markets (using current weights).

[1]The high rate of loss in 'competitive' share shown in Table 8.5 for France between 1929 and 1937 is, however, somewhat inflated. In that period, France lost a considerable amount of export trade as a result of the development of rayon goods which ousted the traditional French silk trade in many European markets. Since this switch occurred within a single commodity group, it is counted here as a loss of share, and not as due to a change in the commodity pattern of trade.

Table 8.5. *Changes in the volume of exports of manufactures attributable to changes in the size of the world market, in the pattern of world trade and in market shares, 1899–1959*

$ billion at constant prices

	United Kingdom	France	Germany	Other Western Europe	Canada	United States	India	Japan	Total
1899 exports	1.33	0.50	0.78	0.46	0.02	0.42	0.11	0.06	3.68
Change to 1913 attributable to:				*(Values at 1913 prices)*					
(a) Size of world market	+1.02	+0.39	+0.60	+0.35	+0.01	+0.32	+0.08	+0.04	+2.82
(b) Area and commodity pattern of trade	−0.02	−0.07	+0.02	−0.05	0	+0.17	−0.03	−0.01	—
(c) Share of individual markets	−0.36	−0.03	+0.33	+0.07	+0.01	−0.07	−0.01	+0.06	—
Total	+0.63	+0.29	+0.95	+0.37	+0.02	+0.43	+0.04	+0.09	+2.82
1913 exports	1.96	0.79	1.73	0.83	0.04	0.85	0.15	0.15	6.50
Change to 1929 attributable to:									
(a) Size of world market	+0.74	+0.30	+0.65	+0.31	+0.02	+0.32	+0.06	+0.06	+2.44
(b) Area and commodity pattern of trade	−0.01	−0.03	−0.09	−0.08	+0.02	+0.26	−0.04	−0.02	—
(c) Share of individual markets	−0.86	−0.01	−0.43	+0.26	+0.24	+0.65	+0.03	+0.14	—
Total	−0.14	+0.25	+0.12	+0.49	+0.27	+1.22	+0.05	+0.18	+2.44
1929 exports	1.82	1.04	1.85	1.32	0.31	2.07	0.20	0.33	8.94
				(Values at 1955 prices)					
1929 exports	5.18	2.76	4.76	3.95	0.93	5.09	0.42	0.76	23.84
Change to 1937 attributable to:									
(a) Size of world market	−0.86	−0.46	−0.79	−0.65	−0.15	−0.84	−0.07	−0.13	−3.94
(b) Area and commodity pattern of trade	+0.21	−0.08	−0.10	−0.05	0	−0.04	+0.02	+0.06	—
(c) Share of individual markets	−0.50	−1.07	−0.63	+0.62	+0.38	−0.13	+0.10	+1.20	—
Total	−1.14	−1.61	−1.52	−0.08	+0.23	−1.02	+0.05	+1.13	−3.94

1937 exports	4.03	1.15	3.24	3.87	1.16	4.08	0.48	1.89	19.90
Change to 1950 attributable to:									
(a) Size of world market	+1.00	+0.29	+0.80	+0.96	+0.29	+1.00	+0.12	+0.47	+4.92
(b) Area and commodity pattern of trade	−0.09	−0.08	+0.16	−0.26	0	+0.91	−0.20	−0.43	—
(c) Share of individual markets	+1.58	+1.11	−2.39	−0.12	+0.04	+0.74	+0.15	−1.12	—
Total	+2.49	+1.32	−1.43	+0.58	+0.32	+2.65	+0.06	−1.07	+4.92
1950 exports	6.52	2.47	1.81	4.45	1.48	6.73	0.54	0.82	24.82
Change to 1955 attributable to:									
(a) Size of world market	+2.51	+0.95	+0.70	+1.71	+0.57	+2.59	+0.20	+0.31	+9.55
(b) Area and commodity pattern of trade	−0.42	−0.05	+0.18	+0.14	+0.12	+0.28	−0.10	−0.14	—
(c) Share of individual markets	−1.93	−0.29	+2.56	+0.47	−0.10	−1.30	−0.17	+0.76	—
Total	+0.17	+0.61	+3.44	+2.32	+0.59	+1.57	−0.07	+0.93	+9.55
1955 exports	6.69	3.08	5.25	6.77	2.07	8.30	0.47	1.75	34.37
Change to 1959 attributable to:									
(a) Size of world market	+1.76	+0.81	+1.38	+1.78	+0.54	+2.18	+0.11	+0.46	+9.03
(b) Area and commodity pattern of trade	−0.33	+0.09	+0.43	+0.32	+0.39	−0.78	−0.05	−0.08	—
(c) Share of individual markets	−0.84	+0.22	+1.29	+0.51	−0.65	−1.35	+0.01	+0.82	—
Total	+0.59	+1.12	+3.10	+2.61	+0.28	+0.05	+0.07	+1.19	+9.03
1959 exports	7.28	4.20	8.35	9.38	2.35	8.35	0.54	2.94	43.40

Sources: Tables A.70–72 and A.75–77; and corresponding data for 1959.

smaller countries of Western Europe, and decreases for the United States, Britain and Japan. Germany benefited from the change in trading pattern, though the major beneficiary was the United States ; both Britain and Japan lost ground as a result of the slower growth in their main markets (in the Sterling Area, and in Asia, respectively) than in North America or Western Europe.

In the latter part of the 1950's, the major shift in trading pattern was the boom in the intra-trade of Western Europe, which particularly benefited West Germany and the smaller European countries. The United States lost ground as a result of the slow growth in the Canadian market, while Britain continued to lose as a result of balance of payments difficulties in several of her important Sterling markets. West Germany also made impressive gains in ' competitive ' share (this element accounted for 40 per cent of the increase in her global share from 1955 to 1959), as Japan did also. Both Britain and the United States continued to lose ground, relatively, in their ' competitive ' shares.

For Britain, the competitive loss of share has been continuous in each period since 1899—the only exception being the period 1937-50, spanning World War II. Immediately after the war, Britain gained much of the shares previously held by Germany and Japan : but this was all lost, and the downward trend in her share was resumed by the early 1950's. None of the other exporting countries has lost competitively so steadily or for so long. Japan is in the opposite position: she gained competitively in every period except 1937-50.

The economic factors affecting changes in market shares

These various trends in market shares reflect numerous influences at work both in the industrial exporting countries themselves, and in the main import markets for manufactured goods. First, there are those influences which express essentially the competitive element in the trends in market shares, particularly the movement in the range and quality of goods available for export, in relative costs and prices, in relative delivery delays, in credit terms, and in other less tangible factors—such as marketing or advertising techniques—which can be included in the concept of ' competitive power '.

Changes in the import markets themselves have also had their effect on the trend in shares of the world market for manufactures of the main supplying countries. These changes are of two types : changes in the relative trends of demand for imports of different kinds of manufactured goods by the different markets ; and institutional and other changes in particular markets which effectively discriminate against imports from certain supplying countries. Such changes in discrimination can result from changes in government policies (for example, in import licensing regulations) ; they can also result from changes in tastes or in buyers' preferences for goods from particular sources.

For many of these factors no quantitative measurement can be arrived at, either because they are intangibles, such as changes in tastes, or because the relevant data are not available. It is possible, however, to bring together statistical information on some factors, such as relative costs and prices, and such information as is available is considered below. But it must be remembered that even if such data were accurate and fully comparable between countries — which they are not—they can at best be only a partial explanation of a complex and changing situation.

Moreover, even if one succeeded in ' explaining ' trends in market shares by trends in, say, relative costs and prices, the range and quality of goods available for export, and some of the other elements of ' competitive power ' mentioned above, this would take us little further forward unless we had some hypothesis about the causal forces affecting these competitive elements. The elaboration of such an hypothesis and its empirical testing fall, strictly speaking, outside the scope of the present study. But a tentative hypothesis which could be examined in a brief fashion would be that the long-term trend in competitive power depends on a country's rate of economic growth. But before this hypothesis can be discussed further, it is necessary to see to what extent those elements of competitive power which can reasonably well be measured do, in fact, contribute to explaining the movement in market shares. At this stage, it is useful to distinguish the price from the non-price factors.

3. THE INFLUENCE OF PRICE ON MARKET SHARES

Price is an essential element of the concept of competitive power, and it might therefore seem self-evident that changes in relative export prices will have a direct impact on market shares. But this is not necessarily how the international economy works. For one thing, we can measure only the prices of goods *actually* exported, whereas it would in this case be more meaningful to measure the prices of goods which are *available* for export, whether or not they are actually sold abroad. Again, it could be argued that, insofar as the world market is a fully competitive one, export prices of all countries must move together, apart possibly from short-run deviations.

A situation could therefore arise—assuming a fully competitive world market —when the cost structure of one exporting country was undergoing some inflationary pressure, so that the costs (and prices) of goods *available* for export were rising relatively to those of other countries. Now, since we are assuming perfect competition, this local inflation would not *per se* affect the world price. Instead, the exports of the inflating country would fall by eliminating all those exporters who were unable or unwilling to reduce their export prices (by cutting margins and other costs) to the world price level. In this case, then, an index of *actual* export prices for the inflating country would show no change and so would not help to explain the falling off in exports.

However, in the real world imperfect, rather than perfect, competition is the rule in the world market for manufactured goods. In this respect, manufactures are very different from primary commodities, such as coffee, jute, wool, oilseeds and many others, for which a single world market can be said to operate; here, the export prices of similar qualities of the same commodity will tend to be equal for all producing countries (after allowing for transport and other marketing costs). But for manufactured goods, export prices can, and do, diverge from one country to another. The divergence can be particularly sharp at a time of currency revaluations, but even in more ' normal ' periods significant changes in the relative export prices of competing industrial countries do occur.

There are, however, formidable statistical difficulties in the way of any attempt to measure the movement in relative expoit prices over any long period. First, it is not possible to construct genuine *price* indices based on quotations for closely specified qualities or varieties of the different commodities entering international trade ; such quotations either do not exist or, at best, cover only a relatively few commodities. Instead, indices must be based on *unit values* derived from the trade statistics for those headings for which both value and quantity data are published. The difficulty here is that many statistical headings cover several varieties or types of goods, so that changes in unit values may be due to changes in the proportion of the different varieties traded as well as to changes in prices. Moreover, it is never certain that changes in prices of goods for which no quantity data are available do, in fact, move in the same way as prices of those included in the unit value calculation. Where, however, the ' coverage ' is high (that is, a large proportion of the total trade can be included in the calculation), and/or the variance of the component unit value indices is small, the unit value index can generally be accepted as indicating the movement in average export prices within some reasonable margin of error[1].

A second difficulty is that changes in quality can never adequately be allowed for in indices based on a standard list of statistical headings[2]. Since there is probably a long-term tendency for the quality of manufactured goods to improve[3], there is likely to be a corresponding upward bias in the unit value indices. Moreover, this bias cannot be assumed to apply equally to all countries. The average quality of products made is likely to rise more rapidly in some countries than in others ; if the general hypothesis advanced earlier is right, then we might expect quality to be related to the general rate of economic growth in the exporting country. If so, the export price indices of the more

---

[1]For a statistical analysis of the effects of 'coverage' and of the variance of the component indices on the standard error of the final index, see A. Maizels, 'Trends in Production and Labour Productivity in Australian Manufacturing Industries': *Statistical Annex, Economic Record*, Vol. 33, No. 65, August 1957.   See also R. E. Lipsey, *Price and Quantity Trends in the Foreign Trade of the United States*, National Bureau of Economic Research, Princeton, 1962, Chapter 5.

[2]This can be overcome, to some extent, by an increasing elaboration of the statistical headings; but there are clearly practical limitations to this.

[3]Where fashion considerations become important, however, products may be made less durable than formerly and, in this sense, quality may deteriorate.

Table 8.6. *Unit values of exports of manufactures from the main industrial countries and from their competitors (in terms of $ U.S.), 1899–1959*

Indices, 1899 = 100[a]

Exporting country	1913	1929	1937	1950	1955	1959
France
1 Exports	112	143	137	238	295	293
2 Exports from competing countries[b]	115	162	141	251	296	312
1 as % of 2	97	88	97	95	100	94
Germany
1 Exports	108	147	(127)[c]	219	267	273
2 Exports from competing countries[b]	113	163	143	243	292	317
1 as % of 2	96	90	(89)[c]	90	92	86
United Kingdom
1 Exports	125	189	170	253	321	346
2 Exports from competing countries[b]	111	149	122	225	263	282
1 as % of 2	113	127	140	113	123	123
Other Western Europe
1 Exports	100	126	108	214	233	238
2 Exports from competing countries[b]	117	165	148	254	313	330
1 as % of 2	85	76	73	84	75	72
United States
1 Exports	112	134	126	221	269	309
2 Exports from competing countries[b]	109	134	134	217	260	275
1 as % of 2	103	97	94	102	103	112
Japan
1 Exports	111	160	91	230	264	272
2 Exports from competing countries[b]	122	187	150	285	325	337
1 as % of 2	91	86	61	81	82	81

Sources: Tables B.1–B.5 and related data.

[a]For each link of years, the indices were weighted by values in the later years, the resulting indices being 'chained' to 1899 as the comparison base. The indices for exports from 'competing countries' using the weights of a specified country were based on unit value indices for each main commodity group (own weights), weighted by the values of exports from the specified country in each commodity group in the later of each pair of years linked.

[b]Countries in the following list, other than the country specified in the table:—Belgium-Luxembourg, France, Germany (West Germany in 1950–59), Italy, Netherlands, Sweden, Switzerland, United Kingdom; Canada, United States; India and Japan.

[c]Very approximate; based on evidence that the Reichsmark used in export transactions was over-valued in 1937 by about 30 per cent. The evidence is not, however, conclusive and would also support a somewhat different assumption (*see* C. P. Kindleberger, *op. cit.,* pp. 115–122).

rapidly expanding countries will have an upward bias in relation to those growing less rapidly.

Third, there are difficulties caused by differences in the commodity-patterns of exports from the different countries. These differences operate at all levels, from the individual statistical ' item ' to the relative sizes of the major commodity groups. Even if we can measure satisfactorily the movement in export prices of, say, textile fabrics or engineering products for different countries, we are still faced with the difficulty of comparing different collections of items within these headings. Such difficulties are, in the last resort, insuperable and, if we are to proceed further, we must assume that the proportionate movement in export prices of all items within each of our commodity groups is the same. That this cannot be so in practice inevitably introduces a margin of error into any price comparison.

Differences in the relative importance of the main commodity groups in the exports of different countries are, however, likely to be of much greater importance in their effect on the export price indices than are the differences within each group. This is because prices of the products of different industries (textiles, chemicals and engineering goods, for example), tend to move more variously over a long period, than do prices of the products of the same industry (different types of cotton goods, or different types of machine tools, for example). This particular source of non-comparability can, however, be eliminated by the construction, for any given exporting country, of an index of ' competitors' prices '. Such an index is based on the movement in export prices of competing countries, by combining the indices for the different commodity groups by using the given country's pattern of exports as weights.

Indices of competitors' prices

Indices of this type have been constructed for each main industrial country, or country group, based on export unit value indices for seven main commodity groups (see Appendix B). To avoid the additional weighting complications which would arise if comparisons were made over very long periods, these indices were computed separately for each successive pair of years included in the trade network tables[1], and the resulting indices were then linked to 1899 as the comparison base (Table 8.6).

---

[1]For each successive pair of years, the index for a given country of competitors' export prices is, using current weights :—

$$P = \frac{\Sigma(p_1 q_1)}{\Sigma\left(\dfrac{P_0 Q_0}{P_1 Q_0} \cdot p_1 q_1\right)}$$

where small letters denote exports from the given country, and capitals exports from competing countries, the aggregations being made over the various commodity groups. The subscripts $_0$ and $_1$ represent the base and current periods, respectively. Thus, the index of relative export prices, current weighted, for a given country can be expressed as:—

$$\frac{Px}{P} = \frac{\Sigma\left(\dfrac{P_0 Q_0}{P_1 Q_0} \cdot p_1 q_1\right)}{\Sigma(p_0 q_1)}$$

Several broad movements are apparent in relative export prices in the sixty-year period, as can be seen from Fig. 8.3. First, British relative export prices have risen considerably more than those of other industrial countries. The deterioration appears to have been both marked and continuous up to 1937 (though there was some improvement when sterling was devalued in 1938). Britain's export prices were becoming uncompetitive in the late 1940's, but the 1949 devaluation brought a sharp improvement. In the decade which followed, some of this improvement was eroded as a result mainly of the more rapid growth in productivity in competing countries (particularly West Germany, France, Italy and Japan), and of the devaluations of the French franc in 1958 and 1959.

Second, there has been an equally marked downward long-term trend in the relative export unit values of Japan and of the smaller European industrial countries. Even before 1929 Japanese export prices were becoming more competitive as Japanese manufacturing industry developed, and the sharp depreciation of the yen in the 1930's resulted in an extraordinarily large gain in competitive power (and was a major reason for the rise in British relative export prices in this period)[1]. Since 1950, Japan has been developing her export trade on a very different basis from that of the inter-war period. Textiles and clothing are now much less, and machinery and transport equipment and light electrical goods are much more, important than they were before the war in Japanese export trade[2]. Since the war Japan has undergone a large-scale cost inflation, and Japanese wage rates in the post-war period, though still much below Western levels, are considerably higher than they were pre-war. Nevertheless, Japanese export prices, relatively to those of her competitors, remained somewhat below the 1929 level during the 1950's.

Export unit values of the smaller European countries have also shown a strong downtrend relatively to those of other exporters of manufactures. In the period up to 1929, this was due, to a substantial degree, to the slow rise in Italian textile prices, while in the late 1930's these failed to recover to the same extent as world textile prices generally[3]. Italy was also partly responsible for the rise in relative export prices in this group of countries between 1937 and 1950. From 1950 to 1955 there was only a slight rise in Italian, and a fall in Swiss, export prices and together these accounted for a further decline in relative export prices of the smaller European industrial countries. The decline continued from 1955 to 1959; Belgian, Dutch and Swiss export prices

[1]By 1934, the yen had been devalued to 36 per cent of its 1929 gold parity, compared with a devaluation to 60–62 per cent of parity for Britain and the United States.

[2]Export of textiles and clothing fell from 59 per cent of total Japanese exports of manufactures in 1937 to 40 and 38 per cent, respectively, in 1955 and 1957; at the same time, the proportion represented by machinery and transport equipment rose from 9 to 14 and 25 per cent (see Table A.68). Japanese exports of radios and other durable consumer goods are discussed in Chapter 12.

[3]See Tables B.2 and B.3.

Fig. 8.3.   Relative unit values[a] of exports from the main industrial
countries, 1899–1959

Indices, 1899 = 100, in terms of U.S. dollars

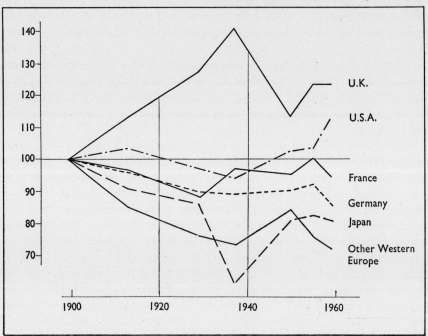

[a]Export unit value index for each country expressed as percentage of unit value index
of exports from competing countries (adjusted for differences in commodity patterns).

rose only marginally, while Italian fell by 5 per cent in this period.

France, Germany and the United States are in an intermediate group insofar
as there had been no very marked trend, in either direction, in their relative
export prices over the past half-century up to about 1955.   There was a fall in
United States relative prices between 1913 and 1937; this was essentially a
result of the great expansion in mass production of machinery and transport
equipment, which allowed exports to rise considerably with lower real unit
costs.   Since 1955, United States export prices have risen relatively to those of
other countries.   French export prices had become more competitive during
the 1920's, but in the 'thirties' the reverse movement dominated as a result of
the delayed devaluation of the franc[1].   For the greater part of the 1950's,
French relative export prices were rising, with adverse effects on the French
export trade.   After two devaluations—in 1957 and 1958—French relative
export prices in 1959 were some 10 per cent below the 1955 level.   German
export prices, in general, moved very closely with French up to 1929, but the

[1]The devaluation of the French franc was not begun until the autumn of 1936.

true movement in the later 1930's is uncertain because of the complex system of multiple currency arrangements and export subsidies practised by the German government. There was little change in West Germany's relative export prices from 1950 to 1955, but in the following four years they fell by much the same proportion as the French.

Taking the period as a whole, therefore, there have been several very large changes in relative export prices, as measured by the unit value indices in Table 8.6, and it seems reasonable to assume that these changes reflect, in part at least, actual changes in relative prices and that they do not result in the main from the purely statistical difficulties of comparison which were discussed earlier. Indeed, one of the previous arguments was that the export price index of more rapidly growing countries would tend to have an upward bias, whereas those of less rapidly growing countries would be biased downwards. If there is any justification for this argument it would reinforce the conclusion that the divergent index movements indicated in Fig. 8.3 relate to real price differences and not to a statistical illusion. If quality changes could be allowed for, the British relative price index would presumably have risen more steeply, and that for 'Other Western Europe' would have fallen more steeply, than they are shown to do in Fig. 8.3.

Indices of world trade

There is, therefore, some justification for seeing whether these changes in relative export prices can account for changes in each country's share of world trade in manufactures. The movement of *total* world trade in manufactures is not, however, a good indicator of the movement in world demand for the exports of a given country. This is because the industrial countries have developed special trading links (through 'spheres of influence', monetary blocs, political associations, etc.), with particular areas of the world; and also—though this is not so important—because they tend to some extent to specialise in different commodities. Thus, a change in import demand in Latin America will primarily affect the market for United States exports; equally a change in the Sterling Area will have its major impact on the United Kingdom's export trade. By the same token, a world recession—or boom—in textiles would influence the demand for Indian and Japanese exports by a far greater extent, proportionately, than exports from other countries.

The influence of changing area and commodity patterns on the exports of the main industrial countries has, however, already been separated out (see Table 8.5) and, using these results, an index of world 'import demand' can readily be calculated for each main industrial country. This index does not purport to measure demand schedules in the Marshallian sense, but simply to indicate how the volume of exports from each country would have changed had it been affected only by changes in (a) the total volume of world trade in manufactures and (b) the area and commodity pattern of trade[1]. Differences in the movement of the 'import demand' index and of actual exports of manufactures thus reflect changes in the exporting country's shares of individual markets, which is the nearest one can get statistically to the change in the underlying competitive position.

The resulting indices (see Table 8.7) show several major divergencies, which reflect different movements in the pattern of world demand for the exports of the different countries[2]. The outstanding one is the sharp—and lasting—shift in the area/commodity pattern of imports in favour of the United States. The 'import demand' index for that country in 1959 was 7.4 times that in 1899, compared with only 4.4 times for world trade in manufactures as a whole; compared with 1937, also, the pattern has shifted in favour of the United States. The main reason has been the great expansion in Canadian imports of manufactures, most of which come from the United States. The 'import demand' index for Japan, by contrast, has risen appreciably less than total world trade in manufactures over the whole period; since 1950, also, the pattern of world demand has moved adversely for Japan as a result of the sluggish growth in imports in South-East Asia, one of Japan's major export markets.

For Britain, with a wide country dispersion of exports, changes in world trading patterns have had, on balance, relatively little effect on the volume of overseas demand for the products which she exports, but West Germany has benefited considerably since 1950 from the relatively fast rate of growth in trade in Western Europe: from 1950 to 1959, her 'import demand' index doubled, whereas total world trade in manufactures rose by about 75 per cent. The smaller industrial countries of Western Europe also benefited from the asymmetrical pattern of trade growth in the 1950's (their 'import demand' index rising by 85 per cent from 1950 to 1959), though over the entire period since 1899 they suffered a net loss, relatively, from the change in the trading pattern. For France, the pattern of trade moved somewhat adversely in the inter-war period, but in the 1950's the change in trading pattern had no significant effect, on balance, on the demand for French exports.

---

[1] Using our previous notation, the index of ' import demand ' is:

$$D = \frac{\Sigma s_0 v_1}{\Sigma s_0 v_0}$$

the aggregations being made over the various commodity/market groups.

[2] Since changes due to the expansion of the world market are common to all the 'import demand' indices, they can differ only because of differences in the 'pattern of trade' component. Since the 'import demand' index is not a measure of demand as such, but merely a statistical device to isolate the effects of changes in the area and commodity pattern of trade on the volume of exports from particular countries, it must of course be recognised that changes in 'import demand' for a country's exports are not entirely independent of that country's competitive push. For example, the expansion of 'import demand' for Germany arising from the fast growth of intra-European trade must owe something to German ability and readiness to supply.

Table 8.7. *Volume of exports of manufactures in relation to 'import demand',[a]*
1899–1959

					Indices, 1899 = 100		
Exporting country		1913	1929	1937	1950	1955	1959
France							
1 Exports		156	206	86	185	230	314
2 Import demand		163	217	176	208	283	365
	1 as % of 2	96	95	49	89	81	86
Germany[b]							
1 Exports		221	236	161	90	260	414
2 Import demand		179	236	191	248	370	500
	1 as % of 2	123	100	84	36	70	83
United Kingdom							
1 Exports		148	137	107	173	177	193
2 Import demand		175	240	211	260	343	415
	1 as % of 2	85	57	51	67	52	46
Other Western Europe							
1 Exports		181	288	282	324	493	682
2 Import demand		166	212	174	205	291	381
	1 as % of 2	109	136	162	158	169	179
United States							
1 Exports		200	490	392	647	798	803
2 Import demand		216	363	301	442	632	739
	1 as % of 2	93	135	130	146	126	109
Japan							
1 Exports		251	541	1,348	582	1,243	2,100
2 Import demand		159	197	179	183	221	270
	1 as % of 2	158	275	752	318	563	778
TOTAL EXPORTS OF MANUFACTURES[c]		180	242	200	250	346	436

Sources: Tables A.6, A.80 and 8.5

[a]For definition of 'import demand', see text.
[b]West Germany in 1950–59.
[c]Including exports from Canada and India.

Regression analysis

If price changes are, in fact, an important element in the competitive position of the industrial countries in the world market for manufactures, then there should be an inverse association between the indices of relative export prices, as given in Table 8.6, and the share of each country in world exports of manufactures, after adjustment has been made for changes in the trading pattern. The association can be expressed in any of a number of different functional relationships, each of which would yield its own estimate of demand elasticity. Two alternative relationships were, in fact, used, as follows :

$$X = \alpha_0 D^{\alpha_1} \left(\frac{Px}{P}\right)^{\alpha_2} \qquad .. \qquad .. \qquad .. \qquad .. \qquad .. \quad (1)$$

$$\frac{X}{D} = \beta_0 \left(\frac{Px}{P}\right)^{\beta_1} e^{rt} \qquad .. \qquad .. \qquad .. \qquad .. \qquad .. \quad (2)$$

where X represents the volume index of exports of manufactures from a given country, D is its 'import demand' index, Px is its export unit value index and P the index of competitors' export unit values. In the first equation, α_2 represents a price-substitution elasticity of demand for exports, while α_1 indicates whether the country's share of world trade tends to rise ($\alpha_1 > 1$) or fall ($\alpha_1 < 1$) when the total volume of that trade increases[1]. The second equation implies that a country's share is not related to the movement in total world trade as such, but is affected by a long-term trend factor, which would include, *inter alia*, those elements of productivity competitiveness (such as range and variety of products) which are excluded from the unit value calculations.

It must, however, be recognized that the application of these equations to the data in Tables 8.6 and 8.7 involve some important qualifications, the first of which is that the new series presented here relate to only a limited number of years, spread over a long period of time. This is not necessarily a major disadvantage when estimating income-elasticities, for example, where the elasticity is not expected to vary greatly, but it is likely that the elasticity of demand for exports will change significantly with changes in the trading pattern and with the development of import-substitution in overseas markets.

A second limitation is that no explicit allowance is made for the influence of supply factors on the volume of goods available for export ; it may be that the ease or difficulty of selling in the home market, for example, would affect the willingness of manufacturers actively to seek new export orders, apart from any indirect influence through changes in export prices. Thirdly, it must perforce be assumed that the export volume in any of our selected years is related to relative prices and the volume of world trade in the same year. Since the new series used here are based on the detailed Trade Network tables, it was not possible to compute them on an annual basis, so that no allowance could be made for the time lags in responses to changes in prices and demand conditions which undoubtedly exist in the real world.

Finally, a purely statistical objection raised against this type of analysis is that it tends to result in biased estimates of the elasticities. The classic case

---

[1]This is seen if the equation is re-written as:
$$\frac{X}{D} = \alpha_0 D^{\alpha_1 - 1} \left(\frac{Px}{P}\right)^{\alpha_2}$$

here, as stated by G. H. Orcutt[1], rests on the fact that the historical data reflect changes in both demand and supply conditions, and a ' line of best fit ' to the data does not therefore represent a demand curve. The objection can be overcome by allowing explicitly for the simultaneous interaction of supply and demand. Where different time lags on the demand and supply sides can be demonstrated, or can reasonably be assumed, the Orcutt objection has less force.

Moreover, Orcutt's objection is less potent if we are considering, not changes in exports from a single country, but the *share* of those exports in total world trade, or the *relative volume* of exports from one country, compared with another. In the present analysis, the volume of exports from each country is related, in effect, to competing exports from other industrial countries considered *en bloc*, so that the elasticity concept is more nearly a price-substitution elasticity than a demand elasticity. Both equations set out above imply that changes in income in overseas markets affect each exporting area equally; and that changes in supply conditions occur independently and do not affect the price elasticity estimates.

Nonetheless, in view of these various limitations, the results of the present analysis should be regarded as tentative approximations based on one possible method of approach. The justification for the computations is that the new series in Tables 8.6 and 8.7 are much more appropriate to an analysis of the influence of price in international trade than have been any of the corresponding series available previously[2].

The statistical results obtained by applying equation (1) above gave generally better results than did equation (2), and Table 8.8 summarises the regression results obtained from the former. Though the goodness of fit, as indicated by the value of R^2, is generally high, only four of the co-efficients of Px/P are greater than their standard errors, and of these only two are more than double their standard errors. Nonetheless, all the Px/P co-efficients (excluding the

---

[1]G. H. Orcutt, 'Measurement of Price Elasticities in International Trade', *Review of Economics and Statistics*, Vol. 32, No. 2, May 1950. For a more optimistic view of the possibility of estimating elasticities in international trade from time-series, see S. J. Prais, 'Econometric Research in International Trade: A Review', *Kyklos*, Vol. 15, 1962, Fasc. 3.

[2]For example, T. C. Chang (*Cyclical Movements in the Balance of Payments*, Cambridge, 1951) computed an index of the export prices of Britain's competitors by taking a weighted average of export prices of France, Germany, Japan and the United States, with no allowance for differences in commodity patterns. H. Neisser and F. Modigliani (*National Incomes and International Trade*, Urbana, 1953) similarly did not adjust their export price series to allow for commodity patterns (*ibid.*, pp. 309–315). J. J. Polak (*An International Economic System*, London, 1954) is, perhaps, exceptional in using Schlote's index of British export prices as, in effect, an index of world prices of manufactures for the period 1920–29. This appears to explain why Polak found that Britain's relative export prices, compared with 'world prices' had no significant effect on British export volume. On this point, and on the general conceptual and statistical difficulties of constructing indices of competitors' prices, see S. F. Kaliski, 'Some Recent Estimates of 'the' Elasticity of Demand for British Exports', *Manchester School*, Vol. 29, No. 1, January 1961.

Table 8.8.   *Results of regressions[a] of export volume on 'import demand' (D)
and relative export unit values (Px/P)*

		Co-efficient of		R^2
		D	Px/P	
France		0.90 (± 0.31)	− 1.25 (± 2.90)	0.730
Germany/West Germany[b]	A	0.70 (± 0.17)	− 0.87 (± 0.92)	0.919
	B	0.81 (± 0.27)	0.27 (± 2.84)	0.895
United Kingdom		0.50 (± 0.03)	− 1.85 (± 0.11)	0.995
Other Western Europe[c]		1.28 (± 0.30)	− 1.49 (± 1.08)	0.960
United States		1.18 (± 0.10)	− 1.31 (± 0.10)	0.973
Japan		2.53 (± 0.38)	− 2.72 (± 0.77)	0.961

Sources: Tables 8.6 and 8.7.

[a]Based on data for 7 selected years, 1899–1959.

[b]Regression A is based on official exchange rate in 1937, while regression B assumes that rate to have been overvalued by 30 per cent; both exclude data for 1950.

[c]Belgium-Luxembourg, Italy, Netherlands (except in 1899 and 1913), Sweden and Switzerland.

results for Germany) are within a range which accords with *a priori* expectations.

The computation for Germany is complicated by the uncertainty surrounding the measurement of export prices during the 1930's. Two regression equations were therefore fitted to the German data, the first based on the official rate of exchange in 1937 and the second based on the tentative estimate given in Table 8.6, which assumes that the official exchange rate in that year was over-valued by about 30 per cent. The first regression yielded a negative price co-efficient, though with a high standard error, but the second—in principle, the more accurate—yielded a positive co-efficient to which no meaning can be attached. The implication of these results may be that changes in the non-price elements of the competitive position have generally been more important than relative price changes in the secular trend in German exports in the period covered.

Of the corresponding seven regressions based on equation (2), the co-efficient of Px/P again exceeded the standard error for the same four countries[1] ; in each case, the co-efficient was not significantly different from that derived from equation (1).

It is difficult to compare these results with other estimates of the elasticity of demand for exports of manufactured goods, partly because of differences in the concept of elasticity used, and partly because other estimates using time series have been based, as already mentioned, on defective unit value indices. An interesting calculation of the demand elasticity for exports has,

[1]The results for these four countries were:

	Co-efficient of		
	Px/P	t	R^2
United Kingdom	−1.40 (±0.36)	−0.003 (±0.001)	0.951
Other Western Europe ..	−0.78 (±0.43)	0.004 (±0.001)	0.961
United States	−1.42 (±1.03)	0.003 (±0.001)	0.557
Japan	−2.43 (±0.80)	0.010 (±0.002)	0.930

however, recently been put forward by Professor Harberger[1] ; using estimates of price-substitution elasticities prepared by MacDougall and Zelder[2]. Harberger's estimates are : France, -1.85 ; Germany, -1.30 ; United Kingdom, -1.45 ; United States, -1.90 ; and Japan, -1.47. In his later paper[3], Harberger concludes that the elasticity of demand for British exports is at least -1.35, and that for United States exports at least -1.64. Though these estimates are both within the margin of error of the corresponding co-efficients in Table 8.8, the concepts of elasticity on which they are based are not strictly comparable.

The regressions presented in Table 8.8 cover an unusually long time period for this type of calculation. For all the exporting countries, the commodity-pattern of trade has radically altered, as was seen in Chapter 7, and the co-efficient of Px/P is, perhaps, best considered as a mean of the elasticities for the different commodity groups. In view of the large changes that have taken place in the commodity pattern of exports, a high value for R^2 does not necessarily indicate that the elasticities for the main commodity groups are of similar orders of magnitude. Thus, the co-efficients in Table 8.8 are descriptive, rather than structural, parameters; they help to explain the past secular trends, but are not necessarily applicable to the future, in which a different commodity pattern is likely to emerge.

The co-efficient of D in Table 8.8 would be unity if a country's share of the world market did not vary with changes in the volume of world exports. This is very nearly the case both for France and the United States. For Britain, however, it appears that, on average, an increase in world trade in manufactures has, by itself, been associated with a fall in her share of the total. The regression results indicate that a 10 per cent rise in the volume of trade (as measured by the 'import demand' index) was associated with a 5 per cent fall in Britain's share of the total export market. But the reverse was also true; that is, Britain's share tended to rise by 5 per cent for every 10 per cent fall in the volume of world 'demand', after allowing for any changes in relative prices[4].

[1] A. C. Harberger, 'Some Evidence on the International Price Mechanism', *Journal of Political Economy*, Vol. 65, No. 6, December 1957; and *Review of Economics and Statistics*, Vol. 40, No. 1, Part 2, Supplement, February 1958.

[2] G. D. A. MacDougall, 'British and American Exports: A Study suggested by the Theory of Comparative Costs', *Economic Journal*, Vols. 61 and 62 (December 1951 and September 1952); R. E. Zelder, 'Estimates of Elasticities of Demand for Exports of the United Kingdom and the United States, 1921–1938', *Manchester School*, Vol. 26, No. 1, January 1958.

[3] *Review of Economics and Statistics*, February 1958.

[4] This appears to be consistent with the results of some previous studies. For example, Hinshaw and Metzler found a regression co-efficient of 0.78 when correlating British export volume with world real income for the period 1932–37 (R. Hinshaw and L. Metzler, 'World Prosperity and the British Balance of Payments', *Review of Economic Statistics*, Vol. 27, No. 4, November, 1945), while Polak derived a regression co-efficient of 0.75 for a regression of British export volume of manufactures on volume of world trade in manufactures for 1924–38 (J. J. Polak, *An International Economic System*, London, 1954). For the United States, the Polak co-efficient was 1.6 for exports of manufactures; for France it was .072, and for Japan (total exports) 1.1.

This implies that, in some sense, Britain's supply of manufactures available for export is less responsive to changes in overseas demand than are supplies from competing countries. This appears to have been the case in Sterling Area markets during the 1950's[1]. By contrast, Japan has a high co-efficient for D, over 2.5, which implies that Japanese exports represent marginal supplies in most import markets, so that they tend to fluctuate more than the total trade volume.

4. THE INFLUENCE OF NON-PRICE FACTORS

Though quantitative information about the various competitive factors other than price is extremely limited, there seems little doubt that, collectively, they play a major role in the changing competitive position of the main industrial countries. It is not possible to assess the relative magnitude of these non-price factors, but probably the most important are the relative delivery delays between acceptance of an order and its execution, the amount and conditions of credit offered to potential overseas buyers, and the energy with which manufacturers push their sales in overseas markets.

In the period since 1950, there have been persistent reports about the long delivery delays for British ships and other engineering products, relatively to those of competing countries, particularly Germany. The average time of ship construction in Britain in 1951 was 18 months, as against only 7 in West Germany and 6 in Japan ; in 1958, the figures were 20, 8 and 9 months, respectively[2]. In the early 1950's, the British engineering industry as a whole had a heavy order book, while the sharp increase in defence orders in 1951-2 seriously extended delivery periods quoted for export orders. At that time West Germany had a light order book and could quote fairly short delivery, dates. The difference in delivery dates was undoubtedly a major factor in stimulating expansion in German engineering exports in the following years. Another factor was the more rapid expansion in capacity in West Germany than in Britain, which allowed the German industry to keep its delivery quotations relatively short, while allowing output to increase at rapid rate[3]. British delivery quotations have been falling, on average, since 1956[4], though the fall

---

[1]See R. S. Gilbert and R. L. Major, 'Britain's Falling Share of Sterling Area Imports', *National Institute Economic Review*, No. 14, March 1961.

[2]G. F. Ray, 'British Imports of Manufactured Goods', in *National Institute Economic Review*, No. 8, March 1960. The average time of construction is the number of months it would take to complete the tonnage under construction at the beginning of a year, at the rate of completion during the year.

[3]The volume of production in West German investment goods industries rose by 85 per cent between 1954 and 1960, whereas the ratio of new orders to deliveries rose by 20 per cent, most of the increase in this ratio occurring in 1960.

[4]The volume of orders on hand in the British engineering and electrical goods industries at the end of 1960 was virtually the same as at the end of 1955, but production rose by nearly 20 per cent over this period. (See *Board of Trade Journal*, 1961, p. 1518).

has not been continuous, so that the gap between German and British delivery delays has narrowed appreciably in this period.

Statistical information about other non-price elements in exports sales is equally scarce. For the greater part of the 1950's, it seems that West Germany was offering longer credit facilities on exports of capital goods than most other countries, particularly Britain. Long-term credit facilities have proved an important selling point for many under-developed countries with limited foreign exchange resources. As a result of successive changes in credit arrangements in Britain—particularly as regards facilities offered by the Export Credit Guarantees Department—it seems probable that the competitive advantage held by West Germany in this respect had been very largely eliminated by 1960.

5. COMPETITION AND ECONOMIC GROWTH

It was suggested earlier that changes in the competitive positions of the different industrial countries may reflect changes in their rates of economic growth. However, since exports are an important part of total demand for final output in most industrial countries, a change in competitive power—which implies a change in shares of the world export market and thus a change in the volume of exports—will itself affect the rate of growth in industrial production. Thus, the development of exports tends to interact in a dynamic manner with the rate of growth in the whole economy.

Economic growth is normally associated both with an extension of the capital stock and with the introduction of new and improved techniques of production, and with new and improved products. This process can thus affect the competitive position in two ways. The first is by an increase in productivity in traditional lines of production, as a result of the introduction of new techniques. The second is by the development of quite new products, the emergence of which enables a wider range of goods to be offered for export.

The pervasiveness of this second aspect of competitiveness has hitherto not been adequately recognised. Conceptually, there are several distinct ways in which the development of a wider range of goods can affect the competitive position. First, a country hitherto specializing in a narrow range of products can extend its range into other, traditional, products. The expansion of the Japanese textile industry is an outstanding example here. Second, the quality of existing products can be improved (for example, by better design, or by use of better materials), and rapid economic growth is likely to afford more opportunities here than a relatively slow general expansion. Third, faster growth tends to be associated with the introduction of new products resulting from technological developments, some of which will displace the traditional products being offered for sale by countries growing more slowly. Indeed, by creating a new trend in demand, as the United States has done with cars, films, and consumer durables, and Japan more recently with transistor radios, the faster-growing country may significantly shift the pattern of world demand in its own favour. Such new technical developments can be made not only in the relatively expanding industries (for example, transistor radios, radar and electronic industrial equipment), but also in those which are relatively declining (for example, synthetic fibres and synthetic finishes for traditional fibres in the textile industry).

Elements of all three types of improvement in quality and range of output can be found in most countries and should, strictly speaking, be regarded as increases in productivity. However, it is not possible in practice to allow for most quality changes, or for changes in the variety of goods produced, in the statistical measurement of physical output in different countries.

Changes in productivity which are calculated from national indices of production and employment therefore relate very largely to the first aspect of productivity—changes in production per head, or per man-hour, in traditional activities. If, as is argued here, such changes are normally associated with productivity in the second sense—improved quality, variety and types of products—then indices of productivity based on statistics currently available will tend to understate the disparities between countries in their rates of productivity growth.

For this reason, the statistical indices must be interpreted with some caution, even apart from the differences in definitions between countries and over time.

Table 8.9. *Changes in productivity and wage cost in relation to the growth of total production in manufacturing industries,* 1953–60

Indices for 1960 (1953 = 100)

	Total employ- ment	Production per man-hour	Wages per hour[a]	Wages per unit of output[a]	Total production
Japan	154	174	148	85	280
West Germany	132	147	164	112	185
Italy	136	135	137	101	184
France	106	155	120[b]	78[b]	169
Netherlands	111	143	156	109	159
Belgium	104	132[c]	138	105	137
Sweden	104	129[c]	149	115	134
United Kingdom	109	118	140	115	133
Canada	97	124	130	105	118
United States	95	126	129	103	117

Sources: Monthly Bulletin of Statistics, United Nations, New York; *Statistical Bulletins,* O.E.E.C., Paris.

[a]In terms of U.S. dollars. The figures relate to average earnings, including bonuses and overtime pay, except for France, Netherlands, Belgium and the United Kingdom, for which the figures relate to average rates of wages.

[b]In terms of national currency, wages per hour in France rose by 68 per cent from 1953 to 1960, and wages per unit of output rose by 8 per cent.

[c]Production per man-year.

For recent years—when such definitional differences have not been major ones— there has been a definite positive association between productivity growth (as measured by production per man-hour in manufacturing) and the growth of manufacturing production, as can be seen from Table 8.9[1]. In the period 1953-60, Japan grew fastest, of the ten countries shown, both in total output and in productivity. West Germany, Italy, France and Holland all grew relatively fast, and their productivity rise also exceeded the average. In the Soviet Union (not included in Table 8.9) both total manufacturing output and productivity also rose considerably faster than the average. Canada and the United States, at the other extreme, grew relatively slowly, both in productivity and in total output. Britain's productivity index rose by less than one-fifth in this period, much less than that of any other country shown, though her total output rose by one-third[2].

The trend in manufacturing costs depends, of course, not only on real productivity changes, but also on changes in wage costs, materials costs and gross margins. Reliable and comprehensive data for a range of countries are not available for the two latter elements of cost. A recent survey of costs of production of American firms operating both at home and abroad revealed substantial variation between countries in materials costs and overhead costs per unit of output for the same year. However, for a small sample of firms for which data were collected for both 1956 (or 1957) and 1960, there was little change in the cost differentials over this period[3]. It would, however, be unwise to generalize from these results. Insofar as the industrial countries are generally dependent on imports for their supplies of a particular commodity, their materials costs are likely to change in similar proportion ; but there are many materials to which this would not apply. Equally, it cannot be assumed that gross margins will move proportionately in all countries, but statistical data are not available to press the argument further.

For wage costs, however, considerable statistical information is available. For the period 1953-60, the data indicate that, while increases in earnings do, of course, differ from country to country, the variation is not nearly so much as in productivity which, as already indicated, tends to vary with the rate of growth in total output. Thus, wage costs per unit of output also show considerable variation and tend to be negatively associated with productivity (see Table 8.9)[4]. Of the main industrial countries, Britain had the lowest rate of productivity increase from 1953 to 1960 and one of the highest increases in wage costs

[1] The co-efficient of correlation between these two series is $r = 0.90$.
[2] The comparison should, strictly speaking, be made in terms of output per unit of input of *all* factors of production. Unfortunately, comparable international statistics are not available on this basis.
[3] T. R. Gates and F. Linden, *Costs and Competition: American Experience Abroad*, National Industrial Conference Board, New York, 1961.
[4] The correlation co-efficient in this case is $r = -0.64$, if the wage series is measured in national currencies.

Table 8.10.   *Shares of production and exports of manufactures, 1899–1959*

	Series[b]	1899	1913	1929	1937	1950	1955	1957	1959
								Percentage[a]	
France	P	11.6	12.3	10.2	8.2	5.9	6.0	6.8	7.1
	E	13.6	12.0	11.5	5.8	9.9	8.9	8.0	9.7
Germany[c]	P	15.1	18.1	13.2	15.3	6.5	9.5	10.0	10.6
	E	20.4	25.6	20.0	16.3	7.3	15.3	17.4	19.2
United Kingdom	P	20.8	15.8	12.1	14.7	13.1	12.0	11.3	11.2
	E	38.3	31.8	21.7	20.3	26.3	19.5	18.0	16.8
Other Western Europe	P[d]	8.8[e]	8.9[e]	8.7	9.1	8.1	8.6	9.0	9.1
	E	13.0[e]	13.9[e]	16.6	19.4	17.9	19.7	19.7	21.6
Canada	P	1.9	3.0	2.9	2.7	3.7	3.3	3.2	3.1
	E	0.5	0.9	3.9	5.8	6.0	6.0	5.5	5.4
United States	P	40.6	40.9	51.1	47.0	61.5	58.5	56.8	55.4
	E	10.5	12.0	21.3	20.5	27.1	24.1	24.1	19.3
Japan	P	1.2	1.0	1.8	3.0	1.2	2.1	2.9	3.5
	E	1.4	2.0	3.2	9.5	3.3	5.1	5.8	6.8
TOTAL	P[d]	100[e]	100[e]	100	100	100	100	100	100
	E[f]	100[e]	100[e]	100	100	100	100	100	100

Sources: Tables A.46 to A.69 and working sheet for Table 8.11.
[a]Based on U.S. dollar values at 1955 prices.
[b]P = net value of manufacturing production, excluding food, beverages and tobacco.
   E = value of exports of manufactures.
[c]West Germany in 1950–59.
[d]Excluding Switzerland.
[e]Excluding Netherlands.
[f]Including India.

per unit of output; Japan, at the other extreme, had the sharpest rise in productivity, combined with a fall in wage costs per unit of output.   Changes in unit wage costs are, of course, a major factor in changes in export prices discussed earlier.

Though no systematic information is available about the range and quality of production, it seems likely that the rate of improvement in these is higher in countries with relatively fast growth rates.   It is now generally accepted that the quality of Japanese goods exported since the early 1950's has been well up to ' Western ' standards, though this was not the case before the war.   The very fast rate of economic growth in Japan in the past decade has been closely bound up with a high rate of investment, technical innovation and improvement in skills.   Moreover, the range of products in which Japan offers serious competition in world markets has widened appreciably[1].   West Germany is another case of

[1]Particularly great advances have been made in exports of some durable consumer goods (transistor radios, sewing machines, etc.), plywood, ships and certain types of electrical machinery.

Fig. 8.4. Shares of world production and exports of manufactures, 1899–1959

Percentage of total values of production or
exports of industrial countries, at 1955 prices

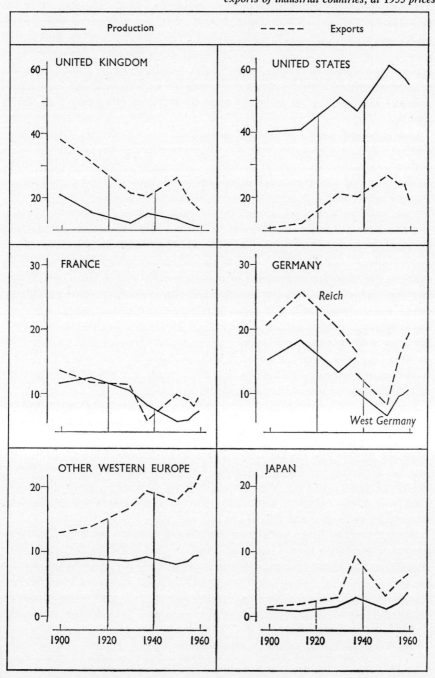

rapid growth, which has been associated with technical advance over a wide front.

The relationship cannot, however, be a rigid one. In all countries, there will be industries (or, rather, individual plants) where innovations are being introduced, and where quality is being improved. Even Britain, with its slow rate of growth, is famous for many new technical developments. Nevertheless, a general environment of persistent slow growth is unlikely to stimulate innovation, or to be associated with improvements in quality, or with widening the range of products available, to the same extent as an economy enjoying a fast rate of growth.

Insofar as differences in rates of growth are associated with differences in productivity and unit costs, and with differences in the range and quality of output, one would also expect to find a relationship between changes in the relative share of world manufacturing production held by a given country and changes in its relative share of the world market for manufactured goods.

There has, in fact, been a remarkably close relationship over the past 60 years in the movements of shares of production and exports of manufactures for each of the main industrial countries (see Table 8.10 and Fig. 8.4). There are, of course, some years in which the relationship was abnormal as, for example, the high Japanese share of exports in 1937 (when the Yen exchange rate was abnormally low), the low German shares in 1937 (when an autarkic policy was being pursued), and again in 1950 (when West German recovery was just beginning), and the consequentially high British and United States shares in the latter year. From this point of view, it appears that the much sharper rise in West Germany's share of world exports of manufactures since 1950 than in world manufacturing production is, to a large extent, a reversion to the position of Germany in the world economy before the 1930's.

For Britain, on the other hand, there has been a secular change in the relationship between the two share percentages. Whereas at the beginning of the century, Britain's share of world exports was almost double her share of world manufacturing production, by 1959 the ratio was little more than $1\frac{1}{2}$ to 1. The opposite tendency has been in evidence for the smaller industrial countries of Western Europe ; in 1913, their combined share of world exports of manufactures was about $1\frac{1}{2}$ times their share of world manufacturing production[1], whereas by 1959 the ratio was 2.3 to 1.

While there may be an underlying relationship between the rate of economic growth, competitive power and the share of the world market, the causal connection—as already mentioned—may also work in the other direction. For countries exporting a substantial proportion of their output of manufactures, a high (or low) rate of growth in exports will in itself tend to accelerate (or retard) the general rate of growth of the economy. For Britain, the relative

[1]The percentage for production excludes Switzerland.

share of exports in production fell off sharply in the 1930's, from nearly two-fifths in 1929 to one-fifth in 1937, and has remained at about one-fifth in the post-war period (see Table 8.11). The relative stagnation of British exports in the inter-war period had a major retarding effect on the growth of the British economy. At the same time, the retardation in growth itself reacted adversely on Britain's relative competitive position.

In West Germany, the proportion of production exported has risen in the past decade : from one-eighth in 1950 to one-fifth in 1955 and one-quarter in 1959. The ' leading ' role of exports stimulated growth in other sectors, and—if the general hypothesis advanced earlier is right—this in itself assisted in enhancing Germany's competitive position in this period. The same trends, though not so pronounced, can also be seen in the smaller countries of Western Europe.

The United States is exceptional among the industrial countries in exporting only a marginal proportion of production of manufactures ; in this case, it cannot be argued that the growth in exports has been a major determinant of

Table 8.11. *Proportion of production of manufactures^a exported, 1899–1959*

Percentage^b

	1899	1913	1929	1937	1950	1955	1957	1959
France	33	26	25	12	23	18	15	18
Germany	31	31	27	15	..	..	..	..
West Germany	—	—	—	17	13	19	23	23
United Kingdom	42	45	37	21	23	19	21	19
Other Western Europe^c	17	18	23	21	17	18	19	21
Canada	4	4	17	21	13	15	15	14
United States	5	5	6	5	5	4	5	4
Japan	25	40	29	40	29	26	24	23
TOTAL	19	18	15	12	10	10	11	11

Sources: Tables A.46 to A.69 and Table E.3. For this calculation, the f.o.b. values of exports have been reduced by 8 per cent to allow, approximately, for costs of transport, services, etc. from factory to port. Production of manufactures for this purpose has been valued on a gross basis, free of duplication, and excluding food, beverages and tobacco; for method of calculation, see Appendix E.

^{a}Excluding manufactured foods, beverages and tobacco.
^{b}Based on U.S. dollar values at 1955 prices. It should be noted that the exchange rates used for production differ from those used for exports (see Appendix F for details). In general, this has the effect of reducing the percentages of production exported for countries other than the United States. For example, the proportion of production of non-food manufactures exported by the United Kingdom in 1955 was 26 per cent in terms of sterling, compared with the 19 per cent shown here. The corresponding percentages in national currencies for other countries and years can be derived, if required, by multiplying the percentages given here by the ratio of the purchasing power parity rate to the official exchange rate in 1955.
^{c}Belgium-Luxembourg, Italy, Netherlands and Sweden.

economic growth generally. Yet the association between the relative share of production and the relative share of world trade in manufactures appears to be as strong for the United States as for other industrial countries. This tends to support the general hypothesis advanced that the rate of economic growth is a major factor determining changes in competitive power.

The connection between economic growth and competitive power can also work through changes in government policy. Countries which are growing at a relatively fast rate will also tend to have a relatively fast rate of growth in imports. Such countries will also need to expand their exports relatively rapidly to maintain balance of payments equilibrium. This export expansion may derive primarily from the causal process already mentioned, namely the increase in productivity (and the associated relative reduction in export prices of traditional products), and the development of new and better products. It may, however, derive primarily from changes in policy—currency devaluation being an extreme case—designed to improve the competitive position of the export trades. In either case, there would be a close connection between the relative growth rate of an industrial country and its share of world exports of manufactured goods.

6. THE RELATIVE IMPORTANCE OF COMPETITION AND IMPORT-SUBSTITUTION

Changes in the volume of exports of manufactures from any given country have, so far, been considered as due to three factors : changes in total world trade in manufactures, changes in the commodity and area pattern of trade, and changes in that country's share of a number of individual markets. However, a change in the volume of world trade in manufactures can itself be considered a resultant of the process of economic growth in the importing countries. More specifically, a given change in imports can be subdivided into one (positive) part attributable to the growth in consumption of manufactures and one (usually negative) part attributable to the substitution of home-produced goods for imports[1].

This process of import-substitution can have a greater adverse effect on the exports of one country than of another, if the exports of the first country are more highly concentrated on markets in which large import-substitutions are taking place. Moreover, insofar as the rate of economic growth of the exporting country is retarded by such import-substitution, this may—for reasons already discussed—adversely affect its relative competitive position in export markets generally.

The importance of import-substitution as an influence on the trend of exports of manufactures from the main industrial countries can be seen from Table 8.12, which relates to the period from 1913 to 1959. The change in the value of

[1]See pages 150–1.

exports from each country, at constant prices, to industrial and semi-industrial markets, is divided into three parts[1] :

(a) the change corresponding to the proportionate increase in the consumption of manufactures in each market (termed 'expansion in demand' in Table 8.12);

(b) the change corresponding to the proportionate reduction in the import-content of supplies of manufactures in each market (the effect of import-substitution); and

(c) the change corresponding to the change in the given country's share of total imports of manufactures into each market (the effect of ' competitive share' changes).

For exports to the rest of the world, consisting mainly of non-industrial countries, the distinction between (a) and (b) could not be made. Insofar as the expansion in exports since 1913 has been to countries in which industrialization has played a minor role in economic development, the import-substitution element would be correspondingly small.

Separate calculations have been made for the four main industrial countries— Britain, France, Germany and the United States—and for the group of smaller Western European countries taken together. Comparable calculations were not made for Canada, India and Japan because of the relatively narrow commodity range of their export trade[2].

[1]The change from one year to another in exports from a given country can be written as:
$$\Sigma e_1 S_1 - \Sigma e_0 S_0$$
where e represents that country's share of total supplies of manufactures available for consumption in a given export market, S the total supplies of manufactures in that export market, the subscripts $_0$ and $_1$ representing the base and current periods, respectively, the aggregations being made over a number of individual markets. This change can be divided into the following elements:

$$\Sigma e_1 S_1 - \Sigma e_0 S_0 = \left\{ \Sigma e_0(S_1 - S_0) \right\} + \left\{ \Sigma e_0 S_1\left(\frac{m_1}{m_0} - 1\right) \right\} + \left\{ \Sigma S_1\left(e_1 - e_0 \cdot \frac{m_1}{m_0}\right) \right\}$$

where m = the import-content of supplies of manufactures in each market.

The first term on the right-hand side measures the change attributable to the movement in total supplies of manufactures in each market; the second, that attributable to import-substitution (using base weights); and the third, that attributable to changes in competitive shares of imports into each market (using current weights).

The first term could be further sub-divided, as follows :

$$\Sigma e_0(S_1 - S_0) = \left\{ \Sigma e_0 S_0\left(\frac{\Sigma S_1}{\Sigma S_0}\right) - \Sigma e_0 S_0 \right\} + \left\{ \Sigma e_0 S_1 - \Sigma e_0 S_0\left(\frac{\Sigma S_1}{\Sigma S_0}\right) \right\}$$

where the first term on the right-hand side measures the change attributable to the movement in aggregate consumption (or, more strictly, supplies) of all markets considered, while the second indicates the effect of changes in the market pattern of consumption. This further sub-division has not, however, been computed since the primary object of the calculation was to isolate the import-substitution effect.

[2]The calculation of the effect of import-substitution on the exports of a single supplying country should, strictly speaking, be based on an analysis of consumption and trade by commodity group. As, however, comprehensive data for consumption by commodity group were not available, the calculation was based on the movement in supplies and 'imports' of total manufactures in each industrial and semi-industrial country. The method

The burden of import-substitution has fallen very unequally on the different industrial countries. The main burden of import-substitution in the industrial countries themselves since 1913 fell on France and Germany; Britain's loss was a relatively small one. A major factor was the contraction of the British market after the Import Duties Act of 1932, which had particularly severe repercussions on French and German exports of manufactures, while German autarkic policy in the later 1930's was also of importance in the general contraction of trade among Western European countries in this period. Britain's relatively small loss from import-substitution was, however, greatly added to by a substantial decline in her competitive share. On the other hand, Germany, which had the largest import-substitution loss here, managed to offset this very largely by an improvement in her competitive position (see Fig. 8.5).

Fig. 8.5. Effects of import-substitution and of changes in competitive shares on exports of manufactures from selected industrial countries, 1913–59

$ *billion, f.o.b. at* 1955 *prices*

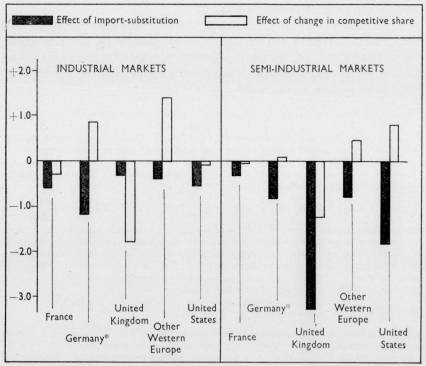

*West Germany in 1959.

thus assumes that the effect of a given import-substitution can be allocated among the supplying countries in proportion to their relative shares of the particular market for manufactured goods as a whole. The bias in the result is minimised for countries whose exports cover a wide commodity range, but it was felt that for Canada, India and Japan this method might produce misleading results.

Table 8.12. *Effect of expansion in demand, import-substitution and changes in competitive shares on exports of manufactures from selected industrial countries, 1913–59*

$ billion, f.o.b. at 1955 prices

| Exports from | Total in 1913 | Changes attributable to | | | | Total in 1959 |
		Expansion in demand	Import-substitution	Competitive share	Total	
FRANCE						
To: Industrial countries	1.37	+ 1.52	− 0.67	− 0.35	+ 0.50	1.87
Semi-industrial	0.24	+ 0.42	− 0.31	− 0.06	+ 0.06	0.30
Rest of world	0.50	+ 1.21		+ 0.33	+ 1.54	2.04
Total	2.11	+ 2.18		− 0.08	+ 2.10	4.21
GERMANY						
To: Industrial countries	2.35	+ 2.75	− 1.22	+ 0.80	+ 2.33	4.68
Semi-industrial	0.63	+ 1.35	− 0.90	+ 0.11	+ 0.56	1.19
Rest of world	1.46	+ 1.31		− 0.29	+ 1.02	2.48
Total	4.44	+ 3.29		+ 0.62	+ 3.91	8.35
UNITED KINGDOM						
To: Industrial countries	1.81	+ 3.05	− 0.37	− 1.82	+ 0.86	2.67
Semi-industrial	2.32	+ 4.28	− 3.34	− 1.31	− 0.36	1.96
Rest of world	1.46	+ 2.44		− 1.25	+ 1.19	2.65
Total	5.59	+ 6.07		− 4.38	+ 1.69	7.28
OTHER WESTERN EUROPE						
To: Industrial countries	1.48	+ 3.50	− 0.42	+ 1.35	+ 4.42	5.90
Semi-industrial	0.36	+ 1.12	− 0.88	+ 0.40	+ 0.63	0.99
Rest of world	0.62	+ 1.50		+ 0.36	+ 1.87	2.49
Total	2.46	+ 4.81		+ 2.11	+ 6.92	9.38
UNITED STATES						
To: Industrial countries	1.36	+ 3.47	− 0.66	− 0.09	+ 2.72	4.08
Semi-industrial	0.33	+ 2.58	− 1.86	+ 0.76	+ 1.49	1.82
Rest of world	0.43	+ 1.85		+ 0.17	+ 2.02	2.45
Total	2.12	+ 5.38		+ 0.85	+ 6.23	8.35

Sources: Tables A.8, A.10, A.12, A.15-A.38, and E.5 and corresponding data for 1959.

In the markets of the semi-industrial countries, on the other hand, Britain was easily the main loser from the process of import-substitution. Over the whole period since 1913, her loss in these markets substantially exceeded the aggregate loss of Continental Western Europe, and was about four-fifths greater than that suffered by the United States. In the period up to the last war, Britain's major loss from import-substitution was in India and Latin America; since then, her main loss has been in Australia, New Zealand and South Africa. The market pattern of import-substitution against British exports is discussed further below.

The United States—the second largest loser from import-substitution in the semi-industrial countries—suffered mainly in Latin America, though she also

Table 8.13.   *Effect of import-substitution and changes in competitive shares on exports of manufactures from selected industrial countries in four periods*, 1913–59

$ billion, f.o.b., at 1955 prices

Exports from	Effect of import-substitution			Effect of changes in competitive shares		
	Industrial markets	Semi-industrial markets	Total	Industrial markets	Semi-industrial markets	Total
FRANCE						
1913–29	− 0.25	− 0.10	− 0.35	+ 0.06	− 0.11	− 0.05
1929–37	− 0.81	− 0.06	− 0.87	− 0.56	− 0.08	− 0.64
1937–50	− 0.12	− 0.05	− 0.17	+ 0.18	+ 0.18	+ 0.36
1950–59	+ 0.51	− 0.10	+ 0.41	−·0.03	− 0.05	− 0.08
GERMANY						
1913–29	− 0.33	− 0.28	− 0.61	− 0.53	− 0.15	− 0.68
1929–37	− 0.92	− 0.21	− 1.13	− 0.50	+ 0.04	− 0.46
1937–50	− 0.33	− 0.27	− 0.60	− 0.83	− 0.58	− 1.41
1950–59	+ 0.35	− 0.14	+ 0.21	+ 2.66	+ 0.80	+ 3.46
UNITED KINGDOM						
1913–29	− 0.50	− 0.64	− 1.14	− 0.89	− 0.77	− 1.66
1929–37	− 0.60	− 0.83	− 1.43	− 0.03	− 0.21	− 0.24
1937–50	− 0.05	− 0.58	− 0.63	+ 0.18	+ 0.40	+ 0.58
1950–59	+ 0.79	− 1.29	− 0.50	− 1.07	− 0.73	− 1.80
OTHER WESTERN EUROPE						
1913–29	− 0.30	− 0.16	− 0.46	+ 0.45	+ 0.06	+ 0.51
1929–37	− 0.94	− 0.18	− 1.12	+ 0.43	+ 0.03	+ 0.46
1937–50	− 0.39	− 0.24	− 0.63	+ 0.09	+ 0.06	+ 0.15
1950–59	+ 1.12	− 0.30	+ 0.82	+ 0.38	+ 0.25	+ 0.63
UNITED STATES						
1913–29	− 0.11	− 0.07	− 0.18	+ 0.67	+ 0.82	+ 1.49
1929–37	− 1.07	− 0.43	− 1.50	+ 0.04	− 0.07	− 0.03
1937–50	− 0.39	− 0.42	− 0.81	+ 0.36	+ 0.37	+ 0.73
1950–59	+ 0.91	− 0.94	− 0.03	− 1.15	− 0.35	− 1.50

Sources: As for Table 8.12.

had a considerable loss in South Africa since the second World War as a result of secondary industry development in that country.

The influence of import-substitution in the semi-industrial markets has generally been greater than the net gain (or loss) suffered by any single industrial country, or group of countries, from increased (or reduced) competitiveness, as measured by the changing shares of total imports into these markets[1]. Britain suffered the greatest loss in market share over the period from 1913 to 1959, as well as the greatest loss resulting from import-substitution. The United States, by contrast, offset a good proportion of her import-substitution loss by a gain in competitive share—again, mainly in Latin America.

Import-substitution in the semi-industrial countries has been important in each of the four periods shown in Table 8.13. Though the greater part of the decline in British exports attributable to this factor since 1913 occurred in the period up to 1950, the *annual* rate of import-substitution during the 1950's appear to have been greater than before. For the United States and the smaller industrial countries of Western Europe, also, the annual rate of import-substitution has risen since 1950.

While import-substitution in the semi-industrial countries reflects the growth of domestic secondary industries, import substitution in the industrial areas has tended to be more a reflection of import restrictions. Thus, in the period since 1950, the faster rise in imports into the industrial countries than in their industrial output, reflecting the increased liberalization of trade, has resulted in a reversal of the import-substitution process: this is best considered in conjunction with the adverse movement in the period from 1929 to 1950, when trade was artificially restricted by government regulations. Curiously enough, comparing 1959 with 1929—both years when trade was relatively free from restrictions in the industrial markets—the United Kingdom was the only country shown which did not suffer in the intervening period from import-substitution in these markets. The main reason for this asymmetry was that in the period 1937-50 the United Kingdom had itself substituted domestic production for imported manufactures on a much larger scale than had other industrial countries. During the 1950's, Britain's import restrictions were progressively

---

[1]The effect on exports of changes in shares of individual markets as shown in Table 8.12 is not quite the same as that shown in Table 8.5. The latter is based on an analysis by commodity group as well as by broad groups of markets, whereas the results in Table 8.12 relate to shares of total manufactures—with no commodity subdivision—into each market for which separate figures were available. The use of commodity detail in one case, but not in the other, inevitably produces a difference in the result, though the broad picture is substantially the same. If the calculation for Table 8.5 had been based on totals for individual markets, rather than on commodity groups by broad market areas, the result would, in principle, be identical with that shown in Table 8.12, since in that case sv (in the notation used in the footnote on pages 198–9) would be equivalent to eS, and

$$\Sigma s_1 v_1 - \Sigma s_0 v_1 = \Sigma s_1 \left(e_1 - e_0 \cdot \frac{m_1}{m_0} \right)$$

relaxed, but the gain to other industrial countries did not offset the import-substitution loss of the previous period.

The market pattern of import-substitution

Since Britain was the principal loser from import-substitution, it is of interest to compare the relative contribution made to the loss by import-substitution in each main market. This is done in Table 8.14, which also shows the corresponding changes in British exports of manufactures attributable to Britain's changing share of each market. In the semi-industrial countries, the most important single post-war factor affecting import-substitution against British exports has been the industrial expansion of Australia; this alone accounted for about half the total import-substitution effect on British exports to the semi-industrial countries in the 1950's. Before the second World War, however, the development of the Indian textile industry—with the consequent sharp contraction of a main market for United Kingdom cotton textiles— had been the major influence. In the period since 1950, the effect of loss of competitive share on United Kingdom exports to the Southern Dominion added

Table 8.14. *Effect of import-substitution and changes in competitive shares on United Kingdom exports of manufactures: relative importance of major markets in four periods, 1913–59*

Percentage

	1913–29		1929–37		1937–50		1950–59	
	A	B	A	B	A	B	A	B
INDUSTRIAL MARKETS								
North America	17	40	24	−35	36	61	− 61	15
Western Europe	48	40	61	−50	33	−162	− 38	87
Japan	35	20	15	185	31	1	− 1	−2
Total	100	100	100	100	100	−100	−100	100
SEMI-INDUSTRIAL MARKETS								
Southern Dominions	16	34	35	24	58	− 88	69	62
India/Pakistan	39	30	47	64	9	− 28	16	17
Other semi-industrial countries	45	36	18	12	33	16	15	21
Total	100	100	100	100	100	−100	100	100

Sources: As for Table 8.12.

Note: A denotes effect of import-substitution, B the effect of changes in the United Kingdom's share of imports into each market. Negative figures indicate *increases* in United Kingdom exports attributable to import-substitution, or to changes in the United Kingdom share of the market, in the areas shown.

considerably to the loss due to import-substitution. In the industrial markets, Britain's main gain due to imports rising faster than home output was in North American markets, while her main loss in competitive shares was in Western Europe.

The relatively severe loss suffered by Britain in the semi-industrial markets may well have had an important indirect influence on her competitive position generally. In 1913, these markets accounted for about 40 per cent of British exports of manufactures, compared with only 10–15 per cent for the other main industrial countries. Moreover, the loss of markets by import-substitution, both in the inter-war period and again since 1950, has been considerably greater in absolute terms for Britain than for any of the other industrial countries. Thus, for both reasons, the impact of secondary industrial development in the primary-producing areas has been a much sharper one in Britain, and over the period as a whole it undoubtedly has had an important depressing influence on the British economy. If, as was argued earlier, a slowly growing economy is likely to be relatively less competitive in overseas markets than fast growing economies, it would seem that part of the loss in Britain's competitive share of world exports may have been an indirect result of import-substitution. The United States, on the other hand, though also suffering a large import-substitution loss, improved its competitive position on balance over the period. In this case, the major factor was the rapid expansion of the United States economy which, because exports were very small in relation to total output of manufactures (see Table 8.11), was not significantly retarded by the import-substitution overseas.

CHAPTER 9

METALS

The volume of exports of metals (iron and steel and non-ferrous metals)[1] from the main industrial countries has tended to grow since the late 1930's at a somewhat slower rate than exports of manufactured goods as a whole[2]. This is true not only of world trade in the aggregate, but also of the trend in imports of metals and other manufactures into the industrial countries themselves, which are the largest import market for metals. Before the 1930's, however, the trend was the other way: world trade in metals tended to rise faster than in other manufactures[3]. One of the reasons for this change in trend relationships has been the development of steel production in a considerable number of industrializing countries. Technological development in the industrial countries has also been important insofar as the consumption of metal per unit of engineering output has tended to be reduced. Finally, in some uses, there has been some substitution of other materials, notably plastics, for metal.

Exports of metals from the industrial countries consist very largely of semi-finished and finished steel products; only Canada and Norway, among these countries, are large exporters of non-ferrous metals. An important part of the industrial countries' imports of non-ferrous metals comes from non-industrial countries—mainly copper from Chile, Northern Rhodesia and the Congo and tin from Malaya and Bolivia. Compared with 1929, exports since the war have risen more sharply from the non-industrial, than from the industrial countries (see Table 9.1); but this was because there was a big switch in sources of supply during the 1930's in favour of the non-industrial countries. Since 1937 (or 1950), the volume of exports of metals from the industrial countries has increased more rapidly than those from other areas.

Between 1937 and 1950 there was a major decline in the ratio of world trade to world production of metals. The early 1950's were a period of steel shortage and in some years, particularly during and immediately after the Korean War, non-ferrous metals were also in acutely short supply. The rise in world steel production, on the other hand, had been very largely in the United States[4], where foreign trade in steel is relatively marginal. Since 1950, trade has tended to grow faster than production, reflecting the more rapid economic growth in Western Europe and Japan than in North America (the stagnation in world metals production from 1955 to 1959 was largely due to the United States).

---

[1] Metal goods (screws, nuts, bolts, etc.) are not included in 'metals', but are discussed separately in Chapter 14.

[2] See the movement in the relative volume indices in Table 7.4.

[3] Table 7.4.

[4] United States' steel production rose by 36 million tons between 1937 and 1950, out of a total rise in all (non-Soviet) countries of 40 million tons in this period.

Table 9.1. *World trade in metals in relation to world manufacturing production,*
1899–1959

$ *billion at constant prices, and index numbers,* 1929 = 100

	Values at 1955 prices[a]			Values at 1913 prices[b]					
	1899	1913	1929	1929	1937	1950	1955	1957	1959
EXPORTS OF METALS									
From main industrial countries	0.38	0.89	1.12	3.74	3.28	3.69	5.15	6.10	6.20
Index	34	80	100	100	88	99	138	163	166
From other countries[c]	..	..	..	0.98	1.23	1.34	1.53	1.82	2.13
Index	..	..	..	100	125	137	156	186	217
Total	..	..	..	4.72	4.51	5.03	6.68	7.92	8.33
Index	..	..	..	100	96	106	141	168	177
WORLD MANUFACTURING PRODUCTION									
Total	36	61	100	100	115	190	252	272	294
of which									
Metals	29	63	100	100	102	135	180	187	184
Metal goods[d]	20	47	100	100	104	202	292	318	345

Sources: Tables A.70, A.80 and national trade statistics; *Statistical Yearbooks,* United
Nations, New York; *Industrial Statistics, 1900–1959,* O.E.E.C., Paris, 1960.

[a]Excluding exports from the Netherlands.
[b]Including exports from the Netherlands.
[c]Mostly non-ferrous metals (Chile, Northern Rhodesia, Malaya and the Congo being
the most important exporting countries).
[d]Engineering products and metalwares (tools, cutlery, etc.).

Trends in demand for metals, and in their production in both industrial and
other countries, are examined in the next sections, followed by an appraisal of
the main trends in international trade.

1. THE DEMAND FOR METALS

Steel

Apparent steel consumption per head of population varies widely between
countries at different stages of industrialization. Latin America, the most
steel-intensive Continent outside the economically advanced areas, uses less
than one-fifth of the per caput steel consumption of Western Europe, and only
7–8 per cent of that of North America (see Table 9.2). At the extreme end
of the scale, the countries of the Far East (other than Japan) consume steel at
only one-quarter of the Latin American rate.

Table 9.2.   *Trends in steel consumption by area, 1913–57*

	Apparent consumption[a] per head					Apparent utilization[b] per head
	Indices				Total	
	1929	1936–38	1951	1957	1957	1957
	(1913 = 100)				*(kg.)*	*(kg.)*
North America	128	91	177	166	553	537
Oceania	84	97	148	160	225	267
Eastern Europe	100	228	313	574	224	227
Western Europe	126	130	142	218	229	207
Japan	275	436	339	760	139	124
Latin America	66	71	120	158	41	62
Africa	144	155	247	306	20	35
Middle East	130	184	328	410	20	32
Rest of Far East						
Including China[c]	130	140	190	310	10	..
Excluding China	..	..	..	..	10	14

Sources: Based on Tables 4 and 11 of *Long-Term Trends and Problems of the European Steel Industry*, United Nations Economic Commission for Europe, Geneva, 1959.

[a]Production plus net imports of steel, in terms of crude steel equivalent.

[b]Apparent consumption plus approximate crude steel equivalent of net imports of metal products.

[c]Rounded indices.

Nonetheless, remarkable progress has been made in the under-developed areas since the 1930's in their steel consumption per head.   By 1957, this was double, or more than double, the 1936–38 average in all four under-developed areas shown in Table 9.2, compared with increases of two-thirds to four-fifths in the industrial areas, except for Eastern Europe where per caput steel consumption in 1957 was $2\frac{1}{2}$ times pre-war.   The general increases in steel consumption reflect the economic growth that has taken place since before the war.   In particular countries, the relation between steel consumption and economic growth depends greatly on whether the expansion is directed to more steel-intensive sectors (like engineering), rather than to, say, housebuilding, agriculture or textiles, which require relatively little steel per unit of output.   But this does not vitiate the fact, as will be seen later, that a fairly close relationship exists in the long-term between economic growth and steel consumption.

The disparity between the developed and the under-developed areas in per caput consumption levels is smaller if account is taken of the export of engineering products from the former areas to the latter.   In 1957, per caput apparent steel utilization, defined as apparent consumption plus the steel equivalent of net imports of metal products, exceeded per caput apparent consumption in the less developed areas by proportions varying from 40 per cent in the Far East to 75 per cent in Africa[1]. Nonetheless, the disparity between the different areas, even on the utilization basis, remains very considerable.

Non-ferrous metals

The expansion in world industrial output, and particularly in that of engineering goods, has carried with it a growing demand for the various non-ferrous metals. In the first decade of the century, lead was far and away the most used non-ferrous metal. It was overtaken by copper in the 1930's, and by both aluminium and zinc in the 1950's (see Table 9.3). Indeed, by 1959, the quantity of aluminium consumed in the world (4 million tons) exceeded for the first time that of any of the other major non-ferrous metals.

Table 9.3. *World[a] consumption of the five major non-ferrous metals, 1901–59*

Annual averages

	Aluminium	Copper	Lead	Tin	Zinc
		(Thousand metric tons)			
1901–10	17	686	981	104	673
1921–30	176	1346	1390	147	1107
1931–40	390	1595	1468	156	1337
1951–59	2796	3019	2117	166	2461
1959	3989	3590	2378	185	2881
Change from		*(Percentage)*			
1901–10 to 1921–30	+935	+96	+42	+41	+64
1921–30 to 1931–40	+122	+18	+ 6	+ 6	+21
1931–40 to 1951–59	+716	+90	+44	+ 6	+84

Sources: *Metal Statistics, 1949–1958* and *1950–1959*, Metallgesellschaft A.G., Frankfurt.
[a]Including the Soviet countries.

These very different trends are the result of a variety of causes, of which four in particular stand out. First, technological developments have had an important influence on demand for non-ferrous metals in some uses. The introduction of electrolytic tinning methods, for example, has meant a considerable reduction in the quantity of tin required per ton of tinplate. Again, the development of new plastic materials during and since the last war, and their adaptation to many uses formerly the exclusive preserve of one or other of the non-ferrous metals, for example, plastic piping for lead or copper pipes,

[1]For some countries, imports of engineering products consist largely of ships and to this extent the utilization total may appear abnormally high in relation to the general level of economic development (see also *Long-Term Trends and Problems of the European Steel Industry*, Economic Commission for Europe, Geneva, 1959, p.13).

has led to a significant amount of substitution of plastics for non-ferrous metals[1].

Second, within the non-ferrous group itself, there have been substantial substitutions of one metal for another as a result of divergent trends in their relative prices. Aluminium has become increasingly attractive to the prospective user since the 1920's, for two reasons: its price has fallen considerably in relation to other non-ferrous metals prices over the period; and it has remained relatively free from short-term price fluctuations, in contrast to the violent price movements in the other metals[2]. Comparing 1959 with 1929, for example, aluminium prices in New York had fallen by one-third in relation to prices of standard grades of copper, lead and zinc in the same centre (see Table 9.4). The price advantage of aluminium has been an important incentive to substitute it for copper and other non-ferrous metals in many uses[3].

A third reason for the different trends in consumption of the various non-ferrous metals has been the very different rates of growth of the industries in which each metal finds its main usage. Thus, an important end-use of copper is for making electric wires and cables, and the rapid development of electricity networks in the industrial countries since the 1920's has played a large part in the growth in world demand for this metal. Again, the rapid growth of the aircraft and road vehicle industries, and the trend towards increased packaging of food and other light consumer products, probably explain a good part of the rapid growth in demand for aluminium.

Finally, the proportion of demand which is met by the production of 'secondary' metal from scrap varies considerably from one non-ferrous metal to another, and this naturally affects the demand for virgin metal with which we are primarily concerned. The consumption figures considered earlier relate solely to virgin metal, and it can be assumed that international trade also consists essentially of virgin production. The production of secondary metal is important for lead and copper, where world secondary production is probably about two-thirds of total primary output, but so far it has been of minor significance for aluminium.

It seems likely that the broad trends in consumption discussed above will continue in the future. The demand for aluminium, for example, will probably

[1]For the industrial areas as a whole, the increase from 1950–52 to 1955–57 in the weight of plastic materials consumed was about half as big again as the increase for aluminium; by value, the rise in plastics consumption was greater than that of all five major non-ferrous metals in total (see J. A. Rowlatt and F. T. Blackaby, 'The Demand for Industrial Materials, 1950–57', *National Institute Economic Review*, No. 5, Sept. 1959).

[2]The main reason for the short-term instability in prices of copper, lead, tin and zinc appears to be that the futures markets in these commodities reflect the swings in traders' and speculators' views, which usually move together in one direction or the other (see P. Lamartine Yates, *Forty Years of Foreign Trade*, London, 1959, page 147).

[3]Some of the main substitutions in this field in the United States during the 1950's were aluminium for bronze and brass as general all-purpose non-corrosive metals, for zinc in die-casting, for copper in electrical wiring, and for tin in packaging.

Table 9.4. *Relative price movements of the five major non-ferrous metals,*
1913–59

	Aluminium	Copper	Lead	Tin	Annual averages Zinc
			(Indices, 1913 = 100)		
1913	100	100	100	100	100
1925	115	92	206	131	139
1929	101	119	156	102	118
1937	85	86	138	123	119
1950	75	139	304	216	252
1955	113	246	346	214	224
1959	114	204	279	230	208
			($ per ton)		
1959	591	687	269	2251	252

Source: Metal Statistics, 1950–1959, Metallgesellschaft A.G., Frankfurt. The series used
were: *Aluminium*, 99.5% ingot, New York; *Copper*, electrolytic, wirebars, United States;
Lead, common grade, New York; *Tin*, Straits (99% for 1913), New York; *Zinc*, Prime
Western, East St. Louis.

continue to rise faster than that for the other main non-ferrous metals. This
will probably be so even if military aircraft production is cut back sharply as
a result of the development of ballistic missiles (or of the conclusion of an
international disarmament agreement), because the trend towards the substitution of aluminium for other metals on price grounds is likely to continue to
be important, while technological development may well find new outlets for
aluminium where lightness and strength need to be combined with non-corrosive
properties.

Total base metals

For a comparison of the movement in world trade in metals with that in
consumption (which will be made later in this chapter), it is necessary to
combine the data given above for the consumption of steel with those for the
major non-ferrous metals. There are various ways in which this could be done.
The most relevant for comparison with trade movements is to value the quantity
of each metal consumed in the various years by a constant average price[1].
The calculation made here was based on typical foreign trade unit values in
1955 for metal at the ingot stage. The results (see Table 9.5) inevitably contain
some margin of error, though the broad trends over time and the relation of
consumption in the different areas can be taken as generally valid.

Metal consumption in the industrial countries rose by about 80 per cent
from 1937 to 1959, but total world consumption rose even faster—by some

[1]The alternative measurements would be by weight or by cubic capacity; either would
give less importance to non-ferrous metals, in relation to steel, than does the value basis.

120 per cent. Growth was particularly rapid in the semi-industrial countries and in the Soviet area and, among the Western industrial countries, in Canada. The general rise in per caput consumption since pre-war reflects in the main the increase in steel consumption discussed earlier (on the value basis, steel represents over 75 per cent of total metal consumption in most areas).

Table 9.5.   *Apparent consumption of metals by area, 1929–59*

	Total				Per head			
	1929	1937	1955	1959	1929	1937	1955	1959
INDUSTRIAL COUNTRIES	($ *billion at* 1955 *prices*[a])				($ *at* 1955 *prices*[a])			
France	1.05	0.81	1.36	1.52	26	20	32	34
Germany[b]	1.83	2.22	2.68	3.10	28	33	53	59
United Kingdom	1.19	1.75	2.67	2.50	26	37	52	48
Other Western Europe[c]	0.97	1.13	2.09	2.37	14	15	25	28
Canada	0.35	0.28	0.70	0.80	35	25	44	46
United States	6.98	6.11	12.90	11.35	57	47	78	64
Japan	0.41	0.87	0.90	1.85	7	12	10	20
Total	12.78	13.17	23.30	23.50	31	30	47	45
SEMI-INDUSTRIAL COUNTRIES								
Southern Dominions	0.18	0.28	0.67	0.69	12	15	27	25
India/Pakistan	0.23	0.16	0.33	0.47	0.7	0.4	0.7	1.0
Latin America	0.24	0.24	0.65	0.79	3	3	5	6
Total	0.65	0.68	1.65	1.95	1.5	1.4	2.7	3.0
SOVIET COUNTRIES								
U.S.S.R.	0.61	2.03	5.07	6.83	4	12	26	33
Eastern Europe[d]	0.42	0.44	1.63	1.95	5	5	17	20
China	0.07	0.12	0.38	1.60	0.2	0.3	0.6	2.3
Total	1.10	2.59	7.08	10.38	1.6	4	8	10
REST OF WORLD[e]	0.41	1.02	1.60	2.48	1	2	2.5	3.5
WORLD TOTAL	14.94	17.46	33.63	38.30	7	8	12	13

Sources: Statistical Yearbooks, United Nations, New York; *Metal Statistics, 1928–1937, 1946–1955* and *1950–1959*, Metallgesellschaft A.G., Frankfurt; *Minerais et Métaux: Statistiques*, Paris, 1956; *Long-Term Trends and Problems of the European Steel Industry*, United Nations Economic Commission for Europe, Geneva, 1959; *Statistical Yearbook, 1956*, International Tin Study Group, The Hague, 1957; I. Svennilson, *Growth and Stagnation in the European Economy*, United Nations, Geneva, 1954.

[a]Based on typical prices at the ingot stage.
[b]West Germany in 1955 and 1959.
[c]Belgium-Luxembourg, Italy, Netherlands, Norway, Sweden and Switzerland.
[d]Excluding in 1929 and 1937 former German territories now in Eastern Europe.
[e]Totals are residuals; per head figures are approximate.

Regression analysis

A more useful way of describing these various trends in metal consumption is to relate them to the concurrent movements in real income. This has been done, for the Western industrial and semi-industrial countries separately, in a series of time-series regressions of per caput apparent consumption on per caput real income[1]. The results, shown in Table 9.6, indicate a considerably sharper rate of growth in consumption in the semi-industrial, than in the industrial, countries in both steel and non-ferrous metals for a given percentage increase in real income. The margin of error is considerably greater for the co-efficients shown for the semi-industrial countries, implying that there is great variation in the way in which economic growth in the earlier stages of industrialization impinges on the demand for metals.

Table 9.6. *Growth co-efficients for metals consumption*

Regression[a]	Steel[b]	Non-ferrous metals[c]	Total[c]
TIME SERIES			
(apparent consumption per head)			
1. Industrial countries (1913–59)			
Growth co-efficient	1.08 (± 0.08)	1.39 (± 0.01)	1.12 (± 0.07)
R^2	0.767	0.736	0.822
2. Semi-industrial countries (1913–59)			
Growth co-efficient	1.81 (± 0.48)	3.85 (± 0.89)	2.61 (± 1.05)
R^2	0.488	0.538	0.277
CROSS-COUNTRY			
3. Apparent consumption per head (1955)			
Growth co-efficient	1.58 (± 0.14)	2.33 (± 0.31)	1.63 (± 0.16)
R^2	0.832	0.670	0.812
4. Apparent utilization per head (1957)			
Growth co-efficient	1.15 (± 0.09)	..	..
R^2	0.872	..	..

[a]For the time-series regressions, 11 industrial countries (54 'observations') and 6 semi-industrial countries (15 or 16 'observations') were included. In the cross-country regressions, 31 countries (industrial, semi-industrial and non-industrial) were included for apparent consumption and 32 for apparent utilization.
[b]In terms of quantity.
[c]In terms of value at 1955 prices.

The other general relationship brought out by the regression results is that the consumption of non-ferrous metals (measured on a constant price basis) has increased at a considerably faster rate than has steel consumption. For the industrial countries, the growth co-efficient[2] for non-ferrous metals exceeds

[1]Double logarithmic equations were used (see page 51).
[2]The 'growth co-efficient' expresses the ratio of the rate of growth in consumption of metals per head to the rate of growth in total real product per head.

that for steel by about 30 per cent, while for the semi-industrial countries the non-ferrous metals co-efficient is rather more than double that for steel. The main reason for this difference is the exceptionally rapid increase in aluminium consumption in this period. As aluminium comes into more general use, however, the rate of growth in its consumption must be expected to decline.

A higher growth co-efficient for non-ferrous metals than for steel was also obtained from a cross-country regression for a recent year (lower part of Table 9.6). As expected, the growth co-efficient is much smaller for steel utilization than for steel consumption, as a result of international trade in engineering products. Since, however, this chapter is concerned essentially with trade in metals as such—trade in engineering products is examined in some detail in Chapter 10—the statistics of apparent consumption alone are used, where relevant, for comparison with the production and trade in metals.

2. METAL PRODUCTION

The industrial areas—North America, Western Europe and Japan—account for by far the greater part of world steel production outside the Soviet countries, and for most of the refining of the main non-ferrous metals. Not only are the industrial countries themselves large producers of metalliferous ores, but they also import and refine a substantial proportion of ores mined in the less-developed areas. Excluding the Soviet group, the proportion of world metal output in 1959 produced in the industrial countries ranged from 50–60 per cent for copper and tin metal up to 95 per cent for steel and aluminium (see Table 9.7).

Table 9.7.   *Metal production in the industrial and non-industrial areas, 1929 and 1959*

					Million metric tons	
	Steel	Aluminium	Copper	Lead	Tin	Zinc
Industrial countries[a]						
1929	110	0.27	1.74	1.17	0.06	1.16
1959	200	3.14	1.74	1.14	0.06	1.96
Change	+ 90	+ 2.87	—	− 0.03	—	+ 0.80
%	+ 82	+1062	—	− 3	—	+ 69
Rest of world[b]						
1929	2	—	0.28	0.54	0.12	0.08
1959	12	0.15	1.34	0.55	0.06	0.30
Change	+ 10	+ 0.15	+ 1.06	+ 0.01	− 0.06	+ 0.22
%	+500	..	+ 378	+ 2	− 50	+ 275

Sources: Statistical Yearbook, 1960, United Nations, New York, 1961; *Long-Term Trends and Problems of the European Steel Industry*, United Nations Economic Commission for Europe, Geneva, 1959; *Collected Statistics*, Metallgesellschaft A. G., Frankfurt, 1956.

[a]North America, Western Europe and Japan.
[b]Excluding Soviet countries.

Over the past thirty years, several countries outside the industrial areas have developed aluminium industries, while the entire increase in world copper production over the period has come from the non-industrial countries (particularly Central Africa and Chile). The proportion of world output accounted for by the industrial countries has also fallen for zinc, but it has increased for tin as a result of the decline in Malayan production.

Steel

Almost all the crude steel production outside the industrial countries and the Soviet group is concentrated in a small number of semi-industrial countries: Australia, India, South Africa, Brazil, Chile, Colombia and Mexico. These countries produced in total about 10 million tons in 1959, or about 5 per cent of the output of the Western industrial countries. All these countries have adequate reserves of iron ore and access to sufficient local or imported sources of coking coal to support a considerable further expansion in steel output. The iron ore output of these seven countries in 1959 was, however, only some 16 million tons (ferrous content) out of a total of 40–45 million tons produced in that year outside the industrial areas and the Soviet countries.

Of the non-industrial countries which mine iron ore but have as yet no blast furnaces or steelworks, easily the most important is Venezuela, where iron ore production has doubled in the past five years (see Table 9.8)[1]. Other important ore producing countries with no steel industry are Malaya, Peru, Algeria[2] and Liberia. In some of these, if not in all, the use of local ore for blast furnaces must be expected to begin with the development of industrialization. Venezuela is in a particularly favourable position, for she possesses high-quality iron ore in abundant amount and great reserves of natural gas which could be used as fuel[3].

Recent developments in iron ore prospecting in the former French territories of West and Equatorial Africa indicate that this area will become a major supplier of ore to the industrial countries in the near future[4]. However, it is unlikely that any large-scale production of steel will be undertaken there for some time to come.

Steel production need not, however, be tied to local supplies of iron ore, if pig iron or scrap can be imported and combined with home supplies of coking coal and power. In Western Europe, there is a large interchange of pig iron

[1]Venezuelan iron ore production rose to 12.7 million tons, ferrous content, in 1960.

[2]A small steel plant has, however, recently been erected in Algeria.

[3]The Economic Commission for Europe has estimated Venezuelan steel output to rise from nil at present to 3 million ingot tons in 1972–75 (see *Long Term Trends and Problems of the European Steel Industry*, Geneva, 1959, p. 143).

[4]Known reserves in Mauretania and Gabon have recently been assessed at about 150 million tons, ferrous content, in each country. By the late 1960's, iron ore production in Mauretania is likely to reach 5–6 million tons, and in Gabon over 10 million tons a year.

Table 9.8.   *Iron ore and pig iron production in selected semi-industrial and non-industrial countries[a], 1948, 1955 and 1959*

Million metric tons

	Iron ore[b]			Pig iron and ferro-alloys		
	1948	1955	1959	1948	1955	1959
AFRICA						
Algeria	1.02	1.87	1.00	—	—	—
Liberia	—	1.16	1.83	—	—	—
Morocco	0.68	0.77	0.73	—	—	—
Sierra Leone	0.57	0.78	0.90	—	—	—
Tunisia	0.38	0.63	0.53	—	—	—
Union of South Africa	0.70	1.26	1.84	0.65	1.30	1.81
LATIN AMERICA						
Argentina	0.02	0.04	0.05	0.02	0.04	0.03
Brazil	1.07	2.30	3.87	0.55[c]	1.09	1.48
Chile	1.68	0.94[d]	2.49	0.01[c]	0.26[c]	0.29[c]
Colombia	—	0.15	0.17	—	0.10	0.13
Mexico	0.23	0.43	0.54	0.18[c]	0.31[c]	0.47[c]
Peru	—	1.06	2.09	—	—	—
Venezuela	—	5.40	10.15	—	—	—
ASIA						
India	1.48	2.83	4.84	1.49	1.93	3.11
Malaya	—	0.83	2.14	—	—	—
Philippines	0.01	0.82	0.69	—	—	—
Portuguese India	0.00	1.22	1.77	—	—	—
Turkey	0.12	0.48	0.57	0.10	0.20	0.24
OCEANIA						
Australia	1.36	2.34	2.75	1.15[c]	1.83[c]	2.54[c]

Source: Statistical Yearbook, 1960, United Nations, New York, 1961.

[a]All countries outside North America, Europe, China and Japan producing $\frac{1}{2}$ million tons or more of iron ore (ferrous content) in 1959.

[b]Ferrous content.

[c]Excluding ferro-alloys.

[d]Average production in 1954–56 was 1.27 million tons.

and scrap but in the less-developed areas only a few countries rely mainly on imported steel-making materials.   Argentina is the outstanding example of a steel industry based mainly on imported pig iron[1], while Mexico has relied heavily on imports of scrap from the United States (see Table 9.9).   Mexico has large reserves of iron ore—though their mountainous location involves heavy transport costs—and an adequate supply of coking coal, so that steel production can be expected to increase substantially in the next 10–15 years[2].

[1]A blast furnace with an output of over 500 thousand tons a year began operations in Argentina in 1961.

[2]An output of $3\frac{1}{2}$ million tons by 1972–75 is forecast for Mexico by the Economic Commission for Europe (see *Long Term Trends and Problems of the European Steel Industry*, Geneva, 1959, p. 143).

A number of countries with little reserves of iron ore, or reserves of low metal-content, produce steel from imported pig iron and scrap. Pakistan, whose iron ore and coal are both low-grade, is a case in point (Table 9.9), while Egypt's steel industry, established in 1948 to convert scrap iron into steel products, has now developed to the processing of local ore.

Table 9.9. *Imports of pig iron and iron and steel scrap in relation to crude steel production in selected countries, 1937, 1955 and 1959*

Thousand metric tons

		Production		Imports	
		Crude steel	Pig iron	Pig iron	Scrap
Argentina	1937	2	—	52	0
	1955	218	35	191	—
	1959	214	32	138	..
Mexico	1937	106	58	2	57
	1955	510	312	5	234
	1959	1016[a]	473	—	387
Pakistan	1955	11	2	21	..
	1959	9	..	69	0
Egypt	1955	86	3	3	3
	1959	173	120	12	7

Sources: Statistical Yearbook, 1960, United Nations, New York, 1961; *Yearbook of International Trade Statistics, 1959,* United Nations, New York, 1960; *Long-Term Trends and Problems of the European Steel Industry,* United Nations Economic Commission for Europe, Geneva, 1959; *Statistical Summary of the Mineral Industry, 1954–1959,* Overseas Geological Surveys, London, 1961; *Mineral Trade Notes,* United States Bureau of Mines.

[a]Not comparable with previous figures owing to change in method of estimation.

The countries of Eastern Europe appear to be in a unique position inasmuch as they are developing their steel industries on the basis of imported iron ore[1]. In 1959, the proportion of pig iron output based on imported ore ranged from about 55 per cent for East Germany and Rumania to 85–90 per cent for Czechoslovakia, Hungary and Poland (see Table 9.10). East Germany is also heavily dependent on imported pig iron as well as on imports of Soviet ingots and semis. All these countries are planning for further large increases in steel production.

Though the sharpest rates of growth in steel production in the next decade or two are likely to come in the less-developed countries—particularly, of course, where new steel industries are based on local ore production—the

[1]Supplied by the Soviet Union.

largest contribution to the expansion in world output will inevitably be made by the Western industrial countries and the Soviet group[1]. Nonetheless, an expansion in steel production in the less-developed countries—which are the main net-importing areas—is likely to result in a slower rate of growth in world import trade in steel. This is discussed further in the next section.

Table 9.10. *Imports of steel-making materials in relation to crude steel production in Eastern Europe, 1937, 1955 and 1959*

Million metric tons

		Production		Imports		
		Crude steel	Pig iron[a]	Iron ore[b]	Pig iron[a]	Scrap
Czechoslovakia	1937	2.30	1.68	..	0.06	0.26
	1955	4.47	2.98	2.32	0.18	—
	1959	6.14	4.24	3.78	0.17	0.02
East Germany	1955	2.51	1.52	0.73	0.29	—
	1959	3.21	1.90	1.00	0.64	..
Hungary	1937	0.67	0.36	0.25	0.03	0.06
	1955	1.63	0.88	0.80	0.12	..
	1959	1.76	1.12	1.00	0.06	..
Poland	1937	1.46	0.72	..	0.01	0.64
	1955	4.43	3.11	2.61	0.01	..
	1959	6.16	4.38	3.67	0.09	..
Rumania	1937	0.24	0.13	..	0.01	0.02
	1955	0.77	0.57	..	0.02	—
	1959	1.42	0.85	0.48	..	..

Sources: As for Table 9.9, and national statistics.

[a]Including ferro-alloys in some cases.

[b]Ferrous content.   Figures are based on estimated average ferrous content of 60 per cent; or East Germany, the 1959 ferrous content figure has been officially published.

Non-ferrous metals

As already mentioned, the large increases in production outside the main industrial areas over the past 30 years have been in aluminium, copper and zinc (Table 9.7). Bauxite, the main ore from which aluminium is made, is one of

[1]The Economic Commission for Europe estimate world steel output in the period 1972–75 in the region of 630 million tons.   This is more than double the 1959 total (305 million tons).   One-half of the increase from 1959 to 1972–75 is attributable to North America, Western Europe and Japan, and one-third to the Soviet countries.   Even if the estimates for 1972–75 for individual countries prove wide of the mark, the general conclusion—that the less-developed countries will play a relatively small part in the global expansion—seems inescapable.

the most widely distributed minerals geographically, the limiting factor in aluminium production being the availability of abundant quantities of low-cost electric power. Several under-developed countries with large bauxite deposits have already developed sufficient hydro-electric power to support aluminium production on an economic basis, and in other countries similar schemes are well advanced. India and Brazil have both become sizeable producers in recent years (19 thousand tons each in 1960/1), but a much bigger development is in process in West Africa. The Republic of Cameroun, which began the production of aluminium in 1957, has increased its output from 8 thousand tons in that year to 44 thousand tons in 1960/1[1], and both Ghana and Guinea (which has one of the largest bauxite deposits in the world) are planning future production on a fairly large scale[2].

Production of the other major non-ferrous metals is much more highly localised. Over 90 per cent of the copper produced in the non-industrial areas, for example, is accounted for by Chile, the Congo Republic and Northern Rhodesia, over 80 per cent of the output of refined tin comes from Malaya, while about 85 per cent of the lead is produced in Australia, Mexico and Peru. Since this configuration of output depends on the geographical disposition of ore, it is not likely to change substantially in future. More important for the economic prospects of the producing countries would be the long-term changes in world demand for particular non-ferrous metals which were discussed above.

3. METAL CONSUMPTION AND TRADE

Western Europe has been by far the largest import market for steel over the whole period since before the first World War (see Table 9.11). In 1913, Western Europe took 40 per cent of the total; in 1957, 38 per cent. The shares of the other economically advanced areas (North America, Japan and Oceania), however, have fallen since 1913, a particularly notable decline taking place for Oceania (from 7 per cent in 1913 to 2 per cent in 1957).

Of the less-developed areas, exports to the Middle East have expanded considerably since the 1930's with the development of oilfields in that region, while shipments of steel for the Venezuelan oilfields explain about half the rise in the total for Latin America between 1950 and 1957. China was a considerable steel importing country in the late 1930's, taking some 600,000 tons in 1937, though her share has declined considerably since 1950 with the rapid growth in home steel production. India is now the main steel importing country in the Far East, the rise in Indian imports from 1950 to 1957 accounting for some two-thirds of the expansion in steel imports into this area.

---

[1]Cameroun production is based on alumina imported from France, using cheap local hydro-electric power.

[2]For both Ghana and Guinea, future development depends heavily on the availability of foreign capital investments.

The relationship between the growth of trade and the consumption of metal is, however, obscured if the analysis is confined to broad geographical areas. Since the impact on trade depends heavily on the degree to which an increase in demand can be met from home metal output, a more useful picture of how

Table 9.11. *World exports of semi-finished and finished steel by area of destination, 1913–57*

					Million metric tons
Exports to	1913	1929	1937	1950	1957
Western Europe	4.77	7.90	5.75	5.55	11.76
North America	1.57	1.63	0.91	2.19	2.89
Japan	0.56	0.96	0.90	0	0.96
Oceania	0.85	0.56	0.33	1.01	0.58
Sub-total	7.75	11.05	7.89	8.75	16.19
Far East (except Japan)	1.48	2.38	2.04	1.87	3.84
Middle East	0.10	0.29	0.47	0.97	1.13
Africa	0.57	0.93	0.90	1.23	1.74
Latin America	1.68	2.12	2.12	2.14	4.11
Sub-total	3.83	5.72	5.53	6.21	10.82
Eastern Europe*a*	0.31	0.70	0.64	0.71	3.30*c*
TOTAL*b*	12.02	17.90	14.45	15.85	30.77

Source: Long-Term Trends and Problems of the European Steel Industry, United Nations Commission for Europe, Geneva, 1959.

aIncluding U.S.S.R.
bIncluding exports which could not be allocated by destination.
cOf which, 2.08 million tons of intra-trade between Eastern European countries.

economic development affects trade in metals can be obtained by separating the net-importing from the net-exporting countries and, within the former group, separating those countries which produce metal from those that do not.

An analysis of trends in production, consumption and net trade in steel, which has been made on this basis (see Table 9.12), shows that of the expansion in net imports from 1929 to 1959 into the countries which are net importers of steel, the greater part occurred in imports into the non-producing countries. Part of this increase resulted from the development of the oilfields in the Middle East and Venezuela. Exports of steel to four oil-producing countries (Iran, Iraq, Saudi Arabia and Venezuela), rose from 0.3 million tons in 1929 and 0.4 million tons in 1937 to 1.5 million tons in 1959. In addition, there have been heavy shipments of French equipment for the new Algerian oilfields in recent years; in 1959, apparent steel consumption in Algeria amounted to 0.45 million tons, and imports of steel pipes and tubes to about 0.15 million tons ingot-equivalent. Allowing also for imports of oil pipe into the Persian Gulf Sheikhdoms, total imports of steel into the main oil-producing countries in 1959 would have been in the region of 1¾ million tons, ingot-equivalent, or about 20–25 per cent of all steel imports into the non-producing countries in that year.

The larger part of the increase to the non-producing countries since pre-war was in exports to a wide variety of countries in the less-developed areas, particularly in the Middle and Far East and in Africa. It is not possible to identify all the end-uses of this trade in steel, but one of the important ones is the shipment of tinplate for use in local meat and fruit canning industries in countries like Malaya, Hong Kong and the Philippines. Such uses, together

Table 9.12. *Production, net trade and apparent consumption of steel in net-exporting and net-importing countries, 1929–59*

			Million metric tons[a]		
	1929	1937	1950	1955	1959
1. NET-EXPORTERS OF STEEL[b]					
Production	105.0	105.2	139.1	183.7	179.2
Net exports (−)	− 13.6	− 13.4	− 15.1	− 19.5	− 19.8
Apparent consumption	91.4	91.8	124.0	164.2	159.4
2. NET-IMPORTERS OF STEEL[c]					
Steel producers[d]					
Production	6.6	7.9	14.1	23.5	32.5
Net imports (+)	+ 9.8	+ 8.3	+ 9.2	+ 12.6	+ 10.5
Apparent consumption	16.4	16.2	23.3	36.1	43.0
Non-producers					
Net imports (+)[e]	+ 3.5	+ 4.5	..	+ 8.1	+ 7.9
3. SOVIET COUNTRIES					
Production	9.2[f]	22.9[f]	35.7	62.1	92.6
Net imports (+)	+ 0.3	+ 0.6	..	− 1.2	+ 1.4
or net exports (−)					
Apparent consumption	9.5[f]	23.5[f]	..	60.9	94.0
WORLD PRODUCTION	121	136	189	269	305

Sources: Statistical Yearbook, 1960, United Nations, New York, 1961; *Long-Term Trends and Problems of the European Steel Industry*, United Nations Economic Commission for Europe, Geneva, 1959.

[a]In terms of ingot-equivalent.

[b]Net exporters in 1955 (Austria, Belgium-Luxembourg, France, Germany—West Germany in 1955 and 1959—Saar, United Kingdom, United States and Japan).

[c]Net importers in 1955.

[d]Denmark, Finland, Italy, Netherlands, Norway, Spain, Sweden, Switzerland and Yugoslavia; Australia, Canada, Southern Rhodesia (the Federation of Rhodesia and Nyasaland in 1955 and 1959) and the Union of South Africa; India and Pakistan; Argentina, Brazil, Chile, Colombia and Mexico; Taiwan and Turkey.

[e]Residue obtained by deducting the aggregate of apparent consumption in other areas from total world production.

[f]Excluding those areas of Germany now in Eastern Europe.

with steel used for construction and on the railways, make up most of the demand for steel in this group of countries. Where there is no local steel industry, the fabrication of steel into engineering products—a major use in the industrial countries—tends not to exist, or to require only small quantities of metal.

Table 9.13. *Production, net imports and apparent consumption of steel in net-importing, steel-producing countries, 1929–59*

Millions metric tons[a]

	1929	1937	1950	1955	1959
WESTERN EUROPE[b]					
Production	3.95	3.73	5.99	11.29	15.64
Net imports	+ 3.57	+ 3.99	+ 4.25	+ 5.68	+ 5.10
Apparent consumption	7.52	7.72	10.24	16.97	20.74
N.I. per cent A.C.	*48*	*52*	*41*	*33*	*24*
AUSTRALIA, CANADA AND SOUTH AFRICA					
Production	1.88	2.90	5.18	7.94	10.71
Net imports	+ 2.63	+ 1.45	+ 2.17	+ 2.05	+ 0.54
Apparent consumption	4.51	4.35	7.35	9.99	11.25
N.I. per cent A.C.	*58*	*33*	*29*	*20*	*5*
INDIA/PAKISTAN					
Production	0.59	0.91	1.47	1.74	2.48
Net imports	+ 1.29	+ 0.51	+ 0.54	+ 1.37	+ 1.29
Apparent consumption	1.88	1.42	2.01	3.11	3.77
N.I. per cent A.C.	*69*	*36*	*27*	*44*	*34*
OTHER COUNTRIES[c]					
Production	0.15	0.31	1.46	2.37	3.34
Net imports	+ 2.09	+ 2.13	+ 1.86	+ 3.06	+ 3.22
Apparent consumption	2.24	2.44	3.32	5.43	6.56
N.I. per cent A.C.	*93*	*87*	*56*	*56*	*49*

Sources: As for Table 9.12.

[a]In terms of ingot-equivalent.
[b]Denmark, Finland, Italy, Netherlands, Norway, Spain, Sweden, Switzerland and Yugoslavia.
[c]Argentina, Brazil, Chile, Mexico and Turkey only.
Note: N.I. = net imports; A.C. = apparent consumption.

In the other groups of countries, steel consumption has risen very much more, in absolute terms, than in the non-producing countries. In the industrial countries which are net exporters of steel, consumption rose by 68 million tons (75 per cent) from 1929 to 1959, the increase being supported wholly by the rise in production. Throughout the period, the greater part of the steel export trade in this group has been accounted for by Western Europe. The Soviet countries, taken in total, have only a marginal net trade in steel, virtually the entire expansion in consumption since pre-war coming from production within the group.

While the non-producing countries accounted for the larger part of the expansion in world imports from 1929 to 1959, their net steel imports showed a decline in the most recent period. In the other net importing countries, too, there has been a reduction in steel imports since 1955. This latter reduction was very largely concentrated in Australia, Canada and South Africa (see Table 9.13). Steel production in all three countries has expanded, the increase in Australia between 1955 and 1959 (over 50 per cent) being particularly sharp. Moreover, all three countries have recently developed an export trade in semi-finished steel products, and by 1959 Australia had become a net steel-exporting country. South Africa seems likely to become a net exporter also in the near future.

In both the Western European steel-producing and -importing countries, and in India, there were also reductions in steel imports in the latter half of the 1950's. In the West European group, production rose by 4.3 million tons (nearly 40 per cent) between 1955 and 1959, of which 3.1 million tons resulted from expansion in the Netherlands and in Italy. In the Netherlands, the rise in production exceeded that in consumption by 0.5 million tons, this being virtually the whole of the decline in net imports for this group of countries as a whole.

Almost all the steel consumption shown for the Indian sub-continent in Table 9.13 relates to India, consumption in Pakistan in 1959 amounting to only 0.24 million tons. India's steel requirements mounted sharply with the introduction of the first two Plans, the production target for the end of the Second Plan period (i.e. 1960/61) being 6.5 million ingot tons. Actual production in 1961/61 was, however, only half that amount—3.3 million tons—which, in itself, was a notable increase on the pre-Plan level. The steel target for the end of the Third Plan (1965/66) is 9.5 million ingot tons actual output (capacity to be installed is planned to exceed 10 million tons), giving 6.9 million tons of finished steel against estimated requirements of 7.3 million tons[1]. Even if there is a substantial shortfall in the trend of steel output, compared with the Plan, India's imports of steel are unlikely to rise much over recent levels because of her continuing balance of payments difficulties.

The 'other countries' in Table 9.13 are mostly in Latin America, the whole of the increase in net steel imports between 1955 and 1959 being in Argentina and Brazil. Chile's imports of steel have been drastically reduced with the expansion in home production, and there was also a decline in imports into Mexico from 1955 to 1959. Net imports into Turkey rose only slightly from 1950 to 1959, almost the entire increase in consumption being met from the expansion in local output.

[1] *Third Five Year Plan: A Draft Outline*, Government of India, Planning Commission, New Delhi, 1960.

Thus, in all areas of the world where countries are in a position to develop steel industries, their dependence on imports is reduced, at a greater or lesser speed, as their steel requirements rise with their economic growth.   The process is shown graphically in Fig. 9.1 for some of the separate countries or groups of countries included in Table 9.13.   The rate of decline in the import proportion has been particularly great for some of the smaller industrial countries of

Fig. 9.1.   Import-content of steel consumption in relation to steel consumption per head in selected countries, 1929–59

Semi-logarithmic scale

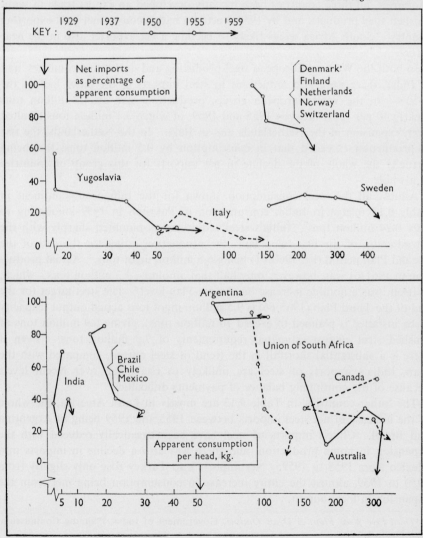

Western Europe (except Sweden), for the semi-industrial countries of Latin America (except Argentina) and for Australia and South Africa. In Sweden, the level of consumption has risen extremely rapidly, necessitating an expansion in imports; the relative stagnation in Argentina, on the other hand, had little effect on the import proportion because home output is marginal.

A similar, though more detailed, study of trends in world trade in steel products recently made by the Economic Commission for Europe reaches much the same conclusion[1]. In this study, a distinction is made between 'deficit-covering' trade and 'exchange'. The former arises in areas where steel supply is in deficit compared with demand, so that total deficit-covering trade is equal to the aggregate net imports of all countries. The latter consists of trade between countries able to produce in total all or most of the steel needed to meet domestic requirements; such trade derives from differences in comparative advantage in the production of particular types and qualities of steel. Since 1913, the volume of 'exchange' in steel products has tended to grow faster than deficit-covering trade. This has been particularly true of the period since 1950, 'exchange' in 1957 being three and a half times the 1950 volume (mainly as a result of growing economic integration in both Western and Eastern Europe), whereas the rise for deficit-covering trade was only 60 per cent (reflecting the growth in local steel production in the net-importing countries).

Total trade in metals

Steel represents, however, little more than one-half of the total value of world trade in base metals. In 1955, total exports of steel (other than from Soviet countries) amounted to $3.6 billion—virtually all from the industrial countries— and of non-ferrous metals to $3.0 billion (of which $1.8 billion were exported by the industrial countries). Copper is easily the most important single non-ferrous metal in world trade; in 1959, the percentages by value were, approximately: copper, 65; aluminium, 16; lead and tin, $7\frac{1}{2}$ each; zinc, 5 of the total for all five metals.

Since 1929, the outstanding changes in world trade in non-ferrous metals have been an eight-fold rise for aluminium and a doubling of trade in copper; at the same time, world exports of zinc rose by one-quarter (Table 9.14). The volume of trade in lead has not yet recovered the 1929 peak level, though it has been rising since 1950, but there seems to be a long-term decline in world trade in tin. These diverse movements reflect broadly the trends in consumption of each metal which were discussed earlier, though the proportion of consumption met by imports varies considerably—from about 85 per cent for tin to about 30 per cent for aluminium and zinc.

Taking all base metals together, there is a striking difference between the industrial and the semi-industrial countries in the movement of their imports

[1] *Long-Term Trends and Problems of the European Steel Industry*, Geneva, 1959, pp. 24–26.

Table 9.14. *World trade in non-ferrous metals, 1929–59*

	1929	1937	1950	1955	1959	1959 as proportion of 1929
	(Thousand metric tons)					*(Percentage)*
Aluminium	117	132	546	752	1056	*902*
Copper	1195	1418	1543	1922	2505	*210*
Lead	878	854	801	825	834	*95*
Tin	151	179	135	129	124	*82*
Zinc	544	595	490	654	674	*124*
	($ billion at 1955 prices[a])					
Total	1.85	2.12	2.31	2.79	3.46	..
Index	*100*	*116*	*125*	*151*	*187*	..

Sources: Statistical Summary of the Mineral Industry, Overseas Geological Surveys (pre-war, *Commonwealth Geological Surveys*), London.

[a]Quantities shown valued at typical 1955 unit values for metal at the ingot stage.

in relation to their economic growth (see Fig. 9.2). Comparing 1959 with 1929, apparent consumption of metals in the industrial countries rose by about 85 per cent, while total metal imports were higher by some 70 per cent and the volume of intra-trade by about 60 per cent—only a moderate reduction in the average import-content of consumption. The sharper rise in imports than in consumption in the later 1950's is due to a fall in the apparent consumption of steel in the United States, which has a very much lower import-content than have the other industrial countries[1]. This fall does not indicate a downward trend in steel consumption in the United States; consumption was high in 1955 because of the exceptionally large number of cars produced in that year, whereas in 1959 steel supplies were affected by a strike. By contrast, while apparent consumption in the semi-industrial countries trebled from 1929 to 1959[2], their imports of metals from the industrial countries were only one-sixth higher, mainly as a result of the substitution of home-produced for importedsteel. The metal exports from the industrial countries to the rest of the world (mainly non-industrial countries), however, have risen sharply since 1950, when they were limited by supply restrictions, and by 1959 were double the corresponding 1929 volume (Table 9.15).

The main trends in world trade in metals discussed above can reasonably be expected to continue in future. Certainly, the trend towards a lower import-content of steel consumption in the less-developed countries is likely to

[1]The percentage of 'imports' to apparent consumption was only 15 per cent for the United States in 1959, compared with 29 per cent for Britain, France and West Germany combined, and 63 per cent for the smaller countries of Western Europe.

[2]See Table 9.5.

continue with their further economic growth. The intra-trade of the industrial countries is likely to continue to expand, and there may well be increasing opportunities for profitable specialization by different countries, particularly in the various types of semi-finished and finished steel products. The trend in exports to the non-industrial areas seems also likely to rise, though the rate of growth depends to a considerable extent both on whether or not the rate of exploitation of oil deposits achieved in the past decade can be maintained and on the extent to which the non-oil producing countries can expand their export earnings.

Fig. 9.2.   Apparent consumption and trade in metals, 1899–1959

Semi-logarithmic scale, $ billion at 1955 prices

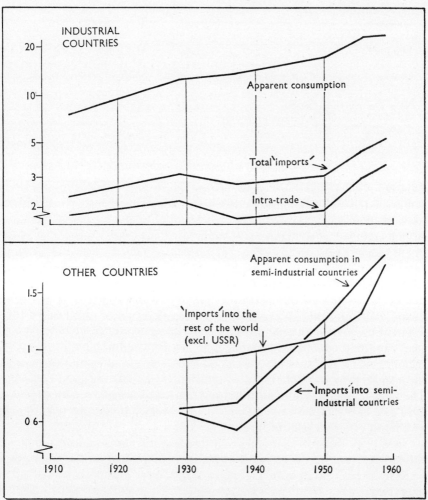

Table 9.15. *World exports of metals by major market, 1929–59*

$ billion, f.o.b. at 1955 prices

Exports to	1929	1937	1950	1955	1959
INDUSTRIAL COUNTRIES					
Intra-trade	2.27	1.79	1.92	3.06	3.67
'Imports' from other countries	0.85	1.09	1.11	1.39	1.69
Total	3.11	2.88	3.03	4.44	5.36
of which					
France, Germany*a*, United Kingdom	1.29	1.21	0.76	1.72	2.04
Other Western Europe	0.86	0.83	0.95	1.31	1.49
North America	0.79	0.60	1.32	1.39	1.75
SEMI-INDUSTRIAL COUNTRIES					
'Imports'*b*	0.62	0.53	0.78	0.86	0.73
REST OF WORLD*c*					
'Imports'*b*	0.81	0.85	0.98	1.22	1.64

Sources: Tables A.70 and A.81; *Commodity Trade Statistics, 1959*, United Nations, New York, 1960; national trade statistics.

aWest Germany in 1950–59.
b'Imports' from industrial countries only
cExcluding U.S.S.R.

4. COMPETITION IN THE WORLD MARKET FOR METALS

Exports of steel have been highly concentrated since the early years of the century in relatively few industrial countries, though the degree of concentration has been diminishing. Five countries—Belgium-Luxembourg, France, Germany, Britain and the United States—accounted for 98 per cent of world steel exports in 1913 and 93 per cent in 1929.   The proportion fell off somewhat (to 86 per cent) in the 1930's with the emergence of Japan as an important exporter, while in the 1950's it fell still further (to 74 per cent in both 1955 and 1957) mainly as a result of the increasing importance of exports from the Soviet Union and from some of the smaller producing countries (see Table 9.16).

In 1913, Germany (which then included Luxembourg) was by far the largest steel exporting country, accounting for nearly two-fifths of the total.   Her relative decline as a steel exporter in the inter-war period can be attributed in the main to the growth of exports from Belgium-Luxembourg and France-Saar. The relative importance of British and United States exports fell off between 1913 and 1929, but the United States share increased in the late 1930's mainly as a result of higher sales to Japan.

Since 1950, Britain's share of world steel exports has continued to fall.   In the early years of the decade, steel was in short supply and exports from Britain were restricted.   Even with the expansion in steel capacity achieved in the later 1950's, the rate of increase in output was insufficient both to feed the

Table 9.16.   *Shares of world exports of semi-finished and finished steel products,*
1913–57

Percentage[a]

Exports from	1913	1929	1937	1950	1955	1957
Belgium-Luxembourg	12.3[b]	23.3	25.8	21.2	21.0	19.1
France[c]	3.8	17.3	10.5	20.7	19.0	13.9
Germany[d]	37.6	21.6	18.6	11.0	9.9	15.7
United Kingdom	22.8	17.8	13.8	15.1	9.8	9.8
United States	21.1	12.6	17.0	16.3	14.2	15.7
Japan	—	0.9	4.2	3.4	6.8	2.9
Eastern Europe[e]	—	4.5	4.5	6.9	10.6	11.0
Other countries[f]	2.4	2.0	5.6	5.4	8.7	11.9
TOTAL	100.0	100.0	100.0	100.0	100.0	100.0
Total in million tons	12.0	17.9	14.4	15.8	26.1	30.8

Source: Long-Term Trends and Problems of the European Steel Industry, United Nations
Economic Commission for Europe, Geneva, 1959.

[a]Based on tonnage exported.
[b]Belgium only.
[c]Including Saar (except in 1913 and 1937).
[d]West Germany in 1950–57; including Saar in 1913 and 1937.
[e]Czechoslovakia, Poland and the Soviet Union.
[f]Austria, Italy, Netherlands, Norway, Sweden, Yugoslavia; Canada and Australia.

growing demand from the home engineering industry and other steel consumers,
and also to attain a substantial increase in exports.   While world trade in steel
virtually doubled between 1950 and 1957, British exports rose by only one-
quarter.   From 1955 to 1959, British steel production rose by only 2 per cent,
whereas West Germany's output increased by 21 per cent and her share of world
steel exports also rose sharply.   The Soviet Union—now the world's second
largest steel producer—has become an important exporter in recent years, with
shipments mainly to Eastern Europe, China and India.

The percentages shown in Table 9.16 are based on the weight of steel products
exported, and thus do not reflect the trends in some countries towards the
export of more highly fabricated products.   In British exports, for example,
tubes and fittings—one of the more expensive types of steel product per ton—
represented only 6 per cent of the total in 1913 and 10 per cent in 1929, but by
1957 had reached 21 per cent.   Similar trends towards a higher proportion of
the more expensive products can be seen in German and American exports.
Exports from Belgium-Luxembourg, on the other hand, are still heavily
dependent on ingots, sections and other semi-processed items.   In 1959, the
unit value of steel products exported from Belgium-Luxembourg was $114 per
ton, compared with $131 for France, $138 for West Germany and $170 for

Britain, so that on a value basis the fall in Britain's share since pre-war would be significantly less than is indicated by the tonnage figures.

There has, nonetheless, been a drastic decline in the British share of steel going to many important markets since 1929—and even more so since 1913. A major decline in Britain's share occurred in Indian imports: Britain supplied about 60 per cent in 1913, 52 per cent in 1929 and 39 per cent in 1937 (on a tonnage basis); by 1955, the percentage was down to 17 and by 1957 to $12\frac{1}{2}$. Japan, West Germany and the Soviet Union were the main steel exporters to India in 1957. Falling British shares since pre-war are also in evidence in the Middle East and Latin America, but Britain has not lost much ground in the main Commonwealth markets (to which preference was given in the years of steel scarcity).

Germany has traditionally been the main steel supplier to other Western European countries, and since the war over half of West Germany's steel exports have gone to this area. Though Germany has been the main beneficiary from the expansion in the intra-trade in steel in Western Europe since 1950, exports from Belgium-Luxembourg and France to other countries in the area also increased substantially. United States exports are fairly highly concentrated in Western Hemisphere markets (in 1957, for example, these took 60 per cent, by weight, of all United States exports of steel products), while most of Britain's shipments abroad go to the Commonwealth countries, apart from tubes and fittings sent to the oil countries. These traditional ties have tended to become weaker to some extent in recent years with increasing competition between the main producing countries and with the effect on trade channels of new institutional arrangements, particularly in Western Europe.

A further trend which might affect the relative position of the main exporting countries is that industrializing countries will tend to begin production in the less-processed forms, such as ingots, sections, etc. They will therefore tend to shift the balance of their import demand towards the more highly-fabricated products, such as tubes, sheets and railway construction accessories. If this trend became pronounced it might well necessitate some re-adjustment of the pattern of output in countries like Belgium-Luxembourg which tend to specialize in the less-fabricated sections of the industry[1].

Aluminium

As already mentioned, the location of aluminium plants depends on the availability of large quantities of low-cost electric power, while the siting of refineries for the other non-ferrous metals is heavily dependent on the relative costs of transporting ore and metal from the ore-producing to the metal-consuming countries. An examination of market shares held by each industrial

[1]There are, indeed, some indications already of greater emphasis in exports from Belgium-Luxembourg on higher quality steel products.

Table 9.17. *Share of world exports of aluminium[a], 1929–59*

Percentage

Exports from	1929	1937	1950	1955	1959[b]
Canada	30	34	57	63	45
Norway	25	15	8	8	13
United States	7	1	3	2	11
France, Germany and United Kingdom	19	25	19	14	14
Other industrial countries[c]	19	25	13	12	11
Other countries[d]	—	—	0	1	6[e]
TOTAL	100	100	100	100	100
Total in thousand metric tons	117	132	546	752	1056

Sources: As for Table 9.14.

[a]Excluding exports from Soviet countries.

[b]Exports in 1959 from the Soviet Union were 88 thousand tons (122 thousand tons in 1958) and from Hungary 5 thousand tons.

[c]Austria, Belgium-Luxembourg, Denmark, Italy, Netherlands, Sweden, Switzerland and Japan.

[d]Australia, Cameroun Republic, Hong Kong, Malaya, Taiwan and Yugoslavia.

[e]Of which, Cameroun Republic 4 per cent.

country therefore has not the same significance for non-ferrous metals as for steel. In aluminium, for example, the proportion of world exports supplied by Canada and Norway—the two low-cost producers—was about one-half before the war, rose to two-thirds or more in the period 1950–55, but has since fallen somewhat (see Table 9.17). From 1955 to 1959 Canadian exports have been virtually stable, while exports from Norway, the United States and the Cameroun Republic increased sharply. With the devaluation of its currency in 1957, and again in 1959, the unit value of Cameroun's exports of aluminium in 1959 fell below even the Canadian and Norwegian export price[1]. Future trends in market shares for aluminium will depend very much on the availability of the large amounts of capital investments required for hydro-electric development; if sufficient capital is forthcoming the prospects in the medium term are for an appreciable increase in West Africa's share of a growing world market.

[1]Export unit values per ton in 1959 were: Canada and Norway, $490; Cameroun Republic, about $430.

CHAPTER 10

CAPITAL GOODS

As was shown in Chapter 7, capital goods[1] have constituted the most dynamic element in the upward trend in trade in manufactures since at least the beginning of the century. Within the total of capital goods, transport equipment (excluding passenger road vehicles) has shown a sharper secular increase than machinery. Taken as a whole, trade in capital goods has roughly doubled in volume every ten years since 1900 if the slump and recovery of the 1930's are excluded.

In the period before 1914, trade in capital goods increased at virtually the same rate as their production. The depression of the 1930's had, however, a severe adverse effect on trade in capital goods, and the recovery in the latter part of the decade was mainly a recovery in home output in the main industrial countries rather than one in imports. The early post-war period, too, saw a more rapid rise in production than trade, but from 1950 to 1959 both trade and production once more increased at the same proportionate rate (Table 10.1).

The general relationship between economic growth and imports of machinery and transport equipment has already been discussed in Chapter 7. In the following sections, the factors influencing the demand for and supply of capital goods are further explored, followed by an examination of the main trends since 1899 in world trade in capital goods.

1. THE DEMAND FOR CAPITAL GOODS

Our first task is to discover whether changes in gross capital investment in machinery and transport equipment can validly be related to industrialization or to economic growth generally. If an underlying relationship of this kind

---

[1]'Capital goods' are defined here as machinery and transport equipment (other than passenger road vehicles); see Appendix D for the detailed definition. This corresponds very broadly with the concept of finished capital assets which enter international trade and which are normally purchased on capital account by firms or Government agencies. Intermediate products, such as constructional steel parts, or building materials, which may eventually form a significant part of gross capital formation in the importing country are, in any case, excluded from the scope of the definition. Trade in prefabricated structures is excluded for statistical convenience; since trade in these is relatively quite small, no harm is done by their exclusion here (they are treated separately in Chapter 14). Of greater significance, perhaps, is that the trade figures for machinery and transport equipment inevitably include minor pieces of equipment and spare parts which may be bought by firms on current account; they would therefore not be comparable in this respect with the statistics of capital formation where these are based on accounting data rather than on commodity flows. Finally, the trade figures include trade in military equipment, such as army trucks or military aircraft; these cannot readily be separated out from the normal commercial trade, except for the large shipments under 'special categories' from the United States, which have been excluded here.

Table 10.1. *World trade^a in capital goods in relation to world manufacturing production, 1899–1959*

$ billion at constant prices, and index numbers, 1929 = 100

	Values at 1913 prices^b			Values at 1955 prices^c				
	1899	1913	1929	1929	1937	1950	1955	1959
WORLD TRADE								
Machinery	0.28	0.68	1.07	4.07	3.18	5.38	7.67	9.69
INDEX	26	64	100	100	78	132	188	238
Transport equipment (excluding passenger road vehicles)	0.10	0.24	0.94	1.52	1.39	2.63	3.58	4.35
INDEX	11	26	100	100	91	173	234	284
Total, capital goods	0.38	0.92	2.01	5.59	4.57	8.01	11.25	14.04
INDEX	19	46	100	100	82	143	202	251
WORLD MANUFACTURING PRODUCTION								
Total index	36	61	100	100	115	190	252	294
of which								
Metal goods^d	20	47	100	100	104	202	292	345

Sources: Tables A.6 and A.80; *Industrial Statistics, 1900–1959*, O.E.E.C., Paris, 1960; *Statistical Yearbooks*, United Nations, New York.

^{a}Exports from twelve main exporting countries.
^{b}Excluding exports from the Netherlands.
^{c}Including exports from the Netherlands.
^{d}Not strictly comparable in scope with the index for trade in capital goods, since it includes passenger road vehicles and metalwares (tools, cutlery, etc.).

does exist, and if it can be quantified, this would constitute a large part of any explanation of the trend in international trade in capital equipment. The relation being sought here is between economic growth and *gross* investment in plant, machinery and vehicles, since trade in capital equipment cannot be subdivided according to whether it is intended for replacement of obsolescent plant or for extension of the capital stock.

The difficulties involved are twofold. First, from the theoretical viewpoint, there is no necessary, unique, relationship between gross investment and economic growth. Second, the task of finding whether there is, in practice, any general long-term relationship between the two is bedevilled by numerous statistical difficulties.

Economic growth, in the sense of increasing real income per head, and investment in fixed capital, are inter-related and re-act upon each other. Though increased investment is normally associated with an increase in output per head, the causal relationship is not a simple one. It is now generally accepted that technical progress is a major cause of increases in productivity, and this can be distinguished in principle from the accumulation of capital as such. The latter may be either 'capital extending' or 'capital deepening', according to whether it results in increased total output (with no rise in productivity) or in increased productivity (irrespective of the effect on total output). But even capital-deepening investment could, in principle, take place without technological progress; simply by providing more machinery per worker of the type already in use, it is probable that output per worker would be increased. However, insofar as new plant embodies technological improvements, the capital-deepening process will result in greater productivity for this reason also.

Apart from capital accumulation and technological progress, increases in output per head can also result from an increase in the degree of utilization of the capital stock. Thus economic growth, if measured by increases in output per head, bears no necessarily unique relationship to net investment in capital assets, since this—the increase in capital stock—is only one of many factors affecting total output. It follows that the relation between economic growth over time in any country and its rate of gross investment is also not a unique one.

However, if a long time-period is considered rather than year-to-year changes, variations in output per head due to variations in the degree of utilization of the capital stock are likely to be minimized. With a constant rate of technical progress, the relation between output per head and the capital stock can be expected to be reasonably stable in the longer term. Even so, the rate of growth in net investment will not be uniquely related to the rate of growth in total output except under very special circumstances. Nonetheless, it might be the case that these two rates of growth moved together in practice over a certain range and if this were so it would be a useful rule of thumb to have.

The relationship between investment and economic growth is, however, extremely difficult to demonstrate statistically. First, there is the difficulty of disentangling the effects of capital accumulation from those of technical progress. From some pioneer work in this field on the American and British statistics, it appears that the greater part of the increase in labour productivity in these two countries has been associated with technical progress[1]; but similar studies can be made for very few other countries because of lack of data on the capital stock.

A convenient approach to the problem of the relation between investment and growth, when a number of countries at different stages of development are considered together, is to compare their rates of growth with the corresponding proportions of gross product invested in producers' durable goods. The

[1]R. M. Solow, 'Technical Change and the Aggregate Production Function', *Review of Economics and Statistics*, Vol. 39, No. 3, August 1957; W. B. Reddaway and A. D. Smith, 'Progress in British Manufacturing Industries in the Period 1948–1954', *Economic Journal*, Vol. 70, No. 277, March 1960.

Table 10.2. *Rates of growth in investment in producers' durables^a and gross product, shares of investment in gross product and incremental capital-output ratios, 1950–59*

	Annual rate of growth			Share of investment in gross product^c (*Percentage*)	Incremental capital-output ratio^d
	Invest-ment^a (*Percentage*)	Gross product^b	Ratio		
INDUSTRIAL COUNTRIES					
Austria	9.3	5.7	1.6	12.6	2.2
Belgium-Luxembourg	2.1	2.7	0.8	8.1	3.0
Denmark	3.7	2.7	1.4	9.9	3.7
France	5.8	4.0	1.4	9.8	2.5
Germany^e	9.9	7.5	1.3	13.0	1.7
Italy	5.2	5.7	0.9	10.2	1.8
Netherlands	9.5	4.6	2.1	11.9	2.6
Norway	5.0	3.5	1.4	17.4	5.0
Sweden	3.6	3.3	1.1	8.1	2.5
United Kingdom	4.0	2.4	1.7	8.6	3.6
Canada	2.2	3.9	0.6	9.1	2.3
United States	0.3	3.3	0.1	6.5	2.0
OTHER COUNTRIES					
Argentina	2.7	1.0	2.7	7.9	7.9
Brazil	4.4	6.0^f	0.7	8.4	1.4
Chile	10.4	3.2	3.3	5.8	1.8
Colombia	11.8	4.5	2.6	8.0	1.8
Philippines	14.6	5.6	2.6	3.3	0.6
Union of South Africa	3.0	5.1^f	0.6	8.4	1.6
Venezuela	6.8	8.3	0.8	12.0	1.4

Source: Yearbook of National Accounts Statistics, 1960, United Nations, New York, 1961.

^{a}Gross investment in machinery and transport equipment, valued at constant prices.
^{b}Gross domestic product, valued at constant prices.
^{c}Average for period 1950–59.
^{d}Share of investment in producers' durables in gross product divided by annual rate of growth in gross product.
^{e}West Germany.
^{f}1950–58.

relevant data are summarized in Table 10.2 for the period 1950–59 for some 20 countries, both industrial and other. For the industrial countries, there is a definite positive relationship, which can be seen in Fig. 10.1, between the proportion of gross product invested in producers' durables in this period, and the average rate of growth in the gross product itself. Leaving Norway aside as a special case,[1] the highest proportion of gross product invested was achieved by West Germany, followed closely by Austria and the Netherlands, and these

[1]Norway has an exceptionally large investment per head in ships and in electric power, in both of which the ratio of capital investment to output is relatively high.

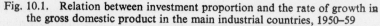

Fig. 10.1.   Relation between investment proportion and the rate of growth in the gross domestic product in the main industrial countries, 1950–59

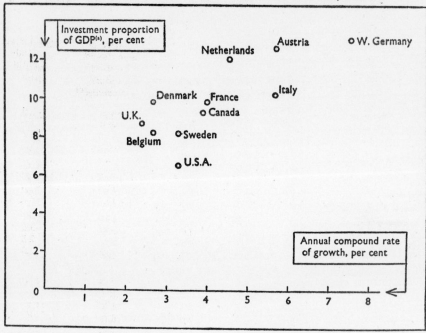

(a)Average for the period 1950–59.

three also had the highest growth rates.   At the other extreme, the United States, Belgium, Sweden and Britain had relatively low investment proportions, and these were among the countries which grew relatively mostly slowly in this period.

At the same time, there is a considerable variation in the investment-growth relationship between the different countries.   Six countries shown in Fig. 10.1 had investment proportions between 8 and 10 per cent of gross product, whereas their rates of growth varied from $2\frac{1}{2}$ to 4 per cent—a much larger proportionate variation.   Again, the investment proportion was much the same in the Netherlands, Austria and West Germany, but the rate of growth was considerably different[1].   Nonetheless, there was a marked tendency for the ratio of the gross investment proportion to the rate of growth (i.e. the 'gross incre-

---

[1]This point—that the differences between countries in the proportion invested in producers' durables is considerably less than the differences in their rates of growth—is reinforced by the fact that the investment proportion differences would be narrowed if allowance were made for the high relative prices of producers' durables in some countries, e.g. Italy and Norway, which tend to inflate their investment proportions, and the low relative prices of such goods in other countries, e.g. Belgium and the United States, which have the reverse effect (see Milton Gilbert and Associates, *Comparative National Products and Price Levels*, O.E.E.C., Paris, 1958).

mental capital-output ratio') to decline as the rate of growth increased; this tendency is also noticeable for the less developed countries shown in Table 10.2.

One possible explanation of the high gross incremental capital-output ratios in the slow-growing countries is that investment had been planned for rather higher rates of growth than in fact were achieved (or were allowed, by government policy, to be achieved). In these countries, some excess capacity developed in this period which tended to be concentrated in particular sectors of the economy; this difficulty would be largely avoided by the fast-growing countries. Second, a rapid expansion of demand tends to stimulate productivity in one way or another, so reducing the incremental gross capital-output ratio[1]. A third reason for the high capital-output ratios in the slow-growing countries is that they tend to devote a higher proportion of their gross investment to replacing obsolescent assets than do the faster growing countries[2].

Another way of considering the relation of gross investment to real output is to compare their respective rates of growth. For the period 1950–59, the ratio of the growth rate of investment to that of real product[3] showed considerable variation, though it exceeded unity for the majority of countries listed in Table 10.2. Such inter-country variations are to be expected over the medium term in the relative rates of growth in investment and real product, for much the same reasons as apply to variations in the incremental gross capital-output ratio.

A corresponding cross-country comparison of growth rates in investment and real product over a long period of time (say 30–50 years) can be made for very few countries. The evidence suggests that here, too, the relationship will differ from country to country, and possibly also from one sub-period to another. For the United States, which has the most detailed historical statistics in this field, a close long-term correlation exists between investment and real product. A regression of the volume of gross capital formation in producers' durables on total real gross national product for the period 1869–1953 yields a co-efficient of 1.3[4]. Recent estimates for Germany show that from 1851 to 1913 the volume of investment rose by 4 per cent per annum, on average, compared

---

[1]See Chapter 8 for a more detailed discussion of the relation between growth and productivity.

[2]This has been demonstrated by A. Lamfalussy (*The United Kingdom and the Six*, 1963), on the assumption that the average length of life of capital assets is the same in each country.

[3]This ratio, η, is related to the incremental capital-output ratio, σ, as follows:—

$$\eta = \sigma . \frac{i}{c}$$

where i is the rate of growth in gross investment and c the proportion of gross product invested.

[4]The regression was based on decade averages given in S. Kuznets, *Capital in the American Economy: Its Formation and Financing*, National Bureau of Economic Research, Princeton, 1961, Table R-12 (variant III of gross national product) and Table R-15. The regression co-efficient (based on a double-logarithmic regression) was 1.28 ± 0.04 ($R^2 = 0.986$).

with a rise of 2.6 per cent per annum in real income, the ratio of the two rates of increase being 1.5[1]. For Denmark, gross investment in machinery and equipment rose at 1.5 times the rate at which the gross domestic product increased from 1870–72 to 1900–01, but from then until 1913–14, the ratio of the two rates of growth increased to 2.2, while for the period 1922–23 to 1938–39, it rose again to 2.5[2].

The conclusion that the relationship between the growth rate of investment in producers' durables and that in the total gross product is likely to be different from country to country, seems to accord with the findings of Professor Kuznets in a careful review of the long period movements in the incremental capital-output ratios for a variety of countries[3]. One of his conclusions is that 'the incremental capital-output ratios . . . differed widely among countries—with average levels for the net domestic ratio ranging from less than 2 to over 5. These ratios tended to show a secular rise, but again the rise was much delayed in some countries, and not observed in others. The rise was less marked but still perceptible in the capital-output ratios derived from capital formation proportions based on totals in constant prices[4]'.

A great deal of further research into long-term investment trends in a large number of countries would be needed before one could establish by this approach whether there is any meaningful long-term relationship and, if so, whether any typical range can be deduced from the statistics. In the next section an indirect approach to the problem is adopted, based on how imports of producers' durables, and the import-content of investment, move with economic growth.

2. THE IMPORT-CONTENT OF INVESTMENT

World production of capital goods is highly concentrated in a few countries though the degree of concentration has not tended to increase since pre-war. The proportion of total world output of metal goods produced in the six large industrial countries was rather more than four-fifths both in 1938 and in 1959 (see Table 10.3); the corresponding proportions for producers' durables

[1]W. G. Hoffmann, 'Long-Term Growth and Capital Formation in Germany', in *The Theory of Capital*, Proceedings of a Conference held by the International Economic Association, London, 1961.

[2]Based on estimates by Kjeld Bjerke ('The National Product of Denmark, 1870–1952', in *Income and Wealth*, Series V, International Association for Research in Income and Wealth, London, 1955).

[3]Simon Kuznets, 'Quantitative Aspects of the Economic Growth of Nations: VI. Long-Term Trends in Capital Formation Proportions', *Economic Development and Cultural Change*, Vol. IX, No. 4, Part II, University of Chicago, July 1961.

[4]*Ibid.*, p. 54.

may well have been higher than this[1].   Moreover, the rise shown since 1955 in the percentages for the 'rest of the world' is due, in large part, to the expansion in production in the relatively well-to-do Southern Dominions, so that the proportion of world output of capital goods that can be attributed to the less-developed countries is still very small—almost certainly under 5 per cent of the world total.

Table 10.3.   *World[a] production of metal goods[b], 1938–59*

	Proportion of world total				Volume change	
					Percentage	
	1938	1948	1955	1959	1938–55	1955–59
Western Europe	58	35	38	39	+110	+ 22
North America	33	59	56	50	+455	+ 6
Japan	3	1	1½	4½	+ 62	+248
Total	94	95	95½	93½	+227	+ 16
of which						
Large industrial countries[c]	81	84	84	82½	+238	+ 16
Small industrial countries	13	11	11½	11	+162	+ 16
Rest of East and South-East Asia	1	1	1	1½	+270	+ 62
Rest of world[a]	5	4	3½	5	+150	+ 58
WORLD TOTAL	100	100	100	100	+223	+ 18

Source: Statistical Yearbook, 1960, United Nations, New York, 1961.

[a]Excluding Soviet countries.
[b]Including passenger road vehicles and metal products other than machinery.
[c]France, Germany, Italy, Japan, United Kingdom and United States.

Much the same conclusion is reached on the basis of relative steel consumption, though not all steel is used in making machinery and vehicles.   In 1959, only four under-developed countries (outside Europe) consumed more than one million tons of steel—India, Argentina, Brazil and Mexico—compared with a world total of some 300 million tons.

This heavy concentration of output in the large industrial countries implies that in all other countries, industrial as well as non-industrial, there is a high degree of dependence on imports for supplies of producers' durables.   For recent years, the degree of dependence on imports can be fairly closely estimated for a number of countries at different stages of economic development (see Table

[1]This comparison excludes production in the Soviet countries.   A crude guide to the relative importance of capital goods production in Soviet and non-Soviet countries is the relative consumption of steel in the two areas which, in 1959, was in the ratio of 3 (Soviet) to 7 (non-Soviet).   Since a negligible proportion of steel is used for passenger cars in the former, whereas cars are important steel consumers in Western countries, the steel ratio under-weights relative Soviet output of capital goods.

10.4). In 1957–59, the import-content of investment in producers' durables averaged only some 7 per cent in five large industrial countries, compared with about 60 per cent in the small industrial countries. Comparable import-content percentages can be obtained for a number of semi-industrial countries, but for only a limited range of non-industrial ones; for the latter the percentages tend to be high; and complete (or virtually complete) dependence on imports for supplies of producers' durables is not uncommon.

There are striking differences in imports of producers' durables per head of population. The smaller industrial countries have far higher imports per head than any other group, while both the larger industrial countries and the non-industrial ones have low per caput imports. The semi-industrial countries tend to be spread between the three other groups (see Fig. 10.2). Australia and New Zealand are exceptional, insofar as they behave in this respect like the small industrial countries, while Colombia behaves like a non-industrial country.

Variations over time from the mid-1950's have generally been fairly small; but large changes cannot be expected over so short a period. Unfortunately,

Table 10.4. *Imports of producers' durables[a] and the import-content of investment in selected countries, 1954–59*

	Total imports		Imports per head		Annual averages Import-content of investment[b]	
	1954–56	1957–59	1954–56	1957–59	1954–56	1957–59
	($ billion, c.i.f.)		($ c.i.f.)		(Percentage)	
LARGE INDUSTRIAL COUNTRIES						
France	0.48	0.66	11	15	12	14
Germany[c]	0.25	0.54	5	10	5	9
Italy	0.31	0.37	6	8	16	16
United Kingdom	0.39	0.60	8	12	10	12
United States	0.45	0.76	3	4	2	3
Total	1.87	2.92	5	8	5	7
SMALL INDUSTRIAL COUNTRIES						
Austria	0.13	0.22	19	31	29	38
Belgium-Luxembourg	0.46	0.48	52	53	63	55
Canada	1.69	1.94	107	114	73	68
Denmark	0.16	0.24	36	53	38	46
Netherlands	0.53	0.69	49	62	56	60
Norway	0.36	0.47	106	133	67	69
Sweden	0.33	0.48	46	65	52	60
Switzerland	0.19	0.27	39	53	35	39
Total	3.85	4.79	62	74	58	59

For footnotes, see next page.

Table 10.4 (cont.)

	Total imports		Imports per head		Import-content of investment[b]	
	1954–56	1957–59	1954–56	1957–59	1954–56	1957–59
	($ billion, c.i.f.)		($ c.i.f.)		(Percentage)	
SEMI-INDUSTRIAL COUNTRIES						
Argentina	0.27[d]	0.32[e]	14[d]	16[e]	63[d]	49[e]
Brazil	0.36[f]	0.50[e]	6[f]	8[e]	58[f]	..
Colombia	0.24	0.14[g]	19	10[g]	100	100[g]
Ireland	0.10	0.11	36	38	100	100
Australia	0.42	0.46	45	47	..	43[h]
New Zealand	0.17	0.17	78	76	46	44
Union of South Africa	..	0.49	..	34	..	84
Yugoslavia	0.10	0.19	5	10	14	21
NON-INDUSTRIAL COUNTRIES						
Burma	0.03	0.05	2	3	58	59
Ceylon	0.03	0.05	3	5	..	100
Cyprus	0.02	0.02	35	35	93	83
Ecuador	0.03	0.03	8	7	..	65
Ghana	0.04	0.05	8	10	100	100
Philippines	0.11	0.15	5	6	76	68
Federation of Rhodesia and Nyasaland	0.12	0.14	16	17	79	79

Sources: Yearbook of National Accounts Statistics, 1960, United Nations, New York, 1961; *Yearbook of International Trade Statistics, 1957* and *1959,* United Nations, New York.

[a] Machinery and transport equipment (excluding passenger road vehicles).

[b] Ratio of imports of machinery and transport equipment (excluding passenger road vehicles) valued c.i.f. in national currency to value of gross investment in machinery and vehicles as recorded in National Accounts data. The investment figures for most countries include business purchases of passenger road vehicles, and to this extent are not comparable with the import figures. See also footnote [1] on page 258.

[c] West Germany.

[d] 1955–56 average.

[e] 1957–58 average.

[f] 1955.

[g] 1957.

[h] 1959.

comparable data for pre-war years are not available except for very few countries, but it can reasonably be assumed that import dependence has fallen as a result of industrial development in the economically advanced countries.

Variations between countries can largely be explained by differences in size and in the degree of industrialization attained. For 18 of the countries included in Table 10.4, a regression of the import-content proportions in 1954–56 on per caput real income and population in 1955 showed that the import-content proportion varied, on average, by some 4 per cent for every 10 per cent variation (in the reverse direction) in per caput real income, and by about 6½ per cent for

Fig. 10.2.   Relation between imports of producers' durables per head and the import-content of investment, 1957–59

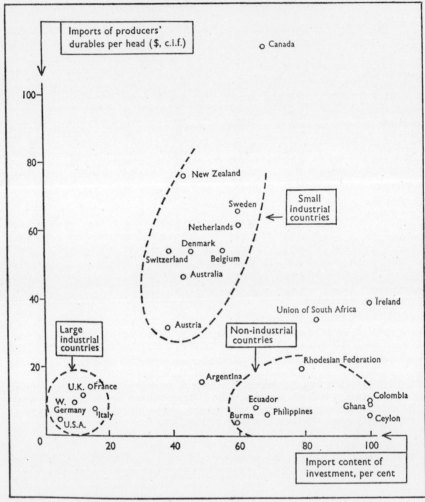

every 10 per cent variation (again in the reserve direction) in total population size[1].

[1]A double logarithmic equation was used, as follows:—

$$\log I = \log \beta_0 + \beta_1 \log Y/N + \beta_2 \log N$$

where I represents the import-content, and Y/N and N the real income per head and total population, respectively.   The co-efficients β_1 and β_2 were calculated as $-0.38\ (\pm 0.13)$ and $-0.66\ (\pm 0.18)$, with $R^2 = 0.766$.   An extra variable for the proportion of exports of goods and services in the gross domestic product was also tried in the regression (cf. Table 6.8), but the resultant co-efficient was not significantly different from zero: $0.12\ (\pm 0.34)$.

If this cross-country result can be taken as a valid indication of how the import proportion changes over time as economies grow[1], it can be combined with the regression results obtained earlier for imports of producers' durables. For the industrial countries, the growth co-efficient for imports of producers' durables was 1.7, while for the semi-industrial countries it was 1.4[2]. Taking the corresponding co-efficient for the import-content of investment as —0.4, the growth co-efficient for investment itself would be 2.1 for the industrial, and 1.8 for the semi-industrial, countries[3]. These two co-efficients are not significantly different, so that for both groups of countries this evidence indicates that, over a long period, gross investment per head in producers' durables tends to grow at about double the rate at which total real income per head increases. However, in view of the evidence given earlier about the ratio of the long-term growth rates of investment and total product in the United States, Germany and Denmark, it seems safer to conclude that, if there is any 'typical' long-term ratio, it is probably in the range of, say, 1.5 to 2.0.

The fact that imports of capital goods per head in the smaller industrial countries are considerably higher than in the other types of economy means that a given rate of economic growth will have a far greater impact on world trade if the growth occurs in these countries than if it takes place elsewhere. An illustrative example (see Table 10.5) makes this clear. The figures are based on the growth co-efficients given earlier (taking the investment growth co-efficient at 2.0), and represent typical countries in each of the four groups shown; they do not purport to be accurate measures or forecasts of how the aggregate of any group of countries will grow in the coming decade.

Assuming that real income per head grows at 3 per cent a year compound between 1957–59 and 1970, and that the growth co-efficients found from past data continue to be applicable in the future, the volume of imports of producers' durables per head would increase by about $50 (at 1957–59 prices) in the smaller industrial countries, compared with $10 or less in the others If we assume a lower rate of growth in the semi-industrial and non-industrial countries (Table 10.5 also shows the results for a 2 per cent per year rate of growth), the discrepancy is, of course, larger. The small industrial countries already

---

[1]Some support for this assumption is provided by the fact that, for all non-food manufactures, the cross-country regression of import proportion on income per head yielded a co-efficient of —0.38, which compared with the corresponding time-series regression co-efficients of —0.38 to —0.53 (see Table 6.8).

[2]Derived by combining the data for 'Machinery' and 'Other transport equipment' in Table 7.14. The full results were:

Industrial countries : 1.72 ± 0.14 ($R^2 = 0.755$).
Semi-industrial countries : 1.43 ± 0.28 ($R^2 = 0.518$).

There were 60 'observations' in the first regression and 33 in the second.

[3]The growth co-efficient for investment (β) can be derived from the equality

$$\beta = \beta_1 - \beta^*_1$$

where β_1 is the growth co-efficient for imports and β^*_1 that for the import-content of investment.

Table 10.5. *Typical patterns of change in investment, production and imports of producers' durables in industrial, semi-industrial and non-industrial countries. 1957–59 to 1970*

	Industrial countries		Semi-industrial countries		Non-industrial countries	
	Large	Small				
GROWTH CO-EFFICIENTS						
Investment	2.0	2.0	2.0		2.0	
Imports	1.7	1.7	1.45		2.0	
	(Annual percentage change (compound))					
Assumed rate of growth in total real income per head, 1957–59 to 1970			A	B	A	B
	3.0	3.0	2.0	3.0	2.0	3.0
APPROXIMATE POSITION IN 1957–59	*($ per head at 1957–59 prices)*					
Investment	115	125	25		7	
Imports	8	75	15		7	
Production for home use	107	50	10		—	
APPROXIMATE POSITION IN 1970			A	B	A	B
Investment	210	230	40	45	11	13
Imports	14	130	20	25	11	13
Production for home use	196	100	20	20	—	—
CHANGE FROM 1957–59 TO 1970						
Investment	+95	+105	+15	+20	+4	+6
Imports	+ 6	+ 55	+ 5	+10	+4	+6
Production for home use	+89	+ 50	+10	+10	—	—

Sources: Yearbook of National Accounts Statistics, 1960, United Nations, New York, 1961; Yearbook of International Trade Statistics, 1957 and 1959, United Nations, New York.

import a larger total volume of capital goods than do any of the other groups of countries (see Table 10.4), and their share of world imports seems likely to increase still further.

As Fig. 10.2 shows, the groups are not entirely clear-cut and, with further economic growth, the typical semi-industrial country can be expected to increase its imports per head, and so move nearer to the position now occupied by the small industrial countries; as mentioned earlier, Australia and New Zealand have already developed in this way.

3. THE PATTERN OF WORLD TRADE IN CAPITAL GOODS

Main export markets

Several major trends stand out in the period since 1899. First, Western Europe has made a large contribution to the expansion of world imports of capital equipment; over the sixty years up to 1929, and again from 1937 to 1955,

Table 10.6. *Changes in exports of capital goods by major market, 1899–1959*

$ billion at 1955 prices

Exports to	Total in 1899[a]	Change from 1899[a] to 1929	1929 to 1937	1937 to 1955	1955 to 1959	Total in 1959
INDUSTRIAL COUNTRIES[b]	0.62	+ 1.71	− 0.80	+ 3.07	+ 1.48	6.08
France, Germany[c] and United Kingdom	0.34	+ 0.42	− 0.25	+ 0.46	+ 0.48	1.45
Other Western Europe	0.20	+ 0.60	− 0.24	+ 1.26	+ 0.48	2.30
Canada	0.03	+ 0.51	− 0.23	+ 1.02	+ 0.05	1.38
United States	0.02	+ 0.09	− 0.05	+ 0.33	+ 0.38	0.76
SEMI-INDUSTRIAL COUNTRIES[d]	0.22	+ 1.15	− 0.17	+ 1.73	+ 0.14	3.06
Southern Dominions	0.08	+ 0.28	+ 0.09	+ 0.50	− 0.08	0.86
India/Pakistan	0.05	+ 0.17	− 0.06	+ 0.34	+ 0.14	0.64
Latin America	0.08	+ 0.65	− 0.22	+ 0.64	+ 0.08	1.23
RUSSIA/U.S.S.R.	0.15	+ 0.06	− 0.07	− 0.04	+ 0.04	0.14
REST OF WORLD	0.23	+ 1.45	+ 0.02	+ 1.92	+ 1.12	4.75
TOTAL	1.22	+ 4.37	− 1.02	+ 6.68	+ 2.78	14.03

Sources: Tables A.6 to A.39 and A.81.

[a] Including passenger road vehicles.
[b] Including Japan.
[c] West Germany in 1955 and 1959.
[d] Including Palestine/Israel, Turkey and Yugoslavia.

one-quarter of the total increase in world exports of capital goods went to the main industrial countries of Western Europe (see Tables 10.6 and 10.7); from 1955 to 1959 the proportion was even higher (one-third). Second, Canada has contributed more than any other single country to the expansion in import demand, even allowing for the contraction in Canadian capital goods imports from 1955 to 1959. Third, the semi-industrial countries have also played a major role in the total growth in the world market (import-substitution being very small for capital goods), except during the later 1950's when many of these countries had to restrict the growth in their imports for balance of payments reasons. Fourth, Russia was an important market for capital goods before the first World War, but since then the Soviet Union has taken only a small fraction of exports from the Western industrial countries; indeed, the Soviet Union is now a substantial exporter of capital equipment. Finally, the miscellaneous group of countries included in the 'rest of the world' in Tables 10.6 and 10.7 accounted for a varying but substantial proportion of the increase in imports of capital goods in the different periods considered here.

Within Western Europe, imports into the three largest industrial countries—Britain, France and Germany—have increased relatively slowly, taking the

Table 10.7. *Contribution of each importing area to expansion in world market for capital goods and their shares of total import market, 1899–1959*

Percentage

Market	Contribution to change in volume of world trade in capital goods			Share of total import market			
	1899*a* to 1937	1937 to 1955	1955 to 1959	1899*a*	1937	1955	1959
INDUSTRIAL COUNTRIES*b*	27	46	53	46	36	41	44
France, Germany*c* and United Kingdom	5	7	17	21	12	9	10
Other Western Europe	11	19	17	15	14	16	16
Canada	8	15	2	3	7	12	11
United States	1	5	14	1	1	3	6
SEMI-INDUSTRIAL COUNTRIES*d*	30	26	5	19	28	26	22
Southern Dominions	11	8	− 3	6	10	8	6
India/Pakistan	3	5	5	5	4	5	5
Latin America	13	9	3	8	12	10	9
RUSSIA/U.S.S.R.	0	− 1	2	12	3	1	1
REST OF WORLD	43	29	40	23	33	32	33
TOTAL	100	100	100	100	100	100	100
Total in $ billion				0.36	2.11	11.25	16.18

Sources: Tables A.5 to A.39 and A.81; national trade statistics.

*a*Including passenger road vehicles.
*b*Including Japan.
*c*West Germany in 1955 and 1959.
*d*Including Palestine/Israel, Turkey and Yugoslavia.

period as a whole, while those into the smaller industrial countries increased much faster. Though the 'big three' together took one-fifth of all capital goods imports in 1899, they contributed only 5 per cent of the increase in imports from then up to 1937, and little more than this in the subsequent period up to 1955. The small growth shown for the earlier period was very largely due to the sharp contraction in German imports of capital equipment in the 1930's—part of the German policy of autarky in preparation for war[1]. Since 1950, imports into West Germany have risen fairly rapidly, as have those into Britain since 1955. The rise in French capital goods imports in the post-war period has been much less than in British or German imports.

The Canadian economy grew rapidly in the early years of this century, supported by a great increase in immigration and a wave of investment in prairie

[1]Exports of capital equipment to Germany by 1937 were only one-third the 1929 volume.

agriculture and railways[1]. This growth was mirrored in the figures of capital goods exports to Canada, which rose from $12 million in 1899 to $60 million in 1913 (both figures at 1913 prices). A second spurt came during the first World War and in the 1920's as a result of increased world demand for Canadian primary products and the industrial diversification of the economy. From 1913 to 1929, Canadian imports of capital goods rose by nearly $220 million (at 1913 prices), or by $3\frac{1}{2}$ times the 1913 volume, and in this period Canada contributed as much as 20 per cent of the expansion in world imports of capital goods. During the 1930's, Canada experienced a severe and lasting recession, Canadian capital goods imports by 1937 being still some 40 per cent below the 1929 peak, compared with a shortfall of about 20 per cent for world trade in capital goods as a whole. A third wave of investment and growth occurred under the pressures of World War II and continued in the post-war period. Comparing 1955 with 1937 (Table 10.7), Canada was once again a major area of growth for capital goods imports, accounting for 15 per cent of the increase in the world total. The Canadian recession in the years 1957–59 affected imports of capital goods as well as home investment, but seems unlikely to affect significantly the longer-term upward trend.

The semi-industrial countries were extremely important areas of growth in the world market in the period up to the depression of the 1930's, and they have also been of major importance since the second World War. In the early post-war years many countries were able to finance increased imports of capital goods by drawing on reserves of foreign exchange accumulated during the war, but by 1955 reserves had generally been run down (after the post-Korean War price falls) and imports had generally to be restricted for balance of payments reasons. Exceptionally, India was able to achieve a considerable expansion in capital goods imports from 1955 to 1959, with the help of foreign loans and aid and by severe restriction of consumer goods imports.

The importance of the Russian market before 1914 has already been mentioned. Exports to Russia dwindled to virtually zero in the post-Revolutionary period up to the launching of the First Five-Year Plan in 1928. In 1929 and the early 1930's, the Soviet Union was a fairly important market for industrial plant and machinery, but Soviet imports of capital goods fell off in the later 1930's, partly as a result of the expansion in home production. Since the war, the Soviet Union has taken only a negligible proportion of world imports of capital equipment, and has instead become a large exporter, a high proportion of her exports now going to other Soviet countries and to the under-developed areas.

About one-quarter of the expansion in exports of capital goods to the 'rest of the world' from 1955 to 1959 is accounted for by the petroleum exporting

---

[1] R. E. Caves and R. H. Holton, *The Canadian Economy: Prospect and Retrospect* Cambridge, Mass., 1959, pp. 337 *et. seq.*

countries of Venezuela, Iran, Saudi Arabia, Iraq and the Persian Gulf Sheikh-doms. Though comparable detail is not fully available for pre-war, it seems that these petroleum countries also accounted for about one-quarter of the increase shown for the 'rest of the world' from 1929 to 1955. For both periods, the increase in exports to the petroleum countries represented about one-tenth of the total growth in world trade in capital goods.

Exports of capital goods to East European countries (other than the Soviet Union) and to some West European countries are also included in the mis-cellaneous heading of 'rest of the world'. Exports to East Europe in 1959 were relatively small (under $200 million), but those to the West European countries —Austria, Denmark, Finland and Spain—amounted to about $1 billion, or one-fifth of the total for the 'rest of the world' in that year. Exports to under-developed countries outside Europe and the petroleum countries represented about 60 per cent of the total in recent years.

Commodity groups

Three countries—Britain, Germany and the United States—account for a large proportion of world exports of capital equipment[1], so that a good approximation to the changes in the commodity-pattern of world trade can be obtained by analysing the exports from these three countries. This has been done in some detail for 1913, 1937 and 1955 (see Table 10.8), and a corresponding comparison of 1955 with 1959 has been based on exports from all the main industrial countries. The striking feature of Table 10.8 is the general stability of the commodity pattern of trade; substantial changes have occurred in relatively few of the commodity groups shown.

Since 1913, non-electric machinery has fallen slightly in relative importance, while electric machinery and transport equipment have both increased relatively. Mechanical engineering products are, however, still the main group, being over half the total, while electrical engineering goods are still under one-quarter. The relatively small percentage changes in these broad groups took place before 1937, but within the groups some continuing trends can be seen. The outstanding ones have been a downward trend in the relative importance of railway vehicles and textile machinery, and an uptrend—interrupted in the later 1950's—in road vehicles and construction, etc. machinery. In railway and road vehicles the major relative changes took place in the inter-war period. The fall in the percentage for ships from 1913 to 1937 reflects the sharp cutback in ship replace-ments during the Depression of the 1930's, which was only slowly made good towards the end of the decade; the subsequent rise in the percentage for ships is due to the growth in world petroleum consumption and the consequent demand for new tankers. There were, of course, numerous other trends of significance,

[1]See Table 10.9.

including a relative growth in trade in radio, telephone and telegraph equipment, in agricultural machinery and tractors, and in electric power-generating equipment.

These various trends reflect to a large extent the development of new products, such as commercial vehicles, radio and many types of construction machinery, and the decline of older products, such as railway equipment and textile

Table 10.8. *Exports of capital goods by main commodity group,* 1913–59

Percentage

	Exports from United States, United Kingdom and Germany[a]			Exports from 10 industrial countries[b]	
	1913[c]	1937[c]	1955	1955	1959
NON-ELECTRIC MACHINERY	60.0	55.3	53.3	53.0	53.5
Power generating machinery	9.7	6.7	7.1	7.0	7.9
Agricultural machinery and tractors	7.5	5.9	8.8	8.2	7.4
Office machinery	2.6	3.3	2.3	2.6	3.0
Metal-working machinery	5.0	9.2	5.4	4.8	5.4
Construction and mining machinery	2.2[d]	5.4	8.5	7.4	7.2
Textile machinery	7.2	5.5	3.8	3.8	3.1
Other machinery	25.8	19.3	19.4	19.2	19.5
ELECTRIC MACHINERY	16.8	18.5	18.5	19.7	19.8
TRANSPORT EQUIPMENT	23.2	26.2	26.2	27.3	26.7
Railway vehicles	10.9	3.8	3.2	3.8	2.2
Road vehicles	4.7	15.1	15.8	14.1	12.5
Aircraft	.	3.9	3.0	2.7	3.5
Ships and boats	7.6	3.4	4.2	6.7	8.6
TOTAL	100.0	100.0	100.0	100.0	100.0
Total in $ billion at 1955 prices	2.14	3.41	8.46	10.90	13.58

Sources: Foreign Trade Statistical Bulletins, Series IV and Series B, O.E.E.C., Paris; national trade statistics.

[a] West Germany in 1955.

[b] Belgium-Luxembourg, France, Italy, Netherlands, Sweden, United Kingdom and West Germany; Canada and United States; Japan.

[c] Because of the different commodity classifications of the three exporting countries, the percentages for commodity groups can only be approximately accurate.

[d] Mining machinery only.

machinery.   Even so, the classification used is too broad to reveal more than a few of the main changes in trend.   Within the electrical engineering field, for example, radio communication equipment, including radar, and transistorised radio sets, have both grown fairly rapidly in recent years, while new mechanical developments in nuclear power plant and electronic engineering and automation indicate that trade in these fields may well be substantial in the next decade or two.

4. COMPETITION IN THE WORLD MARKET
FOR CAPITAL GOODS

The supply of capital equipment on the world market has remained considerably more concentrated in the hands of the 'big three' industrial countries—the United States, Britain and Germany—than has that of other manufactures. In 1913, for example, some four-fifths of all capital goods exports came from the big three, and the proportion was the same in both 1929 and 1937; by 1950 it had fallen to three-quarters, and there was a further small fall, to 70 per cent, by 1959. By contrast, the proportion of other manufactures exported by the big three was only two-thirds in 1913 and fell to one-half by 1959. Only large industrial countries export a full range of capital equipment on a substantial scale. Exports from the smaller industrial countries tend to be more specialized; for example Swiss machine tools of advanced design, or Swedish electrical apparatus.

The relative position of each of the big three has, however, changed considerably since the beginning of the century (see Table 10.9). Britain's preeminent position was fast being whittled away in the decade before 1914 by the expansion in German engineering exports. The further loss of ground by Britain in the 1920's was, however, due to the great expansion in exports by the United States, which virtually doubled her share of world trade in this category between 1913 and 1929, most of the increase occurring during the first World War. Germany's share was also reduced for the same reason in this period. Changes between 1929 and 1937 were relatively small, but in the early post-war years up

Table 10.9. *Exports of capital goods by country of origin, 1899–1959*

							Percentage
Exports from	1899a	1913a	1929	1937	1950	1955	1959
United Kingdom	44.2	31.1	20.0	19.3	27.5	23.0	20.4
France	6.2	6.1	5.0	2.6	5.4	5.4	5.4
Germany	17.2	30.1	21.7	24.4	..	..	..
West Germany	—	—	—	18.2	6.3	17.7	21.2
Other Western Europeb	9.9	10.3	11.7	14.2	15.3	14.9	15.9
United States	22.5	20.8	39.2	35.3	41.4	34.5	29.9
Canada	—	1.4	1.9	1.8	2.9	2.4	2.4
Japan	—	0.2	0.5	2.4	1.2	2.1	4.8
TOTALc	100.0	100.0	100.0	100.0	100.0	100.0	100.0
Total in $ billion	0.36	0.92	2.48	2.11	6.39	11.25	16.18

Sources: Tables A.46 to A.68 and A.80.

aExcluding estimated value of exports of passenger road vehicles.
bBelgium-Luxembourg, Italy, Netherlands (except in 1899 and 1913), Sweden and Switzerland.
cIncluding India.

to 1950 the absence of Germany from the world market, and the needs of post-war reconstruction in other Continental countries, allowed both Britain and the United States to increase their shares very considerably. The outstanding feature of the subsequent decade was the rapid comeback of West Germany in the world capital goods market: by 1957, her share had recovered to the comparable pre-war percentage, while by 1959 the latter had been comfortably exceeded.

Apart from the early 1950's, when special export opportunities were available, Britain's share remained essentially unchanged for the 30 years up to 1959. By that year, the United States share had fallen to the lowest probably since the mid-1920's. The rise of Japanese exports in recent years is also of importance as indicating a possible future trend.

Area patterns of trade

The different rates of growth in demand for imported capital goods by different areas of the world will affect the share of world exports from each of the main industrial countries, insofar as these have special trading links with particular areas. Britain, for example, has traditionally relied on Commonwealth markets for the greater part of her overseas demand for capital equipment, whereas the United States has, since the first World War, relied chiefly on Western Hemisphere markets, and Germany on Europe and the Middle East.

The market pattern of exports before the first World War was, however, very different from that subsequently. In 1899, as much as one-quarter of German exports went to Russia, which also took one-eighth of Britain's exports; by 1929, the proportions had fallen to 7 and 2 per cent, respectively. After the first World War, the expanding Canadian market took a much larger proportion of America's exports (one-quarter in 1929, only one-tenth in 1899), while the proportion of Britain's exports directed to the overseas Dominions also increased considerably. It was during the period up to 1929, in fact, that the subsequent pattern of market shares was substantially established.

The fall in Britain's share of the trade in capital goods from over 40 per cent to 20 per cent, from 1899 to 1929, was almost entirely due to large reductions in her shares of almost all the main import markets over this period. The United States' gain (23 to 39 per cent), however, was mainly due to the fact that her principal markets (Canada and Latin America) were expanding faster than those elsewhere. Germany gained an increasing share of the West European import market, but this was partly offset by an adverse shift in the area pattern of trade (due to some extent to the contraction in Russian imports mentioned earlier).

Since 1929, Britain has continued to lose ground—particularly to Germany—in India and Pakistan, and in several other semi-industrial and non-industrial markets; offsetting increases in shares were, however, achieved in a number of industrial countries, especially Germany and North America, and in the

Table 10.10.   *Relative shares of main markets for capital goods*, 1929 *and* 1959

Exports from

Exports to		United King-dom	Ger-many[a]	Other Western Europe[b]	United States	Total[e]	Total[e] ($ billion at 1955 prices)
				(Percentage)			
INDUSTRIAL COUNTRIES							
United Kingdom	1929	—	23	20	55	100	0.31
	1959	—	29	44	22	100	0.45
France	1929	19	38	16	26	100	0.30
	1959	15	43	25	17	100	0.52
Germany[a]	1929	12	—	38	49	100	0.15
	1959	19	—	58	21	100	0.48
Other Western Europe	1929	15	41	28	16	100	0.80
	1959	15	42	30	11	100	2.30
United States	1929	18	46	19	—	100[d]	0.10
	1959	22	17	17	—	100[d]	0.76
Canada	1929	11	1	—	88	100	0.54
	1959	10	2	2	85	100	1.38
Total[e]	1929	13	24	18	44	100	2.33
	1959	14	24	24	31	100	6.08
SEMI-INDUSTRIAL COUNTRIES							
Southern Dominions	1929	49	5	3	36	100	0.35
	1959	53	11	9	24	100	0.86
India/Pakistan	1929	71	7	5	14	100	0.22
	1959	46	25	10	13	100	0.64
Other semi-industrial countries	1929	17	16	10	54	100	0.80
	1959	10	17	18	52	100	1.56
Total	1929	34	12	8	43	100	1.37
	1959	30	17	14	35	100	3.06
REST OF WORLD	1929	18	26	23	30	100	1.90
	1959	23	20	23	24	100	4.89
TOTAL	1929	20	22	17	39	100	5.59
	1959	20	21	21	30	100	14.03

Sources: Foreign Trade Statistical Bulletins, 1959, Series B and C, O.E.E.C., Paris, 1960; *Yearbook of International Trade Statistics, 1959*, Vol. II, United Nations, New York, 1960; national trade statistics.

[a]West Germany in 1959.
[b]Belgium-Luxembourg, France, Italy, Netherlands, Sweden and Switzerland.
[c]Including Canada, Japan and India.
[d]Of which, the share held by Canada rose from 14 per cent in 1929 to 30 per cent in 1959, while Japan's share rose from 2 to 14 per cent over the period.
[e]Including Japan.

Southern Dominions (see Table 10.10). Germany has made some notable gains in India, Pakistan and the Southern Dominions, again comparing 1959 with the position thirty years earlier, but lost heavily in the United States import market, mainly because of sharp increases in the Canadian and Japanese shares. The smaller countries of Western Europe have generally gained ground, a particularly large increase in import share being achieved in the British market. The United States, by contrast, suffered big reductions in her share in the main industrial countries of Western Europe, and in the Southern Dominions, but has continued to dominate the Canadian market.

Table 10.11. *Changes in the volume of exports of capital goods attributable to changes in size, area pattern and shares of the world market[a], 1929–59*

	United Kingdom	United States	Germany[b]	Other countries[c]	Total
				$ *billion at* 1955 *prices*	
1929 exports	0.97	2.02	1.10	1.50	5.59
Change from 1929 to 1937 attributable to change in					
(a) Size of world market	− 0.17	− 0.37	− 0.20	− 0.27	− 1.02
(b) Area pattern of demand	+ 0.05	− 0.06	− 0.01	+ 0.02	0
(c) Share of individual market areas	− 0.09	+ 0.25	− 0.08	− 0.08	0
Total	− 0.22	− 0.18	− 0.29	− 0.34	− 1.02
1937 exports	0.75	1.84	0.82	1.16	4.57
Change from 1937 to 1955 attributable to change in					
(a) Size of world market	+ 1.09	+ 2.70	+ 1.19	+ 1.70	+ 6.68
(b) Area pattern of demand	+ 0.01	+ 0.20	− 0.02	− 0.20	0
(c) Share of individual market areas	+ 0.74	− 0.86	0	+ 0.13	0
Total	+ 1.84	+ 2.04	+ 1.17	+ 1.63	+ 6.68
1955 exports	2.59	3.88	1.99	· 2.79	11.25
Change from 1955 to 1959 attributable to change in					
(a) Size of world market	+ 0.64	+ 0.96	+ 0.49	+ 0.69	+ 2.78
(b) Area pattern of demand	− 0.10	− 0.02	+ 0.06	+ 0.06	0
(c) Share of individual market areas	− 0.28	− 0.88	+ 0.48	+ 0.68	0
Total	+ 0.26	+ 0.06	+ 1.03	+ 1.43	+ 2.78
1959 exports	2.85	3.94	3.02	4.22	14.03

Sources: Based on Table A.74 and related data.

[a]For method of calculation, see page 199.
[b]West Germany in 1955 and 1959.
[c]Belgium-Luxembourg, France, Italy, Netherlands, Sweden, Switzerland; Canada; Japan.

By combining the information about changing shares of particular import markets, as in Table 10.10, with data about changes in the relative size of these markets, the effect of these two elements on the volume of exports from each industrial country can be estimated[1]. The results of this computation (Table 10.11) show that over the whole period since 1929 the changing area pattern of imports of capital goods was generally of little significance in explaining changes in the volume of exports. For each country, or country group, changes in exports resulting from shifts in the competitive position in particular markets were generally the decisive factor—apart from the general upward trend in the total—in determining the volume of exports.

Commodity patterns of trade

Some part of the changes in the share of the world market is also due to the shifts in the commodity-pattern of trade which have already been discussed. In 1913, about three-quarters of exports of capital goods from the United States consisted of non-electric machinery, but by the late 1930's the pattern had been considerably modified in favour of transport equipment and, to a lesser extent, electrical machinery, both of which had expanded at a faster rate on the world market than had non-electric machinery. Britain's pattern of exports also showed a considerable shift towards electrical machinery between 1913 and 1937, but this was entirely at the expense of transport equipment—the other rapidly expanding group[2].

The contrast between the British and American experiences here was due essentially to Britain's relative specialisation in railway vehicles and ships, for which world demand was on a downtrend in the inter-war period; whereas, the United States specialized in commercial road vehicles, which underwent a large secular expansion. The decline in Britain's share of the total market in the inter-war period was confined to non-electric machinery and transport equipment; in electric machinery, Britain gained ground relatively to Germany, comparing 1937 with 1913 (see Table 10.12). The rise in the American share in this period was a general one, and was particularly marked in transport equipment. In the 1930's, the United States was pre-eminent in the export of agricultural machinery and tractors, office machinery and commercial vehicles, but in each of these Britain and West Germany have made considerable inroads into the United States' share since the war; in several cases, the successful British or German exporters were subsidiaries of American companies. In aircraft, Britain's share is considerably higher than pre-war, mainly as a result of the restrictions imposed in this field on the German industry. Nonetheless,

[1] The method used has been described on page 199.
[2] Electrical machinery rose from 12 per cent of Britain's exports of capital goods in 1913 to 23 per cent in 1937; for transport equipment (other than passenger road vehicles), the proportions fell from 36 to 24 per cent.

British exports of aircraft and parts also gained ground from the United States industry between 1955 and 1959. By contrast, Britain's competitive weakness in shipbuilding is revealed by the sharp fall in her share of exports in the latter half of the 1950's.

Changes in relative shares of trade in particular commodity groups have generally been of far greater importance in influencing the global market shares than have changes in the commodity-pattern of world trade, as is shown in Table

Table 10.12. *Exports of capital goods from the United States, United Kingdom and Germany by main commodity group, 1913–59*

Percentage[a]

	United States				United Kingdom				Germany[b]			
	1913	1937	1955	1959	1913	1937	1955	1959	1913	1937	1955	1959
NON-ELECTRIC MACHINERY	31	43	47	44	34	24	28	27	35	33	25	29
Power-generating machinery	12	29	31	31	59	38	45	47	29	33	24	22
Agricultural machinery and tractors	71	77	55	53	14	12	29	32	15	11	16	15
Office machinery	85	71	55	51	0	7	21	19	15	22	24	30
Metal-working machinery	36	42	44	40	13	8	17	15	51	50	39	45
Other non-electric machinery	24	37	49	46	36	30	25	23	40	33	26	31
ELECTRIC MACHINERY AND APPARATUS	19	31	36	34	28	30	37	30	53	39	27	36
TRANSPORT EQUIPMENT	13	59	50	43	60	23	34	32	27	18	16	25
Railway vehicles	18	23	37	33	44	45	42	37	38	32	21	30
Road vehicles (except for passenger)	24	83	61	52	40	14	29	26	36	3	10	22
Aircraft	..	52	56	40	..	24	44	56	..	24	0	4
Ships and boats	2	2	11	22	91	36	42	26	7	62	47	52
TOTAL	25	45	46	42	39	25	31	28	36	30	23	30

Sources: Foreign Trade Statistical Bulletins, Series IV, and Series B, O.E.E.C., Paris; national trade statistics.

[a]Percentage of total exports of each commodity from the three countries.
[b]West Germany in 1955 and 1959.

10.13. Exceptionally, the changing commodity-pattern from 1937 to 1955 significantly favoured the United States and was detrimental to Germany; it had virtually no influence on Britain's share. The main factor here appears to have been American predominance in the export of tractors, construction and mining machinery and commercial vehicles, in all of which world trade grew faster than for other types of capital equipment[1]. In all three, too, Germany's

[1]See Table 10.8.

contribution has tended to be small, while in some of her specialities (particularly machine tools and ships) the growth in world trade was lower than the average. The main change, however, between 1937 and 1955 was the gain in Britain's share, largely at Germany's expense. This loss was more than made good by West Germany after 1955, though the major loser was the United States and not Britain, West German success in selling road vehicles abroad being a major reason for these changes.

These various changes in market shares since before the first World War appear to reflect essentially the underlying changes in the relative competitive position of the main industrial countries; only a small part can be explained by shifts in the area and commodity patterns of world trade. A number of diverse forces were operating on the competitive position in this period. Some of these can be considered as quite general in character, affecting the whole economy of particular countries. In this category would be included the effects of inflationary and deflationary policies, or the effects of the different rates of economic growth in the main industrial countries on their productivity, and on the variety

Table 10.13. *Effect of changing commodity-pattern on shares of world market[a] in capital goods*, 1913–59

Percentage of total exports[a] of capital goods

Change attributable to	United Kingdom	United States[b]	Germany[c]
1913[d] to 1937			
(a) Commodity-pattern of trade	+ 0.9	− 0.9	0
(b) Share of trade in each commodity group	− 14.4	+ 20.2	− 5.8
Total	− 13.5	+ 19.3	− 5.8
1937 to 1955			
(a) Commodity-pattern of trade	+ 0.4	+ 2.7	− 3.1
(b) Share of trade in each commodity group	+ 5.7	− 1.6	− 4.1
Total	+ 6.1	+ 1.1	− 7.2
1955 to 1959			
(a) Commodity-pattern of trade	+ 0.4	− 0.4	0
(b) Share of trade in each commodity group	− 2.5	− 3.6	+ 6.1
Total	− 2.1	− 4.0	+ 6.1

Source: Based on working sheets for Table 10.12.

[a]Taking total exports of capital goods from the United Kingdom, United States and Germany as the ' world market' for this purpose.

[b]Excluding 'special category' exports in 1955 and 1959.

[c]West Germany in 1955 and 1959.

[d]Excluding estimated value of exports of passenger road vehicles.

and range of equipment they are able to offer for sale abroad. This latter type of effect has been discussed in Chapter 8, and little needs to be added here, except perhaps that the erosion of competitive power which might result from a slow rate of economic growth might well be more severe in the capital goods industries than in other sectors.

Secondly, there are underlying trends, or changes of a relatively long-term nature, in the engineering industry itself which directly affect the competitive position of the main producing countries. Such trends may be either techno-logical as, for example, leadership in design or technical performance, or financial, such as relative trends in wages or materials costs.

In another category are those changes—again affecting the supply side—which are of a temporary character or specific to a particular period. Perhaps the outstanding example in the post-war period was the British rearmament programme adopted in 1951 following the Korean War. This placed a heavy additional burden on the engineering industries which were already working to long order-books for both home and export markets. The rapid expansion of engineering exports from West Germany in the subsequent decade probably owes a good deal to the diversion of much of Britain's effort elsewhere.

Exports from Soviet countries

The discussion of changes in market shares has so far been confined to the main industrial countries of the West. There has, however, been a growing volume of exports of capital equipment from Eastern Europe to non-Soviet countries since the early 1950's, though this trade is still very small in relation to the world total. About nine-tenths of the exports of machinery and transport equipment from Soviet countries has consisted of intra-trade within the group (see Table 10.14), exports from the Soviet Union to China having risen substantially in the period up to 1959[1].

A major trend in recent years has been an increasing proportion of capital goods exports directed to the under-developed areas. In 1955, such exports from the Soviet countries represented under 2 per cent of total capital goods exports to these areas, but by 1959 the proportion had risen to $3\frac{1}{2}$ per cent. For many individual countries, such as India, Cuba (from 1960), Egypt and various other countries in the Middle East and South-East Asia, the relative importance of Soviet supplies was considerably greater than this. This trade has developed on the basis of bilateral trade and payment agreements, in many of which long-term credits advanced by the Soviet Union and other East European countries

---

[1]There was, however, a sharp reduction in exports from the Soviet Union to China in 1960 as a result of China's economic difficulties in that year and her consequent reduced ability to pay for imports.

have been of major importance. Prospects here are considered further in Chapter 15.

Table 10.14. *Exports of machinery and transport equipment[a] from Soviet and other developed countries, 1955 and 1959*

$ *billion, f.o.b.*

	Exports from					
Exports to	Soviet countries		Other developed countries[b]		Total	
	1955	1959	1955	1959	1955	1959
Soviet countries—						
Eastern Europe	1.57	2.20	0.25	0.54	1.82	2.74
China[c]	0.64	0.93	0.01	0.06	0.65	0.99
Other countries—						
Developed[b]	0.11	0.18	7.96	12.11	8.07	12.29
Under-developed[d]	0.09	0.25	5.19	6.99	5.28	7.24
Total	2.41	3.56	13.41	19.70	15.82	23.26

Source: Monthly Bulletin of Statistics, March, 1961 (Special Table E), United Nations, New York.

[a]Including passenger road vehicles, but excluding special category exports from the United States.
[b]North America, Western Europe, Japan and the Southern Dominions.
[c]Including Mongolian People's Republic, North Korea and North Viet-Nam.
[d]All other countries.

CHAPTER 11

CHEMICALS

Since the early years of the century, world trade in chemicals and allied products has increased in volume at a considerably faster rate than world trade in manufactured goods as a whole. From 1899 to 1929, trade in chemicals rose by 170 per cent in volume, as against a rise of about 120 per cent for other manufactures. In the Great Depression, chemicals suffered little by comparison with other commodities, and by 1937 their volume had recovered to only some 7 per cent below the 1929 peak (see Table 11.1), whereas trade in other manufactures was still about 17 per cent lower. In the 1950's chemicals have again been one of the more dynamic sectors of world trade. From 1950 to 1959, their volume rose by 150 per cent, compared with an increase of 65–70 per cent for all other manufactures in the aggregate.

This buoyancy of trade in chemicals reflects several distinct developments. First, because chemicals in one form or another are essential materials in the production process of almost every important manufacturing industry, world demand has expanded with the growth of the world economy and of world manufacturing activity. To a large extent, this is a derived demand, reflecting a technical relationship between the input of chemicals and the output of various types of manufactured product. A second trend, particularly in the post-war period, has been the extended application of existing techniques in various uses; the outstanding example here is the rapid growth in the use of fertilizers by farmers in both the under-developed and more advanced countries. Finally, the development of a new technology in the field of synthetic fibres and synthetic rubber, in petroleum chemicals and in other new chemical products, has opened up a large range of new products and has stimulated new areas of demand. The importance of these new products is discussed in some detail later in this chapter, but it is worth emphasizing at this stage that by the mid-1950's they were already playing a major role in the growth of world trade in chemicals.

Though the volume of trade in chemicals has outpaced that in other manufactures in total, it has grown less rapidly than world production of chemicals (see Table 11.1). The latter, at the same time, has grown more rapidly than manufacturing production as a whole, reflecting the faster growth in world demand for chemicals than for all other manufactures taken together. This disparity in rates of growth in production is a marked feature of industrial development in the economically advanced countries[1]. Of the nine countries listed in Table 11.2, the rate of growth in chemical production was $1\frac{1}{2}$ times or more that in total manufacturing in seven countries in the period 1950–59,

---

[1] The point has already emerged in the discussion in Chapter 2 of the general pattern of industrial growth (see pp. 52–5).

Table 11.1. *World trade[a] in chemicals in relation to world manufacturing production, 1899–1959*

| | $ billion at constant prices, and index numbers, 1929 = 100 | | | | | | | |
| | Values at 1913 prices[b] | | | Values at 1955 prices[c] | | | | |
	1899	1913	1929	1929	1937	1950	1955	1959
WORLD TRADE								
Chemical intermediates	0.20	0.41	0.44	0.94	0.87	1.28	2.35	3.79
Finished chemical and allied products	0.07	0.19	0.30	0.68	0.64	1.03	1.56	1.96
Total	0.27	0.59	0.74	1.62	1.51	2.30	3.91	5.75
INDEX	37	81	100	100	93	142	241	356
WORLD MANUFACTURING PRODUCTION								
Total index	36	61	100	100	115	190	252	294
of which								
Chemicals and allied products	23	43	100	100	127	275	430	570

Sources: Tables A.6 and A.80; *Industrial Statistics, 1900–1959,* O.E.E.C., Paris, 1960; *Statistical Yearbooks,* United Nations, New York.

[a]Exports from twelve main exporting countries.
[b]Excluding exports from the Netherlands.
[c]Including exports from the Netherlands.

Table 11.2. *Change of manufacturing production and production of chemicals in the industrial countries, 1913–59*

Percentage

| | Total Manufacturing | | | Chemicals | | | Ratio | | |
	1913–1937	1937–1950	1950–1959	1913–1937	1937–1950	1950–1959	1913–1937	1937–1950	1950–1959
Belgium-Luxembourg	+ 43	+ 18	+ 40	+149	+ 21	+ 83	3.47	1.17	2.08
France	+ 20	+ 10	+ 72	..	+ 25	+123	..	2.50	1.71
Germany[a]	+ 39	− 1	+129	..	+ 17	+186	..	..	1.44
Italy	+ 63	+ 22	+106	+343	+ 37	+238	5.44	1.68	2.25
Netherlands	..	+ 63	+ 67	..	+131	+ 92	..	2.08	1.37
Sweden	+125	+ 63	+ 25	+200	+135	+ 47	1.60	2.14	1.88
United Kingdom	+ 64	+ 36	+ 33	+ 83	+108	+ 70	1.30	3.00	2.12
Canada	..	+108	+ 29	..	+136	+ 48	..	1.26	1.66
United States	+100	+ 92	+ 36	+256	+148	+ 64	2.56	1.61	1.78

Source: Industrial Statistics, 1900–1959, O.E.E.C., Paris, 1960.

[a]West Germany in 1950 and 1959.

while the same was true of six out of eight for the period 1937–50. Though only limited data are available for the less-developed areas, the evidence suggests that in the industrializing countries in these areas also, the chemicals industry tends to expand at a faster pace than the general average[1].

The following sections consider briefly the demand for chemical products, and the relative shares of the industrial and semi-industrial countries in world output, as a prelude to a more detailed discussion of trends in world trade in chemical products.

1. THE DEMAND FOR CHEMICALS

The heterogeneous character of the group makes any generalization about demand subject to many qualifications. A major difficulty is that different groups of chemical products find their way into very different uses (for example fertilizers for agriculture, plastic materials for industrial use, dyestuffs for textiles and drugs for the medical services or for retail sale), and the proportions directed to the different end-uses are liable to substantial change over a long period. The movement in total chemicals consumption is thus in part a resultant of (possibly divergent) movements in demand in the different sectors of the economy. Moreover, since the relative importance of agriculture and industry (particularly the textile industry), and of medical expenditure, varies considerably between countries, we must also expect variation in the relationship between chemical consumption and total gross product.

As Fig. 11.1 shows, even allowing for the inevitable margin of error in the estimates, there is considerable variation in the ratio of chemical consumption to gross product in the different countries. West Germany, Belgium and the Netherlands, for example, appear to consume more than the average amount of chemicals in relation to their gross domestic products, while New Zealand, Pakistan and Turkey consume less than average. These differences are large and are probably related to differences in industrial structures, in relative usage of fertilizers in agriculture, of drugs in the health services, and so on. The slope of the fitted regression line is 1.39 ($\pm$0.10), implying that a country having a real product per head 10 per cent greater than another in 1955 would tend to have a per caput consumption of chemicals about 14 per cent greater[2].

It would, however, be misleading to use the cross-country relationship as indicating the way in which the consumption of chemicals grows over time as the economy expands[3]. That this is not so can be seen from Fig. 11.2, which shows the corresponding movements from 1929 to 1957 for eleven economically advanced countries. For each country, the rate of growth in chemical consump-

---

[1]See pages 53–4.
[2]A double logarithmic regression equation was used ($R^2 = 0.879$).
[3]Cf. the discussion on the divergent result of cross-country and time-series regressions in Chapters 2 and 7.

Fig. 11.1. Chemicals consumption per head in relation to gross domestic
product per head, 1955

Double logarithmic scale

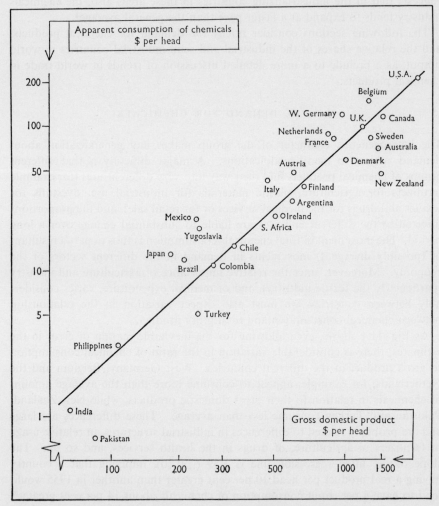

tion in relation to real product exceeds that implied in the cross-country comparison. For all eleven countries taken together, a regression of per caput
chemicals consumption on per caput real product over time shows an elasticity
of 2.11 ($\pm$0.11), or some 50 per cent higher than the cross-country result[1].

For the less-developed countries, insufficient data are available for a regression
analysis (see Table 11.3); however, the income elasticity of demand for chemicals

[1] A double logarithmic form of equation was used (see footnote [3] to page 51). The
regression related to the selected years from 1913 to 1957 for which data were available
(see Table 11.3), and 61 'observations' were included in the calculation ($R^2 = 0.882$).

in the industrializing countries in the less-developed areas may not be very different from that in the industrial countries of Western Europe and North America.

Fig. 11.2. Changes in chemicals consumption per head in relation to gross domestic product per head, 1929–57

Double logarithmic scale

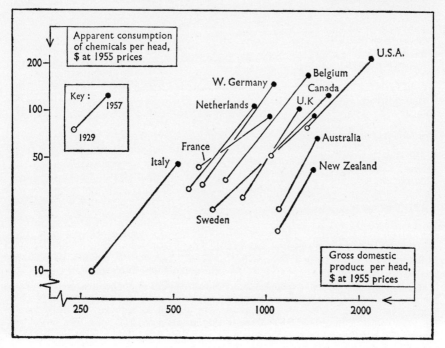

2. CHEMICAL PRODUCTION

Since the beginning of the century, the outstanding change in world chemical production (outside the Soviet Union) has been the vast expansion of the industry in the United States. Not only does the United States dominate world production in terms of sheer output of the majority of chemical products, but it has achieved a very considerable technological leadership as well. A major spurt in American chemical output occurred during the second World War, when the basis for large-scale production of chemical synthetics and petroleum chemicals was firmly established, as well as a large expansion of basic chemical products. By 1950, output was $2\frac{1}{2}$ times the volume achieved in 1937, the immediate pre-war peak, while by 1959 the industry's output was

U   WT

Table 11.3. *Apparent consumption^a of chemicals and allied products per head
of population in selected industrial and semi-industrial countries, 1913–59*

Gross values, $ at 1955 prices

	1913	1929	1937	1950	1955	1957	1959
INDUSTRIAL COUNTRIES							
Belgium-Luxembourg	24	38	45	95	158	169	154
France	..	45	46	57	81	97	117
Germany	..	34	41	71	123	145	177
Italy	5	10	14	19	41	47	61
Netherlands	..	32	29	67	90	102	112
Sweden	14	24	32	67	83	94	97
United Kingdom	23	29	36	71	98	103	115
Canada	..	51	56	108	116	122	126
United States	33	77	88	167	207	216	234
Japan	..	..	10	8	13	19	22
SEMI-INDUSTRIAL COUNTRIES							
Australia	20	24	30	50	62	67	73
New Zealand	15	17	19	29	44	45	..
Argentina	..	..	16	27	28	30	28
Yugoslavia	..	..	..	..	19	26	36
India	..	..	..	..	1.3	1.5	1.7

Sources: For production indices—*Statistical Yearbooks*, United Nations, New York;
A. Maizels, 'Trends in Production and Labour Productivity in Australian Manufacturing
Industries', *Economic Record*, Vol. XXXIII, No. 65, August 1957; national statistics and
estimates.   For trade series—Appendix A.   For population—Table E.7.

aEstimated gross values of chemical, etc. production, free of duplication, were estimated
for 1955 by multiplying net values by gross : net ratios derived from input-output tables.
Corresponding gross values for other years were derived by applying volume indices to
the 1955 values.   Imports (f.o.b. values at 1955 prices *plus* 10%) were then added, and
exports (f.o.b. values at 1955 prices *less* 8%) were deducted.   For a fuller description of
the method, see Appendix E.

Note: Estimates of apparent consumption of chemicals per head in 1955 for a selection
of other countries are as follows, in $:—
AFRICA: Union of South Africa, 24.
AMERICA: Brazil, 12; Chile, 15; Colombia, 11; Mexico, 23.
ASIA: Pakistan, 0.7; Philippines, 3; Turkey, 5.
EUROPE: Austria, 47; Denmark, 61; Finland, 40; Ireland, 24.

over five times that in 1937.   The United States produced about one-third of
world chemical output (outside the present Soviet area) in the later 1930's—
much the same proportion as in 1913 (see Table 11.4).   The wartime and post-
war expansion brought the proportion to about one-half in the early 1950's, but
thereafter the re-expansion of German and Japanese production resulted in a
fall in the United States share.

West Germany's share of world chemicals production has risen considerably
in recent years, though it is still well below the comparable pre-war proportion.

Britain's share of the total has shown a definite secular decline. It was 11–12 per cent in 1913, under 10 per cent in 1938 and only about $7\frac{1}{2}$ per cent by 1959. The French share has also declined, taking the period as a whole, but France—unlike Britain—has improved her relative position since 1953. From 1953 to 1959, French chemical production doubled—a considerably greater increase than that for the O.E.E.C. countries in total (75 per cent), or for the world as a whole outside the Soviet group (60 per cent)[1].

The estimates for the Soviet Union and Eastern Europe shown in Table 11.4 must be accepted with some reserve[2]. For what they are worth, they indicate that in 1954 the Soviet Union was producing one-third of the volume of output of the United States chemical industry, or about the same as Britain and West Germany combined. As a proportion of total world chemical output, these estimates put Soviet production at 8 per cent in 1938 and 13–14 per cent in 1954. More recent estimates, however, give a somewhat lower proportion: 6 per cent for 1938 and 11 per cent for 1960[3].

Outside the industrial areas, chemical production has also increased rapidly in recent years. In the semi-industrial countries, the rate of growth in chemical production from 1953 to 1959 exceeded that in the industrial countries (outside the Soviet group), though in total they still produce less than one-tenth of world chemical output. In this period of six years, the greatest increases in output were in Yugoslavia (210 per cent), and Australia and India (about 75 per cent each).

The expansion in the semi-industrial countries has generally tended to be greater in basic chemical products (including fertilizers) than in the more complicated processes, such as petro-chemicals and plastic materials. There are several reasons for this trend in development[4]. First, many of the basic chemicals are bulky, heavy goods which attract high transport charges so that, compared with the lighter, more processed products, they are more economical to produce in countries in an early stage of industrial development. Second, the technical processes involved in the production of most basic chemicals are unlikely to change—or, at any rate, to change substantially—for a considerable time, so that such investment is likely to be more profitable than investment in

[1]The percentages shown in Table 11.4 for 1953 and 1959 are based on United Nations series for chemicals, including coal and petroleum products. For 1959, rather different estimates of chemicals production, excluding coal and petroleum products, are published by the O.E.C.D. for member countries. These estimates show value added in chemicals production in the United Kingdom in 1959 as about 87–88 per cent of that in West Germany, compared with only 79 per cent as shown in Table 11.4 (see *The Chemical Industry in Europe, 1960–1961*, O.E.C.D., Paris, 1962).

[2]They are derived from estimates in A. Metzner, *Die Chemische Industrie der Welt*, Düsseldorf, 1955.

[3]*Chemische Industrie*, Düsseldorf, December, 1961, p. 755.

[4]The more important factors behind this trend were discussed in a paper on *International Competition in the Chemical Industry* by S. P. Chambers, then Deputy Chairman (now Chairman) of Imperial Chemical Industries, Ltd., read before the Plastics Institute, London, 12th March, 1959.

Table 11.4. *World chemical production, 1913–59*

	Based on total sales				Based on value added	
					Approximate percentages	
	1913	1927	1938	1954	1953	1959
INDUSTRIAL COUNTRIES	*94.2*	*93.4*	*91.4*	*85.7*	*87.0*	*8.5*
United States	35.6	44.4	33.8	52.0	51.0	44.9
Germany[a]	25.2	16.9	23.6[b]	7.0	8.2	9.5
United Kingdom	11.5	10.8	9.7	8.9	8.4	7.5
France	8.9	7.1	6.3	4.7	4.6	5.9
Japan	1.6	2.5	6.3	4.0	2.9	4.2
Other countries[c]	11.4	11.7	11.7	9.1	11.9	13.0
SEMI-INDUSTRIAL COUNTRIES[d]	*5.8*	*6.6*	*8.6*	*14.3*	*6.3*	*7.0*
REST OF WORLD					*6.7*	*8.0*
WORLD, EXCLUDING SOVIET COUNTRIES	100.0	100.0	100.0	100.0	100.0	100.0
SOVIET COUNTRIES[e]						
U.S.S.R.	3	4	9	17	..	..
Eastern Europe	..	c.2[f]	3.4[g]	7	..	..

Sources: I. Svennilson, *Growth and Stagnation in the European Economy*, Economic Commission for Europe, Geneva, 1954; A. Metzner, *Die Chemische Industrie der Welt*, Düsseldorf, 1955; *Statistical Yearbook, 1959*, United Nations, New York, 1960; *Monthly Bulletin of Statistics*, United Nations, New York; national statistics and estimates.

[a] West Germany in 1953, 1954 and 1959.
[b] Of which, about 8.5 represents the production in areas now in Eastern Europe.
[c] Belgium-Luxembourg, Canada, Italy, Netherlands, Switzerland and Sweden.
[d] Australia, New Zealand, South Africa; Argentina, Brazil, Chile, Colombia, Mexico; Turkey, Yugoslavia and India.
[e] Percentage of world total above.
[f] Estimate for Czechoslovakia and Poland only.
[g] Excluding German territory now in Eastern Europe.

newer chemical products where the process installed may prove to be obsolete in several years. Finally, in under-developed countries whose governments are influencing the direction of new investment, it is often a matter of major policy to develop the production of basic chemicals[1].

[1] In the Indian second Five-Year Plan, for example, increased production of heavy chemicals, including nitrogenous fertilizers, was given equal priority with the development of the iron and steel, heavy engineering and machine building industries (*Second Five Year Plan*, Ch. XIX, Government of India, New Delhi, 1956). Government priority for heavy chemicals has also been a feature of industrial development in some economically advanced countries at certain times; the French Monnet Plan, for example, included fertilizers among its basic production targets.

It is, unfortunately, not possible to trace these trends in detail for more than a few countries owing to the lack of relevant production data. In both Australia and New Zealand—where annual statistics of output are available over a considerable period—the relative importance of industrial chemicals has increased since before the war, as the chemical industries in these countries have widened their range of production; conversely, the relative importance of the more traditional products, such as soap and fertilizer, has decreased. In India, on the other hand, chemical fertilizer production has been expanded considerably in relative importance since 1950.

For certain basic chemicals some general comparisons can be made of production in the semi-industrial countries with the world total. For the six or seven semi-industrial countries for which the figures are available (see Table 11.5), production of sulphuric acid in 1957 was about three times the 1937 level, production of caustic soda was 4 or 5 times as great, superphosphate output was double, while that of nitrogenous fertilizers was nearly 60 per cent up. Chile is in a special position as a producer of natural fertilizer from guano,

Table 11.5. *Production of four basic chemical products in semi-industrial countries, 1937–57*

			Thousand metric tons	
	1937	1948	1955	1957
SULPHURIC ACID (100% H_2SO_4)				
World total[a]	15,130	21,300	34,000	36,430
Semi-industrial countries[b]	c.550	c.725	1,302	1,496
Percentage of world output	c.3.6	c.3.4	3.8	4.1
CAUSTIC SODA (NaOH)				
World total[a]	..	..	c.7,300[f]	c.8,300
Semi-industrial countries[c]	40–50	c.90	c.165–170	c.200
Percentage of world output	..	..	c.2.3	c.2.4
SUPERPHOSPHATES (P_2O_5)				
World total[a]	3,392	4,155	5,150	5,050
Semi-industrial countries[d]	c.345	c.430	750	c.750
Percentage of world output	c.10	c.10.3	14.7	c.15.0
NITROGENOUS FERTILIZERS (N)				
World total[a]	2,600	3,300	6,700	7,900
Semi-industrial countries[e]	235	302	302	367
Percentage of world output	9.1	9.1	4.5	4.6
(of which, Chile)	(8.6)	(8.2)	(2.6)	(2.9)

Sources: Statistical Yearbook, 1958, United Nations, New York, 1959; *Annual Review of World Production and Consumption of Fertilizers,* Food and Agriculture Organization, Rome.

[a]Excluding the U.S.S.R.
[b]Australia, Argentina, Mexico, Turkey, Yugoslavia and India.
[c]As in b *plus* Chile.
[d]Australia, New Zealand, Union of South Africa, Mexico, Turkey, Yugoslavia and India.
[e]Australia, New Zealand, Brazil, Chile, Mexico, Turkey and India.
[f]Estimates.

which now makes only a marginal contribution to world supplies as a result of the great expansion of low-cost synthetic production. Excluding Chile, the output of nitrogenous fertilizers in the semi-industrial countries in 1957, at about 130,000 tons, was over ten times the 1937 total.

Since 1957, there have been further increases in production of basic chemicals in several of the semi-industrial countries, particularly in India. However, apart from superphosphates, the production of basic chemicals in these countries has remained at under 5 per cent of the world total.

3. CHEMICAL IMPORTS AND ECONOMIC GROWTH

We have already seen, in Chapter 7, that imports of chemical products tend to increase at a more rapid rate than does the total real product. This has been so both in the industrial countries and in the semi-industrial ones; in the former group, the growth co-efficient was 1.48, and in the latter 1.19[1]. Though these co-efficients for imports are among the highest for the different commodity groups, they are well below the chemicals consumption elasticity of 2.11 which was given earlier in this chapter. This divergence in rates of growth implies that the proportion of chemicals consumption which is met from imports tends to decline with economic growth.

This general conclusion also follows from the fact that world chemical production has risen much faster than world trade in chemicals[2]. However, the global comparison exaggerates the tendency of the import-content of consumption to fall, since a large percentage of the increase in world output has been in countries having a low import-content. This is particularly the case for the United States which, since the first World War, has imported only about 1 per cent of its chemical requirements (see Table 11.6). Indeed, in all the four major producing countries, i.e. the United States, Germany, Britain and France, the import-content[3] has been under 5 per cent since 1950. For Britain, this represented a substantial reduction in dependence on imported supplies compared with pre-war, particularly with the pre-1932 position; for the other three, the import-content appears to have been small even in the inter-war period, and probably back at least to the beginning of the century.

For the smaller industrial countries, the import proportion was considerably reduced during the first World War, and again in the 1930's, but since 1950 the trend has, if anything, been an upward one. The same tendency of the import proportion first to decline and then to rise is also apparent for Australia and New Zealand. It may be that the underlying tendency of the import

[1] See pp. 180–4, and Table 7.14.
[2] See Table 11.1.
[3] Table 11.6 shows the import-content of supplies of chemicals available either for home use or for export. It was not possible, with existing data, to calculate the corresponding percentages of imports in apparent consumption of chemicals, but the trends over time would be unlikely to differ significantly from those shown here.

Table 11.6.   *Imports of chemicals as proportion of total supplies, 1913–59*

Percentage

	1913	1929	1937	1950	1955	1957	1959
INDUSTRIAL COUNTRIES							
Belgium-Luxembourg	35	21	14	8	10	11	14
France	..	3	3	3	4	5	4
Germany*a*	..	4	2	2	2	3	3
Italy	27	11	5	8	7	8	7
Netherlands	..	24	17	13	15	15	16
Sweden	23	16	16	11	15	17	18
United Kingdom	14	10	7	4	4	4	5
Canada	..	14	11	12	14	15	15
United States	4	1	1	1	1	1	1
Japan	..	..	9	6	8	10	10
SEMI-INDUSTRIAL COUNTRIES							
Australia	30	22	18	12	17	18	22
New Zealand	50	50	42	30	39	41	..
Argentina	..	..	16	9	12	11	10
Yugoslavia	..	..	..	..	7	8	9
India	..	..	..	..	25	27	27

Source: As for Table 11.3.

aWest Germany in 1950–59.

Note: Corresponding estimates for the year 1955 have also been made for a number of other countries, as follows:—
AFRICA: Union of South Africa, 24.
AMERICA: Brazil, 17; Chile, 19; Colombia, 49; Mexico, 19.
ASIA: Pakistan, 57; Philippines, 65; Turkey, 27.
EUROPE: Austria, 16; Denmark, 28; Finland, 34; Ireland, 51.

proportion of chemicals supplies (or consumption) to decline with economic growth has been overlaid since the last war with the expansionary effects on demand of the various new technological developments mentioned earlier. Since there is always a time lag between the commercial exploitation of a new technique in the most advanced countries, and its spread on a large scale to the less industrial (or smaller) countries, it can reasonably be assumed that the new demand has tended to spill over into imports in all but the large industrial producing countries.   If so, the downtrend in the import proportion could be expected to re-assert itself if the lag in technique were reduced.   But the chemical industry in the advanced industrial countries can be expected to continue to innovate at a rapid pace, and the time lag of the other countries in the exploitation of such innovations may not, in fact, be reduced substantially.

The implication of this general argument is that the demand for chemical imports is likely in future to rise at a faster rate in relation to economic growth than the average rate so far achieved this century; if this came about, it would, of course, reinforce the tendency for the volume of world trade in chemicals to expand at a faster rate than world trade in manufactures in the aggregate.

4. THE PATTERN OF WORLD TRADE IN CHEMICALS

Main export markets

Even in countries undergoing a rapid process of industrialization, including a marked expansion in chemical production, the demand for imported chemicals has tended to rise. Between 1937 and 1955, for example, the volume of chemicals exported to the semi-industrial countries rose by two-thirds, this expansion accounting for 20 per cent of the total increase in world chemical exports in the period (Table 11.7). Again, from 1955 to 1959, exports of chemicals to this group of countries rose further by nearly 30 per cent, though this represented only about 10 per cent of the increase in the world total. In absolute terms, the largest increases in this latter period were in exports to Australia, India, Mexico and Yugoslavia.

The major part of the expansion in world imports of chemicals since pre-war has, however, come from the industrial countries. Among these, the growth in demand by the smaller industrial countries in Western Europe has been the

Table 11.7. *Changes in exports of chemicals by major market, 1899–1959*

$ *billion at* 1955 *prices*

Exports to	Total in 1899	Change from				Total in 1959
		1899 to 1929	1929 to 1937	1937 to 1955	1955 to 1959	
INDUSTRIAL COUNTRIES[a]	0.38	+ 0.45	− 0.16	+ 1.12	+ 0.97	2.75
France, Germany[b] and United Kingdom	0.20	+ 0.10	− 0.08	+ 0.29	+ 0.27	0.78
Other Western Europe	0.10	+ 0.16	− 0.04	+ 0.43	+ 0.45	1.10
North America	0.07	+ 0.12	− 0.01	+ 0.36	+ 0.14	0.67
SEMI-INDUSTRIAL COUNTRIES	0.08	+ 0.15	+ 0.06	+ 0.47	+ 0.23	0.98
Southern Dominions	0.03	+ 0.04	+ 0.01	+ 0.12	+ 0.07	0.27
India/Pakistan	0.01	+ 0.03	+ 0.03	+ 0.08	+ 0.04	0.18
Other semi-industrial countries	0.04	+ 0.09	+ 0.01	+ 0.27	+ 0.12	0.53
REST OF WORLD	0.14	+ 0.40	− 0.01	+ 0.82	+ 0.65	2.02
TOTAL	0.60	+ 1.00	− 0.11	+ 2.40	+ 1.84	5.75

Source: Tables A.6 to A.38, and A.81 and related data.

aIncluding Japan.
bWest Germany in 1955 and 1959.

largest single element in the increase. Imports of chemicals into Italy in 1955, for example, were about four times the 1937 volume, those into Switzerland were $3\frac{1}{2}$ times, while Belgium, Netherlands, Norway and Sweden all took about $2\frac{1}{2}$ times the pre-war amount. Import demand from Canada and the United States also expanded very considerably between these two years; together, their imports of chemicals in 1955 were three times the 1937 total. Even Britain, France and Germany showed substantial increases in chemical imports from 1937 to 1955; in this respect chemicals were exceptional, since in most other groups of manufactures there was a decline in imports into these three countries in this period.

Much the same pattern of growth in imports can be seen during the period 1955–59. Imports of chemicals into the smaller countries of Western Europe rose by two-thirds in volume, those into Britain, France and West Germany combined rose by one-half, but for North America the increase was only one-fifth.

Detailed information about trends in imports of chemicals is not available for countries included in the heading 'Rest of world' in Table 11.7. Among the more important destinations, however, exports to the Soviet group increased by some $100 million from 1955 to 1959, and probably those to West European countries not included under 'Industrial countries' in the table increased by at least that amount. There were also increases to the Middle East (about $90 million), to other Latin American countries ($70 million), and to countries in Central Africa ($50 million).

Commodity groups

Basic chemicals as such constitute only about one-quarter of the total value of world trade in chemicals and allied products (see Table 11.8). In this context, basic chemicals include the organic chemicals, such as ethyl alcohol, glycerine, benzene, phenol, acid anhydrides and naphthalene, as well as the inorganic chemicals, such as caustic soda, soda ash and sulphuric acid. In recent years, the miscellaneous group of 'other general chemicals' (which includes insecticides and disinfectants, starches, glue and a large variety of chemical materials and products), and drugs and medicines, have each accounted for about one-seventh of the total. The relative importance of drugs and medicines has increased considerably since 1913, though the percentage has fallen somewhat since 1950.

The outstanding expansion, however, has been in plastic materials, trade in which was relatively very small before the second World War. By 1950, the exports of plastic materials from the four main industrial producers represented about 7 per cent of their total chemical exports, and this proportion had grown to nearly 11 per cent by 1955. Since then, plastic materials have increased further in relative importance, and by 1959, were the third largest of the groups shown in Table 11.8; in 1950, they were only the sixth largest.

By contrast, world trade in paint, pigments, etc. in the 1950's was considerably less important, relatively, than in 1913. There were also reductions in the relative importance of perfumery, cosmetics and soap, of essential oils, and of explosives, though none of these reductions were as marked as for paint. World trade in dyestuffs has declined in relative importance since 1950, though the percentage is still higher than in 1913.

Table 11.8.   *Exports of chemicals and allied products : main groups, 1913–59*

Percentage

	Exports from four main industrial countries[a]			Exports from ten countries[b]		
	1913	1950	1955	1955	1957	1959
Organic and inorganic chemicals[c]	43.9 {	23.8	28.9	27.5	27.1	27.8
Other general chemicals[d]	{	9.6	13.1	14.9	14.5	14.4
Medicinal and pharmaceutical preparations	6.9	21.9	16.2	14.0	14.8	13.6
Manufactured fertilizers	10.2	10.4	8.4	13.3	13.5	12.6
Plastic materials	0.8	6.8	10.6	10.1	11.8	14.3
Pigments, paints, etc.	19.7	10.3	7.1	6.2	5.5	5.3
Perfumery, cosmetics, soap, etc.	7.9	6.3	6.1	5.1	5.0	4.8
Coal tar dyestuffs and dyeing and tanning extracts	2.0	6.2	4.9	4.3	3.7	3.6
Essential oils	3.3	3.2	2.4	2.5	2.3	2.1
Explosives	5.3	1.5	2.3	2.1	1.8	1.5
TOTAL	100.0	100.0	100.0	100.0	100.0	100.0
Total in $ billion	0.50	1.59	2.81	3.69	4.53	5.16

Sources: Statistical Bulletins, Series IV and Series B, O.E.E.C., Paris; national trade statistics.

[a]France, West Germany (whole of Germany in 1913), United Kingdom and United States.
[b]Belgium-Luxembourg, Canada, Italy, Japan, Netherlands and Sweden, in addition to those listed in [a].
[c]S.I.T.C. 511 and 512.
[d]S.I.T.C. 521 and 599 (except 599–01).

These changes in the relative sizes of the main groups of chemicals reflect in part the bias, noted earlier, in the development of chemical production outside the main industrial countries. The concentration of new chemical production on basic chemicals, fertilizers and dyestuffs in many of the main importing countries has led to a change in the structure of their imports in favour of other chemical products, particularly plastic materials, and drugs and medicinal products. At the same time, the vast new technological developments in petro-chemicals and synthetics and in new forms of drugs, have themselves provided the opportunity for a large extension in the area of demand.

Chemicals which can readily be identified as technically new products developed during, or since, the last war accounted for some 20 per cent of world trade in chemicals in 1955, 22 per cent in 1957 and 24 per cent in 1959 (see Table 11.9). Of these, plastic materials have grown most rapidly in recent years[1], followed closely by synthetic detergents, though the latter are much smaller in total value. Export trade in the new drugs has increased rather slowly in value, but as prices have tended to fall with improving methods of production, the rise in volume terms has been greater than is indicated by the value figures. Trade in vitamins and in tetra-ethyl lead, on the other hand, has been virtually static since 1955.

Table 11.9. *Exports of new and traditional chemical products from five industrial countries[a], 1937–59*

$ million, f.o.b.

	1937	1955	1957	1959
NEW PRODUCTS				
Antibiotics, sulphonamides and hormones[b]	—	163	211	210
Vitamins	—	52	58	53
Anti-knock compounds (tetra-ethyl lead)	—	58	49	52
Synthetic detergents	—	29	44	53
Total	—	302	362	368
MAINLY NEW PRODUCTS				
Plastic materials	18[c]	301	443	624
Total	18[c]	603	805	992
TRADITIONAL CHEMICAL PRODUCTS[d]	742	2,290	2,789	3,074
TOTAL	760	2,893	3,594	4,066

Sources: National trade statistics; *Statistical Bulletins*, Series B, 1959, O.E.E.C., Paris, 1960.

[a]France, United Kingdom, West Germany (whole of Germany in 1937), United States and Japan.

[b]Including exports of compounds or mixtures containing antibiotics or sulphonamides. Includes approximate estimates for West German exports in 1955 and 1957.

[c]Approximate.

[d]Residue.

Further increases in the share of plastic materials in the total can be expected. Production in the industrial countries more than doubled between 1950 and 1955, and there was a further increase of 70 per cent between 1955 and 1959 (Table 11.10), a much faster rate of growth than for world chemical production

[1]Production and trade in plastic materials is overwhelmingly in the new thermoplastic and thermosetting varieties. Before the war, the small volume of trade was mainly in casein, celluloid and a limited range of thermosetting plastics.

Table 11.10. *Production and trade of industrial countries in plastic materials,*
1950–59

	1950	1953	1955	1957	*Thousand metric tons* 1959
PRODUCTION	*1,349a*	*1,962a*	*3,032*	*3,773*	*5,133*
United States	975	1,260	1,761	1,961	2,533
West Germany	99	251	430	535	779
United Kingdom	158	213	322	400	509
Japan	28	80	136	286	426
Canada	..	..	80b	120b	155b
Other industrial countriesc	89	158	303	471	731
EXPORTS	*140*	*225*	*414*	*622*	*949*
Intra-traded	82	143	248	400	625
Exports to non-industrial countriese	58	82	166	222	324

Sources: Industrial Statistics, 1950–1959, O.E.E.C., Paris, 1960; *Chemical Statistics Handbook, 1955*, Manufacturing Chemists' Association, Inc., Washington, D.C.; *Japanese Economic Statistics*, Economic Planning Agency, Tokyo; *Yearbooks of International Trade Statistics*, United Nations, New York.

aExcluding Canadian production, estimates for which are not available for these years.

bEstimated.

cAustria, Belgium-Luxembourg, Denmark, France, Ireland, Italy, Netherlands, Norway, Sweden and Switzerland.

dActually, total imports into O.E.E.C. countries, Japan and the United States, *plus* exports from O.E.E.C. countries and the United States to Canada.

eResidue.

as a whole. Over one-third of the expansion since 1955 has been in the United States, most of the rest being in Western Europe, though Japanese production has been increasing rapidly. Production outside the industrial areas is significant only in Australia (67 thousand metric tons in 1960/61) and Brazil (41 thousand metric tons in 1959). World trade in plastic materials tripled from 1950 to 1955, and more than doubled from then to 1959. In each period, the greater part of the increase has been in the intra-trade of the industrial countries; exports to non-industrial countries have also risen rapidly, though at a lower rate than the intra-trade.

For chemical fertilizers, on the other hand, the prospects are that these will continue to decline as a proportion of total trade in chemicals, though in absolute terms the volume of trade should expand. As already mentioned, fertilizers have been a major field of industrial expansion in many of the semi-industrial countries. This expansion has been particularly marked in the less-developed countries of Asia, where chemical plant nutrient production was increased by almost 300 thousand metric tons (7 or 8 times) between 1950/51

Table 11.11. *World production, consumption and trade in chemical fertilizers[a]: pre-war, 1950–51, 1956–57 and 1958–59*

	Series[c]	*Thousand metric tons of plant nutrients[b]*			
		1937–39 average	1950–51	1956–7	1958–9
United States and Canada	P	1,186	4,505	6,404	7,514
	C	1,435	4,700	5,739	6,738
	C–P	+249	+195	−665	−776
Europe	P	5,512	8,081	11,893	13,745
	C	5,238	6,977	10,126	11,669
	C–P	−274	−1,104	−1,767	−2,076
Latin America	P	272	381	320	400
	C	132	277	697	635
	C–P	−140	−104	+377	+235
Japan	P	469	647	1,153	1,315
	C	609	773	1,388	1,420
	C–P	+140	+126	+235	+105
Rest of Asia	P	163[d]	40	204	327
	C	311	269	865	1,086
	C–P	+148	+229	+661	+759
Africa	P	58	137	330	325
	C	191	256	552	631
	C–P	+133	+119	+222	+306
Oceania	P	343	490	616	676
	C	384	525	729	803
	C–P	+ 41	+ 35	+113	+127
WORLD TOTAL[a]	P	8,002	14,282	20,927	24,300
	C	8,299	13,778	20,097	22,980

Sources: Food and Agriculture Organization, *World Fertilizer Production and Consumption and Targets for the Future*, 1946; *Fertilizers—a World Report on Production and Consumption*, 1952; and *An Annual Review of World Production and Consumption of Fertilizers*, 1957 and 1959, F.A.O., Rome.

[a]Excluding Soviet countries.

[b]In terms of $N + P_2O_5 + K_2O$.

[c]P—production; C—consumption. The residue (C–P) represents not only the net trade but also changes in recorded stocks.

[d]Including China.

and 1958/59 (see Table 11.11). India alone accounted for some 95 thousand tons of this expansion. Production in Africa (mainly North Africa and the Union of South Africa) rose by 190 thousand tons (about $1\frac{1}{2}$ times) in this period, while the increase for Oceania was about 190 thousand tons (two-fifths). Net imports of chemical fertilizers into these areas have expanded at the same time to meet the large increase in demand, but the rate of growth in world trade in fertilizers has been very much less than in plastic materials, and less than in chemical products as a whole.

Table 11.12. *Exports of chemicals by country of origin*, 1899–1959

Percentage

Exports from	1899	1913	1929	1937	1950	1955	1959
U.K.	19.6	20.0	17.5	16.0	17.9	16.7	15.0
France	13.1	13.3	13.5	9.9	10.1	9.2	8.6
Germany[a]	35.0	40.2	30.9	31.6[b]	10.4	17.4	20.2
Other Western Europe[c]	13.1	13.1	15.3	19.4	20.5	19.6	21.1
United States	14.2	11.2	18.1	16.9	34.6	28.3	27.4
Canada	0.4	0.9	2.5	2.9	5.2	6.3	4.4
Japan	0.4	1.0	1.8	3.0	0.8	2.4	3.1
India	4.2	0.3	0.4	0.3	0.5	0.1	0.2
TOTAL	100.0	100.0	100.0	100.0	100.0	100.0	100.0
Total in $ billion	0.26	0.59	1.04	0.98	2.17	3.91	5.48

Sources: Tables A.46 to A.68 and A.80.

[a]West Germany in 1950–59.

[b]For the present area of West Germany, the 1937 percentage would be approximately 26–27.

[c]Belgium-Luxembourg, Italy, Netherlands (except in 1899 and 1913), Sweden and Switzerland.

Both dyestuffs and explosives are also likely to form a declining proportion of world trade in chemical products in future. Local production of dyestuffs in many industrializing countries must be expected to increase to meet the requirements of their expanding textile industries. India is an important example of this. A similar growth in local production of explosives has also been taking place over the past decade in Australia, India and South Africa. For drugs and medical preparations, the upward trend in demand in the main importing countries in recent years has more than offset the effects of import-substitution (which in many countries has resulted from the establishment of branch or subsidiary companies by the larger North American or West European firms). Though local production, including tabletting and packaging of imported bulk preparations, is likely to increase outside the main industrial countries, it seems probable that world trade in drugs and medical preparations will continue to expand. The extension of health services in the less-developed countries, and the constant introduction of new types of drug, appear likely to be the main factors making for such an expansion.

5. COMPETITION IN THE WORLD CHEMICAL MARKET

There has been a sharp reversal in the relative importance of Germany and the United States as exporters of chemical products since pre-war. Before 1914, Germany dominated the world export market, accounting for some two-fifths of world exports of chemicals (see Table 11.12). The German share fell to about one-third of the inter-war period mainly as a result of the growth

Table 11.13. *Share of exports of chemicals and allied products: main groups, by countries, 1955–59*

Percentage

		United King- dom	United States	France	Ger- many	Other industrial countries[a]	Total
Organic and inorganic	1955	15	29	10	25	21	100
chemicals[b]	1959	14	29	9	26	22	100
Other general chemicals[c]	1955	19	30	5	13	33	100
	1959	19	29	6	19	27	100
Medical and pharmaceutical	1955	21	44	13	10	12	100
preparations	1959	17	41	12	14	16	100
Manufactured fertilizers	1955	2	14	9	23	52	100
	1959	2	12	8	21	57	100
Plastic materials	1955	20	36	5	18	21	100
	1959	17	36	5	23	19	100
Pigments, paints, etc.	1955	26	47	4	11	12	100
	1959	27	40	4	15	14	100
Perfumery, cosmetics, soap,	1955	38	23	23	7	9	100
etc.	1959	29	25	24	11	11	100
Coal tar dyestuffs and	1955	19	16	11	41	13	100
dyeing and tanning extracts	1959	21	12	8	50	9	100
Essential oils	1955	10	31	31	2	26	100
	1959	10	34	28	4	24	100
Explosives	1955	44	25	8	10	13	100
	1959	37	20	9	17	17	100
TOTAL[d]	1955	18	30	10	18	24	100
	1959	16	29	9	21	25	100

Sources: Statistical Bulletins, Series IV, and Series B, O.E.E.C., Paris; Japanese trade statistics.

[a] Belgium-Luxembourg, Italy, Netherlands and Sweden; Canada and Japan.

[b] S.I.T.C. 511 and 512.

[c] S.I.T.C. 521 and 599 (except 599-01).

[d] These percentages differ slightly from those in Table 11.12 because they exclude exports from Switzerland and India.

in American exports. In the immediate post-war years, the chemical industry in West Germany was considerably smaller than that of the old Reich; about one-third of the 1938 output had been in areas now in Eastern Europe. The West German industry has, however, grown with great rapidity since 1950, and exports of chemicals from the Federal Republic in 1959 were three times

Table 11.14. *Selected countries' share of exports of new and traditional chemicals in the exports from five industrial countries[a], 1955 and 1959*

	United Kingdom		United States		West Germany		Percentage Five countries[a]	
	1955	1959	1955	1959	1955	1959	1955	1959
Antibiotics, sulphonamides and hormones	18	14	68[b]	62[b]	7[c]	18[c]	100	100
Vitamins	16	14	63	59	10	11	100	100
Anti-knock compounds (tetra-ethyl lead)	57	68	43	32	..	..	100[d]	100[d]
Synthetic detergents	65	34	31	34	4	17	100	100
Plastic materials	25	20	44	44	23	27	100	100
Traditional chemical products	21	20	35	34	26	29	100	100
TOTAL	23	20	38	37	24	27	100	100

Sources: Statistical Bulletins, Series B, 1959, O.E.E.C., Paris, 1960; national trade statistics.

[a]France, United Kingdom, West Germany, United States and Japan.
[b]Including exports of compounds or mixtures containing antibiotics or sulphonamides.
[c]Approximate estimates.
[d]Excluding exports from West Germany and Japan, for which data are not available.

as great in volume than were those from the Reich in 1937[1]. This expansion nevertheless failed to keep pace with that of the United States, exports from which were five times as great in 1959 as in 1937. Though West Germany's share has risen rapidly since the early 1950's, by 1959 it was still less than the comparable pre-war percentage. The shares held by both Britain and France have been falling since 1950, while the relative importance of the smaller West European exporters has been increasing.

The increase in West Germany's share of world trade since 1955 affected all but one of the main groups of chemicals (Table 11.13), indicating that the German chemical industry achieved a general increase in its relative competitive power in the period. The fall in Britain's share since 1955 has been mainly in drugs and medicines, and in plastic materials, among the large commodity groups, while for the smaller industrial countries, the gains were mainly in fertilizers and drugs, partly offset by losses in general chemicals and plastic materials.

The fall in Britain's share of world exports of plastic materials appears to be typical also of her export performance in the 'new' chemical products generally; her fall in share since 1955 has been particularly marked in synthetic detergents as a result of rapidly increasing German competition (see Table 11.14). For all the new chemicals together, Britain's share fell from 27 to 22 per cent between

[1]Or about 4½ times the volume of exports in 1937 from the present area of West Germany.

1955 and 1958, while Germany's share rose from 15 to 22 per cent. Though the United States share also fell somewhat (from 52 to 47 per cent), she remains easily the largest exporter of the new drugs and vitamins, and of plastic materials.

Prospects here depend very much on the relative ability of each producing country to expand its range of newer products. This in turn largely depends on the resources invested in research and development work. Trade in the more traditional products will, of course, continue to be important, though here the competitive position will probably depend much more on price and quality than on other factors.

CHAPTER 12

DURABLE CONSUMER GOODS[1]

In general the importance of consumer goods in world trade is declining; but
this is not true of durable consumer goods[2]. From 1937 to 1950 this group

Table 12.1. *World trade^a in durable consumer goods*, 1937–58

$ million

Exports of	1937	1950	1955	1957	1958
Passenger road vehicles, including chassis	353	857	1665	2046	2325
Household durables	249	561	1095	1337	1369
Total	602	1418	2760	3383	3694
As percentage of world exports of manufactures^b					
Passenger road vehicles, including chassis	3.8	4.1	4.8	4.7	5.5
Household durables	2.7	2.7	3.2	3.1	3.2
Total	6.5	6.8	8.0	7.8	8.7

Sources : National trade statistics.
^a Exports from twelve main exporting countries.
^b Defined as S.I.T.C. sections 5 to 8, inclusive.

held its share of total trade in manufactured goods at about 7 per cent; from
1950 to 1957 the figure rose to 8 per cent; and in 1958—mainly because of a
sharp rise in shipments of cars from Europe to the United States, a trend which
was reversed in 1960—it went up to nearly 9 per cent (Table 12.1).

The two main sub-groups of durable consumer goods are road passenger
vehicles and household durables. Trade in road vehicles has risen the faster
of the two, whether 1958 is compared with pre-war or with 1950. Table 12.2
sets out the main items in more detail. The figures are at current prices, but

[1] This chapter is a revised version of an article published in the *National Institute
Economic Review*, No. 6, Nov. 1959. The data presented in that article related generally
o the post-war period up to 1958, and though some of the production tables have now
been brought up to 1959, it was not possible to make similar revisions to the detailed
trade tables.

[2] The term is used here to cover passenger road vehicles—passenger cars, motor cycles
and bicycles—and those household durables produced by the metal and engineering
industries. Books, jewellery, toys, boats, sports gear, glassware, crockery, furniture, floor
coverings and similar items—which might be included in a more comprehensive definition
of durable consumer goods—are not included here. The figures for passenger road vehicles
necessarily include those for business use. The 'household durables' category is not part
of the main commodity classification used in this book, but is rather a convenient cross-
classification of particular items. For this reason, some of these durables are referred
to in Chapter 14 ('Miscellaneous Manufactures') also.

the ratios in the final columns can be taken as rough guides to the changes in the relative importance of the different items. Passenger cars, gramophones and record players, washing machines, heating and cooking apparatus and miscellaneous electrical appliances have all done better than average throughout—comparing 1958 with either 1950 or 1937. Cutlery, motor cycles and pedal

Table 12.2. *World trade[a] in durable consumer goods: separate items,*
1937–58

	1937	1950	1955	1957	1958	$ million 1958 as ratio of 1937	1950
PASSENGER ROAD VEHICLES	353	857	1665	2046	2325	6.6	2.7
Passenger cars and chassis[b]	274	708	1436	1804	2120	7.7	3.0
Motor cycles, motor scooters and cycles[c]	80	149	229	242	205	2.6	1.4
RADIOS, TELEVISION SETS AND GRAMOPHONES	55	85	225	325	390	7.1	4.6
Radios and radiograms	50 } 67		140	167	203 } 5.8		4.3
Television receivers	—		27	64	87		
Gramophones, record players, tape recorders, etc.	5	18	58	94	100	20.0	5.6
DOMESTIC ELECTRICAL APPLIANCES	67	182	367	421	442	6.6	2.4
Sewing machines	27	60	105	117	117	4.3	2.0
Refrigerators	20	55	104	113	135	6.8	2.5
Cooking apparatus	8 } 19		27	27	23 } 7.1		3.0
Heating apparatus (including irons)			28	33	34		
Vacuum cleaners and floor polishers	8	16	26	30	31	3.9	1.9
Washing machines	2	22	47	61	60	30.0	2.7
Other portable mechanical appliances, electrically operated	2	10	30	40	42	21.0	4.2
Total, excluding sewing machines	40	122	262	304	325	8.1	2.7
OTHER ITEMS	126	296	502	591	537	4.3	1.8
Watches and clocks	78	212	328	389	344	4.4	1.6
Cutlery (including safety razors)	28	46	82	91	92	3.3	2.0
Cameras (excluding cine-cameras)	17	19	55	70	63	3.7	3.3
Gas water heaters, water softeners, etc.	2	14	28	33	29	14.5	2.1
Lawn mowers	1	5	9	8	9	9.0	1.8
TOTAL, ALL ITEMS	602	1418	2760	3383	3694	6.1	2.6
TOTAL, EXCLUDING PASSENGER ROAD VEHICLES	249	561	1095	1337	1369	5.5	2.4

Sources : National trade statistics.

[a]Exports from twelve main exporting countries.
[b]S.I.T.C. 732-01 and 04.
[c]S.I.T.C. 732-02 and 07 ; 733-01 and 02.

cycles, sewing machines, vacuum cleaners and floor polishers, and watches and clocks have all done worse than average in both comparisons. Trade in cutlery and motor cycles has probably not risen at all in volume terms since before the war. Exports of sewing machines and of watches and clocks have risen comparatively slowly since 1950, the first partly because of increased

Table 12.3.   *Consumer goods ownership, 1957–58[a]*

Numbers per 1,000 *population*

	Passenger cars	Motor cycles[b]	Bicycles	Radio sets	Television sets	Refrigerators	Washing machines
NORTH AMERICA							
Canada	187	2	31	563	180	178	173
United States	315	3	143	890	288	265	235
WESTERN EUROPE							
Austria	21	47	215	256	7	65	34
Belgium	54	23	325	249	25	53	151
Denmark	50	28	447	318	47	50	40
Finland	20	15	303	251	2	28	69
France	70	41	190	233	22	49	56
West Germany	36	48	315	277	39	39	45
Ireland	46	10	..	159	8	14	20
Italy	18	43	145	131	23	20	6
Netherlands	25	16	450	264	35	10	104
Norway	36	22	231	280	0	73	112
Portugal	11	..	36	60	1	..	..
Spain	5	3	62	63	1	..	..
Sweden	88	43	478	348	33	187	119
Switzerland	54	31	365	252	10	98	39
United Kingdom	72	26	175	282	172	37	97
Yugoslavia	1	1	17	40	0	..	..
EASTERN EUROPE							
Czechoslovakia	..	26	..	249	24	15	63
U.S.S.R.	..	4	..	148	14	..	..
OCEANIA							
Australia	146	13	80	223	41	197	104
New Zealand	170	11	149	238	—	132	144
LATIN AMERICA							
Argentina	18	2	205	158	11	..	..
Brazil	7	0.5	17	61	11	11	1
Chile	7	..	9	98	..	..	..
Colombia	6	..	6	44	10	..	..
Cuba	25	..	11	155	49	..	..
Mexico	12	0.2	20	84	12	11	6
Peru	6	..	21	61	..	..	
Venezuela	25	2	20	123	32	..	

For footnotes, see next page.

Table 12.3 (cont.)

	Passenger cars	Motor cycles*b*	Bicycles	Radio sets	Television sets	Refrigerators	Washing machines
FAR EAST							
Ceylon	..	..	34	18	—	..	..
India	0.5	0.1	15	3	—	..	..
Indonesia	0.8	..	12	4	—	..	..
Japan	2	6	166	149	17	27	4
Pakistan	0.3	0.1	..	1	—	..	..
Philippines	3	..	..	10	1	..	..
MIDDLE EAST							
Egypt	3	..	13	36	—	..	..
Israel	..	..	17	181	..	..	..
Turkey	..	0.7	4	42	0	..	..
AFRICA							
Belgian Congo	1.9	..	..	1.4	..	..	..
Nigeria	0.5	..	95	2	—	..	..
Union of South Africa	49	2	..	56	..	32	9

Sources : Statistical Yearbook, 1960, United Nations, New York, for passenger cars and radio and television sets ; F. Knox, 'Some International Comparisons of Consumers' Durable Goods', *Bulletin of the Oxford Institute of Statistics*, Vol. 21, No. 1, February 1959, for motor cycles, refrigerators and washing machines; British Cycle and Motor Cycle Industries' Association, Ltd., for bicycles.

[a]The figures for passenger cars, motor cycles, refrigerators and washing machines relate to 1957, and those for television sets to 1958. For bicycles and radio sets the figures relate in most cases to 1957 but for some countries for which 1957 figures were not available the corresponding figures for 1955 or 1956 were used.
[b]Includes motor scooters and motor-assisted bicycles.

local production in many import markets, and the second partly because of an increase in the United States import duty.

The relatively rapid increase in world trade in durable consumer goods has two major causes. First, demand for them has generally risen faster than income. Secondly, production of many important items in the group is still concentrated in a few industrial countries, so that a rise in world demand necessarily means an increase in trade—although there is a small group of industrializing countries whose imports have risen little, because they are developing their own production or assembly. At the same time there has been a big increase in the interchange of these goods between the industrial countries themselves, which accounted for half the rise in trade from 1950 to 1955 and for two-thirds of the increase from 1955 to 1957.

1. THE DEMAND FOR CONSUMER DURABLES

A number of studies have recently been made of the demand for consumer durables in different countries. For passenger cars, all investigations have shown that demand for them has risen much faster than disposable income. In the United States, for instance, the rise in demand for new cars has been more than three times as great as the rise in real disposable income, after allowing for the influence of changes in the relative prices of cars and other consumer goods[1]. In most west European countries, too, the demand for cars since 1950 has been rising considerably faster than real expenditure on consumer goods as a whole; in Britain and France, the same is true for the main household durables[2]. In these and other countries, however, the recent rapid rise in the demand for consumer durables is not simply the result of the rise in income; the extension of hire purchase facilities also explains some of it.

Another method of studying the way in which demand rises with income is to look at the level of ownership of the main consumer durables in countries with different levels of real income, since so far as ownership does depend on the relative real income of consumers over a period of years, rich countries should obviously show much higher ownership figures than poor ones[3]. Ownership figures are given in Table 12.3 for seven consumer durables for a recent period. Over forty countries at very different stages of economic development are included, though ownership figures for all seven items are not available for all countries. Many of the figures are estimates, based in some instances on numbers of licences (there may, of course, be considerable evasion of licence regulations in some countries); small differences between countries cannot therefore be regarded as significant.

The relationship between real income per head[4] and the level of ownership for some of these durables is shown in Fig. 12.1. Passenger car ownership appears to vary fairly closely with income. Much of the variation of particular countries from the straight line—the position above the line of the United States and Canada, for example—no doubt results from the price factor. In the United States the retail price of a car (including tax) is much lower, compared with the prices of other goods, than it is in Europe[5]. There are, of course,

[1]A recent calculation shows income-elasticities of demand for the periods 1929–41 and 1949–56 varying from 3.80 and 4.59 according to assumptions made (see D. B. Suits, 'The Demand for New Automobiles in the United States 1929–1956', *Review of Economics and Statistics*, Vol. 40, No. 3, August 1958). Income-elasticities exceeding 2.0 have also been found by other investigators.

[2]*Economic Survey of Europe in 1958*, ch. 5, p. 19. Several studies of family budget data and of time series have found that the demand for consumer durables tends to rise at least twice as fast as real income, other things being equal. See, for example, the articles by J. R. N. Stone and D. A. Rowe, 'Dynamic Demand Functions: Some Econometric Results', *Economic Journal*, Vol. 68, June 1958; and J. Aitchison and J. A. C. Brown, 'A Synthesis of Engel Curve Theory', *Review of Economic Studies*, Vol. 22 (1), No. 57, 1955.

[3]Demand for new durables must depend on the existing stock as well as on the income level (which affects the desired stock), on the rate of depreciation of the existing stock and on relative prices. Thus, the change in demand for new durables in a given year may be influenced by whether demand was high or low in previous years, as well as by the income change in the current year and the expected income change in the succeeding year.

[4]See Table E.2.

[5]See *Economic Survey of Europe in 1958*, United Nations, Geneva, 1959, ch. 5, pp. 21–23.

Fig. 12.1. Relation between ownership per head and gross domestic product per head for selected durable consumer goods, 1957–58

Double logarithmic scale

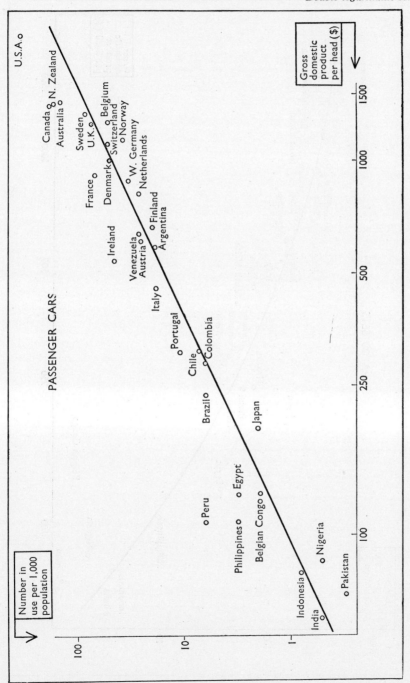

Fig. 12.1 (Continued)

Double logarithmic scale

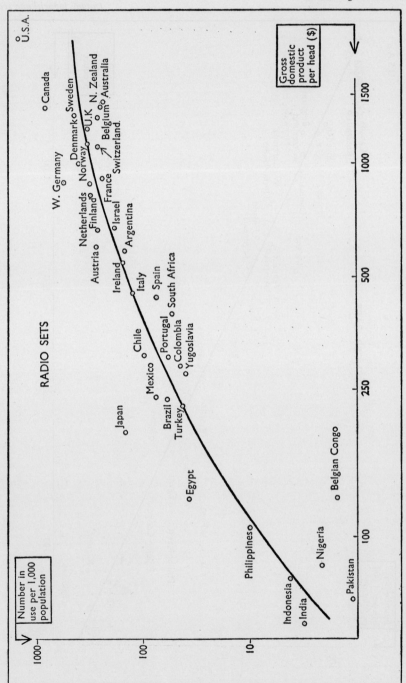

Fig. 12.1 (Continued). Relation between ownership per head and gross domestic product per head for selected durable consumer goods, 1957–58

Double logarithmic scale

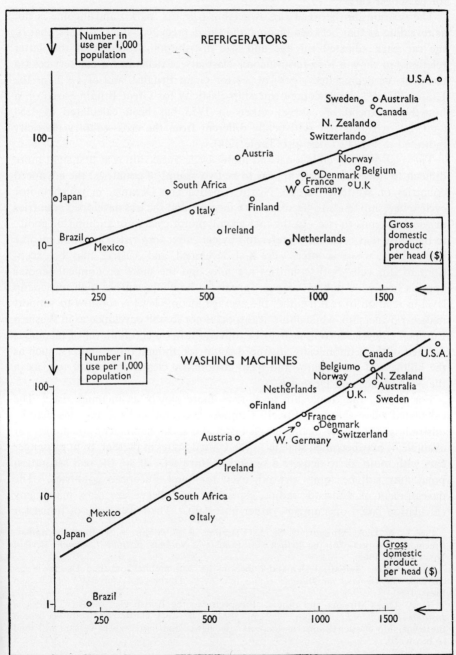

many other factors at work—such as the adequacy of public transport. The chart suggests that there is no effective 'saturation level' in sight in the demand for passenger cars.

The relationship between car ownership (the car 'park') and income is not as revealing as that between income and the depreciated 'stock' of cars, that is, the car park adjusted for age and size distribution. Studies of this latter relationship show a long-term income elasticity of demand for car services (in terms of the depreciated stock) of 2.4 for Great Britain[1], and of $1\frac{1}{2}$–2 for the United States[2]. An income-ownership elasticity for Great Britain based on a household expenditure survey taken in 1953 has been calculated at 1.58 (± 0.12)[3], which is not statistically different from the cross-country elasticity indicated in Fig. 12.1 (see also Table 12.4).

The relation between income and motor cycle ownership is at first sight more difficult to interpret. There appear to be two groups of countries; the advanced countries of Western Europe, North America and Oceania, in which motor cycle ownership tends to decrease with income, and the less developed countries in which it tends to rise. In the first group, motor cycles are an 'inferior good', in the sense that consumers prefer to buy cars after they reach a certain income level. Italy, where scooters were first developed, and Austria, may be exceptions to this rule; both countries are hilly and the more economical scooter appeals to a wide public. Japan appears to be unique in her high ownership level in relation to real income; the average income level is too low to support mass car ownership, while public transport is not so well developed as in Western Europe. Bicycles also appear to be 'inferior' after a certain level of income is reached in the economically advanced countries, though other matters, such as the hilliness of the country and local custom are clearly important too, as in the Netherlands and Denmark.

For radios, the ownership level rises more slowly as incomes rise. The calculated curve shown in Fig. 12.1 implies a saturation level, but this may be misleading. At higher income levels tastes and social habits tend to change; for example, it may become usual, as in the United States at present, to fit passenger cars with radio, or to acquire a second or third set. If so, the real saturation point may still be some way off, even for West European countries. The development of transistor radios, especially the 'pocket size' sets, makes any calculation based on numbers rather uncertain. The lower price of transistor

[1]See L. A. Dicks-Mireaux, C. St. J. O'Herlihy, R. L. Major, F. T. Blackaby and C. Freeman, 'Prospects for the British Car Industry', *National Institute Economic Review*, No. 17, Sept. 1961.

[2]G. C. Chow, 'Statistical Demand Functions for Automobiles and their Use for Forecasting', *The Demand for Durable Goods* (ed. A. C. Harberger), University of Chicago Press, 1960.

[3]L. A. Dicks-Mireaux and others, 'Prospects for the British Car Industry', *National Institute Economic Review*, No. 17, Sept. 1961. The stock elasticity will always exceed the ownership elasticity, since as incomes rise, newer and more expensive cars will tend to be owned.

radios, compared with other sets, and their greater convenience in use, is likely to extend the area of demand considerably.

For television receivers it may still be too early to draw any conclusions about the relationship between ownership and income. In some of the countries included, widespread television transmission began only a few years ago, while in others such as Britain, Canada and the United States, regular transmission services began before 1954, so that these countries have had time to absorb a large number of sets. Refrigerators and washing machines are both relatively new items in the consumer's stock of durable goods. Even in the advanced countries of Western Europe, ownership did not reach a mass scale until the 1950's, and in many under-developed countries sales of these goods are only just beginning. There are clearly factors other than income which determine the ownership of these two items.

Ownership appears to rise throughout the range of incomes for all the items except motor cycles and bicycles; for these two, the proportion of people owning the article tends to fall after a certain level of income is reached, since consumers can afford to switch to a superior product. In general, it appears that income is the main determinant of ownership, but that there are a large number of other factors. Price is clearly an important one; ownership is higher where the price of the goods, relative to other prices, is low. Other factors which are likely to influence ownership levels are local habits and customs; the ease or difficulty with which hire purchase facilities are available; changes in the distribution of income between different economic and social groups; and—insofar as electrically operated durables are concerned—the availability of public electricity supply. Table 12.4 gives the ownership-elasticities derived from least-squares equations based on cross-country data relating ownership levels to real income per head[1]. Where the elasticity falls off as real income rises, values are given for various income levels. Although the relationship between ownership and income is only a first approximation to the relationship between demand in a particular year and income[2], these results are generally consistent with those of the more detailed studies, mentioned earlier, of the behaviour of demand, or of the 'stock' of consumer durables, as income changes. They do not, of course, describe how demand for the different kinds of consumer durables will in fact evolve as incomes rise in particular countries.

---

[1] Ownership figures in 1957–8 (Table 12.3) were related to income per head estimates for 1957 (Table E.2).

[2] The ownership elasticity with respect to income will approximate to the corresponding demand elasticity only if (a) replacement demand is small in each country (or is the same proportion of the total stock); (b) ownership elasticity is the same in all countries at given levels of income; and (c) the rate of growth in real income is the same everywhere. Though the first two conditions may be approximately true, for some consumer durables, the third will not hold. However, it is unlikely that variations in growth rates are systematically related to per caput income levels, so that this factor would not seriously distort the relationship between the average ownership and income elasticities.

Table 12.4   *Ownership elasticity for consumer durables*[a]

	Ownership elasticity	R^2
PASSENGER CARS	1.66	0.926
MOTOR CYCLES		
Non-industrial countries	1.46	0.935
Industrial countries		
Average income per head at		
$500	0.93	
$750	−0.77	
$1000	−1.80	0.568
$1500	−3.25	
BICYCLES		
Average income per head at		
$100	1.27	
$250	0.81	
$500	0.48	
$750	0.28	0.419
$1000	0.14	
$1500	−0.07	
RADIO RECEIVING SETS		
Average income per head at		
$100	2.53	
$500	1.29	0.879
$1000	0.75	
REFRIGERATORS	1.16	0.548
WASHING MACHINES	2.09	0.864

Sources: Tables 12.3 and E.2.
[a] Based on cross-country regressions.

2. TRENDS IN PRODUCTION

Durable consumer goods can conveniently be divided into two groups: the traditional household goods, such as kitchenware, which can easily be produced in small factories or by artisans, and the newer products of large-scale mechanical and electrical engineering. In this second group, however, the products vary considerably in complexity, and consequently in the degree of organization and skill required in production. Bicycle production, for example, is comparatively simple to organize in a less-developed country. Car production, with more numerous and more complex component parts, is more difficult, and so also is the production of watches and cameras, which requires skilled craftsmanship.

World production of passenger cars is still highly concentrated; seven industrial countries, in 1959, produced all but 4 per cent of total world output. The assembly of cars from imported parts and components is, however, becoming increasingly important in many overseas countries. Altogether, about 450,000 cars a year were assembled in 1959 outside the main industrial areas[1].

[1] Australia is easily the most important car assembly country in this group.

The development of assembly work enables the local labour force to acquire engineering skills, so that eventually full production may be undertaken. The proportion of bicycles produced outside the industrial areas is rising. In 1955, about 8 per cent of world production outside Western Europe was located in five semi-industrial countries; the proportion rose to about 11 per cent in 1957 because of a large increase in production in India. Since 1955, bicycle production has fallen sharply in Britain, mainly because of a fall in exports, and has risen considerably in Japan, mainly to satisfy higher home demand[1].

Production of radio sets is almost as highly concentrated in the industrial areas as the production of cars. In several important markets, however, European or United States firms have established branches or subsidiaries, and there local production and assembly are advancing rapidly. The outstanding development in recent years has been the expansion of Japanese output, particularly of transistor radios[2]. So far, the production of television receivers has been either nil or negligible outside the main industrial countries, except for Australia where over 300,000 sets were produced in 1959.

Of the other important consumer durables, production of domestic sewing machines has grown in the industrial areas since 1950—Japanese and Soviet output rose particularly fast—and there has been some expansion in India and Australia too. Outside the industrial areas, production is mainly confined to the assembly of imported components and parts (particularly machine heads); an integrated sewing machine industry is only possible where the workers become sufficiently skilled to do the necessary precision work. Production of domestic electric refrigerators has been falling in the United States since 1955 (only about 13 per cent of homes in that country have no refrigerator). In Australia and New Zealand it was only slightly higher in 1958 than in 1957, though substantially higher than in 1950. In Britain, production rose by over 50 per cent between 1957 and 1958, and after a boom year in 1960, fell off in 1961 when production was, however, nearly 60 per cent above the 1958 level. In Japan and Argentina there have also been big increases in output in the last few years. There was no marked trend, one way or the other, in the production of electric washing machines and domestic vacuum cleaners in Britain and the United States between 1955 and 1960. Japanese production of washing machines, however, has risen considerably since the early 1950's; almost a million were produced in 1958 and 1½ million in 1960. Australia and New Zealand in recent years have raised their output of washing machines, but not of vacuum cleaners.

Some general, though tentative, conclusions emerge from these various production statistics. First, production of durable consumer goods has made

---

[1] The relative importance of home and export demand since the early 1950's is discussed in greater detail at the end of this chapter.

[2] Japanese production of radio sets rose from 1.8 million sets in 1955 to 13.7 million in 1961.

considerable strides in many overseas markets since the early 1950's; in particular, there has been rapid development in the economically more advanced countries, such as Australia and New Zealand, and also more recently in some Latin American countries, such as Argentina and Mexico. Secondly, these countries have concentrated on the less complex products, such as bicycles and refrigerators, and also on those which are suitable for large-scale assembly operations such as motor cars and sewing machines. But most under-developed countries are unlikely for some years to have enough skilled workers to begin local production of such items as cameras and watches, though the development of transistors and printed circuits should facilitate the growth of local assembly of radio sets.

Table 12.5. *Production and imports of passenger cars and bicycles in semi-industrial countries, 1938–57*

					Thousands
	Series	1938	1950–52 average	1953–54 average	1955–57 average
PASSENGER CARS					
A. Australia, India, New Zealand and South Africa	Production, incl. assembly[a]	99	156	209	295
	Imports				
	Complete	44	47	35	34
	For assembly	95	114	120	184
B. Argentina, Brazil and Mexico[b]	Imports complete	51	42	16	16
BICYCLES					
A. Australia, Brazil and India	Production[c]	126[d]	246	438	878
	Imports	173[e]	423	182	112
B. Argentina, Mexico, New Zealand and South Africa	Imports	40[f]	161	73	43

Sources: National trade and production statistics. Pre-war figures for India relate to the whole of the Indian sub-continent; post-war figures to Republic of India only.

[a] For Australia, the figures include assembly of motor car chassis only.
[b] These countries also assemble cars from imported parts. In 1955–1957, about 16,000 cars (annual average) were so assembled in Mexico and about 2,000 in Brazil, but figures for most earlier years are not available.
[c] Assembly from imported parts might be included.
[d] Australian production only.
[e] Excluding imports into Brazil.
[f] Excluding imports into South Africa.

3. PRODUCTION AND IMPORTS

This rise in local production in overseas markets outside the main industrial areas has led in some instances to a decline in imports. Table 12.5 compares the trends in production and imports of passenger cars and bicycles for two groups of markets: countries for which the production figures are available (group 'A'), and those for which they are not (group 'B').

Imports of complete passenger cars into group 'A' countries have been below pre-war since 1953–54, but imports in completely-knocked-down form have increased considerably as a result of the development of local assembly plants. A similar development appears to have begun in several important Latin American markets; though the statistics of local assembly output are inadequate it seems that in Latin America more cars are now being locally assembled than are imported complete.

Table 12.6. *Production and imports of selected consumer durables in semi-industrial countries, 1938–57*

					Thousands
	Series	1938	1950–52 average	1953–54 average	1955–57 average
RADIO RECEIVING SETS					
A. Australia, India and New Zealand	Production	239	512	491	663
	Imports[a]	51	30	17	7
B. Mexico and South Africa	Imports	97	70	108	153
DOMESTIC SEWING MACHINES					
A. Argentina, Australia and India	Production[b]	19	85	147	254
	Imports	147	168	90	93
B. Mexico, New Zealand and South Africa	Imports	71	159	124	188
DOMESTIC REFRIGERATORS					
A. Argentina, Australia and New Zealand	Production	30	240	328	468
	Imports	8[c]	27	6	3
B. India and South Africa	Imports	29	23	18	32
DOMESTIC WASHING MACHINES					
A. Australia and New Zealand	Production	..	88	164	205
	Imports	..	87	36	16
B. South Africa	Imports	..	20	19	17
DOMESTIC VACUUM CLEANERS					
A. Australia and New Zealand	Production	..	98	8.	100
	Imports	45	116	32	43
B. South Africa	Imports	14	23	22	31

Sources: As for Table 12.5.

[a]Excluding imports into Australia (6,000 units in 1957).
[b]Including approximate estimates for Argentina.
[c]Excluding imports into New Zealand which were not recorded separately.

For bicycles, India has been substituting locally-produced machines for the foreign product. In 1950, Indian production was 103,000 complete bicycles and imports (1950/51) were 166,000; production rose rapidly after 1953, to 490,000 in 1955, 912,000 in 1958 and 1,050,000 in 1960, while imports were reduced to 7,000 by 1958 and to only 200 in 1960. Brazil, too, is a clear case of import-substitution; imports had been as high as 181,000 in 1952, when local production was only 10,000, but by 1956 imports were negligible while production had reached 200,000. Bicycle imports into group 'B' countries declined after 1950–52 mainly because Mexico and South Africa reduced their imports. No official production figures are available for either country, but estimates by the trade put Mexican production in 1957–58 at about 95,000 bicycles a year, with negligible imports, whereas in 1950–51 imports averaged 92,000 bicycles a year.

A similar comparison of local production and imports can be made for five other durable consumer goods—radio sets, sewing machines, refrigerators, washing-machines and vacuum cleaners (Table 12.6). For all five, imports into group 'A' countries have declined as local production has risen; in particular, local production of sewing machines has replaced imports in India and Argentina, and local production of washing machines has done the same in Australia. For the non-producing countries[1], however, imports of four of the five items have risen since 1950–52.

This process of substitution has been generally fostered by government fiscal policies. In the semi-industrial countries, import duties on consumer durables are usually imposed for protective, rather than for revenue, purposes and they are generally higher than the tariff levels in force in the main industrial countries. Moreover, there is generally a lower rate of duty on components and parts than on the complete article. Tariff rates[2] appear to be extremely high in Brazil, for example; passenger cars not exceeding 1,600 kilogrammes are charged at 80 per cent *ad valorem*, and most other household durable goods are charged at least 100 per cent. In Argentina, a rate of 40 per cent is common, though radio sets and smaller motor bicycles carry only 25 per cent; Colombia charges 40 per cent on imports of complete passenger cars. India, which is attempting to create a car production industry, imposes a tariff of 75 per cent on complete cars and rates ranging from 25 to 50 per cent on unassembled cars, chassis and parts. In the industrial countries, tariffs on complete cars are generally lower, ranging from free entry for British cars into the Canadian market ($17\frac{1}{2}$ per cent on United States cars), and $10\frac{1}{2}$ per cent on all cars entering the United States, to 30 per cent for France and Britain[3] and 40 per cent for Japan.

Apart from import duties a number of other devices have been used to protect local production: for instance multiple exchange rate systems, which include

[1]There may, of course, be some production carried on though not officially recorded.
[2]The rates quoted are those in force in 1959.
[3]Since purchase tax is chargeable on the value of imports including the duty, the effective rate of protection for home-produced cars in Britain in 1959 was 45 per cent.

Table 12.7. *Exports[a] of durable consumer goods by area of destination,*
1950–57 $ *million*

	Passenger road vehicles			Household durables[b]			Total[b]		
	1950	1955	1957	1950	1955	1957	1950	1955	1957
INDUSTRIAL COUNTRIES	318	674	957	242	508	649	560	1182	1606
France, United Kingdom and West Germany	23	71	87	31	70	86	54	141	173
Other Western Europe[c]	196	405	438	87	204	264	283	609	502
United States	25	103	316	82	146	201	107	249	217
Canada	71	87	109	40	82	93	111	169	702
Japan	3	8	7	2	6	5	5	14	12
SEMI-INDUSTRIAL COUNTRIES	262	318	363	117	150	144	379	468	507
Australia, New Zealand and South Africa	171	205	213	43	77	69	214	282	282
India	13	24	24	6	14	11	19	38	35
Other semi-industrial countries[d]	78	89	126	68	59	64	146	148	190
REST OF WORLD	277	673	726	181	386	490	458	1059	1216
WORLD TOTAL	857	1665	2046	540	1044	1283	1397	2709	3329

Increase	1950–55	1955–57	1950–55	1955–57	1950–55	1955–57
INDUSTRIAL COUNTRIES	+356	+283	+266	+141	+622	+424
of which						
Western Europe	+257	+ 49	+156	+ 76	+413	+125
United States	+ 78	+213	+ 64	+ 55	+142	+268
SEMI-INDUSTRIAL COUNTRIES	+56	+ 45	+ 33	− 6	+ 89	+ 39
REST OF WORLD	+396	+ 53	+205	+104	+601	+157
WORLD TOTAL	+808	+381	+504	+239	+1312	+620

Sources: National trade statistics; total exports of principal exporting countries, as in Table 12.1.

[a]Exports from twelve main exporting countries.

[b]Excluding exports of radio and television sets from the Netherlands, for which statistics by country of destination are not published.

[c]Belgium-Luxembourg, Italy, Netherlands, Norway, Sweden and Switzerland.

[d]Argentina, Brazil, Chile, Colombia, Mexico, Turkey and Yugoslavia.

unfavourable rates for cars and other durable consumer goods, bilateral quotas, and restrictions temporarily imposed for balance of payments reasons. In general, consumer durables are regarded as 'less essentials' by the governments of most semi-industrial countries, and when foreign exchange is scarce it tends to be reserved for 'development goods', such as capital equipment, fuel and industrial raw materials; this, too, has stimulated local production.

It is not surprising, therefore, that exports of durable consumer goods to the semi-industrial countries have risen little in recent years (Table 12.7), and that their share in the total of world exports of these goods has fallen sharply. The big expansion in trade in durable consumer goods has been between the industrial nations themselves. From 1950 to 1955 they accounted for about half the rise in exports of both cars and household durables; there was a particularly big rise in exports to West European countries (including, of course, trade between them) as demand recovered there. From 1955 to 1957 the industrial countries took nearly three-quarters of the rise in world car exports—there was a remarkable increase in European exports to the United States over this period, which proved to be largely a temporary phase—and the intra-trade accounted for nearly 60 per cent of the rise in exports of household durables. In both periods, non-industrial countries accounted for nearly all the rest of the rise in exports, and the semi-industrial countries for hardly any of it.

4. COMPETITION IN THE WORLD MARKET

Passenger road vehicles

There has been a sharp reversal in the relative share of the world market in passenger cars supplied by the main producing countries since pre-war. The United States, which started mass-producing cars during and immediately after the first World War, dominated world trade in passenger cars during the 1920's. It was not until the mid-1930's that the small European car emerged as a successful competitor; by 1937, the United States share of world exports of all passenger cars had fallen to about 50 per cent (Table 12.8).

Table 12.8.   *Share of the world market in passenger cars and chassis, 1937–58*

| | | | | *Percentage of value* | |
Exports from	1937	1950	1955	1957	1958
West Germany	10.4ᵃ	7.9	28.8	33.8	34.8
United Kingdom	16.7	46.1	23.9	24.6	25.0
France	7.5	11.6	10.6	12.7	14.5
United States	49.6	26.4	26.9	17.0	12.5
Italy	3.6	2.7	4.0	5.1	6.2
Sweden	1.6	0.8	1.5	2.1	2.7
Belgium-Luxembourg	2.9	1.1	2.4	2.5	2.3
Canada	5.8	2.6	0.9	1.3	0.9
Other countriesᵇ	1.9	0.8	1.0	0.9	1.1
TOTAL	100.0	100.0	100.0	100.0	100.0

Sources: National trade statistics.

ᵃExports from the whole of Germany.
ᵇNetherlands, Switzerland and Japan.

X2

In the post-war period the British car industry has conducted a vigorous export drive. In 1950, Britain's exports amounted to almost one-half, by value, of the world total, as against only one-sixth in 1937. The subsequent recovery of the West European industries and the success of their export efforts has reduced Britain's share in recent years to about one-quarter of the world total—still larger than pre-war. The United States share has continued to fall, and in 1958 was only one-eighth of the total trade.

In the earlier post-war period the low United States share was largely explained by the restrictions which many countries imposed on imports from dollar sources: though discrimination against 'dollar' cars was much less widespread in the later 1950's, it was still enforced, to a greater or lesser degree, in many markets[1]. Dollar discrimination does not, however, explain why the United States share has continued to fall in recent years. The main reason for this appears to be that the more economical European car has a wider appeal than the larger American vehicle[2].

Since 1955 West Germany has increased her share further, to one-third of the world total, while the French car industry has nearly doubled its pre-war share. A substantial part of the increase in French car exports from 1950 to 1957 went to the associated territories in the French Union, and little more than half of it went to the more competitive markets of the industrial countries; over this period, three-quarters of the increase in British and West German exports went to the industrial areas. Germany concentrated her export effort on the expanding markets of Western Europe and the United States. The United Kingdom lost to Germany and the United States part of her share of the imports into the Southern Dominions—Australia, New Zealand and South Africa; imports of American cars into this area rose as discrimination was relaxed.

Exports of motor cycles and motor scooters have risen rapidly since 1950, though they fell from 1957 to 1958 (Table 12.9). There is little doubt that it is the motor scooters which account for most of the rise; Italy, which has specialised in motor scooters, has increased her share of the total market in both motor cycles and scooters from 7 per cent in 1950 to 33 per cent in 1958. Britain's share in 1958 was lower than before the war.

World exports of bicycles have been falling since 1955. Primary-producing countries have been developing their own production, as noted earlier, and the United States, which was a very big importer in 1955, has raised its tariff since

[1]This statement relates to the position up to about 1959. As from November 1959, however, the United Kingdom abolished import restrictions on United States cars.

[2]A small part of the decline in the United States share of world exports since 1950 is explained by the substantial increase in its imports of cars during this period. This automatically reduces its share and increases that of other countries. But even if all exports of passenger road vehicles to the United States are excluded from the world total the United States share still shows a fall from 23.0 per cent in 1950 to 17.9 per cent in 1957 and 14.8 per cent in 1958.

then and has reduced its imports of bicycles substantially. Although Britain's share of the market has fallen, it was still over 50 per cent in 1958 and was higher than pre-war.

Table 12.9. *Exports of motor cycles, bicycles, and parts,[a] and shares of the world market, 1937–58*

	1937	1950	1955	1957	1958
MOTOR CYCLES[b] AND PARTS					
World exports ($ *million*)	28	45	103	124	102
Percentage shares					
West Germany	67[c]	27	43	42	34
Italy	1	7	18	27	33
United Kingdom	24	54	23	17	16
BICYCLES AND PARTS					
World exports ($ *million*)	50	95	129	107	92
Percentage shares					
United Kingdom	45	66	62	56	57
West Germany	31	10	16	17	16
Japan	16	6	7	8	7

Sources: National trade statistics; exports from twelve main exporting countries.

[a]For France, excludes parts. German figures of parts do not separately distinguish bicycle and motor cycle parts; the separate figures have been estimated for 1955, 1957 and 1958.

[b]Including motor scooters and motor-assisted bicycles.

[c]Exports from the whole of Germany.

Household durables

Before the war, Germany was easily the biggest exporter of household durables; in 1937 she accounted for one-third of total exports from the main industrial countries (Table 12.10). Switzerland and the United States each held about one-fifth of the total market, while Britain came a long way behind with one-tenth. In the earlier post-war period, both Switzerland and Britain benefited from the absence of many German firms, but since the early 1950's West Germany has been regaining ground. By 1958 she had established a clear lead, supplying one-quarter of the world total—still substantially less, however, than the pre-war share held by the old Reich. Britain's share in 1958, though less than in the early 1950's, was still larger than pre-war. Japan and France have also improved their positions. The United States share in 1958 was a good deal lower than it was pre-war.

The different movements in world trade for the specialities of the different producing countries account for some of these changes. In the earlier post-war years, there were widespread import restrictions on consumer durables, while the absence of traditional suppliers (especially German industry) from the

Table 12.10. *Shares of the world market in household durables, 1937–58*

Percentage

Exports from	1937	1950	1955	1957	1958
West Germany	32.4[a]	11.6	23.5	25.5	26.3
Switzerland	22.6	33.0	25.8	25.4	21.7
United States	19.9	20.0	16.0	14.4	14.2
United Kingdom	10.3	17.3	15.4	12.6	12.8
Japan	2.1	2.3	4.4	6.2	7.9
Netherlands	6.6	4.5	6.1	5.7	6.6
France	1.5	4.9	3.1	4.0	4.6
Belgium-Luxembourg	0.5	1.3	2.0	1.9	2.3
Italy	0.6	1.5	1.3	1.5	1.7
Sweden	2.9	2.9	2.2	2.2	1.6
Canada	0.7	0.7	0.3	0.5	0.3
TOTAL	100.0	100.0	100.0	100.0	100.0

Sources: National trade statistics.

[a]Exports from the whole of Germany.

export market also distorted the trading pattern, which showed marked changes compared with pre-war.   World trade in watches and clocks, for instance, rose faster than average from 1937 to 1950, and this explains about half the rise in Switzerland's share during this period.   The United States also benefited from the shift in the pattern of trade, particularly from the relative increase in trade in electric washing machines, gas water heaters and water softeners.   By contrast, the changes in the pattern of world trade worked to the disadvantage of the Netherlands and West Germany.   Radio sets and other radio equipment were a large part of Dutch exports in 1937; trade in this group rose less than average from 1937 to 1950, and so the Dutch share in world trade in household durables fell.   Relatively low trading volume in cameras, radio sets and cutlery explain about one-third of the fall in Germany's share over these years; but it may be that one reason why world trade in cameras, for instance, rose only slowly was that the German article was not on the market.

Since 1950, the changing pattern of world trade in household durables has again benefited the United States, because of the big rise in trade in radios, television sets and record players; it has also helped Britain and the Netherlands. Trade in watches and clocks has risen comparatively slowly, to Switzerland's disadvantage.

Table 12.11 gives detailed figures for individual household durables.   For a number of them, the most important change since 1950 has been West Germany's re-entry into the world market; in particular, her trade in electrical goods recovered substantially, in spite of the fact that, before the war, an appreciable

Table 12.11   *Shares of the world market for selected household durables,*
1937–58

Percentage

Exports from	1937	1950	1955	1957	1958
CUTLERY					
West Germany	55[a]	31	35	32	32
United Kingdom	21	32	34	27	27
Japan	6	3	8	16	15
United States	11	15	9	8	8
France	2	9	6	6	7
Value of U.K. exports ($ m.)	5.9	14.7	27.6	24.8	24.8
SEWING MACHINES					
Japan	0	15	32	35	35
United Kingdom	33	28	26	27	23
West Germany	38[a]	23	12	9	17
Switzerland	0	11	12	10	9
Italy	1	9	10	9	8
United States	24	7	4	3	3
Value of U.K. exports ($ m.)	9.0	16.8	27.2	31.4	26.5
ELECTRIC WASHING MACHINES					
West Germany	—	—	25	34	29
United States	98	42	30	28	28
United Kingdom	—	49	33	24	27
France	—	1	5	7	8
Canada	1	8	2	2	2
Value of U.K. exports ($ m.)	—	10.6	15.5	14.8	16.5
RADIOS, RADIOGRAMS AND TELEVISION SETS					
West Germany	27[a]	7	33	39	34
Netherlands	32[b]	31	30	23	22
United States	32	25	12	12	12
Japan	1	0	1	5	12
Belgium-Luxembourg	1	9	10	8	8
United Kingdom	5	11	7	4	3
Value of U.K. exports ($ m.)	2.6	7.7	11.1	10.0	9.9
ELECTRIC COOKING AND HEATING APPLIANCES (INCLUDING IRONS)					
West Germany	55[a]	10	29	36	32
United States	12	29	29	24	27
United Kingdom	22	46	32	24	25
France	5	7	5	4	5
Sweden	1	2	1	1	2
Value of U.K. exports ($ m.)	1.7	8.7	17.4	14.4	14.2
DOMESTIC REFRIGERATORS					
United States	67	60	50	45	36
West Germany	15[a]	4	17	24	27
United Kingdom	4	22	21	15	21[c]
France	1	4	5	7	9
Italy	—	0	0	2	5
Sweden	11	7	6	6	..
Value of U.K. exports ($ m.)	0.7	12.2	21.3	16.9	28.0[c]

For footnotes, see next page.

Table 12.11 (cont.).

Exports from	1937	1950	1955	1957	1958
GRAMOPHONES, RECORD PLAYERS, TAPE-RECORDERS, ETC.					
United Kingdom	48	21	24	23	25
United States	5	51	33	27	24
West Germany	9a	1	18	23	22
Netherlands	1	9	15	13	15
Switzerland	14	13	7	5	5
Belgium-Luxembourg	0	0	2	4	5
Japan	22	2	1	1	2
Value of U.K. exports ($ m.)	2.5	3.8	14.2	21.7	24.7
CAMERAS (EXCLUDING CINE-CAMERAS)					
West Germany	89a	59	71	61	56
Japan	—	4	9	17	21
Switzerland	1	10	13	14	14
United States	5	7	2	2	3
United Kingdom	3	12	3	2	2
France	1	6	1	2	2
Value of U.K. exports ($ m.)	0.5	2.2	1.9	1.4	1.0
WATCHES AND CLOCKS					
Switzerland	70	80	77	78	76
West Germany	20a	7	16	15	17
France	2	6	3	3	3.
Value of U.K. exports ($ m.)	0.6	3.9	4.5	5.4	5.0

Sources: National trade statistics. Countries listed in order of importance in 1958 export trade. Listing is confined to countries accounting for 5 per cent or more of the world total in any one of the years shown.

aExports from the whole of Germany.

bApproximate estimate. Complete radio receiving sets were not separately distinguished in the Netherlands export returns until 1948, when they accounted for 52 per cent of the heading 'radio products and parts thereof, n.e.s.'. The corresponding proportion in 1950 was 60 per cent. It has been assumed here that complete radio receiving sets accounted for 55 per cent of the combined heading in 1937.

cThe figure for 1958 is not completely comparable with those for earlier years.

part of Germany's light electrical industry was in an area now in East Germany. By 1958, her share in the market for washing machines, refrigerators and gramophones and record players was bigger than that of the old Reich in 1937. However, her share in the trade in sewing machines and cameras fell from 1950 to 1958, mainly because of competition from Japan.

The United States share of a number of items has fallen considerably since pre-war. The trade in electric washing machines was virtually an American monopoly then; by 1958, Britain and West Germany together exported 55 per cent of the world total. The United States also no longer dominates the domestic refrigerator market as she did; in sewing machines, too, her share has come down drastically, mainly because of the rapid rise in Japanese sales, but also partly as a result of the post-war success of Swiss and Italian makes. In electric

Table 12.12.   *Proportion of exports of consumer durable goods going to the industrial areas, 1950–57*

| | Percentage | |
Exports from	1950	1957
United Kingdom	26	36
United States	33	42
Japan	50	60
Switzerland	60	54
West Germany	53	60

cooking and heating apparatus, however, the United States has held her own since 1950.

Japan's share of the world market in household durables has risen fast from 1950 to 1958; domestic sewing machines and radio sets explain about two-thirds of the rise, and cameras and cutlery the rest.   Japanese sewing machines, which were a negligible export before the war, now account for one over-third of total world exports.   Japan has also launched a successful export drive in the past few years in small transistor radio sets (the United States is a major market for these), and she is now the second largest exporting country for cameras, specializing in precision-built miniatures.

Though Britain's share of the total market for household durables in the past two years just exceeded the pre-war figure, there was a noticeable fall from 1950 to 1958, in particular in washing machines and electric cooking and heating apparatus, but also in cutlery, sewing machines, radio sets and cameras.   Since the commodity pattern of world demand changed in Britain's favour in this period, her loss in share has to be explained in other ways.   One explanation is that demand has grown more slowly in the primary producing countries (to which most of Britain's exports go) than in the industrial countries (which are the main markets for West Germany, Switzerland and Japan).   Table 12.12 gives the proportion of exports of household durables going to the main industrial markets[1] in 1950 and 1957.

Nonetheless, it is not likely that this shift in the area pattern of world trade is the whole explanation of the fall in Britain's share.   Both Germany and Japan, with intensive export drives, have gained ground at Britain's expense in a number of markets.   In both these countries, the industries making consumer durables succeeded in raising their exports substantially at the same time as they were meeting a large unsatisfied home demand.   In Britain, however, the expansion in home demand has failed to carry with it a corresponding increase in exports.

5.   EXPORTS AND THE HOME MARKET

In addition to the shift in the area pattern of world trade, and fierce competition from Japan and Germany, a third reason is often given for Britain's loss of

[1]Taking these as the countries listed in Table 12.10, plus Norway.

share in the world market for durable consumer goods since 1950: that is, the pull of the home market. It is argued that industries cease to concern themselves with exports when the pull of the home market is too strong, and conversely that those industries are successful in exporting which cannot sell in the home market and are consequently forced to look for markets abroad. To throw some light on this question, some new index numbers have been prepared of home and export deliveries of passenger road vehicles and of household durables (Table 12.13) and the experience of this and other countries in home and export markets for particular items has been examined (Table 12.14 and Fig. 12.2).

Table 12.13.   *Home and export deliveries*^{a} *of consumer durables in the United Kingdom, 1950–60*

	Passenger road vehicles			*Volume index numbers*, 1950 = 100 Household durables^b			
Year	Home	Export	Total	Home (Ex. T.V.)		Export	Total (Ex. T.V.)]
1950	100	100	100	100	100	100	100 100
1951	93	97	95	113	105	132	119 115
1952	90	88	89	90	64	93	91 75
1953	142	82	108	122	82	81	109 82
1954	190	95	136	170	145	84	144 121
1955	231	99	156	210	159	78	169 128
1956	165	89	122	163	118	81	138 103
1957	196	108	146	203	142	75	164 116
1958	219	134	171	233	174	74	184 135
1959	254	155	197	331	247	68	250 177
1960	313	148	219	292	248	87	229 185

Source: Computed from quantity data in *Monthly Digest of Statistics*, Central Statistical Office, using 1955 factory values as weights.

The export indices are based on statistics of deliveries by manufacturers and do not necessarily reflect corresponding changes in actual exports as recorded in the Trade Accounts. Nevertheless, it is not thought that the general trend in exports since 1950 is distorted by the use of the delivery statistics. The advantage in using delivery figures is that they relate to precisely the same items as are included in the home sales index numbers.

^{a}Production or deliveries by manufacturers.
^{b}Radios and radiograms, television sets, domestic refrigerators, domestic hand-operated laundering machinery, electric vacuum cleaners, dry shavers, domestic electric washing machines, electric irons and portable typewriters.

Television sets account for a large part of the increase in sales of household durables in Britain: they explain nearly 60 per cent of the rise in home deliveries from 1952 to 1955, and 50 per cent of the rise from 1956 to the peak in 1959. The British manufacturer who wishes to export television sets is confronted by a

Fig. 12.2.   Changes in exports and home market sales of selected durable
consumer goods from 1950–52 to 1956–58

Thousands

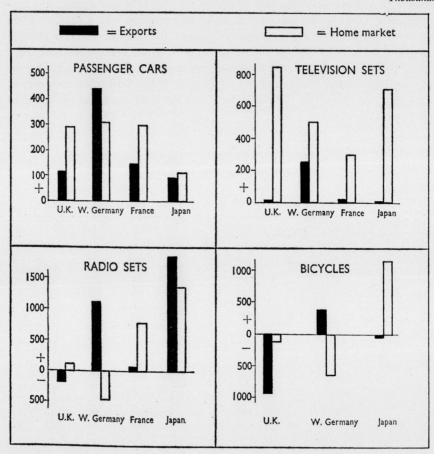

major technical obstacle—the difference between the British picture definition
standard and those in use abroad[1].   Because of this, export models have to be
built to different specifications from models for the home market, and this means
higher production costs.   British exports of television sets have in fact been
negligible, while both Holland and West Germany export them on a substantial
scale.   How far the technical difficulties explain this difference, and how far the
British television industry would in any event have concentrated on the home
market, it is not possible to say.   If television set production is omitted from

[1]In Britain, television reception is based on 405-line definition, while on the Continent,
apart from France, 625-line definition is standard.   France uses 819-line, while the United
States uses 525-line, as does the rest of the American Continent and most countries in the
Middle East.

Table 12.14. *Exports and production for the home market of selected durable consumer goods, 1950–52 and 1956–58*

Annual averages, thousand units

	1956–58		Change from 1950–52 to 1956–58	
	Exports[a]	Home market[b]	Exports[a]	Home market[b]
PASSENGER CARS				
France	230	524	+ 142	+ 298
Italy	116	207	+ 96	+ 103
United Kingdom	443	438	+ 103	+ 290
United States	149	5247	− 10	− 35
West Germany	528	468	+ 444	+ 301
BICYCLES, COMPLETE				
Italy	47	271	+ 29	− 27[c]
Japan	63	2038	− 42[d]	+ 1150
Netherlands	87[e]	421[e]	− 19	0
United Kingdom	1650	870	− 970	− 160
West Germany	428	542	+ 397	− 623
RADIOS AND RADIOGRAMS				
France	199	1392	+ 66	+ 553
Japan	1832	1986	+ 1828	+ 1344
United Kingdom	296	1464	− 200	+ 150
United States	266	9113	− 132	+ 810
West Germany	1530[e]	1457[e]	+ 1127[g]	− 499[g]
TELEVISION RECEIVERS[f]				
France	14	309	+ 13	+ 282
Japan	7	703	+ 7	+ 703
United Kingdom	18	1752	+ 12	+ 845
United States	182	6068	+ 75	+ 69
West Germany	179[e]	604[e]	+ 160	+ 494
DOMESTIC SEWING MACHINES				
Italy	154	301	+ 41	+ 93
Japan	1659	371	+ 1072	− 156
United Kingdom[h]	706[i]	125	+ 100[i]	+ 43
West Germany	85[e]	506[e]	− 81[g]	+ 112[g]
DOMESTIC ELECTRIC WASHING MACHINES				
United Kingdom	194	526	− 96	+ 235
United States	90	2916	+ 31	+ 1335
VACUUM CLEANERS				
Netherlands	174	210	+ 86	+ 74
United Kingdom	226	978	− 91	+ 271
United States	99	3273	+ 78	+ 261

Sources: National production and export statistics.

[a]Actual exports, except for the United Kingdom, the figures for which are for manufacturers' production, or deliveries, for export; exceptionally, exports of sewing machines from the United Kingdom are actual exports.

[b]Production or deliveries for the home market; or total production less exports.

[c]Change from 1953–1955 average.

[d]Although there was a fall in exports of complete bicycles from Japan, this was more than offset by an expansion in exports of bicycle parts over the same period.

[e]1957.

[f]Changes shown are from 1952 (W. Germany from 1954).

[g]Change from 1952.

[h]The figures for the later period are an average for 1956–57.

[i]Including exports of industrial sewing machines.

the figures, the index of home deliveries increases much more slowly up to 1958, while the index of export deliveries is unchanged.   There was a home market boom in both television sets and other household durables (particularly washing machines) in 1959, but in 1960 a sharp recession in sales in all consumer durables, except radio sets, occurred mainly as a result of hire purchase restrictions. Even excluding television sets from the comparison, the contrast between rising home sales and stagnant export sales in the decade 1950–60, though smaller, is still striking.

It does not follow, however, that exports would have risen more if the rise in home sales had been restrained; the year-to-year movements in home sales and exports of household durables do not suggest any such connection. Further, the rise in home sales of passenger cars from 1950 to 1960 was rather greater than the rise in home sales of household durables; but export sales of cars over this period rose appreciably, while exports of household durables fell. Indeed, from 1956 to 1959 exports of cars rose faster than home sales.

In Britain, the car industry has certainly been more successful in export markets than the household durable industries, particularly since 1956.   It is difficult, however, to point to any single cause for this difference in experience. One major influence may be the fact that the car industry was obliged by Government action to export a substantial proportion of its production in the early post-war period, and that later it came under pressure to sell in the highly competitive American market.   The industry has thus developed since 1945 in an 'export-minded' way and considerable capital has been invested in export sales organisations and in service depots in foreign markets.   For household durables, on the other hand, the big rise in production came after the setting of export targets for industries had been abandoned, and the household durable industries have, since 1950–1952, concentrated on the home market; in general they have not acquired the habit—as the car industry has done in the post-war period—of looking to export markets for an appreciable proportion of their sales.

The experience of other industrial countries also does not suggest any systematic connection between the movement of home and export sales. Table 12.14 and Fig. 12.2 compare the annual averages of 1956–58 with 1950–52. For some items and in some countries, a fall in home sales was accompanied by a rise in exports: this was true, for instance, for radios and radiograms in West Germany and for sewing machines in Japan.   Also, in a number of instances, home sales rose and exports fell—Japanese bicycles and United States radios and radiograms are examples.   But, more commonly, home and export sales both rose, and often substantially.   For instance, Japanese home deliveries of radios rose by over a million, and so did their export sales; West German home sales of television sets rose by nearly half a million, and export sales rose by 160,000.   Dutch home sales and exports of vacuum cleaners both rose by about 80,000.   For passenger cars, home sales rose by about 300,000 in France,

West Germany and Britain—suggesting that in the three countries the pull of the home market was about the same; but during this period the French increase in exports was 40 per cent bigger than the British, and the German increase was four times as great.

CHAPTER 13

TEXTILES AND CLOTHING

The dramatic decline in the share of textiles in world trade in manufactures over the past half-century has already been commented upon. In this chapter, the decline in the textile market will be examined in more detail and we shall be particularly concerned with the impact on that market of the development of textile manufacturing in the main importing countries.

Taking the period as a whole, two distinct divergencies stand out. First, world demand for textile products has risen much more slowly than that for other manufactured goods. From 1899 to 1929, for example, world textile production increased by about 60–70 per cent, whereas total manufacturing output rose by some 175 per cent (Table 13.1). Again, comparing 1929 with 1959, the divergence is equally marked, textile production increasing by about 55 per cent against a rise of over 190 per cent in the total. This differential movement implies a corresponding divergence in the rates of growth in consumption of textiles and of other manufactured goods. The relatively slow rate of growth in textile consumption has already been mentioned (see Chapter 2), and it is discussed further below. Second, in the period up to 1929 world trade in textiles and clothing increased with the growth in world textile output, though at a somewhat slower rate, indicating that the exporting countries were meeting a large proportion of the increase in world textile requirements; but after 1929 while world textile production continued to rise, world trade in textiles was reduced (see Fig. 13.1).

Thus, since 1929 the growth in world textile requirements has been met in the main from the development of industries serving local markets. This seems to point to the financial difficulties and trade restrictions of the early 1930's as the initiating factors in this process. While this was undoubtedly so in many countries, particularly in Western Europe, a further development of major importance has been—as will be seen later—the impetus to local textile production provided by the industralization of numerous under-developed countries.

The sharp contraction in world trade in textiles during the 1930's affected all three sections distinguished in Table 13.1, though by 1937 yarns had recovered to a much greater extent than fabrics, and had also come nearer the 1929 peak than had made-up goods. The relative stagnation of trade in fabrics has continued in the post-war period. From 1950 to 1959, the volume of trade in fabrics rose by only one-sixth, while trade in yarns rose by one-quarter and in made-up goods by over one-half. The divergent trends of trade in fabrics and made-up goods are particularly striking: by 1959, trade in the latter was some 20 per cent above 1929, whereas in the former it was about 16 per cent lower. Trade in yarns had virtually recovered the 1929 level by 1959.

Table 13.1. *World trade[a] in textiles and clothing in relation to world manufacturing production, 1899–1959*

$ *billion at constant prices, and index numbers, 1929 = 100*

	Values at 1913 prices[b]			Values at 1955 prices[c]				
	1899	1913	1929	1929	1937	1950	1955	1959
WORLD TRADE								
Textile yarns	0.37	0.42	0.40	1.01	0.88	0.78	0.85	0.98
Textile fabrics	0.96	1.38	1.33	3.46	2.87	2.48	2.65	2.91
Total	1.33	1.80	1.73	4.47	3.75	3.26	3.50	3.89
INDEX	77	104	100	100	84	73	78	87
Textile made-up goods and clothing	0.34	0.42	0.49	1.20	1.00	0.94	1.09	1.45
INDEX	69	86	100	100	83	78	91	122
Total, textiles and clothing	1.67	2.22[d]	2.22	5.67	4.75	4.20	4.59	5.34[e]
INDEX	75	100	100	100	84	74	81	94
WORLD MANUFACTURING PRODUCTION								
Total index	36	61	100	100	115	190	252	294
of which								
Textiles	60	97	100	100	112	128	142	156

Sources: Tables A.6 and A.80; *Industrial Statistics, 1900–1959*, O.E.E.C., Paris, 1960; *Statistical Yearbooks*, United Nations, New York.

[a]Exports from twelve main exporting countries.
[b]Excluding exports from the Netherlands.
[c]Including exports from the Netherlands.
[d]In addition, exports from other large textile exporters amounted to $0.15 billion (Austria-Hungary, $90 million; Russia, 25; China, 30).
[e]In addition, exports in 1959 from other large textile exporters outside the Soviet area amounted to about $440 million (Hong Kong, $242 million ; Austria, 93; Portugal, 47; Egypt, 37; and Mexico, 20).

The failure of trade in textiles and clothing during the 1950's to recover to the 1929 level was due essentially to the development of textile industries in numerous import markets, and the consequent substitution of home produced for imported textiles.   Even without such import-substitution, however, the growth in world trade in textiles would have lagged behind that in other manufactures because of the lower income-elasticity of demand for textile products.   Britain, the largest exporter of textiles in the inter-war period, was the most adversely affected by the import-substitution process; in addition, her share of the reduced world import market was eroded by vigorous competition from other textile exporting countries.   These several aspects of the development of the world textile market are considered in turn below.

Fig. 13.1.   World trade in textiles and clothing in relation to world
manufacturing production, 1899–1959

Volume indices, 1899 = 100,
semi-logarithmic scale

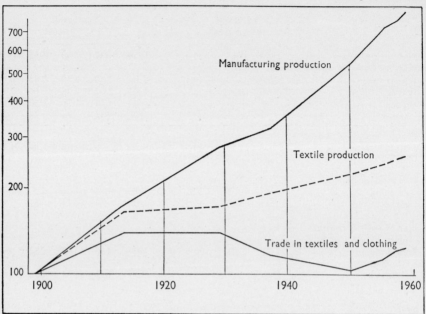

1.   THE DEMAND FOR TEXTILES AND CLOTHING

As was shown in Chapter 2, empirical studies have demonstrated that the income-elasticity of demand for textiles and clothing is significantly lower than that for other manufactured goods in total[1].   The available estimates of the income-elasticity for textiles and clothing do, however, differ among themselves and some are more relevant than others to an appraisal of trends in world trade.

The income-elasticities discussed in Chapter 2 were generally divided into three groups: those based on regressions covering consumption in many countries in a single year; those based on family expenditure surveys within different countries; and those based on the relative movements over time in consumption and real income.   For textiles and clothing, however, more than perhaps for any other group of manufactures, the position is complicated by the fact that changes in the level of consumption can be measured in several quite distinct ways.   There are three main methods which can be used to calculate consumption levels, and as each can be used in combination with one of several alternative regression approaches, there are consequently a variety of possible

[1]See page 41.

alternative bases of estimating the requisite income elasticity.

Two of the three methods of calculating consumption levels have been in general use for many years. The first of these is the use of the *gross weight* of textile fibres available for domestic consumption to represent the movement in the *quantum* of textile consumption. Estimates of income elasticities using the gross weight of fibre recently made by the Food and Agriculture Organization are summarized in the upper part of Table 13.2. These estimates cover a large number of countries, but relate only to a short period of time and, moreover, make no allowance for changes in textile and clothing prices relatively to consumer prices generally. In the period 1953–57, there was a fall in relative textile and clothing prices, and this appears to be a major reason for the elasticity co-efficients based on time series (the 'average within countries') being systematically higher than those based on cross-country relationships (the 'average within years'). Even apart from price changes, however, the time-series elasticity might be expected to exceed the cross-country one, insofar as there is a trend over time to economize in raw materials per unit of output[1].

Table 13.2. *Estimates of income-elasticity of demand for textiles and clothing[a]*

		Basis of estimate	Income-elasticity	Standard error	R^2
TEXTILE FIBRES[b]					
28 countries[c]	1953/57	Average within countries	0.84	± 0.06	0.63
		Average within years	0.52	± 0.02	0.82
19 countries[d]	1953/57	Average within countries	0.78	± 0.16	0.24
		Average within years	0.53	± 0.04	0.68
CLOTHING[e]					
9 European countries	1950/57	Average within countries	0.76	± 0.03	0.91
		Average within years	0.91	± 0.08	0.68

Source: 'Report by the F.A.O. Secretariat on Fiber Consumption Trends' in *Studies of Factors Affecting Consumption of Textile Fibers*, International Cotton Advisory Committee, Washington, 1960.

[a]The co-efficients shown are those derived from double logarithmic functions. The F.A.O. study also gives co-efficients derived from semi-logarithmic functions.
[b]Weight of per caput fibre consumption.
[c]Income figures based on estimated purchasing power parity rates with the U.S. dollar in 1950.
[d]Income figures based on official exchange rates.
[e]Consumers' expenditure.

[1]Mr T. S. Robertson, of the Food and Agriculture Organization, in commenting on the results, suggested that 'the disparity between the two average co-efficients could be bridged by apportioning one half to price reduction and one half to favourable trends in technology, tastes, etc.' (*Studies of Factors Affecting Consumption of Textile Fibers*, International Cotton Advisory Committee, Washington, 1960, p. 31).

The use of gross fibre weights is, however, open to the objection that it is not meaningful to count equivalent weights of, say, nylon and wool or nylon and cotton as equivalent units of consumption. The synthetic fibres have distinct technical advantages in many uses over the natural fibres: for example, greater tensile strength and longer life, while they are considerably lighter for a given surface area. The use of a given weight of synthetic fibre for apparel would thus displace a much greater weight of natural fibre. Since the proportion of synthetic in total fibre consumption has grown markedly over the past decade, particularly in the high-income countries, regressions based on gross fibre weights (whether time-series or cross-country) are likely to under-estimate the true income-elasticity for textiles as a whole.

The second method of approach to a calculation of the *quantum* of consumption is *via* the measurement of consumers' money expenditures. Most countries publish official estimates of the value of consumers' expenditure at constant prices, and these usually distinguish expenditure on clothing. Direct information on such expenditure can be obtained from sample household enquiries. In either case, clothing expenditures per head can be related to total consumer expenditure per head, allowing for family size when household expenditures are analysed, or for relative price changes in the analysis of time series. The lower half of Table 13.2 summarizes some recent estimates of the income elasticity of demand for clothing based on consumer expenditure estimates. The average cross-country elasticity of 0.91 is somewhat higher than that based on time-series, 0.76, presumably because in the richer countries expenditure on clothing is inflated by the cost of providing better fitting and finish, more stylish clothes, and more elaborate distributive services, than can be obtained in poorer countries. These results compare with an average income elasticity for clothing of 1.2 based on household surveys in a number of different countries[1]; a cross-country income elasticity of 0.84 calculated in a recent O.E.E.C. study[2] and one of 1.22 using the same method but based on a wider range of countries[3].

The use of money expenditure figures very largely avoids the objection raised to the use of gross fibre weights, because differences in the technical characteristics of the different fibres are reflected—along with other factors—in their relative prices. However, there is a major drawback to this approach

---

[1]H. S. Houthakker, 'An International Comparison of Household Expenditure Patterns, Commemorating the Centenary of Engel's Law', *Econometrica*, Vol. 25, No. 4, October 1957. See also Table 2.1.

[2]M. Gilbert and Associates, *Comparative National Products and Price Levels*, O.E.E.C., Paris, 1958. See also Table 2.1.

[3]T. Watanabe, 'A Note on an International Comparison of Private Consumption Expenditure', *Weltwirtschaftliches Archiv*, Band 88, Heft 1, 1962. Watanabe's calculation was based on the estimated dollar value, at purchasing power equivalents, of per caput consumers' expenditure on clothing in 22 countries in a single year (which differed from country to country). A double logarithmic regression of per caput consumption on per caput income was used.

also, insofar as it applies to the analysis of international trade. This is that, as already mentioned, the proportion of expenditure devoted to fit, finish, styling and services tends to rise with the level of real income. The higher the level of income, the greater is likely to be the difference between total expenditure on clothing and the value of the textile materials used. Thus, at medium and high income levels, an income elasticity based on expenditure figures is likely to over-estimate the rate at which demand for textile fibres as such will rise with the rise in income. At low income levels, on the other hand, the difference is not likely to be important.

A third approach, which attempts to avoid both the objections mentioned, would be to combine the consumption of the different fibres on the basis of their total values. This can be done by valuing the gross weight figures by the relevant price per unit of each fibre. An illustrative calculation on this basis which was made for Western Europe for the period 1953–60 showed an income elasticity of 0.74 ($\pm$0.09) at the 1960 level of consumption[1]. The corresponding calculation using the gross weight of fibre as the indicator of consumption gave an income elasticity of 0.67 ($\pm$0.05). While there is no significant difference between these two elasticities derived from data for recent years, the two approaches are likely to yield very different results for the 1960's, if the proportion of synthetic fibres in the total continues to increase substantially.

2. GROWTH OF TEXTILE PRODUCTION IN IMPORTING COUNTRIES

We have already seen that the development of local textile industries is very often a major feature of the earlier stages of industrialization[2]. This is particularly true of cotton textile production in the countries where raw cotton is grown. Such countries—spread across a wide belt of tropical and semi-tropical latitudes—would turn to the production of cotton goods as a natural development of cotton growing if they were intent on a programme of secondary industry expansion. The capital investment required is modest in relation to, say, chemicals or engineering production and it can often be started off on the basis of second-hand looms and other equipment, while the skills involved can be readily acquired by unskilled labour in a fairly short training period. Moreover, in countries in which handicraft production of textiles has traditionally been

[1]The weights used were cotton, 1.0; wool, 3.5; rayon. 1.4; synthetic fibres, 5.0; these correspond approximately to relative (wholesale) prices per unit weight in Western Europe in 1960. A regression of the average (weighted) per caput consumption in Western Europe on the logarithms of per caput real income for the same area was computed. The income series was derived by weighting the per caput real income series for individual countries by their estimated value of textile fibre consumption in 1960. The regression result was $C = 25.77 \log Y - 61.53$ ($R^2 = 0.895$), where C represents the weighted value of fibre consumption per head, and Y the estimated dollar value of gross national product per head in 1960 prices.

[2]See the discussion on patterns of industrial growth in Chapter 2.

important, the existence of local skills in the technical processes, and possibly also a highly organised merchanting system, would appreciably facilitate the development of production on a factory basis.

This is not to imply, of course, that cotton-growing countries can produce cotton textiles as cheaply as the large industrial countries. In practice, all these industrializing countries have found it necessary to protect their cotton textile industries by tariffs or quotas against competing imports[1], even though the imports would carry transport costs on the raw cotton as well as on the finished textiles. Another way in which raw cotton growing countries have been able to protect their own cotton textile industries is by means of export duties on raw cotton, which keep the cost of the raw material to their mills below the world market price.

The position is very different for wool and for the man-made fibres. In the case of raw wool, the major producing countries, though they have expanded their wool textile industries vigorously since the end of the war, have a limited home market—in contrast with many of the major raw cotton producing countries, which are heavily populated—and tend to have relatively high labour costs. The production of man-made fibres (but not their processing) requires considerable capital investment per unit of output and, for this reason, progress has so far been relatively slow in the under-developed areas.

Growth of the textile industries

This asymmetrical development in the textile industries outside Europe and North America is examined in greater detail below. But it is important to bear it in mind when considering the growth of the textile industries in different parts of the world. In 1955, the textile industries (excluding clothing) employed some 5.8 millions in the industrial areas (Western Europe, 3.2 million; North America, 1.7 million; Japan 1.0 million), as against perhaps 2.5 millions in the rest of the world outside the Soviet countries (of which India, 1.0 million excluding handicraft workers; Latin America, 0.9 million; Australia, New Zealand and South Africa together, 0.1 million)[2]. A comparison of numbers employed is, however, misleading since the output per person employed is considerably higher in the industrial areas than in the non-industrial ones. In terms of physical production, the textile output of the non-industrial countries amounted in 1955 to perhaps some 20 per cent of world textile production (excluding the Soviet countries), whereas their employment represented about 30 per cent of the world total.

Nonetheless, the pace of expansion in textile production has been considerably more rapid in the semi-industrial countries of Latin America, in

---

[1] See Chapter 7, page 180, and Table 7.13.
[2] See *The Textile Industry in Europe, Statistical Study, 1955–1956*, O.E.E.C., Paris, March 1957; *Year Book of Labour Statistics*, International Labour Office, Geneva, 1957.

India and Pakistan and in the three Southern Dominions[1] than it has been in the industrial areas (see Table 13.3). By 1937, output in the semi-industrial countries was probably more than twice as great as in 1913, when local production must have been fairly small, whereas in the industrial areas the rise was only marginal in this period. Again, from 1937 to 1957, the textile output of the semi-industrial countries expanded by some 60 per cent, compared with only 20–25 per cent in the industrial areas. There was little change in the relative textile output of the two groups of countries between 1957 and 1960, though there were some substantial changes in several countries in each group. As already mentioned, the textile industry has been developed in the semi-industrial countries on the basis of tariff protection against competing imports; in some countries, also, import quotas of a very restrictive character have been used to foster the growth of the local industry.

Table 13.3. *Textile production in industrial and semi-industrial countries, 1900–59[a]*

	1900	1913	1929	1937	1950	1955	1957	1959	Value added in 1957 ($ billion)
		(*Volume indices, 1929 = 100*)							
INDUSTRIAL COUNTRIES	63	100	100	110	123	129	135	138	9.95
United Kingdom	79	128	100	117	109	107	106	99	1.45
France	87	101	100	88	86	84	100	90	0.92
Germany	84	115	100	102	68	103	113	138	1.41
United States	43	100	100	113	188	182	178	201	3.90
Japan	27	45	100	155	56	115	151	159	0.76
Other net exporters[c]	52	81	100	92	102	104	114	114	1.11
Net importers[d]	59	88	100	147	253	223	233	231	0.40
SEMI-INDUSTRIAL COUNTRIES	..	65–70	100	158	183	245	255	..	2.18
Southern Dominions[e]	..	65	100	147	212	295	300	..	0.35
India, including Pakistan	..	65–70	100	167	140	225	245	..	1.03
Latin America[f]	..	..	100	150	225	255	250	233	0.80

Sources: Statistical Yearbook, 1960, United Nations, New York, 1961; *Industrial Statistics, 1900–1959,* O.E.E.C., Paris, 1960; national production statistics and estimates by the author.

[a]Indices relate to actual boundaries of countries in years specified.
[b]Approximate value added in textile production at 1955 prices.
[c]Belgium-Luxembourg, Italy and Netherlands.
[d]Canada, Norway and Sweden.
[e]Australia, New Zealand and Union of South Africa.
[f]Argentina, Brazil, Chile, Colombia and Mexico.

[1]Textile production has also expanded rapidly in the Middle East, which is excluded from Table 13.3.

Trade in textiles

The impact of the expansion in output on the demand for imports of textiles can be seen from Table 13.4, which relates to trade in yarns and fabrics only. Before 1913, both production and imports of textiles were expanding, not only in the industrial countries, but in the rest of the world also. The first check to the growth in trade came during the first World War and in the early 1920's with the development of mill production in India, China and other import markets. By 1929 the volume of imports into both industrial and semi-industrial countries was still lower than in 1913. Between 1929 and 1937, a considerable amount of import-substitution took place in both groups of countries, but the major reduction was in the imports of the industrial countries, which accounted for almost 90 per cent of the contraction in the world import

Table 13.4.   *World trade in textile yarns and fabrics by major trading countries,*
1899–1955

	Values at 1913 prices[a]			Values at 1955 prices			
	1899	1913	1929	1929	1937	1950	1955
INDUSTRIAL COUNTRIES							
United Kingdom							
'Imports'	148	190	154	308	117	160	117
Exports	669	834	533	1994	1435	988	764
France							
'Imports'	47	43	28	71	47	70	38
Exports	177	239	297	644	264	469	435
Germany							
'Imports'	128	135	107	290	173	143	203
Exports	156	222	195	288	224	97	277
United States							
'Imports'	109	159	140	310	250	205	283
Exports	36	50	63	188	84	324	393
Japan							
'Imports'	20	16	11	34	12	2	10
Exports	37	78	177	438	858	296	542
Other net exporters							
'Imports'	142	176	190	442	239	318	334
Exports	194[c]	277[c]	363[c]	735	667	712	784
Net importers[d]							
'Imports'	25	72	88	244	229	276	320
Exports[e]	2	3	6	15	19	21	24
Total, industrial countries							
'Imports'	619	791	718	1699	1067	1174	1305
Exports	1272	1703	1633	4301	3553	2908	3218
Intra-trade[e]	608	752	660	1600	974	1063	1183
Net exports	664	951	973	2701	2579	1845	2035

For footnotes, see next page.

Table 13.4 (cont.)

	Values at 1913 prices[a]			Values at 1955 prices			
	1899	1913	1929	1929	1937	1950	1955
SEMI-INDUSTRIAL COUNTRIES							
Southern Dominions[f]							
'Imports'	47	67	86	282	318	397	407
India, including Pakistan							
'Imports'	146	215	147	462	251	134	78
Exports	55	91	97	176	201	350[g]	278[g]
Latin America[h]							
'Imports'	91	132	156	439	332	109	90
Total, semi-industrial countries[i]							
'Imports'	308	467	422	1206	996	676	631
REST OF WORLD							
'Imports'	400	536	590	1572	1691	1408	1560
WORLD TOTAL							
Exports	1327	1794	1730	4477	3754	3258	3496

Sources: Tables A.6 to A.69.

[a]'Import' figures exclude 'imports' from the Netherlands.
[b]Belgium-Luxembourg, Italy, Netherlands and Switzerland.
[c]Excluding exports from the Netherlands.
[d]Canada, Norway and Sweden.
[e]Canada and Sweden only.
[f]Australia, New Zealand and Union of South Africa.
[g]Republic of India only.
[h]Argentina, Brazil, Chile, Colombia and Mexico.
[i]Including Palestine (1929 and 1937), Israel (1950 and 1955), Turkey and Yugoslavia (1929 onwards) as well as countries listed in the table.

trade in yarns and fabrics in the period. Imports into the semi-industrial countries in 1937 were about 20 per cent lower than in 1929 as a result of substantial cuts by India and the Latin American countries; by contrast, imports into both the Southern Dominions and the non-industrial areas had recovered by 1937 to above the 1929 peak.

Since 1950, imports of textiles into the industrial countries have been expanding with the growth in incomes and with the progressive liberalization of trade, yet by 1955 imports were still nearly one-quarter below the 1929 peak. Imports into the semi-industrial countries continued their downward trend, but those into the rest of the world were increasing (see Fig. 13.2). The main trends in the period 1955–59 can be estimated from export data for the industrial countries.

Fig. 13.2.   Production and trade in textile yarns and fabrics, 1899–1957

$ billion, at 1955 *prices,*
semi-logarithmic scale

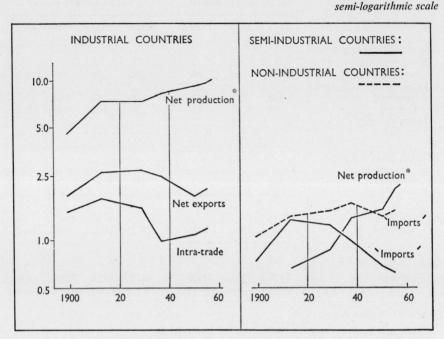

*Value added in manufacturing.

In this period, exports of yarns and fabrics to the industrial countries themselves rose sharply—by about 30 per cent in volume terms—the main increases being in imports by the United States, West Germany and the United Kingdom. Exports of yarns and fabrics to the rest of the world taken as a whole, on the other hand, fell by about 12 per cent, indicating that the process of import-substitution was still continuing.

The virtual collapse of the import market for textiles in China (included in the 'rest of the world' in Table 13.4), has been a major element in the fall in world demand for imports of textiles since the second World War. The position is in strong contrast with that before 1914, when China was one of the largest markets in the world for imported textiles. In 1913, China took 6 per cent of total shipments of yarns and fabrics from the industrial countries, while the fall in exports to China from 1913 to 1955 was as much as one-quarter of the total decline in world trade in these goods over this period (Table 13.5). If only exports to markets outside the industrial areas are considered, the contraction in the Chinese import market accounted for as much as one-half of the total contraction ($290 million out of about $580 million[1]). As the result

[1] This figure can be derived from Table 13.4.

of industrialization since 1950, China has expanded her textile industries considerably and has become an important exporter of piece goods since 1958.

Excluding China, exports to the 'rest of the world' have risen appreciably over the past 40–50 years. The countries included are, in the main, non-industrial countries with—generally speaking—only small-scale production of textiles, including handicraft industries in some countries, as in Latin America. For these countries, a rise in incomes, and in the demand for textiles and clothing, will tend to result directly in an increase in imports.

Table 13.5. *'Imports' of textile yarns and fabrics into China, 1913–55*

	1913	1955	Change	
	\$ *billion at* 1955 *prices*			*percentage*
'Imports' into				
China	0.29	0	− 0.29	..
Rest of world	4.35	3.49	− 0.86	−20
TOTAL	4.64	3.49	− 1.15	−25

Sources: Table 13.4 and national trade statistics.

Production in relation to trade

From 1937 to 1955, textile production in the industrial countries and their intra-trade in textiles have expanded at about the same rate. Thus, the structural discontinuity in their relationship which occurred in the early 1930's was maintained in the post-war period up to the mid-1950's. This discontinuity was general among the industrial countries, but it seems to have been sharpest, and most persistent, in the United Kingdom. Indeed, the reduction in Britain's imports of yarns and fabrics between 1929 and 1955 accounted for almost one-half of the total contraction in the intra-trade during this period. The major part of the decline in Britain's textile imports occurred after the sterling devaluation of 1931 and the imposition of the Import Duties Act, 1932. A particularly sharp decline occurred in imports of cotton and wool manufactures, and though there was some recovery after 1935, except for silk goods, imports of textiles in 1937 were still only one-half of the 1930 volume[1]. Among the industrial countries, the net importers of yarns and fabrics (Canada, Norway and Sweden) were the only group to show greater imports in 1955 than in 1929.

[1]Volume indices of United Kingdom imports in 1937 (1930 = 100) were: Cotton goods, 47; Wool goods, 33; Silk and artificial silk goods, 42; Other textiles, 76. The combined index for these four groups was 51.

The post-war developments in the semi-industrial countries continue the trends apparent in the 1930's. Since the end of the second World War, the textile industries have been considerably expanded in these countries. The one major halt was in Indian production of jute goods in the first few years following Partition in 1948 (this accounts for the fall in the textile production index for India/Pakistan between 1937 and 1950). This growth in local textile output has caused a considerable further substitution against imports. Thus, between 1937 and 1955, the contraction in imports into the semi-industrial countries amounted to some $350–400 million (1955 prices), and this was only partly offset by a recovery of about $200 million in the intra-trade of the industrial countries.

3. EFFECTS OF IMPORT-SUBSTITUTION AND OF THE GROWTH IN HOME DEMAND

The inter-relationship between the expansion of local textile industries and import-substitution can be more directly illustrated by the estimates in Table 13.6, which are based on the production and trade series already discussed. For this purpose, import-substitution over a given period has been defined as the difference between the actual change in imports over the period, and the change that would have occurred if the share of imports in home consumption had remained unchanged[1]. The growth of home industry does not, on this definition, count as import-substituting unless it results in a falling share of imports in home consumption. The trend in home consumption of textiles can be estimated by adding net imports (from Table 13.4) to estimates of the gross value of home output (free of the duplication of inter-firm transactions[2]). The calculation of the effect of the growth in home output on imports can then be estimated in the way described in Chapter 6[3]. The resulting estimates inevitably contain a considerable margin of error, and small changes shown are probably of no significance. Nonetheless, several major trends appear to emerge from the calculation.

In the whole period from 1913 to 1937, the substitution of home output for imports by the industrial countries was at least as important, quantitatively, as that by the semi-industrial countries; indeed, in the 1930's, it was significantly greater (see Fig. 13.3.) In both the 1920's and 1930's, the main import-substituting country was India, but between 1929 and 1937 the import-substitution by the United Kingdom was almost as great as India's. Since 1937, however, the major substitution against imports has taken place in the semi-industrial countries; from 1937 to 1955 the reduction in imports which can be attributable

---

[1]See discussion of the concept of import-substitution on pages 150–1.

[2]Gross values were estimated by applying gross : net ratios based on input-output tables to the value added figures for different countries. For further details of the method used, see the discussion in Appendix E.

[3]See page 151.

to the growth of local industry in these countries amounted to some $600 million at 1955 prices, or about 60 per cent of their total yarn and fabric imports in 1937. For the industrial countries, the corresponding amount of substitution was in the region of $100 million (10 per cent of their 1937 level of imports).

Since before the war, the major import-substituting region has been Latin America, followed by India and Pakistan. In the three Southern Dominions, on the other hand, the effect of import-substitution has been more than offset

Table 13.6. *Estimates of effect of import-substitution[a] and of changes in home demand on imports of textile yarns and fabrics, 1913–55*

$ billion at 1955 prices

	1913 to 1929			1929 to 1937		
	Import substi- tution	Home demand	Total	Import substi- tution	Home demand	Total
INDUSTRIAL COUNTRIES	− 0.29	+ 0.11	− 0.18	− 0.84	+ 0.22	− 0.63
United Kingdom	− 0.09	+ 0.02	− 0.07	− 0.39	+ 0.21	− 0.18
France	− 0.03	− 0.01	− 0.04	− 0.02	0	− 0.02
Germany[b]	− 0.03	− 0.05	− 0.08	− 0.12	0	− 0.12
United States	− 0.03	− 0.01	− 0.04	− 0.10	+ 0.04	− 0.06
Japan	− 0.07	+ 0.05	− 0.02	− 0.03	+ 0.01	− 0.02
Other net exporters[c]	− 0.05	+ 0.08	+ 0.03	− 0.12	− 0.08	− 0.20
Other net importers[d]	+ 0.01	+ 0.03	+ 0.04	− 0.06	+ 0.04	− 0.02
SEMI-INDUSTRIAL COUNTRIES	..	..	− 0.14	− 0.65[e]	+ 0.37[e]	− 0.26
Southern Dominions	− 0.04	+ 0.10	+ 0.06	− 0.03	+ 0.07	+ 0.04
India, including Pakistan	− 0.26	+ 0.05	− 0.21	− 0.42	+ 0.21	− 0.21
Latin America	..	..	+ 0.04	− 0.20	+ 0.09	− 0.11
Other semi-industrial countries	..	..	− 0.03	..	..	+ 0.02
NON-INDUSTRIAL COUNTRIES	..	..	+ 0.14	..	..	+ 0.16
TOTAL						
All areas	..	..	− 0.17	..	..	− 0.73
Special areas[f]	− 0.59	+ 0.26	− 0.33	− 1.49	+ 0.59	− 0.91

	1937 to 1950			1950 to 1955		
INDUSTRIAL COUNTRIES	− 0.19	+ 0.30	+ 0.11	+ 0.08	+ 0.06	+ 0.14
United Kingdom	0	+ 0.05	+ 0.05	− 0.04	0	− 0.04
France	+ 0.03	− 0.01	+ 0.02	− 0.03	0	− 0.03
Germany[b]	+ 0.02	− 0.05	− 0.03	0	+ 0.06	+ 0.06
United States	− 0.20	+ 0.15	− 0.05	+ 0.08	0	+ 0.08
Japan	0	− 0.01	− 0.01	+ 0.01	0	+ 0.01
Other net exporters[c]	+ 0.04	+ 0.04	+ 0.08	+ 0.01	+ 0.01	+ 0.02
Other net importers[d]	− 0.08	+ 0.13	+ 0.05	+ 0.05	− 0.01	+ 0.04

For footnotes, see next page.

Continued

Table 13.6 (cont.)

	1937 to 1950			1950 to 1955		
	Import substitution	Home demand	Total	Import substitution	Home demand	Total
SEMI-INDUSTRIAL COUNTRIES	− 0.36^e	+ 0.10^e	− 0.32	− 0.25^e	+ 0.18^e	− 0.05
Southern Dominions	− 0.03	+ 0.11	+ 0.08	− 0.07	+ 0.08	+ 0.01
India, including Pakistan	− 0.04	− 0.08	− 0.12	− 0.15	+ 0.09	− 0.06
Latin America	− 0.29	+ 0.07	− 0.22	− 0.03	+ 0.01	− 0.02
Other semi-industrial countries	..	..	− 0.06	..	..	+ 0.02
NON-INDUSTRIAL COUNTRIES	..	..	− 0.28	..	..	+ 0.16
TOTAL						
All areas	..	..	− 0.50	..	..	+ 0.23
Special areas^f	− 0.55	+ 0.40	− 0.15	− 0.17	+ 0.24	+ 0.07

Sources: Based on Tables 13.3 and 13.4.

[a] Defined as in text.
[b] West Germany for 1950 and 1955.
[c] Belgium-Luxembourg, Italy, Netherlands and Switzerland.
[d] Canada, Norway and Sweden.
[e] Totals excluding 'other semi-industrial countries'.
[f] Special areas cover only areas for which separate estimates can be made of effect of import-substitution and home demand.

by the growth of home demand. Thus, historically it is not correct to assume that the development of textile industries in importing countries *necessarily* leads to a reduction in competing imports. The actual trend of imports depends heavily on the movement in the capacity to import, as well as on the growth in home textile output. The divergent trends in textile imports by the different groups of semi-industrial countries can largely be explained by the application of economic development programmes in India, Pakistan and several Latin American countries, in conjunction with their chronic shortage of foreign exchange in the period since 1950. This has generally forced these countries to restrict their imports of 'less essentials', among which textiles are usually included. Though the Southern Dominions have also been through periods of foreign exchange difficulties, their limitation of imports has tended to be more of a temporary nature than have the restrictions imposed by the other industrializing countries. Moreover, the price support policy for raw cotton, operated by the United States Government up to 1956, had the effect of subsidizing the cotton textile industries of countries like India, which grow their own cotton.

Apart, however, from these general factors arising in part from differences in the development of the capacity to import and in part from differences in government action, there are also important differences relating specifically

Fig. 13.3. Effects of import-substitution and of expansion in demand on 'imports' of textile yarns and fabrics, 1913–55

$ *million, at* 1955 *prices*

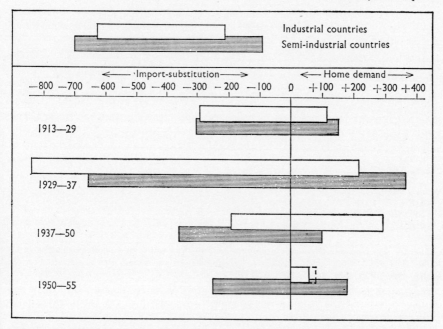

Note. The broken line for the period 1950–55 indicates that imports into the industrial countries rose faster than home output.

to the textile industries. As Table 13.7 shows, the greater part of the contraction in textile imports since 1938 into India, Pakistan and Latin America[1] has been in cotton goods (the same is true of imports into China); simultaneously, the growth in local production has been largely based on the use of locally-grown cotton. The Southern Dominions, however, have had to rely mainly on imported raw cotton and cotton yarn for the development of their cotton textile industries, which have expanded to only a small extent compared with the growth since 1938 in India/Pakistan and Latin America.

There has also been a considerable growth in Latin American production of wool and rayon textiles since 1938. In wool, local development has substituted for imports, and in rayon, too, imports have been reduced since the early 1950's as a result of the growth in home output. In the Southern Dominions, all major raw wool producers, wool is the most important sector of the textile industries; the fall in imports since the early 1950's has been mainly in wool

[1] Including non-industrial as well as semi-industrial countries in Latin America and the caribbean.

Table 13.7.   *Production and net imports of major textile products in selected semi-industrial areas*, 1938–60

Thousand metric tons, annual averages

	Latin America		India/Pakistan		Southern Dominions	
	Produc-tion[a]	Net imports	Produc-tion[a]	Net imports	Produc-tion[a]	Net imports
Cotton goods						
1938	253	106	622	52	7	56
1959–51	423	52	751	− 33	22	74
1958–60	584	52	1118	−129	38	74
Rayon goods[b]						
1938	6	16	—	13	—	16
1949–51	50	33	1	29	—	39
1958–60	97	27	37	20	7	47
Wool goods[c]						
1938	33	15	10	2	22	11
1949–51	76	3	10	3	37	10
1958–60	84	−12	12	6	45	−6

Sources: Per Caput Fiber Consumption Levels, F.A.O., Commodity Series, Nos. 25 and 31, Rome, 1954 and 1960; *Monthly Bulletin of Agricultural Economics and Statistics*, F.A.O., Rome, Dec. 1956, Dec. 1957 and Jan. 1962.

[a]For cotton goods, mill consumption of raw cotton; for rayon, production of staple and continuous filament; for wool goods, estimated consumption of raw wool, clean basis.
[b]Including trade in staple fibre.
[c]Including trade in tops, noils and waste.

fabrics and made-up goods, while at the same time both Australia and South Africa have developed their export trade in tops.

Thus, the pace of development in import-substitution of textiles appears to be closely related to each country's status as a producer of the raw fibre.   It is possible to extend this type of analysis in a systematic way to cover the development of textile production and trade in the majority of countries.   In the following sections, the trends in world production and trade in cotton, rayon and wool textiles are separately considered.

Cotton textiles

The shift in the balance of cotton textile production (as indicated by mill consumption of raw cotton) away from the industrial areas of Western Europe and North America has been a very marked one since 1913 (see Table 13.8). These areas accounted for some 85 per cent of world cotton textile output outside Russia before the first world war, but for only 70 per cent in 1936–38 and 57 per cent in 1954–56.   The greatest proportionate increases in production have been in the main cotton-growing areas of India, China, Latin America and, in recent years, Pakistan. It is true that some countries dependent wholly or in part on raw cotton imports for their yarn and cloth production have been able to expand their cotton processing activities, but their growth has been considerably smaller in absolute terms than in the major cotton-growing countries.

The relationship between the growth in local cotton textile output and the movement of trade is also shown in Fig. 13.4. Before the first world war, the United Kingdom supplied about one-half of total world exports of cotton textiles, Europe and Japan being the other main exporters. The principal markets at that time were China, the raw cotton exporters and the raw cotton importers[1]. The Indian sub-continent was also an important net importer. Developments since that time in China, India and the raw cotton exporters have been remarkably similar, as can be seen from Fig. 13.4; all these areas have moved downwards and to the right on this Figure, India becoming a net exporter of cotton textiles in the 1930's and China in the 1950's. By the late 1950's, the group of raw cotton exporters had become marginal net exporters of cotton textiles, instead of a major net import market for them, as they were even a decade previously. In this group, both Egypt and Pakistan now export substantial amounts of cotton yarn, while Mexico, Brazil and Turkey have also become net yarn exporters.

The movement shown for the raw cotton importers and for African countries (the latter are not included in Fig. 13.4) is in marked contrast to that for the raw cotton exporters. Though the former group of countries have been expanding their local production, there has been relatively little change in their net imports over the long period from 1926–28 to 1958–60. This group includes not only the three Southern Dominions discussed earlier, but also other important markets in America, Africa and South-East Asia. In an intermediate position are the countries which rely on both home and imported growths for their industrial consumption of raw cotton; in these countries, taken as a whole, production of cotton textiles has expanded at roughly the same rate as in the raw cotton importing countries but, in this case, the increase in local output has tended—at least since the early 1930's—to substitute for imports, though the substitution has been much less marked than for the raw cotton exporters.

The extent to which imports are replaced by the development of local cotton textile production thus depends largely on whether or not that development is based on supplies of locally-grown cotton. Where development is wholly or partly based on imported cotton (and/or on imported yarns), there appear to be important limitations coming into play on the extent of import-substitution that is practicable or profitable. One explanation may be that in most of the semi-industrial and non-industrial cotton importing countries, there is a general

[1]See footnotes to Table 13.8 for the countries included in the two latter groups.

Table 13.8. *Production[a] and trade in cotton textiles by area, 1910-60*

Thousand metric tons, annual averages

		Mill con-sumption of raw cotton	Net exports (−) or net imports (+) of cotton goods			Apparent con-sumption of cotton goods[c]
			Yarn	Fabrics, etc.[b]	Total	
A. NET EXPORTERS OF COTTON GOODS[d]						
1. United Kingdom	1910–13	950	−95	−655	−750	200
	1926–28	665	−80	−405	−485	180
	1936–38	600	−70	−200	−270	330
	1949–51	455	−25	− 75	−100	355
	1958–60	278	0	+ 29	+29	309
2. United States	1910–13	1090	0	−40	−40	1050
	1926–28	1495	−10	−55	−65	1430
	1936–38	1495	0	−20	−20	1475
	1949–51	1970	−10	−100	−110	1860
	1958–60	1867	− 3	−28	−30	1837
3. Europe[e]	1910–13	1385	+20[f]	−160[f]	−140[f]	1245
	1926–28	1300	+10	−200	−190	1110
	1936–38	1090	−15	−155	−170	920
	1949–51	1140	−30	−175	−205	935
	1958–60	1538	−13	−151	−164	1374
4. Japan	1910–13	320	−65	−45	−110	210
	1926–28	590	−30	−185	−215	375
	1936–38	715	−25	−315	−340	375
	1949–51	245	−10	−125	−135	110
	1958–60	579	−19	−166	−185	394
5. India	1910–13	365	−65	+110[g]	+45	410
	1926–28	390	+5	+20[g]	+25	415
	1936–38	625	−5	−100[g]	−105	520
	1949–51	700	−20	−110	−130	570
	1958–60	898	−10	98	−108	790
B. NET IMPORTERS OF COTTON GOODS[d]						
1. Raw cotton importers[h]	1910–13	75	+15	+255	+270	345
	1926–28	95	+25	+315	+340	435
	1936–38	140	+45	+330	+375	515
	1949–51	245	+50	+320	+370	615
	1958–60	325	+68	+285	+353	678
2. Raw cotton growers/ importers	1910–13	20	+20	+90	+110	130
	1926–28	60	+45	+115	+160	220
	1936–38	150	+50	+75	+125	275
	1949–51	170	+15	+45	+60	230
	1958- 60	332	+16	+48	+64	396

For footnotes, see next page.

Table 13.8 (cont.)

		Mill con-sumption of raw cotton	Net exports (−) or net imports (+) of cotton goods			Apparent con-sumption of cotton goods[c]
			Yarn	Fabrics, etc.[b]	Total	
3. Raw cotton exporters (a) African countries (excluding Egypt)	1910–13	—	0	+45	+45	45
	1926–28	5	0	+50	+50	55
	1936–38	5	0	+75	+75	80
	1949–51	15	0	+85	+85	100
	1958–60	21	+7	+77	+84	105
(b) Other raw cotton exporters[j]	1910–13	125	+25	+285	+310	435
	1926–28	130	+25	+280	+305	435
	1936–38	305	+25	+260	+285	590
	1949–51	505	+35	+105	+140	645
	1958–60	982	−27	+ 17	−10	972
C. CHINA AND RUSSIA/ U.S.S.R. 1. China	1910–13	70	+140	+135	+275	345
	1926–28	430	+5	+90	+95	525
	1936–38	475	−5	+45	+40	515
	1949–51	662	−11	−13	−24	638
	1958–60	1781	−9	−63	−72	1709
2. Russia/U.S.S.R.	1910–13	365	0	−5	0	365
	1926–28	360	+5	0	+5	365
	1936–38	765	−5	−10	−15	750
	1949–51	754	0	−5	−5	750
	1958–60	1313	−4	−9	−13	1300

Source: Based on data supplied by the Statistical Department of the Cotton Board, Manchester.

[a] As measured by mill consumption of raw cotton.

[b] Trade in piece-goods *plus* 20 per cent to allow for trade in other cotton manufactures and for waste loss in production.

[c] In terms of raw cotton-equivalent. The figures exclude consumption of cotton goods made from hand-spun yarn.

[d] Net exporters, or net importers, in 1954–56; excluding China and the U.S.S.R.

[e] Excluding Scandinavia, Irish Republic and Balkan States.

[f] Adjusted to allow for changes in frontiers after 1918.

[g] Estimated for present area of Republic of India by assuming that consumption in the two parts of the sub-continent was proportional to respective populations.

[h] Countries entirely (or almost entirely) dependent on raw cotton imports for their industrial requirements. Countries included are Scandinavia and Irish Republic; five British Dominions (Australia, Canada, New Zealand, South Africa and Rhodesia); and non-cotton growing countries in Africa, South America (Chile, Cuba, Uruguay, etc.), and in Asia (Ceylon, Hong Kong, Indonesia, Philippines, etc.).

[i] Countries dependent on both imported and home grown raw cotton for their industrial requirements. Countries included are Balkan States; Colombia, Ecuador, Venezuela; Korea, Indo-China and Thailand.

[j] Countries entirely (or almost entirely) dependent on home grown raw cotton for their industrial requirements. Countries included are the raw cotton exporters in South America (Argentina, Brazil, Mexico, Peru, etc.) and Asia (Iran, Pakistan and Turkey), and Egypt.

Fig. 13.4.   Raw cotton consumption and net trade in cotton goods,
1910–60

Thousand metric tons

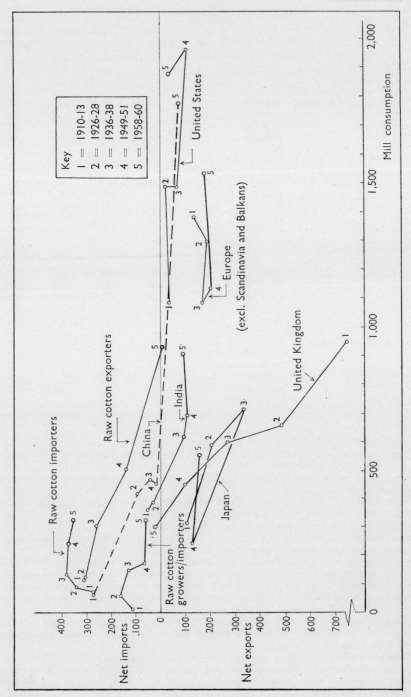

scarcity of investment capital, and investment in secondary industry tends in the first place to be attracted to the processing of local raw materials, in order to minimize the foreign exchange cost of industrialization. A further factor of importance is that in the earlier stages of development of a cotton industry there is likely to be a concentration on coarse and medium quality goods and the finer qualities are likely to continue to be imported. This is particularly important in high-income countries, such as the Southern Dominions, where a growing sector of demand would be in the better-quality goods. In most of the raw cotton exporting countries, on the other hand, demand is likely to be much more concentrated on the lower quality range, which is readily satisfied by the home mills.

Rayon goods

Before the war, the major rayon producers were Germany, Italy and Japan; they developed their rayon industries rapidly during the 1930's to lessen their dependence on imported raw cotton for autarkic reasons. They also dominated world trade in rayon yarns and piece-goods, and still do so. Total imports of rayon goods into the net importing countries in 1938 were divided about equally into imports by rayon-producing countries and imports by countries which did not themselves produce rayon (see Table 13.9). The development since 1938 has, however, been strikingly different in these two groups of markets. The rayon-producing countries which are still net importers of rayon goods (group B.1) expanded their rayon production very substantially during and after the war to meet the increase in home demand (which was, in part, a substitution against imports of cotton textiles); consequently, their net imports of rayon fabrics and other finished goods in 1949–51 were not greatly above the 1938 level, though there was a sharp rise in yarn imports to meet local production requirements. Between 1949–51 and 1958–60 yarn imports fell off somewhat as local production expanded further. In the non-producing countries[1], however, imports rose substantially in the 1950's.

Rather less than half the expansion in rayon production between 1949–51 and 1958–60 in the net importing countries in group B.1 occurred in countries which were already producing rayon before the war (Argentina, Brazil, Canada, Spain and Sweden). The rest of the increase was spread over a great many countries, particularly in the less-developed areas. This spread of the newer techniques involved in the production of rayon has been a noteworthy feature of recent progress in industrialization. Among the more important 'new' rayon producers since the early 1950's are Colombia, Cuba, Mexico, India and Egypt.

[1]Defined as countries not producing rayon in the mid-1950's.

Table 13.9.   *Production and net trade in rayon goods by area*, 1938–60

Thousand metric tons, annual averages

		Rayon production	Net exports (−) or net imports (+)[a]				Available for home use
			Staple	Yarn	Tissues	Other rayon goods	
A. NET EXPORTERS OF RAYON GOODS							
1. United Kingdom	1938	60	−6	−3	−4	+1	47
	1949–51	154	−5	−8	−16	−3	123
	1958–60	187	−15	−17	−4	−1	150
2. United States	1938	130	+10	−1	−2	0	139
	1949–51	537	+29	−5	−37	0	523
	1958–60	488	+32	−4	−19	0	497
3. Germany, Italy and Japan	1938	586	−11	−34	−79	−4	458
	1949–51	377	−21	−33	−42	−3	278
	1958–60	767	−82	−65	−136	−10	474
4. Other net exporters[b]	1938	55	−1	−12	−4	−1	37
	1949–51	191	−36	−28	−12	−1	114
	1958–60	268	−53	−46	−20	−2	148
B. NET IMPORTERS OF RAYON GOODS							
1. Rayon producers[c]	1938	17	+4	+26	+15	+2	63
	1949–51	135	+3	+53	+26	+2	219
	1958–60	297	−10	+24	+16	+15	331
2. Other countries (a) Importers of staple fibre and/or yarn[d]	1938	—	0	+7	+31	0	38
	1949–51	—	+8	+15	+30	+1	53
	1958–60	19	+30	+43	+47	+2	140
(b) Rest of world	1938	—	—	+1	+14	+1	15
	1949–51	—	0	+3	+34	+1	38
	1958–60	2	+7	+18	+115	−6	149
C. SOVIET COUNTRIES							
1. U.S.S.R. and Eastern Europe	1938	27	+3	+8	—	..	38
	1949–51	152	+11	+3	—	..	166
	1958–60	437	+88	+26	+2	−1	551
2. China	1938	—	—	+4	+18	..	22
	1949–51	—	+3	0	—	..	3
	1958–60	6	+5	+8	0	—	19

Sources: As for Table 13.7.

[a]Actual weight as recorded or estimated.   No allowance is made for gains or losses in manufacture.

[b]Austria, Belgium-Luxembourg, France, Netherlands and Switzerland.

[c]Finland, Norway and Sweden; Australia and Canada; Argentina, Brazil, Chile, Colombia, Cuba, Mexico, Peru, Uruguay and Venezuela; Greece, Portugal, Spain and Turkey; Egypt and India.

[d]Countries each importing over 1,000 metric tons of staple and yarn in 1955: Denmark, Ireland and Yugoslavia; Ecuador; Indonesia, Iran, Iraq, Palestine/Israel, Lebanon, Pakistan (post-war) and Syria; Belgian Congo and Union of South Africa.   The 1954–56 totals also include Taiwan, Hong Kong and South Korea.

Among the countries classified as non-producers of rayon, two groups of countries can be distinguished: those which are developing a rayon weaving or knitting industry on the basis of imported staple fibre or rayon yarn, and those which are not. The development in the first group of countries is a good illustration of the tendency of countries first to import fabrics, then yarns, and then staple as the processing stages of the local industry are developed one by one; indeed, by the late 1950's some of these countries had begun to produce rayon themselves[1]. Imports of both staple and yarn into this group have risen appreciably since 1949–51 and this, if continued, may well presage a slowing down in the future rate of growth in imports of fabrics. In the second group of countries, however, imports of fabrics have expanded considerably since 1949–51.

Eastern Europe, including the Soviet Union, has been a net rayon-importing area since pre-war. These countries have, however, greatly expanded their rayon production since the early 1950's, and published plans for the period up to 1965 indicate a further appreciable increase[2]. It seems probable that, if anything, net imports of rayon into these countries will decline over the next decade as their home production of rayon and synthetic fibres expands.

Wool goods

Wool textile production has remained heavily concentrated in the industrial areas of Western Europe and North America; including Japan, where wool textile production has expanded rapidly since the early 1950's, the industrial areas accounted for 84 per cent of total world raw wool consumption outside the present Soviet area in 1938, 78 per cent in 1949–51, and 77 per cent in 1958–60 (see Table 13.10).

The development of the wool textile industry in the non-industrial areas has thus been slow and modest, in relation to that in cotton and rayon. This is partly because per caput consumption of wool textiles in most of these countries is relatively small, compared with cotton and rayon, and partly also because the expensive and complicated processes involved in blending, topmaking and finishing tend to prevent the spread of the industry on a large scale outside the traditional centres. This latter difficulty can be partly overcome, however, by importing tops for worsted spinning[3]. The development of the local industry in the three Southern Dominions since 1938 has been relatively small, and has not prevented a rise in imports, though during the 1950's imports were curtailed

[1]As mentioned earlier, the classification of countries was based on the position in the mid-1950's.

[2]*Prospective Trends in Consumption of Textile Fibers*, Part IV, International Cotton Advisory Committee, Washington, 1962.

[3]Both Egypt and India, for example, depend on imported tops for a substantial part of their wool textile supplies.

Table 13.10.   *Production and net trade in wool textiles by area*, 1938–60

Thousand metric tons, annual averages

		Estimated consumption of raw wool (clean basis)	Net exports (−) or net imports (+)[a]				Available for home use
			Tops	Yarn	Tissues	Other wool goods	
A. NET EXPORTERS OF WOOL GOODS[b]							
1. United Kingdom	1938	200	−15	−11	−20	− 4	150
	1949–51	213	−28	− 6	−25	−16	138
	1958–60	217	−40	− 8	−20	− 7	142
2. Belgium-Luxembourg,	1938	165	−22	−18	−16	− 5	104
France and Italy	1949–51	192	− 9	−26	−19	−13	125
	1958–60	241	−13	−37	−45	−14	132
3. Japan	1938	40	—	− 4	− 8	..	28
	1949–51	18	+ 1	− 1	− 1	..	18
	1958–60	100	0	− 3	− 6	− 7	84
4. India and Iran	1938[c]	14	+ 1	+ 1	+ 1	− 3	14
	1949–51	14	+ 3	+ 1	+ 2	− 4	15
	1958–60	18	+ 7	+ 1	+ 1	− 3	24
B. NET IMPORTERS OF WOOL GOODS[b]							
1. Major raw wool exporters							
(a) Australia, New	1938	22	− 2	+ 1	+ 6	+ 8	33
Zealand and	1949–51	37	− 3	+ 1	+ 8	+11	53
South Africa	1958–60	45	−12	+ 1	+ 4	+ 6	44
(b) Argentina and	1938	16	—	+ 1	+ 5	0	22
Uruguay	1949–51	43	− 4	+ 2	0	..	41
	1958–60	41	−12	0	0	—	29
2. Major raw wool importers							
(a) United States and	1938	138	+ 5	+ 1	+ 5	+ 2	151
Canada	1949–51	238	+ 9	+ 2	+ 7	+ 6	262
	1958–60	171	+ 6	+ 3	+16	+14	210
(b) Western Europe[d]	1938	111	+12	+14	− 3	0	134
	1949–51	85	+11	+15	+10	+ 3	124
	1958–60	91	+22	+33	+24	+ 5	175
3. Other countries (excluding Soviet countries)							
(a) Importers of tops	1938	21	+ 3	+ 8	+10	+ 2	43
and/or yarn[e]	1949–51	32	+10	+10	+ 8	+ 4	64
	1958–60	28	+19	+ 7	+ 6	+ 2	62
(b) Rest of world	1938	56	+ 2	+ 5	+ 8	+ 4	74
	1949–51	80	+ 4	+ 6	+ 8	+ 8	105
	1958–60	111	0	+ 3	+12	+ 8	134

For footnotes, see next page.

Table 13.10 (cont.)

		Estimated consumption of raw wool (clean basis)	Net exports (−) or net imports (+)[a]				Available for home use
			Tops	Yarn	Tissues	Other wool goods	
C. SOVIET COUNTRIES							
1. U.S.S.R. and	1938	154	+13	− 2	− 2	− 2	161
Eastern Europe	1949–51	133	+ 3	0	− 3	0	133
	1958–60	278	+ 5	+ 2	+ 2	− 7	280
2. China	1938	10	0	+ 1	+ 5	− 1	14
	1949–51	20	+ 2	—	—	—	22
	1958–60	42	+10	—	− 4	− 4	44

Sources: As for Table 13.7.

[a]Actual weight as recorded or estimated. No allowance has been made for losses or gains in manufacture.

[b]Other than wool tops.

[c]Including present area of Pakistan.

[d]Austria, Netherlands, Sweden, Switzerland and Western Germany.

[e]Countries importing 1,000 metric tons or more of tops and yarn in 1955: Denmark, Finland, Greece, Norway and Yugoslavia; Colombia; Hong Kong, Pakistan and South Korea; Egypt.

by quantitative restrictions. In Argentina and Uruguay, the other main raw wool-growing and exporting countries, however, the local industry has grown at the expense of imports of wool tissues, which were reduced almost to zero by the mid-1950's. Uruguay, indeed, has in recent years become a major exporter of wool tops, her exports having been aided by a differential exchange rate.

There was a very large expansion in United States' raw wool consumption in the immediate post-war period, followed by a contraction after 1948 caused in part by the rapid increase in the use of synthetic fibres. Wool is less competitive in relation to synthetics in the United States than in most other industrial countries, because of the tariff on raw wool imports and the incentive price paid to domestic raw wool producers. Nevertheless, imports of wool textiles into both the United States and Canada have remained well above the 1938 level. The main countries of Western Europe which are net importers of wool textiles are Austria, Netherlands, Sweden, Switzerland and Western Germany. Imports into this group have risen substantially, while raw wool consumption in 1958–60 was still below the pre-war total (which included the large Silesian textile area). These European countries and, to a lesser extent, North America are the only areas where the demand for imported wool textiles is expanding to any substantial extent; the United States has, however, a high level of protection against imports of wool textiles.

In the rest of the non-Soviet world, raw wool consumption is considerably above the 1938 level.   The increases have been well spread over a number of countries, the more important being in Latin America (Brazil, Chile and Mexico) and Western Europe (Spain and Ireland).   For the countries which are developing their local industries by using imported tops and/or yarns, there is a noticeable switch away from imports of wool tissues.

Since consumption of wool textiles per head is many times greater in the economically advanced countries than in the less-developed areas, it must be expected that further growth in world imports is likely to be concentrated in the former group of countries.   If past trends continue, the expansion in demand in the main wool-growing areas is likely to be met, either wholly or in greater part, by the further growth in local output.   In the other non-industrial areas, imports seem unlikely to expand much unless there is a substantial growth in real income.

Synthetic fibres[1]

World consumption of synthetic fibres has grown at a much faster pace since the early 1950's than that of the other textile fibres. In 1950, world synthetic consumption was only 70 thousand metric tons; by 1960, it had grown to about 700 thousand metric tons.   In the same period, world consumption of cotton rose by nearly 50 per cent, wool rose about 20 per cent, and rayon about 60 per cent.   By the end of the 1950's, synthetics accounted for about one-fifth of world consumption of all man-made fibres (see Table 13.11).

International trade in synthetic textiles has also been growing relatively fast, though it still represents only a small proportion of total trade in textile products. The greater part of the trade so far has been between the industrial countries themselves.

Since production of synthetic fibres requires relatively large capital investment

Table 13.11.   *World consumption and world exports of synthetic and other man-made textiles, 1950–60*

				Thousand metric tons	
	1950	1955	1957	1959	1960
World consumption					
Synthetics	70	268	412	577	709
Percentage of all man-made fibres	4	11	14	19	21
World exports[a]					
Synthetics	3	20	29	83	120
Percentage of all man-made fibres	1	5	6	11	14

Sources: As for Table 13.7.

[a]Yarns, fabrics and other manufactures.

[1]I.e. all man-made fibres other than rayon.

per unit of output, it is unlikely that the less-developed areas will be able to produce substantial quantities for a considerable time to come. Up to 1960, only four primary-producing countries—Australia, Argentina, Brazil and Mexico—were producing more than one thousand metric tons of synthetic fibres a year, the combined output of these countries being only 10 thousand metric tons in that year, or little more than 1 per cent of the world total. Nor is it likely that exports of synthetic textiles will expand substantially in the medium-term to the less-developed areas of the world, unless further technical developments result in a sharp fall in their price. Otherwise, the prospects for synthetics in the less-developed areas may continue to be restricted by the fact that their uses are largely industrial. Probably small inroads will continue to be made by the synthetics in the export trade to the more advanced countries at the expense of the other main fibres.

Import-substitution by type

The major part of the substitution of home for imported textiles since pre-war has occurred in cotton textiles, though the substitution process has also been important in rayon goods (see Table 13.12). Taking only those countries which are net importers of cotton, rayon and wool goods, respectively[1], it can be estimated that, had imports risen in the same proportion as home consumption between pre-war and 1958–60, the level of imports into these countries in the later period would have been about 40–50 per cent above pre-war for cotton

Table 13.12. *Effects of import-substitution and of growth in home demand on imports of textiles into net importing areas[a], pre-war to 1956*

Thousand metric tons

	Cotton goods[b]	Rayon goods[c]	Wool goods[d]
Imports into net importing countries			
Pre-war[e]	715	100	60
1954–56	410	275	50
Difference	−305	+175	−10
attributable to			
Import-substitution[f]	−625	−245	−40
Home demand[f]	+320	+430	+30

Sources: As for Table 13.7.

[a] Areas outside Europe, North America and the Soviet countries (see Tables 13.8, 13.9 and 13.10).   The figures for cotton, however, include Scandinavia and the Balkans.
[b] Actual weight.
[c] Gross imports, excluding staple.
[d] Excluding tops.
[e] 1936–38 for cotton goods, 1938 for rayon and wool goods.
[f] Calculation as in Table 13.6.

[1] I.e. the countries included in the general heading 'net importing countries' in Tables 13.8, 13.9 and 13.10, excluding the industrial countries and the Soviet area.

and wool textiles; in fact, net imports of cotton goods into these countries were substantially reduced, while there was a marginal reduction for wool textiles. On the other hand, for rayon goods the rise would have been more than four-fold, had net imports expanded in proportion to consumption, and in fact the rise was nearly double the pre-war total.

Though the proportionate effect of import-substitution since pre-war has been greatest in rayon, the impact in absolute terms on world trade in textiles has been greatest in cotton textiles, as can be seen from Table 13.12. An approximate valuation of these changes in terms of 1959 unit values in world trade indicates that, in 1958–60, the additional world exports which would have taken place had there been no import-substitution since pre-war in net-importing countries outside the industrial areas would have amounted to roughly $2½ billion, or about one-half of actual world exports of textiles and clothing in 1959. About two-thirds of this total 'loss' from import-substitution was in cotton textiles, most of the remainder being in rayon goods.

4. COMPETITION IN THE WORLD TEXTILE MARKET

The contraction in the volume of world trade in textiles after 1929–30 was accompanied by greatly intensified competition among the principal exporting countries. Britain's share of the total had suffered severely from Japanese competition even in the 1920's, but British exports in the following decade were further curtailed under the dual pressure of the fall in world demand and the sharp depreciation of the Japanese yen[1].

British textile and clothing exports before the first World War accounted for some 40 per cent of world exports (Table 13.13), but the proportion was reduced considerably by 1929 to one-third. In value terms, Britain's share was the same in 1937 as it was in 1929, but this reflected a marked 'stickiness' in prices in a period when export prices of competing countries, and particularly Japan's, had fallen drastically. By volume, British exports in 1937 were lower than in 1929 by nearly 30 per cent, whereas the decline in total world trade in textiles and clothing was only about 15 per cent (see Table 13.4). Meanwhile, Japanese exports had been expanding rapidly; by 1937 they were double their 1929 volume. In the post-war period, Britain's share of the world market has continued to fall; Japanese exports have no more than regained their 1937 share, but there has been a remarkable increase in the United States' share of the world total, the increase being concentrated in the Canadian market and in synthetic materials in which the United States industry had invested heavily during and after the war. Exports from India, which had risen to one-seventh of the world total in 1950 fell off by 1957–59 to under one-tenth, mainly as a result of increased competition from Japan.

[1]See page 207.

Table 13.13. *Shares of the world market in textiles and clothing, 1899–1959*

Percentage

Exports from	1899	1913	1929	1937	1950	1955	1959
United Kingdom	41.9	42.8	33.1	33.2	27.0	20.9	15.3
Japan	2.4	4.3	9.5	19.0	8.5	15.1	18.9
United States	2.3	3.0	5.5	4.1	11.6	11.7	10.7
France	16.6	14.9	15.1	6.6	12.9	11.6	11.3
India	4.0	6.1	6.3	7.5	13.8	9.3	8.4
Germany[a]	16.6	14.6	11.8	10.7[b]	2.3	7.7	8.4
Belgium-Luxembourg	3.6	3.5	3.8	5.0	7.2	7.1	7.3
Italy	6.3	5.8	8.5	7.6	9.0	6.9	8.9
Netherlands	..	..	2.6	2.6	3.8	5.0	5.9
Switzerland	6.1	4.8	3.4	2.8	3.0	4.0	3.9
Canada	0.1	0.1	0.2	0.6	0.6	0.4	0.4
Sweden	0.1	0.1	0.2	0.3	0.3	0.3	0.6
TOTAL	100.0	100.0	100.0	100.0	100.0	100.0	100.0
Total in $ billion	1.26	2.22	3.51	2.00	4.13	4.59	5.09

Sources: Tables A.46 to A.68 and A.80.

[a]West Germany in 1950–59.

[b]For the present area of West Germany, the 1937 percentage would be about 5–6.

The area pattern of demand

To some extent, these changes in relative shares reflect the different rates of change in import demand by the different markets.   Britain's traditional textile markets have been in the overseas Sterling Area, particularly in India, the Southern Dominions and the British Colonies, while both North and South America have been important buyers of British wool textiles.   The sharp secular contraction in the Indian import market (see Table 13.14) had a severe adverse effect on Britain's export trade in cotton textiles, but this was offset by buoyancy in other markets, such as the Southern Dominions, in which Britain's share of trade was large.   Similarly, the contraction in Latin American imports had a relatively severe effect on the British wool textile trade, especially since the last war.

Over half France's textile exports, on the other hand, are sold in Western Europe, and the sharp decline in intra-European trade in the 1930's hit France with particular severity; by 1937, French textile exports were about 20 per cent lower, in volume, than they were in 1913.   There were, however, two additional influences in the French decline.   The first was that the traditional export of silk fabrics was facing a secular decline as a result of competition from other textiles, especially cotton and rayon; the second was the long struggle to preserve the franc from devaluation, which resulted in French export prices becoming seriously uncompetitive by the middle 1930's[1].

[1]The devaluation of the franc extended from the autumn of 1936 to the summer of 1937.

Table 13.14. *'Imports' of textiles and clothing into major markets*, 1913–59

Percentage changes in volume

Market	1913–29	1929–37	1937–55	1955–59
Industrial countries	− 4	−36	+28	+38
Semi-industrial countries	−10	−18	−39	−28
of which				
Southern Dominions	+17	+12	+ 4	−20
India/Pakistan	−29	−44	−72	−51
Latin America	+ 5	−28	−71	−34
Rest of world[a]	+16	+ 8	− 4	+14
TOTAL	0	−16	− 3	+16

Sources: Tables A.76 and A.80.
[a]Including U.S.S.R. and China.

The greater part of Japanese cotton and rayon exports find their markets in the semi-industrial and non-industrial countries, though for wool textiles the United States is Japan's most important single market. Since the war, the contraction in the Indian import market[1] has been a major adverse factor in the development of Japan's export trade (Japan suffered even more heavily here than did Britain), while the balance of payments difficulties and import restrictions of many South-East Asian countries also tended to affect Japan more than other textile exporters.

Nonetheless, taking the period since 1913 as a whole, these changes in the area pattern of demand for textiles have generally been much less important in influencing each exporting country's share of the world textile trade, than have the changes in shares of individual markets. This can be seen from Table 13.15. The changes in the value of textile exports (at 'constant' prices) are divided into three parts, attributable to: (a) the change in the size of the world import market for textiles and clothing as a whole; (b) the change in the area pattern of trade; and (c) the change in the share of each exporting country in each market[2].

Changes due to the variation in shares of individual markets have in general been the most important element in the changes in the volume of textile exports from each country. The British experience of the 1930's is the outstanding exception to the general rule; by 1937, the decline in British exports from the 1929 peak can be attributable in rather greater measure to the decline in world import demand than to a decline in Britain's share of her overseas markets. Nevertheless, the decline in shares has been by far the most important factor for Britain over the period as a whole; from 1913 to 1959, about 95 per cent of the con-

---

[1]Part of the fall in India's demand for Japanese textiles resulted from the fact that before the war India and Japan had a barter agreement under which India exchanged 600 thousand bales of raw cotton for 60 million yards of cotton cloth a year from Japan.

[2]The method used in distinguishing these three elements is described in Chapter 8 (see page 199).

traction in British exports can be attributed to loss of share of individual markets. Moreover, the loss of share of individual markets was still the major element in Britain's export position even in the latest of the periods shown. In value terms, the fall in exports from 1913 to 1959 amounted to \$2.75 billion at 1955 prices, of which 2.6 was due to loss of share, while only 0.3 can be attributable to the decline in world import demand; in addition, the area pattern of import demand in 1959 was more favourable to British exports than in 1913, and this alone contributed an *increase* of some \$0.2 billion in the British total.

Over the whole period, the largest gain in market share was achieved by Japan, most of the increase occurring in the 1930's. From 1937 to 1955, the Japanese share fell off sharply, partly because of discriminatory import restrictions against Japanese textiles in many markets. This loss was, however, largely made good in the later 1950's, when discrimination against Japan was being reduced. The United States has also achieved a notable increase in its share of the world market since 1937, in spite of minor setbacks since 1955, while the smaller European exporters—particularly Belgium and Holland—gained considerably in their share both from 1937 to 1955 and since 1955.

The commodity pattern of trade

It is not possible to make a comprehensive analysis of the effect of the changing pattern of trade in different types of textiles and clothing on the share of each exporting country in the world market. However, a division of the export trade in yarns and fabrics according to the main types of fibre used has been made for selected years from 1913 to 1955 (see Table 13.16). The outstanding change has been the rise of man-made fibre products, first rayon and, in recent years, the synthetic fibres. In 1955, rayon and the synthetics accounted for one-quarter of world trade in all textile yarns and fabrics, whereas in 1913 they were negligible. Trade in cotton goods fell, relatively, from 1937 to 1955, but there was some increase in the relative proportion of wool manufactures.

Taking account of the commodity-pattern of each country's exports, the effect of the changing pattern of world demand on market shares can be calculated in the same way as for the area pattern. The results (Table 13.17) show fairly conclusively that, up to 1955, the changing pattern of demand by type of fibre had relatively little effect, in the majority of cases, on the global market shares[1].

Relative price changes

Since the major part of the changes in market shares has not been due to variations in area and commodity patterns, it is reasonable to assume that such

---

[1] It is possible, of course, that a more detailed commodity analysis, distinguishing different items within each type of fibre, might show that the changing commodity pattern had more effect on market shares than is shown here.

Table 13.15. *Changes in volume of exports of textiles and clothing attributable to changes in size, area pattern and shares of the world market[a], 1913–59*

$ million at constant prices

	United Kingdom	France	United States	Japan	India	Other countries[b]	Total
			(Values at 1913 prices)				
1913 exports	950	330	65	95	135	640	2215
Change from 1913 to 1929 attributable to change in							
(a) Size of world market	0	0	0	0	0	0	+ 5
(b) Area pattern of demand	+ 30	− 10	0	+ 5	+ 5	− 30	0
(c) Share of individual market areas	−335	+ 40	+ 40	+115	+ 20	+120	0
Total	−305	+ 30	+ 40	+120	+ 25	+ 90	+ 5
1929 exports	645	360	105	215	160	730	2220
			(Values at 1955 prices)				
1929 exports	2420	780	320	500	320	1340	5680
Change from 1929 to 1937 attributable to change in							
(a) Size of world market	−400	−130	− 55	− 85	− 55	−210	−935
(b) Area pattern of demand	+ 85	− 75	+ 25	+ 25	0	− 60	0
(c) Share of individual market areas	−350	−285	−130	+595	+110	+ 60	0
Total	−665	−490	−160	+535	+ 55	−210	−935
1937 exports	1755	290	160	1035	375	1130	4745
Change from 1937 to 1955 attributable to change in							
(a) Size of world market	− 65	− 10	− 5	− 35	− 15	− 30	−160
(b) Area pattern of demand	+ 55	+ 10	+ 15	−135	+ 5	+ 50	0
(c) Share of individual market areas	−785	+245	+370	−175	+ 55	+290	0
Total	−795	+245	+380	−345	+ 50	+310	−160
1955 exports	960	535	540	690	425	1440	4585
Change from 1955 to 1959 attributable to change in							
(a) Size of world market	+155	+ 85	+ 85	+110	+ 70	+250	+755
(b) Area pattern of demand	− 65	+ 20	− 10	− 10	− 15	+ 80	0
(c) Share of individual market areas	−250	+ 5	− 45	+160	− 40	+170	0
Total	−160	+110	+ 30	+260	+ 15	+500	+755
1959 exports	800	645	570	950	435	1940	5340

Sources: Based on Table A.76 and related data.

[a]For method of calculation, see text, page 199.
[b]As listed in Table 13.13.

Table 13.16. *World exports[a] of textile yarns and fabrics, 1913–55*

Percentages

	1913	1929	1937	1955
Cotton	53.9	51.0	52.0	41.5
Wool	17.6	19.1	18.5	20.3
Silk	17.8 ⎱	21.0[b]	5.4	2.2
Rayon (including new synthetics)	0.6 ⎰		14.0	26.5[c]
Linen	4.6	2.3	3.4	2.5
Jute	4.3	5.3	5.2	5.2
Other textiles	1.2	1.3	1.5	1.8
TOTAL	100.0	100.0	100.0	100.0
Total in $ billion	1.70	2.54	1.45	3.03

Sources: National trade statistics.

[a]Exports from nine major exporting countries (Belgium-Luxembourg, France, Germany/West Germany, Italy, Switzerland, United Kingdom, United States, Japan and India).

[b]Separate figures for silk and rayon goods are available only for exports from France and the United Kingdom for 1929. In that year, the bulk of French exports of the combined heading consisted of silk fabrics, while the greater part of British exports were rayon.

[c]Mostly rayon (see also Table 13.11).

changes reflect, to a substantial extent, the relative competitive position of the different exporting countries and, in particular, their relative export prices.

Changes in relative export prices are, in any case, extremely difficult to measure at all precisely from trade statistics, because unit values based on such data are affected by changes in commodity composition as well as by price movements[1]. However, as we have seen, changes in the broad commodity-pattern of exports have generally been a minor influence on the movement in relative exports of textiles and clothing from the main industrial countries; thus, unit values can reasonably be used in lieu of price indices and can be correlated with the volume figures to give estimates of price elasticity. The general relationship between the unit value and volume changes can be seen from Fig. 13.5, which shows scatter diagrams for four periods since 1913[2]. For each period, the volume change can be expressed as a function of the unit value change: Table 13.18 gives the results of calculations of price-substitution elasticity for each period, a double-logarithmic function being used for each. The results must not be accepted without qualification, particularly as the country indices have not been adjusted for differences in commodity patterns. Taken very broadly, however, the results—which show an elasticity between −2 and −4 according to the period selected—are of some interest. During the Great Depression, the calculated

[1]See Chapter 8 (pages 203–6) for some discussion of the limitations of unit value indices in this context.

[2]These diagrams are based on Appendix tables A.46–A.69 and B.1–B.5.

Table 13.17.   *Effect of changing commodity pattern of world trade on the volume of exports of textile yarns and fabrics, 1913–55*

Percentages

Change attributable to	United Kingdom	France	United States	Japan	India	Other countries[a]
1913 to 1929						
(a) Commodity-pattern of demand	− 9	+ 7	− 9	− 1	+ 18	+ 8
(b) Share of trade in each commodity group	− 19	+ 10	+ 94	+125	− 10	+ 2
1929 to 1937						
(a) Commodity-pattern of demand	+ 1	− 5	+ 4	+ 2	+ 8	− 3
(b) Share of trade in each commodity group	− 10	− 42	− 40	+ 95	+ 24	+ 7
1937 to 1955						
(a) Commodity-pattern of demand	− 8	+ 9	− 2	− 3	− 8	+ 18
(b) Share of trade in each commodity group	− 29	+ 61	+290	− 20	+ 58	+ 5

Sources: Based on national trade statistics.

[a]Belgium-Luxembourg, Germany (West Germany in 1955), Italy and Switzerland.

substitution elasticity was rather smaller than in other periods[1]; this was probably due, in part at least, to the widespread imposition of discriminatory restrictions on imports, affecting Japanese textile exports particularly adversely. Some of this discrimination was eliminated in the latter half of the 1950's, and the results for the period 1955–59 may thus overstate the long-term substitution relationship to some extent. On balance, the evidence suggests that a 10 per cent change in relative export prices (unit values) resulted on average in an inverse change in relative export volume of the order of some 30 per cent.

These results do not, of course, imply that relative prices are the only important element in the competitive position of the major textile industries; in fact,

Table 13.18.   *Estimates of price-substitution elasticities for exports of textiles*

	Number of countries	Elasticity	Standard error	R^2
1913–29	7	−2.45	±0.49	0.832
1929–37	10	−2.02	±0.79	0.453
1937–50	9	−3.04	±1.27	0.451
1937–55	9	−3.54	±0.97	0.657
1955–59	10	−3.96	±1.30	0.536

Sources: Based on Tables A.46–A.69 and B.1–B.5, and related data.

[1]The French unit value index for 1937 shown in Fig. 13.5 is 71 (1929 = 100). This index was calculated by assuming a time-lag of 3 months between the date of receipt of an export order and the date of shipment. This seems a more realistic figure to take in this context than the unit value index for 1937 calendar year of 66, as given in the Appendix, in view of the substantial devaluations of the franc in 1936 and 1937.

Fig. 13.5. Relation between volume and unit value changes of exports of
textiles and clothing, 1913–55

*Indices, earlier year = 100,
double logarithmic scale*

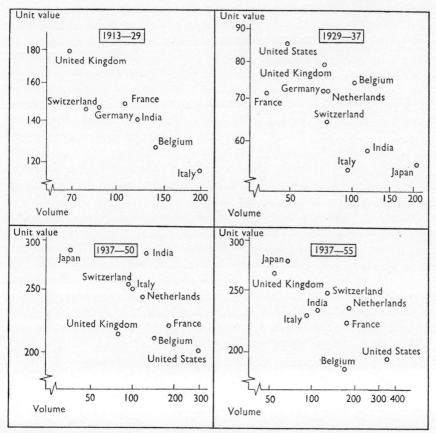

movements in relative export unit values appear to account for only about half
the variance in the volume of textile exports from the main producing countries
since 1929.   Other factors such as quality, design, delivery delays, advertising,
arrangements for credit, the availability of stocks in foreign markets, etc., though
not susceptible to statistical analysis—and therefore excluded from the previous
discussion—all play an important part in the shifting pattern of relative competitive power and, in some cases, they may well outweigh the effects of the
price factor[1].

[1]This conclusion seems to be supported by a detailed analysis by B. Vitkovitch of the
quantity and unit value of imports of particular items of cotton cloth into Canada and
Sweden in the period 1935–38 and 1948–52 (B. Vitkovitch, 'The U.K. Cotton Industry,
1937–54', *Journal of Industrial Economics*, Vol. III, No. 3, July 1955).   For a more general
discussion of the non-price elements in competitive power, see Chapter 8 (pages 202–3).

Exports from low-cost producers

The analysis so far has been concerned with export competition among the major textile producing countries, both 'high wage' countries like the United States and Britain, and 'low wage' countries like India and Japan. Since, however, textiles—particularly cotton textiles—tend to be developed rather early in the industrializing process, an increasing supply of textile goods for export must be expected from a number of industrializing countries in the less-developed areas. Labour productivity in cotton textiles in such countries is likely to be considerably lower than the levels attained in Western Europe (though Hong Kong is probably an exception); but their wage levels are even lower, in relation to European countries, than their labour productivity. Thus, the problem of 'low cost' competition in the world textile market is likely to grow more acute in the future.

Since the war, both Hong Kong and China have achieved a considerable increase in exports of low-cost textile fabrics and made-up goods. Exports from Hong Kong have gone mainly to Britain and the United States (exports to Britain are, however, limited by voluntary agreement between the cotton textile industries of the two countries[1]), while exports from China have made inroads into Japanese markets in South-East Asia. Among other countries which are developing their own textile industries, Pakistan and Egypt have already been mentioned as becoming important exporters of cheap cotton textiles, while Taiwan, South Korea, Israel and Turkey were beginning to export cotton textiles in significant quantities by 1959. It is likely that these, and other, industrializing countries will in future play an important part in the total supply of cheap cotton textiles on the world market.

Hitherto, the protectionist policies of the industrial countries of Western Europe and North America have acted as a brake on the cotton textile exports of the less-developed areas, as well as of those of India and Japan[2]. If these policies are continued in future, textile exports from industrializing countries are likely to be directed to the low-income markets in the less-developed areas themselves, where such exports are likely to continue to displace exports from the industrial countries.

[1] Voluntary agreements also cover cotton textile exports to Britain from India and Pakistan.
[2] Japanese exports of both wool and cotton textiles are subject to quantitative restrictions in many Western European countries.

CHAPTER 14

MISCELLANEOUS MANUFACTURES

It is useful for many purposes to distinguish the metal products included in this very heterogeneous group from the non-metallic manufactures. In fact, trends in world trade in the two categories have been very different, as can be seen from Table 14.1.

In the period up to 1929, world trade in metal goods expanded considerably; in that year, the volume was more than double that in 1899. The economic depression of the early 1930's and the accompanying network of trade restrictions resulted in a drastic curtailment of trade. 'Metal goods' consist to a large extent of relatively simply-fabricated products, such as wire and hand tools, which were particularly vulnerable to import restrictions imposed at that time on 'less essential' goods. By 1937, the immediate pre-war peak year, trade in metal goods was still some 30 per cent less than in 1929. The sluggishness has continued into the post-war period; only by the end of the 1950's was the volume of world trade in metal goods virtually back to the 1929 level.

By contrast, trade in the remaining miscellaneous groups of manufactures had recovered the 1929 peak level by the early 1950's, and by 1959 had exceeded

Table 14.1. *World trade^a in metal goods and miscellaneous manufactures in relation to world manufacturing production, 1899–1959*

$ *billion at constant prices, and index numbers, 1929* = 100

Trade^b or production	Values at 1913 prices^c			Values at 1955 prices				
	1899	1913	1929	1929	1937	1950	1955	1959
WORLD TRADE								
Metal goods	0.24	0.42	0.53	1.75	1.25	1.35	1.64	1.68
INDEX	45	80	100	100	72	78	94	96
Miscellaneous manufactures								
Intermediate products	0.17	0.34	0.54	1.49	1.29	1.41	2.11	2.68
INDEX	31	63	100	100	87	95	142	180
Finished manufactures	0.57	1.00	1.21	3.01	2.47	2.78	4.05	5.13
INDEX	47	83	100	100	82	92	134	170
WORLD MANUFACTURING PRODUCTION INDEX	36	61	100	100	115	190	252	294

Sources: Tables A 6 and A.80; *Industrial Statistics, 1900–1959*; O.E.E.C., Paris, 1960; *Statistical Yearbooks*, United Nations, New York.

^{a}Exports from twelve main exporting countries.
^{b}For definitions of these commodity groups, see Appendix D.
^{c}Excluding exports from the Netherlands.

it by some 75 per cent. Trade in intermediate products has tended to rise somewhat faster than trade in finished goods, both in the period up to 1929 and since 1950. The trends in each of the three groups are considered below in greater detail; because of the heterogeneous character of these groups, however, the discussion is mainly directed to a small number of the more important items included.

1. METAL GOODS

As already mentioned, these consist essentially of simply-processed metal manufactures ; their other common characteristic is that—except for ordnance —they contain no machinery or electrical equipment. The main items included are shown for a recent year in Table 14.2, which relates to exports from Britain, Germany and the United States, the three largest exporters. Again apart from ordnance, the pattern of exports is very similar in each country. Hand tools, etc., the largest single item, represented in 1957 about one-fifth of the total exports from the three countries, excluding ordnance, while another one-third comprised goods like structural metal parts, hardware, nails and stoves intended essentially for use in building and construction. Other main items which can be

Table 14.2. *Exports of metal goods from United Kingdom, United States and West Germany, 1957*

	United Kingdom	United States	West Germany
		(Percentage)	
Hand tools, tools for machines and hand implements	19	14	24
Finished structural parts	16	16	8
Wire cables, ropes, netting, fencing, etc.	9	8	10
Metal containers	8	11	6
Hardware (locks, etc.)	6	9	9
Nails, bolts, nuts, etc.	7	6	8
Cutlery	7	2	10
Household utensils	3	8	4
Stoves, furnaces, etc.	3	6	3
Other metal goods (except ordnance)	22	20	18
Total of above	100	100	100
		($ million)	
Total of above	360	390	391
Ordnance	109	7[a]	4
TOTAL	469	397	395

Sources: Foreign Trade Statistical Bulletins, Series B, Jan.-Dec. 1959, O.F.E.C., Paris, 1960; national trade statistics.

[a]Excluding special category exports, amounting to $239 million.

separately distinguished were cables and ropes, metal containers and cutlery[1].

Ordnance has been included here because it is a product of the metal-using industries; its movement over time cannot, however, be expected to have any relation to the forces normally operating on the level of trade. Though the relatively large United States exports of ordnance are excluded[2], British exports are not; these have been relatively important in the total exports of metal goods from Britain[3], but too small to have had much influence on the trend in total world trade in the group.

Table 14.3. *Exports of metal goods by country of origin, 1899–1959*

Percentage

Exports from	1899	1913	1929	1937	1950	1955	1959
United Kingdom	29.3	31.6	20.4	17.6	29.0	28.2	21.1
France	11.9	8.5	9.0	5.8	10.7	7.6	8.3
Germany[a]	33.5	35.4	37.8	42.4[b]	15.8	19.0	21.3
Other Western Europe[c]	8.7	7.6	11.5	13.2	18.3	21.2	23.9
United States	16.1	16.0	18.5	15.3	22.6	19.1	17.6
Japan	0	0.5	1.4	4.0	2.1	3.7	6.2
Other countries[d]	0.5	0.4	1.4	1.7	1.5	1.2	1.6
Total	100.0	100.0	100.0	100.0	100.0	100.0	100.0
Total in $ billion	0.22	0.42	0.72	0.60	1.02	1.64	1.94

Sources: Tables A.46 to A.68 and A.80.

[a]West Germany in 1950–59.

[b]For the present area of West Germany the 1937 percentage would be about 39.

[c]Belgium-Luxembourg, Italy, Netherlands (except in 1899 and 1913), Sweden and Switzerland.

[d]Canada and India.

Before 1914, Britain and Germany were the principal exporters of metal goods; together, they accounted for some two-thirds of the world total (Table 14.3). Then, as now, a great variety of goods were exported. Germany had an important export trade in partly-worked ferrous castings in 1913, and also in cutlery and copper manufactures, while Britain supplied a wide range, from hardware and cutlery to wire, cables and anchors. Britain's share fell off considerably, however, during the inter-war period, but recovered in the early 1950's to almost the 1913 proportion; there was a further fall in Britain's share

[1]World trade in cutlery has already been discussed in Chapter 12 (see also footnote 2 on page 306).

[2]Virtually all United States exports of ordnance are classified as 'special category', so that they are excluded from the definition of 'manufactures' used here (see Appendix A).

[3]Exports of arms and ammunition in 1929, for example, represented one-tenth of British exports of metal goods in that year.

from 1955 to 1959. Though West Germany's share has been increasing since 1950, by 1959 her share was little more than half that of the comparable 1937 percentage. The big change has been a marked increase in the share held by the smaller countries of Western Europe, largely as a result of higher exports from Belgium and Italy.

Only one-third of the expansion in the volume of trade in metal goods from 1899 to 1929 was in the intra-trade of the industrial countries. Imports into Germany failed to rise significantly in the period up to 1913, and in 1929 they were lower than at the turn of the century[1]. Imports into Britain rose, but at a slower rate than for most other industrial countries[2]. In both Germany and Britain, there was a substantial substitution of home output for imports. There was a relatively severe contraction in the intra-trade in metal goods during the 1930's. The expansion in the market from 1937 to 1955 presented a very different pattern from that in previous periods, the North American market expanding most (one-half the increase in the world total), and there was also an increase in exports to the smaller European countries. Imports into Britain, France and West Germany in 1955, however, were 60 per cent below the 1929 peak[3]. Though world trade in metal goods showed only a marginal rise in volume between 1955 and 1959, imports into these three industrial countries rose by some two-thirds in this period—but, even so, they were still considerably less than in 1913.

Other declines have occurred in exports to the less-developed industrializing countries. Exports to India/Pakistan in 1955 were slightly less than those to undivided India in 1929, while there was a 40 per cent reduction in exports to the miscellaneous group of semi-industrial countries. The greater part of this decline occurred in the 1930's; it was particularly severe in imports into Latin America, where the substitution of home output for imports could be carried much further for light metal products than for capital equipment. Even in exports to the 'rest of the world', which includes the non-industrial countries, the ground lost in the 1930's had still not been fully made good by 1955.

Metal goods are likely to continue to be an important field for the substitution of home output for imports, particularly in the semi-industrial countries which, in 1955, accounted for one-fifth of world imports. Imports into the industrial countries—apart, perhaps, from Britain, France and Germany—are likely to continue to expand as real incomes rise.

2. MISCELLANEOUS INTERMEDIATE PRODUCTS

Two main items—paper and board, and leather and furs—have dominated this very mixed group. Together, they represented about 80 per cent of the

[1]See Table A.17.
[2]See Tables A.6 and A.23.
[3]Even if allowance is made for the territorial changes in Germany, there was a clear reduction in the volume of metal goods imports into the three countries in this period.

total in 1913, though by 1959 the proportion had fallen to some 60 per cent (see Table 14.4). A considerable diversification has, in fact, taken place since the inter-war years, with marked increases in the relative importance of veneers and plywood, of mineral manufactures other than glass and of silver, and platinum group metals. Taking the period as a whole, however, the outstanding

Table 14.4. *Exports of miscellaneous intermediate products*, 1913–59

Percentage

	1913[a]	1929	1955	1957	1959
Paper and paper board					
Newsprint	2.5[b]	19.2	33.3	31.1	29.4
Other paper and board	23.5	22.0	20.4	19.7	19.3
Leather and furs	53.4	35.2	7.6	9.3	11.1
Veneers, plywood, etc.	0.1	0.8	8.7	7.9	9.7
Precious and semi-precious stones and pearls	0.4	10.6	8.1	7.9	9.6
Glass[c]	16.5	5.0	7.7	6.5	8.4
Other mineral manufactures	1.3	4.0	6.5	6.9	6.4
Silver, and platinum group metals	1.1	2.2	5.6	8.5	3.6
Rubber fabricated materials	1.2	1.0	2.1	2.2	2.5
Total[c]	100.0	100.0	100.0	100.0	100.0
Total in $ billion	0.34	0.85	2.11	2.74	2.83

Sources: Foreign Trade Statistical Bulletins, Series IV and Series B., O.E.E.C., Paris; national trade statistics.

[a]Excluding exports from the Netherlands.
[b]Approximate.
[c]Including some exports classified as miscellaneous finished manufactures.

features have been the relative growth in paper and board and the sharp relative decline in leather and furs. Within the paper group, newsprint has been the dynamic element; trade in other paper and board has, indeed, tended to fall off somewhat relatively to the group total.

The rapid expansion in exports of newsprint reflects in the main the growth of Canadian supplies. Canada's production was negligible at the beginning of the century; her entry into the world newsprint market dates from the mid-1920's and by 1929 she accounted for one-fifth of world exports of all the miscellaneous intermediate manufactures included here. There was a further large expansion in Canadian supplies after the second World War, and by 1950 two-fifths of world exports of all miscellaneous intermediates came from Canada. Since then the proportion has fallen (to one-third in 1959). The other major change in sources of supply since 1913 has been the contraction in the French and German shares of the total; the main reason has been the decline in the international leather trade, France and Germany being the principal leather exporters before the first World War.

On the demand side, the outstanding feature has been the expansion in imports by the United States. From 1913 to 1929, and again from 1937 to 1955, the United States was the major expanding import market; in both periods, Canadian supplies (mostly newsprint) were mainly drawn upon. Western Europe has played only a minor role in the development of world demand in these intermediate products. To a large extent, this was due to a reduction in British imports, falling mainly on imports of leather from India[1], which partly offset increases in imports by Continental countries.

Taken as a group, the industrial countries remain by far the largest area of demand for these intermediate products, and this dependence on industrial markets must be expected to continue in future. Much will depend on the trend of demand for newsprint, which has hitherto tended to dominate the expansion in the group.

Newsprint

Though world newsprint consumption now greatly exceeds the pre-war level, the trends have been very different in some of the main consuming areas. Consumption in the United States, which now accounts for over half the world total outside the Soviet area, has virtually doubled since pre-war, but consumption in Britain in the early post-war period was restricted and even after the control was lifted, in 1956, newsprint consumption remained below the pre-war total until 1959[2]. Consumption in other industrial countries and in the rest of the world is now well above pre-war levels and is continuing to rise (see Table 14.5).

Table 14.5.   *World consumption of newsprint*, 1927–59

	Total				Annual averages Per head
	1927–29	1935–39	1950–54	1955–59a	1955–59
	(*Million metric tons*)				(*Kg.*)
United States	3.27	3.21	5.47	6.20	36
Canada	0.19	0.19	0.35	0.41	25
United Kingdom	0.80	1.24	0.70	1.01	20
Other Europeb	0.92	1.23	1.32	1.91	7
Japan	0.25	0.39	0.29	0.55	6
Rest of worldb	0.45	0.64	0.94	1.31	1
Totalb	5.88	6.90	9.06	11.39	6

Sources: Newsprint Association of Canada; *Monthly Bulletin of Statistics*, United Nations, New York.

aIncluding provisional figures for 1959.
bExcluding Soviet countries.

[1]There has been a substantial substitution of rubber and plastic materials for leather in Britain since 1950.

[2]British newsprint consumption rose from 1.16 million metric tons in 1959 to 1.29 in 1960 (25 kg. per head), the same per caput level as in 1939.

The demand for newsprint depends both on the number of newspapers sold and on their average size. The number sold depends on a variety of factors. On the demand side, perhaps the most important are the average income of the potential readers, the relative cost of the newspaper, the degree of literacy in the population, and the general interest taken in current affairs and sport. On the cost side, the overwhelming factor—at least in the well-to-do capitalist societies—is the amount of revenue derived from advertisements. Until the advent of commercial television, advertising revenue generally increased with the level of real income, but the greater potency of television as a mass advertising medium has resulted in a serious loss of revenue for the newspapers in the United States and Britain. The average size of newspapers is also highly dependent on revenues from advertisements, which support a larger size than would otherwise be economic.

Various studies of newsprint consumption per head in different countries have established that the income-elasticity generally exceeds unity, and that it tends to fall off as the level of income rises[1]. This implies that at some level of per caput income a saturation point is reached, beyond which per caput newsprint consumption will not rise[2]. Estimates based either on past historical trends or on cross-country relationships all show that a considerable expansion in world newsprint consumption is probable over the period up to 1975/80. A recent study by the United Nations' Food and Agriculture Organization, for example, estimates that newsprint demand in the non-Soviet world will rise from 10.6 million tons in 1955 to 16.0 million tons in 1965 and to 22.9 million tons in 1975[3]. Similar results were arrived at by the Royal Commission on Canada's Economic Prospects, which envisages world newsprint demand (outside the Soviet countries) increasing by about 10 million tons (90 per cent) between 1955 and 1980[4]. Even allowing for the possibility of faster rates of economic expansion in the less-developed countries, the bulk of this increase in demand would arise in North America and Western Europe.

These estimates inevitably contain a considerable margin of error as a number of imponderables are involved, apart altogether from the assumed rates of growth of the economies of the main net importing countries. For one thing, many countries may not have sufficient foreign exchange to finance increases in newsprint imports on the scale envisaged in these estimates. Another uncertainty is the extent to which advertising revenues will be switched in future

[1]See *Pulp and Paper Prospects in Latin America*, United Nations, New York, 1955; and *World Demand for Paper to 1975*, Food and Agriculture Organization, Rome, 1960.

[2]The recent study by the Food and Agriculture Organization puts the saturation level at 60 kg. per head, or two-thirds above the United States level in the period 1955–59 (*World Demand for Paper to 1975*, p. 8).

[3]*World Demand for Paper to 1975*, p. 51.

[4]*The Outlook for the Canadian Forest Industries*, Royal Commission on Canada's Economic Prospects, Ottawa, 1957; the estimate of future demand in the United States was based on the trend in the index of newspaper page circulation per adult and on the probable increase in the adult population.

away from newspapers to television and other mass media; any spread of this tendency, now a marked one in the United States and Britain, to other countries seems bound to put an upper limit to the demand for newsprint. But, even if the estimates now current prove to be somewhat optimistic, it seems evident that world trade in newsprint is likely to continue to be the most rapidly expanding item in the whole group of miscellaneous intermediates.

3. MISCELLANEOUS FINISHED MANUFACTURES

The main items in this group in recent years have been scientific instruments, fabricated building materials and paper manufactures (over 10 per cent each of the group total), rubber goods and watches and clocks (see Table 14.6). The

Table 14.6. *Exports of miscellaneous finished manufactures, 1913–59*

Percentage

	1913[a]	1929	1955	1957	1959
CAPITAL ITEMS					
Scientific, etc. instruments	3.5	3.6	12.6	12.4	12.9
Fabricated building materials, pre-fabricated buildings and sanitary, etc. fittings and fixtures	5.3	7.2	12.9	11.9	10.5
Total	8.8	10.8	25.5	24.3	23.4
CONSUMER ITEMS					
Paper and paperboard manufactures and printed matter	11.4	9.5	10.5	10.6	11.0
Rubber manufactures, including tyres and tubes	9.1	13.1	8.7	9.5	8.6
Watches and clocks	5.6	5.2	8.6	8.5	6.7
Glassware and pottery	9.2	13.1	7.3	6.5	6.4
Fur clothing and footwear	3.5	3.7	3.1	3.9	5.4
Musical instruments	3.9	4.4	3.5	4.1	4.6
Photographic, etc. supplies and cine film	2.8	3.1	4.5	4.4	4.4
Furniture, etc.	1.7	1.5	2.9	3.0	3.0
Jewellery, etc.	5.8	2.8	2.5	2.6	2.6
Wood and cork manufactures	9.7	7.5	2.6	2.6	2.3
Leather manufactures	8.2	4.6	0.7	0.6	0.6
Other manufactures	20.3	20.7	19.6	19.4	21.0
Total	91.2	89.2	74.5	75.7	76.6
TOTAL[b]	100.0	100.0	100.0	100.0	100.0

Sources: Foreign Trade Statistical Bulletins, Series IV and Series B., O.E.E.C., Paris; national trade statistics.

[a]Excluding exports from the Netherlands.
[b]Excluding some exports of finished manufactures shown in Table 14.4.

first two are really different in kind from the rest, being normally purchased on capital account by firms or government agencies. The other items in Table 14.6 are largely sold direct to consumers ; the only major exception may be rubber tyres and tubes, to the extent that these are sold for incorporation in new vehicles.

Trade in the two 'capital' items, scientific instruments and fabricated building materials[1], has expanded much more since pre-war than has trade in the various consumer manufactures. From 1929 to 1955, the two capital items more than tripled in volume, while the increase in the consumer group as a whole was only 12 per cent—indeed, for some consumer items (for example, leather goods and wood and cork manufactures) the volume of trade is now considerably less than in 1929 or before the first World War. However, since 1955, trade in these miscellaneous consumer manufactures has been expanding at a somewhat faster rate than that in the two capital items.

Several distinct influences have been at work over the period since 1929. First, the degree to which the consumer items have been subject to quantitative import restrictions, or exchange controls, has varied greatly. Trade in 1929 was generally free of such restrictions, but in the 1930's restrictionism had a severe depressing influence on the level of trade. Since the war, the only major relaxations have been made by the economically advanced countries (the liberalization of this sector of trade in O.E.E.C. countries took place mainly from 1955 to 1958); most of the less-developed industrializing countries, however, have continued to restrict severely the import of 'less essential' consumer goods, a category which usually includes the majority of consumer items listed in Table 14.6. Increasing liberalization of trade in Western Europe appears to be a major reason for the expansion of trade in this group of items from 1955 to 1959.

A second factor has been the growth of local production substituting for imports in many of the more important markets outside the industrial areas. In addition, new materials—particularly synthetics—have come into use to replace traditional ones; the substitution of plastics for leather, and of metals and plastics for wood, for example, are probably only the most obvious examples of a more general process in this field. Finally, the general shift in the pattern of world demand, particularly the expansion in engineering and constructional requirements in relation to consumer expenditures, must have played a part in stimulating the growth of trade in scientific instruments and building materials.

Changes in the shares of world exports held by the different industrial countries have little meaning here, because of the heterogeneous character of the commodities considered, and because some countries tend to specialize in certain items. The Canadian specialization in newsprint has already been

---

[1]'Scientific instruments' include medical, optical, measuring and controlling instruments and apparatus, while 'fabricated building materials' consist largely of cement, bricks, tiles and sanitary fittings, though in recent years some prefabricated buildings are also included.

mentioned (Canadian exports of other paper and board and of plywood and veneers are also important); other major specializations are Switzerland in watches and clocks[1], Belgium in diamonds, Sweden in paper and board, India in leather goods and Japan in plywood and veneers.

Among the industrial countries, the trend in imports into Britain, France and Germany has been falling since 1913. The major reduction was in British imports, which in 1955 were only one-third of the 1913 volume. West German imports in 1955 were one-fifth lower than those of the Reich in 1929, but French imports in 1955 had recovered to the 1929 level. Comparable statistics with these are not available for a later year than 1955, but the official import returns indicate a substantial increase in West German imports between 1955 and 1959 in paper and board and in a variety of other miscellaneous finished goods, and smaller increases in British and French imports in this period.

By contrast, imports into the smaller industrial countries of Western Europe and into Canada and the United States rose considerably from 1937 to the 1950's. There was also a substantial increase in shipments to the non-industrial areas over this period. The semi-industrial countries, however, took less in 1955 than they had in 1929 ; evidently, the progress of import-substitution, combined with the shortage of foreign exchange available for imports of 'less essentials' in the post-war period, more than offset any increase in demand for the 'capital' items in this commodity group. This has been particularly true of Argentina and India.

Cement and scientific instruments

Since the expansion in world trade has been so highly concentrated in the two 'capital' items, they merit some more detailed consideration. An important part of the trade in fabricated building materials is in cement[2]. World cement production has expanded considerably since the war. By 1948 the total, at 103 million metric tons, was already 27 per cent above the 1937 level; by 1952, the total reached 160 million, by 1955, 217 million, and by 1959, 292 million metric tons. The sharpest relative expansion, compared with pre-war, has been in the countries (mainly non-industrial) classified in the 'rest of the world' (see Table 14.7). Among these, the largest producers of cement in 1959 in the less-developed continents were Venezuela (1.87 million tons), Egypt (1.78 million tons) and Taiwan (1.07 million tons); numerous other under-developed countries were producing over half a million tons in that year. Rapid expansion in cement production has also taken place in a number of the semi-industrial countries, as well as in the Soviet area.

[1] See Table 12.11 for figures of exports of watches and clocks from Switzerland and West Germany.
[2] In 1955, cement accounted for about 38 per cent of the total; sanitary, heating, etc. fixtures and fittings for 34 per cent; bricks, tiles, etc. for 24 per cent; and prefabricated buildings for 5 per cent.

This growth in cement production outside the industrial areas is not a surprising development. Cement is a heavy, bulky and low-cost product which attracts heavy freight charges in relation to its *ex works* price, so that it is most economically produced in close proximity to the consuming area. This is usually technically feasible, as the raw material is fairly abundant in most countries; moreover, though more capital-intensive than light consumer industries, cement production does not involve a complicated technical process, nor highly specialized know-how.

Table 14.7. *World production of cement, 1937–59*

	1937	1955	1957	1959	1959 as ratio of 1937
		(Million metric tons)			
INDUSTRIAL COUNTRIES	60.5	135.1	144.9	160.0	2.6
United States	20.1	53.0	52.6	56.8	2.8
Other countries[a]	40.4	82.1	92.3	103.2	2.6
SEMI-INDUSTRIAL COUNTRIES	7.0	28.3	33.6	38.5	5.5
Southern Dominions[b]	1.7	4.7	5.3	5.9	3.5
India/Pakistan	1.1	5.3	6.8	8.0	7.3
Latin America[c]	2.4	8.5	10.1	11.0	4.6
Other countries[d]	1.8	9.8	11.4	13.6	7.6
SOVIET COUNTRIES	10.8[e]	40.6	51.7	70.7	6.5
REST OF WORLD	2.7	14.0	16.0	23.0	8.5
WORLD TOTAL	81	217	247	292	3.6

Sources: Statistical Yearbook, 1958 and *1959*, United Nations, New York; *Monthly Bulletin of Statistics*, United Nations, New York.

[a] Austria, Belgium-Luxembourg, Canada, Denmark, France, Germany (West Germany in 1955–59), Italy, Japan, Netherlands, Norway, Sweden, Switzerland and United Kingdom.
[b] Australia, New Zealand and the Union of South Africa.
[c] Argentina, Brazil, Chile, Colombia and Mexico.
[d] Finland, Greece, Ireland, Portugal, Spain, Turkey and Yugoslavia.
[e] Excluding China.

World trade in cement more than doubled from 1937 to 1957 (Table 14.8). The percentage increase in exports to industrial countries exceeded the percentage increases in their production but, in any event, imports form only a marginal proportion of their supplies. Exports to the semi-industrial countries were two-fifths (300,000 tons) lower in 1957 than in 1937, while their own production was up by over 30 million tons ; imports are now of little significance in meeting the cement requirements of these countries. For the 'rest of the world', however, imports still form a significant fraction of total cement supplies, though the proportion has been reduced from almost one-half before the war to one-fifth in 1957. It seems doubtful whether more than marginal amounts of imported cement will be taken by the semi-industrial countries in the future; for exports to the two other groups of countries, the prospects seem to be for a moderate rate of growth.

For scientific instruments, the prospects seem brighter. Over half world exports go to industrial markets, mainly in Western Europe; about one-tenth goes to Latin America and the same proportion goes to Sterling markets outside

Table 14.8   *World exports[a] of cement, 1937–57*

Destination[b]	1937	1955	1957	1957 as ratio of 1937
	(Million metric tons)			
INDUSTRIAL COUNTRIES	0.88	3.11	2.83	3.2
SEMI-INDUSTRIAL COUNTRIES	0.71	0.47	0.41	0.6
Southern Dominions	0.06	0.26	0.02	0.3
India/Pakistan	0.06	0.07	0.08	1.3
Latin America	0.18	0.05	0.09	0.5
Other countries	0.41	0.09	0.22	0.5
REST OF WORLD[c]	2.27	5.10	5.15	2.3
TOTAL	3.86	8.68	8.39	2.2

Sources: Foreign Trade Statistical Bulletins, Series IV, O.E.E.C., Paris; *Japanese Economic Statistics*, Economic Planning Agency, Tokyo; and national trade statistics.

[a]Exports from Belgium-Luxembourg, Denmark, France, Germany (West Germany in 1955 and 1957), Japan, United Kingdom and United States.
[b]Definition of areas as in Table 14.7.
[c]Including Soviet countries.

Europe. It is unlikely that local production in the semi-industrial countries can replace imports of most of these instruments and appliances for a considerable time to come. West Germany and the United States together accounted for about 60 per cent of the total trade in 1959, the American share having risen sharply since pre-war mainly at Britain's expense.

Taking the group of miscellaneous finished manufactures as a whole, it is evident that most items are well suited to local production in substitution for imports. Further substantial growth in trade may be possible but such growth is likely to be at a considerably lower rate than industrial growth in the world economy or in the main import markets.

CHAPTER 15

PAST TRENDS AND FUTURE PROSPECTS

In earlier chapters, we have explored some of the long-term relationships between the growth of real income in countries at various stages of industrial development and the growth and changing structure of their import trade in manufactures. On reasonable assumptions about the future growth of real income, some assessment can be made of how world trade in manufactures might develop in the next decade or so, and of the kind of problems for economic policy which might arise. Such an assessment is attempted in this chapter which is, in a sense, a special application of some of the more general trends and relationships discussed previously. Allowance must be made for the development of new influences on world trade. One recent development is the trend towards regional economic integration, the outstanding example being the formation of the European Economic Community ; a second is the emergence of the Soviet countries as major exporters of manufactures—particularly of capital equipment—to many countries in the under-developed areas. Both are discussed further below.

There are two main issues around which a discussion of past trends and future prospects of international trade in manufactures can usefully be focussed. The first concerns the total volume of such trade : can we reasonably expect the trade volume to continue to expand at the high rate achieved in the past decade, or not ? If not, what would be a more likely rate of growth ? What are the implications for the economic progress of the less-developed areas ? This first group of questions, concerned essentially with overall totals of income, trade and international payments, forms the subject matter of the first part of this chapter. The second group of questions, discussed later, relates to changes in the commodity and area pattern of world trade in manufactures. What kind of commodity pattern is likely to emerge, and will this be significantly affected by differential changes in the rates of growth of the main importing areas ? Finally, the implications of these trends for the economic policies of the industrial countries are considered, with particular reference to the problem of increasing the rate of economic progress in the less-developed areas.

1. A QUANTITATIVE ASSESSMENT

A quantitative assessment of the prospects for exports of manufactures from the industrial countries, however approximate, is useful as a framework for discussion of the main trends and of possible policy changes. Such an assessment can be made on the basis of assumed rates of change in total population and in real income per head in the different groups of countries; and of estimates of consumption or supplies of manufactured goods corresponding to the assumed level of real income, and of the probable import-content of these supplies.

The estimates presented below relate to an average for the period 1970–75. Estimates of the *total population* of each country in 1970 and in 1975 have been made by the United Nations, and an average of the estimates for these two years has been used here. In the industrial countries, total population is estimated to rise by one-seventh between 1959 and 1970–75 (or by 1.1 per cent per annum, compound), compared with a much greater increase (one-third, or 2.1–2.2 per cent per annum, compound) for the semi-industrial and non-industrial areas.

The estimates of future trends in *real income per head* are not forecasts, but assumptions on which a discussion of the changing patterns of trade can reasonably be based. During the 1950's, the average annual rate of growth in real income per head was 2.6 per cent in the large industrial countries, and 2.2 and 2.0 per cent, respectively, in the small industrial countries and the semi-industrial countries; though no very reliable estimates can be made for the non-industrial areas, it seems probable that their annual rate of growth was little more than 1 per cent per head.

In the present calculations, it is assumed that income per head in the large industrial countries will grow, on average, at much the same rate as in the recent past—by some 2½–3 per cent per annum. The small industrial countries are assumed, arbitrarily, to increase their rate of growth to 3 per cent per annum, while for the semi-industrial and non-industrial areas alternative assumptions—either 2 or 3 per cent per annum—are used. The higher rate assumed for the latter two areas would represent a considerable economic achievement compared with past performance[1].

In the following sections, the trade prospects of the main groups of countries are considered separately.

The intra-trade of the industrial countries

During the 1950's the volume of intra-trade in manufactures among the industrial countries increased very fast. From 1950 to 1959, its average rate of growth was 9.4 per cent per annum, compound, while non-food manufacturing production in the same group of countries rose by only 5.0 per cent a year. This much faster rate of growth in trade than in production is unprece-

---

[1]The main aim of the Development Decade, launched in December 1961 by the General Assembly of the United Nations is to achieve 'in each under-developed country a substantial increase in the rate of growth, with each country setting its own target, taking as the objective a minimum rate of growth of aggregate national income of 5 per cent at the end of the Decade' (General Assembly resolution 1710 (XVI)). In a recent report by the Secretary-General, this objective of a 5 per cent increase in aggregate income is stated to correspond with an increase of only 1½–2 per cent in per caput income (*The United Nations Development Decade: Proposals for action*, United Nations, New York, 1962).

dented in the historical development of Western Europe and North America since the beginning of the century. Possibly half the growth in the intra-trade in manufactures from 1950 to 1959 can be attributed to the reduction or elimination of trade and payments restrictions (as indicated by the rising proportion of imports in the industrial countries' markets), the other half reflecting the growth of the economies of the industrial countries[1]. Other things being equal, therefore, intra-trade might be expected to rise at only about half the rate achieved in the 1950's, in relation to the rate of economic growth in the industrial countries. But this relationship might be affected by the trend towards economic integration in Western Europe.

One would expect, on *a priori* grounds, that closer economic union between two or more countries would result in a higher ratio of trade to output than before the union was effected. A reduction in trade barriers is likely to result in a greater degree of specialization among the countries concerned. Within each country, the effect of increased specialization would be to stimulate the transfer of resources from industries which are relatively less competitive in the wider international market to those which are relatively more competitive. Total gross product in each country would increase to the extent that resources were, on average, more efficiently used, but this increase is likely to be considerably smaller, proportionately, than the increase in trade between the partner countries resulting from the increase in specialization. In the field of consumer goods alone, increased specialization through differences in styling, quality, brand names, etc. can be of considerable importance in stimulating the flow of international trade between countries at a high level of income. In the longer run, however, there may be some offset to the expansion in trade, insofar as producers in the less efficient industries rationalize their production techniques or invest in new techniques and thus raise their competitive level.

The differential rates of economic growth in the main industrial countries may be equally important. Since the import-content of consumption of manufactures is lower in the United States than in the other large industrial countries, and is considerably lower in all the large industrial countries than in the small ones, the impact on trade of a given rate of economic growth will depend heavily on where the growth takes place. During the past decade, the low average rate of growth in the United States, with its low import proportion, in relation to the rapid economic growth in Continental Western Europe, has tended to inflate the ratio of intra-trade to the total gross product of the industrial countries. It seems unlikely that these disparities in rates of growth will be quite as large in the near future, if only because of the 'once-for-all' factors which stimulated growth in West Germany in the 1950's. More specifically, if the United States rate of growth increases while that of the European Economic Community declines somewhat—which is not an unreasonable assumption—

[1]See page 153.

this alone would significantly reduce the overall ratio of the intra-trade to the gross product.

In Table 15.1, which relates to the *large* industrial countries only, an attempt is made to quantify the difference in total trade in manufactures which could result from different assumed rates of growth. At one extreme, alternative I assumes the same (3 per cent) rate of growth in each large industrial country; this implies, in effect, that the United States will achieve a distinct improvement

Table 15.1. *Alternative patterns of growth in real income and 'imports'[a] of manufactures in the large[b] industrial countries, 1959 to 1970–75*

	Alternative I	Alternative II			Alternative III		
	Total	United States	Others	Total	United States	Others	Total
		(Annual percentage change (compound))					
ASSUMED RATES OF GROWTH 1959 TO 1970–75							
Population	1.1	1.3	0.9	1.1	1.3	0.9	1.1
Real income per head	3.0	2.5	4.0	3.0	2.0	4.5	2.5
Import-content of supplies of manufactures[c]		*(Percentage)*					
1959	3.9	2.9	5.5	3.9	2.9	5.5	3.9
1970–75	4.1–4.8	2.8–3.3	7.0–8.0	4.7–5.4	2.8–3.3	7.0–8.0	4.9–5.7
Supplies[d] of manufactures		*($ per head at 1955 prices)*					
1959	685	1080	445	685	1080	445	685
1970–75	1220	1600	850	1140	1450	930	1130
'Imports' of manufactures, f.o.b.							
1959	27.0	31.3	24.5	27.0	31.3	24.5	27.0
1970–75	50–58	45–53	60–68	54–62	41–48	65–74	55–64
Total 'imports' of manufactures, f.o.b.		*($ billion at 1955 prices)*					
1959	12.7	5.6	7.1	12.7	5.6	7.1	12.7
1970–75	27–31	10–11	20–23	30–34	8½–10	21½–24	30–34
Rate of growth in total 'imports' of manufactures		*(Annual percentage change (compound))*					
1950 to 1959	11.5	11.6	11.5	11.5	11.6	11.5	11.5
1959 to 1970–75	5.7–6.8	4.4–5.1	8.0–9.1	6.6–7.6	3.1–4.4	8.6–9.4	6.6–7.6

Sources: Tables 6.4 and A.81; *Yearbook of International Trade Statistics, 1959,* United Nations, New York, 1960; *The Future Growth of World Population,* United Nations, New York, 1958 ('medium' assumption); *Monthly Bulletin of Statistics,* United Nations, New York, 1961.

[a]'Imports' from 11 main industrial countries. 'Imports' from India are not included.
[b]France, Italy, United Kingdom, West Germany, United States and Japan.
[c]Ratio of 'imports', f.o.b. to supplies; for ratio of 'imports', c.i.f., to supplies, see Table 6.4.
[d]As defined in footnote [a] in Table 6.4.

on its rate of growth in recent years, and that the rate of growth in Continental Western Europe will slow down. At the other extreme, alternative III assumes that the rates of growth in the United States and in the other large industrial countries will continue to diverge in much the same way as in the recent past.

The relationship between the growth in real income per head and in the consumption of manufactured goods of all kinds was explored in Chapter 6, where it was shown that there was a high degree of correlation between the two[1]. The correlation between real income and supplies (i.e. production plus imports) of manufactures is, equally, a very close one, and this relationship is used here to project the level of supplies per head in the period 1970–75 on the basis of the assumptions made about the growth in real income. The results, shown in Table 15.1, indicate that *supplies of manufactures* per head in the large industrial countries would rise between 1959 and 1970–75 by about four-fifths on alternative I and by about two-thirds on alternatives II and III.

Estimates of the *import-content of supplies* in 1970–75 are much more speculative. In the United States, the import-content has varied between 2 and 3 per cent for each of the selected years since 1899[2]; however, since the latter part of the 1950's an upward trend in the import-content has been noticeable, mainly as a result of the 'export drives' of a number of European countries (particularly in passenger cars and other consumer goods) and of some relaxation in United States import restrictions. The import-content of supplies in 1959 can be estimated at almost 3 per cent[3], and little change has been assumed to occur in the period up to 1970–75.

In the other large industrial countries, the future average import-content of supplies might fall within a wide range. The proportion of imports in the main constituent countries has recovered sharply since 1950, as can be seen from Fig. 15.1; but even by 1959 the low 1937 level (just under 6 per cent) had not been exceeded. It could be argued, in principle, that the average 1929 import-content (about 10–11 per cent) more nearly reflects the 'normal' level for this group of countries when trade restrictions are minimal. However, it also seems likely that the average import-content would have fallen in any event in some of these countries from the 1929 level. In Japan, for example, the import-content would probably have fallen as the industrial structure became more diversified; in Britain, too, not all the import-substitution effected by protection in the 1930's is likely to be recovered. If some offset is to be allowed on this score, the upper limit for the import-content in 1970–75 seems unlikely to exceed 9 per cent.

Much depends, of course, on the trade-creating effects of economic integration in Western Europe. If the tariff reductions now in progress within the

[1]See pages 132-3 and Tables 6.2 and 6.3.
[2]See Table 6.4 (which is on a c.i.f. basis).
[3]The United States import-content fell somewhat in 1960-61, largely as a result of reduced imports of passenger cars.

Fig. 15.1.   Import-content of supplies of manufactures in large industrial
countries (excluding the United States)[a], 1899–1975

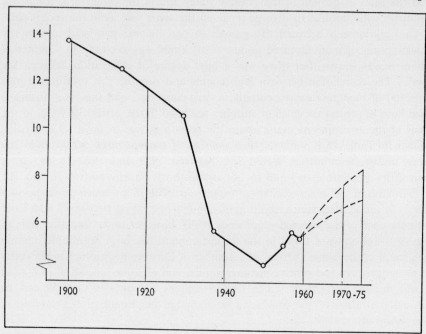

Percentage

[a]France, Italy, United Kingdom, West Germany and Japan.

European Economic Community increase the ratio of trade to production as
much as did the reduction of quantitative restrictions in the 1950's, then the
import-content of manufacturing supplies in the large industrial countries other
than the United States might rise to around 7–8 per cent, as shown by the
broken curves in Fig. 15.1.   The relaxation of quantitative restrictions on
imports of Japanese goods into Western European countries would work in the
same direction, though this is not likely to affect the overall import percentages
more than marginally.   This projection for 1970–75 may be optimistic, since
some allowance must be made for trade-diversion (for example, a fall in the
United States' share of these countries' imports), while Japan—which is also
in this group—is not likely to raise its own import-content of supplies of
manufactures so sharply as seems probable in Western Europe.

The application of these several assumptions about the import-content of
supplies to the projections for total supplies gives a range of estimates for the
probable increase in the volume of imports of manufactures into the large
industrial countries, as shown in Table 15.1.   If real income per head in all
the constituent countries grows at the same rate (3 per cent per annum), total

imports of manufactures would rise from 1959 to 1970–75 at 6–6½ per cent a year (mid-point of range). A higher rate of growth (7 per cent a year) would occur if the United States grew more slowly than the other large industrial countries, as in the 1950's, though the overall rate of growth in real income

Table 15.2. *Typical patterns of change in ' imports '[a] of manufactures into small industrial, semi-industrial and non-industrial countries, 1959 to 1970–75*

	Small industrial countries[b]	Semi-industrial countries[c]		Non-industrial countries[d]	
ASSUMED RATES OF GROWTH 1959 TO 1970–75	(*Annual percentage change (compound)*)				
Population	0.9	2.2		2.1	
		A	B	A	B
Real income per head	3.0	2.0	3.0	2.0	3.0
Import-content of supplies of manufactures[e]	(*Percentage*)				
1959	19.6	16.2		45–50	
1970–75	21–23	11–15		40–45	
Supplies[f] of manufactures	(*$ per head at 1955 prices*)				
1959	845	65		30–35	
1970–75	1,350	90	105	42–48	48–56
'Imports' of manufactures, f.o.b.					
1959	163	10.5		15.7	
1970–75	290–320	10–14	12–16	17–22	19–25
Total 'imports' of manufactures, f.o.b.	(*$ billion at 1955 prices*)				
1959	11.5	7.9		9.5	
1970–75	23–25	10–14	12–16	14–18	15–20
Rate of growth in total 'imports' of manufactures	(*Annual percentage change (compound)*)				
1950 to 1959	7.5	1.9		4.0	
1959 to 1970–75	5.3–5.9	1.8–4.3	3.1–5.4	2.9–4.8	3.4–5.7

Sources: Tables 6.4 and A.81; *Yearbook of International Trade Statistics, 1959*, United Nations, New York, 1960; *The Future Growth of World Population*, United Nations, New York, 1958 ('medium' assumption); *Monthly Bulletin of Statistics*, United Nations, New York, 1961.

[a]'Imports' from 11 main industrial countries; 'imports' from India are not included.
[b]Including Austria, Denmark and Finland.
[c]Including Greece, Ireland, Portugal and Spain.
[d]Excluding Soviet countries.
[e]Ratio of 'imports', f.o.b., to supplies; for ratio of imports, c.i.f., to supplies, see Table 6.4.
[f]As defined in footnote a in Table 6.4.

Note: In this and the following tables it is assumed that real income per head in the small industrial countries will rise by 3 per cent per annum, compound, between 1959 and 1970–75, and by either 2 per cent (assumption A), or 3 per cent (assumption B), per annum, compound, in the other countries.

per head remained at 3 per cent. A reduction in the overall rate of growth, to 2½ per cent a year, combined with a lower growth rate in the United States and a higher one in other large industrial countries (alternative III) yields the same rate of growth in imports of manufactures as does alternative II. On all these alternatives, the volume of per caput imports of manufactures into the United States in the early 1970's would be much less than in the other large industrial countries, whereas in the late 1950's the United States figure was higher.

For the small industrial countries, the various estimates for 1970–75 are shown in the first column of Table 15.2. Their average import-content of supplies was essentially unchanged, at about 20 per cent, in the latter half of the 1950's, but it seems probable that there will be some rise over the next ten years, reflecting the tariff reductions within the Common Market. Imports of manufactures per head are estimated almost to double between 1959 and 1970–75 on the assumptions made. Both Tables 15.1 and 15.2 show fairly wide ranges for the projected rates of growth in imports of manufactures; the uncertainties in these flows of trade are too great for more precise estimates to be made.

The semi-industrial and non-industrial countries

Exports of manufactures from the industrial to the semi-industrial countries have grown slowly in the post-war period. This reflects very largely the 'lag' in exports of primary produce from the semi-industrial group which has been discussed in Chapter 5. These countries have increased their supply of manufactured goods by industrial growth at home rather than by greater international exchange of primary produce for manufactures.

Since 1929, the semi-industrial countries have become much less dependent on imports for their supplies of manufactures, but it is unlikely that the past rate of reduction in the import-content of supplies will be maintained. Before the war their imports contained a large proportion of textiles and other consumer goods which could readily be replaced by the products of local industry, whereas now their imports consist in the main of capital equipment, chemicals and other metal products which it is more difficult to develop locally. At the same time, unless these countries can considerably expand their export trade and their capital inflow (the prospects of this are discussed below), they are likely to remain in balance of payments difficulties, which would place an upper limit on the rate of growth in their volume of imports of manufactures. The growth in real income per head in these primary-exporting countries is thus likely to depend heavily on further industrialization, and the import-content of supplies of manufactures will continue to fall.

To emphasize the area of doubt, rather a large range is assumed for the import-content of supplies of the semi-industrial countries in 1970–75. At the upper limit, the decline is only marginal; the lower limit implies a substantial further degree of import-substitution.

'Imports' of manufactures by the non-industrial countries showed a rapid rate of growth in the 1950's, due partly to increased investment in the oil industry in a few countries, but mainly to a better export performance than was achieved by the semi-industrial group and to an increased flow of loans and aid. Though these countries are termed 'non-industrial', they all produce manufactured goods of some kind and some, for example Egypt and Southern Rhodesia, already have a fairly well-developed industrial sector. In future, it must be expected that such countries will generally tend to follow the phases of development experienced earlier by the present semi-industrial group. Thus the import-content of supplies of manufactures in this group must be expected to fall in the future as the process of industrialization develops in a number of countries. However, it does not seem likely that the import-content will be substantially reduced over the next decade or so for this group of countries in the aggregate, and in Table 15.2 only a marginal decline has been assumed.

At the lower rate of growth assumed for real income per head (2 per cent a year), supplies of manufactures per head would increase from 1959 to 1970–75 by some two-fifths in both the semi-industrial and non-industrial countries (taking the mid-points of the ranges shown for the latter group), or at $2\frac{1}{2}$ per cent a year. Similarly, on the higher growth assumption (real income per head rising by 3 per cent a year), supplies of manufactures per head in each group of countries would rise by some $3\frac{1}{2}$ per cent a year. By contrast, the corresponding increases in 'imports' of manufactures per head would be markedly different, because of the possibility of further substantial import-substitution in the semi-industrial countries. On the lower growth assumption, the annual rate of change in 'imports' per head would range from $-\frac{1}{2}$ to $+2$ per cent for the semi-industrial countries, compared with a range of $+1$ to $+3$ per cent for the non-industrial group; on the higher growth assumption, the difference would be equally great ($+\frac{1}{2}$ to $+2\frac{1}{2}$ per cent a year for the former and $+1\frac{1}{2}$ to $+3\frac{1}{2}$ a year for the latter).

Taking all four groups of countries together, the expansion in total 'imports' of manufactures from 1959 to 1970–75 is estimated, on the various assumptions made, at some \$40–45 billion[1]; the annual average in the later period would thus be approximately double the 1959 volume (\$42 billion)[1]. The rise projected for imports by the industrial countries would account for the bulk (between two-thirds and three-quarters) of the total expansion—marginally less than during the 1950's (see Table 15.3). Even on the lower growth assumption, these estimates show an appreciable increase in the relative contribution of the semi-industrial countries to the expansion in world imports of manufactures, compared with the 1950's; on the higher growth assumption, the relative contribution of this group of countries would double—though it should be remembered that these higher figures assume that no serious external payments

[1]Valued at 1955 f.o.b. prices.

difficulties would arise. Little change is projected in the relative share of the non-industrial areas in the expansion in world imports of manufactures on the lower growth assumption, though at the higher rate of growth there would be a marginal rise in their share.

Table 15.3. *Changes in 'imports' of manufactures into industrial, semi-industrial and non-industrial countries, 1959 to 1970–75*

	Industrial countries		Semi-industrial countries		Non-industrial countries^b		Total^b	
	Large	Small						
			($ billion, f.o.b., at 1955 prices)					
Change from								
1950 to 1959	+ 8.0	+ 5.5	+ 1.2		+ 2.8		+ 17.5	
1959 to 1970–75^a								
Alternative			A	B	A	B	A	B
I	+16½	+12½	+4	+6	+6½	+8	+39½	+43
II and III	+19½						+42½	+46
			(*Percentage of total*)					
Change from								
1950 to 1959	46	31	7		16		100	
1959 to 1970–75								
Alternative								
I	38–42	29–32	10–14		16–19		100	
II and III	42–46	27–30	9–13		15–18		100	

Sources: Tables 15.1, 15.2, A.6, A.13 and A.81.
^aTaking the mid-points of the estimates in Tables 15.1 and 15.2.
^bExcluding Soviet countries.

The effect on the estimates of changing the assumptions about the future level of the import-content of supplies would be much greater for the large industrial countries than for the other groups; a change of one percentage point in the import-content would make a difference of $5–6 billion in the estimates for total 'imports' for the former, but of only $1 billion for each of the other country groups. Thus, if the import-content in the large industrial countries in 1970–75 was no higher than in 1959, the increase over the period in their total 'imports' of manufactures would be only some $11–12 billion on assumption I and $15 billion on assumptions II and III. Even so, the expansion in the intra-trade of the industrial countries would still be the dominant feature of world trade.

Changes in the assumptions about the rates of growth in the different areas would also affect the estimates significantly. The difference made to the estimate of total 'imports' of manufactures by changing from a 2 per cent to a 3 per cent annual rate of growth, for example, would be about $4–5 billion for the large industrial countries, compared with $3 billion for the small industrial countries, $2 billion for the semi-industrial and $1–2 billion for the non-industrial.

Various combinations of these assumptions would yield a greater or lesser expansion in the import trade of the industrial countries compared with that of the rest of the world. On balance, though, it seems reasonable to conclude that the trade development of the 1960's is likely to be similar to that of the 1950's, insofar as trade between the industrial countries will be the main dynamic sector. However, the disparities in the rates of growth in the different sectors of world trade are not likely to be so great as in the recent past.

2. ECONOMIC GROWTH AND THE BALANCE OF PAYMENTS PROBLEM OF THE PRIMARY-PRODUCING AREAS

The increase in the imports of manufactures by the semi-industrial and non-industrial areas which would be required, on the various assumptions made, to support even a rate of growth as low as 2 per cent per head a year, is substantial, compared with the 1950's, and the implications of such an increase need further consideration in the light of the balance of payments position and prospects of these areas.

Table 15.4. *Exports of primary products and manufactures from industrial, primary-producing and Soviet countries, 1953–60*

	Exports in 1960 from			Change from 1953		
	Industrial countries[a]	Primary-producing countries	Soviet countries	Industrial countries	Primary-producing countries	Soviet countries[b]
	($ billion, f.o.b.)			(Percentage)		
Food	11.5	10.5	2.6	+ 44	+ 10	..
Industrial materials	8.4	8.4	2.2	+ 71	+ 24	..
Fuels	3.3	7.7	1.7	+ 23	+ 63	..
Total, primary products	23.2	26.6	6.5	+ 49	+ 26	..
Manufactures	55.3	4.4	8.4	+ 93	+ 41	..
TOTAL[c]	79.6	31.3	15.0	+ 76	+ 28	+ 90
of which, exports to:						
Industrial countries	52.4	21.8	2.8	+ 86	+ 24	+134
Primary-producing countries	23.9	7.6	1.3	+ 51	+ 23	+195
Soviet countries	2.8	1.4	10.8	+218	+243	+ 76

Source: International Trade, 1961, G.A.T.T., Geneva, 1962.

[a]North America, Western Europe and Japan.
[b]Commodity detail for 1953 is not available.
[c]Including exports not classified by commodity group.

Since 1950, the semi-industrial countries have, without exception, been in balance of payments difficulties for some part, if not the whole, of the period and imports have had to be limited in one way or another by most of them. In volume terms, imports of manufactures per head by the semi-industrial countries in 1959 were no higher than in 1950. If we assume that in the coming decade or so these semi-industrial countries will have to restrict imports for balance of payments reasons to the same degree as in the past decade, then the expansion in their imports would essentially reflect the increase in their population[1]. On this basis, the total in 1970–75 would be $10\frac{1}{2}$ billion, an increase of $2\frac{1}{2}$ billion (one-third) from the 1959 level. It might, however, rise to about $14 billion (mid-point of range in Table 15.2) if they could support a 3 per cent a year rate of growth. A similar calculation for the non-industrial group would put their 1970–75 average level of imports at some $12\frac{1}{2}$ billion, if imports per head were restricted to the 1959 level for balance of payments reasons. This would, however, be too pessimistic, since this group includes the oil countries (some of which have no foreseeable payments problems) as well as many countries whose staple export products enjoy reasonably high rates of growth in demand.

The possibility of supporting such increases in imports depends essentially on the prospects of expanding exports to the industrial countries and of receiving more loans and grants from them. The next section examines the export prospects of the primary-producing countries as a preliminary to an assessment of the amount of aid required to support a given rate of economic growth.

Imports by the industrial countries

Over the past decade, exports from the primary-producing areas have grown slowly relatively to other sectors of world trade. This reflects not only the unusually rapid increase in world trade in manufactures, but also the slower growth in exports of primary products from the primary-producing than from the industrial countries. In the period 1953–60, for example, exports of primary products from the industrial areas rose in value by 50 per cent, whereas only half that rate of growth was achieved by the primary-producing countries themselves (Table 15.4). The same relationship held for manufactures: exports from the industrial countries rose by some 90 per cent, while the small exports from other countries rose by little more than 40 per cent. In food and industrial materials—the principal exports of the majority of non-industrial countries —the margin in favour of exports from the industrial countries has been exceptionally great; in food, for instance, the industrial countries expanded

[1] It is not suggested that population is a determinant of imports independently of income; but, for illustrative purposes, an actual reduction in imports per head below the 1950 level can be taken as some kind of lower limit.

their exports from 1953 to 1960 by over 40 per cent as against only 10 per cent for the other countries. Thus, by 1960 the industrial countries exported more food, about as much industrial materials, but less than half the oil, than did the primary-producing countries.

Taking food and industrial materials together, exports from the primary-producing countries rose by only 15 per cent in value from 1953 to 1960; if manufactures, but not fuels, are included the increase is somewhat higher, 20 per cent. The striking development in the period has been the growth in the trade in oil, which accounted for over 40 per cent of the increase in exports from the primary-producing countries in these seven years. Fuels are exported by relatively few countries, and their inclusion in the figures obscures the magnitude of the export problem which faces the majority of the primary-producing countries. For the latter, the vital question is whether their export performance during the 1950's can be substantially improved upon. The export prospects for the main non-fuel commodities are considered below.

(a) *Food and industrial materials.* A detailed analysis of changes in the volume of commodity exports from the primary-producing to the industrial countries during the 1950's has shown that three distinct factors have been at work within the industrial countries, all of which have tended to retard the growth in their imports of primary products[1]. The first has been a shift in the pattern of demand with economic growth. In foodstuffs, the higher level of real incomes has meant an increased demand for meat—particularly in the United States—in relation to foods such as tropical beverages; and since meat has a low import-content compared with, say, coffee and cocoa, this has reduced the proportion of consumers' expenditure which ultimately goes to the primary-producing countries. In the industrial sphere, too, the changing pattern of demand consequent on economic growth has worked adversely for the primary-producers. The principal change in pattern, as was shown in Chapter 2, is the relatively fast rate of growth in demand for capital goods, chemicals and durable consumer goods, all of which have a low import-content, while the demand for textiles and clothing, with a high content of imported materials, tends to grow relatively slowly. These, and similar, changes in the pattern of demand in the industrial countries, insofar as they are associated with rising standards of living, must be expected to continue in future.

The second factor at work has been technological change, particularly the development of synthetic substitutes for natural materials. Synthetic detergents have made great inroads into the market for vegetable oils for soap;

---

[1] A. Maizels, *Recent Trends in World Trade*, a paper presented to a Conference on 'Trade in a Developing World', held by the International Economic Association, 1961. See also K. Jones, A. Maizels and J. Whittaker, 'The Demand for Food in the Industrial Countries, 1948–1960', *National Institute Economic Review*, No. 20, May 1962; *Economic Survey of Europe in 1957* (Chapter IV), United Nations, Geneva, 1958; *World Economic Survey, 1958*, United Nations, New York, 1959; and recent annual reports of G.A.T.T.

plastics have been substituted for non-ferrous metals, leather and other natural products; and synthetic fibres have displaced cotton and wool[1]. Technical developments have also found new uses for aluminium, which has been substituted for the traditional non-ferrous metals, as well as for steel and other materials; since bauxite imports represent only a small fraction of the value of aluminium production, this substitution has had an unfavourable effect on the exports of non-ferrous ores and metals from non-industrial countries. An important element in extending the market for these 'new' products has been their relative price stability, compared with the price fluctuation experienced for most agricultural and mineral products. Again, one must expect this general trend to continue. Technological development may well speed up, rather than diminish; while the process of substituting synthetic for natural products, which so far has gone much further in the United States than elsewhere, is likely to spread much more in the other industrial countries during the 1960's (even if the process comes to a halt—which is unlikely—in the United States).

Finally, the fiscal and protectionist policies of the industrial countries have had an important retarding effect on the growth of their imports of foodstuffs and manufactured goods. In foodstuffs, all the industrial countries protect their farmers from competing imports; the particular technique of protection varies considerably—import quotas, tariffs, subsidies and price support schemes are all involved—but the general effect is to shift a substantial proportion of world output of temperate-zone products to the industrial countries from the primary-producing areas. The most important commodities affected are cereals, sugar, oils and oilseeds and dairy products. In addition, several industrial countries impose duties for purely fiscal reasons on tropical beverages, which significantly restrict the consumption of these products. There has also been a considerable amount of substitution resulting from such protectionist and fiscal measures. Perhaps the most important single example is the United States price-support policy for soya-beans, which has encouraged a large increase in output and a major substitution of soya for oilseeds from the less-developed areas.

(b) *Manufactures.* The relatively slow expansion in exports of manufactures from the primary-producing countries (see Table 15.4) is only partly explicable by the fact that a large part of these exports consists of textiles for which demand in the industrial countries has been expanding at a slower rate than for other manufactures. A second factor has been that most industrial countries impose import duties or quotas on such 'low cost' imports[2]. Britain has been exceptional in allowing free entry of textiles from India, Pakistan and Hong

---

[1]See J. A. Rowlatt and F. T. Blackaby, 'The Demand for Industrial Materials, 1950-57', *National Institute Economic Review*, No. 5, September 1959.

[2]See the more detailed discussion of trends in exports of manufactures from the semi-industrial countries on pages 75–8 and page 370.

Kong, but imports of cotton goods have been limited in recent years by voluntary agreements between the industries concerned, while imports of jute manufactures have been subject to a price 'mark up' to prevent them undercutting the Dundee product.

Taken together, exports of food, industrial materials and manufactures from the primary-producing to the industrial countries rose by 12 per cent in value from 1953 to 1960. In volume terms, the rise was probably about 20 per cent, compared with a rise of some 30 per cent in total real incomes in the industrial countries[1]. As already indicated, the long-term influences retarding the rate of growth of exports (other than oil) from the primary-producing countries are partly technological and structural, and partly a result of government policies. Such technological and structural changes must be expected to continue and, unless there is a drastic relaxation in the protectionist policies of the industrial countries, it seems reasonable to conclude that the volume of non-oil exports from the primary-producing to the industrial countries will continue to increase at an average rate only about two-thirds as fast as real incomes in the latter group. This conclusion is generally supported by some detailed estimates of the probable increase in the industrial countries' imports of primary commodities published by the United Nations[2].

The balance of payments prospect

These general assessments of the probable trends in the foreign trade of the non-oil primary-producing countries can be used in constructing a tentative balance of payments statement for them. It will be useful, to begin with, to review the main trends during the 1950's. The first three columns in Table 15.5 show how the main elements in the balance of payments of these countries changed from 1953[3] to 1958–60.

On the debit side, there was an increase of nearly $5 billion in imports of manufactures, accounting for the bulk of the increase in the total. From 1953 to 1958–60, total imports of primary products, as shown in Table 15.5, rose in value by 28 per cent, or by about two-thirds of the percentage rise in imports of manufactures (nearly 45 per cent). These primary products cover three separate classes of trade: commercial shipments, Commodity Aid and petroleum

---

[1] If the increases in real incomes in North America and Western Europe are weighted by their respective values of imports from primary-producing countries, the overall rise from 1953 to 1960 was 35 per cent.

[2] The Economic Commission for Europe estimated the volume of primary product imports (excluding fuels but including base metals) into North America and Western Europe in 1975 as 47 or 62 per cent above the 1954–6 level, according to the assumptions made about rates of economic growth. These two percentages are both about two-thirds of the corresponding percentage increases assumed in the real product of these two areas. (See *Economic Survey of Europe, 1957*, United Nations, Geneva, 1958, Ch. V.)

[3] 1953 is the first year for which a detailed trade table is available on this basis.

Table 15.5. *Trade and payments position of the primary-producing areas (excluding petroleum-exporting countries)[a], 1953, 1958–60 and 1970–75*

	1953	1958–60	Change from 1953 to 1958–60	1970–75		Change from 1958–60 to 1970–75	
	($ billion)			($ billion at 1958–60 prices)			
				A	B	A	B
DEBITS							
Imports, f.o.b. from the industrial countries[b]							
Manufactures	11.0	15.8	+ 4.8	26[c]	29½[c]	+10	+13½
Primary products[d]	4.7	6.0	+ 1.3	9	10	+ 3	+ 4
Net payments for freight and insurance, interest on foreign investments and other services	1.7	1.9	+ 0.2	3	3½	+ 1	+ 1½
Total	17.4	23.7	+ 6.3	38	43	+14	+19
CREDITS							
Exports, f.o.b. to the industrial countries	15.0	16.8	+ 1.8	25[e]	25[e]	+ 8	+ 8
Net long-term capital receipts and official grants	3.5		+ 1.9⎱				
Other net capital receipts and balancing items	− 0.2[g]	1.5	+ 1.7⎰	13[f]	18[f]	+ 6	+11
Drawings on reserves	− 0.9	—	+ 0.9	—	—	—	—
Total	17.4	23.7	+ 6.3	38	43	+14	+19

Sources: Table 15.2; *International Trade, 1961*, G.A.T.T., Geneva, 1962; *Balance of Payments Yearbook*, Vol. 13, International Monetary Fund, 1962; *International Economic Assistance to the Less Developed Countries*, United Nations, New York, 1961; *The Flow of Financial Resources to Countries in Course of Economic Development, 1956–1959*, O.E.E.C., Paris, 1961; *Development Assistance Efforts and Policies in 1961*, O.E.C.D., Paris, 1962; *International Financial Statistics*, International Monetary Fund, monthly, 1962.

[a]Outside Europe and the Soviet countries.
[b]Western Europe, North America and Japan.
[c]Based on mid-points of estimates shown in Table 15.2.
[d]Including imports of petroleum from countries in Latin America and the Middle East ($2.0 billion in 1953 and $2.6 billion in 1958–60), and Commodity Aid (about $1.4 billion in 1958–60).
[e]Assuming an increase over 1958–60 of two-thirds the rate of growth in real income in the industrial countries (i.e. 48 per cent as against 70 per cent).
[f]Residual.
[g]Including the monetary equivalent of Commodity Aid.

imported from non-industrial countries. Commodity Aid, which averaged $1.4 billion in 1958–60, is included since some allowance must be made for the probability of an appreciable further expansion, particularly in the shipment of surplus grains from North America and some countries in Western Europe; the monetary counterpart is included under 'Other net capital receipts'. Petroleum is purchased from the international oil companies, whether it is shipped from the producing countries in Latin America and the Middle East, or routed for refining through the industrial countries; in either case, the credit accrues, in effect, to the industrial countries.

On the credit side, the expansion in exports—nearly $2 billion—financed less than one-third of the increase in imports of goods and services, the remaining two-thirds being met by borrowing from the industrial countries (including loans from the international agencies) and by gifts in money or as Commodity Aid.

The implications for the balance of payments of the primary-producing areas of the increases in imports of manufactures envisaged in Table 15.2 can be assessed if specific assumptions are made about the other debit items and about exports. In the last four columns of Table 15.5 a possible balance of payments account is constructed on this basis.

The figures for imports of manufactures in 1970–75 are those given in Table 15.2, allowing for exports to the oil countries and for some increase in prices between 1955 and 1958–60. For primary products, the rise between 1958–60 and 1970–75 has been assumed to be two-thirds as fast as in manufactures (as it was during the 1950's), while net invisible payments are assumed, arbitrarily, to rise at the same rate as total merchandise imports. Total debits, on these assumptions, would rise by $14 billion at constant prices (about 60 per cent) over the period, on assumption A, and by $19 billion (80 per cent) on assumption B.

It was argued earlier that the volume of exports from this group of countries might expand at an average rate of some two-thirds of that in real income in the industrial countries. On this basis, exports would rise by about 50 per cent—not far short of the percentage increase in debits on assumption A, but considerably below that on assumption B. It can reasonably be assumed that monetary reserves will not in general be large enough to make a significant contribution to closing the payments gap, which is shown in the table as being met entirely by foreign loans and grants.

On assumption A (2 per cent a year increase in real income per head), the net inflow of loans and grants in 1970–75 would need to be virtually double the average level of 1958–60 ($13 billion as against almost $7 billion), if short-term finance and Commodity Aid are included as well as long-term capital. On the higher growth assumption, B, of 3 per cent a year, net capital requirements would rise to $18 billion, or 2½ times the 1958–60 level. These estimates are presented purely to illustrate possible orders of magnitude on various assumptions.

A major unknown, which has not so far been discussed, is the future movement in the terms of trade of the primary-producing areas. From 1953 to 1958–60, average export prices of the non-oil primary-producing countries fell by about 8 per cent, while their import prices rose by about 6 per cent. If export prices recovered, by 1970–75, to the 1953 level, this would add another $2 billion to their export earnings in that period provided, of course, that the price rise had no adverse repercussions on the quantity sold. It is not very likely, however, that their import prices would fall if primary product prices were rising. Moreover, any substantial improvement in the terms of trade above the 1953 level seems improbable, unless the rate of income growth in the industrial countries considerably exceeds that assumed here, or unless the rate of growth in world supplies of primary produce falls off drastically. The operation of international commodity agreements is likely to mitigate any deterioration in primary commodity prices that may occur, but they cannot be expected to lead to a sustained swing in the other direction.

The other major uncertainty concerns the level of exports to the industrial countries. If technological and scientific progress intensifies, the rate of substitution of synthetic for natural materials might increase. Moreover, a faster rate of growth in the industrial countries than assumed here, if achieved, might well be associated with a sharper shift in demand and output patterns away from the traditional export products of the primary-producing countries. If their exports were to rise only *half* as fast as real incomes in the industrial countries, instead of the two-thirds assumed here, this alone would worsen their payments position by $2 billion a year in the early 1970's.

These various estimates all assume that government restrictions in the industrial countries on imports from the primary-producing countries are continued in much the same degree as in 1958–60. A substantial relaxation here would have a major beneficial effect on the payments position of the developing countries. The implications of such a relaxation are further considered at the end of this chapter.

Trade with the Soviet countries

The discussion so far has excluded the small, but growing trade between the primary-producing countries and the Soviet group. Exports of manufactures from the Soviet countries to the rest of the world, though expanding quite fast in recent years, are still only a small proportion of world trade. In 1960, for example, such exports represented only about 4 per cent of world exports of manufactures, if the intra-trade among the Soviet countries is excluded, or 12 per cent if that intra-trade is included (see Table 15.4). The prospects for expanding trade between the Soviet countries and the underdeveloped areas depend on several factors. The first is the extent to which changes in the pattern of demand and output in the Soviet group influence the trend of their imports[1]. Another question is how far the Soviet countries will absorb increasing quantities of the simpler types of manufactures from the less-developed countries. Again, this is a question of adapting an existing industrial structure to 'low-cost' imports, but insofar as their rate of economic growth is higher, this should be less difficult for the Soviet group than for the Western industrial countries. Finally, much will depend on the willingness of the Soviet countries to extend long-term credits for the purchase of capital equipment. Since 1956, the Soviet Union has granted a series of long-term credits in conjunction with economic agreements with a number of under-developed countries, and a further expansion in long-term credit facilities seems probable to finance an expansion in this trade[2].

3. TRENDS IN THE COMMODITY PATTERN OF WORLD TRADE IN MANUFACTURES

Changes in the broad commodity pattern of world trade in manufactures since the beginning of the century have been definite and unambiguous. As shown in Chapter 7, the main commodity groups can readily be divided into the three categories of 'expanding', 'stable' and 'declining', by fitting a straight-line trend to the movement in the percentage share of each group in the total current value of trade in manufactures, or to that in the relative volume index for each group[3]. The two methods give broadly the same picture, with some important exceptions, of which the outstanding one is that chemicals are 'stable' on current value, but are 'expanding' if the volume basis is used. Such differences are due essentially to an association between technological progress and industrial growth. Industries like chemicals and transport equipment, which have been growing much more rapidly than others, also tend to be the industries where technological progress is most rapid, and where output prices tend to fall, in the long run, in relation to the output prices of other industries.

---

[1]Published plans for the period up to 1965 for the Soviet Union and several other East European countries indicate large increases in the production of many agricultural products, including tea, rice, oils and oilseeds and sugar, as well as of synthetic rubber (see *Economic Survey of Europe in 1960*, United Nations, Geneva, 1961).

[2]Economic assistance by the Soviet countries to the under-developed countries in Africa, Asia and Latin America under bilateral agreements increased substantially between 1955 and 1960. In both 1959 and 1960, the total of new credits announced exceeded $950 million, most of which were for India, Indonesia, Iraq, Egypt, Cuba and Ethiopia (see *International Flow of Long-term Capital and Official Donations, 1951–1959*, United Nations, New York, 1961). Actual annual drawings on credits would be considerably less than the total credits extended.

[3]The relative volume index is the volume index for a commodity group expressed as a percentage of the volume index for all manufactures (see page 167 and Table 7.5).

Value pattern

Since these past trends have been so marked, there is some point in projecting them into the future. This can be done in a purely mechanical way to start with, in order to derive an hypothetical pattern of trade. Table 15.6 shows the hypothetical patterns for the period 1970–75 on both the value and volume bases, derived by applying the trend co-efficients for the period 1937–57 to the position in 1959. On the value basis, the main changes—if the past trends in pattern continued in the future—would be that by 1970–75 one-half of total trade in manufactures would consist of machinery and transport equipment, compared with two-fifths in 1959; and that textiles and clothing, which had fallen from one-fifth in 1937 to one-tenth in 1959, would decline still further, to only 5 per cent, by 1970–75.

Table 15.6.   *Commodity pattern of world trade[a] in manufactures, 1937 to 1970–75*

	Proportion of current value			Relative volume[b]		
	1937	1959	1970–75[c]	1937	1959	1970–75[c]
	(Percentage)			*(Indices, 1929 = 100)*		
Metals	15.3	13.5	13–14	106	90	83
Machinery	16.0	24.8	30	94	131	157
Transport equipment	10.5	16.5	20	105	155	189
Other metal goods	6.5	4.2	3	87	53	35
Chemicals	10.6	12.0	12–13	112	196	237
Textiles and clothing	21.5	11.1	5	101	52	19
Other manufactures	19.5	17.9	16–17	101	96 ·	91
TOTAL	100.0	100.0	100	100	100	100

Sources: Tables 7.1, 7.4 and 7.5.

[a]Exports from 12 main exporting countries.
[b]Volume index for each group as percentage of index for total manufactures.
[c]Based on regression co-efficients for the period 1937–57, as given in Table 7.5.

It is unlikely, however, that the past trends will continue unmodified in the future. The reduction since 1937 in the share of textiles, for instance, resulted largely from import-substitution in the semi-industrial countries[1], which now import very small quantities indeed. The scope for further large-scale substitution against textile imports is thus greatly reduced. Moreover, it may well be that the intra-trade of the industrial countries in textiles will increase rather than decline. The 1970–75 percentage is therefore likely to be higher than the 5 per cent shown by the mechanical projection; indeed, if the past trend continued unchanged the percentage for textiles and clothing would be reduced to zero around the year 1975, which does not seem a plausible result.

[1]See page 346.

Equally, the percentage shown for machinery and transport equipment in 1970–75 (50 per cent) may turn out to be too high. A mechanical projection of the trend shows that these two groups would account for the whole of trade in manufactures by the year 2050. Again, this is not plausible, but the change in trend may well begin after 1970–75 rather than before it.

Volume pattern

A more useful assessment of the probable changes in trading pattern can be made from the trends in volume. These show (second part of Table 15.6) a sharp increase in the relative volume of trade in chemicals, as well as in machinery and transport equipment; and an even sharper relative decline in textiles. These indices can be translated into value figures only by making an assumption about the movement in the total volume of trade in manufactures. In the discussion of the probable future trend, total exports from the industrial countries (other than to the Soviet countries) were estimated to rise from about $42 billion in 1959 to $74–88 billion in 1970–75 on alternative I for the large industrial countries and assumption A for the semi-industrial and non-industrial countries, and $80–95 billion on alternatives II and III and assumption B, respectively. Exports of manufactures from the main Western industrial

Table 15.7. *Changes in the volume of world trade*[a] *in manufactures by main commodity group, 1937 to 1970–75*

| | | | | $ billion at 1955 prices | |
| | | | | Change from | |
	1937	1959	1970–75[b]	1937 to 1959	1959 to 1970–75
Metals	3.3	6.2	11½	+ 2.9	+ 5½
Machinery	3.2	9.7	24	+ 6.5	+14
Transport equipment	2.1	6.9	17	+ 4.8	+10
Other metal goods	1.2	1.7	2½	+ 0.5	+ 1
Chemicals	1.5	5.7	14½	+ 4.2	+ 9
Textiles and clothing	4.4	5.0	3½	+ 0.6	− 1½
Other manufactures	3.7	7.7	15	+ 4.0	+ 7
TOTAL[c]	19.4	42.9	88	+ 23.5	+45

Sources: Tables 15.6, A.6 and A.80.

[a]Exports from 11 main industrial countries.

[b]Estimates based on relative volume indices in Table 15.6, assuming total exports of manufactures from the 11 main industrial countries in 1970–75 average about $88 billion at 1955 prices.

[c]Including exports to Soviet countries.

countries to the Soviet countries in 1959 totalled rather more than $1 billion. The size of this trade in the early 1970's cannot be estimated by examining past trends, or current indicators.   There is undoubtedly scope for a large increase in the volume of East-West trade, both in manufactures and in primary products.   For present purposes, however, it suffices to make an arbitrary assumption that exports of manufactures to the Soviet countries in 1970–75 will be in the range of $3–5 billion (at 1955 prices).   Taking also assumption A as probably the more realistic for the economic growth of the primary-producing areas, and either alternative II or III for the industrial countries, total exports of manufactures from the main industrial countries in 1970–75 can be put at about $88 billion at 1955 prices (with a margin of error of perhaps 10 per cent either way).

The application of the relative volume indices for 1970–75 given in Table 15.6 to a total trade of $88 billion results in a set of estimates of the value of trade in each commodity group (see Table 15.7).   On this basis, machinery and transport equipment together would contribute about 50–55 per cent of the total expansion in trade in manufactures from 1959 to 1970–75, as against rather less than 60 per cent between 1937 and 1959.   The relative contribution of chemicals would also rise, though slightly, and that of most of the other groups would fall.   The relative importance of the different groups in 1970–75 would be broadly similar to that shown for current values in Tables 15.6, except that chemicals would represent about one-sixth of the total on the volume basis, compared with only one-eighth in terms of current values.

Area and commodity patterns

An alternative approach to the problem is to consider the pattern of imports into different groups of countries separately.   The distinction could be of some importance since, as was shown earlier, the proportion of capital goods in the imports of the semi-industrial countries, for example, is considerably greater than in those of the other areas, while the corresponding proportion is relatively small for the large industrial countries[1].   There are other significant differences in the commodity pattern of imports of the various groups of countries.

The pattern of 'imports' of manufactures in 1959 is set out in Table 15.8 for five main groups of manufactures and four groups of countries.   The projections to 1970–75 could not, however, be made on the same basis as those in Tables 15.1 and 15.2, since estimates of consumption of manufactures could not be made for all the separate commodity groups.   Instead, the import growth co-efficients presented in Table 7.14, which show the average past long-term relationship between imports in each commodity group and real income per head, have been used to project the 1970–75 import levels by commodity group.

[1]See pages 174–8

This approach has two main limitations, which together tend to produce a rather larger margin of error than the method used earlier. First, the commodity regressions summarised in Table 7.14 relate to a long period of time, during much of which the level of international trade was artificially restricted. The resulting import growth co-efficients are therefore generally too low to apply to trading conditions in the 1960's. For all manufactures, for example, the import growth co-efficient for the industrial countries in Table 7.14 was 1.01, whereas for the period 1959 to 1970–75 the corresponding co-efficients implied in Table 15.1 for the large industrial countries are 2.05, 2.35 and 3.05 for alternatives I, II and III, respectively, while for the small industrial countries, the implied co-efficient (in Table 15.2) is 1.79[1]. For the semi-industrial countries, the difference from the previous result is also large, the import growth co-efficient in Table 7.14 being 0.22, whereas Table 15.2 implies co-efficients of 0.48 (assumption A) and 0.67 (assumption B).

A purely mechanical solution of the difficulty would be to inflate the separate commodity co-efficients in the same ratio as the total co-efficients; for example, by the ratio 1.79 : 1.01 for the small industrial countries. However, it is probable that an increase in the overall rate of growth would also widen the disparities between the various commodity co-efficients; trade in capital goods and chemicals, for example, would then probably grow faster in relation to trade in, say, metals than would be indicated by the relevant co-efficients. Moreover, it has been argued earlier that the rate of import-substitution against textiles is likely to be considerably less in future than it has been in the past. Clearly, no infallible solution is possible; the procedure used was to begin with a mechanical inflation of the commodity co-efficients as suggested above, and then to adjust the 'inflated' co-efficients arbitrarily in the light of the other considerations mentioned. As will be seen later, the adjustments made to the co-efficients for textiles make a big difference to the projection for trade in this group in 1970–75. For the large industrial countries, the co-efficients were adjusted to be consistent with the earlier calculations for alternative II.

The second limitation is that, owing to lack of data on real income, import growth co-efficients could not be calculated for the non-industrial countries. The overall co-efficient for this group implied by the calculations in Table 15.2 is 0.8 (on both assumptions A and B) which lies between the unadjusted co-efficient for the industrial countries, and the adjusted one for the semi-industrial countries. A set of co-efficients was then selected for the non-industrial countries which appeared to be consistent with those for the other country groups, and which also gave a total volume of imports consistent with the projections in Table 15.2.

The results of this computation are summarized in percentage form in

---

[1] These co-efficients are simply the ratios of the percentage increases in imports per head taking mid-points of ranges) to percentage increases in real income per head.

Table 15.8. *Typical commodity-patterns of ' imports ' into industrial, semi-industrial and non-industrial countries, 1959 and* 1970–75

	Metals	Capital goods	Chemi-cals	Textiles and clothing	Other manu-factures[b]	Total
		Percentage of total 'imports' of manufactures[a]				
Large industrial countries						
1959	18.8	23.8	11.1	10.0	36.3	100
1970–75 (Alternative II)	18	29	13	8	32	100
Small industrial countries[c]						
1959	11.6	37.0	11.4	10.7	29.3	100
1970–75	10	45	13	7	25	100
Semi-industrial countries[d]						
1959	10.6	48.1	13.4	7.3	20.6	100
1970–75 A	8	56	14	6	16	100
B	8	58	15	5	14	100
Non-industrial countries[e]						
1959	9.3	35.9	12.5	17.1	25.2	100
1970–75 A	8	41	14	15	22	100
B	8	43	14	13	22	100
TOTAL[e]						
1959	13.1	34.8	12.0	11.3	28.8	100
1970–75[f]A	12	41	13	9	25	100
B	12	42	13	8	25	100

Sources: Tables 7.14, 15.1 and A.81.

[a] Valued at 1959 prices.
[b] Including passenger road vehicles and 'other metal goods'.
[c] Including Austria, Denmark and Finland.
[d] Including Greece, Ireland, Portugal and Spain.
[e] Excluding Soviet countries.
[f] Using mid-points of estimates for the four groups of countries in Tables 15.1 and 15.2 s weights.

Table 15.8. This shows that the commodity pattern of world trade[1] in 1970–75 would be unlikely to vary significantly according to whether the rate of growth in the semi-industrial and non-industrial areas is taken at 2 per cent or 3 per cent per annum. In either case, capital goods would probably make up about two-fifths of the total, chemicals one-eighth, and textiles and clothing under one-tenth, on the assumptions made.

The increase in the proportion of capital goods and chemicals in the total seems likely to hold good for all four groups of countries. Moreover, the higher the rate of growth assumed, the greater is likely to be the relative

[1] The calculations exclude 'imports' by Soviet countries, but this is not likely to distort the results significantly.

importance of capital goods and chemicals in the total. An exception to this latter relationship could, however, arise in the semi-industrial countries, if they were still experiencing balance of payments difficulties in the early 1970's sufficient to prevent them from achieving a rate of growth in excess of 2 per cent per annum. In that case, they might choose to restrict or reduce their imports of consumer goods so as to maximise their supplies of capital equipment, chemicals and other 'essentials'. If, on the other hand, their balance of payments allowed them a more rapid rate of growth, their import policy might well be less restrictionist, so that the relative importance of capital goods and chemicals would be less, not more, than if their rate of economic growth were lower. In either case, the relative importance of these two 'development goods' categories is likely to be substantially higher in the imports of the semi-industrial countries than elsewhere.

The estimates in Table 15.8 for the commodity pattern of world trade in manufactures in the early 1970's also depend very much on whether the growth rate in the industrial countries averages 3 per cent per annum; and, even more, whether, and to what extent, the rate of growth diverges from the average in particular countries. As mentioned earlier, a faster rate of growth in the United States relatively to that in the other industrial countries would reduce the impact on trade of a given rate of economic growth. It would also reduce the relative importance of capital goods and chemicals in the imports of the industrial areas as a whole[1]. A higher rate of growth in the small, than in the large, industrial countries would, however, accentuate the present general trends in the commodity pattern of world trade.

Patterns of production and export

Though somewhat different commodity patterns can be arrived at according to the different assumptions made, the general pattern is essentially a continuation of the previous trend, with the possible exception of the trade in textiles. The pattern of manufacturing production in the industrial countries must also be expected to change, and this change is likely to be similar to that in their exports of manufactures. The relation between economic growth in the industrial countries and their output by major industry group was examined in Chapter 2, where growth co-efficients were calculated for five non-food industries[2]. If these co-efficients are applied to an assumed increase of 70 per cent[3] in total real income from 1959 to 1970–75, the increase in the volume of production in each industry over this period is obtained. The method assumes, once again, that past relationships can be projected into the

---

[1]See the commodity pattern of imports of manufactures into the main industrial countries in Table 7.10.

[2]See Table 2.5.

[3]Corresponding to a 3 per cent annual compound rise in real income per head, and an increase of 1 per cent annually in total population.

future ; the assumption here is, in fact, more reasonable than the corresponding one for imports[1].

The calculation (see Table 15.9) shows that the changes in the pattern of manufacturing output are likely to bear a close resemblance to those envisaged in the pattern of exports. In volume terms, however, the growth in production may well significantly exceed that in exports for the chemicals group. The likely pattern of change in exports is broadly the same—apart from textiles— whether the previous trends are assumed to continue, or a more detailed and less 'mechanical' set of assumptions are used for the various groups of countries. For textiles and clothing, however, the results of the two approaches diverge widely. It seems most unlikely that the sharp relative rate of decline in this group which occurred in the past will continue unchanged in the future. On the other hand, exports from the main industrial countries will undoubtedly be subject to increasing competitive pressure from countries like Hong Kong, Pakistan and China. On balance, it seems probable that the volume of textile exports from the main industrial countries will increase, in the coming decade,

Table 15.9. *Relative rates of growth in production and exports of manufactures in the main industrial countries by commodity group, 1959 to 1970–75*

	Production			Exports	
	Proportion of total		Volume index for 1970–75	Volume index for 1970–75[a]	
	1959	1970–75		(a)	(b)
	(Percentage)		*(1959=100)*	*(1959=100)*	
Metals	8.7	8.5	200	185	190
Capital goods[b]	33.5	37.5	230	245	245
Chemicals	13.6	16.5	250	245	205
Textiles and clothing	12.7	9.0	150	75	140
Other manufactures[c]	31.5	28.5	185	200	185
TOTAL	100.0	100.0	205	200	200

Sources: Production—*Statistical Yearbook, 1960,* United Nations, New York, 1961; *Federal Reserve Bulletin; The Engineering Industries in Europe, 1960,* O.E.E.C., Paris, 1961; Table 2.5.

Exports—Tables 7.14, 15.1, 15.2, 15.7 and 15.8.

[a]Estimate (a) is based on Table 15.7, while estimate (b) is based on Table 15.8 (including an arbituary allowance for exports to Soviet countries).
[b]Machinery and transport equipment *less* passenger road vehicles.
[c]Including passenger road vehicles and 'other metal goods'.

[1]This is because the production regressions gave a much closer fit to the past data than did the import regressions.

but it does not seem possible to make any reliable estimate from past trends.

A discussion pitched in terms of broad commodity groups can, of course, give only general indications of the important developments which may lie ahead. A deeper insight would require an analysis in terms of new techniques and processes and the development of products based on new materials, or catering to new needs. Such new products can arise in the 'declining' as well as in the 'expanding' industries[1], and their exploitation may well play some part in modifying the long-term trends in the broad commodity groups to which the present discussion has had to be confined.

4. THE POLICY ISSUES FOR THE INDUSTRIAL COUNTRIES

Since changes in the pattern of world trade in manufactures seem likely to correspond generally with changes in output patterns they would not, in themselves, raise any new major policy issues for the industrial countries, except for the trade in textiles. Here the problem is essentially one of competition from 'low cost' less-developed countries in a framework of contracting or slowly-expanding world trade, and it is part of the more general issue of the freedom of access of manufactured exports from such countries to the markets of the economically advanced areas. This is discussed further below.

The shift in the pattern of demand within the industrial countries is, however, likely to continue to react adversely in the future, as it has done previously, on the exports of the primary-producing countries. The same is true of technological developments in the industrial countries. Neither of these forces can be expected to come to a halt, much less to be reversed; nor would it be sensible to consider policy changes which would have this effect. Moreover, any substantial alleviation of the balance of payments problems of the primary-producing areas from a swing in the terms of trade in their favour appears to be unlikely, for the reasons mentioned earlier. Certainly, no reliance can be placed on the chances of such a swing taking place.

There are, however, three fields of action in each of which policy changes by the industrial countries would have beneficial effects on the balance of payments position of the primary-producers and would allow them to increase their rate of economic growth. These three possible lines of policy—increasing the rate of growth in the industrial countries; relaxing restrictions on imports both of primary produce and of manufactures; and providing capital on more favourable terms—are discussed in turn below.

(a) *The rate of growth.* It is not possible to make exact estimates of the effects of an additional 1 per cent rate of growth in the industrial countries on their imports of primary products. As already mentioned, much depends on whether

---

[1]See the general discussions of the relation between economic growth and the development of new products in Chapter 8, and the more detailed discussion of trends in production and trade in new chemical products in Chapter 11.

the assumed increase in the rate of growth is evenly spread, or is concentrated in one country or another. Taking the industrial countries as a single aggregate, it was shown earlier in this chapter that the volume of exports, other than fuels, from the primary-producing countries rose between 1953 and 1960 at about two-thirds the rate of growth in the real income of the industrial countries. If this general relationship held for any assumed marginal expansion in the industrial countries, a very approximate order of magnitude can be arrived at for the increase in the export earnings of the primary-producing countries associated with any given increase in growth in the industrial countries.

An additional 1 per cent rate of growth per year in real income per head in the industrial countries implies an additional increase in total real income of about 25 per cent over the period 1959 to 1970–75. If the resulting increase in imports from the primary-producing areas were two-thirds of this proportion, this would add some $3 billion, at 1958–60 prices, to the export earnings of the primary-producing areas in the later period. This would represent almost half the extra finance required, above the 1958–60 level, to sustain the 2 per cent a year growth rate illustrated in assumption A of Table 15.5.

Policy measures designed to increase the rate of economic growth have been in force—with varying degrees of success—in many, but not in all, the main industrial countries over the past decade. If such measures can be successfully reinforced and the average rate of growth improved, the benefit will accrue to the primary-producing areas no less than to the industrial countries themselves.

(b) *Import restrictions.* These are of two kinds: import restrictions (usually tariffs or quotas) designed to protect home agriculture or manufacture, and taxes on imported goods imposed purely for revenue purposes.

A substantial relaxation by the industrial countries of their present *protectionist* measures against imports from primary-producing countries would involve compensating adjustments in their pattern of output. Such adjustments would be economically beneficial to the industrial countries by allowing a more rational allocation of resources to be made. However, adjustments on any large scale are always politically difficult to make because of temporary unemployment that may be caused. Such temporary difficulties would, however, be minimized if the adjustments were spread over a number of years, and were made in a period of economic expansion such as is envisaged here for the period up to the early 1970's.

Quantitative estimates of the effect of relaxations in import restrictions are inevitably surrounded by a considerable margin of error. However, very broad orders of magnitude can be established. In 1958, the import-content of supplies of food and feeding stuffs in North America and Western Europe together has been estimated at about 9–10 per cent[1]. If import restrictions were progressively relaxed so as to allow the import-content to rise by only $\frac{1}{2}$ percentage point a year, the proportion of supplies met by imports in 1970–75 would be

[1]*International Trade, 1959*, G.A.T.T., Geneva, 1960.

16–17 per cent. A relaxation of this order, had it been fully effective in 1958–60, would have allowed an additional $5–6 billion of export earnings by primary-producing countries. At the higher level of food consumption which can be expected by 1970–75, the additional earnings resulting from the same degree of import relaxation would be about $8 billion. This by itself would meet all the additional finance required to sustain a 2 per cent a year growth rate.

Protection against imports of primary products is generally greater for processed foods and processed industrial materials than it is for the crude produce. Examples can readily be found in the tariff systems of all the main industrial countries. The common external tariff of the European Economic Community has a considerable duty preference, for example, on cocoa beans compared with processed cocoa, on oilseeds, nuts and kernels compared with vegetable oils, on natural rubber compared with rubber manufactures, and on raw cotton compared with cotton yarn. Such examples can be multiplied from the tariff schedules of Britain, the United States and Japan.

The large-scale processing of their own primary produce by the less-developed countries could be an important means of increasing their export incomes, as well as a ready avenue of expanding their manufacturing activities[1]. However, the demand prospects for processed primary produce are little better than those for crude foodstuffs and materials, so that the increase in export earnings would be largely a 'once for all' gain. Nevertheless, this gain might well make a substantial contribution to meeting the payments gap of the less-developed countries. One recent estimate puts the probable increase in the import capacity of these countries if they processed their own materials at between 10 and 20 per cent[2]; on this basis, the export earnings of the primary-producing countries shown in Table 15.5 would be higher in 1970–75 by some $2½–5 billion.

The other main area in which the primary-producing countries are adversely affected by import restrictions is in manufactured goods (excluding base metals). The spread of industrialization in the primary-producing areas will mean that, in time, a wider range of manufactured goods will become available for export. Not only textiles, but simply-processed engineering goods, such as some electrical appliances and some types of machinery, might well become important and these would have much better long-term prospects than textiles or, indeed, most primary commodities provided, of course, that they could gain free access to the markets of the industrial countries. Though manufactures will not supersede primary products as the major export of most of the present under-developed countries in the foreseeable future, expanding exports of manufactures could nevertheless help to increase the rate of economic growth in these countries. Exports of manufactured goods, other than base metals, from the primary-producing to the industrial countries averaged rather more than $1

[1]The establishment of processing plants would, however, normally involve additional imports of capital equipment and ancillary materials.
[2]See *Economic Survey of Europe in 1960*, United Nations, Geneva, 1961, Chapter V.

billion in 1958–60. The possible gain from import relaxations of the order envisaged above for foods could well be in the region of $½ billion at the 1958–60 level of consumption in the industrial countries, and as much as $1 billion at the higher level implied for 1970–75.

Relaxations in the protectionist policies of the industrial countries could thus make a major contribution to closing the prospective payments gap of the primary-producing areas. The further gain which would accrue from reductions in purely *revenue duties* would, however, be relatively small. It has been estimated, for example, that the abolition of import duties and internal taxes on coffee in Western Europe would have increased total coffee imports into this area in 1958 by 10 per cent of actual coffee imports in that year[1]. If the same percentage increase can be assumed to hold at the higher level of consumption in 1961, the value of this notional increase would probably be about $100 million.

Import relaxations of the size mentioned would be marginal to the economies of the industrial countries. Yet they would add more to the earnings of the primary-producing areas than would a 1 per cent increase in the rate of growth in the industrial countries—an objective which would be considerably more difficult to achieve.

(c) *The capital flow.* There are two separate aspects of the flow of capital investment and aid from the industrial to the primary-producing countries to be considered. The first, which has been widely discussed in recent years, relates to the policies designed to increase the total flow to the less-developed areas. In 1958–60 the net capital outflow from the industrial countries represented about 1 per cent of their total gross national product. Even if this proportion is not increased, the expansion in total real income assumed in the industrial countries would imply an addition by 1970–75 of some $6 billion (at 1958–60 prices) to the total capital outflow that can otherwise be assumed. If the proportion could be raised to 1½ per cent of gross national product, a further $6 billion would be made available. An increase of this magnitude would appear to be the minimum necessary if this is to be the chief method of helping the primary-producing countries attain a significant rise in real income per head.

The second aspect is the probability that interest payments on the mounting total of capital investments will themselves become so large as to threaten the external viability of the developing countries. A reduction of interest charges below market rates is, in effect, another form of aid. Yet some concerted effort, possibly of an international character, seems required to minimize the future burden of interest on the less-developed countries.

The prospects for economic growth in the less-developed areas would be greatly improved if the policies of the main industrial countries were re-aligned in some of the ways indicated above. This would allow for both a fuller use of the resources of the less-developed areas and a more rational allocation of

[1] *The World Coffee Economy,* Commodity Bulletin No. 33, F.A.O., Rome, 1961.

existing resources in the industrial countries. A breaking down of the present barriers to trade between the industrial countries and the rest of the world is an essential element of such a general re-alignment of economic policies. Indeed, in this wider context of world economic development, the relaxation of these restrictions seems a more important objective than economic integration among the industrial countries themselves. However, in the longer term, even a free import market combined with rapid economic growth in the industrial countries would not ensure a fast rate of growth in many of the less-developed countries, especially as some of the benefits of free trade in primary products would inevitably go to the often more efficient agricultural and mining sectors of Europe and North America. A broader industrial development, in addition to export growth, thus appears to be necessary in most of the less-developed countries if they are to achieve a continuous rise in their real incomes.

CHAPTER 16

CONCLUSIONS

Several major conclusions can be drawn from the detailed analysis made in this study. Before reviewing these, however, it seems useful to draw together the qualifications attaching to the results, which have been made where relevant at various points in the book. This serves not only to place the conclusions in a better perspective, but also to indicate fruitful areas of further research.

One important qualification arises from the limitations inherent in the basic statistical data. An obvious example is the calculation of the gross domestic product in constant prices and United States dollars for a variety of countries, both developed and under-developed. The estimates used here do not pretend to be more than first approximations to the truth; the range in real product per head is, however, so wide among the different countries that even first approximations suffice for the type of general analysis used. Nonetheless, this is an area in which more accurate estimates are urgently needed; but the scale of the statistical investigation is so considerable that probably only the United Nations Organization can be expected to tackle it successfully.

The limitations attaching to the volume series of foreign trade have already been explained in Chapter 8. Though these series are inevitably surrounded by some margin of error, it is believed that they provide a good representation of the secular trends in world trade; small changes in the figures have little or no significance. The volume series were arrived at by 'deflating' value figures by computed unit value indices; the latter were also used to indicate the movement in the relative prices of exports from different countries. Here again there is an important field for statistical improvement, particularly in the development of indices of export *prices*—as distinct from export unit values— for detailed commodity categories. It was argued earlier that the prices of goods *actually* exported are not, strictly speaking, so relevant to the problem of price competition in international trade as are the prices of goods *available* for export[1]. A major step forward in the provision of data suitable for the analysis of price elasticities in international trade would be taken if statistical series were compiled for comparable commodity groups of 'available exports' in competing countries.

A further qualification arises because the analysis was essentially confined to a number of 'years of good trade' from 1899 to 1959; as already explained, this was done to keep the large amount of statistical extraction and computing work within reasonable bounds. In most of the regression calculations in previous chapters, seven or eight years were included for any single country; this small number of 'observations' was, however, generally offset by including a number of different countries in each of the time regressions.

[1]See page 203.

A second general qualification—which arises directly out of the first—is that the lack of annual series prevented a more sophisticated statistical analysis being used, such as the inclusion of time lags of different periods for the different quantifiable variables, the calculation of separate long-term and short-term elasticities, or the use of a more general model. This type of analysis, using lags, and based on a general econometric model, should however be much more possible in the future, in view of the wealth of comparable statistical data in the fields of international trade and of national accounts now being published by various international organizations.

In spite of these various qualifications, some general conclusions emerge from the preceding analysis. First, as regards the main theme of the study—the impact of industrial growth on trade in manufactures—it seems that the industrialization of primary-producing countries is generally associated, in the long run, with an expansion in the volume of their total imports of manufactured goods. Industrialization has a two-fold effect on imports of manufactures. The first, positive, effect arises insofar as industrialization implies greater capital investment and results in an increase in real incomes. The second, negative, effect arises from the import-substituting character of industrial production itself. That the positive effect will more than offset the negative one is quite clear for capital equipment and other 'sophisticated' manufactures; but for consumer goods, the net impact of industrialization on the volume of imports is much less certain. There are, admittedly, examples of industrialization where the volume of imports of manufactures in total has not expanded, and even some where the volume of imports has contracted. But viewed in historical perspective, these examples appear as particular exceptions to the general rule.

Whether industrialization will also be accompanied by an expansion in exports depends on external forces in the world market as well as on the more immediate impact of industrialization on the export sector of a primary-producing country. The major restraint on the growth of imports arises, not from the industrialization process as it normally develops, but from these external forces. Industrialization in the primary-producing areas could no doubt be considerably extended without any very appreciable expansion in their exports of primary products or in their imports of manufactures, if none of the policy changes discussed in the previous chapter were made, or if the rate of import-substitution in the industrial countries against the traditional exports of the primary-producing areas were increased appreciably. But such a development could not reasonably be regarded as a consequence of the initial industrialization.

Moreover, the further industrial growth of the more advanced economies of Western Europe, North America and Japan would also normally be associated with an expanding volume of trade in manufactures between them. This is not simply a question of the rise in incomes creating a new demand—for example, for capital equipment—which can be met only by imports. Further factors which come into play are the diversification of consumer demand at high levels of income; continual technical progress, accompanied by the introduction of new products; and the structural factor of specialization by the smaller industrial countries in particular ranges of manufactured goods.

Rapid, and necessarily uneven, technical progress implies a continual process of adjustment in the comparative advantages enjoyed by any one industrial country in its various lines of manufacturing production. This, combined with an increasing diversification of demand, is likely to result in a complex and shifting commodity-pattern of intra-trade among the industrial countries. It may also result in a higher volume of trade, in relation to production, than would have been the case without such technical progress or diversification of demand. In conditions of relative freedom of trade from government restrictions, the intra-trade of the industrial countries is likely to remain the most dynamic sector of world trade.

Moreover, on any reasonable assumptions based on present policies, the future rate of economic growth of the industrial countries—as well as their future rate of trade expansion—at present seems certain to exceed that of the primary-producing areas taken as a whole. Given that technological changes, together with secular shifts in demand, both tend to reduce the requirements of the industrial countries for primary produce in relation to their total income, an urgent condition for ensuring even a modest rate of economic growth in most of the primary-producing areas is a combination of substantially increased aid (both financial and technical) with reduced protectionist restrictions on trade.

Within these movements in total trade in manufactures, changes must be expected in the commodity pattern of trade. Over a long period, these changes are very large but have generally followed a fairly unambiguous pattern. Even so, it is not possible to make accurate predictions about the future commodity-pattern of trade. A major uncertainty surrounds any estimate of the probable level of trade in textiles; as was shown in the previous chapter, if past trends were, in fact, to continue unchanged, international trade in textiles would disappear quite soon. But this seems in fact unlikely to happen, partly because technical developments continually extend the area within which fruitful international specialization can take place. Yet there seems little doubt that in the final quarter of this century international trade in manufactures is likely to be largely, or even mainly, in the 'development sector' of engineering and chemical products. The extent of this further shift in the pattern of trade will depend partly on the rate of economic growth in the world economy—particularly on how fast the main trading countries grow—and partly on the success of industrializing countries in substituting home production for imports of the more highly fabricated products, as well as of the simpler types of manufactures.

The second, subsidiary, object of the present study was to analyse the main factors affecting the relative export performances of the principal industrial countries. Changes in relative export performance reflect changes in competitive power which, in turn, appear to be closely related to the general rates of economic growth in the different industrial countries. For countries with a large export trade, a circular connexion tends to be set up. A weak competitive position results in a loss of exports and a retardation of general economic growth which, in turn, further weakens the external competitive position. A strong initial competitive position would tend to set in motion the reverse cycle.

In Britain, an additional factor has influenced the 'vicious circle' of slow economic growth combined with the erosion of competitive power, namely, the import-substitution engendered by the industrialization of the primary-producing areas. Such substitution has borne disproportionately on British exports. Britain has traditionally been a major supplier of manufactures to the primary-producing countries—particularly to those connected by political or currency ties; moreover, at least up to the last War, Britain tended to concentrate more than most other industrial exporting nations on textiles and other consumer goods which were among the first to be hit by the import-substitution process.

The effect on British exports of import-substitution as the primary-producing countries industrialize will probably continue to be disproportionately high, though the dramatic results of the industrialization of a single very large market (India) are unlikely to be repeated. Continual adaptation in Britain's export industries to the changing pattern of world demand, together with a faster general rate of economic growth, will be required to prevent a repetition of the past experience when import-substitution exacerbated an underlying decline of competitive power.

APPENDIX A

THE TRADE NETWORK TABLES

The primary objective of this set of tables was to arrive at long-term series representing imports of different classes of manufactured goods, as well as a total for all manufactures, for a wide range of countries in different stages of development. An essential condition, from the viewpoint of analysing the results, was that the commodity groupings chosen for the trade of each country should be identical, so far as the limitations of the trade statistics permitted. This condition in effect ruled out an analysis of the import returns of the countries to be covered, since this would have involved an enormous task of reclassifying the detailed import headings of each of 30–40 countries on to a comparable basis. Apart from the labour involved, it is somewhat doubtful whether in fact the results would have been comparable for many countries, especially for the earlier part of the century. There were, in addition, other difficulties which made the approach from the import side unattractive[1].

On the other hand, a compilation from the export returns of the main industrial countries offered several advantages. Since 12 countries account for some 90 per cent of world exports of manufactures, the trend in their aggregate shipments to any country can reasonably be taken as indicating the trend in the latter's imports of manufactures. On this basis, the commodity reclassification is very considerably reduced compared with what would have been necessary had the import approach been adopted. Apart from this, the analysis of export returns provided a set of network tables which show not only the total exports of manufactures to individual countries, but also the share of each market held by each supplying country. The same tables thus provide a basis for an analysis of competition between the main industrial countries in the world market, and also a statistical basis for analysing the long-term relation between industrial growth and imports of manufactures.

Exporting countries

The countries whose export statistics were used for these network tables were: Belgium-Luxembourg, France, Germany, Italy, Netherlands, Sweden, Switzerland and the United Kingdom; Canada and the United States; India and Japan.

[1]For example, several important countries recorded imports at official valuations up to fairly recent years (Argentina did so up to 1941); while in others, multiple exchange rate practices make conversions to a common currency unit rather dubious (e.g. Chile). For a discussion of these technical difficulties, see *International Trade Statistics* (ed. R. G. D. Allen and J. E. Ely), 1953, Chs. 5 and 18.

No attempt has been made to adjust the recorded figures for boundary changes. For example, the pre-war figures for Germany relate to exports from the pre-war area of the Reich; those for post-war are exports from West Germany only. Similarly, the post-war figures for India relate to exports from the Republic of India, whereas the pre-war ones were exports from undivided India.

The most important exporting countries not included in the detailed network tables of trade in manufactures are some of the smaller countries of Western Europe (Austria, Denmark and Finland), the Soviet Union, the African copper-exporting countries (Rhodesia and the Congo) and Hong Kong. However, exports from these countries are discussed separately at various appropriate places in the text.

Countries of destination

In order to limit the labour of extracting and assembling a mass of detailed statistics, countries of destination were selected mainly so as to include countries 'representative' of different stages of development. It was also thought desirable to include a number of colonial territories as well as independent countries in the under-developed areas. The countries selected have been grouped into the three broad categories of industrial, semi-industrial and non-industrial countries distinguished in Chapter 3. It has not, however, been possible to compile results for other kinds of country groupings, such as the currency blocs (the Sterling area, the Franc area, etc.); nor were the present members of the Soviet area distinguished as a group, though separate information for the Soviet Union has been extracted.

The countries of destination included are:—

1. *Industrial countries:* The exporting countries mentioned above (except India), plus Norway.
2. *Semi-industrial countries:* Australia, New Zealand and the Union of South Africa; India, including Pakistan; Argentina, Brazil, Chile, Colombia and Mexico; Palestine/Israel; Turkey and Yugoslavia.
3. *Russia/U.S.S.R.*
4. *Non-industrial countries:*
   Africa: Belgian Congo, Egypt, French Morocco, Nigeria, Southern Rhodesia.
   Asia: Indonesia, Iran and the Philippines.
   Latin America: Cuba, Peru and Venezuela.
   Others: All other countries, as a group, can be obtained as a residue after deducting the figures for the selected countries from the world total. This group includes some European countries (such as Austria, Denmark and Finland, and Czechoslovakia and East Germany), as well as non-industrial primary-producing countries.

Once again, boundary changes have been ignored. In particular, no attempt has been made in the trade network tables to adjust the pre-war figures for exports to Germany to the present territory of West Germany; estimates of trade in manufactures by pre-war Germany, adjusted to post-war territory are, however, given in Chapters 8, 11, 13 and 14. Similarly, Japanese shipments to Formosa and Korea before the last war were excluded from the Japanese export statistics (being considered internal trade), but similar shipments since the war have been included. In all, 37 separate countries of destination are distinguished and together they accounted for 77 per cent of the total exports of manufactures from our 12 exporting countries in 1955.

Before the first World War, some countries recorded their exports according to the country of shipment, rather than the country of consignment or ultimate destination. The United Kingdom was, perhaps, the most important example, the shipment basis being in use until 1904. Before that date, shipments destined for land-locked countries were recorded as exports to the country in which the goods were unshipped. British exports to Switzerland, for example, were recorded as exports to Belgium, France, Germany or the Netherlands, according to the foreign port involved. Thus, exports to the four latter countries shown in the trade network tables for 1899 are inflated in comparison with the figures for 1913 and later years.

Commodity classification

Exports of manufactures from each of the 12 countries of origin to each of the separate countries of destination were classified into seven major groups and nine sub-groups. The major groups were metals, machinery, transport equipment*, other metal goods, chemicals*, textiles and clothing* and other manufactures*. The four asterisked groups were divided into two or three sub-categories. The complete classification is set out in Appendix D[1], which also gives the definition of each group and sub-group. The totals correspond as nearly as possible to Sections 5 to 8 inclusive of the United Nations' *Standard International Trade Classification*[2], excluding 'special category' exports from the United States. This is the definition of 'manufactures' which is now generally accepted[3].

Exports relate to 'special trade', that is to exports of goods manufactured or processed in the exporting country, and exclude re-exports.

[1] See page 518.
[2] *Statistical Papers*, Series M, No. 10, 2nd ed. (1951); indexed edition (1953); United Nations, New York. The revised edition (Series M, No. 34), which was published in 1961, was not used here.
[3] This is, for example, the definition used by the United Nations Statistical Office in computing an index of the volume of world trade in 'manufactures'.

Choice of years

In view of the amount of statistical work involved, the compilation of network tables on an annual basis would have been completely outside the resources available. The choice of selected years to represent a long-term trend is inevitably an invidious one. No individual year is fully representative of its immediate period, and a 'boom' year in one period may not, in fact, be really comparable with a 'boom' year in another, if the degree of utilization of resources is significantly different, for example, or if there is a substantial difference in the extent of restrictions on the free movement of trade. Nevertheless, a choice had to be made, and it seemed preferable to select years of prosperous trade rather than ones of recession.

The years chosen were 1899, 1913, 1929, 1937, 1950 and 1955. For each of these years a detailed set of trade network tables has been assembled. These have been supplemented in certain cases by adding comparable figures for 1957 and 1959, taken from United Nations' publications. The first two years reasonably represent the trend in the period prior to the first World War; 1929 was the peak year of the boom before the world economic depression, and 1937 the peak year of the recovery of the late 1930's. 1950 is included in the series as perhaps the first reasonably 'normal' year following a period of post-war reconstruction, while 1955, 1957 and 1959 were all years of expanding world trade.

A major qualification, however, needs to be made at the outset. World trading conditions were very different in 1937 and, to some extent also in 1950, from those in the other years selected. The depression of the 1930's had been followed by an extensive system of import restrictions, exchange controls, multiple currency practices and various other measures of trade control and restriction, all of which were in full operation in 1937. In 1950, too, many countries operated quantitative import restrictions, usually of a discriminatory character, to protect their external payments positions. Moreover, in that year there were still significant supply shortages, particularly in metals and many types of engineering equipment. The Korean War, which began in the summer of 1950 did not, however, seriously distort the pattern of world trade until the following year.

By contrast, trading conditions in 1955 were generally more favourable than in any previous post-war year. The campaign in O.E.E.C. for trade liberalization had been largely completed and restrictions against dollar imports had by then also been significantly reduced both in Western Europe and in many other non-dollar areas. In these respects, therefore, world trade in the period 1955–59 was much more comparable with that in 1929 than with any of the intervening years. A comparison of 1955–59 with 1929, rather than with 1937, is thus more revealing of the underlying long-term trend in world trade; the particular conditions of the world economy in 1937 must always be borne in mind when comparisons involving that year are made.

For the industrial and semi-industrial countries as defined earlier, the trade network tables were constructed for all the selected years back to 1899. By deduction of these two groups from the world total, a table for the 'rest of the world' has also been constructed for each selected year. For the eleven separate countries distinguished as 'non-industrial' (see above), the network tables were carried back only to 1929.

All but two of the tables in this Appendix relate to the selected years up to 1955 or 1957. Comparable data for 1959 were compiled in summary form only, and are given in the last two tables (A.80 and A.81).

Valuation

All the trade network tables were first expressed in terms of current United States dollars, using the mean rates of exchange in force in each of the selected years[1]. In addition, a set of tables has been constructed in terms of 'constant' dollars, so that changes in the volume of trade can be revealed.

The construction of any volume series from trade statistics is an operation which by its nature cannot produce unique answers, but only a range of probabilities. The range is inevitably widened the longer the period covered. The difficulty is inherent to some extent in the nature of the trade statistics themselves, insofar as the 'unit value' of an individual statistical heading may change not only because of a change in price, but also because of a change in the relative importance of the different items included. In addition, there is the usual difficulty of index number construction, that of the changing relative importance of the statistical headings themselves.

The latter difficulty can be overcome to a large extent by changing the weighting system with the period to be compared. However, when the period extends over half a century, as in the present case, and includes five or six links of years, a complete investigation of volume changes would require two weighting systems for each link, i.e. ten or twelve sets of calculations at 'constant' prices. Moreover, the problem of linking through the various results to give a continuous volume series for the whole period would present many difficulties, particularly of consistency between commodity and country detail. On the other hand, to revalue the trade of each year by the weights of a single year would certainly involve some distortion in the results. In the end, a compromise was adopted whereby a comparison of the years 1899, 1913 and 1929 was made at 1913 prices; and a separate comparison of 1929 with the later years was made at 1955 prices. This greatly simplifies the presentation of the tables, though it may have resulted in some small distortions of the

[1] See Appendix F, Exchange Rates, page 545, for the rates of exchange used.

movements between 1929 and 1937[1].

One other discontinuity in the series should be mentioned here. Before 1919, the Netherlands recorded foreign trade at official valuations which were established in 1845 and added to in subsequent years[2]; moreover, the export figures were considerably inflated by the inclusion of goods in transit. For 1899 and 1913, the recorded figures were undoubtedly substantially higher than the true current valuations[3]. Accordingly, the network tables for the two earlier years exclude exports from the Netherlands. For purposes of comparison, Netherlands exports are also excluded from the 1929 totals whenever these are linked to 1913.

Unit value series

The network tables in current values were converted into tables at 'constant' values by using a series of unit value index numbers. The series used are given in Appendix B.

Exports, imports and 'imports'

It was mentioned above that one of the advantages of the network form of table was that it yielded totals representing, in effect, world exports of manufactured goods to individual countries. The movement in this total can reasonably be taken to represent the movement in total imports of manufactures (or of particular classes of manufactures) into each of the countries of destination distinguished. However, the total arrived at in this way is not the same as the true import figure, and the total arrived at from the network table is here denoted by the term 'imports', the quotation marks being used to distinguish this concept from the actual import total.

'Imports' as now defined may differ from true imports for several reasons. In the first place, 'imports' come only from the twelve exporting countries included in the network analysis. It is true that these twelve account for some 90 per cent of world exports of manufactures; but the coverage may be significantly lower in particular commodity groups (metals being the outstanding case) and for particular countries of destination (the United Kingdom being especially affected). Second, since 'imports' of one country are arrived at from the export returns of other countries, the valuation is on an f.o.b.

---

[1]Separate revaluations of the trade in 1929 at 1937 prices, and of 1937 at 1929 prices, were also made, and some of the summary results are given in Appendix C, pages 515-6.

[2]See the discussion on the pre-1919 Netherlands trade returns in C. P. Kindleberger, *The Terms of Trade: A European Case Study*, 1956, pp. 330 and 359.

[3]P. L. Yates, *Forty Years of Foreign Trade*, 1959, p. 201, postulates that the overvaluation in 1913 may have been of the order of 25 per cent.

basis, whereas imports are normally valued c.i.f.[1]. Third, there is always some time-lag between the export of a commodity and its recording as an import in the receiving country.

---

[1]Except for a minority of countries, including Canada and the United States, where imports are valued f.o.b., or near-equivalent of f.o.b.

Table A1. Total exports from the industrial countries, at current prices

$ million, f.o.b.

Exports from / Exports to	Industrial countries				Semi-industrial countries				U.S.S.R.	Rest of World	World Total
	United Kingdom	Continental Western Europe	North America	Total (including Japan)	Southern Dominions	India (including Pakistan)	Other Semi-Industrial Countries	Total			
United Kingdom											
1899	—	368	124	530	165	153	92	410	57	291	1288
1913	—	640	259	970	329	342	257	928	88	572	2558
1929	—	744	390	1199	527	381	305	1213	30	1110	3552
1937	—	497	291	810	490	177	189	856	39	870	2575
1950	—	1125	669	1801	1296	386	349	2031	32	2215	6079
1955	—	1599	906	2542	1653	467	232	2352	64	3177	8135
1957	—	1893	1235	3206	1538	590	315	2443	105	3556	9310
France											
1899	240	303	49	594	2	4	43	49	8	165	816
1913	283	555	86	927	3	9	92	104	16	312	1359
1929	297	750	153	1209	11	18	100	129	10	615	1963
1937	110	324	67	507	6	5	44	55	4	386	952
1950	282	893	140	1319	47	25	194	266	3	1491	3079
1955	353	1509	232	2107	57	55	241	353	36	2304	4800
1957	278	1622	277	2199	54	73	169	296	45	2507	5047
Germany											
1899	191	321	96	618	12	16	46	74	95	215	1002
1913	343	729	184	1285	24	36	178	238	210	672	2405
1929	311	1145	256	1770	46	52	252	350	84	1005	3209
1937	174	813	97	1131	48	60	302	410	47	786	2374
1950	86	1003	113	1210	48	27	189	264	—	502	1976
1955	245	2700	442	3428	167	170	542	879	27	1801	6135
1957	335	3748	696	4892	222	308	601	1131	60	2492	8575
Other Western Europe											
1899a	172	479	57	712	4	11	38	53	19	127	911
1913a	264	791	118	1181	20	25	129	174	49	275	1679
1929a	416	961	273	1675	37	55	196	288	16	585	2564
1929	579	1321	310	2238	49	68	221	338	17	771	3364
1937	436	1133	248	1847	56	38	152	246	32	749	2874
1950	661	2728	521	3929	158	105	470	733	67	1553	6282
1955	1052	4647	899	6653	269	144	623	1036	67	2600	10356
1957	1143	5812	1076	8110	262	200	703	1165	115	3130	12520

Canada											
1899	85	3	39	127	2	—	1	3	—	7	137
1913	170	12	140	323	9	—	3	12	2	19	356
1929	274	134	493	939	52	10	32	94	3	116	1152
1937	381	86	470	963	62	5	18	85	1	61	1110
1950	443	158	1920	2540	84	38	80	202	0	197	2939
1955	778	346	2581	3797	138	31	87	256	3	281	4337
1957	752	518	2969	4382	119	41	111	271	11	383	5047
United States											
1899	506	372	86	981	35	4	51	90	9	124	1204
1913	592	758	397	1805	66	11	177	254	26	344	2429
1929	842	1152	902	3156	251	56	557	864	87	1050	5157
1937	530	639	491	1949	185	44	352	581	47	722	3299
1950	511	1900	1995	4822	247	242	1466	1955	1	3221	9999
1955	915	2478	3134	7169	513	242	1820	2575	0	3741	13485
1957	1090	3695	3826	9838	551	552	2470	3573	4	5061	18476
Japan											
1899	6	18	33	57	1	3	0	4	2	50	113
1913	16	53	95	164	4	15	1	20	5	126	315
1929	29	33	434	496	28	91	7	126	8	339	969
1937	48	44	194	286	42	86	27	155	8	466	915
1950	26	58	198	282	54	76	28	158	1	379	820
1955	61	101	493	655	92	129	143	364	1	984	2004
1957	73	194	658	925	100	130	61	291	9	1624	2849
TOTAL											
1899[a]	1200	1864	484	3619	221	191	271	683	190	979	5471
1913[a]	1668	3538	1279	6655	455	438	837	1730	396	2320	11101
1929[a]	2169	4919	2901	10444	952	663	1449	3064	238	4820	18566
1929	2332	5279	2938	11007	964	676	1474	3114	239	5006	19366
1937	1679	3536	1858	7493	889	415	1084	2388	178	4040	14099
1950	2009	7865	5556	15903	1934	899	2776	5609	104	9558	31174
1955	3404	13380	8687	26351	2889	1238	3688	7815	198	14888	49252
1957	3671	17482	10737	33552	2846	1894	4430	9170	349	18753	61824

[a] Excluding goods consigned from the Netherlands.

Table A2. *Total exports from the industrial countries, at constant prices*

$ million, f.o.b.

Exports from	Exports to	Industrial countries				Semi-industrial countries				U.S.S.R.	Rest of World	World Total
		United Kingdom	Continental Western Europe	North America	Total (including Japan)	Southern Dominions	India (including Pakistan)	Other Semi-Industrial Countries	Total			
United Kingdom	*a* 1899	—	452	148	643	206	204	118	528	65	386	1622
	1913	—	640	259	970	329	342	257	928	88	572	2558
	1929	—	458	249	751	349	235	201	785	19	722	2277
	b 1929	—	1271	686	2078	954	716	556	2226	52	1949	6305
	1937	—	997	596	1638	992	351	400	1743	78	1754	5213
	1950	—	1353	810	2170	1650	489	433	2572	42	2689	7473
	1955	—	1599	906	2542	1653	467	232	2352	64	3177	8135
	1957	—	1737	1134	2942	1411	542	289	2242	96	3261	8541
France	*a* 1899	270	344	55	671	2	4	47	53	9	196	929
	1913	283	555	86	927	3	9	92	104	16	312	1359
	1929	219	582	110	919	8	13	75	96	13	509	1537
	b 1929	465	1458	243	2191	18	31	193	242	23	1159	3615
	1937	199	564	116	891	11	10	89	110	8	738	1747
	1950	299	981	161	1445	57	30	245	332	5	1748	3530
	1955	353	1509	232	2107	57	55	241	353	36	2304	4800
	1957	257	1502	257	2037	50	67	157	274	42	2321	4674
Germany	*a* 1899	216	360	105	691	13	19	52	84	106	240	1121
	1913	343	729	184	1285	24	36	178	238	210	672	2405
	1929	225	844	188	1302	34	40	185	259	62	751	2374
	b 1929	596	2406	468	3587	90	112	569	771	185	2019	6562
	1937	280	1524	165	2041	78	98	505	681	79	1342	4143
	1950	98.	1173	137	1416	63	33	234	330	—	607	2353
	1955	245	2700	442	3428	167	170	542	879	27	1801	6135
	1957	316	3514	656	4592	216	300	588	1104	56	2337	8089
Other Western Europe	*a* 1899c	187	527	62	780	5	13	42	60	20	119	979
	1913c	264	791	118	1181	20	25	129	174	49	275	1679
	1929c	312	735	203	1269	39	46	159	244	15	493	2021
	b 1929	1015	2426	552	4056	98	137	408	643	35	1584	6318
	1937	932	2454	524	3975	126	83	347	556	78	1749	6358
	1950	711	3048	585	4366	175	111	524	810	80	1776	7032
	1955	1052	4647	899	6653	269	144	623	1036	67	2600	10356
	1957	1086	5479	1013	7653	248	188	660	1096	107	2945	11801

		1	2	3	4	5	6	7	8	9	10	11
Canada	*a* 1899	102	4	47	153	3	0	1	4	0	9	166
	1913	170	12	140	323	9	—	3	12	2	19	356
	1929	217	99	355	699	46	9	26	81	3	92	875
	b 1929	538	265	1002	1877	114	23	71	208	8	236	2329
	1937	877	195	1139	2275	151	12	44	207	3	142	2627
	1950	525	183	2232	2962	98	45	93	236	0	225	3423
	1955	778	346	2581	3797	138	31	87	256	3	281	4337
	1957	733	507	2884	4264	115	40	105	260	11	366	4901
United States	*a* 1899	722	509	113	1366	46	4	63	113	10	172	1661
	1913	592	758	397	1805	66	11	177	254	26	344	2429
	1929	647	911	721	2485	213	47	468	728	66	845	4124
	b 1929	1217	1717	1534	4855	437	104	1038	1579	147	1764	8345
	1937	995	1237	979	3769	393	91	750	1234	98	1662	6763
	1950	570	2121	2299	5429	293	273	1759	2325	2	3627	11383
	1955	915	2478	3134	7169	513	242	1820	2575	0	3741	13485
	1957	1018	3453	3576	9194	515	516	2308	3339	4	4730	17267
Japan	*a* 1899	6	21	38	65	1	3	0	4	2	68	139
	1913	16	53	95	164	4	15	1	20	5	126	315
	1929	21	24	333	378	19	60	4	83	6	241	708
	b 1929	62	77	1269	1408	48	148	12	208	18	639	2273
	1937	168	147	699	1014	130	250	83	463	25	1425	2927
	1950	27	72	248	347	67	83	45	195	1	429	972
	1955	61	101	493	655	92	129	143	364	1	984	2004
	1957	65	179	630	874	97	128	58	283	9	1575	2741
TOTAL	*a* 1899c	1503	2217	568	4369	276	247	323	846	212	1190	6617
	1913c	1668	3538	1279	6655	455	438	837	1730	396	2320	11101
	1929c	1641	3653	2159	7803	708	450	1118	2276	184	3653	13916
	b 1929	3893	9620	5754	20052	1759	1271	2847	5877	468	9350	35747
	1937	3451	7118	4218	15603	1881	895	2218	4994	369	8812	29778
	1950	2230	8931	6472	18135	2403	1064	3333	6800	130	11101	36166
	1955	3404	13380	8687	26351	2889	1238	3688	7815	198	14888	49252
	1957	3475	16371	10150	31556	2652	1781	4165	8598	325	17535	58014

a Values at 1913 prices.
b Values at 1955 prices.
c Excluding goods consigned from the Netherlands.

Table A3. *Exports of manufactures from the industrial countries and India, at current prices*

$ million, f.o.b.

Exports from / Exports to	Industrial countries				Semi-Industrial countries				U.S.S.R.	Rest of World	World Total
	United Kingdom	Continental Western Europe	North America	Total (Including Japan)	Southern Dominions	India (including Pakistan)	Other Semi-Industrial Countries	Total			
United Kingdom											
1899	—	251	98	387	144	143	79	366	42	236	1031
1913	—	365	194	624	289	316	205	810	47	479	1960
1929	—	448	306	815	470	347	267	1084	20	816	2735
1937	—	286	190	494	457	159	160	776	26	639	1935
1950	—	881	511	1396	1247	362	315	1923	31	1750	5100
1955	—	1252	688	1968	1564	405	211	2180	54	2484	6686
1957	—	1443	1012	2509	1454	547	288	2289	83	2832	7713
France											
1899	148	118	35	302	2	3	30	34	4	106	446
1913	199	242	60	502	4	7	72	83	7	195	787
1929	217	445	119	790	10	11	85	105	7	424	1327
1937	59	135	35	234	5	3	36	44	4	259	541
1950	128	442	98	671	41	23	168	232	2	1089	1993
1955	145	830	163	1149	50	44	219	313	24	1591	3077
1957	133	931	212	1295	48	68	148	264	45	1820	3424
Germany											
1899	131	185	64	388	10	13	43	67	59	183	697
1913	246	512	139	925	22	33	163	218	154	429	1726
1929	268	814	201	1339	42	48	234	324	73	767	2504
1937	164	592	77	879	47	58	287	391	47	704	2021
1950	53	639	96	795	47	26	177	250	—	418	1462
1955	219	2124	395	2777	160	168	531	859	27	1587	5250
1957	308	2998	651	4061	213	305	587	1105	58	2247	7471
Other Western Europe											
1899a	89	192	30	313	2	10	27	39	14	72	438
1913a	152	302	52	514	14	23	103	140	26	149	829
1929a	263	523	155	967	32	50	167	249	15	424	1654
1929	307	590	171	1094	38	57	178	273	16	577	1960
1937	211	519	134	886	45	33	127	205	30	577	1700
1950	297	1518	369	2190	127	86	376	589	66	1227	4074
1955	441	2778	688	3939	236	129	540	905	49	1880	6773
1957	491	3527	879	4964	235	190	613	1038	88	2271	8361

	Year											
Canada	1899	5	0	4	10	1	—	0	1	0	1	12
	1913	6	3	19	28	7	—	3	10	1	3	42
	1929	47	20	225	304	43	9	30	82	2	39	427
	1937	138	16	173	344	51	4	15	70	0	34	447
	1950	105	40	905	1051	54	31	50	136	0	80	1266
	1955	292	101	1384	1782	91	27	72	191	—	96	2069
	1957	316	158	1463	1963	88	29	100	217	2	168	2349
United States	1899	85	99	45	236	22	3	45	70	6	50	362
	1913	127	211	185	535	44	7	86	137	23	151	846
	1929	238	364	527	1212	159	43	432	635	51	593	2491
	1937	163	240	283	798	142	29	297	468	35	479	1780
	1950	179	739	1161	2121	206	121	1199	1526	0	1880	5526
	1955	333	1092	2331	3896	399	164	1301	1864	0	2536	8296
	1957	331	1383	2850	4986	421	216	1759	2396	1	3634	11016
Japan	1899	4	5	7	17	1	1	—	2	1	28	48
	1913	13	16	19	48	3	7	1	11	1	93	153
	1929	18	16	45	79	25	88	7	120	5	272	476
	1937	21	21	58	99	36	81	25	143	7	396	645
	1950	19	39	135	195	52	72	29	154	0	349	697
	1955	33	61	385	479	85	126	140	351	1	917	1748
	1957	31	138	553	719	94	127	58	279	9	1532	2538
India	1899	17	3	9	31	4	—	3	7	0	35	73
	1913	21	4	42	69	13	—	16	29	0	56	154
	1929	49	11	79	150	22	—	30	52	0	78	280
	1937	45	4	39	95	13	—	13	26	—	76	196
	1950	97	25	99	223	49	19	26	94	—	335	652
	1955	80	13	90	185	47	10	25	82	—	204	471
	1957	87	23	176	289	45	4	23	72	6	240	607
TOTAL	1899a	479	853	292	1680	186	173	227	586	126	716	3108
	1913a	763	1653	711	3248	400	394	654	1448	259	1543	6497
	1929a	1100	2641	1657	5656	803	596	1252	2651	173	3415	11895
	1929	1144	2708	1673	5783	809	603	1263	2675	174	3569	12201
	1937	801	1813	989	3829	796	367	960	2123	149	3165	9266
	1950	878	4323	3374	8642	1823	733	2348	4904	99	7126	20771
	1955	1542	8245	6127	16172	2632	1072	3038	6742	155	11298	34367
	1957	1695	10598	7795	20783	2599	1487	3576	7662	292	14742	43479

ᵃExcluding goods consigned from the Netherlands.

Table A4. *Exports of manufactures from the industrial countries and India, at constant prices*

$ million, f.o.b.

Exports to Exports from	Industrial countries				Semi-industrial countries				U.S.S.R.	Rest of World	World Total
	United Kingdom	Continental Western Europe	North America	Total (including Japan)	Southern Dominions	India (including Pakistan)	Other Semi-Industrial Countries	Total			
United Kingdom											
a 1899	—	318	118	479	182	192	103	477	48	323	1327
1913	—	365	194	624	289	316	205	810	47	479	1960
1929	—	293	202	537	317	216	180	713	13	558	1821
b 1929	—	862	570	1547	875	669	504	2048	38	1543	5176
1937	—	608	410	1056	931	318	347	1596	54	1328	4034
1950	—	1116	657	1776	1602	466	400	2468	41	2238	6523
1955	—	1252	688	1968	1564	405	211	2180	54	2484	6686
1957	—	1375	964	2389	1384	521	275	2180	79	2691	7339
France											
a 1899	168	132	39	341	2	3	33	38	5	120	504
1913	199	242	60	502	4	7	72	83	7	195	787
1929	155	344	83	590	6	8	62	76	11	362	1039
b 1929	387	1016	197	1624	17	22	173	212	19	901	2756
1937	125	290	70	495	10	7	77	94	8	554	1151
1950	148	539	120	809	51	28	220	299	4	1354	2466
1955	145	830	163	1149	50	44	219	313	24	1591	3077
1957	123	862	196	1199	45	63	137	245	41	1699	3184
Germany											
a 1899	149	210	70	437	11	16	48	75	66	204	782
1913	246	512	139	925	31	33	163	227	154	420	1726
1929	193	597	147	981	31	37	172	240	54	572	1847
b 1929	486	1562	327	2489	80	102	478	660	157	1456	4762
1937	254	961	114	1399	75	93	464	632	79	1133	3243
1950	63	791	119	980	62	32	220	314	—	519	1813
1955	219	2124	395	2777	160	168	531	859	27	1587	5250
1957	302	2939	638	3981	209	299	575	1084	57	2180	7302
Other Western Europe											
a 1899c	92	197	31	323	3	12	30	45	13	76	457
1913c	152	302	52	514	14	23	103	140	26	149	829
1929c	200	412	116	748	26	42	136	205	14	350	1317
b 1929	555	1192	317	2120	78	118	337	533	33	1261	3947
1937	462	1142	282	1933	103	72	296	471	74	1391	3869
1950	285	1633	407	2329	139	89	415	643	79	1400	4451
1955	441	2778	688	3939	236	129	540	905	49	1880	6773
1957	469	3349	837	4719	226	182	590	998	83	2167	7967

		(1)	(2)	(3)	(4)	(5)	(6)	(7)	(8)	(9)	(10)	(11)
a	1913	6	3	19	28	7	—	3	10	1	3	42
	1929	34	15	146	207	39	8	24	70	2	33	312
b	1929	100	45	485	655	97	21	65	183	6	86	930
	1937	338	42	480	899	127	10	36	173	1	82	1155
	1950	133	47	1055	1236	63	37	58	158	0	88	1482
	1955	292	101	1384	1782	91	27	72	191	—	96	2069
	1957	301	151	1393	1869	84	28	94	206	2	153	2230
United States a	1899	103	106	53	272	27	3	53	83	6	62	423
	1913	127	211	185	535	44	7	86	137	23	151	846
	1929	182	305	433	990	142	37	372	551	38	494	2073
b	1929	480	756	1076	2483	325	88	885	1298	103	1208	5092
	1937	346	532	611	1734	317	64	653	1034	77	1232	4077
	1950	225	912	1432	2619	250	147	1481	1878	1	2233	6731
	1955	333	1092	2331	3896	399	164	1301	1864	0	2536	8296
	1957	290	1213	2500	4373	369	190	1543	2102	1	3229	9705
Japan a	1899	4	5	7	16	1	1	—	2	1	42	61
	1913	13	16	19	48	3	7	1	11	1	93	153
	1929	13	11	34	58	17	58	4	79	4	189	330
b	1929	28	25	74	127	39	139	12	190	9	433	759
	1937	64	59	177	300	107	231	75	413	21	1156	1890
	1950	18	48	168	233	64	78	45	187	0	396	816
	1955	33	61	385	479	85	126	140	351	1	917	1748
	1957	30	132	542	704	92	125	56	273	9	1496	2482
India a	1899	22	5	14	43	7	—	2	9	0	54	106
	1913	21	4	42	69	13	—	16	29	0	56	154
	1929	33	9	58	107	16	—	22	39	0	53	199
b	1929	80	20	104	223	32	—	39	71	0	127	421
	1937	101	12	86	212	38	—	29	67	—	196	475
	1950	83	21	84	192	39	16	20	75	—	271	538
	1955	80	13	90	185	47	10	25	82	—	204	471
	1957	86	22	174	285	45	4	23	72	6	240	603
TOTAL a	1899c	545	977	338	1923	234	227	271	732	139	884	3677
	1913c	763	1653	711	3248	408	394	654	1456	260	1533	6497
	1929c	810	1985	1220	4212	592	407	972	1971	136	2617	8936
b	1929	2115	5480	3150	11272	1543	1159	2497	5198	365	7006	23841
	1937	1692	3643	2230	8031	1709	796	1977	4482	314	7068	19895
	1950	953	5109	4041	10176	2269	892	2860	6022	125	8498	24821
	1955	1542	8245	6127	16172	2632	1072	3038	6742	155	11298	34367
	1957	1600	10043	7244	19521	2454	1412	3294	7160	278	13853	40812

a Values at 1913 prices.
b Values at 1955 prices.
c Excluding goods consigned from the Netherlands.

Table A5. *Exports of manufactures to all countries, at current prices*

$ million, f.o.b.

	1899ᵃ	1913ᵃ	1929ᵃ	1929ᵇ	1937ᵇ	1950ᵇ	1955ᵇ	1957ᵇ
By commodity								
METALS AND ENGINEERING	943	2345	4970	5091	4482	10947	19707	26120
Metals	358	891	1436	1449	1423	2674	5152	6746
Machinery	249	678	1652	1722	1483	4296	7670	10438
Passenger road vehicles	10	110	441	442	353	857	1665	2046
Other transport equipment	108	242	736	758	622	2096	3577	4959
Other metal goods	218	424	705	720	601	1024	1643	1916
CHEMICALS	258	594	996	1040	983	2174	3911	4795
Intermediates	194	408	595	620	572	1169	2349	3096
Finished chemicals	64	186	401	420	411	1005	1562	1699
TEXTILES AND CLOTHING	1261	2217	3414	3505	1996	4127	4590	5123
Yarns	279	416	592	607	382	778	849	929
Fabrics	720	1378	2077	2137	1192	2533	2647	2937
Made-up goods	262	423	745	761	422	816	1094	1257
OTHER MANUFACTURES	646	1342	2515	2565	1805	3523	6157	7440
Intermediates	145	339	826	852	594	1204	2111	2738
Finished goods	501	1003	1689	1713	1211	2319	4046	4702
TOTAL	3108	6497	11895	12201	9266	20771	34367	43479
By country								
UNITED KINGDOM	1031	1960	2735	2735	1935	5100	6686	7713
FRANCE	446	787	1327	1327	541	1993	3077	3424
GERMANY	697	1726	2504	2504	2021	1462	5250	7471
OTHER WESTERN EUROPE	438	829	1654	1960	1700	4074	6773	8361
Belgium/Luxembourg	172	323	656	656	610	1282	2212	2580
Italy	112	213	452	452	311	759	1149	1627
Netherlands	..	..	..	306	279	607	1299	1498
Sweden	29	89	211	211	239	579	912	1217
Switzerland	125	204	335	335	261	847	1201	1439
UNITED STATES	362	846	2491	2491	1780	5526	8296	11016
CANADA	12	42	427	427	447	1266	2069	2349
JAPAN	48	153	476	476	645	697	1748	2538
INDIA	73	154	280	280	196	652	471	607

ᵃExcluding ⎫
ᵇIncluding ⎬ goods consigned from the Netherlands.
　　　　　 ⎭

Table A6. *Exports of manufactures to all countries, at constant prices*

$ *million, f.o.b.*

	Values at 1913 prices[a]			Values at 1955 prices[b]				
	1899	1913	1929	1929	1937	1950	1955	1957
By commodity								
METALS AND ENGINEERING	999	2345	4229	12051	9879	14139	19707	23794
Metals	379	891	1138	3782	3304	3697	5152	6098
Machinery	276	678	1065	4067	3183	5382	7670	9301
Passenger road vehicles	}105	352	1498	932	752	1077	1665	1973
Other transport equipment				1524	1388	2630	3577	4684
Other metal goods	239	424	528	1746	1252	1353	1643	1738
CHEMICALS	274	594	736	1618	1513	2302	3911	4826
Intermediates	203	408	441	935	872	1276	2349	3114
Finished chemicals	71	186	295	683	641	1026	1562	1712
TEXTILES AND CLOTHING	1670	2217	2224	5675	4749	4197	4590	5054
Yarns	369	416	398	1014	879	778	849	913
Fabrics	958	1378	1332	3463	2875	2480	2647	2901
Made-up goods	343	423	494	1198	995	939	1094	1240
OTHER MANUFACTURES	735	1342	1747	4498	3755	4183	6157	7138
Intermediates	169	339	540	1486	1290	1407	2111	2631
Finished goods	566	1003	1207	3012	2465	2776	4046	4507
TOTAL	3677	6497	8936	23841	19895	24821	34367	40812
By country								
UNITED KINGDOM	1327	1960	1821	5176	4034	6523	6686	7339
FRANCE	504	787	1039	2756	1151	2466	3077	3184
GERMANY	782	1726	1847	4762	3243	1813	5250	7302
OTHER WESTERN EUROPE	457	829	1317	3947	3869	4451	6773	7967
Belgium/Luxembourg	172	323	539	1413	1328	1429	2212	2324
Italy	129	213	408	731	795	775	1149	1601
Netherlands	..	..	..	639	632	692	1299	1478
Sweden	27	89	143	401	553	755	912	1160
Switzerland	129	204	227	763	561	800	1201	1404
UNITED STATES	423	846	2073	5092	4077	6731	8296	9705
CANADA	18	42	312	930	1155	1482	2069	2230
JAPAN	61	153	330	759	1890	816	1748	2482
INDIA	106	154	199	421	475	538	471	603

[a]Excluding ⎫
[b]Including ⎭ goods consigned from the Netherlands.

Table A7.   *Exports of manufactures to industrial countries, at current prices*

$ *million, f.o.b.*

	1899[a]	1913[a]	1929[a]	1929[b]	1937[b]	1950[b]	1955[b]
By commodity							
METALS AND ENGINEERING	478	1128	2251	2284	1787	4284	8994
Metals	225	536	861	872	767	1409	3056
Machinery	131	290	714	724	534	1635	3321
Passenger road vehicles	} 37	142	423	131	91	317	674
Other transport equipment				299	214	622	1275
Other metal goods	85	160	253	258	181	300	668
CHEMICALS	159	344	520	541	448	913	1789
Intermediates	131	267	360	377	317	610	1287
Finished chemicals	28	77	160	164	131	303	502
TEXTILES AND CLOTHING	656	998	1423	1461	636	1554	1828
Yarns	176	241	335	345	146	371	372
Fabrics	327	550	734	752	323	859	933
Made-up goods	153	207	354	364	167	323	523
OTHER MANUFACTURES	387	778	1454	1489	953	1858	3556
Intermediates	97	221	588	607	391	840	1539
Finished goods	290	557	866	882	562	1018	2017
TOTAL	1680	3248	5656	5783	3829	8642	16172
By country							
UNITED KINGDOM	387	624	815	815	494	1396	1968
FRANCE	302	502	790	790	234	671	1149
GERMANY	388	925	1339	1339	879	795	2777
OTHER WESTERN EUROPE	313	514	967	1094	886	2190	3939
Belgium/Luxembourg	124	206	431	431	389	839	1475
Italy	72	96	189	189	82	312	498
Netherlands	..	..	..	127	114	318	759
Sweden	20	60	122	122	134	270	519
Switzerland	97	152	225	225	167	451	688
UNITED STATES	236	535	1212	1212	798	2121	3896
CANADA	10	28	304	304	344	1050	1782
JAPAN	17	48	79	79	99	195	479
INDIA	31	69	150	150	95	223	185

[a]Excluding } goods consigned from the Netherlands.
[b]Including

Table A8.   *Exports of manufactures to industrial countries, at constant prices*

$ *million, f.o.b.*

	Values at 1913 prices[a]			Values at 1955 prices[b]			
	1899	1913	1929	1929	1937	1950	1955
By commodity							
METALS AND ENGINEERING	500	1128	1874	5580	3908	5516	8994
Metals	233	536	677	2305	1808	1924	3056
Machinery	126	290	469	1711	1067	2013	3321
Passenger road vehicles	} 47	142	540	283	197	404	674
Other transport equipment				618	462	787	1275
Other metal goods	94	160	188	663	374	388	668
CHEMICALS	168	344	381	841	675	962	1789
Intermediates	139	267	261	577	486	662	1287
Finished chemicals	29	77	120	264	189	300	502
TEXTILES AND CLOTHING	812	998	959	2231	1431	1548	1828
Yarns	219	241	232	581	340	365	372
Fabrics	400	550	486	1118	727	809	933
Made-up goods	193	207	241	532	364	374	523
OTHER MANUFACTURES	443	778	994	2605	2011	2111	3556
Intermediates	115	221	383	1074	885	928	1539
Finished goods	328	557	611	1531	1126	1183	2017
TOTAL	1923	3248	4212	11272	8031	10176	16172
By country							
UNITED KINGDOM	479	624	537	1547	1056	1776	1968
FRANCE	341	502	590	1624	495	809	1149
GERMANY	437	925	981	2489	1399	980	2777
OTHER WESTERN EUROPE	323	514	748	2120	1933	2329	3939
Belgium/Luxembourg	128	206	351	878	817	918	1475
Italy	79	96	165	295	186	310	498
Netherlands	..	..	..	227	252	363	759
Sweden	18	60	81	240	314	310	519
Switzerland	98	152	151	480	364	428	688
UNITED STATES	272	535	990	2483	1734	2619	3896
CANADA	14	28	207	655	899	1236	1782
JAPAN	16	48	53	127	300	233	479
INDIA	43	69	107	223	212	192	185

[a]Excluding } goods consigned from the Netherlands.
[b]Including

Table A9. *Exports of manufactures to semi-industrial countries, at current prices*

$ *million, f.o.b.*

	1899[a]	1913[a]	1929[a]	1929[b]	1937[b]	1950[b]	1955[b]
By commodity							
METALS AND ENGINEERING	176	550	1211	1216	1104	3059	4426
Metals	52	172	254	254	240	556	857
Machinery	46	151	398	399	412	1271	1935
Passenger road vehicles	23	106	378	145	129	272	324
Other transport equipment				236	177	701	990
Other metal goods	55	121	181	182	146	259	320
CHEMICALS	33	79	158	162	181	475	750
Intermediates	20	45	77	79	102	257	441
Finished chemicals	13	34	81	83	79	217	309
TEXTILES AND CLOTHING	279	584	847	857	510	816	781
Yarns	20	42	96	98	104	158	171
Fabrics	200	425	583	590	303	500	460
Made-up goods	59	117	168	169	103	158	150
OTHER MANUFACTURES	98	235	433	438	325	543	781
Intermediates	16	40	91	94	79	135	248
Finished goods	82	195	342	344	246	408	533
TOTAL	586	1448	2651	2675	2123	4904	6742
By country							
UNITED KINGDOM	366	810	1084	1084	776	1923	2180
FRANCE	34	83	105	105	44	232	313
GERMANY	67	218	324	324	391	250	859
OTHER WESTERN EUROPE	39	140	249	273	205	589	905
Belgium/Luxembourg	13	54	84	84	80	113	177
Italy	21	59	108	108	53	200	285
Netherlands	..	..	..	24	15	59	159
Sweden	—	9	23	23	30	106	122
Switzerland	5	18	34	34	27	111	162
UNITED STATES	70	137	635	635	468	1526	1864
CANADA	1	10	82	82	70	136	191
JAPAN	2	11	120	120	143	154	351
INDIA	7	29	52	52	26	94	82

[a]Excluding ⎫
[b]Including ⎬ goods consigned from the Netherlands.

Table A10.   *Exports of manufactures to semi-industrial countries,*
at constant prices

$ million, f.o.b.

	Values at 1913 prices[a]			Values at 1955 prices[b]			
	1899	1913	1929	1929	1937	1950	1955
By commodity							
METALS AND ENGINEERING	186	556	1026	2668	2287	3949	4426
Metals	55	174	206	618	528	779	857
Machinery	50	151	247	887	825	1613	1935
Passenger road vehicles	} 22	108	452	285	266	333	324
Other transport equipment				480	369	875	990
Other metal goods	59	123	121	398	299	349	320
CHEMICALS	38	79	117	251	280	513	750
Intermediates	22	45	56	105	156	287	441
Finished chemicals	16	34	61	136	124	226	309
TEXTILES AND CLOTHING	392	585	526	1503	1256	888	781
Yarns	27	42	60	168	218	162	171
Fabrics	281	426	362	1038	778	514	460
Made-up goods	84	117	104	297	260	212	150
OTHER MANUFACTURES	116	236	302	772	656	659	781
Intermediates	20	40	60	163	162	156	248
Finished goods	96	196	242	609	494	503	533
TOTAL	732	1457	1971	5198	4482	6022	6732
By country							
UNITED KINGDOM	477	810	713	2048	1596	2468	2180
FRANCE	38	83	76	212	94	299	313
GERMANY	75	227	240	660	632	314	859
OTHER WESTERN EUROPE	45	140	205	533	471	643	905
Belgium/Luxembourg	14	54	70	204	185	130	177
Italy	27	59	96	170	123	208	285
Netherlands	..	..	..	43	32	70	159
Sweden	—	9	15	41	71	138	122
Switzerland	4	18	24	75	60	97	162
UNITED STATES	83	137	551	1298	1034	1878	1864
CANADA	2	10	70	183	173	158	191
JAPAN	2	11	79	190	413	187	351
INDIA	9	29	39	71	67	75	82

[a]Excluding } goods consigned from the Netherlands.
[b]Including

Table A11. *Exports of manufactures to the rest of the world, at current prices*

$ *million, f.o.b.*

	1899[a]	1913[a]	1929[a]	1929[b]	1937[b]	1950[b]	1955[b]
By commodity							
METALS AND ENGINEERING	289	667	1508	1591	1591	3604	6287
Metals	81	183	321	323	415	709	1239
Machinery	72	237	541	599	538	1390	2414
Passenger road vehicles	} 58	104	376	166	133	268	667
Other transport equipment				223	231	773	1312
Other metal goods	78	143	270	280	274	464	655
CHEMICALS	66	171	319	337	354	786	1372
Intermediates	43	96	159	163	152	302	621
Finished chemicals	23	75	160	174	202	484	751
TEXTILES AND CLOTHING	326	635	1143	1187	850	1758	1981
Yarns	83	133	161	164	133	249	306
Fabrics	193	403	759	795	566	1174	1254
Made-up goods	50	99	223	228	151	335	421
OTHER MANUFACTURES	161	329	628	637	527	1122	1820
Intermediates	32	78	146	150	125	230	324
Finished goods	129	251	482	487	402	892	1496
TOTAL	842	1802	3588	3743	3314	7225	11453
By country							
UNITED KINGDOM	278	526	836	836	665	1781	2538
FRANCE	110	202	431	431	263	1091	1615
GERMANY	242	583	840	840	751	418	1614
OTHER WESTERN EUROPE	86	175	439	593	607	1293	1929
Belgium/Luxembourg	35	63	141	141	141	330	560
Italy	19	58	155	155	176	246	366
Netherlands	..	..	..	154	149	230	381
Sweden	9	20	66	66	75	202	271
Switzerland	23	34	77	77	66	285	351
UNITED STATES	56	174	644	644	514	1880	2536
CANADA	1	4	41	41	34	80	96
JAPAN	29	94	277	277	403	349	918
INDIA	35	56	78	78	76	335	204

[a]Excluding } goods consigned from the Netherlands.
[b]Including

Table A12. *Exports of manufactures to the rest of the world, at constant prices*

$ *million, f.o.b.*

	Values at 1913 prices[a]			Values at 1955 prices[b]			
	1899	1913	1929	1929	1937	1950	1955
By commodity							
METALS AND ENGINEERING	313	661	1329	3799	3803	4674	6287
Metals	91	181	255	859	968	994	1239
Machinery	100	235	349	1469	1291	1756	2414
Passenger road vehicles	} 36	104	506	364	289	340	667
Other transport equipment				426	557	968	1312
Other metal goods	86	141	219	685	579	616	655
CHEMICALS	68	171	238	526	558	827	1372
Intermediates	42	96	124	243	230	327	621
Finished chemicals	26	75	114	283	328	500	751
TEXTILES AND CLOTHING	466	634	739	1941	2062	1761	1981
Yarns	123	133	106	265	321	251	306
Fabrics	277	402	484	1307	1370	1157	1254
Made-up goods	66	99	149	369	371	353	421
OTHER MANUFACTURES	176	328	441	1121	1088	1413	1820
Intermediates	34	78	97	249	243	323	324
Finished goods	142	250	354	872	845	1090	1496
TOTAL	1023	1794	2753	7371	7382	8623	11453
By country							
UNITED KINGDOM	371	526	571	1581	1382	2279	2538
FRANCE	125	202	373	920	562	1358	1615
GERMANY	270	574	626	1613	1212	519	1614
OTHER WESTERN EUROPE	89	175	364	1294	1465	1479	1929
Belgium/Luxembourg	30	63	118	331	326	381	560
Italy	23	58	147	266	486	257	366
Netherlands	..	..	..	369	348	259	381
Sweden	9	20	47	120	168	307	271
Switzerland	27	34	52	208	137	275	351
UNITED STATES	68	174	532	1311	1309	2234	2536
CANADA	2	4	35	92	83	88	96
JAPAN	43	94	193	442	1177	396	918
INDIA	54	56	53	127	196	271	204

[a]Excluding } goods consigned from the Netherlands.
[b]Including }

Table A13. *'Imports' of manufactures at 1955 prices*

$ million, f.o.b.

	1899[a]	1913[a]	1929	1937	1950	1955	1957
INDUSTRIAL COUNTRIES							
Belgium-Luxembourg	472	762	847	480	754	1111	1336
France	454	907	901	605	702	1121	1447
Germany[b]	924	1295	1110	534	517	1327	1622
Italy	174	472	532	269	525	762	1003
Netherlands	400	639	983	705	1107	1592	1857
Norway	85	149	226	288	455	605	706
Sweden	65	178	348	446	600	977	1106
Switzerland	256	422	533	316	449	750	966
United Kingdom	1331	1945	2115	1692	953	1542	1600
Canada	247	824	1457	903	1903	2867	3252
United States	609	1016	1693	1327	2138	3260	3992
Japan	175	324	527	466	73	258	634
SEMI-INDUSTRIAL COUNTRIES							
Australia	}435	613	811	656	1224	1244	999
New Zealand		149	269	283	357	480	462
Union of South Africa	204	344	462	770	688	908	992
India	}704	1219	1159	796	590	820	1182
Pakistan					302	242	230
Argentina	218	744	1064	725	623	562	645
Brazil	174	429	489	372	757	532	731
Chile	75	193	269	120	124	153	248
Colombia	26	57	153	146	312	456	293
Mexico	155	138	262	293	553	677	789
Palestine/Israel	..	..	19	54	136	150	161
Turkey	95	224	132	147	230	328	225
Yugoslavia	..	..	109	120	125	180	203
U.S.S.R.	376	705	363	314	124	155	278
OTHER SELECTED COUNTRIES							
Belgian Congo	..	..	72	55	145	241	252
Egypt	..	..	285	219	331	315	164
French Morocco	..	..	113	64	203	231	..
Nigeria	..	..	62	94	148	226	..
Southern Rhodesia	..	..	18	28	92	166[c]	198[c]
Indonesia	..	..	484	437	254	320	367
Iran	..	..	41	84	164	204	315
Philippines	..	..	167	201	244	352	404
Cuba	..	..	196	166	379	387	483
Peru	..	..	84	87	131	177	..
Venezuela	..	..	131	158	486	732	1234

Sources: Tables A15–A45.

[a]Computed by multiplying 'imports' in each commodity group at 1913 prices by the ratio of 'imports' in 1929 at 1955 prices (including 'imports' from the Netherlands) to those at 1913 prices (excluding 'imports' from the Netherlands), and aggregating.

[b]West Germany in 1950–57.

[c]Federation of Rhodesia and Nyasaland.

Table A14. *'Imports' of manufactures per head at 1955 prices*

	1899	1913	1929	1937	1950	$ million, f.o.b. 1955	1957
INDUSTRIAL COUNTRIES							
Belgium-Luxembourg	68	96	102	56	85	121	144
France	12	23	22	15	17	16	33
Germany[a]	17	19	17	8	11	26	31
Italy	5	13	13	6	11	16	21
Netherlands	78	105	126	81	110	147	169
Norway	39	62	81	99	138	178	202
Sweden	13	32	57	71	86	134	149
Switzerland	78	108	133	75	96	150	189
United Kingdom	35	46	46	36	19	30	31
Canada	46	111	146	80	139	183	196
United States	8	10	14	10	14	20	23
Japan	4	6	8	7	1	3	7
SEMI-INDUSTRIAL COUNTRIES							
Australia	} 97	130	127	96	149	135	104
New Zealand		135	192	177	188	229	210
Union of South Africa	41	56	58	79	55	66	70
India	} 2	4	3	2	2	2	3
Pakistan					4	3	3
Argentina	46	94	92	51	36	29	32
Brazil	10	17	15	10	15	9	12
Chile	24	54	64	25	20	23	35
Colombia	..	11	20	17	28	36	22
Mexico	12	9	16	16	21	23	25
Palestine/Israel	..	..	19	39	105	88	85
Turkey	..	..	10	9	11	14	9
Yugoslavia	..	..	8	8	8	10	11
U.S.S.R.	..	4	2	2	1	1	1
OTHER SELECTED COUNTRIES							
Belgian Congo	..	..	8	5	13	19	19
Egypt	..	..	20	14	16	14	7
French Morocco	..	..	21	10	26	27	..
Nigeria	..	..	3	5	6	7	..
Southern Rhodesia	..	..	16	22	42	17[b]	19[b]
Indonesia	..	..	8	6	3	4	4
Iran	..	..	..	5	8	11	16
Philippines	..	..	14	13	12	16	18
Cuba	..	..	49	38	69	63	75
Peru	..	..	14	13	15	19	..
Venezuela	..	..	41	46	97	126	202

Sources: Tables A13 and E7.

[a]West Germany in 1950–57.
[b]Federation of Rhodesia and Nyasaland.

Table A15. '*Imports*' of manufactures into Belgium/Luxembourg

$ million, f.o.b.

	Values at 1913 prices[a]			Values at 1955 prices[b]			
	1899	1913	1929	1929	1937	1950	1955
By commodity							
METALS AND ENGINEERING	48	98	160	504	257	433	627
Metals	20	41	46	187	79	71	100
Machinery	15	27	40	166	70	184	247
Passenger road vehicles	} 3	} 13	} 58	45	39	82	131
Other transport equipment				46	40	58	85
Other metal goods	10	17	16	60	29	38	64
CHEMICALS	15	28	26	71	58	68	141
Intermediates	12	21	17	47	45	46	86
Finished chemicals	3	7	9	24	13	22	55
TEXTILES AND CLOTHING	64	66	56	145	73	107	124
Yarns	15	20	24	65	30	36	30
Fabrics	37	35	26	63	26	39	58
Made-up goods	12	11	6	17	17	32	36
OTHER MANUFACTURES	32	61	48	123	91	140	219
Intermediates	6	14	16	41	30	35	60
Finished goods	26	47	32	82	61	105	159
TOTAL	157	251	292	847	480	754	1111
By country							
UNITED KINGDOM	48	37	33	98	66	151	145
FRANCE	60	115	128	384	108	130	171
GERMANY	33	76	60	165	108	121	301
OTHER WESTERN EUROPE	3	11	15	80	82	170	313
Belgium/Luxembourg	—	—	—	—	—	—	—
Italy	0	5	6	13	8	17	36
Netherlands	..	..	..	37	40	80	194
Sweden	1	1	3	8	17	19	32
Switzerland	2	5	6	22	17	54	51
UNITED STATES	11	11	51	109	98	163	158
CANADA	0	1	2	5	4	6	13
JAPAN	0	0	0	1	10	5	6
INDIA	1	1	2	5	4	7	3

[a]Excluding } goods consigned from the Netherlands.
[b]Including

Table A16. *'Imports' of manufactures into France*

$ *million, f.o.b.*

	Values at 1913 prices[a]			Values at 1955 prices[b]			
	1899	1913	1929	1929	1937	1950	1955
By commodity							
METALS AND ENGINEERING	60	151	187	568	359	454	760
Metals	29	65	62	194	136	99	255
Machinery	20	54	62	239	132	267	341
Passenger road vehicles }	4	14	46	13	7	11	26
Other transport equipment }				63	53	60	102
Other metal goods	7	18	17	59	31	17	36
CHEMICALS	17	33	31	58	49	69	151
Intermediates	14	27	22	43	37	54	111
Finished chemicals	3	6	9	15	12	15	40
TEXTILES AND CLOTHING	55	53	36	88	65	87	52
Yarns	16	9	10	25	15	19	14
Fabrics	31	34	18	46	32	51	24
Made-up goods	8	10	8	17	18	17	14
OTHER MANUFACTURES	35	87	75	187	131	91	156
Intermediates	8	32	36	86	40	23	50
Finished goods	27	55	39	101	91	68	106
TOTAL	166	322	328	901	605	702	1121
By country							
UNITED KINGDOM	59	79	57	151	92	120	162
FRANCE	—	—	—	—	—	—	—
GERMANY	31	117	102	277	103	77	266
OTHER WESTERN EUROPE	42	69	88	257	249	279	433
Belgium/Luxembourg	18	37	40	116	140	102	190
Italy	11	11	23	47	14	66	75
Netherlands	..	..	..	15	22	29	55
Sweden	1	3	6	15	19	21	36
Switzerland	12	18	19	64	54	61	77
UNITED STATES	27	46	74	193	137	205	232
CANADA	0	1	2	7	10	14	24
JAPAN	4	10	7	14	11	4	3
INDIA	2	1	1	2	1	2	3

[a]Excluding } goods consigned from the Netherlands.
[b]Including }

Table A17.   'Imports' of manufactures into Germany

$ million, f.o.b.

	Values at 1913 prices[a]			Values at 1955 prices[b]			
	1899	1913	1929	1929	1937	1950[c]	1955[c]
By commodity							
METALS AND ENGINEERING	79	134	168	535	214	179	749
Metals	37	81	88	316	154	74	474
Machinery	26	30	28	112	34	64	191
Passenger road vehicles	} 6	12	43	34	6	14	25
Other transport equipment				42	13	15	36
Other metal goods	10	11	9	31	7	12	23
CHEMICALS	27	44	35	91	53	68	146
Intermediates	22	31	23	63	37	47	112
Finished chemicals	5	13	12	28	16	21	34
TEXTILES AND CLOTHING	139	150	114	310	184	182	248
Yarns	97	98	77	207	110	74	108
Fabrics	31	37	30	83	63	69	95
Made-up goods	11	15	7	20	11	39	45
OTHER MANUFACTURES	44	76	58	172	84	85	184
Intermediates	10	21	23	62	35	32	86
Finished goods	34	55	35	110	49	53	98
TOTAL	292	404	377	1110	534	517	1327
By country							
UNITED KINGDOM	121	121	68	221	127	73	144
FRANCE	40	61	86	279	21	89	273
GERMANY	—	—	—	—	—	—	—
OTHER WESTERN EUROPE	92	130	124	365	311	289	703
Belgium/Luxembourg	28	49	49	119	112	55	233
Italy	27	22	28	50	42	52	91
Netherlands	..	..	..	48	40	83	162
Sweden	6	15	12	36	32	29	61
Switzerland	31	44	35	112	85	70	156
UNITED STATES	35	84	84	210	49	52	174
CANADA	1	1	7	20	12	3	19
JAPAN	1	5	3	6	13	8	13
INDIA	2	2	4	10	3	4	2

[a]Excluding }
[b]including } goods consigned from the Netherlands.
[c]West Germany only.

Table A18. *'Imports' of manufactures into Italy*

$ million, f.o.b.

	Values at 1913 prices[a]			Values at 1955 prices[b]			
	1899	1913	1929	1929	1937	1950	1955
By commodity							
METALS AND ENGINEERING	26	76	95	311	161	371	440
Metals	10	27	33	115	62	118	112
Machinery	9	24	36	135	63	207	244
Passenger road vehicles	} 3	8	14	9	1	2	6
Other transport equipment				10	11	27	30
Other metal goods	4	17	12	42	24	17	48
CHEMICALS	8	21	20	45	33	67	133
Intermediates	7	16	14	31	18	44	91
Finished chemicals	1	5	6	14	15	23	42
TEXTILES AND CLOTHING	17	28	28	64	20	25	44
Yarns	6	7	8	17	4	10	11
Fabrics	9	16	14	33	12	10	26
Made-up goods	2	5	6	14	4	5	7
OTHER MANUFACTURES	11	39	41	111	54	57	145
Intermediates	3	11	16	38	17	12	39
Finished goods	8	28	25	73	37	45	106
TOTAL	63	164	180	532	269	525	762
By country							
UNITED KINGDOM	17	27	24	73	16	95	126
FRANCE	9	25	36	107	25	53	90
GERMANY	21	75	69	185	129	74	251
OTHER WESTERN EUROPE	9	21	25	82	57	93	161
Belgium/Luxembourg	5	8	10	24	15	28	44
Italy	—	—	—	—	—	—	—
Netherlands	..	..	..	7	5	9	21
Sweden	0	1	2	5	5	13	21
Switzerland	4	12	13	46	32	43	75
UNITED STATES	6	15	27	80	36	193	121
CANADA	0	0	1	3	3	6	10
JAPAN	0	1	1	2	2	8	4
INDIA	0	0	0	1	0	1	1

[a]Excluding } goods consigned from the Netherlands.
[b]Including

Table A19. *'Imports' of manufactures into the Netherlands*

$ *million, f.o.b.*

	Values at 1913 prices			Values at 1955 prices			
	1899	1913	1929	1929	1937	1950	1955
By commodity							
METALS AND ENGINEERING	60	108	172	554	385	628	992
Metals	39	62	62	223	177	230	337
Machinery	8	20	39	159	92	197	334
Passenger road vehicles ⎫				20	17	50	94
Other transport equipment ⎭	3	13	41	46	42	77	123
Other metal goods	10	13	30	106	57	74	104
CHEMICALS	12	24	40	72	56	94	152
Intermediates	10	19	25	47	38	57	112
Finished chemicals	2	5	15	25	18	37	40
TEXTILES AND CLOTHING	53	56	81	179	145	227	207
Yarns	15	20	22	57	64	78	74
Fabrics	22	23	32	69	43	104	74
Made-up goods	16	13	27	53	38	45	59
OTHER MANUFACTURES	23	46	82	175	118	151	241
Intermediates	4	9	28	56	35	40	69
Finished goods	19	37	54	119	83	111	172
TOTAL	149	236	377	983	705	1107	1592
By country							
UNITED KINGDOM	45	53	49	148	124	223	242
FRANCE	5	7	29	63	40	92	85
GERMANY	55	96	179	474	254	263	491
OTHER WESTERN EUROPE	20	32	94	230	200	419	584
Belgium/Luxembourg	18	27	76	182	156	344	460
Italy	0	1	5	9	10	13	32
Netherlands	—	—	—	—	—	—	—
Sweden	1	2	5	13	16	38	50
Switzerland	1	2	8	26	18	24	42
UNITED STATES	24	47	23	58	70	91	153
CANADA	0	0	2	6	5	5	14
JAPAN	0	0	1	2	10	7	21
INDIA	0	0	1	2	2	6	4

Table A20.   *'Imports' of manufactures into Norway*

$ *million, f.o.b.*

	Values at 1913 prices[a]			Values at 1955 prices[b]			
	1899	1913	1929	1929	1937	1950	1955
By commodity							
METALS AND ENGINEERING	14	29	51	131	177	322	440
Metals	4	11	12	40	51	66	97
Machinery	5	8	9	27	38	80	116
Passenger road vehicles ⎱				3	11	5	12
Other transport equipment ⎰	2	6	24	40	59	153	182
Other metal goods	3	4	6	21	18	18	33
CHEMICALS	1	5	7	14	16	23	42
Intermediates	1	4	6	12	13	18	33
Finished chemicals	0	1	1	2	3	5	9
TEXTILES AND CLOTHING	11	13	19	46	62	71	73
Yarns	2	3	4	10	14	31	17
Fabrics	6	7	9	24	33	28	40
Made-up goods	3	3	6	12	15	12	16
OTHER MANUFACTURES	5	8	14	36	34	36	50
Intermediates	1	2	3	7	7	13	16
Finished goods	4	6	11	29	27	23	34
TOTAL	31	54	91	226	288	455	605
By country							
UNITED KINGDOM	13	16	24	56	57	162	164
FRANCE	0	1	2	7	9	44	29
GERMANY	15	25	37	82	83	30	130
OTHER WESTERN EUROPE	1	10	19	61	103	169	244
Belgium/Luxembourg	0	2	4	13	22	13	43
Italy	0	0	2	3	4	8	10
Netherlands	..	..	..	5	6	23	30
Sweden	1	7	12	36	66	121	149
Switzerland	0	1	1	4	5	4	12
UNITED STATES	2	2	8	18	31	40	33
CANADA	0	0	0	0	1	4	5
JAPAN	—	—	0	0	4	4	0
INDIA	—	0	0	0	1	1	—

[a]Excluding ⎱ goods consigned from the Netherlands.
[b]Including ⎰

Table A21.   *'Imports' of manufactures into Sweden*

$ million, f.o.b.

	Values at 1913 prices[a]			*Values at 1955 prices*[b]			
	1899	1913	1929	1929	1937	1950	1955
By commodity							
METALS AND ENGINEERING	10	27	65	200	253	365	594
Metals	4	13	20	80	99	105	177
Machinery	3	8	15	56	73	123	190
Passenger road vehicles ⎫	1	3	24	20	30	66	99
Other transport equipment ⎬				20	26	56	93
Other metal goods	2	3	6	24	25	15	35
CHEMICALS	1	8	11	23	33	47	89
Intermediates	1	7	8	17	26	35	65
Finished chemicals	0	1	3	6	7	12	24
TEXTILES AND CLOTHING	8	17	30	62	92	124	151
Yarns	4	5	7	16	29	36	35
Fabrics	3	8	12	25	40	55	72
Made-up goods	1	4	11	21	23	33	44
OTHER MANUFACTURES	3	10	25	63	67	65	143
Intermediates	1	3	5	14	15	19	30
Finished goods	2	7	20	49	52	46	113
TOTAL	22	62	132	348	446	600	977
By country							
UNITED KINGDOM	16	15	22	60	86	225	209
FRANCE	0	1	3	10	20	58	63
GERMANY	4	38	64	168	157	114	370
OTHER WESTERN EUROPE	1	4	11	39	74	114	206
Belgium/Luxembourg	1	2	6	18	41	50	83
Italy	0	0	2	5	5	17	25
Netherlands	..	..	..	6	15	33	57
Sweden	—	—	—	—	—	—	—
Switzerland	0	2	3	10	13	14	41
UNITED STATES	2	5	30	68	94	78	112
CANADA	0	0	1	2	6	4	6
JAPAN	—	0	0	0	8	7	10
INDIA	—	0	0	0	0	1	0

[a]Excluding ⎫
[b]Including ⎬ goods consigned from the Netherlands.

Table A22. *'Imports' of manufactures into Switzerland*

$ million, f.o.b.

	Values at 1913 prices[a]			Values at 1955 prices[b]			
	1899	1913	1929	1929	1937	1950	1955
By commodity							
METALS AND ENGINEERING	25	41	71	236	153	251	406
Metals	12	20	20	85	82	93	143
Machinery	5	11	19	76	32	70	143
Passenger road vehicles ⎫	2	3	21	18	14	48	62
Other transport equipment ⎭				15	6	24	28
Other metal goods	6	7	11	42	19	16	30
CHEMICALS	6	14	16	36	28	50	97
Intermediates	5	11	12	26	20	36	74
Finished chemicals	1	3	4	10	8	14	23
TEXTILES AND CLOTHING	46	66	72	153	69	61	92
Yarns	23	26	31	64	24	14	18
Fabrics	15	29	33	74	36	27	43
Made-up goods	8	11	8	15	9	20	31
OTHER MANUFACTURES	21	39	47	105	65	83	154
Intermediates	5	9	12	28	20	20	40
Finished goods	16	30	35	77	45	63	114
TOTAL	97	160	208	533	316	449	750
By country							
UNITED KINGDOM	..[c]	17	17	56	40	66	60
FRANCE	18	32	61	166	67	72	119
GERMANY	52	85	86	211	128	112	315
OTHER WESTERN EUROPE	27	25	36	78	64	98	134
Belgium/Luxembourg	4	4	13	34	29	47	47
Italy	23	21	22	38	22	27	49
Netherlands	..	..	..	3	7	13	23
Sweden	—	0	1	3	6	11	15
Switzerland	—	—	—	—	—	—	—
UNITED STATES	0	1	8	20	16	89	109
CANADA	—	0	1	2	1	6	10
JAPAN	0	—	0	0	1	4	4
INDIA	—	—	0	0	0	1	0

[a]Excluding ⎱
[b]Including ⎰ goods consigned from the Netherlands.
[c]Not separately recorded (see p. 421).

Table A23. *'Imports' of manufactures into the United Kingdom*

$ million, f.o.b.

	Values at 1913 prices[a]			Values at 1955 prices[b]			
	1899	1913	1929	1929	1937	1950	1955
By commodity							
METALS AND ENGINEERING	85	200	289	926	856	456	814
Metals	45	106	133	469	485	273	475
Machinery	18	39	67	243	231	123	240
Passenger road vehicles	} 4	29	57	34	27	4	20
Other transport equipment				62	44	26	55
Other metal goods	18	26	32	118	69	30	24
CHEMICALS	42	64	62	148	119	134	218
Intermediates	35	54	47	108	92	103	177
Finished chemicals	7	10	15	40	27	31	41
TEXTILES AND CLOTHING	228	263	230	463	205	199	161
Yarns	26	33	26	56	10	31	19
Fabrics	122	157	128	252	107	129	98
Made-up goods	80	73	76	155	88	39	44
OTHER MANUFACTURES	187	237	229	578	511	161	349
Intermediates	64	81	92	263	230	93	206
Finished goods	123	156	137	315	281	68	143
TOTAL	545	763	810	2115	1692	953	1542
By country							
UNITED KINGDOM	—	—	—	—	—	—	—
FRANCE	168	199	155	387	125	148	145
GERMANY	149	246	193	486	254	63	219
OTHER WESTERN EUROPE	92	152	200	555	462	285	441
Belgium/Luxembourg	44	62	99	254	176	112	111
Italy	11	26	41	70	36	64	62
Netherlands	..	..	..	76	81	52	108
Sweden	8	26	27	85	101	29	97
Switzerland	29	38	33	70	68	28	63
UNITED STATES	103	127	182	480	346	225	333
CANADA	7	6	34	100	338	133	292
JAPAN	4	13	13	28	64	18	33
INDIA	22	21	33	80	101	83	80

[a]Excluding ⎱
[b]Including ⎰ goods consigned from the Netherlands.

Table A24. *'Imports' of manufactures into Canada*

$ million, f.o.b.

By commodity	Values at 1913 prices[a]			Values at 1955 prices[b]			
	1899	1913	1929	1929	1937	1950	1955
METALS AND ENGINEERING	37	140	372	901	519	1223	1850
Metals	12	54	66	192	125	213	285
Machinery	10	38	107	323	188	549	895
Passenger road vehicles	} 2	22	170	74	30	88	87
Other transport equipment				218	125	268	437
Other metal goods	13	26	29	94	51	105	146
CHEMICALS	7	16	28	69	67	169	258
Intermediates	5	10	20	48	56	130	186
Finished chemicals	2	6	8	21	11	39	72
TEXTILES AND CLOTHING	22	73	81	245	152	173	223
Yarns	2	5	7	25	22	18	20
Fabrics	8	44	49	144	91	108	136
Made-up goods	12	24	25	76	39	47	72
OTHER MANUFACTURES	21	68	96	242	166	336	530
Intermediates	2	6	12	37	24	49	89
Finished goods	19	62	84	205	142	287	441
TOTAL	85	297	577	1457	903	1903	2867
By country							
UNITED KINGDOM	25	84	92	254	215	377	327
FRANCE	0	3	13	29	7	12	18
GERMANY	4	12	13	31	17	10	53
OTHER WESTERN EUROPE	2	9	16	48	31	48	83
Belgium/Luxembourg	1	3	8	19	13	21	28
Italy	—	0	2	3	3	4	10
Netherlands	..	..	..	8	3	2	10
Sweden	—	0	1	3	5	6	11
Switzerland	1	6	5	15	7	15	24
UNITED STATES	53	185	433	1076	611	1432	2331
CANADA	—	—	—	—	—	—	—
JAPAN	0	1	5	12	13	14	40
INDIA	0	2	5	7	9	11	14

[a]Excluding }
[b]Including } goods consigned from the Netherlands.

Table A25.   *'Imports' of manufactures into the United States*

$ *million, f.o.b.*

	Values at 1913 prices[a]			Values at 1955 prices[b]			
	1899	1913	1929	1929	1937	1950	1955
By commodity							
METALS AND ENGINEERING	21	55	128	381	220	814	1191
Metals	12	30	82	237	142	580	584
Machinery	4	11	22	85	42	139	288
Passenger road vehicles }	0	3	11	1	4	30	104
Other transport equipment }				15	6	21	95
Other metal goods	5	11	13	43	26	44	120
CHEMICALS	27	68	63	128	105	135	275
Intermediates	22	57	44	88	70	84	185
Finished chemicals	5	11	19	40	35	51	90
TEXTILES AND CLOTHING	148	195	197	433	349	287	437
Yarns	7	12	13	31	15	17	23
Fabrics	102	147	127	279	235	188	260
Made-up goods	39	36	57	123	99	82	154
OTHER MANUFACTURES	56	97	255	748	651	896	1357
Intermediates	10	29	134	425	416	590	847
Finished goods	46	68	121	323	235	306	510
TOTAL	253	414	643	1693	1327	2138	3260
By country							
UNITED KINGDOM	93	110	110	316	195	280	361
FRANCE	39	57	70	168	63	108	145
GERMANY	66	127	134	296	97	109	342
OTHER WESTERN EUROPE	30	43	101	268	250	359	605
Belgium/Luxembourg	6	8	38	75	92	142	228
Italy	7	9	32	54	40	42	106
Netherlands	..	..	..	20	29	39	93
Sweden	—	4	9	29	33	22	44
Switzerland	17	22	22	90	56	114	134
UNITED STATES	—	—	—	—	—	—	—
CANADA	6	19	148	485	480	1055	1384
JAPAN	7	18	28	62	164	154	345
INDIA	14	40	53	97	77	73	76

[a]Excluding } goods consigned from the Netherlands.
[b]Including }

Table A26.   *'Imports' of manufactures into Japan*

$ *million, f.o.b.*

	Values at 1913 prices[a]			Values at 1955 prices[b]			
	1899	1913	1929	1929	1937	1950	1955
By commodity							
METALS AND ENGINEERING	35	69	116	333	354	20	131
Metals	9	26	53	167	216	2	17
Machinery	3	20	25	90	72	10	92
Passenger road vehicles	} 17	16	31	12	11	4	8
Other transport equipment				41	37	2	9
Other metal goods	6	7	7	23	18	2	5
CHEMICALS	5	19	42	86	58	38	87
Intermediates	5	10	23	47	34	8	55
Finished chemicals	0	9	19	39	24	30	32
TEXTILES AND CLOTHING	21	18	15	43	15	5	11
Yarns	6	3	3	8	3	1	3
Fabrics	14	13	8	26	9	1	7
Made-up goods	1	2	4	9	3	3	1
OTHER MANUFACTURES	5	10	24	65	39	10	28
Intermediates	1	4	6	17	16	2	7
Finished goods	4	6	18	48	23	8	21
TOTAL	66	117	197	527	466	73	258
By country							
UNITED KINGDOM	42	65	41	114	38	4	28
FRANCE	2	1	7	24	11	3	11
GERMANY	7	28	44	114	69	7	39
OTHER WESTERN EUROPE	4	8	19	57	50	6	32
Belgium/Luxembourg	3	4	8	24	21	4	8
Italy	0	1	2	3	2	0	2
Netherlands	..	..	..	2	4	0	6
Sweden	—	1	3	7	14	1	3
Switzerland	1	2	6	21	9	1	13
UNITED STATES	9	12	70	171	246	51	140
CANADA	0	0	9	25	39	0	5
JAPAN	—	—	—	—	—	—	—
INDIA	2	2	8	19	14	2	2

[a]Excluding } goods consigned from the Netherlands.
[b]Including

Table A27.   *'Imports' of manufactures into Australia*

$ *million, f.o.b.*

	Values at 1913 prices[a]			Values at 1955 prices[b]			
	1899[c]	1913	1929	1929	1937	1950	1955
By commodity							
METALS AND ENGINEERING	45	104	160	376	290	759	742
Metals	18	34	29	73	46	164	146
Machinery	10	26	35	126	114	225	264
Passenger road vehicles	} 4	} 20	} 78	59	52	151	94
Other transport equipment				75	48	162	181
Other metal goods	13	24	18	43	30	57	57
CHEMICALS	10	13	14	31	34	47	90
Intermediates	6	8	8	18	25	32	65
Finished chemicals	4	5	6	13	9	15	25
TEXTILES AND CLOTHING	74	72	86	263	215	275	247
Yarns	2	3	7	26	20	27	35
Fabrics	37	41	49	154	129	140	144
Made-up goods	35	28	30	83	66	108	68
OTHER MANUFACTURES	36	43	54	140	115	142	165
Intermediates	6	8	16	45	39	36	59
Finished goods	30	35	38	95	76	106	106
TOTAL	165	232	316	811	656	1224	1244
By country							
UNITED KINGDOM	122	152	161	450	360	888	769
FRANCE	1	2	5	13	4	32	31
GERMANY	9	20	12	30	24	35	68
OTHER WESTERN EUROPE	3	10	14	40	30	73	109
Belgium/Luxembourg	2	4	3	7	7	18	26
Italy	1	2	4	7	4	21	18
Netherlands	..	..	..	4	3	8	21
Sweden	—	2	2	7	9	19	20
Switzerland	0	2	5	15	7	7	24
UNITED STATES	22	30	87	196	106	96	138
CANADA	2	4	14	35	59	29	40
JAPAN	1	3	11	27	50	35	51
INDIA	5	10	11	21	23	34	40

[a]Excluding } goods consigned from the Netherlands.
[b]Including
[c]Including New Zealand.

Table A28. *'Imports' of manufactures into New Zealand*

$ million, f.o.b.

	Values at 1913 prices[a]			Values at 1955 prices[b]			
	1899[c]	1913	1929	1929	1937	1950	1955
By commodity							
METALS AND ENGINEERING	..	23	56	126	134	182	279
Metals	..	7	9	23	21	38	60
Machinery	..	5	10	36	45	66	102
Passenger road vehicles ⎫				29	34	21	44
Other transport equipment ⎭	..	5	30	22	17	36	46
Other metal goods	..	6	7	16	17	21	27
CHEMICALS	..	4	6	11	12	15	34
Intermediates	..	2	2	4	5	8	18
Finished chemicals	..	2	4	7	7	7	16
TEXTILES AND CLOTHING	..	18	21	71	85	105	97
Yarns	..	0	1	2	4	8	10
Fabrics	..	9	9	33	42	64	62
Made-up goods	..	9	11	36	39	33	25
OTHER MANUFACTURES	..	12	23	59	52	55	71
Intermediates	..	2	4	11	11	14	20
Finished goods	..	10	19	48	41	41	51
TOTAL	..	56	105	269	283	357	480
By country							
UNITED KINGDOM	..	45	61	164	183	309	366
FRANCE	..	—	0	0	0	2	4
GERMANY	..	2	2	5	4	1	18
OTHER WESTERN EUROPE	..	0	2	5	7	7	23
Belgium/Luxembourg	..	—	1	1	1	2	7
Italy	..	0	0	0	0	0	2
Netherlands	..	..	..	0	1	1	5
Sweden	..	—	0	1	3	3	5
Switzerland	..	0	1	3	2	1	4
UNITED STATES	..	5	22	50	37	22	36
CANADA	..	1	16	39	33	11	19
JAPAN	..	—	1	3	14	1	7
INDIA	..	1	2	4	5	4	7

[a]Excluding ⎫
[b]Including ⎭ goods consigned from the Netherlands.
[c]Included in Australia.

Table A29. *'Imports' of manufactures into the Union of South Africa*

$ million, f.o.b.

	Values at 1913 prices[a]			Values at 1955 prices[b]			
	1899	1913	1929	1929	1937	1950	1955
By commodity							
METALS AND ENGINEERING	23	51	88	226	414	386	515
Metals	7	14	19	53	77	65	54
Machinery	8	14	22	79	155	170	232
Passenger road vehicles				42	69	33	67
Other transport equipment }	2	9	32	12	57	75	110
Other metal goods	6	14	15	40	56	43	52
CHEMICALS	4	7	11	23	31	37	75
Intermediates	2	4	4	9	15	20	45
Finished chemicals	2	3	7	14	16	17	30
TEXTILES AND CLOTHING	27	38	42	140	213	187	187
Yarns	0	0	1	4	11	15	23
Fabrics	8	15	19	63	112	143	133
Made-up goods	19	23	22	73	90	29	31
OTHER MANUFACTURES	15	24	29	74	113	76	130
Intermediates	1	2	5	15	25	23	50
Finished goods	14	22	24	59	88	53	80
TOTAL	69	120	171	462	770	688	908
By country							
UNITED KINGDOM	60	92	95	262	388	405	429
FRANCE	1	2	1	4	5	16	15
GERMANY	2	9	17	45	47	26	74
OTHER WESTERN EUROPE	—	4	10	32	68	57	104
Belgium/Luxembourg	—	2	6	17	28	9	27
Italy	—	1	—	—	11	21	19
Netherlands	..	..	..	5	6	5	26
Sweden	—	1	2	4	17	20	19
Switzerland	—	0	2	6	6	2	13
UNITED STATES	5	9	33	79	173	132	225
CANADA	0	2	9	23	35	23	33
JAPAN	—	0	4	9	43	29	27
INDIA	1	2	4	7	11	—	—

[a]Excluding }
[b]Including } goods consigned from the Netherlands.

Table A30. *'Imports' of manufactures into India and Pakistan*

$ *million, f.o.b.*

	Values at 1913 prices[a] India			Values at 1955 prices[b] India				Pakistan	
	1899	1913	1929	1929	1937	1950	1955	1950	1955
By commodity									
METALS AND ENGINEERING	44	119	168	484	323	435	589	133	163
Metals	13	50	57	168	81	67	129	29	36
Machinery	9	28	37	149	118	216	242	40	79
Passenger road vehicles ⎫	9	19	62	28	26	16	24	10	4
Other transport equipment ⎭				72	44	102	157	28	26
Other metal goods	13	22	12	67	54	34	37	26	18
CHEMICALS	8	17	31	62	67	81	114	23	29
Intermediates	5	11	15	29	39	36	68	9	12
Finished chemicals	3	6	16	33	28	45	46	14	17
TEXTILES AND CLOTHING	155	226	160	495	279	26	47	124	41
Yarns	13	16	17	51	57	17	32	28	15
Fabrics	133	199	130	411	194	7	13	82	18
Made-up goods	9	11	13	33	28	2	2	14	8
OTHER MANUFACTURES	20	32	47	119	128	47	71	21	19
Intermediates	6	4	9	25	33	14	20	4	3
Finished goods	14	28	38	94	95	33	51	17	16
TOTAL	227	394	407	1159	796	590	820	302	252
By country									
UNITED KINGDOM	192	316	216	669	318	325	311	141	94
FRANCE	3	7	8	22	7	20	33	7	11
GERMANY	16	33	37	102	93	21	139	11	29
OTHER WESTERN EUROPE	12	23	42	117	73	58	102	31	27
Belgium/Luxembourg	3	9	18	56	31	13	21	8	9
Italy	7	8	18	31	14	16	27	18	5
Netherlands	..	..	..	12	6	5	17	2	4
Sweden	—	2	2	5	11	11	12	2	6
Switzerland	2	4	4	13	11	13	25	1	3
UNITED STATES	3	7	37	88	64	114	130	33	34
CANADA	—	—	8	21	10	28	23	8	4
JAPAN	1	7	58	139	231	23	83	56	43
INDIA	—	—	—	—	—	—	—	16	10

[a]Excluding ⎫
[b]Including ⎭ goods consigned from the Netherlands.

Table A31. *'Imports' of manufactures into Argentina*

$ *million, f.o.b.*

	Values at 1913 prices[a]			Values at 1955 prices[b]			
	1899	1913	1929	1929	1937	1950	1955
By commodity							
METALS AND ENGINEERING	23	111	239	620	387	488	422
Metals	7	34	44	141	123	157	171
Machinery	7	32	65	220	127	173	160
Passenger road vehicles ⎱	2	27	108	67	33	7	18
Other transport equipment ⎰				121	68	126	62
Other metal goods	7	18	22	71	36	25	11
CHEMICALS	4	13	19	42	36	41	62
Intermediates	3	8	9	18	20	32	42
Finished chemicals	1	5	10	24	16	9	20
TEXTILES AND CLOTHING	38	93	107	252	218	42	35
Yarns	3	6	15	35	41	13	9
Fabrics	30	66	84	195	167	28	26
Made-up goods	5	21	8	22	10	1	0
OTHER MANUFACTURES	12	53	60	149	81	51	42
Intermediates	2	8	13	34	22	21	21
Finished goods	10	45	47	115	59	30	21
TOTAL	77	270	424	1064	725	623	562
By country							
UNITED KINGDOM	33	88	86	234	185	121	60
FRANCE	8	31	26	68	40	125	59
GERMANY	13	59	62	174	89	30	90
OTHER WESTERN EUROPE	12	47	65	156	154	131	132
Belgium/Luxembourg	3	16	21	58	74	12	21
Italy	8	23	35	62	41	72	55
Netherlands	..	..	..	12	10	17	33
Sweden	—	3	4	10	14	17	6
Switzerland	1	5	5	14	15	13	17
UNITED STATES	9	30	150	350	185	154	115
CANADA	0	2	15	44	15	14	4
JAPAN	—	1	3	6	36	33	78
INDIA	2	10	18	31	20	16	23

[a]Excluding ⎱
[b]Including ⎰ goods consigned from the Netherlands.

Table A32.   *'Imports' of manufactures into Brazil*

$ million, f.o.b

	Values at 1913 prices[a]			Values at 1955 prices[b]			
	1899	1913	1929	1929	1937	1950	1955
By commodity							
METALS AND ENGINEERING	16	75	117	314	255	549	383
Metals	3	16	19	61	74	73	66
Machinery	4	24	29	108	88	269	188
Passenger road vehicles ⎫	2	16	54	23	15	39	10
Other transport equipment ⎭				71	50	135	99
Other metal goods	7	19	15	51	28	33	20
CHEMICALS	4	9	12	25	31	100	80
Intermediates	2	5	7	13	18	60	48
Finished chemicals	2	4	5	12	13	40	32
TEXTILES AND CLOTHING	28	31	23	68	34	27	12
Yarns	4	7	7	21	17	16	5
Fabrics	19	19	13	39	14	9	5
Made-up goods	5	5	3	8	3	2	2
OTHER MANUFACTURES	11	30	29	82	50	79	59
Intermediates	2	6	5	13	9	15	22
Finished goods	9	24	24	69	41	64	37
TOTAL	59	146	180	489	372	757	532
By country							
UNITED KINGDOM	28	47	34	100	58	143	17
FRANCE	10	13	11	44	13	41	68
GERMANY	12	45	35	101	110	44	72
OTHER WESTERN EUROPE	4	22	22	66	46	142	133
Belgium/Luxembourg	2	13	9	29	24	47	22
Italy	2	6	9	21	7	12	38
Netherlands	..	..	..	3	2	13	24
Sweden	—	—	2	5	6	42	25
Switzerland	0	3	2	8	7	28	24
UNITED STATES	5	18	74	167	122	371	200
CANADA	0	1	3	10	11	14	10
JAPAN	—	—	0	1	12	3	32
INDIA	—	—	0	0	—	0	—

[a]Excluding ⎫
[b]Including ⎭ goods consigned from the Netherlands.

Table A33. *'Imports' of manufactures into Chile*

$ million, f.o.b

	Values at 1913 prices[a]			Values at 1955 prices[b]			
	1899	1913	1929	1929	1937	1950	1955
By commodity							
METALS AND ENGINEERING	7	28	65	156	59	83	109
Metals	2	8	9	31	19	13	15
Machinery	2	9	13	43	23	42	50
Passenger road vehicles }	1	4	36	11	2	2	7
Other transport equipment }				48	6	16	33
Other metal goods	2	7	7	23	9	10	4
CHEMICALS	1	4	5	12	9	14	17
Intermediates	1	2	2	5	6	9	10
Finished chemicals	0	2	3	7	3	5	7
TEXTILES AND CLOTHING	15	25	25	66	35	9	11
Yarns	1	1	2	6	9	3	3
Fabrics	10	16	16	43	22	3	4
Made-up goods	4	8	7	17	4	3	4
OTHER MANUFACTURES	4	12	14	35	16	17	14
Intermediates	0	2	2	5	3	3	3
Finished goods	4	10	12	30	13	14	11
TOTAL	27	69	111	269	120	124	153
By country							
UNITED KINGDOM	12	23	32	75	19	21	12
FRANCE	2	6	6	15	3	6	12
GERMANY	7	21	17	45	36	8	37
OTHER WESTERN EUROPE	2	6	11	28	10	10	19
Belgium/Luxembourg	1	3	4	11	3	1	4
Italy	1	2	5	8	5	2	5
Netherlands	..	..	..	2	0	1	2
Sweden	—	—	1	3	1	2	2
Switzerland	0	1	1	4	1	4	6
UNITED STATES	2	10	38	92	39	75	67
CANADA	0	—	3	6	2	2	3
JAPAN	—	0	1	2	9	0	3
INDIA	1	3	3	7	2	2	2

[a]Excluding }
[b]Including } goods consigned from the Netherlands.

Table A34.   *'Imports' of manufactures into Colombia*

$ *million, f.o.b.*

	Values at 1913 *prices*[a]			Values at 1955 *prices*[b]			
	1899	1913	1929	1929	1937	1950	1955
By commodity							
METALS AND ENGINEERING	1	4	25	72	69	193	306
Metals	0	1	4	14	14	25	40
Machinery	0	1	7	26	28	77	149
Passenger road vehicles ⎱	0	1	9	4	5	13	14
Other transport equipment ⎰				11	10	47	74
Other metal goods	1	1	5	17	12	31	29
CHEMICALS	1	1	4	10	13	42	64
Intermediates	0	0	1	2	4	19	32
Finished chemicals	1	1	3	8	9	23	32
TEXTILES AND CLOTHING	6	11	15	42	46	28	25
Yarns	0	1	1	3	7	13	16
Fabrics	5	8	10	29	33	10	7
Made-up goods	1	2	4	10	6	5	2
OTHER MANUFACTURES	1	4	12	30	19	50	60
Intermediates	0	1	1	3	4	8	16
Finished goods	1	3	11	27	15	42	44
TOTAL	9	20	56	153	146	312	456
By country							
UNITED KINGDOM	4	6	9	30	34	19	21
FRANCE	2	3	2	7	5	6	16
GERMANY	1	3	10	26	20	22	62
OTHER WESTERN EUROPE	0	1	6	15	10	22	44
Belgium/Luxembourg	—	0	2	5	4	6	12
Italy	—	1	3	5	2	4	4
Netherlands	..	..	..	1	1	2	7
Sweden	—	—	0	1	2	4	12
Switzerland	0	0	1	3	1	6	9
UNITED STATES	2	5	28	73	73	235	289
CANADA	0	—	1	2	3	7	17
JAPAN	—	—	—	—	1	1	7
INDIA	—	0	0	0	0	—	—

[a]Excluding ⎱ goods consigned from the Netherlands.
[b]Including ⎰

Table A35. *'Imports' of manufactures into Mexico*

$ *million, f.o.b.*

	Values at 1913 prices[a]			Values at 1955 prices[b]			
	1899	1913	1929	1929	1937	1950	1955
By commodity							
METALS AND ENGINEERING	22	22	64	160	193	378	455
Metals	4	5	9	26	36	58	58
Machinery	9	9	19	58	70	173	229
Passenger road vehicles ⎱	2	2	27	17	17	32	33
Other transport equipment ⎰				29	45	87	111
Other metal goods	7	6	9	30	25	28	24
CHEMICALS	4	6	10	23	27	79	122
Intermediates	2	3	5	11	13	48	73
Finished chemicals	2	3	5	12	14	31	49
TEXTILES AND CLOTHING	21	12	11	31	28	22	20
Yarns	1	1	2	7	13	4	7
Fabrics	18	7	6	16	9	10	8
Made-up goods	2	4	3	8	6	8	5
OTHER MANUFACTURES	10	11	20	48	44	71	80
Intermediates	1	1	2	5	8	12	21
Finished goods	9	10	18	43	36	59	59
TOTAL	57	51	102	262	293	553	677
By country							
UNITED KINGDOM	11	8	7	22	15	16	20
FRANCE	5	7	3	7	6	10	9
GERMANY	5	10	10	26	41	11	37
OTHER WESTERN EUROPE	1	4	4	13	15	20	49
Belgium/Luxembourg	1	1	1	5	4	4	5
Italy	0	1	1	2	3	4	20
Netherlands	..	..	..	1	2	1	5
Sweden	—	1	1	2	2	4	6
Switzerland	—	1	1	3	4	7	13
UNITED STATES	35	21	77	190	201	476	521
CANADA	0	—	1	3	5	14	34
JAPAN	—	0	0	1	10	6	7
INDIA	—	0	0	0	0	1	0

[a]Excluding ⎱ goods consigned from the Netherlands.
[b]Including ⎰

Table A36. *'Imports' of manufactures into Palestine/Israel*

$ *million, f.o.b. at 1955 prices*

	1929	1937	1950	1955
By commodity				
METALS AND ENGINEERING	10	28	103	107
Metals	3	9	36	31
Machinery	3	10	40	39
Passenger road vehicles	1	1	3	1
Other transport equipment	1	3	16	28
Other metal goods	2	5	8	8
CHEMICALS	1	3	7	16
Intermediates	0	1	3	9
Finished chemicals	1	2	4	7
TEXTILES AND CLOTHING	3	13	11	11
Yarns	0	2	4	6
Fabrics	2	8	4	4
Made-up goods	1	3	3	1
OTHER MANUFACTURES	5	10	15	16
Intermediates	1	3	2	7
Finished goods	4	7	13	9
TOTAL	19	54	136	150
By country				
UNITED KINGDOM	6	14	30	21
FRANCE	2	2	10	6
GERMANY	5	18	0	59
OTHER WESTERN EUROPE	4	9	17	22
Belgium-Luxembourg	2	4	3	4
Italy	2	3	3	4
Netherlands	0	0	2	7
Sweden	0	1	4	2
Switzerland	—	1	5	5
UNITED STATES	2	5	74	37
CANADA	—	0	4	3
JAPAN	—	5	0	1
INDIA	0	0	0	—

Table A37. '*Imports*' *of manufactures into Turkey*

$ *million, f.o.b.*

	Values at 1913 prices[a]			*Values at 1955 prices*[b]			
	1899	1913	1929	1929	1937	1950	1955
By commodity							
METALS AND ENGINEERING	5	17	19	59	76	167	231
Metals	1	5	5	16	20	32	33
Machinery	1	4	4	18	20	78	122
Passenger road vehicles ⎫	0	2	6	1	7	4	5
Other transport equipment ⎭				9	12	30	49
Other metal goods	3	6	4	15	17	23	22
CHEMICALS	2	5	2	5	9	18	26
Intermediates	1	2	1	2	5	6	9
Finished chemicals	1	3	1	3	4	12	17
TEXTILES AND CLOTHING	27	58	24	50	50	24	38
Yarns	3	7	3	6	14	8	2
Fabrics	20	45	19	40	32	13	34
Made-up goods	4	6	2	4	4	3	2
OTHER MANUFACTURES	7	14	8	17	14	21	32
Intermediates	2	6	2	4	2	2	3
Finished goods	5	8	6	13	12	19	29
TOTAL	41	94	53	132	147	230	328
By country							
UNITED KINGDOM	15	33	8	25	14	34	36
FRANCE	6	12	9	23	4	17	39
GERMANY	9	21	12	32	71	70	122
OTHER WESTERN EUROPE	11	23	19	38	24	38	67
Belgium/Luxembourg	2	6	5	13	3	5	12
Italy	8	15	12	18	15	17	35
Netherlands	..	..	..	2	1	6	6
Sweden	—	—	1	3	4	6	5
Switzerland	1	2	1	2	1	4	9
UNITED STATES	0	2	4	9	26	66	60
CANADA	—	—	0	0	—	4	1
JAPAN	—	0	1	2	2	0	4
INDIA	0	3	1	1	6	2	1

[a]Excluding ⎫
[b]Including ⎭ goods consigned from the Netherlands.

Table A38. *'Imports' of manufactures into Yugoslavia*

$ million, f.o.b. at 1955 prices

	1929	1937	1950	1955
By commodity				
METALS AND ENGINEERING	65	59	93	125
Metals	9	8	22	18
Machinery	21	27	44	79
Passenger road vehicles	3	5	2	3
Other transport equipment	9	9	15	14
Other metal goods	23	10	10	11
CHEMICALS	6	8	9	21
Intermediates	4	5	5	10
Finished chemicals	2	3	4	11
TEXTILES AND CLOTHING	22	40	8	10
Yarns	7	23	6	8
Fabrics	13	16	1	2
Made-up goods	2	1	1	0
OTHER MANUFACTURES	14	14	14	22
Intermediates	2	3	2	3
Finished goods	12	11	12	19
TOTAL	109	120	125	180
By country				
UNITED KINGDOM	11	8	16	24
FRANCE	7	5	7	10
GERMANY	69	79	35	52
OTHER WESTERN EUROPE	19	25	37	74
Belgium/Luxembourg	—	2	2	7
Italy	14	18	18	53
Netherlands	1	0	7	2
Sweden	0	1	4	2
Switzerland	4	4	6	10
UNITED STATES	2	3	30	12
CANADA	—	0	0	0
JAPAN	—	—	0	8
INDIA	0	—	—	—

Table A39. *'Imports' of manufactures into the U.S.S.R.*

$ *million, f.o.b.*

	Values at 1913 prices[a]			Values at 1955 prices[b]			
	1899[c]	1913[c]	1929	1929	1937	1950	1955
By commodity							
METALS AND ENGINEERING	90	145	107	304	271	119	143
Metals	27	22	15	54	118	17	23
Machinery	42	83	56	181	109	86	51
Passenger road vehicles	7	16	26	6	1	—	—
Other transport equipment				30	29	10	42
Other metal goods	14	24	10	33	14	6	27
CHEMICALS	9	27	12	23	8	2	4
Intermediates	7	19	9	17	7	1	—
Finished chemicals	2	8	3	6	1	1	4
TEXTILES AND CLOTHING	17	31	5	10	17	2	4
Yarns	10	13	1	2	8	—	0
Fabrics	4	13	3	7	7	2	—
Made-up goods	3	5	1	1	2	—	4
OTHER MANUFACTURES	22	58	11	25	18	2	4
Intermediates	5	22	2	4	6	1	—
Finished goods	17	36	9	21	12	1	4
TOTAL	139	260	134	363	314	124	155
By country							
UNITED KINGDOM	48	47	13	38	54	41	54
FRANCE	5	7	11	19	8	4	24
GERMANY	66	154	54	157	79	—	27
OTHER WESTERN EUROPE	13	26	14	33	74	79	49
Belgium/Luxembourg	6	5	2	5	37	24	16
Italy	0	3	3	6	0	22	6
Netherlands	..	..	..	2	28	1	12
Sweden	1	8	8	16	6	28	11
Switzerland	6	10	1	4	3	4	4
UNITED STATES	6	23	38	103	77	1	0
CANADA	0	1	2	6	1	0	—
JAPAN	1	1	4	9	21	0	1
INDIA	0	0	0	0	—	—	—

[a]Excluding ⎱
[b]Including ⎰ goods consigned from the Netherlands.
[c]Russia.

Table A40. *'Imports' of manufactures into Belgian Congo and Egypt*

$ *million, f.o.b. at* 1955 *prices*

	Belgian Congo				Egypt			
	1929	1937	1950	1955	1929	1937	1950	1955
By commodity								
METALS AND ENGINEERING	56	31	101	156	105	81	194	196
Metals	10	6	18	30	28	23	43	38
Machinery	26	14	31	63	30	21	65	90
Passenger road vehicles	0	1	8	11	7	9	10	11
Other transport equipment	13	4	29	31	21	16	39	35
Other metal goods	7	6	15	21	19	12	37	22
CHEMICALS	0	1	6	16	15	17	31	50
Intermediates	0	0	2	6	7	4	10	14
Finished chemicals	0	1	4	10	8	13	21	36
TEXTILES AND CLOTHING	11	19	22	33	129	95	57	32
Yarns	0	0	0	2	7	7	10	6
Fabrics	7	13	15	21	101	74	34	14
Made-up goods	4	6	7	10	21	14	13	12
OTHER MANUFACTURES	4	4	16	37	35	24	43	37
Intermediates	0	0	1	3	6	6	7	8
Finished goods	4	4	15	34	29	18	36	29
TOTAL	72	55	145	241	285	219	331	315
By country								
UNITED KINGDOM	6	4	17	21	89	59	135	69
FRANCE	—	—	—	0	41	13	58	46
GERMANY	3	2	4	20	32	26	23	53
OTHER WESTERN EUROPE	61	30	73	140	72	63	77	87
Belgium/Luxembourg	60	29	67	121	23	19	17	14
Italy	0	0	2	3	37	33	34	28
Netherlands	1	1	4	8	3	3	9	12
Sweden	0	0	1	2	2	4	7	6
Switzerland	—	—	3	6	7	4	10	27
UNITED STATES	1	4	43	47	19	24	28	39
CANADA	0	0	1	1	2	0	1	1
JAPAN	—	13	4	3	21	22	2	11
INDIA	—	1	0	0	8	10	6	8

Table A41. 'Imports' of manufactures into French Morocco and Nigeria

$ million, f.o.b. at 1955 prices

	French Morocco				Nigeria			
	1929	1937	1950	1955	1929	1937	1950	1955
By commodity								
METALS AND ENGINEERING	65	27	129	131	22	18	61	95
Metals	18	5	23	23	10	0	13	7
Machinery	22	8	56	49	4	2	14	28
Passenger road vehicles	5	2	13	23	—	1	0	13
Other transport equipment	10	7	20	23	7	4	22	23
Other metal goods	10	5	17	13	1	11	12	24
CHEMICALS	4	4	9	23	3	3	5	16
Intermediates	1	2	4	0	1	1	1	0
Finished chemicals	3	2	5	23	2	2	4	16
TEXTILES AND CLOTHING	31	23	30	35	35	65	70	79
Yarns	0	1	2	0	1	2	2	0
Fabrics	25	18	23	0	29	52	52	37
Made-up goods	6	4	5	35	5	11	16	42
OTHER MANUFACTURES	11	10	31	42	4	7	12	37
Intermediates	1	2	5	0	1	0	1	0
Finished goods	10	8	26	42	3	7	11	37
TOTAL	113	64	203	231	62	94	148	226
By country								
UNITED KINGDOM	22	2	7	15	58	56	102	136
FRANCE	61	22	162	141	—	—	—	—
GERMANY	3	3	4	22	—	8	4	21
OTHER WESTERN EUROPE	18	14	6	28	—	6	9	7
Belgium/Luxembourg	8	6	1	3	—	—	1	2
Italy	8	5	1	11	—	6	6	—
Netherlands	1	1	1	8	—	—	2	3
Sweden	0	1	2	3	—	—	—	—
Switzerland	1	1	1	3	—	—	0	2
UNITED STATES	7	9	24	25	2	5	2	4
CANADA	1	0	1	—	2	2	0	—
JAPAN	—	14	0	0	—	12	13	42
INDIA	0	—	0	—	0	5	17	17

Table A42. 'Imports' of manufactures into Southern Rhodesia and Indonesia

	Southern Rhodesia $ million, f.o.b. at 1955 prices				Indonesia			
	1929	1937	1950	1955ᵃ	1929	1937	1950	1955
By commodity								
METALS AND ENGINEERING	9	16	57	110	228	146	103	148
Metals	2	4	9	12	61	41	20	41
Machinery	2	4	20	44	73	40	43	43
Passenger road vehicles	0	2	5	17	15	11	3	16
Other transport equipment	4	3	16	26	30	18	22	27
Other metal goods	1	3	7	11	49	36	15	21
CHEMICALS	0	2	3	13	28	27	20	45
Intermediates	0	1	1	3	10	14	12	27
Finished chemicals	—	1	2	10	18	13	8	18
TEXTILES AND CLOTHING	2	9	23	24	163	214	99	87
Yarns	—	—	1	1	7	18	12	24
Fabrics	1	5	12	17	135	169	80	55
Made-up goods	1	4	10	6	21	27	7	8
OTHER MANUFACTURES	6	1	9	19	65	49	32	40
Intermediates	0	0	1	3	5	9	6	11
Finished goods	6	1	8	16	60	40	26	29
TOTAL	18	28	92	166	484	437	254	320
By country								
UNITED KINGDOM	14	23	82	135	81	40	30	30
FRANCE	..	..	—	1	6	8	6	11
GERMANY	..	1	1	5	94	36	15	50
	..	1	2	8	149	131	84	96
OTHER WESTERN EUROPE								
Belgium/Luxembourg	..	0	—	2	16	16	7	19
Italy	..	1	1	1	13	6	3	8
Netherlands	..	0	0	3	110	103	67	59
Sweden	..	..	1	1	4	3	5	6
Switzerland	..	..	0	1	6	3	2	4
UNITED STATES	..	..	4	11	75	49	68	59
CANADA	3	3	1	1	6	1	3	1
JAPAN	..	0	0	1	62	161	46	56
INDIA	..	—	2	2	12	12	4	17

ᵃFederation of Rhodesia and Nyasaland.

Table A43.   'Imports' of manufactures into Iran and the Philippines

$ million, f.o.b. at 1955 prices

	Iran				Philippines			
	1929	1937	1950	1955	1929	1937	1950	1955
By commodity								
METALS AND ENGINEERING	23	61	109	124	68	85	110	158
Metals	8	14	27	34	19	18	27	36
Machinery	6	20	42	36	19	26	37	71
Passenger road vehicles	1	2	5	13	5	8	2	6
Other transport equipment	4	11	19	30	13	16	25	28
Other metal goods	4	14	16	11	12	17	19	17
CHEMICALS	2	4	15	18	14	18	35	40
Intermediates	1	2	9	9	2	4	13	16
Finished chemicals	1	2	6	9	12	14	22	24
TEXTILES AND CLOTHING	10	10	21	35	48	57	47	91
Yarns	2	0	2	4	2	3	4	10
Fabrics	8	9	15	29	36	42	34	68
Made-up goods	0	1	4	2	10	12	9	13
OTHER MANUFACTURES	5	10	20	28	36	42	52	64
Intermediates	0	2	2	3	5	9	13	21
Finished goods	5	8	18	25	31	33	39	43
TOTAL	41	84	164	204	167	201	244	352
By country								
UNITED KINGDOM	19	27	87	48	9	5	6	11
FRANCE	3	2	7	14	3	2	1	5
GERMANY	7	32	12	42	9	8	3	12
OTHER WESTERN EUROPE	1	6	15	27	5	4	7	10
Belgium/Luxembourg	1	1	5	6	3	1	2	4
Italy	0	1	4	11	0	0	3	1
Netherlands	0	1	1	3	0	0	0	2
Sweden	0	3	2	3	0	1	1	1
Switzerland	—	0	3	4	2	2	1	2
UNITED STATES	5	12	39	49	118	135	195	258
CANADA	0	0	1	1	—	2	2	4
JAPAN	—	2	4	22	19	41	27	48
INDIA	5	2	0	2	3	4	2	3

Table A44. *'Imports' of manufactures into Cuba and Peru*

$ *million, f.o.b. at* 1955 *prices*

	Cuba				Peru			
	1929	1937	1950	1955	1929	1937	1950	1955
By commodity								
METALS AND ENGINEERING	74	56	175	199	42	50	85	111
Metals	15	14	29	32	9	9	11	19
Machinery	24	18	62	81	15	16	36	55
Passenger road vehicles	9	7	25	28	4	4	6	7
Other transport equipment	9	9	36	37	6	13	22	18
Other metal goods	17	8	23	21	8	8	10	12
CHEMICALS	19	14	46	44	7	7	14	21
Intermediates	5	5	20	18	2	2	6	9
Finished chemicals	14	9	26	26	5	5	8	12
TEXTILES AND CLOTHING	59	55	77	61	20	15	14	17
Yarns	3	4	7	10	2	2	1	1
Fabrics	34	36	48	33	13	8	8	10
Made-up goods	22	15	22	18	5	5	5	6
OTHER MANUFACTURES	44	40	81	83	16	14	18	28
Intermediates	11	11	18	22	2	3	3	5
Finished goods	33	29	63	61	14	11	15	23
TOTAL	196	166	379	387	84	87	131	177
By country								
UNITED KINGDOM	17	15	10	12	17	10	34	22
FRANCE	8	4	4	8	3	2	4	9
GERMANY	10	8	9	18	11	21	8	22
OTHER WESTERN EUROPE	8	7	14	22	8	10	13	23
Belgium/Luxembourg	4	3	6	10	2	3	3	5
Italy	2	1	1	3	4	5	2	4
Netherlands	1	1	1	3	0	0	2	3
Sweden	1	1	1	2	1	1	3	5
Switzerland	—	1	5	4	1	1	3	6
UNITED STATES	141	122	318	307	39	34	68	88
CANADA	2	2	7	7	2	2	2	4
JAPAN	1	2	5	5	1	5	0	5
INDIA	10	6	11	9	2	2	2	3

Table A45. *'Imports' of manufactures into Venezuela*
$ million, f.o.b. at 1955 prices

	1929	1937	1950	1955
By commodity				
METALS AND ENGINEERING	81	98	300	500
Metals	26	27	45	99
Machinery	28	33	120	205
Passenger road vehicles	7	8	33	60
Other transport equipment	7	16	60	84
Other metal goods	13	14	42	52
CHEMICALS	7	10	40	59
Intermediates	2	3	14	26
Finished chemicals	5	7	26	33
TEXTILES AND CLOTHING	23	28	50	54
Yarns	1	2	6	7
Fabrics	18	22	25	36
Made-up goods	4	4	19	11
OTHER MANUFACTURES	18	23	95	116
Intermediates	2	3	10	22
Finished goods	17	20	85	94
TOTAL	131	158	486	732
By country				
UNITED KINGDOM	22	18	47	63
FRANCE	4	4	8	27
GERMANY	19	29	21	76
OTHER WESTERN EUROPE	10	11	34	80
Belgium/Luxembourg	3	2	8	19
Italy	3	3	10	21
Netherlands	2	3	4	19
Sweden	0	1	4	7
Switzerland	2	2	8	14
UNITED STATES	72	88	357	462
CANADA	2	2	15	11
JAPAN	—	8	4	13
INDIA	0	0	0	—

VALUES AT CURRENT PRICES

Table A46. *Exports of manufactures from Belgium-Luxembourg*

$ *million, f.o.b.*

	1899	1913	1929	1937	1950	1955	1957
METALS AND ENGINEERING	68	140	274	303	666	1337	1558
Metals	32	82	184	224	431	900	1046
Machinery	9	15	30	32	109	173	239
Passenger road vehicles	} 12	25	18	9	14	40	51
Other transport equipment			16	13	34	95	93
Other metal goods	15	18	26	25	78	129	129
CHEMICALS	21	46	44	60	138	187	219
Intermediates	21	37	22	26	45	72	80
Finished chemicals	—	9	22	34	93	115	139
TEXTILES AND CLOTHING	46	77	133	100	298	327	381
Yarns	27	45	40	32	99	106	114
Fabrics	14	24	65	44	144	119	146
Made-up goods	5	8	28	24	55	102	121
OTHER MANUFACTURES	37	60	205	147	180	361	411
Intermediates	7	10	81	80	76	169	235
Finished goods	30	50	124	67	104	192	176
TOTAL	172	323	656	610	1282	2212	2568

Table A48. *Exports of manufactures from France*

	1899	1913	1929	1937	1950	1955	1957
METALS AND ENGINEERING	74	165	382	202	889	1646	1881
Metals	26	48	142	89	333	735	745
Machinery	14	28	86	37	234	428	465
Passenger road vehicles	} 8	53	52	23	98	182	254
Other transport equipment			37	18	115	176	269
Other metal goods	26	36	65	35	109	125	148
CHEMICALS	34	79	140	97	219	360	414
Intermediates	25	48	63	52	102	193	213
Finished chemicals	9	31	77	45	117	167	201
TEXTILES AND CLOTHING	210	330	531	132	535	534	529
Yarns	15	44	109	34	155	163	152
Fabrics	136	195	333	86	316	272	247
Made-up goods	58	91	89	12	64	99	130
OTHER MANUFACTURES	128	213	274	110	350	537	589
Intermediates	31	52	89	35	124	141	160
Finished goods	97	161	185	75	226	396	428
TOTAL	446	787	1327	541	1993	3077	3424

VALUES AT CONSTANT PRICES

Table A47. *Exports of manufactures from Belgium-Luxembourg*

$ *million, f.o.b.*

	Values at 1913 prices			Values at 1955 prices				
	1899	1913	1929	1929	1937	1950	1955	1957
METALS AND ENGINEERING	58	140	243	945	835	848	1337	1356
Metals	30	82	156	540	604	573	900	910
Machinery	7	15	23	231	125	119	173	204
Passenger road vehicles ⎱	6	25	42	53	17	16	40	45
Other transport equipment ⎰				47	23	40	95	82
Other metal goods	15	18	22	74	66	100	129	115
CHEMICALS	26	46	45	52	73	131	187	241
Intermediates	26	37	23	26	31	45	72	88
Finished chemicals	—	9	22	26	42	86	115	153
TEXTILES AND CLOTHING	49	77	106	183	186	266	327	363
Yarns	29	45	32	55	59	89	106	109
Fabrics	15	24	52	89	82	128	119	139
Made-up goods	5	8	22	39	45	49	102	115
OTHER MANUFACTURES	39	60	145	233	234	184	361	364
Intermediates	7	10	57	92	127	77	169	208
Finished goods	32	50	88	141	107	107	192	156
TOTAL	172	323	539	1413	1328	1429	2212	2324

Table A49. *Exports of manufactures from France*

	Values at 1913 prices			Values at 1955 prices				
	1899	1913	1929	1929	1937	1950	1955	1957
METALS AND ENGINEERING	86	165	408	1275	492	1273	1646	1697
Metals	31	48	104	517	232	500	735	665
Machinery	15	28	77	376	112	337	428	415
Passenger road vehicles ⎱	9	53	179	105	40	138	182	237
Other transport equipment ⎰				77	32	160	176	251
Other metal goods	31	36	48	200	76	138	125	129
CHEMICALS	36	79	78	261	165	196	360	406
Intermediates	26	48	35	117	88	91	193	209
Finished chemicals	10	31	43	144	77	105	167	197
TEXTILES AND CLOTHING	244	330	358	778	292	537	534	504
Yarns	18	44	82	202	87	159	163	145
Fabrics	159	195	215	442	177	310	272	235
Made-up goods	67	91	61	134	28	68	99	124
OTHER MANUFACTURES	138	213	195	442	203	460	537	577
Intermediates	34	52	63	142	64	163	141	157
Finished goods	104	161	132	299	139	297	396	420
TOTAL	504	787	1039	2756	1152	2466	3077	3184

VALUES AT CURRENT PRICES

Table A50. *Exports of manufactures from Germany*[a]

$ million, f.o.b.

	1899	1913	1929	1937	1950	1955	1957
METALS AND ENGINEERING	192	695	1105	1074	929	3352	5070
Metals	58	249	271	244	290	582	1115
Machinery	48	231	462	416	344	1516	2255
Passenger road vehicles	} 13	} 65	26	63	77	463	680
Other transport equipment			74	96	56	478	625
Other metal goods	72	150	272	255	162	313	395
CHEMICALS	91	239	321	311	227	681	903
Intermediates	72	190	216	184	143	459	657
Finished chemicals	19	49	105	127	84	222	246
TEXTILES AND CLOTHING	209	324	413	214	97	353	402
Yarns	29	44	72	41	25	58	73
Fabrics	91	178	213	118	65	219	224
Made-up goods	89	102	128	55	7	76	105
OTHER MANUFACTURES	205	468	665	422	209	864	1095
Intermediates	42	149	200	96	32	152	222
Finished goods	163	319	465	326	177	712	873
TOTAL	697	1726	2504	2021	1462	5250	7471

Table A52. *Exports of manufactures from Italy*

	1899	1913	1929	1937	1950	1955	1957
METALS AND ENGINEERING	5	19	54	77	260	503	810
Metals	2	2	3	8	35	85	157
Machinery	1	6	15	15	136	210	316
Passenger road vehicles	} 1	} 8	6	11	24	80	133
Other transport equipment			21	37	48	82	128
Other metal goods	1	3	9	6	17	46	76
CHEMICALS	6	15	30	26	44	127	156
Intermediates	5	13	25	18	27	84	102
Finished chemicals	1	2	5	8	17	43	54
TEXTILES AND CLOTHING	79	129	298	151	373	316	397
Yarns	52	46	85	51	104	81	90
Fabrics	21	66	166	85	225	169	216
Made-up goods	7	17	47	15	44	66	91
OTHER MANUFACTURES	22	50	70	57	82	203	265
Intermediates	9	4	19	6	7	26	40
Finished goods	13	46	51	51	75	177	225
TOTAL	112	213	452	311	759	1149	1627

[a]West Germany in 1950–57.

VALUES AT CONSTANT PRICES

Table A51. *Exports of manufactures from Germany*[a]

$ *million, f.o.b.*

	Values at 1913 prices			Values at 1955 prices				
	1899	1913	1929	1929	1937	1950	1955	1957
METALS AND ENGINEERING	225	695	845	2881	1948	1241	3352	4854
Metals	72	249	220	918	537	418	582	1032
Machinery	65	231	282	1002	670	427	1516	2127
Passenger road vehicles ⎤	9	65	121	34	93	110	463	673
Other transport equipment ⎦				102	146	78	478	619
Other metal goods	79	150	222	825	502	208	313	403
CHEMICALS	74	239	261	446	380	223	681	941
Intermediates	59	190	176	300	225	146	459	685
Finished chemicals	15	49	85	146	155	77	222	256
TEXTILES AND CLOTHING	271	324	283	417	300	104	353	390
Yarns	38	44	49	72	58	26	58	71
Fabrics	118	178	146	216	166	71	219	217
Made-up goods	115	102	88	129	76	7	76	102
OTHER MANUFACTURES	212	468	458	1018	615	245	864	1117
Intermediates	44	149	138	307	139	39	152	226
Finished goods	168	319	320	711	476	206	712	891
TOTAL	782	1726	1847	4762	3243	1813	5250	7302

Table A53. *Exports of manufactures from Italy*

	Values at 1913 prices			Values at 1955 prices				
	1899	1913	1929	1929	1937	1950	1955	1957
METALS AND ENGINEERING	5	19	80	214	298	301	503	808
Metals	2	2	2	4	18	39	85	141
Machinery	1	6	8	58	40	159	210	326
Passenger road vehicles ⎤	1	8	64	32	52	28	80	143
Other transport equipment ⎦				105	174	56	82	138
Other metal goods	1	3	6	15	14	19	46	60
CHEMICALS	6	15	24	50	53	42	127	148
Intermediates	5	13	20	41	37	26	84	97
Finished chemicals	1	2	4	9	16	16	43	51
TEXTILES AND CLOTHING	86	129	257	366	342	341	316	393
Yarns	56	46	73	104	113	93	81	89
Fabrics	23	66	143	204	188	200	169	214
Made-up goods	7	17	41	58	41	48	66	90
OTHER MANUFACTURES	33	50	47	101	102	91	203	252
Intermediates	14	4	13	28	10	7	26	38
Finished goods	19	46	34	73	92	84	177	214
TOTAL	129	213	408	731	795	775	1149	1601

[a]West Germany in 1950–57.

VALUES AT CURRENT PRICES

Table A54. *Exports of manufactures from the Netherlands*

$ million, f.o.b.

	1929	1937	1950	1955	1957
METALS AND ENGINEERING	122	139	260	639	717
Metals	13	45	74	179	199
Machinery	70	68	104	260	312
Passenger road vehicles	1	1	5	14	35
Other transport equipment	22	14	58	141	132
Other metal goods	16	11	19	45	59
CHEMICALS	43	50	106	193	263
Intermediates	24	23	67	125	168
Finished chemicals	19	27	39	68	95
TEXTILES AND CLOTHING	91	51	156	230	262
Yarns	15	13	33	57	63
Fabrics	60	33	84	122	136
Made-up goods	16	5	39	51	63
OTHER MANUFACTURES	50	39	85	237	256
Intermediates	26	20	36	116	112
Finished goods	24	19	49	121	144
TOTAL	306	279	607	1299	1498

Table A56. *Exports of manufactures from Sweden*

	1899	1913	1929	1937	1950	1955	1957
METALS AND ENGINEERING	17	46	116	152	363	598	841
Metals	12	22	35	54	66	136	178
Machinery	3	14	51	52	155	225	329
Passenger road vehicles	} 0	} 3	2	5	8	22	39
Other transport equipment			9	19	86	136	205
Other metal goods	2	7	19	22	48	79	90
CHEMICALS	1	3	8	11	23	45	50
Intermediates	—	3	7	6	15	34	41
Finished chemicals	1	0	1	5	8	11	9
TEXTILES AND CLOTHING	1	2	8	6	13	16	21
Yarns	0	1	2	1	5	2	3
Fabrics	0	1	5	4	5	10	13
Made-up goods	0	0	1	1	3	4	6
OTHER MANUFACTURES	11	38	79	70	180	253	305
Intermediates	3	12	43	42	105	163	229
Finished goods	8	26	36	28	75	90	76
TOTAL	29	89	211	239	579	912	1217

VALUES AT CONSTANT PRICES

Table A55. *Exports of manufactures from the Netherlands*

$ *million, f.o.b.*

| | Values at 1955 prices | | | | |
	1929	1937	1950	1955	1957
METALS AND ENGINEERING	312	323	326	639	707
Metals	29	112	99	179	195
Machinery	216	157	127	260	306
Passenger road vehicles	2	2	6	14	15
Other transport equipment	25	21	71	141	131
Other metal goods	40	31	23	45	60
CHEMICALS	83	109	115	193	253
Intermediates	46	50	73	125	162
Finished chemicals	37	59	42	68	91
TEXTILES AND CLOTHING	160	124	149	230	262
Yarns	18	20	31	57	63
Fabrics	121	94	80	122	136
Made-up goods	21	10	38	51	63
OTHER MANUFACTURES	84	76	102	237	256
Intermediates	43	39	43	116	112
Finished goods	41	37	59	121	144
TOTAL	639	632	692	1299	1478

Table A57. *Exports of manufactures from Sweden*

| | Values at 1913 prices | | | Values at 1955 prices | | | | |
	1899	1913	1929	1929	1937	1950	1955	1957
METALS AND ENGINEERING	15	46	86	218	336	480	598	793
Metals	10	22	25	82	131	89	136	175
Machinery	3	14	38	64	96	195	225	305
Passenger road vehicles ⎫				4	12	11	22	36
Other transport equipment ⎭	0	3	10	24	44	120	136	190
Other metal goods	2	7	13	44	53	65	79	87
CHEMICALS	1	3	7	12	25	27	45	50
Intermediates		3	6	10	14	17	34	41
Finished chemicals	1	0	1	2	11	10	11	9
TEXTILES AND CLOTHING	1	2	5	13	13	14	16	21
Yarns	0	1	1	3	3	5	2	2
Fabrics	0	1	3	8	9	5	10	13
Made-up goods	0	0	1	2	1	4	4	6
OTHER MANUFACTURES	10	38	45	158	179	234	253	296
Intermediates	3	12	24	86	107	137	163	222
Finished goods	7	26	21	72	72	97	90	74
TOTAL	27	89	143	401	553	755	912	1160

VALUES AT CURRENT PRICES

Table A58. *Exports of manufactures from Switzerland*

$ million, f.o.b.

	1899	1913	1929	1937	1950	1955	1957[a]
METALS AND ENGINEERING	11	33	90	83	294	432	516
Metals	1	5	17	16	16	24	29
Machinery	9	21	55	47	244	345	411
Passenger road vehicles	} 0	} 3	3	3	3	6	6
Other transport equipment			2	2	6	7	10
Other metal goods	1	4	13	15	25	50	60
CHEMICALS	6	14	34	44	134	216	258
Intermediates	5	10	23	25	73	104	115
Finished chemicals	1	4	11	19	61	112	143
TEXTILES AND CLOTHING	77	107	120	56	124	182	215
Yarns	19	24	30	15	33	48	50
Fabrics	51	72	61	30	62	82	103
Made-up goods	8	11	29	11	29	52	62
OTHER MANUFACTURES	31	50	92	78	295	371	450
Intermediates	2	3	8	7	16	31	32
Finished goods	29	47	84	71	279	340	418
TOTAL	125	204	335	261	847	1201	1439

Table A60. *Exports of manufactures from the United Kingdom*

	1899	1913	1929	1937	1950	1955	1957
METALS AND ENGINEERING	355	680	1018	835	2908	4143	5012
Metals	127	230	313	248	441	647	866
Machinery	98	190	310	287	1018	1605	1910
Passenger road vehicles	} 66	} 126	62	75	414	446	523
Other transport equipment			186	119	738	982	1244
Other metal goods	64	134	147	106	297	463	469
CHEMICALS	51	119	182	157	390	652	749
Intermediates	28	62	103	89	220	375	534
Finished chemicals	23	57	79	68	170	277	215
TEXTILES AND CLOTHING	529	950	1159	663	1112	960	939
Yarns	100	143	212	141	201	170	197
Fabrics	355	691	742	401	677	594	552
Made-up goods	74	116	205	121	234	196	190
OTHER MANUFACTURES	97	211	376	280	690	930	1013
Intermediates	11	33	88	68	136	223	291
Finished goods	86	178	288	212	554	707	722
TOTAL	1031	1960	2735	1935	5100	6686	7713

[a]Including some approximate estimates.

VALUES AT CONSTANT PRICES

Table A59. *Exports of manufactures from Switzerland*

$ million, f.o.b.

	Values at 1913 prices				Values at 1955 prices			
	1899	1913	1929	1929	1937	1950	1955	1957[a]
METALS AND ENGINEERING	14	33	64	182	137	259	432	493
Metals	1	5	12	21	21	18	24	24
Machinery	12	21	38	134	90	207	345	403
Passenger road vehicles ⎱	0	3	5	9	6	3	6	6
Other transport equipment ⎰				3	3	6	7	10
Other metal goods	1	4	9	14	17	25	50	50
CHEMICALS	4	14	18	55	49	98	216	255
Intermediates	3	10	9	38	28	54	104	114
Finished chemicals	1	4	9	17	21	44	112	141
TEXTILES AND CLOTHING	79	107	83	190	140	120	182	219
Yarns	19	24	21	47	36	31	48	51
Fabrics	52	72	42	97	75	60	82	105
Made-up goods	8	11	20	46	29	29	52	63
OTHER MANUFACTURES	32	50	62	336	235	323	371	437
Intermediates	2	3	5	29	19	16	31	31
Finished goods	30	47	57	307	216	307	340	406
TOTAL	129	204	227	763	561	800	1201	1404

Table A61. *Exports of manufactures from the United Kingdom*

	Values at 1913 prices				Values at 1955 prices			
	1899	1913	1929	1929	1937	1950	1955	1957
METALS AND ENGINEERING	371	680	781	1910	1541	3829	4143	4662
Metals	137	230	259	636	467	617	647	809
Machinery	104	190	165	689	559	1364	1605	1705
Passenger road vehicles ⎱	63	126	243	92	119	509	446	513
Other transport equipment ⎰				277	191	914	982	1220
Other metal goods	67	134	114	216	205	425	463	415
CHEMICALS	64	119	142	261	250	433	652	764
Intermediates	35	62	80	148	141	244	375	545
Finished chemicals	29	57	62	113	109	189	277	219
TEXTILES AND CLOTHING	777	950	647	2422	1756	1386	960	930
Yarns	147	143	119	444	372	230	170	195
Fabrics	522	691	414	1550	1063	758	594	547
Made-up goods	108	116	114	428	321	398	196	188
OTHER MANUFACTURES	116	211	251	583	487	875	930	983
Intermediates	14	33	59	137	119	172	223	283
Finished goods	102	178	192	446	368	703	707	701
TOTAL	1327	1960	1821	5176	4034	6523	6686	7339

[a]Including some approximate estimates.

VALUES AT CURRENT PRICES

Table A62. *Exports of manufactures from Canada*

$ million, f.o.b.

	1899	1913	1929	1937	1950	1955	1957
METALS AND ENGINEERING	3	18	170	211	562	945	1144
Metals	0	4	85	149	346	642	736
Machinery	0	9	29	25	119	166	197
Passenger road vehicles ⎱	0	4	30	16	18	13	24
Other transport equipment ⎰			19	13	66	105	167
Other metal goods	2	1	7	8	13	19	20
CHEMICALS	1	5	26	29	114	246	244
Intermediates	0	—	15	17	66	183	185
Finished chemicals	0	5	11	12	48	63	59
TEXTILES AND CLOTHING	1	1	6	12	23	18	23
Yarns	—	—	—	—	—	3	6
Fabrics	1	1	2	3	11	9	10
Made-up goods	0	0	4	9	12	6	6
OTHER MANUFACTURES	8	18	224	195	567	860	940
Intermediates	2	16	170	148	485	777	866
Finished goods	6	2	55	47	82	83	74
TOTAL	12	42	427	447	1266	2069	2349

Table A64. *Exports of manufactures from the United States*

	1899	1913	1929	1937	1950	1955	1957
METALS AND ENGINEERING	211	526	1702	1272	3574	5477	7594
Metals	94	232	360	300	508	894	1423
Machinery	67	163	603	469	1794	2619	3796
Passenger road vehicles ⎱	16	63	239	137	191	390	309
Other transport equipment ⎰			367	274	850	1261	1669
Other metal goods	35	68	133	92	231	313	397
CHEMICALS	37	67	188	166	752	1106	1402
Intermediates	27	40	109	113	397	681	948
Finished chemicals	10	27	79	53	355	425	454
TEXTILES AND CLOTHING	30	66	192	81	477	539	564
Yarns	—	1	19	3	49	63	67
Fabrics	26	49	94	40	288	330	341
Made-up goods	3	16	79	38	140	146	156
OTHER MANUFACTURES	85	187	409	261	723	1174	1458
Intermediates	25	45	87	53	125	240	310
Finished goods	60	142	322	208	598	934	1148
TOTAL	362	846	2491	1780	5526	8296	11016

VALUES AT CONSTANT PRICES

Table A63.   *Exports of manufactures from Canada*

$ million, f.o.b.

	Values at 1913 prices			Values at 1955 prices				
	1899	1913	1929	1929	1937	1950	1955	1957
METALS AND ENGINEERING	4	18	156	392	522	697	945	1050
Metals	1	4	71	188	369	445	642	694
Machinery	0	9	20	70	61	139	166	168
Passenger road vehicles ⎫	1	4	61	72	40	21	13	21
Other transport equipment ⎭				44	31	77	105	148
Other metal goods	2	1	4	18	21	15	19	19
CHEMICALS	1	5	19	33	44	125	246	246
Intermediates	0	—	11	19	25	72	183	187
Finished chemicals	1	5	8	14	19	53	63	59
TEXTILES AND CLOTHING	3	1	5	10	28	22	19	21
Yarns	—	—	—	—	—	—	3	6
Fabrics	2	1	2	4	7	11	9	9
Made-up goods	1	0	3	6	21	11	6	6
OTHER MANUFACTURES	10	18	132	495	561	638	860	913
Intermediates	2	16	100	380	458	545	777	841
Finished goods	8	2	32	115	103	93	83	72
TOTAL	18	42	312	930	1155	1482	2069	2230

Table A65.   *Exports of manufactures from the United States*[a]

	Values at 1913 prices			Values at 1955 prices				
	1899	1913	1929	1929	1937	1950	1955	1957
METALS AND ENGINEERING	213	526	1522	3611	3064	4528	5477	6476
Metals	88	232	266	787	681	676	894	1259
Machinery	69	163	408	1207	1163	2261	2619	3137
Passenger road vehicles ⎫	16	63	767	528	340	236	390	271
Other transport equipment ⎭				811	680	1055	1261	1464
Other metal goods	40	68	81	278	200	300	313	345
CHEMICALS	47	67	123	328	295	884	1106	1375
Intermediates	35	40	70	169	188	493	681	930
Finished chemicals	12	27	53	159	107	391	425	445
TEXTILES AND CLOTHING	41	66	107	318	157	461	539	575
Yarns	—	1	11	32	6	48	63	68
Fabrics	36	49	52	156	78	276	330	348
Made-up goods	5	16	44	130	73	137	146	159
OTHER MANUFACTURES	122	187	321	835	561	858	1174	1279
Intermediates	35	45	53	177	113	147	240	272
Finished goods	87	142	268	658	448	711	934	1007
TOTAL	423	846	2073	5092	4077	6731	8296	9705

[a] Excluding 'Special category' exports.

VALUES AT CURRENT PRICES

Table A66. *Exports of manufactures from India*

$ million, f.o.b.

	1899	1913	1929	1937	1950	1955	1957
METALS AND ENGINEERING	0	2	22	12	7	—	5
Metals	—	2	19	10	4	—	1
Machinery	—	—	0	0	1	—	3
Passenger road vehicles	}						—
Other transport equipment		—	—	—	—	—	1
Other metal goods	0	0	3	2	2	—	—
CHEMICALS	11	2	4	3	11	5	12
Intermediates	10	2	2	2	8	5	9
Finished chemicals	0	0	2	1	3	—	3
TEXTILES AND CLOTHING	50	135	223	150	569	424	433
Yarns	22	32	7	10	54	25	21
Fabrics	14	59	130	84	369	253	271
Made-up goods	14	44	86	56	146	146	141
OTHER MANUFACTURES	12	15	31	31	67	42	157
Intermediates	12	14	29	27	56	42	129
Finished goods	1	1	2	4	11	—	28
TOTAL	73	154	280	196	652	471	607

Table A68. *Exports of manufactures from Japan*

	1899	1913	1929	1937	1950	1955	1957
METALS AND ENGINEERING	6	19	35	119	234	636	959
Metals	6	15	9	35	130	328	251
Machinery	0	1	10	35	38	123	206
Passenger road vehicles	} 0	1	3	10	5	10	13
Other transport equipment			3	15	39	114	417
Other metal goods	0	2	10	24	22	61	72
CHEMICALS	1	6	19	29	17	94	126
Intermediates	1	3	11	18	7	35	44
Finished chemicals	0	3	8	11	10	59	82
TEXTILES AND CLOTHING	31	95	333	378	352	693	957
Yarns	15	37	16	41	20	74	94
Fabrics	11	41	267	263	289	468	677
Made-up goods	5	17	50	74	43	151	186
OTHER MANUFACTURES	10	33	89	119	96	325	502
Intermediates	1	2	12	15	8	30	112
Finished goods	9	31	77	104	88	295	390
TOTAL	48	153	476	645	697	1748	2538

VALUES AT CONSTANT PRICES

Table A67. *Exports of manufactures from India*

$ million, f.o.b.

	Values at 1913 prices			Values at 1955 prices				
	1899	1913	1929	1929	1937	1950	1955	1957
METALS AND ENGINEERING	0	2	17	45	27	8	—	5
Metals	—	2	15	39	24	4	—	1
Machinery	—	0	0	0	0	1	—	3
Passenger road vehicles ⎫	—	—	—	—	—	—	—	—
Other transport equipment ⎭								1
Other metal goods	0	0	2	6	3	3	—	—
CHEMICALS	14	2	3	8	10	10	5	12
Intermediates	13	2	2	4	7	7	5	9
Finished chemicals	1	0	1	4	3	3	—	3
TEXTILES AND CLOTHING	77	135	159	318	374	459	424	429
Yarns	34	32	4	13	23	44	25	21
Fabrics	21	59	93	163	178	306	253	268
Made-up goods	22	44	62	142	173	109	146	140
OTHER MANUFACTURES	15	15	20	50	64	61	42	157
Intermediates	14	14	18	46	55	51	42	129
Finished goods	1	1	2	4	9	10	—	28
TOTAL	106	154	199	421	475	538	471	603

Table A69. *Exports of manufactures from Japan*

	Values at 1913 prices			Values at 1955 prices				
	1899	1913	1929	1929	1937	1950	1955	1957
METALS AND ENGINEERING	8	19	27	66	355	349	636	893
Metals	8	15	7	20	108	219	328	193
Machinery	0	1	7	20	110	46	123	202
Passenger road vehicles ⎫	0	1	6	6	31	6	10	13
Other transport equipment ⎭				3	43	46	114	430
Other metal goods	0	2	7	17	63	32	61	55
CHEMICALS	2	6	16	26	62	19	94	135
Intermediates	1	3	9	15	38	8	35	47
Finished chemicals	1	3	7	11	24	11	59	88
TEXTILES AND CLOTHING	41	95	216	501	1034	337	693	947
Yarns	27	37	7	24	100	22	74	93
Fabrics	10	41	170	414	758	274	468	670
Made-up goods	4	17	39	63	176	41	151	184
OTHER MANUFACTURES	10	33	71	166	439	112	325	507
Intermediates	1	2	10	19	40	9	30	113
Finished goods	9	31	61	147	399	103	295	394
TOTAL	61	153	330	759	1890	816	1748	2482[a]

[a] The rise of 42 per cent compared with 1955 is greater than is shown by the official Japanese index (35 per cent) because the latter is based on 1953 weighting.

Table A70. Exports of Metals from the industrial countries and India, at constant prices

$ million, f.o.b.

Exports from		Year	Industrial countries				Semi-industrial countries				U.S.S.R.	Rest of World	World Total
			United Kingdom	Continental Western Europe	North America	Total (including Japan)	Southern Dominions	India (including Pakistan)	Other Semi-Industrial Countries	Total			
United Kingdom	a	1899	—	50	15	69	20	10	8	38	11	19	137
		1913	—	42	26	78	42	34	25	101	7	44	230
		1929	—	47	29	84	48	32	28	108	1	66	259
	b	1929	—	114	69	204	118	78	69	265	4	163	636
		1937	—	70	54	133	89	30	45	164	15	155	467
		1950	—	106	77	183	137	34	43	214	2	218	617
		1955	—	128	67	195	142	39	25	206	—	246	647
France	a	1899	7	15	1	23	—	0	0	0	1	7	31
		1913	7	25	1	33	0	0	1	1	1	13	48
		1929	12	61	2	77	0	1	3	4	1	22	104
	b	1929	61	297	12	380	0	4	14	18	3	116	517
		1937	31	82	2	120	1	3	19	23	4	85	232
		1950	25	127	44	196	18	11	86	115	3	186	500
		1955	37	307	37	381	10	18	47	75	10	269	735
Germany	a	1899	9	25	0	35	1	1	3	5	11	21	72
		1913	46	84	8	146	6	10	23	39	11	53	249
		1929	29	73	10	122	3	7	23	33	7	58	220
	b	1929	121	314	39	514	12	31	96	139	31	234	918
		1937	28	183	11	232	12	18	86	116	14	175	537
		1950	22	158	48	228	24	7	44	75	..	115	418
		1955	20	248	39	308	7	12	62	81	8	185	582
Other Western Europe	a	1899c	12	17	0	30	0	1	2	3	2	8	43
		1913c	21	47	5	76	3	4	9	16	3	16	111
		1929c	40	68	11	126	3	12	15	30	1	38	195
	b	1929	140	237	37	437	9	41	52	102	5	132	676
		1937	130	340	44	536	19	13	66	98	62	190	886
		1950	60	312	112	485	18	13	72	103	13	217	818
		1955	71	714	112	902	29	16	77	122	5	295	1324

Region		Year	1	2	3	4	5	6	7	8	9	10	11
(continued)		1913	1	0	2	3	—	—	0	0	—	1	4
		1929	9	10	43	70	1	—	1	2	0	0	71
	b	1929	22	27	113	182	3	1	2	6	0	0	188
		1937	212	33	70	347	6	2	2	10	1	11	369
		1950	109	19	292	420	6	8	7	21	—	4	445
		1955	209	36	350	597	14	5	17	36	—	9	642
United States	a	1899	16	46	7	72	3	1	4	8	2	6	88
		1913	28	120	41	193	3	1	11	15	2	22	232
		1929	37	83	52	186	2	3	23	28	3	49	266
	b	1929	108	245	155	549	7	9	68	84	10	144	787
		1937	74	130	82	413	16	5	82	103	20	145	681
		1950	56	119	163	339	32	14	134	180	—	157	676
		1955	125	246	234	614	36	27	125	188	—	92	894
Japan	a	1899	1	1	0	2	—	—	—	—	—	6	8
		1913	3	2	2	7	1	1	—	1	—	7	15
		1929	1	0	0	1	1	1	—	1	—	5	7
	b	1929	3	0	1	4	0	3	—	3	—	12	20
		1937	1	2	1	4	1	11	3	15	—	87	108
		1950	0	17	53	72	31	9	30	70	—	77	219
		1955	13	16	31	60	22	48	79	149	—	119	328
India	a	1899	—	—	—	—	—	—	—	—	—	—	—
		1913	2	0	0	1	0	—	—	0	—	1	2
		1929	15	2	1	14	0	—	0	0	—	1	15
	b	1929	14	7	3	37	0	—	0	0	—	2	39
		1937	9	0	2	22	0	0	—	0	—	2	24
		1950	1	0	1	2	0	—	—	0	—	2	4
		1955	—	—	—	—	—	—	—	—	—	—	—
TOTAL	a	1899c	45	155	24	233	24	13	17	55	27	64	379
		1913c	106	320	84	536	54	50	69	174	22	159	891
		1929c	133	343	148	677	57	57	92	206	15	240	1138
	b	1929	469	1240	429	2305	149	168	301	618	54	805	3782
		1937	485	840	267	1808	144	81	303	528	118	850	3304
		1950	273	856	793	1924	267	96	416	779	17	977	3697
		1955	475	1695	869	3056	260	165	432	857	23	1216	5152

a Values at 1913 prices.
b Values at 1955 prices.
c Excluding exports from the Netherlands.
Note: For exports of metals from other countries, see Chapter 9.

Table A71. Exports of Machinery from the industrial countries at constant prices

$ million, f.o.b.

Exports from	Exports to	Industrial countries				Semi-industrial countries				U.S.S.R.	Rest of World	World Total
		United Kingdom	Continental Western Europe	North America	Total (including Japan)	Southern Dominions	India (including Pakistan)	Other Semi-Industrial Countries	Total			
United Kingdom	*a* 1899	—	32	4	38	12	8	7	27	19	20	104
	1913	—	39	8	57	26	24	22	72	19	42	190
	1929	—	29	7	43	30	26	14	70	5	47	165
	b 1929	—	122	32	184	124	109	59	292	19	194	689
	1937	—	75	25	109	166	72	40	278	12	160	559
	1950	—	267	57	324	322	162	109	593	38	409	1364
	1955	—	291	113	411	382	161	71	614	29	551	1605
France	*a* 1899	1	6	0	7	0	0	1	1	1	6	15
	1913	1	10	0	11	0	0	3	3	1	13	28
	1929	4	30	1	36	0	0	4	4	1	36	77
	b 1929	20	143	5	175	1	1	16	18	5	178	376
	1937	11	22	1	35	1	0	8	9	1	67	112
	1950	6	51	1	58	2	2	31	35	—	244	337
	1955	11	86	9	107	3	5	68	76	7	238	428
Germany	*a* 1899	3	22	1	27	1	0	3	4	17	17	65
	1913	14	77	7	103	4	1	22	27	41	60	231
	1929	17	100	10	132	4	4	30	38	19	93	282
	b 1929	62	354	37	472	14	13	105	132	67	331	1002
	1937	47	203	10	277	18	15	94	127	49	217	670
	1950	8	201	9	219	11	8	60	79	—	129	427
	1955	69	655	64	800	38	63	211	312	1	403	1516
Other Western Europe	*a* 1899c	2	11	0	13	0	0	1	1	4	5	23
	1913c	4	26	1	32	1	1	8	10	8	6	56
	1929c	9	40	5	56	3	2	11	16	5	30	107
	b 1929	53	205	22	287	12	9	59	80	11	325	703
	1937	36	134	11	189	14	8	42	64	9	246	508
	1950	26	266	19	311	21	12	119	152	48	296	807
	1955	71	467	64	611	39	24	168	231	15	356	1213

Country	Year												Total
Canada	1899	a	0	0	0	0	0	0	0	0	0	0	0
	1913		1	3	0	4	2	—	1	3	1	1	9
	1929		2	1	4	7	3	0	7	10	1	2	20
	1929	b	5	6	13	24	9	0	23	32	4	10	70
	1937		16	2	9	27	15	0	14	29	0	5	61
	1950		2	6	90	98	4	2	20	26	—	15	139
	1955		4	7	109	120	6	5	17	28	—	18	166
United States	1899	a	13	20	8	42	5	0	11	16	2	9	69
	1913		18	30	32	84	12	2	24	38	13	28	163
	1929		34	48	100	191	27	6	79	112	25	80	408
	1929	b	102	139	296	564	81	16	232	329	73	241	1207
	1937		119	99	169	423	99	16	192	307	34	399	1163
	1950		81	400	503	993	100	58	555	713	0	555	2261
	1955		86	299	805	1253	130	46	459	635	—	731	2619
Japan	1899	a	—	—	—	—	—	—	—	—	—	0	0
	1913		—	—	—	0	0	—	—	—	0	1	1
	1929		0	0	1	1	0	0	0	0	0	6	7
	1929	b	0	1	3	4	0	1	0	1	1	14	20
	1937		2	1	5	8	1	7	2	10	4	88	110
	1950		0	—	8	8	1	13	2	16	—	22	46
	1955		0	1	19	20	1	19	24	44	—	59	123
TOTAL[d]	1899c	a	18	91	14	126	18	9	23	50	42	58	276
	1913c		39	182	49	290	45	28	80	153	83	152	678
	1929c		67	248	129	469	67	37	143	247	56	293	1065
	1929	b	243	970	408	1711	241	149	497	887	181	1288	4067
	1937		231	534	230	1067	314	118	393	825	109	1182	3183
	1950		123	1192	688	2013	461	256	896	1613	86	1670	5382
	1955		240	1806	1183	3321	598	321	1016	1935	51	2363	7670

a Values at 1913 prices.
b Values at 1955 prices.
c Excluding goods consigned from the Netherlands.
d Including India.

Table A72. *Exports of Transport Equipment from the industrial countries at constant prices*

$ million, f.o.b.

Exports from	Exports to	Industrial countries				Semi-industrial countries				U.S.S.R.	Rest of World	World Total
		United Kingdom	Continental Western Europe	North America	Total (including Japan)	Southern Dominions	India (including Pakistan)	Other Semi-Industrial Countries	Total			
United Kingdom a	1899	—	10	0	26	5	8	3	16	3	18	63
	1913	—	23	3	41	21	17	16	54	4	27	126
	1929	—	35	20	57	40	33	36	109	1	76	243
b	1929	—	53	31	87	60	51	55	166	2	114	369
	1937	—	31	8	40	99	32	25	156	5	109	310
	1950	—	268	146	415	387	104	106	597	1	410	1423
	1955	—	282	130	417	357	64	37	458	—	553	1428
France a	1899	1	3	—	4	0	—	0	0	0	5	9
	1913	12	18	0	30	0	0	7	7	1	15	53
	1929	10	45	2	58	0	2	11	13	9	99	179
b	1929	10	46	2	59	0	2	11	13	9	101	182
	1937	5	15	0	20	0	0	5	5	0	47	72
	1950	9	71	3	83	5	1	11	17	1	197	298
	1955	7	70	7	86	9	5	33	47	2	223	358
Germany a	1899	0	2	0	2	0	0	1	1	2	4	9
	1913	3	16	2	22	1	1	9	11	7	25	65
	1929	3	36	6	46	2	3	16	21	7	47	121
b	1929	3	41	7	52	3	3	17	23	8	53	136
	1937	6	77	8	94	9	6	38	53	1	91	239
	1950	1	102	1	104	7	2	25	34	—	50	188
	1955	21	352	67	441	32	43	91	166	16	318	941
Other Western Europe a	1899c	0	4	—	4	—	0	0	0	1	2	7
	1913c	4	11	0	15	1	0	12	13	2	9	39
	1929c	5	40	2	47	2	3	14	19	2	53	121
b	1929	13	104	5	123	5	7	35	47	5	129	304
	1937	17	81	2	100	3	2	15	20	2	232	354
	1950	7	167	6	180	2	2	72	76	8	93	357
	1955	22	253	23	298	7	13	88	108	23	194	623

Canada a	1899	0	0	0	0	0	0	0	0	0	1	1
	1913	0	0	0	3	1	—	1	4	—	0	4
	1929	6	1	1	22	9	4	8	35	0	18	61
Canada b	1929	11	1	1	43	16	8	13	67	1	35	116
	1937	6	1	1	42	8	5	8	47	—	16	71
	1950	1	2	7	34	10	18	16	68	—	20	98
	1955	2	9	41	37	52	14	2	53	0	13	118
United States a	1899	3	3	1	1	8	0	3	4	1	3	16
	1913	10	5	20	8	35	1	8	17	1	10	63
	1929	34	114	150	74	325	17	166	257	7	178	767
United States b	1929	59	199	261	129	566	29	291	449	11	313	1339
	1937	38	167	145	124	392	22	205	351	9	268	1020
	1950	13	130	244	43	392	27	340	410	—	489	1291
	1955	24	170	454	99	657	53	302	454	0	540	1651
Japan a	1899	—	—	—	—	—	—	—	—	0	0	0
	1913	—	—	—	—	—	—	—	—	—	1	1
	1929	—	—	—	—	—	0	—	0	1	5	6
Japan b	1929	0	—	—	—	—	0	—	0	1	8	9
	1937	—	—	—	1	1	3	0	4	12	57	74
	1950	—	5	—	0	5	1	0	1	0	46	52
	1955	—	1	—	0	1	19	11	30	0	93	124
TOTAL a	1899c	4	24	2	6	47	9	7	22	7	29	105
	1913c	29	72	25	34	142	19	53	106	16	88	352
	1929c	57	271	181	140	540	62	250	452	26	480	1498
TOTAL b	1929	96	444	308	239	901	100	426	765	36	754	2456
	1937	71	375	165	277	659	70	288	635	30	816	2140
	1950	30	748	407	478	1191	156	574	1208	10	1298	3707
	1955	75	1134	723	542	1949	211	561	1314	42	1937	5242

aValues at 1913 prices.
bValues at 1955 prices.
cExcluding goods consigned from the Netherlands.

Table A73. Exports of Passenger Road Vehicles *from the industrial countries at 1955 prices*

$ million, f.o.b.

Exports from		Industrial countries				Semi-industrial countries				U.S.S.R.	Rest of World	World Total
		United Kingdom	Continental Western Europe	North America	Total (including Japan)	Southern Dominions	India (including Pakistan)	Other Semi-Industrial Countries	Total			
United Kingdom	1929	—	17	1	19	24	10	1	35	0	38	92
	1937	—	10	3	14	46	12	2	60	0	45	119
	1950	—	73	104	178	167	21	18	206	—	125	509
	1955	—	64	63	131	140	10	3	153	0	162	446
France	1929	7	30	—	37	1	—	2	2	—	66	105
	1937	1	9	—	11	1	—	1	2	—	27	40
	1950	3	50	3	56	5	0	8	13	—	69	138
	1955	3	43	7	55	6	0	3	9	—	118	182
Germany	1929	1	10	0	12	0	0	2	2	1	19	34
	1937	3	28	2	35	4	2	17	23	—	35	93
	1950	0	74	1	75	3	1	7	11	—	24	110
	1955	10	189	54	254	19	10	25	54	—	155	463
Other Western Europe	1929	2	8	—	10	—	1	4	5	0	85	100
	1937	4	18	1	23	1	0	5	6	—	60	89
	1950	0	33	0	33	1	0	8	9	0	22	64
	1955	5	84	4	95	3	2	10	15	—	52	162
Canada	1929	10	1	0	11	26	3	11	40	1	20	72
	1937	5	0	0	5	25	2	0	27	0	8	40
	1950	0	1	0	1	18	0	1	19	—	1	21
	1955	0	0	0	0	11	0	0	11	—	2	13
United States	1929	14	92	75	190	80	14	107	201	4	133	528
	1937	14	62	27	111	77	8	61	146	0	83	340
	1950	0	50	9	62	12	4	59	75	0	99	236
	1955	2	75	62	140	25	5	49	79	0	171	390
TOTAL[a]	1929	34	162	75	283	130	28	127	285	6	358	932
	1937	27	125	34	197	155	26	85	266	1	288	752
	1950	4	278	118	404	205	26	102	333	0	340	1077
	1955	20	455	191	674	205	28	91	324	0	667	1665

[a]Including Japan.

Exports to

Exports from	Year	Industrial countries				Semi-industrial countries				U.S.S.R.	Rest of World	World Total
		United Kingdom	Continental Western Europe	North America	Total (including Japan)	Southern Dominions	India (including Pakistan)	Other Semi-Industrial Countries	Total			
United Kingdom	1929	—	158	62	252	160	150	113	423	21	270	966
	1937	—	96	30	135	219	92	63	374	17	224	750
	1950	—	462	99	561	542	245	197	984	39	694	2278
	1955	—	509	180	697	599	215	105	919	29	942	2587
France	1929	23	159	7	197	1	3	25	29	14	213	453
	1937	15	28	1	44	0	0	12	12	1	87	144
	1950	12	72	1	85	2	3	34	39	1	372	497
	1955	15	113	9	138	6	10	98	114	9	343	604
Germany	1929	64	385	44	512	17	16	120	153	74	365	1104
	1937	50	252	16	336	23	19	115	157	50	273	816
	1950	9	229	9	248	15	9	78	102	—	155	505
	1955	80	818	77	987	51	96	277	424	17	566	1994
Other Western Europe	1929	64	301	27	400	17	15	90	122	16	369	907
	1937	49	197	12	266	16	10	52	78	11	418	773
	1950	33	400	25	458	22	14	183	219	56	367	1100
	1955	88	636	83	814	43	35	246	324	38	498	1674
Canada	1929	6	6	14	26	26	5	28	59	4	25	114
	1937	17	3	10	30	32	3	14	49	0	13	92
	1950	3	7	97	107	20	20	35	75	—	34	216
	1955	6	16	150	172	32	19	19	70	—	29	271
United States	1929	147	246	482	940	130	31	416	577	80	421	2018
	1937	143	204	287	704	146	30	336	512	43	584	1843
	1950	94	480	738	1323	131	81	836	1048	0	945	3316
	1955	108	394	1197	1770	204	94	712	1010	0	1100	3880
Japan	1929	0	1	3	4	0	1	0	1	2	16	23
	1937	2	1	4	7	1	8	2	11	16	119	153
	1950	0	5	8	13	1	14	2	17	0	62	92
	1955	0	2	19	21	1	37	35	73	0	143	237
TOTAL	1929	305	1252	641	2329	350	221	796	1367	211	1684	5591
	1937	275	784	361	1529	436	162	596	1194	138	1710	4571
	1950	149	1662	977	2800	734	386	1368	2488	96	2629	8013
	1955	295	2485	1715	4596	935	504	1486	2925	93	3633	11247

Table A75. Exports of Chemicals from the industrial countries and India, at constant prices

$ million, f.o.b.

Exports from		United Kingdom	Continental Western Europe	North America	Total (including Japan)	Southern Dominions	India (including Pakistan)	Other Semi-Industrial Countries	Total	U.S.S.R.	Rest of World	World Total
		Industrial countries				Semi-industrial countries						
United Kingdom	1899 a	—	20	7	28	11	4	4	19	2	15	64
	1913	—	27	15	53	16	9	8	33	2	31	119
	1929	—	15	11	36	20	16	8	44	0	62	142
	1929 b	—	28	20	66	37	30	15	82	1	112	261
	1937	—	34	22	59	46	28	17	91	1	99	250
	1950	—	64	34	98	63	42	41	146	0	189	433
	1955	—	123	43	170	109	58	31	198	0	284	652
France	1899 a	6	16	5	27	0	0	3	3	1	5	36
	1913	11	34	7	52	1	0	6	7	1	19	79
	1929	8	30	7	46	1	1	6	8	0	24	78
	1929 b	26	104	22	155	3	3	20	26	1	79	261
	1937	14	48	12	77	2	2	13	17	2	69	165
	1950	20	50	10	83	3	5	16	24	0	89	196
	1955	31	84	20	144	4	7	25	36	1	179	360
Germany	1899 a	12	18	11	42	1	3	2	6	5	21	74
	1913	27	62	39	135	2	5	12	19	20	65	239
	1929	17	80	30	146	3	8	15	26	8	81	261
	1929 b	30	137	52	252	5	13	27	45	14	135	446
	1937	25	86	32	167	6	17	48	71	3	139	380
	1950	16	88	14	124	3	7	22	32	0	67	223
	1955	43	241	39	343	20	25	61	106	1	231	681
Other Western Europe	1899c a	4	21	3	28	0	0	1	1	1	7	37
	1913c	10	37	6	54	1	2	4	7	2	15	78
	1929c	13	38	8	61	1	2	7	10	2	21	94
	1929 b	39	83	25	153	3	5	15	23	4	72	252
	1937	31	99	26	164	4	5	15	24	1	120	309
	1950	36	142	25	207	7	15	37	59	1	146	413
	1955	58	259	61	390	22	24	65	111	2	265	768

	Year											
Canada												
a	1899	0	0	0	0	0	—	0	0	—	1	1
	1913	1	0	3	4	0	—	—	0	—	1	5
	1929	4	0	11	16	0	0	1	1	—	2	19
b	1929	6	0	20	27	0	0	2	2	—	4	33
	1937	8	0	24	32	2	0	2	4	—	8	44
	1950	10	14	69	93	3	6	3	12	0	20	125
	1955	26	34	142	204	5	1	16	22	—	20	246
United States												
a	1899	16	13	4	33	3	0	5	8	0	6	47
	1913	14	15	10	40	3	—	8	12	1	14	67
	1929	19	20	21	69	6	3	17	26	1	27	123
b	1929	47	50	53	175	16	8	46	70	3	80	328
	1937	39	48	48	154	16	8	38	62	1	78	295
	1950	48	125	149	347	20	28	188	236	0	301	884
	1955	57	204	219	521	37	23	208	268	0	317	1106
Japan												
a	1899	0	0	0	0	0	—	—	0	0	2	2
	1913	1	1	1	3	0	1	1	1	0	2	6
	1929	0	3	3	6	0	1	1	1	0	9	16
b	1929	1	3	5	9	1	2	0	3	0	14	26
	1937	2	6	7	15	0	5	2	8	0	39	62
	1950	0	2	2	4	0	1	2	3	—	12	19
	1955	3	4	7	14	3	4	5	12	—	68	94
TOTAL[d]												
a	1899c	42	87	34	168	14	8	16	38	9	59	274
	1913c	64	177	84	344	24	17	38	79	27	144	594
	1929c	62	186	91	381	31	31	55	117	12	226	736
b	1929	148	410	188	841	65	61	124	251	23	503	1618
	1937	119	326	172	675	77	67	136	280	8	550	1513
	1950	134	486	304	962	99	104	310	513	2	825	2302
	1955	218	951	533	1789	199	143	408	750	4	1368	3911

[a] Values at 1913 prices.
[b] Values at 1955 prices.
[c] Excluding exports from the Netherlands.
[d] Including India.

Table A76. Exports of Textiles and Clothing *from the industrial countries and India, at constant prices*

$ million, f.o.b.

Exports from			Industrial countries				Semi-industrial countries				U.S.S.R.	Rest of World	World Total
Exports to			United Kingdom	Continental Western Europe	North America	Total (including Japan)	Southern Dominions	India (including Pakistan)	Other Semi-Industrial Countries	Total			
United Kingdom	a	1899	—	164	71	251	88	140	68	296	8	222	777
		1913	—	174	102	288	101	197	101	399	9	254	950
		1929	—	113	75	196	92	88	62	242	1	208	647
	b	1929	—	423	281	734	345	330	234	909	4	775	2422
		1937	—	294	219	524	345	100	186	631	17	584	1756
		1950	—	209	179	390	417	47	38	502	—	494	1386
		1955	—	144	156	309	280	21	11	313	1	337	960
France	a	1899	102	50	23	176	1	2	17	20	1	47	244
		1913	117	69	37	224	1	5	29	35	0	71	330
		1929	84	104	40	229	4	2	26	32	0	97	358
	b	1929	181	235	86	504	7	5	57	69	0	205	778
		1937	29	60	27	116	3	0	19	22	—	154	292
		1950	48	123	31	202	10	5	23	38	—	297	537
		1955	22	141	36	199	16	5	13	34	1	300	534
Germany	a	1899	68	73	34	177	3	8	19	30	7	57	271
		1913	65	86	35	190	4	9	35	47	16	70	324
		1929	45	94	30	172	5	3	19	27	1	83	283
	b	1929	66	138	44	252	8	5	27	40	1	124	417
		1937	38	90	5	133	6	3	52	61	—	106	300
		1950	9	51	7	67	2	1	10	13	—	24	104
		1955	11	147	18	176	21	6	34	62	—	115	353
Other Western Europe	a	1899c	48	101	20	170	1	3	16	20	1	24	215
		1913c	62	105	28	196	4	9	39	52	2	65	315
		1929c	74	111	40	227	7	16	66	89	0	135	451
	b	1929	151	222	78	454	18	33	107	158	1	299	912
		1937	56	222	75	354	23	13	103	139	2	310	805
		1950	79	425	63	567	42	28	36	106	—	217	890
		1955	69	484	98	651	73	20	35	128	2	290	1071

Country	Basis	Year	1	2	3	4	5	6	7	8	9	10	11
	a	1913	0	0	1	1	0	0	—	0	0	0	1
	a	1929	0	0	2	2	1	0	0	1	0	2	5
	b	1929	1	0	3	4	3	0	0	3	1	2	10
	b	1937	8	—	3	11	12	0	0	12	0	5	28
	b	1950	1	1	13	15	4	0	—	4	—	3	22
	b	1955	1	3	9	13	1	0	1	2	—	4	19
United States	a	1899	3	1	6	10	1	1	13	15	0	16	41
	a	1913	5	2	16	23	3	1	7	11	3	29	66
	a	1929	8	4	20	32	10	3	20	33	0	42	107
	b	1929	24	12	59	96	29	9	61	99	0	123	318
	b	1937	6	6	18	31	12	2	22	36	—	90	157
	b	1950	2	41	55	100	26	5	38	69	—	292	461
	b	1955	2	40	108	151	48	1	33	82	—	306	539
Japan	a	1899	1	4	5	10	0	1	—	1	0	30	41
	a	1913	7	8	10	25	2	4	1	7	—	62	95
	a	1929	8	5	14	27	14	47	4	65	1	123	216
	b	1929	16	11	30	57	33	113	8	154	3	287	501
	b	1937	28	30	73	131	75	161	51	287	—	616	1034
	b	1950	17	19	43	79	29	51	2	83	—	175	337
	b	1955	10	23	154	187	44	26	10	80	—	426	693
India	a	1899	7	2	10	19	7	—	4	11	—	47	77
	a	1913	8	3	40	52	13	—	16	29	—	54	135
	a	1929	11	4	55	72	16	—	21	37	—	50	159
	b	1929	23	8	96	131	31	—	40	71	—	116	318
	b	1937	40	9	82	132	37	—	28	65	—	177	374
	b	1950	44	16	72	132	38	14	21	73	—	254	459
	b	1955	47	10	87	144	47	10	25	82	—	198	424
TOTAL	a	1899c	228	393	170	812	101	155	137	392	17	449	1670
	a	1913c	263	447	268	998	128	226	231	584	31	603	2217
	a	1929c	230	436	278	959	149	160	217	526	5	734	2224
	b	1929	463	1047	678	2231	474	495	579	1503	10	1931	5675
	b	1937	205	710	501	1431	513	279	464	1256	17	2045	4749
	b	1950	199	884	460	1548	567	150	171	888	2	1759	4197
	b	1955	161	991	665	1828	531	88	163	781	4	1977	4590

aValues at 1913 prices.
bValues at 1955 prices.
cExcluding exports from the Netherlands.

Table A77. *Exports of Other Manufactures (including Other metal goods) from the industrial countries and India, at constant prices*

$ million, f.o.b.

Exports from		Industrial countries				Semi-industrial countries				U.S.S.R.	Rest of World	World Total
		United Kingdom	Continental Western Europe	North America	Total (including Japan)	Southern Dominions	India (including Pakistan)	Other Semi-Industrial Countries	Total			
United Kingdom	*a* 1899	—	41	20	64	47	20	13	80	5	34	183
	1913	—	62	40	110	83	35	33	151	6	78	345
	1929	—	54	59	119	87	20	33	140	4	102	365
	b 1929	—	122	135	270	191	71	71	333	9	187	799
	1937	—	105	82	191	186	55	34	275	3	223	692
	1950	—	201	165	367	276	77	63	416	1	516	1300
	1955	—	281	179	463	294	63	35	392	24	514	1393
France	*a* 1899	49	42	10	102	1	1	13	15	2	50	169
	1913	51	84	15	150	1	2	28	31	3	65	249
	1929	37	69	29	136	1	2	14	17	0	90	243
	b 1929	88	181	68	339	4	7	52	63	1	239	642
	1937	33	56	24	114	2	1	9	12	0	153	279
	1950	37	91	25	153	10	3	41	54	1	390	598
	1955	38	141	54	234	7	5	33	45	3	380	662
Germany	*a* 1899	57	71	24	154	6	4	21	31	24	82	291
	1913	91	187	49	330	13	8	63	81	60	144	618
	1929	81	214	60	361	14	12	72	98	12	209	680
	b 1929	204	579	147	948	38	37	205	280	36	579	1843
	1937	110	321	47	493	25	34	147	206	12	406	1117
	1950	7	190	40	237	15	7	58	80	0	136	453
	1955	55	480	169	710	42	20	71	133	1	333	1177
Other Western Europe	*a* 1899*c*	27	43	6	77	1	7	9	17	5	34	133
	1913*c*	50	78	11	142	6	6	26	38	9	41	230
	1929*c*	58	114	50	227	8	7	25	40	2	80	349
	b 1929	162	338	150	668	31	23	72	126	6	299	1099
	1937	197	262	123	592	41	31	52	124	1	290	1007
	1950	75	322	182	580	49	18	81	148	6	432	1166
	1955	150	598	332	1085	64	31	109	204	3	482	1774

	a	[illegible]	[illegible]	[illegible]	[illegible]	[illegible]	1	0	0	1	0	1	12
		1913	3	0	13	16	2	0	1	3	0	0	19
		1929	15	3	88	107	11	3	6	20	0	9	136
	b	1929	54	11	335	404	39	11	22	72	0	37	513
		1937	89	6	374	475	51	3	18	72	0	35	582
		1950	10	6	583	599	12	2	11	25	0	29	653
		1955	50	13	733	797	29	3	19	51	0	31	879
United States	a	1899	53	24	27	108	14	1	17	32	1	21	162
		1913	52	40	67	162	16	2	28	46	3	44	255
		1929	50	38	91	190	23	6	68	97	1	114	402
	b	1929	140	111	252	534	65	17	188	270	4	305	1113
		1937	70	81	150	322	51	13	116	180	12	247	761
		1950	26	96	318	449	29	16	227	272	0	437	1158
		1955	39	132	511	699	50	14	173	237	0	551	1487
Japan	a	1899	1	0	2	3	0	1	0	1	0	6	10
		1913	3	4	7	14	1	2	0	3	0	18	35
		1929	3	4	15	22	2	8	1	11	1	44	78
	b	1929	8	10	35	53	5	19	3	27	2	101	183
		1937	31	20	92	143	28	45	14	87	3	269	502
		1950	0	5	59	64	4	4	7	15	0	65	144
		1955	7	16	174	197	14	9	12	35	0	154	386
India	a	1899	12	0	2	14	0	—	0	0	0	1	15
		1913	12	0	1	13	0	—	0	0	0	2	15
		1929	15	2	1	19	0	—	0	0	0	3	22
	b	1929	41	5	4	52	0	—	0	0	0	4	56
		1937	50	1	1	53	1	—	0	1	0	13	67
		1950	35	4	9	50	0	—	0	0	0	14	64
		1955	32	3	1	38	0	—	0	0	0	4	42
TOTAL	a	1899[c]	205	226	95	537	70	33	72	175	36	226	974
		1913[c]	263	456	202	938	123	54	182	356	82	387	1766
		1929[c]	261	497	393	1182	156	49	218	423	21	649	2275
	b	1929	696	1356	1127	3268	372	186	612	1170	58	1748	6244
		1937	580	854	894	2385	383	182	390	955	32	1635	5007
		1950	191	915	1381	2499	394	128	486	1008	8	2021	5536
		1955	373	1665	2153	4224	502	145	454	1101	31	2444	7800

[a]Values at 1913 prices.
[b]Values at 1955 prices.
[c]Excluding exports from the Netherlands.

Table A78.   *Exports of manufactures classified by stage of fabrication and end-use: totals for three major importing areas*

	\$ million, f.o.b.						
	Values at 1913 prices[a]			*Values at 1955 prices*[b]			
	1899	1913	1929	1929	1937	1950	1955
TO INDUSTRIAL COUNTRIES							
Intermediate products	706	1265	1553	4537	3519	3879	6254
Finished manufactures	1217	1983	2659	6735	4512	6297	9918
Capital goods	164	383	832	2329	1529	2800	4596
Textile fabrics	400	550	486	1118	727	809	933
Other finished goods	653	1050	1341	3288	2256	2688	4389
TO SEMI-INDUSTRIAL COUNTRIES							
Intermediate products	124	301	382	1064	1064	1384	1717
Finished manufactures	608	1155	1589	4134	3418	4638	5025
Capital goods	72	222	522	1367	1194	2488	2925
Textile fabrics	281	426	362	1033	778	514	460
Other finished goods	255	507	705	1729	1446	1636	1640
TO REST OF WORLD							
Intermediate products	290	489	582	1616	1762	1895	2490
Finished manufactures	733	1306	2171	5755	5620	6728	8963
Capital goods	136	315	628	1895	1848	2724	3726
Textile fabrics	277	402	484	1307	1370	1157	1254
Other finished goods	320	589	1059	2553	2402	2847	3983
TOTAL							
Intermediate products	1120	2054	2517	7217	6345	7158	10461
Finished manufactures	2557	4443	6419	16624	13550	17663	23906
Capital goods	372	920	1981	5591	4571	8012	11247
Textile fabrics	958	1378	1332	3463	2875	2480	2647
Other finished goods	1227	2145	3106	7570	6104	7171	10012
Durable consumer goods[c]	..	..	..	1500	1300	1760	2760

Sources: Tables A6, A8, A10, A12.   The figures for capital goods and other finished goods in 1899 and 1913 contain some minor estimates.

[a]Excluding ⎱ goods consigned from the Netherlands.
[b]Including ⎰

[c]These are also included under 'capital goods' or 'other finished goods'; a detailed subdivision is given in Table 12.2.

Note: For definitions of the commodity groups see Appendix D.

Table A79. *Exports of manufactures classified by stage of fabrication and end-use: world totals by main exporting countries*

$ million, f.o.b.

		France	Germany	United Kingdom	Other Western Europe	Canada	United States	India	Japan
INTERMEDIATE PRODUCTS									
a	1899	109	213	333	208	3	158	61	37
	1913	192	632	468	319	20	318	50	57
	1929	284	583	517	479	182	400	39	33
b	1929	978	1597	1365	1342	587	1165	102	78
	1937	471	959	1099	1579	852	988	109	286
	1950	913	629	1263	1562	1062	1364	106	258
	1955	1232	1251	1415	2542	1605	1878	72	467
	1957	1176	2014	1831	2872	1728	2529	160	446
FINISHED MANUFACTURES									
a	1899	395	569	995	249	15	265	45	24
	1913	595	1094	1492	510	22	528	104	96
	1929	755	1264	1304	838	130	1673	160	297
b	1929	1777	3165	3811	2605	343	3927	319	681
	1937	681	2284	2935	2290	303	3089	366	1604
	1950	1553	1184	5260	2889	420	5367	432	559
	1955	1845	3999	5270	4231	464	6418	399	1281
	1957	2008	5288	5508	5095	502	7176	443	2036
CAPITAL GOODS									
b	1929	453	1104	966	910	114	2018	0	23
	1937	144	816	750	773	92	1843	0	153
	1950	497	505	2278	1100	216	3316	1	92
	1955	604	1994	2587	1674	271	3880	—	237
	1957	666	2746	2925	2095	316	4601	4	632
TEXTILE FABRICS									
b	1929	442	216	1550	519	4	156	163	414
	1937	177	166	1063	448	7	78	178	758
	1950	310	71	758	473	11	276	306	274
	1955	272	219	594	502	9	330	253	468
	1957	235	217	547	607	9	348	268	670
OTHER FINISHED GOODS									
b	1929	882	1845	1295	1176	225	1753	156	244
	1937	360	1302	1122	1069	204	1168	188	693
	1950	746	608	2224	1316	193	1775	125	193
	1955	969	1786	2089	2055	184	2208	146	576
	1957	1107	2325	2036	2393	177	2227	171	734

Sources: Tables A47–A69.

ªValues at 1913 prices, excluding Netherlands.
ᵇValues at 1955 prices, including Netherlands.
Note: For definitions of the commodity groups see Appendix D.

Table A80. Exports of manufactures from the industrial countries and India by commodity group, 1959

$ million, f.o.b.

Exports from	United Kingdom	France	Germany, West	Belgium-Luxembourg	Italy	Netherlands	Sweden	Switzerland	Canada	United States[a]	Japan	India	TOTAL	Total at 1955 prices
METALS AND ENGINEERING	5258	2423	5862	1580	1030	940	956	587	1156	6084	1211	13	27100	24496
Metals	852	890	1165	1008	179	229	204	44	716	634	280	5	6206	6204
Machinery	2229	594	2570	241	375	426	355	462	293	3457	354	4	11360	9689
Passenger road vehicles	703	501	852	74	234	23	58	5	19	266	32	0	2767	2579
Other transport equipment	1065	277	861	113	149	192	246	11	101	1385	424	1	4825	4345
Other metal goods	409	161	414	144	93	70	93	65	27	342	121	3	1942	1679
CHEMICALS	821	472	1105	258	208	319	67	306	243	1502	166	10	5477	5750
Intermediates	589	264	822	94	125	216	56	136	184	1072	60	7	3625	3793
Finished	232	208	283	164	83	103	11	170	59	430	106	3	1852	1957
TEXTILES AND CLOTHING	779	576	429	371	454	302	28	198	23	542	964	426	5092	5342
Yarns	155	150	84	108	104	77	3	49	5	86	71	23	915	975
Fabrics	460	250	235	145	219	153	15	94	11	297	631	283	2793	2913
Made-up goods	164	176	110	118	131	72	10	55	7	159	262	120	1384	1454
OTHER MANUFACTURES	1006	705	1284	521	332	326	334	454	969	1502	691	93	8217	7809
Intermediates	265	180	261	322	43	129	235	33	886	335	77	64	2830	2681
Finished	741	525	1023	199	289	197	99	421	83	1167	614	29	5387	5128
TOTAL	7864	4176	8680	2730	2024	1887	1385	1545	2391	9630	3032	542	45886	—
Total at 1955 prices	7281	4201	8348	2650	2131	1833	1247	1515	2354	8350	2944	542	—	43396

Sources: Foreign Trade Statistical Bulletins, 1959, Series B and C, O.E.E.C., Paris, 1960; Yearbook of International Trade Statistics, 1959, Vol. II, United Nations, New York, 1960; national trade statistics.

[a] Excluding 'Special category' exports.

Table A81. *Exports of manufactures from the industrial countries and India by country of destination, 1959*

$ million, f.o.b.

Exports to	Metals	Capital goods	Passenger road vehicles	Chemicals	Textiles and clothing	Other manu- facturesa	TOTAL	Total at 1955 prices
Belgium-Luxembourg	124	436	150	210	158	376	1454	*1404*
France	337	583	31	195	55	272	1473	*1415*
Germany, West	600	535	127	260	429	564	2515	*2431*
Italy	169	413	23	237	51	258	1151	*1101*
Netherlands	343	593	120	248	255	437	1996	*1921*
Norway	87	409	25	63	82	97	763	*723*
Sweden	171	431	132	135	141	234	1244	*1195*
Switzerland	149	317	78	150	129	326	1149	*1113*
United Kingdom	306	512	46	282	194	544	1884	*1814*
Canada	264	1682	229	316	312	922	3725	*3317*
United States	1053	906	811	327	606	2107	5810	*5661*
Japan	47	227	6	191	8	68	547	*500*
TOTAL INDUSTRIAL COUNTRIES	3650	7044	1778	2614	2420	6205	23711	*22595*
Australia	57	496	82	130	189	222	1176	*1098*
New Zealand	33	118	30	36	73	74	364	*339*
Union of South Africa	33	383	103	90	149	186	944	*884*
India	126	603	24	140	33	102	1028	*971*
Pakistan	33	132	7	27	8	42	249	*235*
Argentina	197	350	10	66	26	66	715	*676*
Brazil	85	449	21	85	2	87	729	*677*
Chile	15	112	7	34	10	41	219	*202*
Colombia	28	136	4	55	6	49	278	*253*
Mexico	31	402	57	155	23	138	806	*726*
Israel	33	93	6	20	8	41	201	*190*
Turkey	37	163	11	46	8	59	324	*308*
Yugoslavia	30	122	9	46	12	35	254	*250*
TOTAL SEMI- INDUSTRIAL COUNTRIES	738	3559	371	930	547	1142	7286	*6809*
U.S.S.R.	155	152	—	22	21	33	383	*372*
REST OF WORLD	1663	5430	618	1911	2104	2779	14506	*13620*
WORLD TOTAL	6206	16185	2767	5477	5092	10159	45886	*—*
World total at 1955 prices	*6204*	*14033*	*2579*	*5750*	*5342*	*9488*	*—*	*43396*

Sources: As for Table A80.
aIncluding 'other metal goods'.

EXPORT UNIT VALUES

As mentioned in Appendix A, the value series of trade at current prices were deflated by a set of appropriate unit value indices to obtain value series at ' constant ' prices. The ideal solution is to deflate separately the value series for each commodity group distinguished for each exporting country. Since there are 12 exporters (11 in 1899 and 1913), 12 commodity groups (excluding group totals where sub-groups are distinguished) and five links of years (excluding 1957 and 1959 for which trade network tables were constructed in a less detailed form), a complete system would involve the use of some 700 unit value index deflators. The compilation of such a large number of indices was clearly beyond the scope of the present study. Fortunately, a recent work by Professor Kindleberger[1] has covered a good proportion of the field, though the Kindleberger indices are confined to European countries and do not relate precisely to the years covered here ; nor are they subdivided into as many commodity groups as are distinguished here. These indices were adjusted to allow for the differences in years and have been used in this study ; in some cases, however, where a particular Kindleberger index looked suspiciously out of line with the corresponding commodity group indices for the majority of countries, a new calculation was made directly from the national export returns.

For the United Kingdom, the Kindleberger indices were not used ; instead, the unit value series were based on the official index numbers published by the Board of Trade. For the United States, for which none of the official series are applicable, the unit value indices were derived in part by special computation from the export returns[2] and in part from the movement in wholesale prices. For both India and Japan, special unit value indices were computed back to 1899 for each commodity group. In all, about 400 separate unit value deflators were used[3].

These unit value indices relate to exports to *all destinations* of a particular commodity group from each exporting country. Since the network tables distinguish countries of destination, it could be argued that different deflators should be used for each. To do this systematically would require something like 20,000 deflators to convert all the network tables to constant prices ! Once again, the sheer magnitude of the task necessitated the use of some simplifying assumption. The assumption made here is that the unit value index for a given commodity group applies equally to every country of

---

[1]Kindleberger, *op. cit.*

[2]For the period 1899–1913, the unit value series were based on detailed commodity indices kindly made available by Mr R. E. Lipsey of the National Bureau of Economic Research, Inc., New York ; see footnote to Table B.1.

[3]For the period 1950–59, the indices for Continental European countries were based on detailed unit value series kindly supplied by the United Nations' Economic Commission for Europe, Geneva.

destination within that group[1]. This assumption was applied throughout, and the calculations were made for each exporting country separately.

The assumption is not an unreasonable one, since it is to be expected that prices at which goods are exported to one destination would move broadly in line with prices of similar goods exported by the same country to another destination. There may, of course, be cases in which this will not occur ; for example, if the exporting country has a monopoly of sale in one market and not in another. But, by and large, the assumption is unlikely to result in much distortion of the true unit value movement over a period of years. Moreover, there is likely to be some offsetting of errors, since the aggregate exports to a single destination consist of totals of commodity groups for twelve exporting countries. Nevertheless, the unit value index for all exports of manufactures to a single destination may well be significantly different from a corresponding series derived from national import statistics.

In the following tables, the majority of the unit value indices have either been specially computed from data in the relevant national export returns, or have been adapted from series published elsewhere. In a minority of cases, however, it was not found practicable to compute indices, for example, for commodity groups for which no quantitative data were available in the export statistics. These were usually cases where exports were relatively small ; assumed indices were used in such cases, and these were based on the indices for countries exporting similar classes of goods. For passenger road vehicles the construction of separate unit value indices was not attempted. Instead, the value series for this group was deflated by the unit value indices for all transport equipment.

[1]For a discussion of the relative merits and demerits of the various assumptions which could be made to derive unit value indices for exports to a given country or area *see* A. Maizels, 'Unit Value and Volume Index Numbers of Inter-Area Trade', *J. Roy. Stat. Soc.*, Series A (General), Vol. 120, Pt. II, 1957.

Table B1. Export unit value indices, 1913 (1899 = 100)[a]

	Belgium-Lux'bourg	France	Germany	Italy	Sweden	Switzerland	United Kingdom	Canada	United States	India	Japan	Total 1899 weights	Total 1913 weights
Metals	93 }	121 }	126	..	85[b]	59	108	161[b]	94	—	124	106	107
Metal goods			108	..	..	..	104	..	116	..	..	109	108
Machinery	78	102	136	126[b]	..	134[b]	106	..	103[c] }	—	..	111	108
Transport equipment	47	105	70[b]	..	..	..	95	143[b]		—	..	89	86
Chemicals	121	106	81	105	..	70[b]	127	182[b]	128	..	141[b]	106	99
Textiles and clothing[d]	109	117	130	109	..	102	147	320[b]	137	154	137	132	131
Other manufactures	105	108	103	146	95	107	120	133	143	..	96	114	112
TOTAL MANUFACTURES 1899 weights	99	113	112	116	93	104	129	143	117	144	127	118	
1913 weights	93	112	108	115	96	101	125	132	112	151	111		114
NON-MANUFACTURES	109	111	112	116	119	135	115	119[e]	147[e]	..	120[e]	124[f]	..
TOTAL EXPORTS	105	112	112	116	110	112	128	121	138	..	123	121[f]	..

a In terms of U.S. dollars.
b Based on small sample.
c This index was based on the preliminary results of Mr Lipsey's investigation (see footnote on page 506). Mr Lipsey's final results indicate that the correct index for machinery and transport equipment in 1913 (1899 = 100) would be about 94. Unfortunately, these final results became available too late for the appropriate amendment to be carried through the Trade Network tables.
d Indices for sub-groups, where available, are as follows (in the order yarns, fabrics, made-up goods): India—151, 151, 154; Japan—185, 92, 91.
e Residual.
f Excluding India.

Table B2. *Export unit value indices, 1929 (1913 = 100)*ᵃ

	Belgium-Lux'bourg	France	Germany	Italy	Sweden	Switzer-land	United Kingdom	Canada	United States	India	Japan	Total 1913 weights	Total 1929 weights
Metals	118	136 }	123 }	130ᵇ	141 }	137	121	120	135	124	112	126	126
Metal goods	120			..		150	129	..	164ᵇ	132	..	133	133
Machinery	128	112	164	192	134	146	188	..	148	—	..	163	155
Transport equipment	81ᵇ	50	83	42	120	..	102	..	79	—	..	84	75
Chemicals	100	181	123	122	106ᵇ	186	128	140ᵇ	153	117	122	135	135
Textiles and clothingᶜ	126	148	146	116	176ᵇ	145	179	110ᵇ	180	140	154	161	153
Other manufactures	141	140ᵇ	145	151	174	148	150	170	127	162	127ᵇ	144	145
TOTAL MANUFACTURES 1913 weights	119	140	137	125	152	150	159	142	140	149	157	145	—
1929 weights	122	128	136	111	147	148	151	136	120	141	144	—	133
NON-MANUFACTURES	141	128	134	126	147	139	179	124ᵈ	130ᵈ	..	130ᵈ	..	137ᵉ
TOTAL EXPORTS	126	128	136	117	147	146	159	128	125	..	136	..	134ᵉ

ᵃIn terms of U.S. dollars.
ᵇBased on small sample.
ᶜIndices for sub-groups, where available, are as follows (in the order yarns, fabrics, made-up goods): India—175, 139, 140; Japan—224, 157, 127.
ᵈResidual.
ᵉExcluding India.

Table B3. *Export unit value indices, 1937 (1929 = 100)*[a]

	Belgium-Lux'bourg	France	Germany[b]	Italy	Nether-lands	Sweden	Switzer-land	United Kingdom	Canada	United States	India	Japan	Total 1929 weights	Total 1937 weights
Metals	108	142	153	67	88	95	94	108	89	98	93	76	115	107
Metal goods	(108)							76	..	97	(93)	63	117	107
Machinery	199	140	135	139	136	68	128	114	..	95	—	73	115	110
Transport equipment	167	116	90	108	77	108	..	94	..	89	—	70	95	93
Chemicals	94	112	115	83	88	70	149	90	85	94	68	65	102	99
Textiles and clothing[c]	74	66	72	54	72	74	64	79	79	85	58	55	71	67
Other manufactures	71	86	106	81	87	79	120	89	77	95	78	50[d]	91	86
TOTAL MANUFACTURES 1929 weights	96	96	116	66	93	81	102	90	84	93	63	55	94	—
TOTAL MANUFACTURES 1937 weights	92	96	113	68	91	82	102	90	84	94	62	57	—	89
NON-MANUFACTURES	87	93	100	67	87	79	74	75	90[e]	69[e]	..	80[e]	79[f]	78[f]
TOTAL EXPORTS	90	94	111	68	89	80	98	84	87	80	..	62	88[f]	84[f]

[a] In terms of U.S. dollars.
[b] Based on the overvalued official rate of exchange in 1937 (*see* Appendix F, page 542).
[c] Indices for sub-groups, where available, are as follows (in the order yarns, fabrics, made-up goods): France—72, 64, ..; India—77, 59, 53; Japan—63, 54, 54.
[d] Based on small sample.
[e] Residual.
[f] Excluding India.

Table B4. *Export unit value indices, 1950 (1937 = 100)[a]*

	Belgium-Lux'bourg	France	Germany	Italy	Netherlands	Sweden	Switzerland	United Kingdom	Canada	United States	India	Japan	Total 1937 weights	Total 1950 weights
Metals	205	173	155	200	190	184	118	134	192	171	182	185[b]	171	170
Metal goods					240			135		167	227	179	161	158
Machinery	356	215	129	233	187	144	221	146	213	167	—	256	156	166
Transport equipment	149	125	105	403	125	165	..	129		200	—	250	176	153
Chemicals	130	188	125	209	200	..	152	144	135	157	357	196	151	152
Textiles and clothing[c]	210	220	130	250	244	200	254	212	233	200	286	289	229	226
Other manufactures	157	142	125	160	161	196	280	137	262	182	217	316[b]	179	176
TOTAL MANUFACTURES 1937 weights	193	180	132	251	198	178	221	163	223	178	294	254	182	—
1950 weights	190	174	132	235	186	172	216	149	215	175	277	253	—	173
NON-MANUFACTURES	175	172	243	148	193	210	212	190	177[d]	170[d]	..	300[d]	189[e]	179[e]
TOTAL EXPORTS	187	173	149	188	190	188	215	155	190	173	..	259	183[e]	174[e]

[a] In terms of U.S. dollars.
[b] Based on small sample.
[c] Indices for sub-groups, where available, are as follows (in the order yarns, fabrics, made-up goods); France—250, 210, . .; Netherlands—167, 294, 189; India—270, 256, 417; Japan—222, 303, 250.
[d] Residual.
[e] Excluding India.

Table B5. *Export unit value indices, 1955 (1950 = 100)[a]*

	Belgium-Lux'bourg	France	Germany	Italy	Nether-lands	Sweden	Switzer-land	United Kingdom	Canada	United States	India	Japan	Total 1950 weights	Total 1955 weights
Metals	133	150	144	112	133	135	112	140	129	133	123	169	138	138
Metal goods	128	126	128	112	122	136	100	143	117	130	..	146	133	131
Machinery	109	144	124	117	122	126	85	134	117	126	..	119	126	124
Transport equipment	118	140	142	117	122	139	95	123	117	124	—	..	126	127
Chemicals	95	90	98	97	109	113	73	111	110	115	87	108	106	103
Textiles and clothing[b]	89	101	108	91	96	113	97	125	94	97	81	96	101	99
Other manufactures	102	131	117	111	120	130	109	127	112	119	92	118	119	118
TOTAL MANUFACTURES 1950 weights	112	124	124	102	114	116	95	128	117	122	83	117	119	—
1955 weights	113	124	122	105	116	130	92	127	117	122	81	115	—	119
NON-MANUFACTURES	101[d]	98[d]	105[d]	100[c]	99[d]	143[d]	100[d]	97[d]	115[d]	104[d]	..	128[d]	107[e]	..
TOTAL EXPORTS	109	113	121	104	106	136	99	120	116	114	..	111	116[e]	..

[a] In terms of U.S. dollars.
[b] Indices for sub-groups, where available, are as follows (in the order yarns, fabrics, made-up goods): France—103, 98, 107; Germany—105, 109, 110; Italy—89, 89, 108; Switzerland—94, 98, 100; United Kingdom—114, 112, 170; United States—98, 96, 98; India—82, 83, 75; Japan—110, 95, 95.
[c] Based on small sample.
[d] Residual.
[e] Excluding India.

Table B6. *Export unit value indices, 1957 (1955 = 100)[a]*

	Belgium-Lux'bourg	France	Germany	Italy	Nether-lands	Sweden	Switzer-land	United Kingdom	Canada	United States	India	Japan	Total 1955 weights	Total 1957 weights
Metals	115	112	108	111	102	102	120	107	106	113	..	130[b]	111	111
Metal goods	112	115	98	127	99	103		113		115	..		111	110
Machinery	117	112	106	97	102	108	102	112	117	121	..	102	113	112
Transport equipment	113	107	101	93	101	108		102	113	114	..	97	106	105
Chemicals	91	102	96	105	104	101	101	98	99	102	..	93	99	99
Textiles and clothing	105	105	103	101	100	101	98[c]	101	106[c]	98	101	101[c]	101	101
Other manufactures	113	102	98	105	100	103	103	103	103	114	..	99	105	104
TOTAL MANUFACTURES 1955 weights	111	107	102	102	101	105	103	105	105	113	101	106	107	—
1957 weights	111	108	102	102	101	105	102	105	105	114	101	102	—	106
NON-MANUFACTURES	101[d]	109[d]	140[d]	129[d]	109[d]	101[d]	87[d]	133[d]	101[d]	99[d]	..	120[d]	..	106[e]
TOTAL EXPORTS	109	108	106	110	105	103	101	109	103	107	..	104	..	107[e]

[a] In terms of U.S. dollars.
[b] Metals and metal products.
[c] Excluding clothing.
[d] Residual.
[e] Excluding India.

EXPORT VOLUME INDICES

The detailed trade network tables given in Appendix A show the movement in the volume of trade in terms either of 1913 prices, or of 1955 prices, and this is also the basis of the various volume series given in the text. As already explained (see page 423), this was essentially a device to reduce the amount of statistical calculation while, at the same time, simplifying the presentation of the results.

The use of only two base years in such a long period might, however, result in some distortion of the volume indices for years far from the base and, as a guide to the possible distortion, volume indices have been computed for each link of years using the weighting, first of the earlier year, and then of the later. These dual series are given in the following two tables for individual country totals of exports of manufactures (Table C1) and for commodity group totals for all countries combined (Table C2).

In addition, for the comparisons of 1929 with 1937 and of 1937 with 1950, indices based on 1955 prices are also shown. In the majority of cases, the differences between the various sets of indices for these two periods were very small—under 2 per cent. Indices of export volume for individual countries in 1957 and 1959 are given in Tables 8.2 and 8.7, and for the main commodity groups in Table 7.2.

Table C1. *Volume indices of exports of manufactures by country*

	Series[a]	1913 (1899 = 100)	1929 (1913 = 100)	1937 (1929 = 100)	1950 (1937 = 100)	1955 (1950 = 100)
Belgium-Luxembourg	E	201	167	102	110	154
	L	189	170	97	109	} 155
	1955	..	..	94	108	
France	E	157	132	42	211	124
	L	156	120	43	205	} 125
	1955	..	..	42	214	
Germany[b]	E	229	107	71	55	294
	L	221	106	69	55	} 290
	1955	..	..	68	56	
Italy	E	166	192	101	104	144
	L	164	171	103	97	} 148
	1955	..	..	109	97	
Netherlands	E	..	..	100	118	171
	L	..	..	98	111	} 174
	1955	..	..	99	109	
Sweden	E	324	160	138	141	121
	L	330	155	139	136	} 135
	1955	..	..	138	137	
Switzerland	E	162	111	76	150	155
	L	157	110	76	146	} 150
	1955	..	..	74	143	
United Kingdom	E	152	93	79	178	103
	L	148	88	79	161	} 103
	1955	..	..	78	162	
Canada	E	256	752	125	132	140
	L	236	699	125	127	} 140
	1955	..	..	124	128	
United States	E	209	245	76	177	123
	L	200	211	77	174	} 123
	1955	..	..	80	165	
India[c]	E	140	129	114	120	89
	L	146	122	112	113	} 88
	1955	..	..	113	113	
Japan	E	287	216	238	43	219
	L	251	198	244	39	} 214
	1955	..	..	249	43	

[a]E = series using weights of earlier year; L = series using weights of later year; 1955 = series using 1955 weights.

[b]West Germany in 1950 and 1955.

[c]Republic of India in 1950 and 1955 (exports of manufactured goods from Pakistan being negligible).

Table C2. *Volume indices of exports of manufactures by commodity group*[a]

	Series[b]	1913 (1899 = 100)	1929 (1913 = 100)	1937 (1929 = 100)	1950 (1937 = 100)	1955 (1950 = 100)
Metals	E	234	128	92	111	139
	L	234	128	85	110	} 142
	1955	..	..	87	112	
Machinery	E	240	157	78	174	144
	L	246	150	75	178	} 143
	1955	..	..	78	169	
Transport equipment	E	347	426	88	192	140
	L	335	400	85	172	} 142
	1955	..	..	87	173	
Other metal goods	E	180	125	78	108	122
	L	179	125	71	106	} 121
	1955	..	..	72	108	
Chemicals	E	232	124	95	145	172
	L	218	124	92	146	} 168
	1955	..	..	94	152	
Textiles and clothing	E	134	100	85	91	112
	L	133	96	82	90	} 109
	1955	..	..	84	88	
Other manufactures	E	185	130	82	111	148
	L	182	130	78	109	} 147
	1955	..	..	84	112	
TOTAL	E	184	138	85	129	139
	L	177	127	81	123	} 139
	1955	..	..	83	125	

[a]Exports from countries included in Table C1.
[b]See footnote [a] to Table C1.

COMMODITY CLASSIFICATION

The definition of ' manufactures ' used in this book is Sections 5 to 8 inclusive of the United Nations' *Standard International Trade Classification* (S.I.T.C.), excluding ' special category ' exports from the United States. Within this total, the definitions of the commodity groups which have been distinguished are given in Table D.1 in terms of the S.I.T.C. (1953) code.

The primary classification of the commodity groups is according to the nature of the component material. The four broad groupings based on this criterion—metals and engineering, chemicals, textiles and clothing and other manufactures—correspond fairly closely to the usual classifications of both trade and production statistics, especially when the sub-divisions of the metals and engineering group are taken into account.

For comparisons of trade with industrial growth, however, a classification based on component material is inadequate for many purposes. This is particularly so when a distinction is required between imports which are complementary to the industrialization process, such as capital equipment and semi-finished goods (or ' intermediate products '), and imports which are competitive with the output of local industry. Some of the groups distinguished on the component material criterion could reasonably be classified as wholly ' intermediates ' or wholly ' finished ', though there may in fact be marginal items which do not conform in this respect. Thus, the machinery and transport groups have been taken as ' finished ', though parts for assembly or for incorporation in machines are also normally included. Similarly, metals are considered as wholly ' intermediates ', though a proportion will not in fact be further processed, e.g. railway lines. The gain in precision from a detailed re-classification of items in the metals and engineering groups would, however, be unlikely to justify the additional effort.

For the other broad commodity groups—chemicals, textiles and clothing and other manufactures—it was necessary to re-classify S.I.T.C. items or groups to distinguish intermediates from finished goods. The main criterion used was whether or not the commodity item or group was in the main normally subject to further processing (including use as components or parts) in non-food manufacturing industry in the main importing countries. Since mining and construction as well as food, beverages and tobacco are excluded from the definition of ' manufacturing ' industry in this book, goods which are normally used as materials by these industries (such as explosives, bricks, cement and cigarette paper) are here considered as finished goods. Equally, fertilizers—as material for agriculture—are also included with finished goods.

In the textiles group, fabrics present a major classification difficulty, since an unknown and varying proportion is purchased for retail sale. In many under-developed countries, virtually all the imported fabric is sold direct to consumers, whereas in economically more advanced countries a substantial proportion is made up into apparel in local factories. Fabrics do not, therefore, fit easily into a classification by stage of manufacture, and accordingly they have been shown separately in all the main tables. For some purposes, however, they have been included in finished goods as being in some ways less inappropriate than inclusion in the ' intermediates ' group.

A further difficulty arises in the case of a commodity which is normally a product of one manufacturing industry and a material used by another. Dyestuffs are an important example, since in principle they could be regarded either as finished products of the chemicals industry or as materials for the textiles, and many other, industries. From the point of view of manufacturing industry as a whole, however, dyestuffs are clearly ' intermediates ', and for this reason they were so classified ; they were also left in the chemicals group to maintain comparability with the series for chemical production. This is admittedly a compromise solution, but it seemed preferable to other possible solutions, each of which raised further difficulties of classification and interpretation.

Table D1. *Definition of commodity groups in terms of the Standard International Trade Classification (S.I.T.C.)*

	Stage of manufacture[a]	S.I.T.C. Code
METALS	I	68
METAL GOODS	F	69
MACHINERY[b]	F	71 and 72 *except* 711–04 and –05 and 721–07
TRANSPORT EQUIPMENT		
Passenger road vehicles	F	732–01, –02 and –04; 733–01 and –02
Other transport equipment[b]	F	Rest of 73, *plus* exclusions from machinery in 711 and 721
CHEMICALS		
Intermediates	I	51, 52, 531, 532, 533–01, 551 and 599 *except* 599–02
Finished chemicals	F	Rest of 5
TEXTILES AND CLOTHING		
Yarns	I	651
Fabrics	F	652, 653, 654 and 655
Made-up goods	F	Rest of 65 *plus* 841
OTHER MANUFACTURES		
Intermediates	I	611, 613, 621, 631–01 and –09, 641, 663, 664, 671 and 672
Finished goods	F	Rest of 6 and 8

[a] I = intermediate products; F = finished goods.
[b] These two groups, when taken together, are considered as 'capital goods'.

APPENDIX E

GROSS DOMESTIC PRODUCT AND THE PRODUCTION AND CONSUMPTION OF MANUFACTURES

In various chapters of this book, the long-term movements in international trade in manufactured goods have been related to the corresponding movements in real product per head, or in production or apparent consumption of manufactures per head, in the importing countries. The full set of estimates used for real product, for manufacturing production, and for apparent consumption of manufactures in the different importing countries is given in the following tables.

Gross product

Estimates of gross domestic product at factor cost for the selected years included in the trade network tables are given in Table E.1 for some 40 countries. These estimates are expressed in terms of U.S. dollars at 1955 prices. There were two stages in the calculations. The first was to convert the value of the gross domestic product of each country in 1955, as expressed in national currency, into U.S. dollars at an appropriate exchange rate. The exchange rates used were computed specially for this purpose and are designed to represent an approximation to relative internal purchasing powers; they are given in detail in Appendix F, which also contains a discussion of the rationale of the method used. The second stage was to extrapolate the 1955 estimates so obtained, to earlier years and to 1957, by means of estimates of the movement in the real domestic product of the different countries which were already available in published form. These time series were in some cases the official estimates published by the governments concerned; in others, they were the result of private research. There are, of course, numerous gaps in the data, especially for the earlier part of the period.

The resulting estimates presented here of the value of the gross domestic product of a wide variety of countries over so long a period—almost 60 years for the industrial countries and 30 years or more for a number of semi-industrial countries—inevitably contain a fair margin of error. The error is likely to be greater in cross-country comparisons than in the movement over time for a single country. Thus, small differences in the figures for different countries should be ignored as of no significance.

The error arises not simply from the statistical difficulty of computing a 'purchasing power parity' rate of exchange from scanty data, but also from the fact that the structure of the economy is so very different in countries at different stages of economic development. Some of the economic activities carried out in an under-developed country, for example, may have no counterpart in a highly industrialized society; and the reverse is also likely to be true.   Comparisons of national product of countries differing widely in economic characteristics are thus, to a considerable extent, of an arbitrary nature, and contain an unavoidable element of error.   Nonetheless, the range of per caput real product over the countries here considered is so great—over 30 to 1—that even approximate calculations, such as those presented here, are useful guides to general trends and relationships.   The estimates for gross domestic product per head at 1955 prices are given in Table E.2.

Manufacturing production

The relative output of manufactured goods of different countries can validly be compared only on the basis of the value added in the manufacturing process. Comparisons on a gross value basis, including the cost of materials used, are likely to give a distorted picture of the relative amounts of productive work done.

There are, however, two alternative approaches which are practicable for a statistical comparison on the 'net' basis.   The first relies on data collected from *establishments* (or factories) at censuses of manufactures; the second is based on the accounts of *business enterprises* and is often used in the compilation of national accounting statistics.   With both methods, a considerable amount of statistical estimation may be involved in arriving at a complete coverage of all manufacturing units.   Censuses of manufactures normally exclude small firms, or firms not using power, to a greater or lesser extent, while the detailed information available about the operations of companies and other business enterprises would usually exclude data concerning unincorporated businesses[1].

However, apart from problems of coverage, the census approach and the 'companies' approach differ in two important respects.   The first reflects the fact that the basic unit of operation is different.   Since census data are built up from individual establishments, these can be sorted into a consistent industrial classification; the 'companies' data, however, cannot be used in this way, since individual companies may cover production in several manufacturing industries, and separate operating data for each industry would not be available.   Any analysis of changes in industry-patterns must therefore of necessity be based on the census approach.

The other major difference relates to the concept of 'net value' of output. At censuses of production, information is normally collected about the selling value of goods produced, and work done, and about the cost of materials and fuel purchased.   The difference between the values of output and of materials

---

[1] A further problem of coverage arises when the 'companies' approach is used, since some companies which are classified as non-manufacturing may, in fact, do some manufacturing work while, on the other hand, some part of the net value of production of companies classified as manufacturing may represent non-manufacturing activities.

and fuel used is known as the *value added* in production. Another way of expressing this is to define the concept as 'output net of physical inputs'. The value added so defined generally includes, however, two further elements which, strictly speaking, should be excluded from the 'net value' of production. These are the value of services purchased from other firms (such as transport, advertising and research work), and the cost of repair and maintenance work done by outside firms[1]. Both these elements can normally be excluded from the concept of 'net value' of production when working from the accounts of business enterprises since the figure used in this case is simply the sum of wages (and other payments to the firms' own employees) and of trading profit.

There is one further important difference which may arise, according to whether depreciation charges in respect of fixed capital assets are included or not. Some countries (e.g. Australia) collect information about depreciation at their censuses of manufactures so that in these cases it would be possible to define 'value added' as net of depreciation. From the companies side, the amount of depreciation is readily available, so that 'net value' can be expressed either 'gross' or 'net' of depreciation. However, it is usually possible to obtain comparability in this respect by not deducting depreciation charges from either the census figure or from that arrived at by the companies approach.

In the present book, the total value of manufacturing production is defined as the net value, inclusive of depreciation, as derived from the accounts of business enterprises. In national accounts terminology, the concept used is the contribution of manufacturing to gross domestic product at factor cost. The advantage of using this, rather than the alternative census definition is that the figures are, in principle, closer to the 'true' contribution of manufacturing industry to the national product, for the reasons given above. Estimates on this basis are now available for a large number of countries as a result of the work of the Statistical Office of the United Nations[2]. A number of adjustments to the published figures, however, had to be made where, for example, the value stated was at market prices rather than at factor cost, or where non-manufacturing sectors (mining, construction or electricity, gas and water) were included. In addition, there were a number of countries which publish their estimates only on a 'net of depreciation' basis, and for these (the United States being the most important case), an estimate of the depreciation has been added to the published total[3].

---

[1]When repair and maintenance work is done by the firm's own staff, the cost of repair, etc. materials would be excluded from the census total of value added, but the wages of the maintenance staff would be included. In this respect, the position is the same as in the approach from the 'companies' side.

[2]See *Yearbook of National Accounts Statistics*, New York, United Nations (annual).

[3]Where the adjustment was from market price to factor cost, or from a 'net domestic product' to a 'gross domestic product' basis, it was assumed that the share of manufacturing in the difference was the same as its share in the total. For the exclusion of non-manufacturing sectors, data published by the United Nations were used (*Patterns of Industrial Growth, 1938–1958*, New York, United Nations, 1960, Part II, Country Tables).

The adjusted estimates of the net value of manufacturing production in different countries in 1955 have been converted into United States dollars by use of the 'purchasing power parity' rates shown in Appendix F. The use of these calculated exchange rates is unlikely to produce a greater error in the estimates for manufacturing than in those for the gross domestic product as a whole. The estimated net values for 1955 were then extrapolated to the other selected years by applying national indices of manufacturing production. The resulting set of estimates is given in Table E.3, while Table E.4 gives the corresponding figures on a per caput basis.

All the estimates in Tables E.3 and E.4 relate to the manufacturing sector as a whole, including the processing of food, beverages and tobacco, and the refining of petroleum. The figures of trade in manufactured goods, on the other hand, exclude both the manufactured products of the food, beverages and tobacco industries and refined petroleum (see Appendix A, page 421). When direct comparisons of values of trade and production are being made, it is therefore necessary to make an adjustment to the production series in Tables E.3 and E.4 to bring them to a comparable basis with the trade statistics.

Apparent consumption of manufactures

It is possible, in principle, to bring together the estimates of the value of production of manufactures (Table E.3 adjusted to exclude the processing of food, beverages and tobacco) and the figures of foreign trade in manufactures (Appendix A), so as to arrive at estimates of apparent consumption, defined as production *plus* imports *minus* exports of manufactured goods other than food.

A major difficulty arises, however, in combining the two sets of figures, since those for production are on a 'net' basis, as explained earlier, whereas the trade figures are valued 'gross', i.e. inclusive of the cost of all materials and services used in their production and transport. The statistical difficulty can be overcome in either of two ways. The trade values can be reduced to their 'net output' content, thus allowing the net value of apparent consumption to be estimated. Alternatively, the estimates of the net value of production can be inflated to their gross equivalents, and the value of apparent consumption can then be estimated on a gross basis.

Conceptually, however, these two methods yield very different results. The movement in net values, when measured at constant prices, reflects changes in the volume of work done in the manufacturing process, whereas the gross value series at constant prices indicate changes in the volume of goods leaving the manufacturing sector and available for consumption domestically or abroad.

The gross value basis—which is the one adopted here—corresponds, in principle, to values in actual transactions and it can therefore be used for making direct comparisons with movements in prices and incomes. For present purposes, the gross value of production is defined as the selling value, excluding taxes, of the final output of the non-food manufacturing sector; thus, sales or intra-firm transfers between factories must be excluded as being duplicated in the selling value of goods leaving that sector. The extent of such duplication can readily be calculated from a table showing inter-industry purchases and sales. In recent years, such tables have been compiled for a number of countries[1], while for the United States and Britain comparable tables are available for both pre-war and post-war periods. For Britain, the ratio of the gross output, free of duplication, to the net output has remained remarkably stable since 1924[2]:—

	1924	1930	1935	1948	1950	1954
All productive industry	1.52	1.40	1.47	..	1.56	1.59
Non-food manufacturing only	..	..	1.45	1.50	1.59	1.58

Over this period a considerable shift occurred in the relative importance of different industries, and the constancy of the overall gross : net ratio is due partly to offsetting changes (chemicals, metals and metal goods other than engineering all have relatively higher gross : net ratios, whereas building materials, printing and the miscellaneous group have relatively low ones); and partly to the fact that the ratio for engineering—the major expanding group— has been close to the overall average.

In the United States, on the other hand, the gross: net ratio has fallen over the past thirty years or so[3]:—

	1919	1929	1947
Non-food manufacturing			
Market price basis	2.17	2.15	1.86
Factor cost basis	2.08	..	1.72

The fall between pre-war and post-war appears to have occurred in each main industry, to a greater or lesser extent.

For most other countries, inter-industry tables are available only for one or

[1]The technique of inter-industry analysis was first introduced by W. W. Leontief (*The Structure of the American Economy, 1919–1929*, Harvard University Press, 1941). A review of recent literature on the subject can be found in H. B. Chenery and P. G. Clark, *Interindustry Economics*, New York, 1959.

[2]For 1924 and 1930, the ratios are based on the official estimates of the gross output, free of duplication, and the net output, of industries in Gt. Britain covered by the Censuses of Production (see *Final Report on the Fourth Census of Production* (1930), Part V); the 1935 ratios were calculated from T. Barna, 'The Interdependence of the British Economy', *J. Roy. Stat. Soc.*, A, CXV, Part I, 1952; those for 1948, 1950 and 1954 from the table on 'Inter-industry relations' in *National Income and Expenditure*, H.M.S.O., London, 1952, 1953 and 1958.

[3]The 1919 and 1929 ratios were calculated from the inter-industry tables in W. W. Leontief, *op. cit.;* those for 1947 were based on W. D. Evans and M. Hoffenberg, 'The Inter-Industry Relations Study for 1947' (*Review of Economics and Statistics*, Vol. 34, No. 2, May 1952).

two post-war years. A selection of these[1] has been used to compute gross : net ratios at factor cost for non-food manufacturing; the results are given below, together with the latest ratios for Britain and the United States:—

		Gross : net ratio			Gross : net ratio
Belgium	1953	1.84[a]	Australia	1955/6	2.12
France	1951	1.32	New Zealand	1952/3	2.42[c]
Italy	1950	1.90		1954/5	2.32[c]
Netherlands	1950	2.27[b]	Argentina	1950	2.02[b]
Norway	1954	1.93	Colombia	1953	1.79
United Kingdom	1954	1.58	Mexico	1950	1.86
Yugoslavia	1955	1.79	Peru	1955	2.02
Canada	1949	2.40	India	1953/4	
United States	1947	1.72	large factories		1.93
Japan	1951	1.73	small factories		1.76
			Total		1.66

[a]Including food processing and construction.
[b]At market prices.
[c]Including food (other than meat and dairy produce), beverages and tobacco.

The considerable differences which emerge from these computations in the gross : net ratios between countries reflect differences in industrial structure, in the stage of industrial development and in internal price relationships.

Industrial structure affects the overall gross : net ratio simply because some industries require large amounts of materials, or capital assets, per worker compared with other industries. Thus, countries which tend to concentrate on, say, smelting of metals—an industry with high materials and fuel costs relative to wage and other costs—would for this reason have a higher gross : net ratio than would countries specializing in, say, precision industries, such as watch-making or cameras where wage costs and overheads are relatively high in

[1]The sources used were: *Cahiers Économique de Bruxelles*, No. 1, Oct. 1958, Université Libre de Bruxelles; *Tableau Economique de l'Année 1951*, Institut National de la Statistique et des Études Économique, Paris, 1957; *The Structure and Growth of the Italian Economy*, U.S. Mutual Security Agency, Rome, 1953; *Een Verkenning der Economische Toekomstmogelijkheden van Nederland, 1950–1970*, Centraal Planbureau, 's-Gravenhage, 1955; *Input-Output Analysis of Norwegian Industries, 1954*, Central Bureau of Statistics, Oslo, 1960; *The Inter-Industry Flow of Goods and Services*, Canada, 1949, Dominion Bureau of Statistics, Ref. Paper No. 72, 1956; *Inter-industry Analysis for the Japanese Economy*, Ministry of International Trade and Industry, Tokyo, 1957 (summarised in H. B. Chenery and P. G. Clark, *Interindustry Economics*, New York, 1959); *Interindustry relations of the Yugoslav economy in 1955*, Federal Statistical Office, Belgrade, 1957; Burgess Cameron, 'Inter-Sector Accounts, 1955–56', *Economic Record*, Vol. 36, No. 74, April, 1960; *Report on the Inter-Industry Study of the New Zealand Economy, 1952–53* and *1954–55*, Department of Statistics, Wellington, 1957 and 1959; *The Economic Development of Argentina*, United Nations, Santiago, 1958; *The Economic Development of Colombia*, United Nations, Santiago, 1957; *La Estructura Industrial de Mexico en 1950*, Banco de Mexico, 1957; *The Industrial Development of Peru*, United Nations, Santiago, 1959; *Inter-Industry Relations of the Indian Economy, 1953–54*, Indian Statistical Institute, Calcutta, 1958.

relation to the cost of materials. Another important reason for a high gross : net ratio is the existence of assembly plants (e.g. for cars) using little local labour but a relatively high value of imported parts and components. The assembly of imported motor vehicle parts in New Zealand, for example, appears to be a major reason for the extremely high gross : net ratio for that country[1]. The assembly in Canada of motor vehicle parts produced in the United States also appears to be of importance in the high Canadian gross : net ratio.

Another 'structural' factor operating in some countries, such as India, is the existence of a handicraft or very small-scale manufacturing sector, operating at a fraction of the productivity in the factory sector proper, while income per head in the two sectors does not differ very greatly. Consequently, the gross : net ratio will be lower in the small-scale sector than in the factory sector and, since the latter normally supplies the former with semi-processed materials, the overall gross : net ratio for both sectors taken together will be lower still, as is the case in India.

The stage of industrial development affects the gross : net ratio insofar as the more developed countries tend to produce manufactures embodying a greater degree of fabrication per unit of materials used than do the less-developed countries. Another aspect of the same process has been the trend to use a decreasing volume of materials per unit of output, which has been a marked one in the main industrial countries over the past half-century at least.

Finally, the gross : net ratio is affected by differences in the relative costs of the factors of production. Countries with relatively high wage costs in relation to labour productivity will, *ceteris paribus*, tend to have lower gross : net ratios than other countries. France is perhaps the clearest example. From 1951 to 1960 output per worker in manufacturing industry rose more rapidly in France than in almost any other industrial country (Japanese productivity rose faster than French but West German productivity did not); on the other hand, wages per head in France did not rise as fast, in this period, as they did in several industrial countries, including Britain. The implication is that French wages were abnormally high in relation to productivity in 1951, and this depressed the gross : net ratio in that year. It seems likely that in the later 1950's the French ratio was much closer to that of the other industrial countries.

Again, where capital is relatively scarce and depreciation rates are high, the ratio will tend to be lower than elsewhere. Conversely, countries having relatively high materials costs (e.g. where some major materials are imported and freight charges are heavy), will tend to have relatively high gross : net ratios. High freight charges are likely to have a significant effect on the gross : net ratio in Australia, New Zealand and in many of the under-developed countries in Latin America, Asia and Africa.

[1] The other reason is that the figures include many food industries using a high value of materials in relation to wages.

These various considerations need not all work in the same direction. Thus, it is possible for a particular under-developed country to have a gross : net ratio as low as, or lower than, a particular industrialized country. But it seems most likely that the less-developed countries will, generally speaking, have higher ratios than the more developed ones, mainly because they tend to have wage levels which are low in relation to their physical productivity per worker, while materials costs per unit of output are unlikely to be so much lower than in the industrial countries as to offset the effect of the wage differential. The under-developed countries also tend to concentrate less in the high-skill industries, such as engineering and precision work, while they do much less fabrication work per unit of materials used ; both these factors will reinforce the tendency for their gross : net ratios generally to exceed those of the industrial countries.

For these reasons, a comparison of the levels of consumption of manufactures in countries at different stages of economic development would seriously under-estimate consumption in the less-developed countries if the comparison were made on the net value basis. Moreover, because of the trend towards a decreasing consumption of materials per unit of output in the industrial countries, the use of net, rather than gross, values would result in an upward bias over time, in the consumption estimates for these countries.

For the estimates presented here, the net values as shown in Table E.3 were adjusted in two stages. First, a deduction was made for the net value of processing food, beverages and tobacco[1]. The 1955 net value was estimated by applying to the total figure (in Table E.3) the appropriate percentage for the food, beverages and tobacco industries[2]. Estimates for other years at 1955 prices were then derived by applying the relevant national indices of physical output to the 1955 net values. Second, the residual figures, relating to non-food manufacturing, were inflated to gross value equivalents. For countries for which gross : net ratios were available, the appropriate ratios were used. For the others, the ratio 1.75 was used for industrial countries, 2.0 for semi-industrial countries and 2.25 for non-industrial countries (except for Pakistan, where the Indian ratio was applied)[3].

Adjustments are also necessary to the foreign trade statistics before they

[1]Strictly speaking, a deduction should also have been made for petroleum refining and for the processing of solid fuels. However, the magnitudes involved were relatively small for most countries, and the calculation, if made, would not have affected the estimates of apparent consumption significantly.

[2]These percentages relate to 1953. They were derived from *Patterns of Industrial Growth, 1938–1958*, United Nations, New York, 1960.

[3]Estimates of the gross and net values of manufacturing production by the G.A.T.T. secretariat for 1958 imply gross : net ratios of 1.16 for North America and Western Europe and 1.36 for the rest of the world outside the Soviet countries (*International Trade, 1959*, Table 4, G.A.T.T., Geneva, 1960). These ratios are considerably lower than those given here because the gross value estimates in the G.A.T.T. report exclude the costs of transport, merchanting and other services used by the manufacturing sector.

can be combined with the estimates of gross value of manufacturing production.
Exports. All the industrial countries of Western Europe, Japan and India value their exports f.o.b., i.e. free on board carrier at a border point of exportation. The United States uses an f.a.s. (free alongside ship) basis for goods exported by vessel, while Canada uses the value at the inland point of consignment for export. To maintain comparability with the production estimates, which generally relate to values *ex factory*, a deduction must be made from the f.o.b. values of exports to allow for transport, merchanting and other costs incurred between factory and port. The percentage deduction will vary considerably from commodity to commodity and from country to country, depending on the relative level of freight, etc. charges, the average length of haul from factory to frontier and the weight or bulk of the commodity in relation to its value.

Some detailed investigations into the appropriate deductions have been made in Britain and the United States. For Britain, an official estimate for 1907 put the deduction for that year at 10-15 per cent of the factory value[1], but this included a large element for the cost of moving coal from pits to ports. A fairly detailed estimate made in the early 1930's—when coal was much less important in British exports—indicated a considerably lower deduction: 6-8 per cent for 1924 and 5-7 per cent for 1930[2]. More direct evidence is available from the 1950 Census of Distribution[3]. In that year, the gross margin of export merchants amounted to 9 per cent of their total receipts. Direct exports by manufacturers would probably carry a smaller charge than this between factory and port; in non-electrical machinery and vehicles, for example, the gross margin of manufacturers' export organizations in 1950 amounted only to 7 per cent of their receipts. Probably, an average for all manufactures exported would lie between 7 and 8 per cent for 1950.

For the United States, an analysis of the expense ratios of exporters and export agents, as recorded at the Census of Distribution for 1929, indicated reduction percentages from export to factory values of $12\frac{1}{2}$ per cent for consumer semi-durables, 3 per cent for consumer durables and $\frac{1}{2}$ per cent for producer durables; for groups for which no calculation was made, a 10 per cent reduction was assumed[4]. More recent information is available from the Census of Business for 1948[5]; in that year, the operating expenses of export merchants, excluding those specialising in farm products, groceries, etc., averaged 8.7 per cent of their sales.

[1] *First Census of Production, 1907*, London, 1912.
[2] G. W. Daniels and H. Campion, *The Relative Importance of British Export Trade* (London and Cambridge Economic Service, Special Memorandum No. 41, Aug. 1935).
[3] *Census of Distribution and Other Services, 1950*, Vol. III, H.M.S.O., London, 1955.
[4] W. H. Shaw, *Value of Commodity Output since 1869*, National Bureau of Economic Research, New York, 1947, p. 271. Though the computation was based on exporters' margins in 1929, the figures quoted were based on exports in 1909.
[5] *U.S. Census of Business, 1948*, Vol. IV, Washington, 1952.

Comparable figures based on censuses of merchanting operations are not available for most other countries. For the industrial countries, generally, it has been assumed that a deduction of 8 per cent is necessary from the f.o.b. value of exports to arrive at a valuation *ex works*. For Britain and the United States, the percentages mentioned earlier were used. For Canada, no deduction is required since, as already mentioned, Canadian exports are valued at inland place of consignment. The corresponding deduction for India is somewhat less. A comparison of the unit value of output and of export, f.o.b., of cotton and jute piece goods in 1957 shows a difference of 5.8 and 4.5 per cent respectively of the f.o.b. unit value. For India, a deduction of 5 per cent has been made from f.o.b. values for all years.

Imports. Since the estimates of manufacturing production are on a gross basis, they will include the value of all materials used, both home-produced and imported. To avoid double-counting, therefore, only imports of *finished* manufactures[1] can be added to the gross value of production to arrive at a total for supplies of manufactures. The figures for finished manufactures, as presented in Appendix A are, as explained previously, generally valued on an f.o.b. basis (apart from the exceptional cases of Canada and the United States mentioned above). For comparison with gross production values, however, it is necessary to value imports c.i.f., i.e. the value at the place of entry in the importing country. The c.i.f. value is, broadly, the f.o.b. value plus the insurance and freight charges incurred in transport from the exporting to the importing country. Where the two countries are contiguous, the f.o.b. and c.i.f. values may be identical.

It is not possible to make a precise calculation of the c.i.f. value of imports from the corresponding f.o.b. values, since the difference depends on the distribution of trade by country of origin and by commodity. The percentage which freight charges form of the f.o.b. value will vary widely according to the route taken, the carrier used[2], the length of haul and the nature of the commodity. A number of countries do, however, make estimates of the freight and insurance element in the c.i.f. value of their total merchandise imports in conjunction with their detailed balance of payments statistics[3], while the United States also provides similar estimates even though her imports are valued f.o.b. or at market price in the exporting country. For the United Kingdom, similar estimates were not published in the official balance of payments statistics until 1961 ; these show freight and insurance payments during the years 1958 to 1960 at 13-14 per cent of the f.o.b. value of imports[4].

---

[1]See Appendix D for the technical definition of finished manufactures.
[2]An increasing proportion of international freight is carried by air, at considerably higher rates than for surface transport.
[3]See *Balance of Payments Yearbook*, annual, International Monetary Fund, Washington.
[4]*United Kingdom Balance of Payments, 1958 to 1960*, H.M.S.O., London, 1961 (Cmnd. 1329).

This accords well with an earlier estimate by Board of Trade statisticians, which put freight and insurance on all imports as 10-13 per cent of the c.i.f. value[1], which is equivalent to 11-15 per cent of the f.o.b. value.

For 16 countries for which the difference between c.i.f. and f.o.b. valuations can be estimated for a recent year (1955), the difference represented between 9 and 13 per cent of the f.o.b. value for 10 countries.

Freight and insurance on total merchandise imports as percentage of f.o.b. value, 1955

%	
7–8	Nicaragua, Norway
9–10	Belgium-Luxembourg, Canada, Denmark, Netherlands, Portugal, Union of South Africa, United States, West Germany
12–13	Greece, Italy
11–15	Australia[2], United Kingdom
19–21	Japan, Peru

The unweighted mean percentage for all 16 countries is 11 per cent.

For those countries for which percentage additions are available, these were used to estimate the c.i.f. equivalents of the f.o.b. figures of imports of finished manufactures derived from Appendix A. It has been assumed that the 1955 percentages also applied to other years. For countries for which no direct information is available, it has been assumed that the percentage addition from f.o.b. to c.i.f. valuation is 10 per cent for European and African countries, and 15 per cent for countries in Asia, Latin America and Oceania.

The resulting estimates of the gross value of apparent consumption of non-food manufactures are given in Table E.5. In view of the many assumptions made, and the fact that figures for individual years may be unduly influenced by changes in stocks, small differences between countries, or over time, clearly have no significance. The corresponding estimates per head of population are given in Table E.6. All the estimates are in terms of U.S. dollars at 1955 prices. It should be remembered that the exchange rates used for production (Table F.2) differ from those used for trade (Table F.1). In general, this has the effect of increasing the relative importance of home production in relation to foreign trade for countries other than the United States.

Population

The population series used to compute estimates of per caput gross domestic product and per caput value of production and apparent consumption of manufactures, are given in Table E.7. The figures have been taken, in almost

---

[1] J. Stafford, J. M. Maton and Muriel Venning, (chapter on 'United Kingdom' in *International Trade Statistics*, ed. R. G. D. Allen and J. E. Ely, New York, 1953).

[2] The Australian proportion averaged 14 per cent for the years 1936/37 to 1938/39 and 13½ per cent for the years 1949/50 to 1951/52. For 1957, the proportion was 15 per cent. (*The Australian Balance of Payments, 1928–29 to 1951–52, and 1957–58*, Commonwealth Bureau of Census and Statistics, Canberra, 1953 and 1959, respectively).

every case, from international compilations so as to achieve the maximum amount of comparability possible. For 1899 and 1913, the reliability of the figures is decidedly lower than for the later estimates for many countries, especially where the taking of a population census is difficult for geographic and/or administrative reasons. The figures shown relate, unless otherwise stated, to the total population of each country within the borders existing in the year specified.

Table E1. *Estimates of gross domestic product[a] for selected countries,*
1899–1957

$ *billion at* 1955 *prices*

	1899	1913	1929	1937	1950	1955	1957
WESTERN EUROPE							
Austria	..	2.30[b]	2.56	2.50	3.12	4.30	4.80
Belgium-Luxembourg	3.32[c]	5.75	6.05[d]	6.87	10.3	12.1	12.8
Denmark	1.03	1.72	2.55	3.11	4.08	4.50	4.84
Finland	..	1.02	1.18	1.55	2.21	2.85	2.96
France	14.0[e]	16.0	25.0	22.4	32.4	40.0	44.8
Germany	29.3[f]	37.5[f]	40.5	46.5	..	..	..
West Germany[g]	..	..	..	30.6	31.8	49.0	55.0
Ireland	..	1.00[h]	1.00	1.10	1.50	1.60	1.60
Italy	6.05[i]	8.00	11.1	11.3	16.7	22.7	25.2
Netherlands	2.20[j]	3.08	4.37	5.20	7.55	9.40	10.1
Norway	0.83[j]	1.15	1.77	2.29	3.23	3.80	4.08
Portugal	..	1.17	..	1.70[k]	2.40	2.75	2.95
Sweden	1.83	2.42	4.00	5.25	8.30	9.70	10.40
Switzerland	1.29	1.86	2.87	2.97	4.80	5.75	6.25
United Kingdom	34.0[l]	42.0[l]	42.0	50.0	54.7	63.5	66.0
Yugoslavia[m]	..	1.80[n]	2.53	2.62	3.25	4.30	5.18
NORTH AMERICA							
Canada	3.42	7.20	10.3	10.1	20.0	24.8	26.5
United States	59.0	97.0	168.0	171.0	294.0	362.5	376.0
OCEANIA							
Australia	3.15[o]	4.50	7.10	7.40	12.3	13.2	14.1
New Zealand	0.52[i]	..	1.53	2.03	2.78	3.05	3.20
LATIN AMERICA							
Argentina	1.60	3.60	6.25	6.90	10.6	11.7	12.0
Brazil	..	..	3.47	5.67	10.2	13.2	15.0
Chile	..	..	1.02	1.82	2.07	2.30	2.24
Colombia	..	..	1.17	1.50	2.55	3.50	3.50
Mexico	..	..	..	4.30	6.00	7.20	8.00
Peru	..	..	..	..	1.24	1.50	1.44
Puerto Rico	..	..	..	0.43[p]	0.81	0.99	1.03
Venezuela	..	..	..	..	3.18	4.75	6.32
ASIA							
India	} ..	..	17.7	19.8	20.2	24.0	24.8
Pakistan					6.35	7.10	7.60
Indonesia	..	..	..	..	..	4.80	..
Israel	..	..	..	..	0.80	1.40	1.70
Japan	2.80	4.80	9.10	12.9	11.1	16.5	19.8
Philippines	..	..	..	..	1.80	2.40	2.70
Turkey	..	..	..	3.40	4.30	5.75	6.50
AFRICA							
Belgian Congo	..	..	..	..	1.10	1.55	1.65
Egypt	..	..	..	..	..	3.20	..
Federation of Rhodesia and Nyasl.	..	..	..	..	..	1.68	2.00
French Morocco	..	..	..	..	1.30	1.54	..
Nigeria	..	..	..	..	..	2.40	2.43
Union of South Africa	..	1.41[q]	2.25	3.10	5.75	7.20	7.90

For sources and footnotes see over.

Sources: For 1955: *Yearbook of National Accounts Statistics, 1959,* United Nations, New York, 1960.

> *For indices of real domestic product: Yearbook of National Accounts Statistics, op. cit.; Statistical Yearbook,* United Nations, New York ; *Statistics of National Product and Expenditure, No. 2,* O.E.E.C., Paris, 1957; C. Clark, *Conditions of Economic Progress,* 3rd edn., London, 1957; *Etudes et Conjoncture,* No. 3, 1960, Paris; P. Jostock, 'The Long-Term Growth of National Income in Germany' (*Income and Wealth,* Series V, International Association for Research in Income and Wealth, London, 1955); O. Aukrust and J. Bjerke, 'Real Capital in Norway, 1900-56' (*Income and Wealth,* Series VIII, International Association for Research in Income and Wealth, London, 1959) ; I. Vinski, 'Rast Nacionalnog Dohotka I Bogatstva Jugoslavije' (*Nasa Stvarnost,* Vol. 14, No. 2, Feb. 1960); O. J. Firestone, *Canada's Economic Development, 1867-1953,* in *Income and Wealth,* Series VII; K. Ohkawa, *The Growth Rate of the Japanese Economy since 1878,* Tokyo, Kinokuniya Bookstore, 1957; K. Mukerji, *A Note on the Long Term Growth of National Income in India* (Second Indian Conference on Research in National Income, Delhi, 1960); *The Economic Development of Argentina* (Statistical Annex), Economic Commission for Latin America, Santiago, 1958; *The Economic Development of Brazil,* United Nations, New York, 1956; *The Economic Development of Colombia* (Statistical Appendix), Economic Commission for Latin America, Santiago, 1957; *Economic Survey of Latin America,* var. years, United Nations, New York.

[a] At factor cost.

[b] 1911–13; estimate for post-1919 area. The gross product of the contemporary territory of Austria in the Austro-Hungarian Empire in 1911–13 was in the region of $3\frac{1}{2}$ times that of the post-1919 area. (See C. Clark, *op. cit.,* pp. 99–100).

[c] 1895.

[d] 1930.

[e] 1895–1905.

[f] Contemporary frontiers. The gross product in 1913 of the post-1918 area of Germany was about 95 per cent of that of the 1913 area.

[g] Excluding West Berlin and the Saar.

[h] Excluding the six northern counties.

[i] 1901.

[j] 1900.

[k] 1938.

[l] British Isles. For 1899, the estimate assumes that the movement in real product from 1899 to 1913 was the same for the British Isles as for Great Britain.

[m] Estimates assume that services amount to about 13 per cent of the gross material product.

[n] 1909–12 estimate for present area of Yugoslavia.

[o] 1901–3.

[p] 1939–40.

[q] 1911–12.

Note: Estimates of gross domestic product for the year 1955 have also been made for a selection of countries not included in the trade network tables. These are, in \$ billion:—

> AMERICA: Bolivia, 0.25; Costa Rica, 0.25; Ecuador, 0.57; Guatemala, 0.47; Honduras, 0.25.
>
> ASIA: Burma, 0.8; Ceylon, 1.4; Iraq, 0.7; Lebanon, 0.4; Thailand, 1.75.
>
> EUROPE: Greece, 2.85; Spain, 13.7.

Table E2.   *Estimates of gross domestic product per head of total population*
for selected countries, 1899–1957[a]

	1899	1913	1929	1937	1950	$ at 1955 prices 1955	1957
WESTERN EUROPE							
Austria	..	340	380	370	450	615	685
Belgium-Luxembourg	480	730	730	800	1150	1315	1375
Denmark	430	615	730	840	950	1025	1075
Finland	..	340	345	430	555	680	690
France	360	400	605	540	775	925	1015
Germany	525	560	625	685	..	..	..
West Germany	—	—	—	775	665	975	1070
Ireland	..	325	345	380	500	550	550
Italy	185	225	275	260	360	. 470	520
Netherlands	430	505	560	600	750	870	920
Norway	375	480	630	790	980	1120	1165
Portugal	..	195	..	230	285	315	330
Sweden	360	430	655	835	1185	1330	1405
Switzerland	390	475	720	705	1020	1150	1225
United Kingdom	830[b]	920[b]	915	1055	1085	1245	1280
Yugoslavia	—	135	185[c]	175	200	245	290
NORTH AMERICA							
Canada	635	975	1030	895	1460	1580	1595
United States	790	1000	1380	1330	1940	2195	2185
OCEANIA							
Australia	850	955	1110	1090	1500	1435	1460
New Zealand	650	..	1095	1270	1465	1450	1455
LATIN AMERICA							
Argentina	350	470	540	510	615	615	605
Brazil	..	..	105	145	195	225	245
Chile	..	..	245	380	340	340	315
Colombia	..	..	155	175	225	275	265
Mexico	..	..	..	230	235	240	255
Peru	..	..	..	..	145	160	145
Puerto Rico	..	..	..	240	370	430	450
Venezuela	..	..	..	..	635	820	1035
ASIA							
India	} ..	} ..	50	50	55	65	65
Pakistan					85	85	90
Indonesia	..	..		..	..	60	..
Israel	—	—	..	..	615	825	895
Japan	65	90	145	185	135	185	220
Philippines	..	..	..	..	90	110	120
Turkey	..	..	..	200	205	240	255
AFRICA							
Belgian Congo	..	..	..	..	95	125	125
Egypt	..	..	..	..	..	140	..
Federation of Rhodesia and Nyasaland	..	..	..	..	..	230	265
French Morocco	..	..	..	..	165	180	..
Nigeria	..	..	..	..	..	75	75
Union of South Africa	..	225	285	315	465	525	555

For sources and footnotes see over.

Sources: Tables E1 and E7.

[a]In some cases, the figures do not refer precisely to the years shown; for details, see foot-notes to Tables E1 and E7.

[b]British Isles.   Excluding Southern Ireland, gross domestic product per head in 1913 was $960.

[c]1929 was an exceptionally good year in Yugoslavia; the average for 1928–31 was about $180 per head, and for 1937–39 $185 per head.

Note: Estimates of gross domestic product per head in 1955 for the countries mentioned in the *Note* to Table E1 are as follows, in $:—

AMERICA: Bolivia, 75; Costa Rica, 260; Ecuador, 150; Guatemala, 150; Honduras, 150.

ASIA: Burma, 40; Ceylon, 160; Iraq, 115; Lebanon, 270; Thailand, 85.

EUROPE: Greece, 360; Spain, 475.

Table E3. *Estimates of net value of manufacturing production[a]
in selected countries, 1899–1957*

$ billion at 1955 prices

	1899	1913	1929	1937	1950	1955	1957
INDUSTRIAL COUNTRIES							
Belgium-Luxembourg	1.18	1.88	2.61	2.67	3.18	4.21	4.49
France	3.88	6.57	8.87	7.89	8.67	11.5	14.4
Germany	6.88	11.9	13.4	16.5	..	..	..
West Germany[b]	—	—	—	10.9	10.9	20.3	23.2
Italy	1.29	2.34	3.44	3.81	4.63	7.25	8.30
Netherlands	..	0.64	1.20	1.26	2.05	2.90	3.10
Norway	0.17	0.29	0.38	0.48	0.81	1.07	1.16
Sweden	0.49	0.82	1.18	1.83	2.98	3.40	3.61
United Kingdom	6.58	8.54	10.6	14.1	19.1	23.4	23.5
Canada	0.76	1.40	2.69	2.80	5.85	6.92	7.36
United States	13.1	23.9	46.5	47.7	91.9	115.0	119.3
Japan	0.45	0.63	1.59	2.75	1.71	4.00	5.84
SEMI-INDUSTRIAL COUNTRIES							
Australia	..	0.72	1.04	1.46	2.50	3.20	3.52
New Zealand	0.05	0.14	0.22	0.31	0.52	0.68	0.74
Union of South Africa	..	0.04	0.22	0.41	1.10	1.57	1.68
India[c]	0.36	0.57	1.08	1.65	2.03	2.80	3.14
Pakistan[c]					0.13	0.43	0.51
Argentina	0.23	0.55	1.12	1.39	2.46	2.72	2.80
Brazil	..	..	..	0.92	2.06	2.80	3.05
Chile	..	..	0.18	0.23	0.35	0.50	0.53
Colombia	..	..	0.07	0.14	0.40	0.55	0.57
Mexico	..	..	..	0.73	1.36	1.75	2.05
Israel	—	—	..	..	..	0.29	0.32
Turkey	..	..	..	0.25	0.43	0.72	0.81
Yugoslavia	—	—	0.51	0.55	1.08	1.50	1.95

For sources and footnotes see over.

Sources: For 1955: *Yearbook of National Accounts Statistics, 1959, op. cit.; Patterns of Industrial Growth, 1938–1958,* New York, United Nations, 1960; V. Paretti and G. Bloch, 'Industrial Production in Western Europe and the United States, 1901 to 1955' (Banca Nazionale del Lavoro, *Quarterly Review,* Rome, No. 39, Dec. 1956).

For indices of manufacturing production: F. Hilgerdt, *Industrialization and Foreign Trade,* League of Nations, Geneva, 1945; *Industrial Statistics, 1900–1957,* O.E.E.C., Paris, 1958; *General Statistics,* O.E.E.C., Paris, 1960; *Statistical Yearbooks,* United Nations, New York; K. S. Lomax, 'Production and Productivity Movements in the United Kingdom since 1900', *J. Roy Stat. Soc.,* A., Vol. 122, Part 2, 1959; *Etudes et Conjoncture, op. cit.;* S. Stajic, 'Real National Income of Yugoslavia' (*Consultation on Statistical Problems concerning National Economic Balances and Accounts,* Yugoslav Statistical Society, Belgrade, 1959); K. Ohkawa, *op. cit.; Economic Survey of Africa since 1950,* United Nations, New York, 1959; Australia and New Zealand Bank, *Quarterly Surveys;* A. Maizels, 'Trends in Production and Labour Productivity in Australian Manufacturing Industries', *Economic Record,* Vol. 33, No. 65, Aug. 1957; K. Mukerji, *op. cit.; The Economic Development of Argentina, op. cit.; The Economic Development of Brazil, op. cit.; The Economic Development of Colombia* (Statistical Appendix), *op. cit.*

[a]Inclusive of depreciation charges.

[b]Excluding West Berlin and the Saar.

[c]At least 90 per cent of the total shown for the years up to 1937 represents production in the present area of the Indian Union.

Note: Estimates of the net value of manufacturing production in 1955 for a selection of other countries are as follows, in $ billion:—

AFRICA: Belgian Congo, 0.19; Egypt, 0.37; French Morocco, 0.22; Nigeria, 0.07; Federation of Rhodesia and Nyasaland, 0.11.

AMERICA: Costa Rica, 0.03; Ecuador, 0.08; Honduras, 0.02; Peru, 0.23; Puerto Rico, 0.20; Venezuela, 0.54.

ASIA: Burma, 0.09; Ceylon, 0.08; Lebanon, 0.05; Philippines, 0.31; Thailand, 0.21.

EUROPE: Austria, 1.80; Denmark, 1.43; Finland, 0.86; Greece, 0.57; Ireland, 0.34; Portugal, 0.84; Spain, 3.00; Switzerland, 2.40.

Table E4. *Estimates of net value of manufacturing production per head
of total population in selected countries, 1899–1957*

$ *at* 1955 *prices*

	1899	1913	1929	1937	1950	1955	1957
INDUSTRIAL COUNTRIES							
Belgium-Luxembourg	170	240	315	310	355	460	485
France	100	165	215	190	210	265	325
Germany	125	180	205	245	..	..	..
West Germany	—	—	—	275	230	405	450
Italy	40	65	85	90	100	150	170
Netherlands	..	105	155	145	205	270	280
Norway	75	120	135	165	245	315	365
Sweden	95	145	195	290	425	465	490
United Kingdom	175	200	230	295	380	460	455
Canada	140	190	270	250	425	440	445
United States	175	245	380	370	605	695	695
Japan	10	10	25	40	20	45	65
SEMI-INDUSTRIAL COUNTRIES							
Australia	..	155	165	215	305	350	365
New Zealand	65	125	155	195	275	325	335
Union of South Africa	..	5	30	40	90	115	120
India	} 1	2	3	4	6	7	8
Pakistan					2	5	6
Argentina	50	70	95	105	145	145	140
Brazil	..	..	..	25	40	50	50
Chile	..	..	45	50	55	75	75
Colombia	..	..	10	15	35	45	45
Mexico	..	..	..	40	55	60	65
Israel	..	..	..	..	..	170	170
Turkey	..	..	..	15	20	30	30
Yugoslavia	..	..	35	35	65	85	110

Sources: Tables E3 and E7.

Note: Estimates of net value of manufacturing production per head in 1955 for the countries
mentioned in the *Note* to Table E3 are as follows, in $:—

AFRICA: Belgian Congo, 15; Egypt, 15; French Morocco, 25; Nigeria, 2; Federa-
ation of Rhodesia and Nyasaland, 15.

AMERICA: Costa Rica, 30; Ecuador, 20; Honduras, 15; Peru, 25; Puerto Rico, 85;
Venezuela, 95.

ASIA: Burma, 5; Ceylon, 10;, Lebanon, 35; Philippines, 15; Thailand, 10.

EUROPE: Austria, 255; Denmark, 325; Finland, 205; Greece, 70; Ireland, 115;
Portugal, 95; Spain, 105; Switzerland, 480.

Table E5. *Estimates of apparent consumption of manufactures in selected countries, 1899-1957*

					\$ billion at 1955 prices		
	1899	1913	1929	1937	1950	1955	1957
INDUSTRIAL COUNTRIES							
Belgium-Luxembourg	1.62	2.68	3.54	3.50	4.64	6.01	6.60
France	2.87	6.03	8.32	8.39	8.18	13.8	18.3
Germany	4.60	9.69	12.2	17.8	..	..	..
West Germany	—	—	—	11.6	11.8	21.9	23.6
Italy	1.50	3.26	4.80	5.11	6.27	10.6	12.2
Netherlands	..	..	1.47	1.32	3.01	4.26	4.59
Norway	..	0.43	0.59	0.75	1.31	1.78	1.92
Sweden	0.78	1.24	1.80	2.87	4.83	5.71	6.01
United Kingdom	5.74	7.53	9.49	15.4	20.9	27.4	26.9
Canada	1.29	3.83	5.69	5.03	11.6	14.1	15.1
United States	20.5	37.4	74.3	76.0	129.3	167.4	173.2
Japan	0.54	0.73	2.05	2.85	1.92	4.89	7.58
SEMI-INDUSTRIAL COUNTRIES							
Australia	..	1.55	2.25	2.80	5.10	6.35	6.75
New Zealand	..	0.35	0.60	0.75	1.20	1.66	1.79
Union of South Africa	..	0.36	0.73	1.37	2.20	3.25	3.55
India	} 0.90	1.50	1.75	2.35	2.62	3.95	4.55
Pakistan					0.44	0.80	0.90
Argentina	..	1.00	2.40	2.48	4.16	4.45	4.59
Brazil	..	..	..	1.62	3.90	4.80	5.35
Chile	..	..	..	0.12	0.34	0.55	0.77
Colombia	..	..	0.20	0.27	0.70	0.98	0.87
Mexico	..	..	..	0.95	2.03	2.75	3.30
Israel	..	..	..	..	..	0.50	0.54
Turkey	..	..	..	..	0.75	1.23	1.29
Yugoslavia	..	..	..	0.87	1.85	2.67	3.38

Sources: Tables A5, A13, E3 and national trade statistics.

Note: Estimates of apparent consumption of manufactures in 1955 for a selection of other countries are as follows, in \$ billion:—

AFRICA: Egypt, 0.87; French Morocco, 0.46; Federation of Rhodesia and Nyasaland, 0.18.

AMERICA: Costa Rica, 0.08; Honduras, 0.06; Peru, 0.43; Venezuela, 1.29.

ASIA: Burma, 0.21; Ceylon, 0.27; Lebanon, 0.15; Philippines, 0.67.

EUROPE: Austria, 2.40; Denmark, 2.10; Finland, 1.28; Greece, 1.09; Ireland, 0.59; Portugal, 1.47; Spain, 4.55; Switzerland, 3.04.

Table E6. *Estimates of apparent consumption of manufactures per head of total population in selected countries, 1899-1957*

$ at 1955 prices

	1899	1913	1929	1937	1950	1955	1957
INDUSTRIAL COUNTRIES							
Belgium-Luxembourg	235	340	425	405	520	655	710
France	75	150	200	200	195	320	415
Germany	80	145	190	260	..	..	..
West Germany	—	—	—	295	250	435	460
Italy	45	95	120	120	135	220	250
Netherlands	..	..	190	150	300	395	415
Norway	..	180	210	260	395	525	550
Sweden	155	220	295	455	690	780	810
United Kingdom	150	175	205	325	415	535	520
Canada	240	520	570	445	850	895	910
United States	275	385	610	590	855	1015	1010
Japan	10	15	35	40	25	55	85
SEMI-INDUSTRIAL COUNTRIES							
Australia	..	330	350	410	620	690	705
New Zealand	..	320	430	470	630	790	815
Union of South Africa	..	60	90	140	175	235	250
India	} 3	5	5	6	7	10	12
Pakistan					6	10	11
Argentina	..	130	205	185	240	235	230
Brazil	..	..	..	40	75	80	85
Chile	..	..	..	25	55	80	110
Colombia	..	..	25	30	60	75	65
Mexico	..	..	..	50	80	95	105
Israel	..	..	..	..	..	295	285
Turkey	..	..	..	..	35	50	47
Yugoslavia	..	..	..	55	115	150	185

Sources: Tables E5 and E7.

Note: Estimates of apparent consumption of manufactures per head in 1955 for the countries mentioned in the *Note* to Table E5 are as follows, in $:—

AFRICA: Egypt, 40; French Morocco, 45; Federation of Rhodesia and Nyasaland, 25.
AMERICA: Costa Rica, 80; Honduras, 35; Peru, 45; Venezuela, 225.
ASIA: Burma, 10; Ceylon, 30; Lebanon, 105; Philippines, 30.
EUROPE: Austria, 345; Denmark, 470; Finland, 300; Greece, 135; Ireland, 200; Portugal, 165; Spain, 155; Switzerland, 610.

Table E7. *Total population of selected countries*, 1899–1957

	1899	1913[a]	1929	1937	1950	1955	Millions 1957
WESTERN EUROPE							
Austria	26.2	29.2[a]	6.7	6.8	6.9	7.0	7.0
Belgium-Luxembourg	6.9	7.9[a]	8.3	8.6	8.9	9.2	9.3
Denmark	2.4	2.8[a]	3.5	3.7	4.3	4.4	4.5
Finland	2.5	3.0	3.4	3.6	4.0	4.2	4.3
France	38.9	39.8[a]	41.2	41.6	41.7	43.3	44.1
Germany	56.0	67.0[a]	64.7	67.8	..	..	..
West Germany	—	—	—	39.4	47.8	50.2	51.5
Ireland	3.2	3.1	2.9	2.9	3.0	2.9	2.9
Italy	32.3	35.2[a]	40.5	43.4	46.6	48.1	48.5
Netherlands	5.1	6.1	7.8	8.7	10.1	10.8	11.0
Norway	2.2	2.4	2.8	2.9	3.3	3.4	3.5
Portugal	5.4	6.0	6.7	7.4	8.4	8.8	8.9
Sweden	5.1	5.6	6.1	6.3	7.0	7.3	7.4
Switzerland	3.3	3.9	4.0	4.2	4.7	5.0	5.1
United Kingdom	37.9[d]	42.5[d]	45.9	47.5	50.3	51.0	51.5
Yugoslavia	2.5[e]	3.0[a e]	13.6	15.2	16.3	17.6	18.0
NORTH AMERICA							
Canada	5.4[b]	7.4[c]	10.0	11.3	13.7	15.7	16.6
United States	74.8	97.2	121.8	128.8	151.7	165.3	172.2
OCEANIA							
Australia	3.7[f]	4.7[c]	6.4	6.8	8.2	9.2	9.6
New Zealand	0.8[f]	1.1[c]	1.4	1.6	1.9	2.1	2.2
LATIN AMERICA							
Argentina	4.5	7.7	11.6	13.5	17.2	19.1	19.9
Brazil	17.3[b]	24.6[g]	33.2[h]	38.7	52.0	58.5	61.3
Chile	3.1	3.6[c]	4.2	4.8	6.1	6.8	7.1
Colombia	..	5.1[g]	7.5	8.5	11.3	12.7	13.2
Cuba	1.6[b]	2.4[c]	4.0[i]	4.4	5.5	6.1	6.4
Mexico	13.4	15.2[j]	16.3	18.7	25.8	29.7	31.4
Peru	..	4.7[c]	6.2[k]	6.7	8.5	9.4	9.9
Puerto Rico	..	1.1[j]	1.5	1.8	2.2	2.3	2.3
Venezuela	2.5[b]	2.7[c]	3.2	3.4	5.0	5.8	6.1
ASIA							
Burma	10.5[b]	12.1[l]	14.7[i]	15.6	18.5	19.7	20.1
India	} 283.9[b]	303.0[l]	338.1[i]	377.6	358.3	382.4	392.4
Pakistan					75.0	82.2	84.5
Indonesia	..	..	59.8	67.4	76.0	81.5	85.1
Iran	..	..	..	16.2	19.3	18.3[m]	19.3[m]
Palestine/Israel	..	..	1.0	1.4[n]	1.3	1.7	1.9
Japan	43.7	51.9	62.9	70.4	82.9	89.0	90.9
Philippines	..	..	12.1	15.4	19.9	21.8	22.7
Turkey	..	..	13.6[k]	16.8	20.9	24.1	25.5
AFRICA							
Belgian Congo	..	..	8.8	10.2	11.3	12.5	13.1
Egypt	10.3[b]	12.1[c]	14.5	16.0	20.4	23.0	24.0
French Morocco	..	..	5.4[i]	6.4	7.8	8.5	..
Nigeria	..	16.9[c]	19.2[i]	20.2	24.3	31.2	32.4
Southern Rhodesia	..	..	1.1[i]	1.3	2.2	{ 2.5 [7.2[o]	2.7 7.6[o]
Union of South Africa	5.0[c]	6.2[c]	7.9	9.8	12.4	13.7	14.2
RUSSIA/U.S.S.R.	..	178.9[p]	165.7[q]	169.0	181.0	197.0	203.0[c]

For sources and footnotes see next page.

Sources: G. Sundbärg, *Aperçus Statistiques Internationaux*, Stockholm, 1906; *Statistique Internationale du Mouvement de la Population*, Ministère du Travail et de la Prévoyance Sociale, Paris, 1907; *Annuaire International de Statistique*, International Statistical Institute, The Hague, 1916 (Vols. I–II), 1919 (Vols. III–V); *Annuaire International de Statistique Agricole*, International Institute of Agriculture, Rome, 1920; *Aperçu de la Démographie des Divers Pays du Monde, 1929–1936*, International Statistical Institute, The Hague, 1939; *Statistical Yearbook, 1938/39*, League of Nations, Geneva, 1939; *Historical Statistics of the United States, 1789/1945*, Department of Commerce, Washington, *1949*; I. Svennilson, *Growth and Stagnation in the European Economy*, United Nations, Geneva, 1954; K. Ohkawa, *The Growth Rate of the Japanese Economy since 1878*, Tokyo, 1957; *Demographic Yearbook* (var. edns.), United Nations, New York; *Monthly Bulletin of Statistics*, United Nations, New York.

[a]Population of 1913 territory. Population in 1913 of post-1918 territory, where different from that of 1913 territory, was as follows: Austria, 6.8 million; Belgium-Luxembourg, 8.0; Denmark, 3.0; France, 41.7; Germany, 60.4; Italy, 36.6; Yugoslavia, 13.0.

[b]1900 or 1901.

[c]Estimate based on census results for previous and subsequent years.

[d]Excluding Southern Ireland.

[e]Serbia.

[f]Population of European origin.

[g]1912.

[h]Based on official estimate for 1932 and annual rate of population increase for 1932–34.

[i]1931.

[j]1910.

[k]1927.

[l]1911.

[m]Estimates based on census results for 1956. Figure for 1950 is unrevised.

[n]Jewish population 0.4 million.

[o]Federation of Rhodesia and Nyasaland.

[p]1914 population, excl. Finland. The population of the inter-war territory was 138.3 million.

[q]1932.

EXCHANGE RATES

International trade

The values shown in the trade tables in this book are expressed in terms of United States dollars. The original statistics, in the national currencies of the exporting countries, were converted into dollars by use of the exchange rates shown in Table F1. In general, these exchange rates are the mean official rates of exchange in the years specified.

A major difficulty exists in the case of the German export returns for 1937, in which year German foreign trade was being conducted by the use of a complex system of multiple exchange rates. It was well known that the official rate of 40 U.S. cents per Reichsmark considerably overvalued the German currency, and a wide variety of estimates were published in the late 1930's of the extent of that overvaluation[1]. The evidence points to an overvaluation in the region of 30 per cent, but there is much uncertainty about it. However, it is also apparent that a substantial proportion of German exports in the later 1930's as recorded in the official trade statistics was also overvalued in terms of Reichsmarks, insofar as the official rate was used in the calculations[2]. Thus, the use of the official rate in converting the German export statistics for 1937 into dollars should largely cancel out the overvaluation known to exist in the German export statistics. For this reason, the official rate, as shown in Table F1, was used.

This procedure, while of importance for arriving at the current dollar value of German exports in 1937, does not affect the *volume* calculation, which is ultimately related to the physical quantum of goods traded. However, if we are interested in the movement of German export *prices* in relation to those of other countries, then allowance must be made for the distortion in the German series caused by the arbitrary nature of the official rate[3].

The exchange rates in Table F1 relate to the years selected for the detailed trade network tables, i.e. years ending in 1955. For 1957 and 1959, where shown in the trade tables, the export figures were taken from the *Commodity Trade Statistics*, United Nations, and O.E.E.C. *Foreign Trade Statistical Bulletins*, in both of which they are given in U.S. dollars, for all the principal exporting countries except Switzerland and India. For these two countries, the national export figures were converted into dollars by the mean exchange rate in each year.

Gross domestic product and manufacturing production

When national products are being compared, either in aggregate or for an

---

[1] C. P. Kindleberger, *op. cit.*, pp. 116–117.

[2] This would certainly have applied to exports paid for in foreign exchange, and to goods exported under clearing agreements; it would probably have applied also to a considerable proportion of other exports.

[3] See, for example, the approximate adjustment made to the German series in Table 8.6.

individual sector, it is inappropriate to use official exchange rates to convert the national currency totals into a common currency unit. This is because, for every country, by far the largest portion of its total product does not enter international trade and is not subject to the same pressures of the world market as are goods which are exported. Consequently, considerable price differences may, and frequently do, emerge between similar goods sold on the home markets of different countries. Such differences must be taken into account if genuine 'volume' comparisons are attempted of the output of different countries, and this can most conveniently be done by the calculation of 'purchasing power parity' rates of exchange. Such rates are, in principle, what the rates of exchange would have to be if the same bundle of commodities produced in different countries were to cost the same in terms of the currency of any one of them.

In statistical terms, the problem of cross-country comparison is precisely analogous to that of comparing movements over time within a single country, and the same index number problems are involved. The construction of a volume index number of the gross product of a country over a given time period involves a choice of weights—i.e. the quantities produced in two years being compared can be valued at the prices of either the earlier or the later year, or of some combination of the two. If the structure of relative prices has changed in the interval, the indices obtained may differ substantially according to the weighting system adopted. In the same way, a detailed revaluation of the output of two countries can be made either at the prices ruling in one country, or in that of the other, or—again—at 'synthetic' prices arrived at by some combination of the price structures of the two countries.

In practice, such detailed cross-country revaluations are extremely difficult to make, not only because of the scarcity of suitable statistical data, but also because the pattern of output may be so different in the countries being compared that the results may be of doubtful validity[1]. Even for countries with similar patterns of output, a systematic study on these lines would necessarily entail the accumulation, classification and analysis of a large amount of statistical and other data. In fact, very few cross-country studies of relative national outputs have so far been made[2], though such studies are now becoming

[1]For a fuller discussion of the limitations of such cross-country comparisons see D. Paige and G. Bombach, *A Comparison of National Output and Productivity of the United Kingdom and the United States*, O.E.E.C., Paris, 1959. See also C. Clark, *The Conditions of Economic Progress*, 3rd edn., London, 1957, Ch. II for a valuable discussion of the relative purchasing power of currencies of both advanced and underdeveloped countries.

[2]The pioneer study in this field was the comparison made by the late Dr L. Rostas of British and United States production and productivity in manufacturing industry (*Comparative Productivity in British and American Industry*, Cambridge University Press, 1948). More recent studies have been made by M. Frankel, *British and American Manufacturing Productivity*, University of Illinois, 1957; J. B. Heath, 'British-Canadian Industrial Productivity', *Economic Journal*, Vol. 67, Dec. 1957; A. Maizels, 'Comparative Productivity in Manufacturing Industry: A Case Study of Australia and Canada', *Economic Record*, Vol. 34, No. 67, April 1958 and D. Paige and G. Bombach, *op. cit.*, 1959.

increasingly possible as more countries develop their statistics of production.

Another approach has been to make comparisons of national expenditures rather than of national outputs, the weighting systems being based on the patterns of consumption, investment, etc. in the countries compared. The only detailed studies so far published on this basis are those by Milton Gilbert and his colleagues of the O.E.E.C. Secretariat[1]. Such comparisons yield implicit purchasing power parity rates of exchange for sectors (private consumption, investment, government consumption, etc.) as well as for the economy as a whole. The O.E.E.C. studies, however, cover only eight European countries and the United States, whereas for our present purposes the corresponding rates of exchange were required for a large number of countries at different evels of economic development.

The method adopted here for estimating such rates of exchange is necessarily a crude one. It was assumed that the official mean rate in 1938 correctly reflected the relative purchasing power of the different currencies; the 1955 rate was then estimated by multiplying the 1938 rate by the ratio of the change in United States prices between the two years to the corresponding price change in the country in question. Wherever possible, the (implicit) price change used for estimating the real gross domestic product was taken as the indicator of changes in internal purchasing power. Where such indices were not available, wholesale or retail price indices were used, as seemed most appropriate. The results of such a calculation cannot pretend to provide more than 'orders of magnitude', and they are subject also to the inherent limitations involved in comparisons between countries at different levels of economic development.

Nevertheless, if comparisons *have* to be made over a wide range of countries, it seems preferable to use such estimates of purchasing power parity rates, rather than to use the present official exchange rates, since much less distortion is likely to arise in the final results. A check on the results of the crude method used here can be made for those countries for which estimates are also available on the basis of detailed price comparisons. In Table F2 the estimated rates used in this book are shown, together with the official rates and those estimated in the detailed O.E.E.C. studies; in almost every case, the crude method yields a rate which is within the range of rates calculated by O.E.E.C. on the basis of expenditure studies. The exceptions are Belgium-Luxembourg, for which the 'crude' rate happens to coincide with the higher of the two O.E.E.C. rates; and the United Kingdom, for which the 'crude' rate of $3.80 to the £ exceeds the higher of the two O.E.E.C. rates on the expenditure basis ($3.68), but is within the range of the O.E.E.C. rates on the output basis ($3.60–$4.50).

The only other country for which an independent check is available is Australia. If estimates of the purchasing power parity rates for manufacturing

---

[1] M. Gilbert and I. Kravis, *An International Comparison of National Products and the Purchasing Power of Currencies*, O.E.E.C., Paris, 1954, and M. Gilbert and Associates, *Comparative National Products and Price Levels*, O.E.E.C., Paris, 1958.

industry in 1950[1] are extrapolated to 1955 by the relative movement of domestic prices in Australia and the United States, the corresponding 1955 rates can be estimated at \$2.55–2.70 to the £A, as against \$2.75 derived by the 'crude' method. The correspondence is, perhaps, closer than might have been expected in view of the different techniques involved and the fact that the detailed basis of estimation related to the manufacturing sector only.

As this book was being prepared for printing, a valuable new study by the United Nations Statistical Office of the pattern of industrial growth in a large number of countries was published[2]. The statistical analysis in this study is carried out entirely in U.S. dollars, purchasing power parity rates being used. These were calculated for the year 1953 by a 'crude' method very similar to the one used here, the main difference being that, for a number of countries, the movement in internal prices since 1938 was measured by an index of unit values of manufacturing production, based on data collected at censuses of production. The 1953 rates calculated in this way by the United Nations are also shown in Table F2. The differences between these, and the ones used in the present study, are not in general excessive, bearing in mind the somewhat different basis of the calculation, and also that there were some significant changes in relative prices between 1953 and 1955.

The rates shown in the last column of Table F2 were used to arrive at valuations in U.S. dollars of the gross domestic product of the countries listed, as well as of the value added in manufacturing production, where such figures were available in national currencies (see Appendix E).

Table F1. *Exchange rates used to convert national export statistics to U.S. dollars*

	Currency unit	1899 and 1913	1929	1937	1950	1955
				U.S. cents per national currency unit		
Belgium-Luxembourg	Franc	19.3	2.78	3.38	2.00	2.00
France	Franc	19.3	3.92	3.98	0.286	0.286
Germany	Mark[a]	23.8	23.8	40.2	23.8	23.8
Italy	Lira	19.0	5.24	5.26	0.16	0.16
Netherlands	Guilder	40.2	40.2	55.0	26.3	26.3
Sweden	Krona	26.8	26.8	25.4	19.3	19.3
Switzerland	Franc	19.3	19.3	22.9	23.3	23.3
United Kingdom	£ stg.	487	487	494	280	280
Canada	\$ Can.	100	100	100	94.3	101.3
India	Rupee	32.5	36.2	37.2	21.0	21.0
Japan	Yen	49.5	46.2	28.8	0.278	0.278

Sources: Balances of Payments, 1913–1927, et seq., League of Nations, Geneva; *International Financial Statistics,* International Monetary Fund, Washington; *Yearbook of International Trade Statistics,* United Nations, New York; C. P. Kindleberger, *op. cit.,* Table A-3.

[a]Mark, Reichsmark or Deutschmark.

[1]A. Maizels, *op. cit.,* p. 18. The rates derived relate Australian output to Canadian. rather than to that of the United States. It is assumed that, for present purposes, the Canadian and U.S. dollars are in effect identical.

[2]*Patterns of Industrial Growth, 1938–1958,* United Nations, New York, 1960.

APPENDIX F

Table F2. *Estimated purchasing power parity rates*, 1953 *and* 1955

U.S. cents per national currency unit

	Currency unit	Official exchange rate (1955)	Estimated purchasing power parity rate		
			O.E.E.C. (1955)a	U.N. (1953)	Present book (1955)
NORTH AMERICA					
Canada	$ Can.	101.3[b]	..	101.7	102
United States	$ U.S.	100	100	100	100
WESTERN EUROPE					
Austria	Schilling	3.85	..	4.68	4.86
Belgium-Luxembourg	Franc	2.00	2.23– 2.66	1.76	2.66
Denmark	Krone	14.48	16.80– 21.90	15.67	17.6
Finland	Markka	0.43	..	0.32	0.35
France	Franc	0.29	0.25– 0.35	0.26	0.28
Germany, West	D. Mark	23.81	28.50– 39.40	26.70	32.0
Ireland	£	280.0	..	352.10	363
Italy	Lira	0.16	0.16– 0.30	0.23	0.19
Netherlands	Guilder	26.32	34.10– 46.10	32.42	35.0
Norway	Krone	14.00	15.20– 20.90	19.56	17.6
Portugal	Escudo	3.48	..	3.37	5.7
Sweden	Krona	19.33	..	20.21	23.4
Switzerland	Franc	23.27	..	23.33	22.5
United Kingdom	£ stg.	280.0	314–368[e]	417.70	380
Yugoslavia	Dinar	0.333	..	0.33	0.25[d]
OCEANIA					
Australia	£A.	224.0	..	248.40	275.0
New Zealand	£ N.Z.	280.0	..	369.70	330.0
LATIN AMERICA					
Argentina	Peso	2.77	..	5.14	8.45
Brazil	Cruzeiro	1.50[e]	..	1.80	2.14
Chile	Peso	0.37[f]	..	0.69	0.24
Colombia	Peso	24.0[e]	..	28.30	33.70
Mexico	Peso	8.00	..	12.00	9.10
Peru	Sole	5.26	..	7.56	5.56
Puerto Rico	$ U.S.[g]	100.00	..	..	100.00
Venezuela	Bolivar	29.85	..	27.50	29.50
ASIA					
India	Rupee	21.0	..	21.34	22.8
Pakistan	Rupee	21.0	..	21.34	22.8[h]
Indonesia	Rupiah	8.77[b]	..	4.77	4.8
Israel	£I	55.5–77.0[i]	..	..	70.0
Japan	Yen	0.2778	..	0.28	0.23
Philippines	Peso	50.00	..	23.70	28.9
Turkey	Lira	35.71[b]	..	34.12	30.0
AFRICA					
Belgian Congo	Franc	2.00	..	1.76	2.79
Egypt	£ E.	287.2	..	325.50	335.0
Union of South Africa	£ S.A.	280.0	..	425.40	335.0

For sources and footnotes see next page.

Sources: Statistical Yearbook, United Nations, New York; *Comparative National Products and Price Levels*, Milton Gilbert *et al.*, O.E.E.C., Paris, 1958; D. Paige and G. Bombach, *A Comparison of National Output and Productivity of the United Kingdom and the United States*, O.E.E.C., Paris, 1959; *Patterns of Industrial Growth, 1938–1958*, United Nations, New York, 1960.

[a]The lower end of the ranges shown are exchange rates based on the United States expenditure pattern; the higher figures are based on the expenditure pattern of the country specified.

[b]Currency conversion factor used for trade statistics by United Nations Statistical Office.

[c]The purchasing power rates estimated for 1954 by Miss Paige and Dr Bombach on the basis of a detailed study of relative output and costs in Britain and the United States are 360 cents per £ on U.S. and 450 cents on U.K. weights. These are unlikely to have changed significantly between 1954 and 1955. These rates relate, however, to factor cost excluding taxes and subsidies, and this probably accounts for a third or more of the difference from the rates obtained in the expenditure study, which are at market prices.

[d]Tourist rate plus 5 per cent.

[e]Free rate.

[f]Mean of buying and selling rates for principal imports and exports.

[g]Trade statistics given in terms of U.S. dollars in United Nations publications.

[h]Assumed equal to the rate for India.

[i]Lower figure represents principal rate ; higher figure is mean of other rates up to 1st October 1955.

LIST OF WORKS CITED

I. OFFICIAL PUBLICATIONS

(1) INTERNATIONAL

FOOD AND AGRICULTURE ORGANIZATION OF THE UNITED NATIONS

Annual Review of World Production, Consumption and Trade of Fertilizers (Rome).
Fertilizers: a World Report on Production and Consumption (Rome, 1952).
Monthly Bulletin of Agricultural Economics and Statistics (Rome).
Per Caput Fiber Consumption Levels, Commodity Bulletin Series, 25 (Rome, 1954).
Per Caput Fiber Consumption Levels, 1948–1958, Commodity Bulletin Series, 31 (Rome, 1960).
'Report by the F.A.O. Secretariat on Fiber Consumption Trends', *Studies of Factors Affecting Consumption of Textile Fibers*, International Cotton Advisory Committee (Washington, 1960).
Statistics of the Volume, Average Unit Value and Total Value of International Trade in Agricultural Products (Rome, 1956).
The World Coffee Economy, Commodity Bulletin Series, 33 (Rome, 1961).
World Demand for Paper to 1975 (Rome, 1960).
World Fertilizer Production and Consumption and Targets for the Future (Washington, 1946).

GENERAL AGREEMENT ON TARIFFS AND TRADE

International Trade (Geneva, annual).
Trends in International Trade (Geneva, 1958).

INTERNATIONAL CUSTOMS TARIFFS BUREAU

Bulletin International des Douanes (Brussels, irreg.).

INTERNATIONAL INSTITUTE OF AGRICULTURE

Annuaire International de Statistique Agricole, 1917 et 1918 (Rome, 192

INTERNATIONAL LABOUR OFFICE

Year Book of Labour Statistics, 1957 (Geneva, 1957).

INTERNATIONAL MONETARY FUND

Balance of Payments Yearbook (Washington).
International Financial Statistics (Washington, monthly).

LEAGUE OF NATIONS

Balances of Payments (Geneva, annual).
Industrialization and Foreign Trade (Geneva, 1945).
Minimum List of Commodities for International Trade Statistics, rev. ed., Studies and Reports on Statistical Methods, 2 (Geneva, 1938).
Statistical Year-book, 1938/39 (Geneva, 1939).

ORGANISATION FOR ECONOMIC CO-OPERATION AND DEVELOPMENT (*formerly* ORGANISATION FOR EUROPEAN ECONOMIC CO-OPERATION)

The Chemical Industry in Europe, 1960–1961 (Paris, 1962).

Development Assistance Efforts and Policies in 1961 of the members of the Development Committee (Paris, 1962).

The Engineering Industries in Europe, 1960 (Paris, 1961).

The Flow of Financial Resources to Countries in Course of Economic Development, 1956–1959 (Paris, 1961).

Industrial Statistics, 1900–1957 (Paris, 1958).

Industrial Statistics, 1900–1959 (Paris, 1960).

Statistical Bulletins: Foreign Trade, Series IV, Series B and *Series C* (Paris, quarterly).

Statistical Bulletins: General Statistics (Paris, 6 times yearly).

Statistics of National Product and Expenditure, No. 2, 1938 and 1947 to 1955 (Paris, 1957).

The Textile Industry in Europe: Statistical Study, 1955–1956 (Paris, 1957).

UNITED NATIONS

Department of Economic and Social Affairs

Economic Survey of Africa since 1950 (New York, 1959).

The Future Growth of World Population, Population Studies, 28 (New York, 1958).

International Economic Assistance to the Less Developed Countries (New York, 1961).

International Flow of Long-term Capital and Official Donations, 1951–1959 (New York, 1961).

Processes and Problems of Industrialization in Under-developed Countries (New York, 1955).

The United Nations Development Decade: Proposals for Action (New York, 1962).

World Economic Survey (New York, annual).

Economic Commission for Asia and the Far East

Economic Bulletin for Asia and the Far East (Bangkok, quarterly).

Economic Commission for Europe

Economic Bulletin for Europe (Geneva, twice yearly).

Economic Survey of Europe (Geneva, annual).

Economic Survey of Europe since the War (Geneva, 1953).

Long-term Trends and Problems of the European Steel Industry (Geneva, 1959).

Economic Commission for Latin America

Analyses and Projections of Economic Development. II. *The Economic Development of Brazil* (New York, 1956). III. *The Economic Development of Colombia* (Geneva, 1957). V. *The Economic Development of Argentina* (Mexico, 1959). VI. *The Industrial Development of Peru* (Mexico, 1959).

Economic Bulletin for Latin America (Santiago, twice yearly).

Economic Survey of Latin America (Mexico, annual).

Economic Commission for Latin America, Food and Agriculture Organization of the United Nations *and* Technical Assistance Administration

Pulp and Paper Prospects in Latin America (New York, 1955).

Statistical Office

Commodity Indexes for the Standard International Trade Classification, Statistical Papers, M 10, indexed ed. (New York, 1953).

Commodity Trade Statistics, Statistical Papers, D (New York, quarterly).

Demographic Yearbook (New York).

Monthly Bulletin of Statistics (New York).

Patterns of Industrial Growth, 1938–1958 (New York, 1960).

Standard International Trade Classification, Statistical Papers, M 10, 2nd ed. (New York, 1951).

Statistical Yearbook (New York).

Yearbook of International Trade Statistics (New York).

Yearbook of National Accounts Statistics (New York).

(2) NATIONAL

AUSTRALIA

Commonwealth Bureau of Census and Statistics
The Australian Balance of Payments, 1928–29 to 1951–52 and *1957–58* (Canberra, 1953 and 1959).
Secondary Industries (Canberra, annual).

CANADA

Dominion Bureau of Statistics
The Inter-Industry Flow of Goods and Services, 1949, Reference Paper, 72 (Ottawa, 1956).
Royal Commission on Canada's Economic Prospects
The Outlook for the Canadian Forest Industries (Ottawa, 1957).

FRANCE

Institut National de la Statistique et des Etudes Economiques
'Structures de Base et Croissance Comparée de la Production Industrielle en Allemagne Occidentale et en Allemagne Orientale', *Etudes et Conjoncture*, No. 3, March 1960, p. 243.
Tableau Economique de l'Année 1951 (Paris, 1957).
Ministère du Travail et de la Prévoyance Sociale
Statistique Internationale du Mouvement de la Population . . . 1905, Statistique Générale de la France (Paris, 1907).

INDIA

Planning Commission
Third Five Year Plan: A Draft Outline (New Delhi, 1960).

JAPAN

Economic Planning Agency
Japanese Economic Statistics (Tokyo, monthly).
Ministry of International Trade and Industry
Inter-industry Analysis for the Japanese Economy (Tokyo, 1957).   In Japanese.

NEW ZEALAND

Department of Statistics
Report on the Inter-industry Study of the New Zealand Economy in 1952–53 and *1954–55*, Supplements to the *Monthly Abstract of Statistics* (Wellington, 1957 and 1959).

NORWAY

Central Bureau of Statistics
Input-output Analysis of Norwegian Industries, 1954, Samfunnsøkonomiske Studier, 9 (Oslo, 1960).

UNITED KINGDOM

Board of Trade
Census of Distribution and Other Services, 1950, Vol. 3.   Wholesale Trades (London, H.M. Stationery Office, 1955).
Final Report on the First Census of Production of the United Kingdom (1907), Cd. 6320 (London, H.M. Stationery Office, 1912).
Final Report on the Fourth Census of Production (1930) (London, H.M. Stationery Office, 5 pts., 1933–35).
Imports and Exports at Prices of 1900, Cd. 2894, 3446, 4115, 4867, 5160, 6314, 6782, 7432 (London, H.M. Stationery Office, annual, 1906–10, 1912–14).
'Orders, Deliveries, Productions and Exports in the Engineering Industries ', *Board of Trade Journal*, Vol. 180, No. 3354, 30 June 1961, p. 1518.
Report on Overseas Trade (London, H.M. Stationery Office, monthly).
'Volume of Imports and Exports', quarterly, *Board of Trade Journal* (London, H.M. Stationery Office, weekly).

Board of Trade. Committee on Industry and Trade
  Survey of Overseas Markets (London, H.M. Stationery Office, 1925).
Board of Trade *and* Central Statistical Office
  Input-output Tables for the United Kingdom, 1954, Studies in Official Statistics, 8 (London, H.M. Stationery Office, 1961).
Central Statistical Office
  Monthly Digest of Statistics (London, H.M. Stationery Office).
  National Income and Expenditure, 1946–51, 1946–52 and *1958* (London, H.M. Stationery Office, 1952, 1953 and 1958).
Overseas Geological Surveys
  Statistical Summary of the Mineral Industry (London, H.M. Stationery Office, annual).
Royal Commission on Population
  Papers, Vol. III. Report of the Economics Committee (London, H.M. Stationery Office, 1950).
Treasury
  United Kingdom Balance of Payments, 1958 to 1960, Cmnd. 1329 (London, H.M. Stationery Office, 1961).

UNITED STATES

Bureau of Mines
  Mineral Trade Notes (Washington, Government Printing Office, monthly).
Bureau of the Census
  Historical Statistics of the United States, 1789–1945 (Washington, Government Printing Office, 1949).
  United States Census of Business, 1948, Vol. 4 (Washington, Government Printing Office, 1952).
Federal Reserve System
  Federal Reserve Bulletin (Washington, monthly).
Mutual Security Agency
  The Structure and Growth of the Italian Economy (Rome, 1953).

YUGOSLAVIA

Federal Statistical Office
  Inter-industry Relations of the Yugoslav Economy in 1955, Studije i Analize, 8 (Belgrade, 1957).

II. BOOKS, ARTICLES AND SERIAL PUBLICATIONS

AITCHISON, J. and BROWN, J. A. C. 'A Synthesis of Engel Curve Theory', *Review of Economic Studies*, Vol. 22, No. 57, 1955, p. 35.
ALLEN, R. G. D. and ELY, J. E. (ed.). *International Trade Statistics* (New York, Wiley, 1953).
ATALLAH, M. K. *The Long-term Movement of the Terms of Trade between Agricultural and Industrial Products* (Rotterdam, Netherlands Economic Institute, 1958).
AUKRUST, O. and BJERKE, J. 'Real Capital and Economic Growth in Norway, 1900–56', *Income and Wealth, Series VIII, The Measurement of National Wealth*, International Association for Research in Income and Wealth, ed. R. Goldsmith and C. Saunders (London, Bowes & Bowes, 1959).
AUSTRALIA AND NEW ZEALAND BANK LTD. *Quarterly Survey* (Melbourne and London).
BALDWIN, R. E. 'The Commodity Composition of Trade: Selected Industrial Countries, 1900–1954', *Review of Economics and Statistics*, Vol. 40, No. 1, Part 2, Supplement, February 1958, p. 50.
BANCO DE MEXICO. *La Estructura Industrial de Mexico en 1950* (Mexico, 1957).
BARGER, H. *Distribution's Place in the American Economy since 1869*, National Bureau of Economic Research, General Series, 58 (Princeton, University Press, 1955).

BARNA, T. 'The Interdependence of the British Economy', *Journal of the Royal Statistical Society*, Series A, Vol. 115, Part 1, 1952, p. 29.

BAUER, P. T. and YAMEY, B. S. *The Economics of Under-developed Countries* (London, Nisbet, 1957; Cambridge, University Press).

BIEDA, K. 'The Causes of the Export Lag of the Industrializing Countries', *Kyklos*, Vol. 15, Fasc. 2, 1962, p. 485.

BJERKE, K. 'The National Product of Denmark, 1870–1952', *Income and Wealth, Series V*, International Association for Research in Income and Wealth, ed. S. Kuznets (London, Bowes & Bowes, 1955).

[*Brussels Trade Classification*] *Conférence Internationale de Statistique Commerciale, Bruxelles, 1913* (Brussels, 1914).

Cahiers Economiques de Bruxelles, No. 1, October 1958, p. 191.

CAIRNCROSS, A. K. 'International Trade and Economic Development', *Kyklos*, Vol. 13, Fasc. 4, 1960, p. 545.

'World Trade in Manufactures since 1900', *Economia Internazionale*, Vol. 8, No. 4, November 1955, p. 715.

CAMERON, B. 'Inter-sector Accounts, 1955–56', *Economic Record*, Vol. 36, No. 74, April 1960, p. 269.

CAVES, R. E. and HOLTON, R. H. *The Canadian Economy: Prospect and Retrospect*, Harvard Economic Studies, 112 (Cambridge (Mass.), Harvard University Press, 1959).

CENTRAAL PLANBUREAU. *Een Verkenning der Economische Toekomstmogelijkheden van Nederland, 1950–1970* (The Hague, 1955).

CHAMBERS, S. P. *International Competition in the Chemical Industry*, Plastics Institute, 10th Annual Lecture (London, 1959).

CHANG, T. C. *Cyclical Movements in the Balance of Payments* (Cambridge, University Press, 1951).

Chemische Industrie (Düsseldorf, monthly).

CHENERY, H. B. 'Patterns of Industrial Growth', *American Economic Review*, Vol. 50, No. 4, September 1960, p. 624.

CHENERY, H. B. and CLARK, P. G. *Interindustry Economics* (New York, Wiley, 1959).

CHOW, G. C. 'Statistical Demand Functions for Automobiles and their Use for Forecasting', *The Demand for Durable Goods*, ed. A. C. Harberger (Chicago, University of Chicago Press, 1960).

CLARK, C. *The Conditions of Economic Progress*, 3rd ed. (London, Macmillan, 1957).

DANIELS, G. W. and CAMPION, H. 'The Relative Importance of British Export Trade', *London and Cambridge Economic Service Special Memorandum*, No. 41, August 1935.

DEVONS, E. 'Understanding International Trade', *Economica, New Series*, Vol. 28, No. 112, November 1961, p. 351.

DICKS-MIREAUX, L. A. and others. 'Prospects for the British Car Industry', *National Institute Economic Review*, No. 17, September 1961, p. 15.

DOMINGUEZ, L. M. *International Trade, Industrialization and Economic Growth*, preliminary draft (Washington, Pan-American Union, 1953).

EVANS, W. D. and HOFFENBERG, M. 'The Interindustry Relations Study for 1947', *Review of Economics and Statistics*, Vol. 34, No. 2, May 1952, p. 97.

FIRESTONE, O. J. 'Canada's Economic Development, 1867–1953', *Income and Wealth, Series VII*, International Association for Research in Income and Wealth (London, Bowes & Bowes, 1958).

FLORENCE, P. SARGANT. *Investment, Location and Size of Plant* (Cambridge, University Press, 1948).

The Logic of British and American Industry (London, Routledge & Kegan Paul, 1953).

FRANKEL, M. *British and American Manufacturing Productivity: a Comparison and Interpretation*, Bulletin 81 (Urbana, University of Illinois, Bureau of Economic and Business Research, 1957).

GATES, T. R. and LINDEN, F. *Costs and Competition: American Experience Abroad* (New York, National Industrial Conference Board, 1961).

GILBERT, M. and KRAVIS, I. *An International Comparison of National Products and the Purchasing Power of Currencies* (Paris, Organisation for European Economic Co-operation, 1954).

GILBERT, M. and Associates. *Comparative National Products and Price Levels* (Paris, Organisation for European Economic Co-operation, 1958).

GILBERT, R. S. and MAJOR, R. L. 'Britain's Falling Share of Sterling Area Imports', *National Institute Economic Review*, No. 14, March 1961, p. 18.

HARBERGER, A. C. 'Some Evidence on the International Price Mechanism', *Journal of Political Economy*, Vol. 65, No. 6, December 1957, p. 506.

'Some Evidence on the International Price Mechanism', *Review of Economics and Statistics*, Vol. 40, No. 1, Part 2, Supplement, February 1958, p. 123.

HEATH, J. B. 'British-Canadian Industrial Productivity', *Economic Journal*, Vol. 67, No. 268, December 1957, p. 665.

HEMMING, M. F. W., MILES, C. M. and RAY, G. F. 'A Statistical Summary of the Extent of Import Control in the United Kingdom since the War', *Review of Economic Studies*, Vol. 26, No. 70, February 1959, p. 75.

HINSHAW, R. and METZLER, L. A. 'World Prosperity and the British Balance of Payments', *Review of Economic Statistics*, Vol. 27, No. 4, November 1945, p. 156.

HOFFMANN, W. G. *The Growth of Industrial Economies* (Manchester, University Press, 1958).

'Long-term Growth and Capital Formation in Germany', *The Theory of Capital*, Proceedings of a Conference held by the International Economic Association, by F. A. Lutz, ed. D. C. Hague (London, Macmillan, 1961).

HOUTHAKKER, H. S. 'An International Comparison of Household Expenditure Patterns, Commemorating the Centenary of Engel's Law', *Econometrica*, Vol. 25, No. 4, October 1957, p. 532.

HUMPHREY, D. D. *American Imports* (New York, Twentieth Century Fund, 1955).

INDIAN STATISTICAL INSTITUTE. *Inter-industry Relations of the Indian Economy, 1953–54* (Calcutta, 1958).

INTERNATIONAL COTTON ADVISORY COMMITTEE. *Prospective Trends in Consumption of Textile Fibers* (Washington, 1962).

INTERNATIONAL STATISTICAL INSTITUTE. *Annuaire International de Statistique, I–V* (The Hague, 1916–19).

Aperçu de la Démographie des Divers Pays du Monde, 1929–1936 (The Hague, 1939).

INTERNATIONAL TIN STUDY GROUP. *Statistical Yearbook, 1956* (The Hague, 1957).

JONES, K., MAIZELS, A. and WHITTAKER, J. 'The Demand for Food in the Industrial Countries, 1948–1960', *National Institute Economic Review*, No. 20, May 1962, p. 40.

JOSTOCK, P. 'The Long-term Growth of National Income in Germany', *Income and Wealth, Series V*, International Association for Research in Income and Wealth, ed. S. Kuznets (London, Bowes & Bowes, 1955).

KALISKI, S. F. 'Some Recent Estimates of the Elasticity of Demand for British Exports', *Manchester School of Economic and Social Studies*, Vol. 29, No. 1, January 1961, p. 23.

KEYNES, J. M. 'National Self-sufficiency', *Yale Review*, Vol. 22, No. 4, June 1933, p. 755.

KINDLEBERGER, C. P. *Economic Development* (New York, McGraw-Hill, 1958).

The Terms of Trade: a European Case Study (New York, Wiley, 1956).

KNOX, F. 'Some International Comparisons of Consumers' Durable Goods', *Bulletin of the Oxford University Institute of Statistics*, Vol. 21, No. 1, February 1959, p. 31.

KUZNETS, S. *Capital in the American Economy: its Formation and Financing*, National Bureau of Economic Research, Studies in Capital Formation and Financing, 9 (Princeton, University Press, 1961).

'Economic Growth of Small Nations', *Economic Consequences of the Size of Nations*, Proceedings of a Conference held by the International Economic Association, ed. E. A. G. Robinson (London, Macmillan, 1960).

'Quantitative Aspects of the Economic Growth of Nations, VI. Long-term Trends in Capital Formation Proportions', *Economic Development and Cultural Change*, Vol. 9, No. 4, Part II, July 1961.

LAMFALUSSY, A. *The United Kingdom and the Six: an Essay on Economic Growth in Western Europe* (London, Macmillan, 1963).

LEONTIEF, W. W. *The Structure of the American Economy, 1919–1929* (Cambridge (Mass.), Harvard University Press, 1941).

LERDAU, E. 'Stabilization and the Terms of Trade', *Kyklos*, Vol. 12, Fasc. 3, 1959, p. 362.

LEWIS, W. A. 'World Production, Prices and Trade, 1870–1960', *Manchester School of Economic and Social Studies*, Vol. 20, No. 2, May 1952, p. 105.

LINDER, S. B. *An Essay on Trade and Transformation* (New York, Wiley, 1961).

LIPSEY, R. E. *Price and Quantity Trends in the Foreign Trade of the United States*, National Bureau of Economic Research, Studies in International Economic Relations, 2 (Princeton, University Press, 1963).

LOMAX, K. S. 'Production and Productivity Movements in the United Kingdom since 1900', *Journal of the Royal Statistical Society, Series A*, Vol. 122, Part 2, 1959, p. 185.

MACDOUGALL, SIR DONALD. 'British and American Exports: a Study suggested by the Theory of Comparative Costs', *Economic Journal*, Vol. 61, No. 244, December 1951, p. 697, and Vol. 62, No. 247, September 1952, p. 487.

The World Dollar Problem: a Study in International Economics (London, Macmillan, 1957).

MAIZELS, A. 'Comparative Productivity in Manufacturing Industry: a Case Study of Australia and Canada', *Economic Record*, Vol. 34, No. 67, April 1958, p. 67.

'The Effects of Industrialization on Exports of Primary-producing Countries', *Kyklos*, Vol. 14, Fasc. 1, 1961, p. 18.

'Recent Trends in World Trade', *Trade in Developing Areas*, Proceedings of a Conference held by the International Economic Association, 1961 (London, Macmillan, in preparation).

'Trends in Production and Labour Productivity in Australian Manufacturing Industries', *Economic Record*, Vol. 33, No. 65, August 1957, p. 162.

'Trends in World Trade in Durable Consumer Goods', *National Institute Economic Review*, No. 6, November 1959, p. 15.

'Unit Value and Volume Index Numbers of Inter-area Trade', *Journal of the Royal Statistical Society, Series A*, Vol. 120, Part 2, 1957, p. 215.

MAJOR, R. L. 'The Common Market: Production and Trade', *National Institute Economic Review*, No. 21, August 1962, p. 24.

MANUFACTURING CHEMISTS' ASSOCIATION INC. *Chemical Statistics Handbook*, 4th ed., 1955 (Washington, 1955).

MEADE, J. E. *Negotiations for Benelux: an Annotated Chronicle, 1943–1956*, Princeton Studies in International Finance, 6 (Princeton, University, 1957).

METALLGESELLSCHAFT A.G. *Collected Statistics* (Frankfurt am Main, 1956).

Metal Statistics (Frankfurt am Main, annual).

METZNER, A. *Die chemische Industrie der Welt* (Düsseldorf, Econ-Verlag, 1955).

MICHAELY, M. *Concentration in International Trade* (Amsterdam, North-Holland Publishing Co., 1962).

MINERAIS ET METAUX S.A. *Statistiques, 1955* (Paris, 1956).

MUKERJI, K. *A Note on the Long Term Growth of National Income in India*, 2nd Indian Conference on Research in National Income (Delhi, 1960).

NEISSER, H. and MODIGLIANI, F. *National Incomes and International Trade: a Quantitative Analysis* (Urbana, University of Illinois Press, 1953).

NURKSE, R. *Patterns of Trade and Development*, Wicksell Lectures, Stockholm, 1959 (Uppsala, Almqvist & Wiksell, 1959).

OHKAWA, K. and others. *The Growth Rate of the Japanese Economy since 1878* (Tokyo, Kinokuniya Bookstore Co., 1957).

ORCUTT, G. H. 'Measurement of Price Elasticities in International Trade', *Review of Economics and Statistics*, Vol. 32, No. 2, May 1950, p. 117.

PAIGE, D. and BOMBACH, G. *A Comparison of National Output and Productivity of the United Kingdom and the United States* (Paris, Organisation for European Economic Co-operation, 1959).

PARETTI, V. and BLOCH, G. 'Industrial Production in Western Europe and the United States, 1901 to 1955', *Banca Nazionale del Lavoro Quarterly Review*, No. 39, December 1956, p. 186.

POLAK, J. J. *An International Economic System* (London, Allen & Unwin, 1954).

PRAIS, S. J. 'Econometric Research in International Trade: a Review', *Kyklos*, Vol. 15, Fasc. 3, 1962, p. 560.

RAY, G. F. 'British Imports of Manufactured Goods', *National Institute Economic Review*, No. 8, March 1960, p. 12.

'British Imports of Manufactures', *National Institute Economic Review*, No. 15, May 1961, p. 36.

REDDAWAY, W. B. and SMITH, A. D. 'Progress in British Manufacturing Industries in the Period 1948–54', *Economic Journal*, Vol. 70, No. 277, March 1960, p. 17.

ROBERTSON, D. H. 'The Future of International Trade', *Economic Journal*, Vol. 48, No. 189, March 1938, p. 1.

ROSTAS, L. *Comparative Productivity in British and American Industry*, National Institute of Economic and Social Research, Occasional Papers, 13 (Cambridge, University Press, 1948).

ROWLATT, J. A. and BLACKABY, F. T. 'The Demand for Industrial Materials, 1950–57', *National Institute Economic Review*, No. 5, September 1959, p. 22.

SCOTT, M. FG. *A Study of United Kingdom Imports* (Cambridge, University Press, 1963).

SHAW, W. H. *Value of Commodity Output since 1869*, National Bureau of Economic Research, Publication 48 (New York, 1947).

SOLOW, R. M. 'Technica Change and the Aggregate Production Function', *Review of Economics and Statistics*, Vol. 39, No. 3, August 1957, p. 312.

SPIEGELGLAS, S. 'World Exports of Manufactures, 1956 vs. 1937', *Manchester School of Economic and Social Studies*, Vol. 27, No. 2, May 1959, p. 111.

STAFFORD, J., MATON, J. M. and VENNING, M. 'United Kingdom', *International Trade Statistics*, ed. R. G. D. Allen and J. E. Ely (New York, Wiley, 1953).

STAJIC, S. 'Real National Income of Yugoslavia', *Consultation on Statistical Problems concerning National Economic Balances and Accounts*, Yugoslav Statistical Society (Belgrade, 1959).

STONE, J. R. N. and ROWE, D. A. 'Dynamic Demand Functions: Some Econometric Results', *Economic Journal*, Vol. 68, No. 270, June 1958, p. 256.

SUITS, D. B. 'The Demand for New Automobiles in the United States, 1929–1956', *Review of Economics and Statistics*, Vol. 40, No. 3, August 1958, p. 273.

SUNDBÄRG, G. *Aperçus Statistiques Internationaux* (Stockholm, 1906).

SVENNILSON, I. *Growth and Stagnation in the European Economy* (Geneva, United Nations, 1954).

TORRENS, R. *An Essay on the Production of Wealth* (London, 1821).

TYSZYNSKI, H. 'World Trade in Manufactured Commodities, 1899–1950', *Manchester School of Economic and Social Studies*, Vol. 19, No. 3, September 1951, p. 272.

VINER, J. *The Prospects for Foreign Trade in the Post-war World* (Manchester Statistical Society, paper read 19 June 1946).

VINSKI, I. 'Rast Nacionalnog Dohotka i Bogatstva Jugoslavije', *Naša Stvarnost*, Vol. 14, No. 2, February 1960, p. 184.

VITKOVITCH, B. 'The U.K. Cotton Industry, 1937–54', *Journal of Industrial Economics*, Vol. 3, No. 3, July 1955, p. 241.

WATANABE, T. 'A Note on an International Comparison of Private Consumption Expenditure', *Weltwirtschaftliches Archiv*, Vol. 88, Heft 1, 1962, p. 145.

YATES, P. LAMARTINE. *Forty Years of Foreign Trade* (London, Allen & Unwin, 1959).

ZELDER, R. E. 'Estimates of Elasticities of Demand for Exports of the United Kingdom and the United States, 1921–1938', *Manchester School of Economic and Social Studies*, Vol. 26, No. 1, January 1958, p. 33.

INDEX

PUBLICATIONS OF THE
NATIONAL INSTITUTE OF ECONOMIC
AND SOCIAL RESEARCH

published by

THE CAMBRIDGE UNIVERSITY PRESS

Books published for the Institute by the Cambridge University Press are available through the ordinary booksellers. They appear in the four series below.

ECONOMIC & SOCIAL STUDIES

*I *Studies in the National Income, 1924–1938*
    Edited by A. L. BOWLEY. Reprinted with corrections, 1944. pp. 256.

*II *The Burden of British Taxation*
    By G. FINDLAY SHIRRAS and L. ROSTAS. 1942. pp. 140.

*III *Trade Regulations and Commercial Policy of the United Kingdom*
    By the RESEARCH STAFF OF THE NATIONAL INSTITUTE OF ECONOMIC AND SOCIAL RESEARCH. 1943. pp. 275.

*IV *National Health Insurance: A Critical Study*
    By HERMANN LEVY. 1944. pp. 356.

*V *The Development of the Soviet Economic System: An Essay on the Experience of Planning in the U.S.S.R.*
    By ALEXANDER BAYKOV. 1946. pp. 530.
    Reprinted 1970 in CUP Library Edition, £5.00 net.

*VI *Studies in Financial Organization*
    By T. BALOGH. 1948. pp. 328.

*VII *Investment, Location, and Size of Plant: A Realistic Inquiry into the Structure of British and American Industries*
    By P. SARGANT FLORENCE, assisted by W. BALDAMUS. 1948. pp. 230.

VIII *A Statistical Analysis of Advertising Expenditure and of the Revenue of the Press*
    By NICHOLAS KALDOR and RODNEY SILVERMAN. 1948. pp. 200. £1.25 net.

*IX *The Distribution of Consumer Goods*
    By JAMES B. JEFFERYS, assisted by MARGARET MACCOLL and G. L. LEVETT. 1950. pp. 430.

*X *Lessons of the British War Economy*
    Edited by D. N. CHESTER. 1951. pp. 260.

*XI *Colonial Social Accounting*
    By PHYLLIS DEANE. 1953. pp. 360.

*XII *Migration and Economic Growth*
    By BRINLEY THOMAS. 1954. pp. 384.

*XIII *Retail Trading in Britain, 1850–1950*
    By JAMES B. JEFFERYS. 1954. pp. 490.

*XIV *British Economic Statistics*
    By CHARLES CARTER and A. D. ROY. 1954. pp. 192.

XV *The Structure of British Industry: A Symposium*
    Edited by DUNCAN BURN. 1958. Vol. I. pp. 403. £2.75 net. Vol. II. pp. 499. £3.15 net.

*XVI *Concentration in British Industry*
    By RICHARD EVELY and I. M. D. LITTLE. 1960. pp. 357.

*XVII *Studies in Company Finance*
    Edited by BRIAN TEW and R. F. HENDERSON. 1959. pp. 301.

XVIII *British Industrialists: Steel and Hosiery, 1850–1950*
    By CHARLOTTE ERICKSON. 1959. pp. 276. £2.25 net.

*At present out of print.

OCCASIONAL PAPERS

*At present out of print.

STUDIES IN THE NATIONAL INCOME AND EXPENDITURE OF THE UNITED KINGDOM

Published under the joint auspices of the National Institute and the Department of Applied Economics, Cambridge.

NIESR STUDENTS' EDITION

THE NATIONAL INSTITUTE OF ECONOMIC AND SOCIAL RESEARCH

publishes regularly

THE NATIONAL INSTITUTE ECONOMIC REVIEW

A quarterly Review of the economic situation and prospects.

Annual subscriptions £3.50, and single issues for the current year £1.00 each, are available directly from N.I.E.S.R., 2 Dean Trench St., Smith Square, London, S.W.1.

Back numbers and reprints are distributed by
Wm. Dawson and Sons Ltd, Cannon House, Park Farm Road, Folkestone, Kent.